PSYCHOLOGY OF TIME

Other psychology titles published by Emerald:

Instructional Psychology: Past, Present and Future Trends (2006)
Trust: Reason, Routine, Reflexivity (Hardcover) (2006)
An Introduction to the Psychology of Hearing, Fifth Edition (2003)

PSYCHOLOGY OF TIME

EDITED BY

SIMON GRONDIN

Université Laval, Québec, Canada

United Kingdom • North America • Japan
India • Malaysia • China

Emerald Group Publishing Limited
Howard House, Wagon Lane, Bingley BD16 1WA, UK

First edition 2008

Reprints and permission service
Contact: booksandseries@emeraldinsight.com

British Library Cataloguing in Publication Data
A catalogue record for this book is available from the British Library

ISBN: 978-0-08046-977-5

Contents

List of Contributors

Richard A. Block	Department of Psychology, Montana State University, Bozeman, MT, USA
Scott W. Brown	Department of Psychology, University of Southern Maine, Portland, ME, USA
Anna D. Eisler	Department of Psychology, Stockholm University, SE-106 91 Stockholm, Sweden
Hannes Eisler	Department of Psychology, Stockholm University, SE-106 91 Stockholm, Sweden
William J. Friedman	Department of Psychology, Oberlin College, Oberlin, OH, USA
Simon Grondin	École de psychologie, Université Laval, Québec, Canada
Åke Hellström	Department of Psychology, Stockholm University, SE-106 91 Stockholm, Sweden
Richard B. Ivry	Department of Psychology, UC Berkeley, Berkeley, CA, USA
Edward W. Large	Center for Complex Systems and Brain Sciences, Florida Atlantic University, Boca Raton, FL, USA
Francisco S. N. Lobo	Centro de Astronomia e Astrofísica da Universidade de Lisboa (CAAUL), Campo Grande, Lisboa, Portugal
Ryota Miyauchi	Research Institute of Electrical Communication, Tohoku University, Sendai, Japan
Yoshitaka Nakajima	Department of Acoustic Design, Kyushu University, Fukuoka, Japan

Trevor B. Penney Department of Psychology, Faculty of Arts and Social Sciences, National University of Singapore, Singapore

Thomas H. Rammsayer Department of Psychology, University of Bern, Bern, Switzerland

Bill Roberts Department of Psychology, University of Western Ontario, Ontario, Canada

Jon E. Roeckelein Mesa College, Fountain Hills, AZ, USA

Rebecca M. C. Spencer Department of Psychology, UC Berkeley, Berkeley, CA, USA

Gert ten Hoopen Cognitive Psychology Unit, Department of Psychology, Leiden University, Leiden, The Netherlands

Latha Vaitilingam Department of Psychology, Faculty of Arts and Social Sciences, National University of Singapore, Singapore

Dan Zakay Department of Psychology, Tel-Aviv University, Ramat-Aviv, Israel

Howard N. Zelaznik Health and Kinesiology, Purdue University, Lambert, IN, USA

Acknowledgements

As a specialist of time perception, I have been asked many questions about time over the past 20 years. Often, I would have liked to refer my colleagues, collaborators, and friends to a single source of information that could answer all of their questions, but there was no such source available. Therein lies the inspiration for this book. I felt that there was a real need, beyond the existing literature on time, to provide potential readers a condensed package on the main theoretical and empirical issues in the field of psychological time.

Many people have contributed to the production of the resulting book. I would like to thank Bruce Roberts for being so receptive to the original book proposal and the anonymous reviewers of the book proposal for their advice, which eventually helped make this book a more coherent whole. I would also like to thank Emma Smith, the Assistant Commissioning Editor for Emerald, for her helpful guiding comments on the publication process.

I would like to extend special thanks to each of the authors, who are all world-renowned experts in their respective fields. The fact that they agreed to contribute was an honor for me, and their diligence and openness to comments were most appreciated. Their texts showed me just how much knowledge there is in the different sub-fields of psychological time, but also how much remains to be learned. The benefit I gained from reading their chapters confirmed my initial impression that there was a need for such an integrative book on psychological time.

Finally, I would like to express recognition to the Natural Science and Engineering Research Council of Canada, which has been providing continuous financial support for my research on time perception since 1991. Without this support, I would not have been able to develop the expertise on time perception that has led to this book. I would also like to thank Lucie McCarthy for her support and encouragement over the past 20 years, as well as Camille, Anne-Marie, and Nicolas, who, through their development, remind me how quickly time flies and, especially, how precious each and every moment is.

Simon Grondin, *Editor*
Université Laval, Québec
July 23, 2008

Introduction: A Tentative Picture of the Ubiquity of Time

Time is a fascinating concept. If only for the simple fact that we are all getting older, it is difficult to avoid facing the passage of time. The best we can usually do is to try to forget about time, but life soon finds a way to remind us: We often find ourselves waiting impatiently for a birthday, for a green light, for snow, or for winter to end — or with nothing to do but to waste time away. The list of impressions we can have about time is long, if not endless, and anyone who takes the time to think about its psychological dimensions remains stunned by its ubiquity, its omnipresence, and its boundless wonder.

In the face of such ubiquity, it is difficult to cover the wide variety of topics that can fall under the heading the *Psychology of Time* all within a single volume. For instance, some readers might be searching for the latest advancements in temporal perspective or orientation, or other time-related social issues that determine cultural differences in the pace of life, while others, more interested in well-being and mental illness, may be searching for information on the temporal distortions involved in neuropsychological or psychiatric disorders. Indeed, psychological time issues can be found on a very large range of the physical time scale (Mauk & Buonomano, 2004; Wackerman, 2007). Even within the scope of experimental psychology alone, the contemporary research avenues on psychological time are too numerous to offer a complete picture in just one volume. Nevertheless, this book has a lot to offer. Recent developments in the field of timing and time perception have not simply multiplied the number of relevant questions regarding psychological time, but they have also helped to provide more answers and open many fascinating avenues of thought.

The present book brings together cutting-edge presentations of many of the main ideas, findings, hypotheses and theories that experimental psychology provides to the field of timing and psychological time. The contributors, selected for their ability to address various specific questions, were asked to discuss what is known in their field and what avenues remain to be explored. As a result, this book should point readers in the right direction and guide them to reflect on the various and most fundamental issues on psychological time. It offers a balanced integration of old and sometimes neglected findings and more recent empirical advances, all presented within the scope of the critical sub-fields of psychological time in experimental psychology.

This book begins and ends with two chapters that go beyond experimental psychology, and even beyond psychology itself. In *Chapter 1*, by Jon Roeckelein, the reader is introduced to the main ideas and conceptions about time that hark back to early literature in philosophy, as well as the earliest perspectives on time in the field of physics (readers eager to learn more about physics and time may wish to jump to Chapter 13). This review sets the stage for the rest of the chapter, which provides an overview of the first century of research on psychological time and rhythm, leading up to 1950. Chapter 1 is slightly longer than other chapters because it encompasses notions from several disciplines, along with the history of early time research in experimental psychology.

Before entering into specific time research avenues, hotly debated issues, or detailed descriptions of mechanisms or findings, *Chapter 2*, by Simon Grondin, guides the reader through the methods used for the empirical investigation of psychological time. Of course, it is not possible to describe all of the methods used to study time in psychology, since there are many methods adapted to specific fields or issues, as readers will note as they read on. Nevertheless, there are certain classical methods that those interested in timing and time perception are likely to encounter when consulting contemporary studies emphasising either a behavioural or neuroscientific approach. These methods are described in the chapter.

In *Chapter 3*, by Hannes Eisler, Anna Eisler and Åke Hellström, the reader is invited to explore very basic empirical findings in the field of time perception and learn how to approach the data quantitatively. Based on a psychophysical approach to timing and time perception, this chapter, which describes fundamental mechanisms, is organized around two main topics. The first involves the comparison of successive (very brief) time intervals, and, the second, the psychophysical function for duration. In other words, basic psychophysical issues like the time-order effect, Weber's law, and the psychophysical law are addressed.

The perceived duration of very brief intervals is known to depend on how much attention one pays to the passage of time. *Chapter 4*, by Scott W. Brown, provides an extensive review of the literature on the impact of attention on the experience of time. This chapter does not only cover studies related to the processing of brief intervals but also addresses matters that are closer to everyday life experiences. Readers will be introduced to many of the numerous methods used to address the question of attention in experimental psychology, while learning about the intricate connections between these approaches and studies on psychological time.

Associating time strictly with the auditory modality, like one might connect space to the visual modality, would certainly be unjust. Nevertheless, since the question of time is so central to auditory-based skills like speech and music, it is not surprising that audition takes centre stage for a portion of this book. *Chapter 5*, by Gert ten Hoopen, Ryota Miyauchi and Yoshitaka Nakajima, is dedicated to timing in the auditory mode and, more specifically, to illusions like "time shrinking", which are based mainly on the temporal organization of auditory events. Classic and more recently discovered illusions are described. Some of these illusions involve a combination of frequency and temporal, or spatial and temporal, characteristics. Many of the illusions presented in this chapter are explained on the basis of a so-called "event construction model". That said, it is not as easy to present an auditory illusion on paper as it is to present a visual illusion. The illusions and parameters must be described in greater detail. Hence, Chapter 5 is also longer than most other chapters.

Time plays such a critical role in music that a chapter dedicated specifically to time and music is indispensable. In *Chapter 6*, by Ed Large, readers are introduced to the multiple approaches to pulse and meter and their main attributes. After the presentation of classical studies on different topics such as synchronization and metrical structure, the chapter describes some theoretical approaches, including one related to nonlinear resonance featuring key notions such as entrainment and self-sustained oscillation. The reader is then guided through several empirical investigations designed to study these theoretical proposals, which include the use of electroencephalography.

Somewhat along the same lines as Chapter 6, the next three chapters take a closer look at questions regarding the mechanisms involved in the perception or production of temporal intervals. *Chapter 7*, by Howard Zelaznik, Rebecca Spencer and Richard Ivry, reviews the main findings in the field of human movement timing and their theoretical impact. Although the review focuses mainly on behavioural analyses used to determine how simple movements are timed, some references to neuropsychological findings further support the argument. To understand how timing is learned and performed, the authors distinguish between rapid timing tasks and the timing of a subject's movement relative to some predetermined standard. The analyses of the different motor timing tasks lead the authors to conclude that people do not possess a single timing module responsible for the support of all motor timing tasks.

Chapters 8 and 9 are dedicated to the cerebral mechanisms involved in the processing of temporal information. *Chapter 8*, by Trevor Penney and Latha d/o Vaitilingam, nicely reviews the main findings from some of the neural imaging techniques, mainly functional magnetic resonance imaging (fMRI), positron emission tomography (PET), functional near infrared spectroscopy (fNIRS) and the event-related optical signal (EROS). The findings presented in the chapter are divided according to the ranges of durations — sub- or supra-second — covered in the reported investigations and describe the potential contribution of cortical and sub-cortical structures to timing and time perception. The chapter does not provide definite answers about the functions of these structures, but it highlights the challenges awaiting time perception researchers who adopt a neuroscientific approach.

Chapter 9, by Thomas Rammsayer, rather emphasises a neuropharmacological approach to human timing for studying specific brain-behaviour relationships. More specifically, the reader is offered a detailed description of the main pharmacological sources (dopaminergic, glutamatergic, noradrenergic and GABAergic) for modulating human timing. This neuropharmacological approach further develops on the conclusion of Chapter 7 by providing evidence for distinct timing mechanisms. In this chapter, it is the range of duration under investigation that is considered the most critical. The author argues for the existence of two distinct — but not completely independent — mechanisms, one subcortical (sensory), associated with the timing of very brief intervals, and one cognitive, used for processing intervals longer than one second. Its conclusion is consistent with Chapter 8.

While previous chapters were centred on issues regarding the nature, types or numbers of time-related mechanisms, either from a behavioural or neuroscientific approach, the next chapters address issues that may capture the attention of an even larger audience. *Chapter 10*, by William Roberts, is about the question of time in animals. This chapter is not a review of the abundant literature on animal timing, as such reviews are available elsewhere. In this chapter, the author rather asks what animals know about time, beyond the fact that they can learn and remember general rules linking unconditioned and conditioned stimuli and the fact that pressing a bar or running a path in a maze leads to a food reward. It has previously been argued that animals were "stuck in time" or could not "mentally time travel", but the author shows that an animal's ability to anticipate the future consequences of its actions has been underestimated and goes beyond its present motivational state. The chapter is interesting in that it shows how the application of clever and patient-testing strategies in experimental psychology is expanding our knowledge of the consciousness of time in the animal world.

Chapter 11, by William Friedman, offers a developmental perspective on the diversity of the human experience of time. Indeed, the experience of time is so diverse that this chapter cannot be a comprehensive review in the field. Nevertheless, it provides a summary of the main findings from many of the approaches that developmental psychologists have taken. The readers will learn much about what children know about time, the different ages at which the various components of the human experience of time emerge and the reasons behind the developmental pattern.

Chapter 12, by Richard Block and Dan Zakay, also takes the reader closer to concerns related to experiencing time on a large scale. In this chapter, the multiple temporal aspects of memory are emphasized. How people estimate the temporal location — or recency — of a past event, how they judge the duration of an episode while it is in progress and how they execute a plan to perform an action at a specific future time are some of the questions addressed in this chapter. In other words, Chapter 12 offers a fine review of the main theories and findings related to the timing of the past, the present and the future.

Anyone who is immersed in the field of psychological time comes to wonder about the physical, or objective, nature of time. In *Chapter 13*, a physicist, Francisco Lobo, takes the reader through the main conceptions about the nature of time in physics, presented in relatively clear and simple terms. After a description of the relativistic aspects of time in special and general relativity, which includes specific reference to the notion of spacetime, the questions of time irreversibility and the arrow of time are addressed in the context of thermodynamics and quantum mechanics. In this book's closing chapter, the reader is finally led to an understanding, through the fundamental notion of causality, of the concepts of timelike curves, time travel and its associated paradoxes.

Books on rhythm (1956) and time (1957) written more than 50 years ago by Paul Fraisse have definitely helped to popularize the field of time perception in experimental psychology. As well, major events like the 1983 New York convention

(Gibbon & Allan, 1984) and the 1991 St. Malo NATO workshop (Macar, Pouthas, & Friedman, 1992), along with the publication of special issues in multiple journals in recent years and of relatively new edited books (see, for instance, Block, 1990; Helfrich, 2003; Levin & Zakay, 1989; Meck, 2003), have contributed to the recent explosion of research in this fascinating field. It is my hope that the present volume will stimulate and guide students interested in experimental psychology and neuroscience, as well as young researchers in these fields. Although admittedly capturing only a modest portion of the ubiquitous and elusive phenomenon of time, this book should help the reader to observe the omnipresence of the temporal requirements of life. I hope this book is modern enough that readers will want to read it as soon as possible, yet classic enough that it will remain useful for decades to come.

References

Block, R. A. (Ed.) (1990). *Cognitive models of psychological*. Hillsdale, NJ: Erlbaum.

Fraisse, P. (1956). *Les structures rythmiques* [*Rhythmic structures*]. Louvain: Studia Psychologica.

Fraisse, P. (1957). *Psychologie du temps* [*Psychology of time*]. Paris: Presses Universitaires de France.

Gibbon, J., & Allan, L. G. (Eds). (1984). *Annals of the New York academy of sciences: Vol. 423, timing and time perception*. New York: New York Academy of Sciences.

Helfrich, H. (Ed.) (2003). *Time and mind II: Information processing perspectives*. Seattle, WA: Hogrefe & Huber.

Levin, I., & Zakay, D. (Eds). (1989). *Time and human cognition: A life span perspective*. Amsterdam, The Netherlands: North Holland.

Macar, F., Pouthas, V., & Friedman, W. J. (1992). *Time, action and cognition: Towards bridging the gap*. Dordrecht, The Netherlands: Kluwer.

Mauk, M. D., & Buonomano, D. V. (2004). The neural basis of temporal processing. *Annual Review of Neuroscience*, *27*, 307–340.

Meck, W. H. (Ed.) (2003). *Functional and neural mechanisms of internal timing*. Boca Raton, FL: CRC Press.

Wackerman, J. (2007). Inner and outer horizons of time experience. *Spanish Journal of Psychology*, *10*, 20–32.

Simon Grondin

Chapter 1

History of Conceptions and Accounts of Time and Early Time Perception Research

Jon E. Roeckelein

This chapter on early conceptions of time and time perception research is organized around the following main rubrics: origins and earliest conceptions of time; prescientific accounts of time by early Greek philosophers; prescientific accounts of time by later philosophers; the scientific revolution and conceptions of time; terminology in psychological time research; scientific studies of reaction time, rhythm, and psychological time (1860–1910); and premodern scientific research on psychological time (1911–1949).

1.1. Origins and Earliest Conceptions of Time

Ever since the early days of humankind, people have speculated about, and studied, the passage of time. The early humans informally approached the notion of time mainly via study of the change of seasons and the development of crude devices for measuring time. More recently, in civilization and human history, philosophers, scientists, and psychologists have attempted to understand the concept of time in more organized and controlled ways. The early Greek, and later, philosophers provided formal, but prescientific, accounts of time. The scientific revolution of the 17th century in the physical and natural sciences gave further impetus to the study of time via the employment of advanced instrumentation and scientific methodologies. Formal, systematic, and scientific research on the topic of time in psychology is a relatively recent phenomenon, beginning around the 1860s. From this period on — through a premodern phase up to about 1950 and continuing up to the present modern scientific age — an enormous number of empirical studies and laboratory experiments have been conducted on psychological time. Generally, in psychology, the conceptual and experiential entity called "time" has become an important

Psychology of Time

DOI:10.1016/B978-0-08046-977-5.00001-6

experimental variable to be defined precisely and controlled in laboratory studies in the areas of psychophysics, attention, motor behavior, perception, sensation, neuropharmacology, learning, memory, cognition, developmental, and physiological psychology, among others.

Questions concerning the concept of time are abundant and continue to be asked today. What is the nature of time (Buccheri, Saniga, & Stuckey, 2003; see Chapter 13)? Is there a special sense organ or part of the brain in humans and animals that accounts for one's experience of time? How is time defined? Are there different types of time appreciation? Is time a discrete variable — like discrete grains of sand falling in an hourglass, or is it a continuous variable — like water flowing in a river? How *do* we experience time? Does time appreciation occur in an unknowable and intuitive fashion or does it occur in a more deliberate and intentional manner as a cognitive construction or mental reconstruction? How reliable and valid are the "natural" (e.g., seasons and solar/lunar events) versus the "man-made" (e.g., mechanical and atomic clocks) units of measured time? How does the psychologist's approach to the study of time differ from the physicist's and the biologist's accounts? Do all psychologists consider time to be a dimension of consciousness, and a way by which we give order to our experiences? Do all physicists regard time as one of the three basic quantities by which the universe is described in physical terms? What is the nature of the diversity among philosophers concerning conceptualizations of time? What are the *theories* of time (Roeckelein, 2000, 2006, pp. 65; 176–77; 224–25; 495–96; 534–35; 599–602)?

Historical accounts of the origins and genesis of time necessarily invoke cosmological factors and concerns. The importance of cosmological and celestial influences on the concept of time is due in origin to the Chaldeans or late Babylonians (c. 1000 B.C.). In antiquity, the word "Chaldean" came to mean simply "astrologer" among the Romans (*cf.*, Daniel 1:4 and Daniel 2:2,10 in the Amplified Bible, 1987). Their astrology was based on the fundamental assumption that all events on earth are influenced by the stars (*cf.*, *astrology* — a form of divination based on the theory that the movements of the celestial bodies affect human affairs and determine the course of events versus *astronomy* — a branch of science that studies the motions and natures of celestial bodies, as well as matter and energy, in the universe at large). Astronomy is reputed to be the oldest of the pure sciences, and the earliest astronomers were priests in an era when no attempt was made to distinguish astronomy from the pseudoscience of astrology. Of course, this situation is changed today and there is a great gulf separating astronomy from astrology.

The separation of the five planets they discovered from the so-called "fixed stars" was one of the Chaldeans' greatest achievements (Whitrow, 1972c). More particularly, when considering cosmology and the modern notion of an "expanding universe" — where the galaxies are thought to be flying away from each other at great speeds — the conceptualizations of time, and its measurement, are obvious focal points for study and debate (Hawking, 1988, pp. 35–51; Whitrow, 1980, pp. 283–302). Additionally, when considering the two general types of cosmological theories — the "big-bang" and the "steady-state" hypotheses or theories — the issue of the origin or genesis of time is most salient. According to the "big-bang" theories, at the beginning of time all the matter and energy in the universe were concentrated in a very small volume that exploded where the resultant expansion continues today (cosmologists estimate this explosion occurred between 8 and 13 billion years ago and the original composition of the universe was pure hydrogen; after millions of years, the expanding universe — at first a very hot gas — thinned and cooled enough to condense into separate and distinctive galaxies and, then, stars). According to the "steady-state" theories, the universe expands, but new matter is created continuously at all points in space left by the receding galaxies. The impact of these cosmological theories on the concept of time is that the theories imply the universe has always expanded — with no beginning or end — at a uniform rate and that it always will expand and maintain a constant density (*cf.*, Western and Aztec "creation stories," Aveni, 1989; and the biblical "creation" story where the origin of human time began with the creation by God of Adam and Eve in the Garden of Eden in the "undatable past," or just before 2000 B.C.).

Current cosmological theories assert that the experimental constants of traditional physics (beginning in the 17th century) are not really fixed but change slowly over very long periods of time as the universe evolves (Fraser, 1982; Landsberg, 1982). With the relatively recent discovery of quasars (starlike objects) and the radio galaxies (star systems), scientists estimate that the energy reaching us on earth *now* from some of these objects was emitted as long as 8 billion years ago — a truly mind-boggling image, proposition, percept, or concept — not long after the creation of the universe itself (assuming that the "big-bang" theory is correct). Essentially, to put it another way, the light and energy from such sources as quasars and radio galaxies may not *now* exist. Thus, to look into the sky and into space is to look into the past. We see such objects *today* as they actually were before the earth was created and before the Milky Way was formed. As one astronomer noted, when the light we see today from our nearest spiral galaxy (called "M31") initially left for earth, there were no humans on our planet, although our ancestors were evolving rapidly to their present form (Sagan, 1980).

In addition to making cosmological speculations on the beginning of time, it is proper to consider the prehistoric, and ancient historic, origins of the notion of time. One may imagine the initial appearance of prehistoric humans on earth, their supposed involvement with time, and the early development of their unique human time sense (Goudsmit & Claiborne, 1980). When the small-brained ape-men (*Australopithecus*) started to make tools (an estimated 2 million years ago), they fashioned crude-stone choppers that probably were improvised for the purpose of meeting the needs of an immediate, sometimes desperate, present and an imagined future. With bigger brains in humans came even greater foresight. About 500,000 years ago, the first humans in China used fire, indicating that they were perspicacious enough to keep supplies of fuel available and to keep the fires burning. Also, at about this same time, humans developed the remarkable tool of language that helped to revolutionize their relationship to the concept of time. Thus, words became the best tools for "moving" things in time, and in the mind, whether it concerned past, present, or future events. The appearance of Neanderthal man (between 100,000 and 40,000 years ago) — with a brain at least as large as the 21st-century human brain — raised human imagination and foresight to near-modern levels. Besides developing their hunting skills and making more sophisticated tools than that of earlier primitive individuals, Neanderthals buried their dead — and also interred tools and food with the bodies — which argues for a sort of belief in an afterlife.

Some investigators (Goudsmit & Claiborne, 1980) assert that humans' innate capacity for dealing with time does not seem to have increased markedly since Neanderthal man walked the earth. By contrast, however, humans' "cultural equipment" for coping with time has evolved immensely. Such views further assert that without a growing consciousness of time and without the tools to measure time — and the concepts to relate it to other things — civilization would be totally impossible. With the development of the behaviors of writing and record keeping (around 6000 B.C.) came techniques for the measurement of time — initially and primarily via the development of calendars and clocks.

In some celebrated accounts of the origin of time, it is suggested that time is a kind of *linear* progression measured by the clock and calendar (Whitrow, 1972a, b, c, 1980). Inasmuch as those of us living in modern civilization are so dominated by the *linear* concept of time, it seems to be taken for granted that it is a necessity for our lives and even of our very thoughts. On the other hand, such a necessity may be far from true: not only do primitive races (such as the Australian aborigines) have only very vague ideas about clocks and calendars, but most civilizations and societies — prior to our own of the last 200–300 years — have tended to consider time as essentially *cyclic* in nature. Although all primitive peoples seem to have some idea of time and some method of time reckoning (*cf.*, the "oral" and "written" modes of early time reckoning; Aveni, 1989), it is usually based on celestial and astronomical observations (e.g., the Australian aborigine will fix the time for a proposed action by placing a stone in the fork of a tree, or some such place, so that the sun will strike it at the appropriate or agreed-upon time; *cf.*, Perkins, 1998).

A sense of *rhythm*, also, was an important factor in primitive humans' intuition of time (Whitrow, 1972a). Before a primitive person had any explicit idea of time, he or she was probably aware of temporal associations that divided time into intervals much like bars in a musical score. Moreover, the principal transitions in nature were thought by primitives to occur suddenly where one's journey through life was seen as a sequence of distinct stages. Even in a culture so advanced as the ancient Chinese civilization (c. 14–15th century B.C.), different intervals of time were regarded as separate or discrete units — so that time, in effect, had a discontinuous nature (*cf.*, "time reckoning" in China; Aveni, 1989). Thus, armed with this viewpoint of time as "boxed," time was split up into "eras," "seasons," and "epochs" by our prehistoric and ancient historic ancestors. Later, in medieval Europe (c. 500–1500 A.D.), the development of the mechanical clock did not arise out of a scientific desire to record the passage of time but rather from the practical monastic demand for accurate determination of the hours when the many religious prayers and offices needed to be recited (Barnett, 1998; Goudsmit & Claiborne, 1980; Hood, 1969).

Humans were aware of different times long before they formulated the concept of time itself. It was a long step from the nonhomogeneity of "magical time" to the modern scientific conception of homogeneous linear time (Whitrow, 1972a, c). Of all the ancient peoples, the Mayan priests of pre-Columbian Central America apparently were the most obsessed with the idea of time as compared, for instance, with the Europeans of antiquity who regarded the different days of the week as being under the influence of the sun, the moon, or various sacred deities. For the Mayas, each day was itself divine and — as their altars and monuments show — they pictured the divisions of time as burdens carried on the backs of *many* hierarchically arranged divine load bearers who by replacing their loads among themselves periodically personified the respective numbers by which the different temporal periods of days, months, and years were distinguished. However, despite the Mayan development of a rather precise astronomical calendar, they seem never to have attained the concept of time as the journey of *one* bearer and his load. Rather, according to the Mayan conceptualization of time, each god's burden came to signify the particular aspect of the division of time in question; for example, one year the burden might be drought, and another year it might be a good harvest. Thus, Mayan time was regarded not as an abstract conceptualization, but according to its impact on the lives of individuals (Aveni, 1998, pp. 314–333; Tedlock, 1982).

In the case of the ancient Greeks — unlike the Mayas — there generally was not a discernible obsession concerning the temporal ordering of things in the world. However, at the dawn of Greek literature, two contrasting viewpoints of time may be found in the poets Homer and Hesiod (c. 8th century B.C.). In Homer's epics (e.g., the *Iliad*), time is never the subject of a verb and, thus, is never personified; Homer was not interested in the origin of things inasmuch as he held no cosmogony or views of the creation of the universe. On the other hand, Hesiod (e.g., in his *Works and Days*) gives an account of the origin of the world; although Hesiod's poem may be regarded as a moralistic study based implicitly on the concept of time, the word "time" never actually appears in it (Whitrow, 1972a).

1.1.1. Development of Calendars

The development of calendars provided systems of reckoning time for the practical purpose of recording past events and calculating dates for future plans. Typically, a calendar is based on noting ordinary and easily observable natural events, such as the cycle of the sun through the seasons with equinox and solstice, and the recurrent phases of the moon. About 5000 years ago, the ancient Sumerians — predecessors to the Babylonians — were the first, apparently, to divide the year into units (a year contained 12 months of 30 days each) as well as to divide the day into units (a day consisted of 12 "danna," each of 30 "ges"). Later, the Egyptians developed the notion of the 24-hour day and the 365-day year. The Egyptian word for "hour" is also the word for "priestly duties" (Goudsmit & Claiborne, 1980). The discrepancy between the years presented one of the major problems for humans since their early days, and great efforts were spent in attempting to reconcile and harmonize solar and lunar reckonings. Reckoning of day and year was considered necessary by practical peoples to determine sacred days, to arrange plans for the future, and to keep a coherent record of the past. There were various ancient attempts to reconcile the count of days and years in solar, lunar, and semilunar calendars extending from the Egyptians and the Greeks to the Chinese and the Mayas. Some calendar historians hold that the moon was human's first means of keeping track of time (e.g., various rock and bone relics from the Paleolithic period of history — containing paintings and scratches that tallied the days of the lunar month — are estimated to be some 35,000 years old). Some historians of astronomy, on the other hand, assert that the stars were more widely used for time reckoning than the moon.

Moreover, throughout history, humans' tendency to worship heavenly bodies as well as to observe them gave calendar making a religious significance. The combination of religion and time reckoning among primitive peoples achieved its most visible and impressive expression in the megalithic or "big stone" cult of northwestern Europe in the regions of England, Brittany, and Scandinavia. Herdsmen and farmers erected large stone structures in the centuries following 2000 B.C. that served as places of worship and time reckoning of the seasons. The largest of these monuments is Stonehenge in southern England, Salisbury Plain, Wiltshire.

The first modern calendar, the *Julian calendar*, was used initially in 45 B.C. by Julius Caesar who decreed that henceforth there should be 3 years of 365 days each, and then one year of 366 days, in a perpetual cycle. This custom of the Julian calendar is still observed today by adding one day to the month of February every fourth year (called "leap year"). Around 527 A.D., Dionysius Exiguus, the abbot of Rome, fixed Christmas at the 25th day of December and, also, began the custom of dating events — via the designations B.C. ("before Christ") and A.D. ("anno domini" or "in the year of the Lord") — based on the birth of Jesus Christ. Even though the Julian calendar was a huge improvement over all previous systems, it was not completely accurate. Because there are approximately 365.25 days in a solar year, the Julian calendar was reasonably satisfactory for many years, but there are not exactly 365.25 days in a year. The exact solar year consists of 365 days, 5 hours, 48 minutes, and 47.8 seconds. The difference of about 11 minutes becomes appreciable over several centuries. The final calendar correction, called the *Gregorian calendar*, was accomplished in 1582 by Pope Gregory XIII. In order to make up for all the days that had accumulated since the beginning of the Julian calendar, Pope Gregory XIII decreed the elimination of 10 days from the year 1582. In many countries, after this was done, the day after October 4, 1582 became October 15, 1582. Pope Gregory XIII also set up the "leap year rule" that is now in effect and which will serve us for more than a thousand years in the future. The Gregorian leap year rule provides for dropping one day from every centurial year (i.e., years ending in 00) whose number cannot be divided by 400. Consequently, a day was dropped in the years 1700, 1800, and 1900 (this meant that these years were *not* leap years, i.e., they had 28 days in February). The day is *not* dropped in the year 2000, so the month of February 2000 has 29 days. The error in our present-day calendar is less than one day in about every 3000-plus years. Thus, although the Gregorian calendar is an improvement over the Julian calendar, it still is not 100% accurate (*cf.*, attempts to develop a "world calendar," most notably by Elizabeth Achelis in 1930; Goudsmit & Claiborne, 1980, p. 63).

The initial adoption of the Gregorian calendar in 1582 was by no means universal. The first countries to adopt the new calendar were primarily Roman Catholic nations, as might be expected. Most Protestant countries did not adopt the Gregorian calendar until much later (England and the American Colonies made the adoption in 1752). It should be noted that a 11-day adjustment was now needed — the Julian calendar having added another day between 1582 and 1752. Dates that preceded the change are sometimes designated "O.S." (for Old Style). Most dates in American history have been converted to "New Style" (N.S.) or Gregorian dates. Other countries have been even slower in adopting the new calendar (e.g., Japan in 1873; China in 1912; Russia in 1918; Greece in 1924; and Turkey in 1927). The establishment of chronology — an associative aspect of calendar-making — is one of the major problems in studying ancient and medieval history (Harris & Levey, 1975). The classic work on chronology is that of the Benedictines, and first appeared in 1750 in a treatise called *L'Art de verifier les dates des faits historiques* (the art of verifying the dates of historical acts).

Belief in the *cyclic* pattern of time (as opposed to the *linear* pattern of time) was a common aspect of many ancient cultures and, in particular, characterized early Greek cosmological ideas, especially in prescientific Hellenistic (c. 776–323 B.C.) times (*cf.*, the temporal concepts of Mithraism and Zoroastrianism, and the "Iranian theory of time" [Whitrow, 1972c]; the "Indo-Iranian Gods of Time"[Macey, 1994]; and "Islamic time" [Goldman, 1981; Stern, 1994]).

1.2. Prescientific Accounts of Time by Early Greek Philosophers

Greek philosophers in the 6th and 5th centuries B.C. identified dual aspects of time (*being* — the Parmenidean continuity aspect, and *becoming* — the Heraclitean transience aspect) that to this day are concepts that are unreconciled. Time extends continuously from the past to the future (the *being* aspect), and things change in time (the *becoming* aspect). In the history of language, words for time are long preceded by words for past, present, and future, and the concept of time makes a relatively late appearance (Nichols, 1891a, b). The first attempt in the world to define and study systematically — albeit naively and nonscientifically — the concept of time (and motion) sprang from the ancient Greeks as early as the 5th century B.C., primarily by the Eleatic school, a pre-Socratic philosophical school at Elea that was a Greek colony in Lucania, Italy (Hyland, 1994). The Eleatic school was founded by Parmenides (c. 515– ? B.C.) whose philosophy denied the reality of change on the ground that things either do, or do not, exist (Note: The notion of *change* is a fundamental assumption in modern-day treatments of temporal experience — see Chapters 4 and 12, and Guyau later in this chapter). Thus, according to Parmenides, there are no in-between or mediating stages, as the notion of change or "becoming" usually implies. This point of view served as an issue of debate among the early philosophers, most notably Heraclitus (c. 535–475 B.C.) who taught that there was no permanent reality except the reality of change, and that permanence was an illusion of the senses. Heraclitus taught, also, that all things carried with them their opposites — that death was potential in life, that being and not-being were part of every whole and, therefore, the only possible real state was the transitional one of "becoming" (Harris & Levey, 1975; Harrison, 1994; Strong, 1891).

Although the early Greek philosophers — even Parmenides and Heraclitus — apparently took time for granted, they generated significant questions concerning the issue of time. In addition to the concept of change and its influence on the concept of time, it is certain that the speculation of Pythagoras (c. 582–507 B.C.) regarding "number" had a direct formative influence later on Aristotle's (384–322 B.C.) philosophy of time, and paradoxical problems such as Zeno's (c. 490–430 B.C.) directed philosophical attention critically toward the concept of time. According to an account by the Greek essayist and biographer Plutarch (c. 46–120 A.D.), when asked what time was, Pythagoras replied that it was the soul, or procreative element, of the universe. The degree to which Pythagoras and his followers were influenced by earlier philosophical conceptualizations (such as Asian and Oriental ideas) is a matter for speculation. However, the Orphic (6th century B.C. religious cult of Greece) conception of *kronos* (or *Cronus* — a Greek legendary figure, probably a god of agriculture of a pre-Hellenic people, who fathered mythologically the great gods Zeus, Poseidon, and Hades, among others) has features in common with the Iranian notion of *Zurvan Akarana* (i.e., infinite or unending time) — in particular, each was depicted as a multiheaded winged serpent. Cronus is equated with the Roman god Saturn, and the concept of "Father Time" is believed to stem from Cronus. Later Greeks referred to him as Chronus, the god of time who — with his sickle — cut down the passing years. Today, "Father Time" symbolizes the end of the year. Apparently, before the 5th century B.C., and the writings of the Athenian tragic poet Aeschylus (525–456 B.C.), the concept of time was relatively unimportant for the Greeks (Goudsmit & Claiborne, 1980; Romilly, 1968; Whitrow, 1972a).

Parmenides' most famous disciples were Zeno of Elea and Melissus of Samos. Zeno used a series of paradoxes to show logically the indefensibility of commonsense notions of reality; for instance, an arrow shot toward a target logically never reaches the target because a moving body — the arrow — can never come to the end of a line — the target — as it must first cover half the line, then half the remainder, and so on *ad infinitum*. Melissus is credited with systematizing the viewpoints of the Eleatic school. The ultimate reality for the Eleatics was an undifferentiated "being" in contrast and opposition to the illusory evidence from the senses. Although the paradoxes of Zeno were primarily concerned with the problem of motion, they raised difficulties both for the notion of time as continuous or infinitely divisible and for the notion of temporal atomicity. Democritus — a pupil of Leucippus, and Xenocrates — one of Plato's students, developed the concepts of "atomism" and "atomic time" that occasionally figured in solutions of Zeno's paradoxes: if time consists of indivisible moments, often referred to as "chrons," then motion consists of imperceptible jerks that may explain how the arrow actually strikes the target. In contrast to the Pythagoreans, who tended to identify the chronological with the logical, Parmenides and Zeno asserted that the two are incompatible (Harrison, 1994; Whitrow, 1972a).

Accounts of the development and treatment of the concept of time by the early Greek, and later, philosophers have been provided most prominently by Baldwin (1901–1905), Cohen (1971), Goudsmit and Claiborne (1980), Nichols (1890, 1891a, b), Reck (1994), and Whitrow (1972a, b, c, 1980, 1989).

1.2.1. From Plato to Aristotle

The Greek philosopher Plato (c. 427–347 B.C.) conceived of time as a reality that is an absolute flowing apart from the events filling it. The influence of Parmenides and Zeno on Plato is apparent in the different treatment of space and time in Plato's various cosmological references: space exists in its own right as a given basis for the visible order of things, whereas time is merely an aspect of that order based on an ideal timeless archetype and involves static geometrical shapes ("eternity") of which time is the "moving image" and is governed by a regular numerical sequence occasioned by the motions of the heavenly bodies (Brann, 1994). Thus, Plato's intimate pairing of time with the universe led him to consider time as being produced essentially by celestial sphere revolutions (*cf.*, Aristotle's approach which rejected the idea that time is identified with any particular form of motion).

Nichols (1891a) indicates the following notions regarding Plato's view and philosophy of time: time is the image of eternity; time belongs wholly to generation; time is measured by the movements of heavenly bodies; there is a time to depart and die; time is short compared with eternity; time is nothing, and is not deserving of the solicitude of an immortal being; time and tune are synonymous with good education. However, Nichols (1891a, p. 453) also notes that *time, per se*, is nowhere psychologically contemplated by Plato. Time is not one of Plato's "five categories" (Being, Rest, Motion, Sameness, and Difference) given in his *Sophist* — a work that discusses the nature of "nonbeing."

The Greek philosopher Aristotle was the first to ask — in a psychological sense — *how* we perceive time. In discussing time, Aristotle argued that motion can be uniform or nonuniform and such concepts themselves are defined by time, whereas time cannot be defined by itself. Although time is not identical with motion, it seemed to Aristotle to be dependent on motion. Perhaps influenced by the Pythagoreans, Aristotle asserted that time is a kind of number — and, possibly, the "numerable aspect of motions" — where it becomes a numbering process that is founded on one's perception of "before" and "after" in motion. Psychologically considered, then, time is an immediate (central) sense perception of the "number of motion." Aristotle regarded time and motion as reciprocal entities. However, he recognized that motion can cease (aside from the unceasing motion and continuity of the heavens) but time cannot (Nichols, 1891a; Whitrow, 1972a).

Aristotle's account of time is from the "physical" point of view. Although Aristotle's original term for motion included qualitative change as well as change of place, the ideas on which his representation of time is based are all suggested by the notion of change of place. The factors of magnitude, motion, and time all go together for Aristotle and he spoke of time as the number of the local movement in which the "now," as it were, is carried along — much like a moving point in space, and is the fundamental generating unit. Thus, Aristotle held that the "now" is in one sense always the same — although in another sense, as it occupies different positions in the series, it is always different. In the identity of the "now," Aristotle found the ground of the self-identity of time taken as a whole and, though relative to motion, time is always changing (Baldwin, 1901–1905; Hintikka, 1973; Hussey, 1983; Inwood, 1991).

Goudsmit and Claiborne (1980, p. 146) refer to "Aristotle's time paradox": we apprehend time only when we have marked motion. Yet, not only do we measure the movement by the time but also the time by the movement, because they define each other. When Aristotle attempted to explain the nature and cause of motion, however, his "commonsense" approach runs into difficulty. He accepted the apparent notion that any moving body has a natural tendency to come to a resting position. Evidently, nothing moves of itself — something must be causing it to move. From this it was a small step to the later theory that the velocity of movement is directly proportional to the force, or push, that causes the movement. Goudsmit and Claiborne also note that Aristotle's mistaken ideas on motion (as on many other topics) dominated philosophical thought and science for centuries after the classical world had declined and fallen. Over the years, however, philosophers and scientists such as Galileo (1564–1642) chipped away bit by bit at Aristotle's naïve and incomplete physical view of the world. Some medieval scholars in the 13th century had taken the crucial scientific step — that Aristotle had never taken — of defining the motion-related idea of velocity in a precise manner: they brought the concept of time into the definition. Thus, a moving object was simply changing its position in space, and velocity was defined as how much an object's position changes in a given amount of time (today, velocity is still expressed in such a way; for instance, so many "kilometers per hour" or "meters per second"). In essence, *time perception* for Aristotle was a direct *sense-perception* — the immediate function of the sentient faculty or soul, whether under the presentation of primary sensation or of memory. Nichols (1891a, p. 458) calls Aristotle's account of time a "remarkable first exposition of time" that is important historically where its essential features have survived in all ages and "that is, even now" (i.e., in 1891) "the accepted theory of prominent psychologists."

The Roman neo-Platonist philosopher Plotinus (205–270 A.D.) observed that time was commonly defined among the Greeks in three ways: (1) as motion (either [a] all motion, or [b] that of the celestial sphere); (2) as the moving sphere itself; or (3) as a determination of motion (more particularly as [a] extent of motion — as expressed by the Stoics [c. 300 B.C.], [b] number of motion — as expressed by Aristotle, or [c] an accompaniment of motion generally — as expressed by Epicurus [341–270 B.C.]). Plotinus complained that none of these ways tells what time — in metaphysical terms — really is (Venable, 1994). Baldwin (1901–1905, pp. 699–700) traces the initial development of time from the three approaches of Plato/Plotinus, Aristotle, and St. Augustine. Plotinus argued that time is generated by the restless energy of the soul seeking to express in matter the infinite and eternal fullness of being. This is accomplished in a successive series of acts, not in a single stroke. Time, according to Plotinus, is the life of the soul much like eternity is the life of intelligible being in its full, unbroken, absolutely unchangeable totality. In this view (which recurs in various modifications in the history of "dynamic idealism," i.e., all reality is the creation of mind or spirit), time is objective only because the object that it qualifies is subjectively determined; but subject and object are both included in a comprehensive unity that is timeless.

1.2.2. From St. Augustine to St. Thomas Aquinas

Cohen (1971) notes the remarkable fact that almost a millennium had to elapse before pure temporal experience was subjected to psychological analysis by the Numidian Christian Church Father St. Augustine (354–430 A.D.). By a process of agonizing introspection, St. Augustine arrived at the idea that time is — by its very nature — subjective (e.g., asking himself, "What do I measure when I say either definitely this is double that or indefinitely this is a longer time than that?" St Augustine answered that "It is in thee, my mind, that I measure times"). In his theological tenets, St. Augustine advanced the idea of a distinctive synthetic reconciliation of the doctrines of the fall, predestination, irresistible grace, and free will. In his philosophical and psychological approach to time, St. Augustine advanced a modern-sounding viewpoint: What does one measure if it is not time in some space? Cohen (1971) states that the question whether the spatialization of time (or the spatial representation of time) reveals time's essential character — or is merely an artifact of humans' cerebral and perceptual mechanisms — remains at the heart of the psychology and physics of time. Baldwin (1901–1905) asserts that no one showed a keener appreciation of the contradictions involved in the purely objective view of time than St. Augustine who agreed with Plato in the notion that time is objective, its having been created by God along with the creation of the world. St. Augustine suggested that time is present in, and measured by, the soul.

Furthermore, according to St. Augustine, there are *not* "properly" three times (a past which is not, a future which is not, and an intermediate present which is a mere point of transition between these two nonentities), but there *is* a present of things present (as in "attention"), a present of things past (as in "memory"), and a present of things future (as in "expectation"). St. Augustine's "paradox of time" is that things in time change in time. That is, do things actually change in time, or do they *appear* to change because we move in time? If we move in time, then we change in time — evidently, temporal location does not exhaust the properties of time (Harrison, 1994; Meagher, 1978, 1994).

The novelty of St. Augustine's view consists in the transference of the reference of time from the world soul to the human soul. Yet, St. Augustine does not rest satisfied with such a view, for he still continued to regard time as an objective, divinely created fact (Baldwin, 1901–1905, p. 700). Moreover, although St. Augustine considered time as being in the soul (or mind), he asserted that it is inconceivable apart from the universe. Time, in St. Augustine's view, implies a universe containing motion and change, and a soul (or mind) that exists in its own right (Callahan, 1948). Although

St. Augustine failed to explain how the mind could be an accurate chronometer for the *external* order of physical events, he may be credited as the great pioneer of the study of *internal* time.

From the time of St. Augustine (354–430) to St. Thomas Aquinas (1225–1274), little advance was made in the historical development of the psychology of time (Note: The *kalam theory of atomic time* — developed by Arab philosophers in the 10th and 11th centuries A.D. — sought to demonstrate the total dependence of the material world on the will of the Supreme Being — the sole agent; it was suggested that atoms are isolated by voids and their configurations are governed not by natural events but by the will of the sole agent. Moses Maimonides, a 12th-century Jewish scholar, serves as a primary source of information on the *kalam theory of atomic time*; Harrison, 1994; Maimonides, 1927). However, most — if not all — of the questions and the viewpoints concerning time that were developed and debated in antiquity reappear in the Middle Ages or Medieval period, a period of European history from 500 to 1500 A.D. (some historians refer to the era from the 5th to the 10th centuries as the "Dark Ages" — a time of decline for science and culture; *cf.*, Caudle, 1994). The school of thought called *scholasticism* embodied the philosophy and theology of Western Christendom in the Middle Ages. There were many scholastic philosophies in the Middle Ages but basic to all such thought was the fusion of reason and faith. Accordingly, the concept of time — during this period — was embedded firmly in this theological salmagundi of reason and faith.

Among the scholastics was St. Albertus Magnus (c. 1206–1280) who was the first Western Aristotelian (i.e., he did much to introduce Aristotle's scientific treatises and methods to Europe), and a student of the natural sciences, as well. Magnus held that natural philosophy — rather than psychology or metaphysics — was the primary discipline in which time is properly studied. He argued that because time is an attribute of the events of the physical world, its mode of being is analogous to motion's mode of being. Magnus asserted that time does not possess *enduring* being (as do rocks, trees, and stars), but it has *successive* being which flows and is always losing what was had and gaining what is to come. Magnus argued, also, that the present moment or "now" — which is all of time that exists — is a flowing reality that is the end of the past and the beginning of the future. Ultimately, Magnus's concern was with the being and nature of time, or "chronos," rather than the measurement of time, or "chronometrics" (Snyder, 1994).

Another leading figure during the Middle Ages was St. Thomas Aquinas (1225–1274), an Italian philosopher, theologian, and Dominican friar, who also — like his mentor Albertus Magnus — attempted to "Christianize Aristotle." Aquinas is one of the principal saints of the Roman Catholic Church (he is the founder of the system declared to be the official Catholic philosophy) and, reputedly, the greatest figure of scholasticism. Characteristic of the discussions of time during Aquinas's life were determinations of the differences between time, eternity, and "aevum" (i.e., an attribute of the heavenly bodies and angels; *cf.*, "eternity" which is predicated only of God). Aquinas's best opinion was that eternity is a totality without the beginning, end, or succession essential to time and capable of being conjoined with (though not essential to) "aevum" (Baldwin, 1901–1905). The most important theme in Aquinas's writings involving the notion of time is a divine eternity or "timelessness." He interpreted the biblical opposition between time and eternity in terms of its elaboration by neo-Platonic authors, notably Boethius and Augustine (White, 1994).

An opponent of St. Thomas was John Duns Scotus (c. 1266–1308), a Franciscan friar, who developed a new scholastic synthesis of reason and faith. He asserted that the essence of things — as well as their existence — depends not on the Divine Intellect but on the Divine Will. According to Duns Scotus, time is regarded as a relation or aspect of motion, the two being "materially" identical and only "formally" distinct (Baldwin, 1901–1905; Wolter, 1994).

Francisco Suarez (1548–1617), a Spanish Jesuit philosopher, was the last of the scholastic philosophers who taught, generally, that one may hold the same doctrine both by science (reason) and faith. In regard to time, Suarez made a distinction between "physical time" that measures the motions of the heavens and "spiritual discrete time" that is composed of the indivisible, successive *instants* of change in the intellections and volitions of the angels and measured by the thought of the Supreme Angel. Suarez suggested that the seemingly successive parts of an action — and hence their real duration — may be conceived as a whole in a form that is nonsuccessive. Suarez also considered the idea of time as a sort of space flowing from eternity as purely imaginary, and the location of a given duration in such a space as a purely mental act. However, Suarez apparently did not grasp the radical conception of time purely as a mental construction (Baldwin, 1901–1905, p. 701).

In general, the orthodox scholastics held that time had a beginning, though neither Aquinas nor Scotus could find convincing reasons for the doctrine — apart from revelation. The scholastics also distinguished between *time* (to which succession was essential) and *duration* (to which succession was not essential, in particular, when applied to God and the angels). This distinction between *time* and *duration* reappears in various forms in the early period of modern philosophy in connection with a subjectivistic — or at least idealistic — view of time. Additionally, the distinction between *time* and *duration* steadily gained ground and definition in modern psychological speculations regarding time (Baldwin, 1901–1905, p. 701).

A great deal happened between the death of St. Augustine (430 A.D.) and the death of St. Thomas Aquinas (1274 A.D.), but not much happened that was of any great importance to the history of science in general, and psychology in particular. Scholasticism became a byword to designate petty debates over the details of a philosophical system whose assumptions were never seriously challenged. During the first three quarters of the 13th century, scholarship was viewed more highly than originality. The papacy emerged as a temporal power — heralding an age of politicians, administrators, and systematizers — and scholasticism embodied an age of adaptation and reinterpretation of the "authorities." Gone were the bold speculation and originality of the Greeks, and Aristotle was now considered to be the Great Philosopher. Although the scholastics disagreed on many points, their disagreements were concerned, mainly, with the correct interpretation of Aristotle (Peters, 1965).

1.3. Prescientific Accounts of Time by Later Philosophers

With the later philosophers — such as Descartes, Hobbes, Spinoza, Locke, Leibniz, Berkeley, Hartley, Hume, Kant, Fichte, Hegel, Schelling, and Herbart — the notions of *succession, duration, intuition, subjectivity, objectivity*, and *consciousness* take on additional meaning and importance for the cumulative, balanced, and ultimate understanding of the philosophical and psychological concept of time.

1.3.1. British Philosophers

The English philosopher Thomas Hobbes (1588–1679) declared that time is "a phantasm produced by a body in motion," and that time "stands for the fact of succession or 'before' and 'after' in motion." In Hobbes' study, the actual word *succession* enters the discussion of the concept of time for the first time. Hobbes is considered to be the "Father of the English School of Association," and his importance in the history of the problem of time rests on his being the first to identify with the doctrine that there is no conception in a man's mind that is not at first totally, or by parts, associated with the organs of sense (Nichols, 1891a, p. 467).

The English philosopher, and founder of British empiricism, John Locke (1632–1704) repudiated the traditional doctrine of innate ideas and asserted, rather, that the mind is born blank (a *tabula rasa*) upon which the world describes itself through the experiences of the senses. Locke taught that knowledge arising from sensation is perfected by reflection, and thus enables one to arrive at ideas such as time, space, and infinity. He distinguished the "primary" qualities of things — such as number, solidity, and extension — from their "secondary" qualities — such as color and sound (Heap, 1994). Locke's view of time was based on the idea of succession that is empirically derived as a result of reflecting on several ideas that are successively presented to consciousness (*cf.*, Ernst Mach, 1838–1916, the Austrian physicist, philosopher, and logical positivist who insisted on the contrary idea that time is given independently of experience). However, it was Locke's empiricism (i.e., knowledge is gained from observation, experience, or experiment rather than from theory or solely by reasoning from "a priori truths") which more than anything else paved the way for the later *experimental* study of the psychology of time. Locke had serious doubts about the conception of an "absolute" time and classified time perception as partly sensation and partly reflection. He developed six propositions concerning time: (1) by observing what passes in our minds, we come to the idea of succession; (2) by observing a distance in the parts of this succession, we get the idea of duration; (3) by sensation and observing certain appearances, we get the ideas of certain lengths or measures of durations as minutes, hours, days, years, etc.; (4) by being able to repeat these measures of time, we can come to imagine duration where nothing does really endure or exist — and thus we imagine tomorrow, next year, or even 7 years hence; (5) by being able to repeat ideas of any length of time, as of a minute, a year, an age, and adding them one to another, we can come to the idea of eternity, etc.; (6) by considering any part of infinite duration (as set out by periodical measures), we come by the idea of what we call time in general (Nichols, 1891a, pp. 463–464). Locke asserted that by reflection one may perceive directly and intuitively the time relation between ideas; and most of the denominations of things received from time are only relations. Thus, according to Locke, time is an intuitive perception of relation between successive durative ideas, and his discussions on the topic show much advancement in the development of the concept of time. In particular, Locke anticipated modern experimentally based generalizations regarding attention and *time perception/time estimation* when he observed that if one fixes one's thoughts intently on a single thing — letting slip out of consideration a good part of that duration — one thinks that that particular time is short (Nichols, 1891a, pp. 464–465).

The Anglo-Irish philosopher and clergyman George Berkeley (1685–1753) argued that both types of Locke's qualities (primary and secondary) are known only in the mind (*cf.*, Locke's assertion that only the secondary qualities arise in the mind). Thus, Berkeley's philosophy was that there is no existence of matter independent of perception (*esse est percipi*), and the observing mind of God makes possible the continued apparent existence of material objects. Berkeley held that qualities, not things, are perceived and the perception of qualities is relative to the perceiver. Nichols (1891a, p. 466) suggests that Berkeley initiated one of the greatest epochs in psychology by being the first to disclose the complex makeup of seemingly elemental sensations. However, Berkeley gave his primary attention to space rather than to time. Berkeley admitted that when abstracted from the succession of ideas in the mind, he could form no idea of time at all. "Time," as Berkeley said, "is nothing" (Baldwin, 1901–1905, p. 703). Berkeley looked upon time perception as an act of reason rather than of sense. Also, for Berkeley, ideas are not innate preconditions (as they were for Descartes), but all thoughts are the direct gift of God.

David Hartley (1705–1757) — the English physician/philosopher and founder or formalizer of "associational psychology" (*cf.*, "laws/principles of association" in Roeckelein, 2006, pp. 40–42) — used Isaac Newton's principle (that impulses in the physical world are vibratory in nature) to explain the operation of the brain and nervous system. Vibrations in the nerves — which he believed to be solid, not hollow tubes as Descartes thought — transmit impulses from one part of the body to another. Such vibrations give rise to smaller vibrations in the brain that Hartley considered to be the physiological counterparts of ideas. Hartley's primary law of association was "contiguity," with which he attempted to explain memory, reasoning, emotion, and voluntary and involuntary actions. Those ideas or sensations that occur together (either successively or simultaneously) become associated so that an occurrence of one results in an occurrence of the other. As regards time, Hartley (who first sought to reduce much of psychology to physiology) conceived of time perception and memory to be fundamental acts of mind (Nichols, 1891a).

The Scottish philosopher and historian David Hume (1711–1776) pressed the philosophical analyses of Locke and Berkeley to the logical extreme of skepticism. Hume could see no more reasons for hypothesizing a substantial soul or mind than for accepting a substantial material world. He also argued that causal relation derives solely from the customary conjunction of two impressions, and the apparent sequence of events in the external world is, in fact, the sequence of perceptions in the mind. From this basis, Hume asserted that one's expectation that the future will be like the past has no foundation in reason — it is purely a matter of belief (Harris & Levey, 1975). Like Berkeley, Hume appealed to experience and refused to recognize the reality of mere abstractions. He denied that time is infinitely divisible but conceived it rather as made up of discrete moments each with the duration of a single idea. Baldwin (1901–1905, p. 702) notes that the general criticism of such a view is that it implies the wholly fictitious representation of experience as made up of trains of discrete ideas. More particularly, successive impressions cannot — of themselves — account for the perception of succession. Successive impressions may be subjectively distinguished without consciousness of time at all. Conversely, mental process without successively distinguished parts is found — when measured by objective standards — to occupy a time interval of appreciable (and theoretically divisible) extent. Hume recognized that perceptions of relation are the essence of cognition, and the perception of time relations, thus, becomes an act of reason — something that is more than sensory impression. Moreover, Hume declared distinctly that time is not a particular impression, rather it arises from the manner of the succession of the impressions. Hume did not quite seem to arrive at the great question whether the *idea* of time is "nothing but ideas succeeding each other," yet no one apparently had more lucidly cleared his mind as to what time perceptions are *not*. Hume was hampered by the traditional notions of "relations" and that all ideas must be "unit representations" and "individual pictures," yet he continually struggled toward the thought that time perception should be explained by succession alone (Nichols, 1891a, p. 468).

The 18th-century Scottish philosopher Thomas Reid (1710–1796) also anticipated subsequent experimentally grounded findings concerning *time perception* and *time estimation* as he stated, "When a man is racked with pain, or with expectation, he can hardly think of anything but his distress and the more his mind is occupied by that sole object, the longer the time appears. On the other hand, when he is entertained with cheerful music, with lively conversation and brisk sallies of wit, there seems to be the quickest succession of ideas, but the time appears shortest" (Whitrow, 1980, p. 50).

Among the many other later 18th- and 19th-century philosophers and thinkers who made contributions to the development of the psychological concept of time, Nichols (1891a) discusses the views of the following so-called "Scottish School" philosophers and psychologists (Boring, 1957, for an account of the influence of this school on "associationism" and psychology's history). Thomas Reid clarified some of the difficulties of the time problem when he declared that it would be impossible to show how we acquire a notion of duration if we had no memory (memory implies a conception and a belief of past duration, and remembrance is a particular act of the mind of which we are conscious); Reid also took John Locke to task for confounding the concept of *succession* with *duration*. Dugald Stewart (1753–1828) advanced the time problem in a general way by forcible analysis of such concepts and issues as *identity*, *association*, *memory*, and *reason*. Thomas Brown (1778–1820) asserted that time is one of the earliest notions of the infant; in his development of the doctrine of association (or "suggestion" as he termed it), Brown added a class of association among "relations": "simple suggestion" and "relative suggestion" where time perception was placed in the class of "relative suggestion." Nichols (1891a, p. 486) observes that such "feelings of time relation" (as developed by Brown) are "essentially kin to the disparate *time sense* of Czermak and Vierordt, and to the *time feeling* of Fichte, Horwicz, and James." Sir William Hamilton (1788–1856) declared with "antique vagueness" merely that time is the necessary condition of every conscious act.

The British philosopher Samuel Alexander (1859–1938) developed a whole philosophical system that grounded ultimate reality in his Space–Time notion (Note: The conjoint interpretation of "space" and "time" is characteristic, also, of many American Indian cultures; Sturm, 1994). Time, for Alexander, is one of the two aspects of Space–Time, the ultimate reality or irreducible stuff out of which all that exists emerges. Time has no reality apart from Space, or Space apart from Time. As separate entities, both are abstractions from the four-dimensional reality. In Alexander's approach, mind is a form of Time; Time is the mind of Space, and Space is the body of Time. Moreover, matter, life, and mind are successive emergent qualities of primordial Space–Time. Alexander may be considered to be a "process" philosopher whereby time is not something that happens to things that exist in space; he asserted that there is nothing that is not temporal, and there is no reality but only that of events. Thus, according to Alexander, the only ultimate reality is the system of events he calls "Space–Time" (Eddis, 1994).

1.3.2. French Philosophers

The French philosopher Rene Descartes (1596–1650) made an advance over Aristotle, in particular, in distinguishing duration from Aristotle's "numbering of motion." Descartes argued that one does not conceive of the duration of things that are moved as being different from the duration of things that are not moved. He also distinguished between two kinds of thoughts: *active* (i.e., the different modes of willing) and *passive* (i.e., thought that includes time perceptions). Yet, time was not for Descartes a *sense* perception as it was for Aristotle. Descartes' *time perceptions* spring innately from the intellect or the soul "alone." Moreover, for Descartes, time — derived from a comparison of the durations of certain regular motions — was simply a way of thinking of duration in general (Baldwin, 1901–1905, p. 701; Kalkavage, 1994; Nichols, 1891a, p. 460).

The French social philosopher Jean-Marie Guyau (1854–1888) shifted his own attention from the formal philosophical problem posed by Kant to consider the actual or empirical development of the concept of time and to relate time experience to human information processing — an approach that closely approximates a modern psychological analysis of time. Guyau (1890) asserted that time *itself* does not exist in the universe, but rather it is produced by the events that occur "in time." He considered time as a purely mental construction from the events that take place. Guyau held that temporal experience is constructed based on the intensity of the stimuli, the number of stimuli, the attention paid to the stimuli, the associations of the stimuli, the extent of the differences between the stimuli, and the expectations called up by the stimuli. Guyau maintained that with more "images," and more changes or more mental content, the experience of duration is lengthened (Ornstein, 1969, pp. 16, 37–38). Thus, Guyau (1890) regarded time not as a prior condition but as a consequence of our experience of the world, the result of a long evolution. He asserted that time is essentially a product of human imagination, memory, and will (Note: This notion is in direct opposition to the English associationist and evolutionist school led by the philosopher Herbert Spencer, 1820–1903, who regarded the idea of time as the source of the idea of space). Guyau maintained that, even though we may use time and space to measure each other, nevertheless they are distinct ideas with their own characteristics; he noted that the idea of space originally developed before the idea of time. Guyau suggested, also, that the idea of time arose when humans became conscious of their reactions toward pleasure and pain, and of the succession of muscular sensations associated with such reactions. Thus, Guyau held that the original source of one's idea of time is an accumulation of sensations that produces an internal perspective directed toward the future (Michon, 1994a; Whitrow, 1980, pp. 51–53).

The French philosopher Henri Bergson (1859–1941) argued that chronological time is merely a symbol of space and is, therefore, distinct from the immeasurable flow of duration that is no less than the essence of life itself. Chronological time is a mere convenience that helps us to organize and rationalize our everyday lives, whereas duration is a continuous progression of time in which past, present, and future dissolve into an unbroken flux. Founded on change, duration leads to perpetual recreation of the self in its immediacy. In proposing a theory of the self as an organic whole, Bergson anticipated some of the tenets of the French and German existentialists and phenomenologists (Lacey, 1989; Mosley, 1994).

1.3.3. German Philosophers

The German philosopher and mathematician Gottfried Wilhelm Leibniz (or Leibnitz) (1646–1716) developed the notion that the ultimate constituents of the universe are "monads" or simple substances, each of which represents the universe from a different point of view (*cf.*, the *kalam time atoms* that are thought to be the conceptual forerunners of Leibniz's "monads"). Monads, as the fundamental components of the world, exist in isolation and their inner worlds are coordinated by "preestablished harmony" — a theory known as *parallelism* (Harrison, 1994; Wolfson, 1976). According to Leibniz, the monads are arranged in an infinitely ascending scale, based on the distinctness with which each represents the universe. All monads have perception (consciousness), but only rational monads have "apperception" (i.e., self-consciousness) (Gale, 1994). Leibniz argued that the soul does not think, feel, or perceive, but those aspects are the soul itself under different forms of activity, and time is one of these forms. Leibniz held, also, that all thoughts are innate and the mind itself is innate. Therefore, according to Leibniz, time is innate and but a "phenomenon" of soul development. Leibniz's other ideas regarding time are as follows: space and time "express possibilities" — they are of the nature of eternal truths that relate equally to the possible and to the existing, and they determine existence in some of its relations and are logically prior to any given form of existence; time (not duration) exists only as events are occurring, and is the relation of their succession; and time is purely relative and ideal. Leibniz provided few psychological details of time, but he was, perhaps, the first of the "later" or modern philosophers to emphasize some requirement for "joining the manifold in one." It may be said that with Leibniz the distinction between *duration* and *time* is prominent where everything has its own duration, but not its own time (the former is an attribute of things which the latter — as something outside of things — serves to measure). To Leibniz, time is of the nature of the "eternal verities" and applicable to the possible as well as to the actual and, therefore, not a mere abstraction from experience. Leibniz's mode and style of writing about time gave rise to the traditional interpretation that time is an obscure representation of a real attribute (Baldwin, 1901–1905; Nichols, 1891a).

The German metaphysician Immanuel Kant (1724–1804) termed his basic insight into the nature of knowledge "the Copernican revolution in philosophy" (Harris & Levey, 1975). Instead of assuming that our ideas (to be true) must conform to an external reality independent of our knowing, Kant proposed that objective reality is known only insofar as it conforms to the basic structure of the knowing mind. Kant argued that objects of experience (phenomena) may be known, but things lying beyond the realm of possible experience ("noumena" or things-in-themselves) are unknowable, although their existence is a necessary presupposition. Moreover, phenomena that can be perceived in the pure forms of time, space, and sensibility must — if they are to be understood — possess the characteristics that constitute our categories of understanding. Such categories — which include causality and substance — are the source of the structure of phenomenal experience. In regard to time, Kant viewed the experience of time as the *a priori* form of inner sensible intuitions that have no existence independently of the mind and are a subjective mode in which phenomena appear (Boodin, 1904). Kant argued that time is the form of intuition appropriate to our internal sense, so that we only conceive our states of mind as being in time in introspection, but that they are not really in time. Although Kant considered that all knowledge begins with experience, he did not regard the concept of time (or space) as derived from experience (Lloyd, 1902; Whitrow, 1980). When Kant conceives of time as an *a priori* form of mind, there is both confusion and contradiction from the outset (Nichols, 1891a, p. 471): Does Kant mean mind as *cause*? Or does he mean mind as *result* or as *content*? Surely, a result or content never is *till* it is. Therefore, the term "a priori" is never in any way applicable to it, yet Kant continually speaks of time as an "a priori intuition" and often classifies intuitions as *content* of mind. Nichols (1891a) concludes that Kant's own conception of an "intuition" of time at best could have been but a vague awareness of succession in general or in the abstract, and serious students of the concept of time must judge for themselves what that could really mean or how much is gained by being told by Kant that time is an "a priori form of mind." This same sort of confusion regarding Kant's approach toward time is discussed by Baldwin (1901–1905, pp. 702–703). In this case, Baldwin interprets Kant on the time problem as really meaning that time is merely a form of perceptual experience, and this form is a function of the constructive synthesis that Kant elsewhere attributes to thought. Accordingly, the essence of the Kantian doctrine is that temporal order is a product of the activity of the subject to which all experience is relative.

Other accounts of time by the German philosophers depend on the ways in which they severally interpret the subjective principle and the total constitution of the experience it determines (Baldwin, 1901–1905; Nichols, 1891a, pp. 476–478). For example, Johann Gottlieb Fichte (1762–1814) considered time to be a "present thought." Friedrich Wilhelm Joseph Schelling (1775–1854) defined time as "the I itself thought in activity." Georg Wilhelm Friedrich Hegel (1770–1831) classified time as a "pure form of sensibility." For Johann Friedrich Herbart (1776–1841), time is a process, not a state, that is purely objective, "the number of change." More specifically, Herbart's notion of "time relation" consists of certain proper successive combinations of ordinary sensations or feelings, or of their reproduced representations. Arthur Schopenhauer (1788–1860) declared that time is the form by which self-consciousness becomes possible for the individual will that originally is without knowledge; for Schopenhauer, "succession is the whole nature of time." Friedrich Wilhelm Nietzsche (1844–1900) held that time consciousness is rooted in succession; he described time as actual and infinite in duration. Nietzsche echoed the Greek philosopher Heraclitus in asserting that time is a river flowing inescapably into its own current.

The German philosophers Edmund Husserl (1859–1938) and Martin Heidegger (1889–1976) speculated, also, on the nature of the concept of time. Husserl was the founder and most prominent exponent of the philosophical movement called *phenomenology* that greatly influenced both the philosophical and psychological thought of the 20th century. Through his phenomenological method (i.e., "bracketing" the data of consciousness by suspending all preconceptions, especially those drawn from the "naturalistic" standpoint, and where objects of pure imagination were examined with the same gravity as data taken from the "objective" world), Husserl attempted to reform philosophy and establish a rigorously scientific philosophy that could provide a firm basis for all other sciences (Derrida, 1973; Misiak, 1994). Consistent with the phenomenological approach, Husserl (1965, 1991) rejected scientific objectivism and argued that the existence of time can be discovered by examining its structure and that God is both the end and the motivating force of consciousness and reason (Aveni, 1998). In another case, Heidegger is considered by many philosophers and psychologists to be the center of existential philosophy of the 20th century, and he is regarded as the bridge between existential philosophy and existential psychology. The central focus of Heidegger's system is that the individual is a "being-in-the-world" (Heidegger, 1962, 1972, 1985, 1992). Human beings alone — of all the mammals — have the capacity to be conscious of their existence.

Humans do not exist as a self in relation to the external world, or as a body interacting with other things in the world, but they exist by "being-in-the-world" and the world has an existence because they are in it. Much like the approach of the Danish philosopher Soren Kierkegaard (1813–1855), Heidegger's philosophy considers humans to be in conflict — they contemplate the thought of inescapable death (and the antithesis between temporal existence and eternal truth) that results in the experience of dread, despair, and anguish (Martin, 1994). People have to accept the fact that death is inevitable and that "nothingness" will follow. Human existence is neither of one's own making nor of one's own choice (Lundin, 1994). Heidegger (1985, 1992) extends Husserl's phenomenological analysis by "subjectivizing" time (Merleau-Ponty, 1962); he "desubstantializes" time by laying heavy accent on the past and viewing all temporal experience as part of the dialectical process of coming into being. Heidegger maintained that rather than viewing oneself as helplessly sliding along a teleological temporal pathway toward death, humans participate in constituting temporality. One "manages" time by taking action, and carrying on, along with others who share a common heritage. One does not exist merely as a moment in the world but exists by bringing oneself into being within, and through, one's chosen tradition (Aveni, 1998).

1.4. The Scientific Revolution and Conceptions of Time

Along with the contributions on time made by the early Greek philosophers starting in the 5th century B.C., and later philosophers (such as the 13th-century scholastics, and the 17th-, 18th-, and 19th-century French, English, Dutch, German, and Scottish philosophers), the scientific revolution in the natural and physical sciences in 17th-century Europe provided concepts, methods, and perspectives that helped to shape the development of the concept of time in psychology. This period serves as a transitional point from the early, prescientific, nonempirical, and nonexperimental approaches of the philosophers to the later, scientific, empirical, and experimental approaches of psychologists and other scientists toward time.

The revolt against scholasticism in philosophy culminated in the 17th century (Peters, 1965). The achievements of the physical scientists challenged the old ways of thought. The Aristotelian contemporaries of Galileo (1564–1642) refused to look through his telescope to test their theories about the moon and the planets. The development of astronomy, mechanics, and optics was accompanied by systematic substitutes for the old Aristotelian explanations. Francis Bacon (1561–1626) and Rene Descartes (1596–1650) expressed the new spirit of confidence in the ability of living men to discover the secrets of nature for themselves. They proclaimed that the way out of the "hallowed wasteland" of forms and species lay through the gateway of *method*. Although both Bacon and Descartes shared the view that method was the key to knowledge, they disagreed about the particular method to be used. Descartes — the rationalist — impressed by the success of the new physical sciences, saw in mathematics the key to knowledge. Bacon — the empiricist — on the other hand, distrusted the axiomatic approach and saw in careful observation of nature, the collection of data, and development of cautious generalizations the only correct ways of arriving at knowledge. The rise of the physical sciences in the 17th century and the dogmatic methodism that accompanied it exerted a great influence on the general development of psychology. Descartes' reflexology modeled on mechanics, Locke's inventory of the mind, and Hume's self-conscious attempt to model psychology on Newtonian physics are examples of such an influence. The later history of psychology is filled with attempts to apply recipes such as those of measurement, operational definitions and techniques, and pure laboratory data to psychological problems and issues.

A historiographical account of the 17th-century scientific revolution in Europe is provided by Cohen (1994) that includes many interpretive and sequential causes of that revolution (Note: For extensive discussions of the definition of "revolution" itself, as well as the concept of revolution as applied to science, *cf.*, Cohen, 1985, and Kuhn, 1962). In elaborating on the range of supposed causal agents regarding the 17th-century scientific revolution, Cohen cites a possible precipitating cause that is related to the scientific conception of time: the invention, development, and use of the *mechanical clock*. It is suggested that it was not so much in the instrument of the mechanical clock itself as it was in its widespread distribution all over Europe. As people became accustomed to more precision in their daily lives — via the clock — they also became aware that the passage of time could be subjected to mathematical treatment. Cohen also discusses the concept of *time* — in what might be called a "meta-temporal" nexus or context — when he raises the issue of the "completion" of science (i.e., the issue that science is open-ended and there is always room for new evidence in scientific inquiry). It may be asked, "Does science belong to the past, as a treasure of knowledge once possessed but since lost? Is it to be envisaged within the confines of our own lifetime? Or is it a matter of the future — a perhaps distant or even indefinite or never-to-be-attained future?" Cohen observes that one remarkable thing about the scientific revolution is that traces of all these three conceptions (past, present, and future) of the place of science in time can be detected in the pronouncements of 17th-century scientists. People's notions about their own position in time are notoriously difficult to reconstruct — these belong to the unspoken and shared beliefs of a period rather than presenting a topic of lively contemporaneous debate. Thus, it may be supposed, this is why no research study has ever appeared concerning the time frame in which 17th-century scientists placed their own occupations (Whitrow, 1972a, b, c, 1980, 1989).

In 1609, the German astronomer Johannes Kepler (1571–1630) published the results of the Danish astronomer Tycho Brahe's (1546–1601) calculations of the orbit of Mars, and which also contained the first two of what became known as "Kepler's laws of planetary motion." Early in the century, Kepler specifically rejected the old quasi-animistic magical conception of the universe and argued, rather, that it was similar to a clock (*cf.*, the analogy made by Nicole Oresme in the 14th century that likened the universe to a vast mechanical clock created and set moving by God so that all the wheels move as harmoniously as possible) and, later, the same analogy was made by the Anglo-Irish physicist and chemist Robert Boyle (1627–1691) and others. Thus, the invention of the mechanical clock — beginning with those developed in the 14th century — played a central role in the formulation of the mechanistic conception of nature that dominated natural philosophy from the time of Descartes to that of the English physicist and mathematician William Thomson Kelvin (1824–1907). It has been asserted that the invention of a satisfactory mechanical clock had an enormous influence on the concept of time itself (Whitrow (1972a): the oldest modes of timekeeping basically were discontinuous — they did not depend on a continuous succession of temporal units, but they merely involved the repetition of a concrete phenomenon occurring within a unit (e.g., the rising of the sun). Even the sundials, sand reckoners, and water clocks of antiquity tended to be more or less irregular in their operation. Not until the invention of a successful pendulum clock (by the 17th-century Dutch mathematician and physicist Christiaan Huygens, 1629–1695) were people provided with an accurate measure of time. This must have influenced tremendously the belief in the homogeneity and continuity of time.

The formal discipline of physics was born in the 17th century and historians place the key date for that birth either in 1638 with the publication of Galileo's greatest work, *Two New Sciences*, or in 1687 with the publication of Newton's greatest work, *Mathematical Principles of Natural Philosophy* (often simply called *Principia*). There is no argument, however, that before Galileo there was no such thing as true science, and that after Newton physics was fully established in its recognizable modern form — so all the cumulative achievements of modern science have been made in a little over 300 years.

The Italian astronomer, mathematician, and physicist Galileo Galilei conducted experiments concerning the laws of bodies in motion that yielded results so contradictory to the accepted teachings of Aristotle (i.e., a moving body eventually stops moving because of exhaustion) that strong antagonism was aroused. Eventually, in his experiments, Galileo found that the acceleration of falling bodies is proportional to time and independent of both weight and density. Moreover, Galileo found that the path of a projectile is a parabola and he is credited with conclusions foreshadowing Newton's laws of motion (Goudsmit & Claiborne, 1980; Gribbin, 1998). Galileo also constructed the first complete astronomical telescope with which he discovered that the moon has an uneven, mountainous surface and that the Milky Way is made up of numerous separate stars. In 1610, he discovered the four largest satellites of Jupiter — the first satellites of a planet other than Earth to be observed. Galileo's studies confirmed his acceptance of the Copernican theory of the solar system (i.e., the first modern European theory of planetary motion that was "heliocentric" — placing the sun motionless at the center of the solar system with all the planets, including Earth, revolving around the sun).

1.4.1. Newton and Time

The English mathematician, natural philosopher, and physicist Isaac Newton (1642–1727) is considered by many to be the greatest scientist who ever lived. Newton's most important discoveries remarkably were made during a 2-year period from 1664 to 1666 (an outbreak of the plague forced Newton away from his studies at Cambridge University) with his accounts of universal gravitation — basically a law of the inverse square (the force of gravity declines inversely as the square of distance), with his accounts of the visible spectrum and the nature of color, and with his invention of integral and differential calculus (Note: An interesting case study in the history of science is that, at one point, Newton had a dispute with the philosopher Leibniz over which of them had first invented calculus [Dampier, 1948; Gribbin, 1998; Harre, 1994]). Newton's *Principia* in 1687 showed how his principle of gravitation explained both falling bodies on Earth and of the motions of planets, comets, and other bodies in the heavens. The first part of *Principia* is devoted to dynamics and includes Newton's famous three laws of motion. The second part of *Principia* is on fluid motion; and the third part is on the system of the world, i.e., the unification of terrestrial and celestial mechanics under the principle of gravitation and the explanation of Kepler's laws of planetary motion. Although Newton used the calculus to discover his results, he explained them in the *Principia* by using the older geometric methods.

The implications of Galileo's mathematical physics were indicated by Newton's teacher, Isaac Barrow (1630–1677). Barrow maintained that space and time are absolute, infinite, and eternal because God is omnipresent and everlasting; space extends without limit continuously, and time flows forever evenly and independently of sensible events. This was the first clear formulation of the ideas of absolute time and space as held by Newton. Time and space were represented by Barrow as being independent of human perception and knowledge, existing in their own right, except in their relation to God. Thus, underlying Newton's discoveries in dynamics and astronomy are the conceptions of absolute time and space (Dampier, 1948; Whitrow, 1972a).

Newton distinguished between "relative" space and time (as measured by our senses in terms of natural bodies and motions) on one hand and "absolute" space (which exists immovably) and time (which flows equally without regard to anything external) on the other hand. The notion of "flow" at this juncture invokes the concept of time as a necessary component for Newton's system (see Chapter 13). However, this definition of time involves an element of circularity, though it served Newton well enough. In general, however, time and space to Newton were — by the Will of God — existent in and by themselves, and independent of the mind which apprehends them and of the objects with which they are occupied.

Cohen (1971) observes that Newton's treatment of time had a theological rather than a truly scientific content — as seems evident from the *General Scholium* that Newton added to the second edition of his *Principia*, in which he somewhat equates time with deity: "God endures forever and is everywhere present. He constitutes duration and space…since every particle of space is always, and every indivisible moment of duration is everywhere, certainly the Maker and Lord of all Things cannot be never and nowhere" (Benjamin, 1966). Cohen infers from Newton's words that he did not recognize any time as worthy of scientific study, or as having any "reality" other than his "absolute" time. The recognition that an inherently subjective (nonabsolute) time is worthy of the attention of philosophers is a notion that derives from John Locke. Moreover, although Newton's time was too absolute for Locke, it was not absolute enough to satisfy Leibniz. In 1715, Leibniz wrote that, "According to Newton, God has to wind up His watch from time to time, otherwise it would cease to go; He lacked sufficient foresight to make it a perpetual motion" (Dampier, 1948; Morris, 1934).

By the end of the 17th century, one arrives at the idea of time that dominated physical science until the advent of Einstein's special theory of relativity (Einstein, 1952). This idea can be summarized in the symbol t that denotes the continuous independent variable of classical dynamics. Although the influence of the 17th-century scientific revolution on the change in people's attitudes toward time — by directing attention away from the past with its orientation on cyclic processes and assumptions, to the future with its prospect of linear advancement — may not have been treated with the attention to detail that its importance demanded, the enlightened leaders of thought in the 18th century, and later, finally abandoned the older biblical chronology that largely excluded the possibility of slow processes of transformations over immense periods of time (Whitrow, 1972a).

1.5. Terminology in Psychological Time Research

Some historians of scientific psychology (Boring, 1957, pp. 275–283) maintain that the German physiologist, physicist, psychophysicist, and philosopher Gustav Theodor Fechner (1801–1887) was the key figure in the formal beginning and foundation of experimental psychology with the publication of his book *Elemente der Psychophysik* in 1860. Others consider the founding of the Leipzig psychological laboratory in 1879 by the German physiologist, philosopher, and psychologist Wilhelm Max Wundt (1832–1920) to be the most significant event in the founding of psychology as an independent science (Schultz, 1981, pp. 56–57). Either way — 1860 or 1879 — scientific experimental research in psychology was clearly underway by the 1880s. At about this same time, the German physiologist and psychologist Hermann von Helmholtz (1821–1894) proposed a modification of Fechner's earlier fundamental formula and analysis of the psychophysical ("mind–body") relationship. Also, at this time, the Austrian physicist and philosopher Ernst Mach (1838–1916) in 1860 began experiments in the area of human *time sense* to test "Weber's law," a law of discrimination elaborated by the German physiologist and psychophysicist Ernst Weber (1795–1878) (see Chapters 2, 3, and others). Further, the German physiologist Karl von Vierordt (1818–1884) — also a pioneer in early scientific psychology — undertook studies of the *time sense* in humans in the light of Fechner's *Elemente der Psychophysik* (Vierordt, 1868, see Chapters 3 and 4).

1.5.1. Time Sense

The term *time sense* — used in the first and original psychological research studies of the concept of time — is a loose term denoting the apprehension of duration, change, order of occurrence, and the temporal aspect of attributes of experience. The term *time sense* (in German, *Zeitsinn*, and in French, *sens du temps*) has been applied generally to "capacity" of apprehending, whereas the term *time perception* refers to specific occurrences of apprehending. In the early research studies of *time sense* it was customary to employ a "time-sense apparatus" — an instrument for determining the accuracy of time estimation — that consisted of a uniformly rotating metal arm, which during rotation came into contact with two (or more) sets of terminals or contacts, producing similar sounds, or other forms of stimulation, separated by a time interval that depended on the rate of rotation and the distance between the contacts (Figure 1.1). In some forms of the time-sense apparatus, a swinging pendulum was used to make the contacts. The best-known apparatus of this kind is the "Leipzig time wheel" (Drever, 1973; Dunlap, 1907; Warren, 1934).

Harriman (1966) equates the term *time sense* with time perception and defines it as proficiency in judging the extent of periods of time or in fractionating temporal intervals (the score being corrected for guessing). Drever (1973) defines *time sense* as one's direct experience of the lapse of time, based on the very definite impression one has of a time interval within the *sensory* or *specious present*. He also defines the term *present* as a period or space of time — psychologically, not a point of time — extending under favorable conditions to about 4 seconds, and characterized by the fact that two experiences (e.g., two taps) with this interval between them seem to give a single, temporarily unitary impression: sometimes spoken of as *specious* or *sensory present* (James, 1890, Vol. 1, p. 609). The definition of *time*, according to Drever (1973), refers to a fundamental directional aspect of experience, based on direct experience of the protensity (duration) of sensation, and on experience of change from one sensory event, or train of thought to another, and distinguishing in experience beginning, middle, and end as well as past, present, and future.

The French experimental psychologist Paul Fraisse (1911–1996) maintained that we have no specific *time sense*; that is, we have no direct experience of time as such but only of particular *sequences* and *rhythms* (Ross, 1914). Thus, it is not time itself, said Fraisse, but what goes on in time that produces temporal effects (Fraisse, 1952, 1963, 1984, 1994).

1.5.2. Time Perception

In 1890, the American philosopher and psychologist William James (1842–1910) devoted an entire chapter of his celebrated book, *The Principles of Psychology*, to the topic of *time perception*. In fact, James devoted *two* chapters to the concept of time: Chapter 15 ("The Perception of Time") and Chapter 16 ("Memory") — where he notes: "for a state of mind to survive in memory it must have endured for a certain length of time" (p. 643). The notion of *time perception*, according to James (1890, Vol. 1, p. 605), is sometimes called "internal perception" and deals with "events that occupy a date therein, especially when the date is a past one — in which case the perception in question goes by the name of *memory*" (English & English, 1958, who define *time perception* as the apprehension of the length of time occupied by a psychological process, or rate of change, of placement in time, of order of

(a)

(b)

Figure 1.1: Two psychological laboratory devices used in early time perception research. (a) Wundtian time-wheel (Meumann, 1894); (b) time-sense apparatus (c. 1903) — photo courtesy of the Archives of the History of American Psychology. The University of Akron, Akron, OH.

occurrence; and Friedman, 1992, who distinguishes between *time memory* and *time perception*). For further discussions of *time* and *memory*, see Albert (1978), Block (1978, 1985, 1986), James (1890), Michon (1975), and Whitrow (1980), as well as Chapters 11 and 12. Also, see Gilliland, Hofeld, and Eckstrand (1946) who use the two terms perception of time/*time perception* and estimation of time/*time estimation* interchangeably, but state that *time estimation* implies a kind of quantification that is not necessarily included in *time perception* (Bindra & Waksberg, 1956).

For Warren (1934), *time perception* is the apprehension of the amount of duration, rate of change, placement in time, order of occurrence, beginning and end, etc., of experiences (Gibbon & Allan, 1984; Nichols, 1894; Stout, 1900). In music, *time perception* is the apprehension of rhythm in a melody. He also distinguishes the term *time perception* from *perception time*; the latter defined as the time that elapses from the presentation of an object to its recognition by the observer less (a) the time spent in overcoming inertia of the receptor and (b) the time of transmission of the nerve impulse from receptor to brain centers (this definition constitutes, also, the essential definition of the term *physiological time* for Warren).

In another case (Wolman, 1973), *time perception* is defined as the attention to, or apprehension of, change through the integration of a series of stimuli and characterized by the ability to conceive of duration, simultaneity, and succession. In this account, the perception of time may be broken down into various categories: conditioning to time which includes the *temporal orientation* of organisms; the periodicity of their behavior in terms of the circadian, or day–night, 24-hour cycle; the perception of the passage of time and duration; the ability to estimate various segments of time (10 seconds, 10 minutes, etc.); control over time that is characterized by an active orientation of the self in time, in the present, the past, and the future; and the experience of time, which includes the differences between "psychological" time and "clock" time and how the individual views and experiences time — its passage, its role in one's life, and what it is.

1.5.3. Present and Moment

The term *psychological moment* is defined by Reber (1995) as a very short period of time within which successive stimuli are integrated and perceived as a whole — a kind of discrete quantum of psychological time; and *specious present* as the psychological sense of the present, of "nowness." The concept of a true *present* in the measurement of time has about the same status as the concept in geometry of a *point* on a line or in space: it exists as a locus relative to other loci. Approached from an introspective basis, it may be said that such a definition does not seem very satisfying nor does it feel correct intuitively. Such a "time-less moment," as it has been called, seems to have temporal duration — brief yet palpable.

The origins of the terms *psychological present* and *specious present* are provided by Whitrow (1980). In 1882, E. R. Clay anonymously wrote in his work, *The Alternative: A Study in Psychology*, that the relation of experience to time has not been profoundly studied; its objects are given as being of the present, but the part of time referred to by the datum is a very different thing from the coterminus of the past and future that philosophy denotes by the name "present." Clay called the finite segment of time that constitutes our immediate experience the *specious present*. James (1890) adopted Clay's term *specious present* on the basis that the "true present" must be durationless, a moment of time sharply dividing past from future and clearly distinct from both. Whitrow notes that the term *specious present* is itself somewhat specious, and it would be preferable to use, instead, a more neutral term such as *psychological present* (Note: It is interesting to observe that in an earlier edition of his work, Whitrow, 1961, p. 78, chose a different "more neutral term," called *mental present*). The term *specious present* as used by psychologists is unfortunately somewhat ambiguous. In its widest sense, it signifies a duration of temporal experience compatible with a certain perspective unification. In a more restricted sense, it may be confined to an interval of time during which events are not recognized as being earlier or later but are confused in an apparent simultaneity.

1.5.4. Time Perspective

The term *psychological time* is viewed by English and English (1958) as time subjectively estimated, i.e., without the aid of clocks and without direct guidance by such external factors as the position of the sun. It includes both the direct awareness of *duration* (considered by some to be an elementary attribute of a sensory process) and *judgment* of time based on the number (to some extent, the kind) of experiences that have intervened (Edgell, 1903). English and English also define *time* (or *temporal*) *perspective* as the improved perspective that comes when events are viewed from a certain distance in time. Earlier, Warren (1934) defined *temporal perspective* as the memory for the relative distance in time of various past experiences from the present moment, and *psychological time* as the subjective impression of the temporal duration of an experience or of the duration elapsing between experiences.

The area of study called *time perspective* attempts to understand how and why people turn their thoughts beyond the present moment. The process of *time perception* may be distinguished from the process of *time perspective* (Kastenbaum, 1994). The hands or numbers on a clock move at a steady rate, but humans' sense of time passage is variable. One's "subjective clock" may be slower or faster than objective time and is influenced, also, by the existing stimulus situation. *Time perception* studies have been conducted for many years (Nichols, 1890, who observed that psychologists often attempt to discover a "time sense" that is comparable or analogous to other sensory modalities), but more than a century of research passed without revealing a clear and definitive sensory system that yields "subjective time." More than likely, according to Kastenbaum, sensing time's passage is not a single, independent function but derives from multiple feedbacks as one responds to both the internal and external environments. Also, the way humans organize and interpret their experiences helps to shape their "perspective" of time. Moreover, the relatively newer term, *time perspective*, may be defined more broadly as the *totality* of a person's views of his or her psychological future and psychological past existing at a given time (Frank, 1939; Israeli, 1936). Thus, the concept of *time perspective* refers to a personal way of viewing the world, is expressed in one's interpretations of the past, present, and future, and is a reflection of one's distinctive position in society and one's distinctive developmental history. Typically, as people grow older, their *time perspective* becomes broader and more complex due to their unique experiences (*cf.*, a similar term, *temporal horizon*, in Fraisse, 1963; and *time horizons* in Krebs & Kacelnik, 1984). The concept of *time perspective* includes several dimensions: protension (the length of time in which thought is projected ahead), retrotension (the length of time in which thought is projected back into the past), density (the number of events thought about in past or future), coherence (the degree of organization within one's past-present-future matrix), and directionality (the sense of perceived rate of movement toward the future). Such dimensions have been summarized, also, by Doob (1971), Kastenbaum (1964, 1994), and Wallace and Rabin (1960). Further generalizations concerning *time perspective* include the following: people tend to project further into the future as they move from childhood into adulthood; the stereotype that older people "live in the past" seems to be refuted; time perspectives tend to shrink when the economy is bleak and jobs are hard to find; and time perspectives seem to become more alert and effective when individuals have a sense of control or efficacy in their lives (Seligman, 1975).

Cohen (1971) argues that the phrase "experience of time" is ill defined (Loewald, 1972). It not only means the capacity for estimating the duration of intervals of clock and calendar time, but also refers to the ontogenesis of our ideas of past, present, and future. Beyond quantifiable judgments of time, it refers also to temporal qualities such as the "pastness" and "since-ness" of an event, to temporally toned affective or cognitive processes (such as hope and nostalgia, expectation, anticipation, intention, recollection, and memory), and to the feeling of the inevitability of aging and death. Cohen maintains that *subjective* or *psychological* time is not a distinctive mental entity, rather it is an ensemble or congeries of phenomena.

Early research on psychological time indicated that humans' *sense of duration* depends on the number of stimuli that are perceived and stored in one's mind: if an interval has many divisions (marked off visually or aurally), it tends to appear longer than an equal interval (objective clock time) that has fewer. On the contrary, when for some reason, there is a reduction in the amount of external information registered by the brain, duration appears to be short. Another factor that affects one's general sense of *temporal duration* is age — as one gets older, time appears to pass more rapidly. The reason for such an apparent speeding up of time is that an individual's processes tend to slow down as she or he grows older so that, compared with such processes, clock and calendar time appears to go even faster.

In attempting to understand the psychological nature of human temporal experience and to consider how concepts of time arise in personal and social development, the terms *temporal orientation* (or *time orientation*) and *time perspective* have appeared relatively recently in the psychological literature on time. Wallace and Rabin (1960) refer to the interchangeable nature and usage of the terms *time perspective* and *time orientation*, both of which differ from *time perception*. *Time perspective* and *time orientation* involve molar approaches (the "units" are usually days, weeks, month, or years) to the problem of temporal behavior, whereas *time perception* deals with relatively brief periods of time (the "units" are usually seconds and minutes). Wallace and Rabin also identify a "new look" in the area of time research that is characterized by an emphasis on the relationships between *temporal experience* and other *personality* correlates both normal and abnormal.

1.6. Scientific Studies of Reaction Time, Rhythm, and Psychological Time (1860–1910)

1.6.1. Reaction Time

A specialized experimental context in both early and modern time research in psychology is the *reaction time* (RT) paradigm. RT is defined as the minimum time between the presentation of a stimulus and the participant's response to it. RT is one of experimental psychology's oldest "dependent variables" and several types have been studied (Drever, 1973; Harriman, 1966; Reber, 1995; Swindle, 1917; Warren, 1934; Wolman, 1973). Historical accounts of the RT experiment are provided by Woodworth and Schlosberg (1965), Woodworth (1938), Boring (1957), and Bergstrom (1900). Additional material on RT may be found in Roeckelein (2000).

1.6.2. Rhythm

Another somewhat specialized term, *rhythm*, also made its appearance early — much like RT — in the experimental psychology literature. The early Greek philosopher Plato defined *rhythm* as "order in movement" and the contemporary French experimental psychologist Paul Fraisse (1994) varied this definition as "order in succession." The psychological theory of rhythm had its beginnings in the work of the German philosopher and educator Johann Friedrich Herbart (1776–1841) who initiated the treatment of rhythm in 1850–1852 as a type of *time perception* and suggested an explanation of its emotional effects. Along with Herbart — who pointed out the effect of a whole rhythmic series in giving rise to an emotion of expectation, haste, or delay — the German physiologist and psychologist Rudolph Hermann Lotze (1817–1881), in 1868, applied the principle to groupings in the rhythm and related the emotional effect of rhythm to alternate feelings of strain, expectation, and satisfaction produced by every repetition of each of the unit groupings. In 1868, Vierordt (see above) conducted the first experimental research on rhythm, determining the period of greatest regularity in the tapping of rhythms (Vierordt, 1868). However, the first significant experiments were carried out by the German physiologist Ernst Wilhelm Brucke (1819–1892) in 1871. By tapping out rhythms on a kymograph — an early psychological laboratory device that made a graphic recording of events by using a moving pen or marker that reacted to pressure applied to it to create a trace on paper wrapped around a slowly revolving drum — Brucke determined the "time equality" of the feet in scanned verse and noted a number of facts concerning the time relations of the different unit groupings. In 1865, Ernst Mach added further observations on the subjective accentuation of an objectively uniform series and, in particular, noted that the entire process is involuntary (Mach, 1865). Mach essentially laid the foundation for later theories of rhythm. His most important contribution was his emphasis on the predominantly motor nature — via his motor theory — of the phenomenon of rhythm.

Although many later theories of rhythm were based on the work of Wilhelm Wundt, his studies on rhythmic series were only incidental to the more focal problems of "span of consciousness" and "synthetic activity of consciousness." Thus, rhythm was considered to be only a special temporal form of such "psychic syntheses" (Wundt, 1873–1874). Wundt and his colleagues identified three different elements — causing a synthesis — in a sound series: qualitative changes, intensive changes, and melodic changes — where intensive changes were viewed as the most important of the elements and constituted the "synthetic power of the rhythm." Also, in early research on rhythm, Thaddeus Bolton at Clark University in 1894 established the essential facts of subjective accentuation and apparent temporal displacement. Bolton laid great emphasis on the motor aspect and "motor accompaniment" of rhythm (*cf.*, Wundt's approach that had little place for the motor factor but, rather, emphasized the "mental activity" aspect of rhythm), but he did not completely cut loose from the Wundtian "apperceptive process" as the primary theoretical factor (Meumann, 1894, 1907–1908, who opposed vigorously the motor emphases of Mach and Bolton, and defended Wundt's theory by insisting that the "mental activity" is always primary and without it there could be no "rhythmization").

Sears (1902) provides a resume of the early research literature on rhythm, citing the experimental contributions of Meumann (1894), Ebhardt (1898), Vierordt (1868), and Shaw and Wrinch (1898–1900). He cites the following results and generalizations, among others, from these studies: musical rhythms contain elements in addition to those found in simple rhythms and are, therefore, more complex; in music, rhythm does not hold the primary place but a coordinate place with other distinctively musical factors; pitch of tones has no effect on the relative length of intervals — for simple intervals without accent the greatest exactness of execution is between 0.4 and 0.7 seconds; accent — increasing the irregularity of the time relations in the group — is the source of a constant error; and in the rendering of a piece of music, musicians probably do not produce the tones in the exact ratio denoted by the written notes (Brown, 1911; MacDougall, 1902, 1903).

Bolton (1894) maintained that rhythm is a universal phenomenon in nature and in involuntary physiological activity (such as the pulse, heartbeat, and respiration), as well as in voluntary speech. He identified cosmic rhythms — the regular alternation of light and darkness due to the rotation of the earth on its axis — as the most fundamental of the natural phenomena that also was the cause of many other rhythms (e.g., "tropisms;" and recurrent periods of sleep waking, growth, and gestation) in plant and animal life. Bolton also discussed the relationship between rhythm and attention/periodicity, speech, time relations and intervals, sound intensity, sound quality, the emotional effects upon savages and children, and its influence in aesthetic forms such as prose, verse, poetry, and music (MacDougall, 1900; Ruckmich, 1913a, b; Stetson, 1903; Swindle, 1913).

More recently, Fraisse (1994) examined rhythm and temporal experience, particularly *temporal order*, in the three areas of cosmology, biology, and perception. Cosmic rhythms include experiences independent in time such as seasonal rhythms, lunar rhythms (which affect tides), and solar rhythms (especially the rhythm of day and night). Biological rhythms include animal, vegetable, and human rhythms; almost all the bodily functions are rhythmical — rhythms of the heart, the brain, respiration, urinary secretions, hormone production, body temperature, and the waking–sleeping cycle. Fraisse's third category of rhythms — perceptual rhythms — provides a basis for answering two essential research questions concerning the concept of time: What are the temporal limits in which succession is perceived? And what is the nature of structures that lend themselves to repetition?

1.6.3. Psychological Time

In America — at the end of the 19th century — the philosopher/psychologist William James was one of the most prominent writers who ushered in the era of the *empirical* analysis and research of the concept of time in psychological terms (Benussi, 1908, 1909; Hall & Jastrow, 1886; McDougall, 1904; Meumann, 1892/1893/1894; Munsterberg, 1889; Schumann, 1893; Squire, 1901; Stevens, 1902; Stevens, 1886; Titchener, 1905; Woodrow, 1909, 1930, 1951; Wundt, 1882, 1897; Yerkes & Urban, 1906). In this respect, James may be viewed as an exemplar or a bridge between the older, rational philosophical tradition and the newer American scientific, empirical approaches to researching phenomena in psychology, including that of timing and time perception.

Even though James essentially published only one article on psychological time, modern psychologists most frequently cite James's discussion on three issues (Block, 1990, 1994a, b, c): (1) the "sensible present" or "specious present" (James, 1890, Vol. 1, pp. 608, 609, 631, 641; Akeley, 1925; Natsoulas, 1992–93); (2) the transition from simultaneity to successiveness (James, 1890, Vol. 1, pp. 628, 636, 637); and (3) the differences between experiences of time passing and time in retrospect (James, 1890, Vol. 1, pp. 624–25). In his celebrated work, *The Principles of Psychology*, James (1890) seems to assume the role of *philosopher* when he speculates on temporal material that has little or no supporting evidence, whereas he seems to assume the role of *psychologist* when he reviews the research on time that was current and available in his day. The following few paragraphs contain descriptions provided by James (1890) of various research studies on time that were conducted in psychology in the late 19th century (Boring, 1942, Chapter 15).

Wundt (1873–1874) studied consciousness and the succession of ideas, but James stated that Wundt's account of consciousness and time was merely an attempt to analyze the "deliverance" of a time perception with no explanation of the manner in which it comes about (Strong, 1896). Wundt and his pupil Dietze (1885) tried to determine experimentally the maximal extent of one's immediate distinct consciousness for successive impressions (Wundt found that 12 impressions could be distinguished clearly as a united cluster, provided they were caught in a certain rhythm by the mind, and succeeded each other at intervals not smaller than 0.3 or longer than 0.5 of a second). Dietze gives from 0.18 to 0.3 seconds apart as the most favorable intervals for apprehension (leading to 12 seconds as the maximum filled duration of which one can be both distinctly and immediately aware). Volkmar Estel (1884) and Max Mehner (1884), also working in Wundt's lab, found the maximum unfilled, or "vacant duration," to lie within the same objective range (as determined by Wundt and Dietze) from 5 or 6 to 12 seconds, and perhaps more (Note: These empirically determined figures may be taken roughly to stand for what E. R. Clay and James called the *specious present*; James, 1890, p. 613, states that the *specious present* has a "vaguely vanishing backward and forward fringe, but its nucleus is probably the dozen seconds or less that have just elapsed").

Sigmund Exner (1873) studied the minimum amount of duration that may distinctly be sensed; on auditory trials, he distinctly heard the "doubleness" of two successive clicks of a "Savart's wheel" (a device used to investigate tonal pitch in relation to vibration frequency), and of two successive snaps of an electric spark when their interval was made as small as 1/500 of a second (0.002 second). Exner remarked that our ears and brain must be wonderfully efficient organs to get distinct feelings from so slight an objective difference. Using the eye and the sense of sight, however, perception was less delicate: two sparks made to fall beside each other in rapid succession on the center of the retina ceased to be recognized as successive by intervals below 0.04 of a second.

James indicated that multitudinous impressions may be felt as discontinuous, though separated by excessively minute intervals of time, and cites data given by Helmholtz (1863) who observed that on the retina 20–30 impressions a second at the very utmost can be sensed as discrete when they fall on the same spot. However, the ear — which begins to fuse stimuli together into a musical tone when they follow at the rate of a little over 30 a second — can still sense 132 of them a second as discontinuous when they take the shape of "beats."

James also cites data from Exner (1873) concerning cross-modality stimulation and the smallest perceptible interval under conditions where the first impression falls on one sense and the second on another (in such cases the perception of the intervening time tends to be less certain and delicate, and depends upon which impression comes first): from sight to touch (0.071 second), from touch to sight (0.053 second), from sight to hearing (0.16 second), from hearing to sight (0.06 second), and from one ear to the other (0.064 second). James provides other data from Exner (with footnoted qualifications) regarding the perception of a time interval as shorter or longer than another interval.

James (1890, Vol. 1, p. 616) notes that the minimum *absolute* difference perceived in such interval-comparison conditions could be about 0.355 of a second, and such a minimum absolute difference increases as the times compared grow long. James states that very interesting *oscillations* in the accuracy of judgment, and in the direction of the error, have been noticed by all who have experimented with the issue of the minimum absolute difference that is perceivable. James describes Karl Vierordt's (1868) concept of an "indifference point" (i.e., an interval that is judged with maximum accuracy — a time or "neutral" value that is estimated as neither longer nor shorter than it really is, and away from which errors in both directions increase their size) and provides average indifference points (using the ear) for various observers: Wundt (0.72 second), Kollert (0.75 second), Estel (0.75 second), Mehner (0.71 second), Stevens (0.71 second), Mach (0.35 second), and Buccola (0.40 second). James observes that such data show in so many men about 3/4 of a second as the interval of time most easy to catch and reproduce; he also suggests that one's sense of time — like other senses — seems subject to the *law of contrast* (e.g., an interval sounds shorter if a long one immediately precedes it, and longer if a short one immediately precedes it) (see Chapter 3).

Various other results, data, conclusions, and observations are provided by James (1890) in his discussion of time perception and these, also, reveal the nature and type of problems or issues that typified the study of time in the psychological laboratory during the period 1860–1910. Among James's (1890, Vol. 1, pp. 618–631) findings and conclusions are the following: (1) like other senses, our sense of time is sharpened by practice; (2) tracts of time filled (with clicks of sound) seem longer than vacant ones of the same duration — when the latter does not exceed a second or two; this becomes reversed when longer times are taken; in accordance with this law, a *loud* sound, limiting a short interval of time, makes it appear longer, a *slight* sound shorter (James cautions that in comparing intervals marked out by sounds, one must be careful to keep the sounds uniform); (3) there is an emotional *feeling* accompanying the intervals-of-time experience, as is well known in music; the sense of haste goes with one measure of rapidity, that of delay with another, and these two feelings harmonize with different mental moods; (4) awareness of *change* is the condition on which our perception of time's flow depends, but there exists no reason to suppose that empty time's own changes are sufficient for the awareness of change to be aroused; the change must be of some concrete sort, an outward or inward sensible series or a process of attention or volition; (5) in the experience of watching empty time flow, we tell it off in pulses; we say "now! now! now!" or we count "more! more! more!" as we feel it bud; this composition out of units of duration is called the "law of time's discrete flow;" the discreteness is, however, merely due to the fact that our successive acts of recognition or apperception of what it is are discrete; the sensation is as continuous as any sensation can be; all continuous sensations are *named* in beats; (6) in general, a time filled with varied and interesting experiences seems shorter in passing but longer as we look back; on the other hand, a tract of time empty of experiences seems longer in passing but in retrospect shorter; (7) the same space of time seems shorter as we grow older — that is, the days, the months, and the years do so; whether the hours do so is doubtful, and the minutes and seconds to all appearance remain about the same; (8) a succession of feelings — in and of itself — is not a feeling of succession; and since — to our successive feelings — a feeling of their own succession is added, and that must be treated as an additional fact requiring its own special elucidation; (9) memory gets strewn with *dated* things — dated in the sense of being before or after each other; the date of a thing is a mere relation of *before* or *after* the present thing or some past or future thing; (10) the original paragon and prototype of all conceived times is the *specious present* (varying in length from a few seconds to probably not more than a minute), the short duration of which we are immediately and incessantly sensible (Stanley, 1900, pp. 286–287, for a dissenting viewpoint); and (11) through Wundt (1873–1874), one may examine a "law of discontinuous succession in time" of percepts to which one cannot easily attend at once and where each percept requires a separate brain process.

James (1890, Vol. 1, pp. 635–637) suggests that there is at every moment a cumulation of brain processes overlapping each other, of which the fainter ones are the dying phases of processes which but shortly previous were active in a maximal degree: "The *amount of the overlapping* determines the feeling of the *duration occupied*; what events shall appear to occupy the duration depends on just *what processes* the overlapping processes are; duration and events together form our intuition of the *specious present* with its content; why such an intuition should result from such a combination of brain-processes I do not pretend to say; all I aim at is to state the most elemental form of the psycho-physical conjunction."

1.7. Premodern Scientific Research on Psychological Time (1911–1949)

Among the many methods that psychologists use for data collection and analysis in their research endeavors is the *experimental* method — a highly desirable approach because it takes place in a well-defined and controlled environment arranged to yield concrete, reliable, valid, and measurable responses from participants. The "ideal experiment" is one involving the procedure of "varied conditions" in which all the factors except for the one or more variables systematically manipulated by the experimenter — called the independent variables (IVs) — are held constant, while the participants' reactions — called the dependent variables (DVs) — are observed, measured, and/or transcribed. The desideratum of the experimental method is to determine the "functional relationships" that exist between IVs and DVs in order to derive cause–effect statements (between IVs and DVs) for the purpose of achieving maximum predictability of future events and variables that may occur under conditions similar to those initially studied (Note: Judging by the absence of usage of the compound terms IV and DV in pre-1911 authoritative sources, the concepts of IV and DV have appeared only relatively recently in the psychological literature).

Historically, in the case of research on the issues of timing and time perception in psychology, the notion or variable of time may be treated as either an IV or a DV, depending on the particular hypotheses and research goals of a given study. For example — in the context of psychological time research — the DV (or response) of "time estimation expressed in seconds" may be measured as a function of the IV (or stimulus) of "the delay between two intervals to be discriminated." As experimental psychology developed, the design and control of its experiments and variables became more rigorous and elaborate. Boring (1954) asserts that formal design first developed in the late 1800s in the area of psychophysics under Gustav Fechner, then progressed in the RT experiments of Wilhelm Wundt, and then developed further in the memory experiments of Hermann von Ebbinghaus (Boring, 1921). More recently, experimental psychologists — especially those under the influence of the British statistician and geneticist Sir R. A. Fisher (1890–1962) — have become more concerned with experimental design, as well as with control and precise measurement of the IVs and DVs employed in their research studies (Fisher, 1935).

Moreover, for present purposes, the IV–DV distinction may be viewed as a formal and convenient approach to use in the categorization, classification, and condensation of research on timing and time perception in psychology (Zelkind & Sprug, 1974). Consistent with this fiat and approach, the following time studies were conducted in psychology during the period 1911–1949, and employed the two categories of IV and DV, thus indicating the nature and characteristics of the temporal variables under study.

The DV of *time–order error* (or "time–order effect," TOE) was investigated by Stott (1935), Woodrow (1935), and Woodrow and Stott (1936). TOE is likely to occur when one stimulus follows another in time — the second being compared with the first. TOE is a tendency to overestimate the second stimulus in relation to the first (Urban, 1907; Woodworth, 1938, pp. 439–449; Woodworth & Schlosberg, 1965, pp. 225–229).

Axel (1924) and Roeckelein (2000) provide references and sources for other studies that involve the DVs of temporal/time discrimination, brightness and pitch discrimination, time estimation, time perspective, time perception, duration estimation, temporal judgment, psychological time, temporal experience, time orientation, time concept, temporal indifference interval, time acceleration, temporal patterns, time comprehension, time sense, and time distortion.

In regard to the stimulus ("antecedent") side of the psychological experiments on time during the period 1911–1949, Table 1.1 shows various types of IVs (stimulus measures manipulated by the experimenter) used in early time research (studies are given in chronological order within each IV category).

In regard to the discussions of *theory* in the area of timing and time perception before 1950, Baldwin (1901–1905, pp. 704–705) describes various *general types of theories* of the apprehension, cognition, or awareness of time (Note: For a turn-of-the-20th-century *specific theory* of time perception, see Montague, 1904, and a review of this theory by Dunlap, 1904; Dunlap notes that Montague's theory — although it depends on a rather artificial view of consciousness — marks a new stage in the analysis of time by its conception of time as change, of the specious present as the relation of old content to new, and of recognition as the resultant of a twofold specious present). Baldwin indicates the following categories: (1) intuitive and *a priori* theories — hold that in some form time (whether duration or succession) is a part of the person's "mental furniture" (i.e., a moment or temporal character is contributed by the mind to the structure of its experience as such); this class of theories is called "nativistic" and may be "nativism of product" (e.g., the theory of innate ideas or *a priori* mental forms such as Kant's theory), "nativism of process" (also called "genetic nativism," a class of views asserting that the awareness of time distinctions

Table 1.1: Types of independent variable used in studies on timing and time perception in psychology during the period 1911–1949.

Type of independent variable	Representative research studies
Boundary stimuli	Woodrow (1928)
Filled vs. empty interval	Spencer (1921), Swift and McGeoch (1925), Triplett (1931), Weber (1933), Gilliland, Hofeld, and Eckstrand (1946), Roelofs and Zeeman (1949a, 1949b)
Hypnosis and dreams	Richardson and Stalnaker (1930), Dooley (1941), Cooper (1948), Gross (1949)
Individual differences	Stewart (1926), Gulliksen (1927), Weber (1933), Woodrow (1933, 1934), Bromberg (1938), Gilliland and Martin (1940), Gilliland and Humphreys (1943), Nitardy (1943), Ames (1946), Bradley (1948)
Interpolated stimuli	Spencer (1921), Philip (1947)
Isolation, monotony, and satiation	MacLeod and Roff (1935), Burton (1943), Berman (1939), Farber (1944)
Kinesthetic force fields	Weber (1927)
Memory–error	Dallenbach (1913), Strong (1913)
Motivation, goals, and needs	Rosenzweig and Koht (1933), Harton (1939b), Filer and Meals (1949)
Physiological factors	Lyon and Eno (1912/1914), Brush (1930), Carrel (1931), Hoagland (1933, 1934, 1943), Gardner (1935), Schaeffer and Gilliland (1938)
Pitch, sound intensity, and interstimulus interval	Woodrow (1911), Anderson (1914), Lifshitz (1933), Needham (1935), Vince (1948)
Practice and task difficulty	Woodrow (1935), Woodrow and Stott (1936), Harton (1938, 1939a, 1942)
Psychodynamic factors	Bergler and Roheim (1946), Schneider (1948), Scott (1948)
Retardation and pathology	A. Lewis (1931-1932), Davidson (1941), Brower and Brower (1947), Straus (1947), Clausen (1949), Gothberg (1949)
Rhythmical intervals	Wallin (1911, 1912), Adams (1915), Woodrow (1918)
Sensory modalities	Gridley (1932), Goodfellow (1934), Gault and Goodfellow (1938), Henry (1948)
Social role factors	Hulett (1944)
Spatial factors	Guilford (1926), Abbe (1936), Sturt (1923, 1925)
Stimulus duration	Brewer (1911), Curtis (1916), Stott (1935), Graham and Cook (1937), Graham and Kemp (1938), Harton (1939c), Kowalski (1943), Turnbull (1944), Stein (1949)

Table 1.1: (*Continued*)

Type of independent variable	Representative research studies
Stimulus features and feedback	Ford (1937)
Temporal order and anchors	Philip (1944), Postman (1944), Mowrer and Ullman (1945), Postman and Miller (1945), Hammer (1949)
Time relationships	Henmon (1911), Dunlap (1915), Moore (1915), Tolman (1917), Carr (1919), Carr and Freeman (1919)

arises by some form of function or reaction of consciousness upon data of a certain character), or "nativism of temporal datum" (where a certain time-extent attribute, or temporality, attaches to experience as such; this view is analogous to the "extensity theory" of the cognition of space); and (2) empirical theories — hold that time cognition is a gradual growth under the conditions of actual experiences of time; bits of time are perceived, cognized, or experienced simply as such or as a property of events; and time is built up by abstraction and generalization as an independent mental object; in this approach, the mind gets time out of its experience instead of contributing time to its experience. Baldwin notes that newer views of psychological function treat the older concept of the dualism of mind and its experience as largely a false dichotomy. He observes that experience is a process, not a doctrine or series of data, and mind is also a process where the two processes are not two but one; hence, all knowledge is in the same sense *both* native and empirical (Notes: For early philosophical theories of time, see Nichols, 1891a, b; also, see Boring, 1942, pp. 575–577, for a brief sketch of the earlier theories of temporal perception; Fraser, 1966, 1975, 1989, for interdisciplinary theories and models of time; and Block, 1990, 1994a, for a discussion of the development of psychological theories of time that fluctuated between the biological and cognitive approaches).

At the turn of the 20th century (1860–1910), several theoretical positions were proposed that established the basic foundations for the psychology of time between the biological–cognitive extremes (*cf*., the "extrapsychological" causal and statistical theories of time in Whitrow, 1980, pp. 323, 327; and the notion of "chronons" as the atoms of time, along with the concepts of "physical, physiological, and perceptual chronons" in Fraser, 1978, pp. 29–44). The most important of the early, pre-1950, psychological time theories were formulated by Jean-Marie Guyau, William James, and Henri Bergson (Michon, 1994b). Guyau (1890) invoked cognitive processes and suggested that time is simply an acquired organization of dynamic mental representations that enable individuals to store and remember past events. In support of his theory, Guyau specified five mechanisms (expressed here in contemporary terms) that allow the person to achieve memory organization that is requisite to temporal appreciation: schema formation, matching, spatial analogy, chunking, and narrative closure (Michon, Pouthas, & Jackson, 1988; Michon, 1994a).

William James (1890) also invoked cognitive processes in his account of time, especially when he characterized thinking as cognitive phenomenal events in time. James's theoretical notions of the "specious present" (or "sensible present"), the transitional processes from simultaneity to successiveness, and the differences between experiences of time in passing and in retrospect still are recognized and cited by contemporary psychologists studying timing and time perception (Block, 1994b, c).

Henri Bergson (1910, 1911, 1920, 1922/1965) developed a relational subjective basis in his approach to time experience and, thereby, reacted against the scientific and mechanistic thought that was prevalent in the late 19th and early 20th century. Bergson distinguished between chronological time — which symbolizes space, and duration — which is apprehended through intuition and identical with the essence of life (Pitkin, 1912).

From about 1910 to 1950, interest, research, and theorizing in the area of psychological time seemed to decline noticeably. For instance, borrowing data from Zelkind and Sprug (1974) — which includes studies on many key time-related topics such as time estimation, time perception, and time sense — I calculated that in the 40 years from 1910 through 1949, there were 128 psychological studies published on time for an average of three studies per year, whereas in the 24 years from 1950 through 1973, there were 1035 studies for an average of 43 studies per year: a 14-fold increase. The decline in studies from 1910 to 1949 was due, perhaps, to the elusive character of many temporal phenomena, to the decline in the introspection method in psychology, and to the increasing influence of behaviorism in North America (Michon, 1994b). After the late 1950s, however, the psychology of time experienced a revival, of sorts, that has stimulated current interest in new research and new methods of investigation. With the recent conceptual and methodological developments in psychology of the "experimental analysis of behavior" — that emphasizes the role of "internal timers," and of the "cognitive revolution" — that emphasizes the symbol processing and semantic factors of mental activity, the study of timing and time perception appears, again, to be a vital and robust area in the mainstream of empirical and experimental psychology.

References

Abbe, M. (1936). The spatial effects upon the perception of time. *Japanese Journal of Experimental Psychology*, *3*, 1–52.

Adams, H. (1915). A note on the effect of rhythm on memory. *Psychological Review*, *21*, 289–298.

Akeley, L. (1925). The problem of the specious present and physical time. *Journal of Philosophy*, *22*, 561–573.

Albert, S. (1978). Time, memory, and affect: Experimental studies of the subjective past. In: J. T. Fraser, N. Lawrence & D. Park (Eds), *The study of time III*. New York: Springer-Verlag.

Ames, L. (1946). The development of the sense of time in the young child. *Journal of Genetic Psychology, 68*, 97–126.

Amplified Bible. (1987). Grand Rapids. MI: Zondervan.

Anderson, D. (1914). The duration of tones, the time interval, the direction of sound, darkness and quiet, and the order of stimuli in pitch discrimination. *Psychological Monographs, 16*, 150–156.

Aveni, A. (1989). *Empires of time: Calendars, clocks, and culture*. New York: Basic Books.

Aveni, A. (1998). Time. In: M. Taylor (Ed.), *Critical terms for religious studies*. Chicago, IL: University of Chicago Press.

Axel, R. (1924). Estimation of time. *Archives of Psychology, 74*, 1–77.

Baldwin, J.M. (Ed.) (1901–1905). *Dictionary of philosophy and psychology*. 4 Vols. New York: Macmillan.

Barnett, J. (1998). *Time's pendulum: The quest to capture time—from sundials to atomic clocks*. London: Plenum.

Benjamin, A. (1966). Ideas of time in the history of philosophy. In: J. T. Fraser (Ed.), *The voices of time*. New York: Brazillier.

Benussi, V. (1908). Zur experimentallen analyse des zeitvergleichs. II. Erwartungszeit und subjective zeitgrosse. *Archiv fur die Gesamte Psychologie, 13*, 71–139.

Benussi, V. (1909). Uber aufmerksamkeitsrichtung beim raum- und zeitvergleich. *Zeitschrift fur Psychologie, 51*, 73–107.

Bergler, E., & Roheim, G. (1946). Psychology of time perception. *Psychoanalytic Quarterly, 15*, 190–206.

Bergson, H. (1910). *Time and free will*. London: Allen and Unwin.

Bergson, H. (1911). *Matter and memory*. London: Allen and Unwin.

Bergson, H. (1920). *Essai sur les donees immediates de la conscience*. Paris: Alcan.

Bergson, H. (1922/1965). *Duration and simultaneity*. Indianapolis, IN: Bobbs-Merrill.

Bergstrom, J. (1900). Reaction-time. *Psychological Review, 7*, 526–529.

Berman, A. (1939). The relation of time estimation to satiation. *Journal of Experimental Psychology, 25*, 281–293.

Bindra, D., & Waksberg, H. (1956). Methods and terminology in studies of time estimation. *Psychological Bulletin, 53*, 155–159.

Block, R. (1978). Remembered duration: Effects of event and sequence complexity. *Memory & Cognition, 6*, 320–326.

Block, R. (1985). Contextual coding in memory: Studies of remembered duration. In: J. Michon & J. Jackson (Eds), *Time, mind, and behavior*. Heidelberg, Germany: Springer-Verlag.

Block, R. (1986). Remembered duration: Imagery processes and contextual encoding. *Acta Psychologica, 62*, 103–122.

Block, R. (Ed.) (1990). *Cognitive models of psychological time*. Hillsdale, NJ: Erlbaum.

Block, R. (1994a). Cognition. In: S. Macey (Ed.), *Encyclopedia of time*. New York: Garland.

Block, R. (1994b). Prospective and retrospective time. In: S. Macey (Ed.), *Encyclopedia of time*. New York: Garland.

Block, R. (1994c). William James as psychologist (1842–1910). In: S. Macey (Ed.), *Encyclopedia of time*. New York: Garland.

Bolton, T. (1894). Rhythm. *American Journal of Psychology, 6*, 145–238.

Boodin, J. (1904). Time and reality. *Psychological Review, Monograph Supplements, 6*, Whole No. 26.

Boring, E. G. (1921). The stimulus error. *American Journal of Psychology, 32*, 449–471.

Boring, E. G. (1942). *Sensation and perception in the history of experimental psychology*. New York: Appleton-Century-Crofts.

Boring, E. G. (1954). The nature and history of experimental control. *American Journal of Psychology*, *67*, 572–589.

Boring, E. G. (1957). *A history of experimental psychology*. New York: Appleton-Century-Crofts.

Bradley, N. (1948). Growth of the knowledge of time in children of school age. *British Journal of Psychology*, *38*, 67.

Brann, E. (1994). Plato (ca. 427–347 B.C.). In: S. Macey (Ed.), *Encyclopedia of time*. New York: Garland.

Brewer, J. (1911). The psychology of change: On some phases of minimal time by sight. *Psychological Review*, *18*, 257–261.

Bromberg, W. (1938). The meaning of time for children. *American Journal of Orthopsychiatry*, *8*, 142–147.

Brower, J., & Brower, D. (1947). The relation between temporal judgment and social competence in the feeble minded. *American Journal of Mental Deficiency*, *51*, 619–623.

Brown, W. (1911). Temporal and accentual rhythm. *Psychological Review*, *18*, 336–346.

Brush, E. (1930). Observations on the temporal judgment during sleep. *American Journal of Psychology*, *42*, 408–411.

Buccheri, R., Saniga, M., & Stuckey, W. M. (Eds). (2003). *The nature of time: Geometry, physics, and perception*. Dordretch, The Netherlands: Kluwer.

Burton, A. (1943). A further study of the relation of time estimation to monotony. *Journal of Applied Psychology*, *27*, 350–359.

Callahan, J. (1948). *Four views of time in ancient philosophy*. Cambridge, MA: Harvard University Press.

Carr, H. (1919). Length of time interval in successive association. *Psychological Review*, *26*, 335–353.

Carr, H., & Freeman, A. (1919). Time relationships in the formation of associations. *Psychological Review*, *26*, 465–473.

Carrel, A. (1931). Physiological time. *Science*, *74*, 618–621.

Caudle, F. (1994). History of psychology. In: R. J. Corsini (Ed.), *Encyclopedia of psychology*. New York: Wiley.

Clausen, J. (1949). Time judgment. In: F. Mettler (Ed.), *Selective partial ablation of the frontal cortex*. New York: Harper.

Cohen, H. F. (1994). *The scientific revolution*. Chicago, IL: University of Chicago Press.

Cohen, I. B. (1985). *Revolution in science*. Cambridge, MA: Harvard University Press.

Cohen, J. (1971). Time in psychology. In: J. Zeman (Ed.), *Time in science and philosophy: An international study of some current problems*. New York: Elsevier.

Cooper, L. (1948). Time distortion in hypnosis. *Bulletin of the Georgetown University Medical Center*, *1*, 214–221.

Curtis, J. (1916). Duration and the temporal judgment. *American Journal of Psychology*, *27*, 1–46.

Dallenbach, K. (1913). The relation of memory error to time interval. *Psychological Review*, *20*, 323–337.

Dampier, W. C. (1948). *A history of science*. New York: Cambridge University Press.

Davidson, C. (1941). A syndrome of time agnosia. *Journal of Nervous and Mental Disease*, *94*, 336–337.

Derrida, J. (1973). *Speech and phenomena*. Evanston, IL: Northwestern University Press.

Dietze, G. (1885). Untersuchungen uber den umfang des bewusstseins bei regelmassig auf einander folgenden schalleindrucken. *Philosophische Studien*, *2*, 362–393.
Doob, L. (1971). *Patterning of time*. New Haven, CT: Yale University Press.
Dooley, L. (1941). The concept of time in defence of ego integrity. *Psychiatry*, *4*, 13–23.
Drever, J. (1973). *A dictionary of psychology*. Baltimore, MD: Penguin.
Dunlap, K. (1904). Time. *Psychological Bulletin*, *1*, 363–365.
Dunlap, K. (1907). A new rhythm and time device. *Science*, *26*, 257–258.
Dunlap, K. (1915). The shortest perceptible time-interval between two flashes of light. *Psychological Review*, *22*, 226–250.
Ebhardt, K. (1898). Zwei beitrage zur psychologie des rhythms und des tempo. *Zeitschrift fur Psychologie und Physiologie der Sinnesorgane*, *18*, 99–154.
Eddis, C. (1994). Samuel Alexander (1859–1938). In: S. Macey (Ed.), *Encyclopedia of time*. New York: Garland.
Edgell, B. (1903). On time judgment. *American Journal of Psychology*, *14*, 418–438.
Einstein, A. (1952). *Relativity: The special and the general theory*. London: Methuen.
English, H., & English, A. (1958). *A comprehensive dictionary of psychological and psychoanalytical terms*. New York: McKay.
Estel, V. (1884). Neue versuche uber den zeitsinn. *Philosophische Studien*, *2*, 37–65.
Exner, S. (1873). Experimentelle untersuchung der einfachsten psychischen processe. *Pflugers Archiv Gesamte Physiologie*, *7*, 601–660.
Farber, M. (1944). Suffering and time perspective of the prisoner. *University of Iowa Studies in Child Welfare*, *20*, 153–227.
Filer, R., & Meals, D. (1949). The effect of motivating conditions on the estimation of time. *Journal of Experimental Psychology*, *39*, 327–331.
Fisher, R. A. (1935). *Design of experiments*. Edinburgh: Oliver & Boyd.
Ford, A. (1937). Perceptive errors in time judgment. *Journal of Experimental Psychology*, *20*, 528–552.
Fraisse, P. (1952). La perception de la duree. *Annee Psychologie*, *52*, 39–46.
Fraisse, P. (1963). *The psychology of time*. New York: Harper & Row.
Fraisse, P. (1984). Perception and estimation of time. *Annual Review of Psychology*, *35*, 1–36.
Fraisse, P. (1994). Rhythm. In: R. J. Corsini (Ed.), *Encyclopedia of psychology*. New York: Wiley.
Frank, L. (1939). Time perspectives. *Journal of Social Philosophy*, *4*, 239–312.
Fraser, J. T. (Ed.) (1966). *The voices of time*. New York: Braziller.
Fraser, J. T. (1975). *Of time, passion, and knowledge: Reflections on the strategy of existence*. New York: Braziller.
Fraser, J. T. (1978). *Time as conflict: A scientific and humanistic study*. Basel, Switzerland: Birkhauser Verlag.
Fraser, J. T. (1982). *The genesis and evolution of time: A critique of interpretation in physics*. Amherst, MA: The University of Massachusetts Press.
Fraser, J. T. (1989). *Time and mind: Interdisciplinary issues. The study of time VI*. Madison, CT: International Universities Press.
Friedman, W. (1992). Time memory and time perception. In: F. Macar & V. Pouthas (Eds), *Time, action, and cognition: Towards bridging the gap*. Dordrecht, The Netherlands: Kluwer.
Gale, G. (1994). Gottfried Wilhelm Leibniz (1646–1716). In: S. Macey (Ed.), *Encyclopedia of time*. New York: Garland.
Gardner, W. (1935). Influence of the thyroid gland on the consciousness of time. *American Journal of Psychology*, *47*, 698–701.

Gault, R., & Goodfellow, L. (1938). An empirical comparison of audition, vision, and touch in the discrimination of temporal patterns and the ability to reproduce them. *Journal of General Psychology*, *18*, 41–47.

Gibbon, J., & Allan, L. (1984). *Timing and time perception*. New York: New York Academy of Sciences.

Gilliland, A., Hofeld, J., & Eckstrand, G. (1946). Studies in time perception. *Psychological Bulletin*, *43*, 162–176.

Gilliland, A., & Humphreys, D. (1943). Age, sex, method, and interval as variables in time estimation. *Journal of General Psychology*, *63*, 123–130.

Gilliland, A., & Martin, R. (1940). Some factors in estimating short time intervals. *Journal of Experimental Psychology*, *27*, 243–255.

Goldman, S. (1981). On the beginnings and endings of time in medieval Judaism and Islam. In: J. T. Fraser, N. Lawrence & D. Park (Eds), *The study of time IV*. New York: Springer-Verlag.

Goodfellow, L. (1934). An empirical comparison of audition, vision, and touch in the discrimination of short intervals of time. *American Journal of Psychology*, *46*, 243–258.

Gothberg, L. (1949). The mentally defective child's understanding of time. *American Journal of Mental Deficiency*, *53*, 441–453.

Goudsmit, S., & Claiborne, R. (1980). *Time*. Alexandria, VA: Time-Life Books.

Graham, C., & Cook, C. (1937). Visual acuity as a function of intensity and exposure time. *American Journal of Psychology*, *49*, 654–691.

Graham, C., & Kemp, E. (1938). Brightness discrimination as a function of the duration of the increment in intensity. *Journal of General Physiology*, *21*, 635–650.

Gribbin, J. (Ed.) (1998). *A brief history of science*. New York: Barnes & Noble.

Gridley, P. (1932). The discrimination of short intervals of time by finger tap and by ear. *American Journal of Psychology*, *44*, 18–43.

Gross, A. (1949). Sense of time in dreams. *Psychoanalytic Quarterly*, *18*, 466–470.

Guilford, J. P. (1926). Spatial symbols in the apprehension of time. *American Journal of Psychology*, *37*, 420–423.

Gulliksen, H. (1927). The influence of occupation upon the perception of time. *Journal of Experimental Psychology*, *10*, 52–59.

Guyau, J.-M. (1890). *La genese de l'idee de temps*. Paris: Alcan.

Hall, G. S., & Jastrow, J. (1886). Studies in rhythm. *Mind*, *11*, 55–63.

Hammer, E. (1949). Temporal factors in figural aftereffects. *American Journal of Psychology*, *62*, 337–354.

Harre, R. (1994). Isaac Newton (1642–1727). In: S. Macey (Ed.), *Encyclopedia of time*. New York: Garland.

Harriman, P. (1966). *Handbook of psychological terms*. Totowa, NJ: Littlefield, Adams.

Harris, W., & Levey, J. (1975). *The new Columbia encyclopedia*. New York: Columbia University Press.

Harrison, E. (1994). Atomicity of time. In: S. Macey (Ed.), *Encyclopedia of time*. New York: Garland.

Harton, J. (1938). The influence of the difficulty of activity on the estimation of time. *Journal of Experimental Psychology*, *23*, 426–438.

Harton, J. (1939a). The influence of the degree of unity of organization on the estimation of time. *Journal of General Psychology*, *21*, 25–49.

Harton, J. (1939b). The investigation of the influence of success and failure on the estimation of time. *Journal of General Psychology*, *21*, 51–62.

Harton, J. (1939c). The relation of time estimates to actual time. *Journal of General Psychology*, *21*, 219–224.
Harton, J. (1942). Time estimation in relation to goal organization and difficulty of tasks. *Journal of General Psychology*, *27*, 63–69.
Hawking, S. (1988). *A brief history of time*. New York: Bantam Books.
Heap, J. (1994). John Locke (1632–1704). In: S. Macey (Ed.), *Encyclopedia of time*. New York: Garland.
Heidegger, M. (1962). *Being and time*. New York: Harper & Row.
Heidegger, M. (1972). *On time and being*. New York: Harper & Row.
Heidegger, M. (1985). *History of the concept of time*. Bloomington, IN: Indiana University Press.
Heidegger, M. (1992). *The concept of time*. Oxford, England: Blackwell.
Helmholtz, H. von (1863). *Die lehre von den tonempfindungen als grundlage fur die theorie der musik*. Leipzig, Germany: Voss.
Henmon, V. A. C. (1911). The relation of the time of a judgment to its accuracy. *Psychological Review*, *18*, 186–201.
Henry, F. (1948). Discrimination of the duration of a second. *Journal of Experimental Psychology*, *38*, 734–743.
Hintikka, J. (1973). *Time and necessity in Aristotle*. Oxford, England: Clarendon Press.
Hoagland, H. (1933). The physiological control of judgments of duration: Evidence for a chemical clock. *Journal of General Psychology*, *9*, 267–287.
Hoagland, H. (1934). Physiological control of judgments of duration. *American Journal of Physiology*, *109*, 54.
Hoagland, H. (1943). The chemistry of time. *Scientific Monthly*, *56*, 56–61.
Hood, P. (1969). *How time is measured*. London: Oxford University Press.
Hulett, J. (1944). The person's time perspective and the social role. *Social Forces*, *23*, 155–159.
Husserl, E. (1965). *The phenomenology of internal time consciousness*. New York: Harper.
Husserl, E. (1991). *On the phenomenology of the consciousness of internal time (1883–1913)*. Leiden, The Netherlands: Kluwer.
Hussey, E. (1983). *Aristotle's physics: Books III and IV*. Oxford, England: Clarendon.
Hyland, D. (1994). Presocratics. In: S. Macey (Ed.), *Encyclopedia of time*. New York: Garland.
Inwood, M. (1991). Aristotle on the reality of time. In: L. Judson (Ed.), *Aristotle's physics*. Oxford, England: Clarendon.
Israeli, N. (1936). *Abnormal personality and time*. New York: Science Press.
James, W. (1890). *The principles of psychology*. 2 Vols. New York: Holt.
Kalkavage, P. (1994). Rene Descartes (1596–1650). In: S. Macey (Ed.), *Encyclopedia of time*. New York: Garland.
Kastenbaum, R. (1964). The structure and function of time perspective. *Journal of Psychological Researches (India)*, *8*, 1–11.
Kastenbaum, R. (1994). Time perspective. In: R. J. Corsini (Ed.), *Encyclopedia of psychology*. New York: Wiley.
Kowalski, W. (1943). The effect of delay upon the duplication of short temporal intervals. *Journal of Experimental Psychology*, *33*, 239–246.
Krebs, J., & Kacelnik, A. (1984). Time horizons of foraging animals. In: J. Gibbon & L. Allan (Eds), *Timing and time perception*. New York: New York Academy of Sciences.
Kuhn, T. (1962). *The structure of scientific revolutions*. Chicago, IL: University of Chicago Press.

Lacey, A. (1989). *Bergson*. London: Routledge.
Landsberg, P. (1982). *The enigma of time*. Bristol, England: Adam Hilger.
Lewis, A. (1931–1932). The experience of time in mental disorder. *Proceedings of the Royal Society of Medicine*, *25*, 611–620.
Lifshitz, S. (1933). Two integral laws of sound perception relating loudness and apparent duration of sound impulses. *Journal of the Acoustical Society of America*, *5*, 31–33.
Lloyd, A. (1902). Professor Fullerton on "The doctrine of space and time". *Psychological Review*, *9*, 174–180.
Loewald, H. W. (1972). The experience of time. *Psychoanalytic Study of the Child*, *27*, 401–410.
Lundin, R. (1994). Martin Heidegger. In: R. J. Corsini (Ed.), *Encyclopedia of psychology*. New York: Wiley.
Lyon, D. & Eno, H. (1912/1914). A time experiment in psychophysics. *Psychological Review*, *19*, 312–336; *21*, 9–22.
MacDougall, R. (1900). Rhythm. *Psychological Review*, *7*, 309–312.
MacDougall, R. (1902). Rhythm, time, and number. *American Journal of Psychology*, *13*, 88–97.
MacDougall, R. (1903). The structure of simple rhythm forms. *Psychological Review*, *4*, 309–411.
Macey, S. (Ed.) (1994). *Encyclopedia of time*. New York: Garland.
Mach, E. (1865). Untersuchungen uber den zeitsinn des ohres. *Sitzungsberichte Akademie Wissenschaft der Wien*, *51*, 135–150.
MacLeod, R., & Roff, M. (1935). An experiment in temporal disorientation. *Acta Psychologica*, *1*, 381–423.
Maimonides, M. (1927). *The guide for the perplexed*. New York: Dover.
Martin, G. (1994). Soren Aabye Kierkegaard (1813–1855). In: S. Macey (Ed.), *Encyclopedia of time*. New York: Garland.
McDougall, R. (1904). Sex differences in the sense of time. *Science*, *19*, 707–708.
Meagher, R. (1978). *Augustine: An introduction*. New York: Harper & Row.
Meagher, R. (1994). Augustine (354–430). In: S. Macey (Ed.), *Encyclopedia of time*. New York: Garland.
Mehner, M. (1884). Zur lehre vom zeitsinn. *Philosophische Studien*, *2*, 546.
Merleau-Ponty, M. (1962). *Phenomenology of perception*. London: Routledge and Kegan Paul.
Meumann, E. (1892/1893/1894). Beitrage zur psychologie des zeitsinns. *Philosophische Studien*, *8*, 431–509; *9*, 264–306; *9*, 270 (Figure 1).
Meumann, E. (1894). Untersuchungen zur psychologie und aesthetik des rhythmus. *Philosophische Studien*, *10*, 249–322; 393–430.
Meumann, E. (1907–1908). *Vorlesungen zur einfuhrung in die experimentelle padagogik*. Leipzig, Germany: Englemann.
Michon, J. (1975). Time experience and memory processes. In: J. T. Fraser & N. Lawrence (Eds), *The study of time II*. New York: Springer-Verlag.
Michon, J. (1994a). Jean-Marie Guyau (1854–1888). In: S. Macey (Ed.), *Encyclopedia of time*. New York: Garland.
Michon, J. (1994b). Psychology of time. In: S. Macey (Ed.), *Encyclopedia of time*. New York: Garland.
Michon, J., Pouthas, V., & Jackson, J. (1988). *Guyau and the idea of time*. Amsterdam, The Netherlands: North-Holland.
Misiak, H. (1994). Edmund Husserl. In: R. J. Corsini (Ed.), *Encyclopedia of psychology*. New York: Wiley.

Montague, W. (1904). A theory of time-perception. *American Journal of Psychology*, *15*, 1–14.
Moore, T. (1915). The temporal relations of meaning and imagery. *Psychological Review*, *22*, 177–225.
Morris, M. (Ed.) (1934). *The philosophical writings of Leibniz*. London: Dent.
Mosley, P. (1994). Henri Bergson (1859–1941). In: S. Macey (Ed.), *Encyclopedia of time*. New York: Garland.
Mowrer, O. H., & Ullman, A. (1945). Time as a determinant in integrative learning. *Psychological Review*, *52*, 61–90.
Munsterberg, H. (1889). *Beitrage zur experimentellen psychologie*. Freiburg, Germany: Mohr.
Natsoulas, T. (1992–1993). The stream of consciousness: II. William James's specious present. *Imagination, Cognition, & Personality*, *12*, 367–385.
Needham, J. (1935). The effect of the time interval upon the time error at different intensive levels. *Journal of Experimental Psychology*, *18*, 530–543.
Nichols, H. (1890). *The psychology of time*. New York: Holt.
Nichols, H. (1891a). The psychology of time. *American Journal of Psychology*, *3*, 453–529.
Nichols, H. (1891b). The psychology of time. *American Journal of Psychology*, *4*, 60–112.
Nichols, H. (1894). Review of recent literature on the perception of time. *Psychological Review*, *1*, 638–641.
Nitardy, F. (1943). Apparent time acceleration with age of the individual. *Science*, *98*, 110.
Ornstein, R. (1969). *On the experience of time*. Harmondsworth, England: Penguin.
Perkins, M. (1998). Timeless cultures: The "Dreamtime" as colonial discourse. *Time & Society*, *7*, 335–351.
Peters, R. S. (1965). *Brett's history of psychology*. Cambridge, MA: M.I.T. Press.
Philip, B. (1944). The anchoring of absolute judgments of short temporal intervals. *Bulletin of the Canadian Psychological Association*, *4*, 25–28.
Philip, B. (1947). The effect of interpolated and extrapolated stimuli on the time order error in the comparison of temporal intervals. *Journal of General Psychology*, *36*, 173–187.
Pitkin, W. (1912). Time and free will. *Psychological Bulletin*, *9*, 176–180.
Postman, L. (1944). Estimates of time during a series of tasks. *American Journal of Psychology*, *57*, 421–424.
Postman, L., & Miller, G. (1945). Anchoring of temporal judgments. *American Journal of Psychology*, *58*, 43–53.
Reber, A. (1995). *The Penguin dictionary of psychology*. New York: Penguin.
Reck, A. (1994). Philosophy of time. In: S. Macey (Ed.), *Encyclopedia of time*. New York: Garland.
Richardson, M., & Stalnaker, J. (1930). Time estimation in the hypnotic trance. *Journal of General Psychology*, *4*, 362–366.
Roeckelein, J. E. (2000). *The concept of time in psychology*. Westport, CT: Greenwood Press.
Roeckelein, J. E. (2006). *Elsevier's dictionary of psychological theories*. Amsterdam, The Netherlands: Elsevier.
Roelofs, C., & Zeeman, W. (1949a). The subjective duration of time intervals. *Acta Psychologica*, *6*, 126–177.
Roelofs, C., & Zeeman, W. (1949b). The subjective duration of time intervals: The influence of order in the estimation of duration of two successive intervals. *Acta Psychologica*, *6*, 289–336.
Romilly, J. de. (1968). *Time in Greek tragedy*. Ithaca, NY: Cornell University Press.
Rosenzweig, S., & Koht, A. (1933). The experience of duration as affected by need tension. *Journal of Experimental Psychology*, *16*, 745–774.

Ross, F. (1914). The measurement of time-sense as an element in the sense of rhythm. *Psychological Monographs*, *16*, 166–172.
Ruckmich, C. (1913a/1915/1918/1924). A bibliography of rhythm. *American Journal of Psychology*, *24*, 508–519; *26*, 457–459; *29*, 214–218; *35*, 407–413.
Ruckmich, C. (1913b). The role of kinaesthesis in the perception of rhythm. *American Journal of Psychology*, *24*, 305–359. (Note: Boring's [1942, p. 587] spelling of this name is "Ruckmick;" Dunlap's [*Psychology Bulletin*, 1914, pp. 169–171] is Ruchmich".)
Sagan, C. (1980). *Cosmos*. New York: Random House.
Schaeffer, V., & Gilliland, A. (1938). The relation of time estimation to certain physiological changes. *Journal of Experimental Psychology*, *23*, 545–552.
Schneider, D. (1948). Time-space and the growth of the sense of reality. *Psychoanalytic Review*, *35*, 229–252.
Schultz, D. (1981). *A history of modern psychology*. New York: Academic Press.
Schumann, F. (1893). Uber die schatzung kleiner zeitgrossen. *Zeitschrift fur Psychologie*, *4*, 1–69.
Scott, W. (1948). Some psychodynamic aspects of disturbed perception of time. *British Journal of Medical Psychology*, *21*, 110–120.
Sears, C. (1902). A contribution to the psychology of rhythm. *American Journal of Psychology*, *13*, 28–61.
Seligman, M. (1975). *Helplessness: On depression, development, and death*. San Francisco, CA: Freeman.
Shaw, M., & Wrinch, F. (1898–1900). A contribution to the psychology of time. *University of Toronto Studies, Psychology Series (No.2)*. Toronto, Canada: The Librarian.
Snyder, S. (1994). Albertus Magnus. In: S. Macey (Ed.), *Encyclopedia of time*. New York: Garland.
Spencer, L. (1921). An experiment in time estimation using different interpolations. *American Journal of Psychology*, *32*, 557–562.
Squire, C. (1901). A genetic study of rhythm. *American Journal of Psychology*, *12*, 492–589.
Stanley, H. (1900). Remarks on time perception. *Psychological Review*, *7*, 284–288.
Stein, M. (1949). Personality factors involved in temporal development of Rorschach responses. *Rorschach Research Exchange and Journal of Projective Techniques*, *13*, 355–413.
Stern, M. (1994). Islam. In: S. Macey (Ed.), *Encyclopedia of time*. New York: Garland.
Stetson, R. (1903). Rhythm and rhyme. *Psychological Review*, *4*, 413–466.
Stevens, H. (1902). The relation of the fluctuations of judgments in the estimation of time intervals to vaso-motor waves. *American Journal of Psychology*, *13*, 1–27.
Stevens, L. (1886). On the time sense. *Mind*, *11*, 393–404.
Stewart, I. (1926). Sex differences in substitution and time estimation. *Journal of Comparative Psychology*, *6*, 243–265.
Stott, L. (1935). Time order errors in the discrimination of short tonal durations. *Journal of Experimental Psychology*, *18*, 741–766.
Stout, G. (1900). Perception of change and duration. *Mind*, *9*, 1–7.
Straus, E. (1947). Disorders of personal time in depressive states. *Southern Medical Journal*, *40*, 254–258.
Strong, C. (1891). A sketch of the history of psychology among the Greeks. *American Journal of Psychology*, *4*, 177–197.
Strong, C. (1896). Consciousness and time. *Psychological Review*, *3*, 149–157.
Strong, E. (1913). The effect of time-interval upon recognition memory. *Psychological Review*, *20*, 339–372.

Sturm, F. (1994). American Indians: Time in outlook and language. In: S. Macey (Ed.), *Encyclopedia of time*. New York: Garland.

Sturt, M. (1923). Experiments on the estimate of duration. *British Journal of Psychology*, *13*, 382–388.

Sturt, M. (1925). *The psychology of time*. New York: Harcourt, Brace & Co.

Swift, E., & McGeoch, J. (1925). An experimental study of the perception of filled and empty time. *Journal of Experimental Psychology*, *8*, 240–249.

Swindle, P. (1913). On the inheritance of rhythm. *American Journal of Psychology*, *24*, 180–203.

Swindle, P. (1917). The term reaction time redefined. *American Journal of Psychology*, *28*, 508–518.

Tedlock, B. (1982). *Time and the highland Maya*. Albuquerque, NM: University of New Mexico Press.

Titchener, E. B. (1905). *Experimental psychology*. New York: Macmillan.

Tolman, E. C. (1917). More concerning the temporal relations of meaning and imagery. *Psychological Review*, *24*, 114–138.

Triplett, D. (1931). The relation between the physical pattern and the reproduction of short temporal intervals: A study in the perception of filled and unfilled time. *Psychological Monographs*, *41*, 187.

Turnbull, W. (1944). Pitch discrimination as a function of tonal duration. *Journal of Experimental Psychology*, *34*, 302–316.

Urban, F. (1907). On systematic errors in time estimation. *American Journal of Psychology*, *18*, 187–193.

Venable, B. (1994). Plotinus (A.D. 205–270). In: S. Macey (Ed.), *Encyclopedia of time*. New York: Garland.

Vierordt, K. (1868). *Der zeitsinn nach versuchen*. Tubingen, Germany: Laupp.

Vince, M. (1948). The intermittence of control movements and the psychological refractory period. *British Journal of Psychology*, *38*, 149–157.

Wallace, M., & Rabin, A. (1960). Temporal experience. *Psychological Bulletin*, *57*, 213–236.

Wallin, J. (1911). Experimental studies of rhythm and time. *Psychological Review*, *18*, 100–131; 202–222.

Wallin, J. (1912). Experimental studies of rhythm and time. *Psychological Review*, *19*, 271–298.

Warren, H. (Ed.) (1934). *Dictionary of psychology*. Cambridge, MA: Houghton Mifflin.

Weber, A. (1927). The properties of space and time in kinesthetic fields of force. *American Journal of Psychology*, *38*, 597–606.

Weber, A. (1933). Estimation of time. *Psychological Bulletin*, *30*, 233–252.

White, K. (1994). St. Thomas Aquinas (1224/25-1274). In: S. Macey (Ed.), *Encyclopedia of time*. New York: Garland.

Whitrow, G. J. (1961). *The natural philosophy of time*. London: Nelson.

Whitrow, G. J. (1972a). Reflections on the history of the concept of time. In: J. T. Fraser, F. Haber & G. Muller (Eds), *The study of time*. New York: Springer-Verlag.

Whitrow, G. J. (1972b). *The nature of time*. New York: Holt, Rinehart and Winston.

Whitrow, G. J. (1972c). *What is time?* London: Thames and Hudson.

Whitrow, G. J. (1980). *The natural philosophy of time*. Oxford, England: Clarendon.

Whitrow, G. J. (1989). Man and time: Some historical and critical reflections. In: J. T. Fraser (Ed.), *Time and mind: Interdisciplinary issues*. Madison, CT: International Universities Press.

Wolfson, H. (1976). *The philosophy of the kalam*. Cambridge, MA: Harvard University Press.
Wolman, B. (Ed.) (1973). *Dictionary of behavioral science*. New York: Van Nostrand Reinhold.
Wolter, A. (1994). John Duns Scotus (ca. 1266–1308). In: S. Macey (Ed.), *Encyclopedia of time*. New York: Garland.
Woodrow, H. (1909). A quantitative study of rhythm: The effect of variation in intensity, rate, and duration. *Archives of Psychology, New York, 2*, 1–11.
Woodrow, H. (1911). The role of pitch in rhythm. *Psychological Review, 18*, 54–77.
Woodrow, H. (1918). Time and rhythm. *Psychological Bulletin, 15*, 111–114.
Woodrow, H. (1928). Behavior with respect to short temporal stimulus forms. *Journal of Experimental Psychology, 11*, 167–193.
Woodrow, H. (1930). The reproduction of temporal intervals. *Journal of Experimental Psychology, 13*, 473–499.
Woodrow, H. (1933). Individual differences in the reproduction of temporal intervals. *American Journal of Psychology, 45*, 271–281.
Woodrow, H. (1934). The temporal indifference interval determined by the method of mean error. *Journal of Experimental Psychology, 17*, 167–188.
Woodrow, H. (1935). The effect of practice upon time order errors in the comparison of temporal intervals. *Psychological Review, 42*, 127–152.
Woodrow, H. (1951). Time perception. In: S. S. Stevens (Ed.), *Handbook of experimental psychology*. New York: Wiley.
Woodrow, H., & Stott, L. (1936). The effect of practice on positive time order errors. *Journal of Experimental Psychology, 19*, 694–705.
Woodworth, R. (1938). *Experimental psychology*. New York: Holt.
Woodworth, R., & Schlosberg, H. (1965). *Experimental psychology*. New York: Holt, Rinehart, & Winston.
Wundt, W. (1873–1874). *Principles of physiological psychology*. New York: Macmillan.
Wundt, W. (1882). *Philosophische studien*. Leipzig, Germany: Engelmann.
Wundt, W. (1897). *Outline of psychology*. Leipzig, Germany: Engelmann.
Yerkes, R., & Urban, F. (1906). Time-estimation in its relation to sex, age, and physiological rhythms. *Harvard Psychological Studies, 2*, 405–430.
Zelkind, I., & Sprug, J. (1974). *Time research: 1,172 studies*. Metuchen, NJ: Scarecrow.

Chapter 2

Methods for Studying Psychological Time

Simon Grondin

The purpose of this chapter is to facilitate the reading of the past and contemporary literatures on psychological time, including some of this book's chapters. More specifically, this chapter reviews and explains some of the traditional methods employed for studying time perception and estimation in experimental psychology. Some methods will be emphasised for their usefulness in contemporary research and for their theoretical implications. Nevertheless, the chapter remains mainly focussed on the description of methods and not on the description of theoretical issues, which are reported in the other chapters of the book.

2.1. Distinguishing Researches

The methods employed in experimental studies are, of course, selected based on the questions to be addressed. Because of the ubiquity of time in behaviour and the relevance of a temporal perspective in regard to living organisms and events, a wide range of questions can be related in some way to psychological time (Glicksohn & Myslobodsky, 2006; Helfrich, 2003; Meck, 2003; Perret-Clermont, 2005; Strathman & Joireman, 2005). Briefly distinguishing the types of research on psychological time, even within the scope of experimental psychology, is a necessary exercise before presenting the mechanics of the most classic methods for investigating time perception.

There are many instances of behaviours involving the encoding of time, but where the involvement is only implicit (Zelaznik, Spencer, & Ivry, 2002; see Chapter 7). Such is the case for motor activities like those involved in speech, catching a ball or practicing scales on piano. In these conditions, the person must make temporal adjustments but is not asked to judge time explicitly. Most of the work on psychological time in experimental psychology, and most of the work presented in this book, is related to conditions where people judge time explicitly.

Psychology of Time

DOI:10.1016/B978-0-08046-977-5.00002-8

Of critical interest in examining the literature on explicit temporal judgments is to consider the range of duration under investigation. This duration range issue makes it difficult to generalise about the mechanisms involved in the processing of time. One can easily imagine that studying phenomena lasting a few milliseconds is not like addressing issues involving minutes. Moreover, some issues, also referred to as "temporal processing", do not concern a temporal interval to be judged. As the reader will see below, these issues are related to the order of occurrence of events (Tallal, Galaburda, Llinas, & von Euler, 1993; Vicario, 2003).

It might also be helpful to keep in mind the distinction, used later in this chapter, between psychophysical, animal and cognitive approaches. Of course, these approaches are not mutually exclusive. Methods for studying psychological time have sometimes found their roots in the development of specific fields of psychology. As described below, this is the case in the first two of these three approaches. Ways of testing capabilities for processing time were adopted from the classical procedures described in psychophysics in contexts where the main purpose was to study a specific sensory modality, or perception within a modality. As well, the general interest in animal behaviours and the understanding of learning eventually led to the development of a variety of methods involving animal responses specifically adapted to time.

As regards the cognitive approach, it generally involves long intervals (several seconds or more). To better understand the results obtained from a cognitive perspective, it is important to distinguish between cases in which people required to make time-related judgments are informed in advance (i.e., before they begin the task) that duration has to be judged, and cases in which participants receive no prior warning about the duration issue (Brown, 1985; Eisler, Eisler, & Montgomery, 2004; Hicks, Miller, & Kinsbourne, 1976). The process involved when participants in experiments are told to make a judgment about time only after a given activity is called *retrospective timing*, while the process in which participants know in advance is referred to as *prospective timing*. As the reader will see in Chapter 4, this distinction might be critical in understanding the role of attention on time perception. In general, retrospective timing is often associated primarily with memory processes, whereas prospective timing is heavily dependent on attention (Block & Zakay, 1997, 2001; Zakay & Block, 1997).

The next three sections are dedicated to the psychophysical, animal and cognitive perspectives, respectively, and will be followed by a brief section on methodological issues related to the other type of temporal processing, which concerned with the ordering of events.

2.2. Methods from a Psychophysical Perspective

There are hundreds of published experiments based on psychophysical methods and, as will be described in detail in the next chapter on psychophysics and in Chapter 5 on auditory temporal processing, these results have led to multiple classical effects, models and important theoretical issues. Only the basic mechanics of main psychophysical methods or procedures are described below.

It is generally recognized that the publication in 1860 of Gustav Fechner's book (Fechner, 1860/1965) on psychophysics marks the birth of this discipline, and psychophysics has certainly contributed to the development of scientific psychology. Psychophysics is the scientific study of the relation between body and mind, or of the link between sensation and stimuli. This section describes some of the methods developed to address two classical issues in psychophysics: the psychophysical law and the Weber's law. The former case involves a category of methods often referred to as scaling; in the latter case, the issue is most often addressed with discrimination tasks (which will be described in detail), but can also be addressed, in the context of psychological time, by a method called continuous tapping.

2.2.1. Scaling

One critical piece of knowledge in psychophysics concerns the psychophysical law, i.e., the relationship between the magnitude of the physical value of a stimulus and the psychological (or subjective) magnitude of this stimulus (Bonnet, 1986). In general, the growth of a stimulus magnitude as a function of the physical magnitude can either be linear, logarithmical or exponential. As stated by Stevens (1975), these relations can be summarized within the so-called power law:

$$E_{\mathrm{T}} = kT^{N} \qquad (2.1)$$

where E_{T} is the estimated time, T the physical time, k a constant related to the intercept and N (the exponent) the signature of the sensory continuum under investigation. When the exponent of this power function is 1, psychological time (when time is under investigation) is veridical with physical time, and when the exponent is less than 1, shorter durations have been overestimated, and longer ones underestimated (and the reverse when the exponent is greater than 1). Moreover, the greater the deviation from one, the greater the mismatch between psychological and physical time. According to the power law, plotting this function in log–log coordinates should result in a straight line, with the slope being 1 if the function is linear, less than 1 if the relationship is logarithmical, and more than 1 if the relationship is exponential (Figure 2.1). Whether the slope of this function for time is 1 or close to 1 is a matter of discussion as different experiments and experimental conditions lead to different results (this issue is discussed in detail in Chapter 3). This slope, or the value of N in Equation 2.1, is usually argued to vary between .9 (Eisler, 1976) and 1 (Allan, 1979).

There are many scaling methods for testing the psychophysical law empirically (Gescheider, 1997). Among these is a classical method called magnitude estimation. In an experiment with this method, an observer is first presented with a standard stimulus (often referred to as a *modulus* — an interval of a certain duration, in the case of time perception) to which the experiment assigns a numerical value. Then, a series of stimuli (intervals) are presented. After the presentation of each stimulus, a numerical value is assigned to it by the observer. The psychophysical function is then

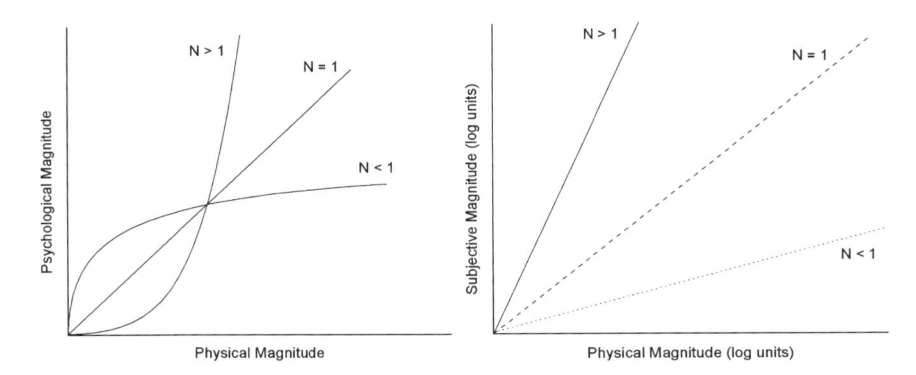

Figure 2.1: Theoretical relationship between the subjective magnitude and the physical magnitude of a stimulus in arbitrary units. Left panel: $E_{\mathrm{T}} = kT^{N}$; right panel shows the same function in log–log coordinates: $\log (E_{\mathrm{T}}) = N \log T + \log K$.

drawn by plotting the numerical values (on the y axis) as a function of the physical value of the stimuli (on the x axis).

There are various versions to this scaling method. Somewhat along the line described in the previous paragraph is *ratio* scaling: Based on the numerical value assigned to a standard stimulus (modulus), an observer might be asked to produce (by pressing on a push button, for instance), instead of estimating, an interval that corresponds to a given numerical value. As well, still in the ratio scaling family, an observer might be asked to estimate the ratio between an interval and the modulus, or to produce an interval according to a ratio of the modulus (1/4, 1/2, ...), known as *fractionation*.

Another family of scaling methods in psychophysics is called *partition* scaling. This includes *category* scaling when stimuli (intervals in the case of experiments on duration) are assigned by an observer to one of a series of pre-defined categories on a scale, and *equisection* scaling where an observer selects a stimulus located midpoint between two stimuli (Gescheider, 1997).

2.2.2. Discrimination

Of fundamental importance in psychophysics and in the study of duration is the notion of difference threshold. Technically, this notion refers to the minimal difference needed to discriminate between two stimuli. In the study of sensation and perception in general, there are several ways of presenting stimuli for assessing discrimination capabilities, and the threshold value will depend on the operational definition adopted within the context of a specific method. Some authors refer to the term *just noticeable difference* (familiarly coined *JND*) to designate the threshold notion.

For the purposes of this chapter, what are usually called stimuli (to be discriminated) will be called intervals, and the stimuli will be the physical signals used to mark the intervals' lengths. Basically, an observer is often placed in conditions where two intervals are presented successively. The task is to judge the relative length of these intervals and to indicate, by pressing the appropriate button, if the second interval was shorter or longer than the first. Technically, more than two intervals may be presented, but presenting two is typical. This case is often referred to as a two-alternative forced-choice method (2AFC). In psychophysics, in some cases, a standard interval is always presented first, followed by a comparison interval (a *reminder* method), while in others, the standard and comparison intervals vary from trial to trial (a *roving* method) (Macmillan & Creelman, 1991).

From this basic 2AFC task, there are two main categories of methods for establishing the discrimination threshold: the method of constant stimuli (MSC) and the adaptive method. In the latter case, the value of the comparison interval is adjusted from trial to trial depending on whether the observer provided a correct or incorrect response. There are several rules adopted to adjust the value of the comparison intervals, with the changes in difficulty levels being fixed steps, as in the staircase method reported by Cornsweet (1962); or adjustable steps as in the parameter estimation by sequential testing — PEST — method of Taylor and Creelman (1967); (Pentland, 1980; for application to time perception, see Keele, Pokorny, Corcos, & Ivry, 1985, or Ivry & Hazeltine, 1995). In addition to deciding about the size of the steps and when to apply a change in direction, the experimenter also has to decide when to stop the experiment. For instance, it could be after a fixed number of trials or after a fixed number of reversals (Kearnbach, 1991; for time perception, see Rammsayer & Lima, 1991).

The case of the MCS is of particular interest as it leads to the drawing of psychometric functions, as do some methods used for studying animal timing. With the MCS, a certain number (usually 6–8) of comparison intervals are determined in advance, and they are presented randomly from trial to trial. Each of the comparison intervals is presented on several occasions, and a psychometric function is traced on the basis of the probability of responding that the comparison interval is judged as being longer than the standard. For instance, an experiment may present a 250 ms standard, with comparison intervals taking the following values: 215, 225, 235, 245, 255, 265, 275 and 285 ms. Figure 2.2 shows the probability, on the y axis, of judging that a given comparison interval is longer than the standard, as a function of the value of the comparison intervals on the x axis.

There are several ways of operationally defining the threshold. On this function, the 0% and 100% cases represent perfect discrimination, and 50% the incapacity to discriminate (note that the point at 50% is often referred to as the *point of subjective equality* — PSE — which equals 247.84 ms in the example reported in Figure 2.2). Researchers often refer to the notion of constant error (CE), which is derived from the PSE with the MCS: CE = PSE – Standard. The threshold,

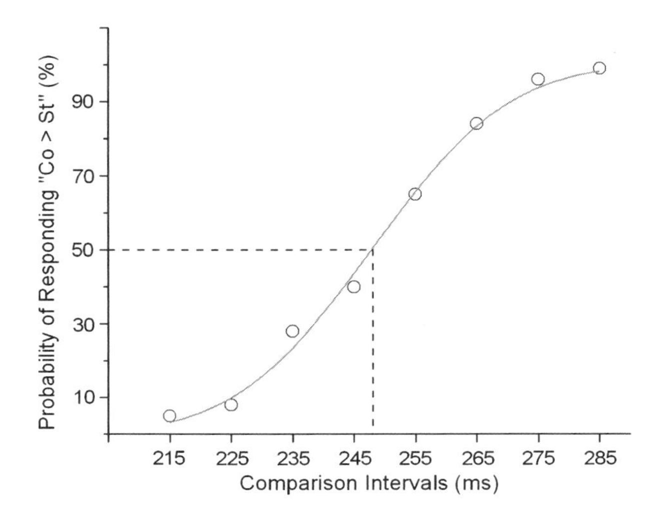

Figure 2.2: Psychometric function used for estimating the difference threshold with the method of constant stimuli. "Co > St" means that the comparison interval is judged as longer than the standard. The model for fitting the data points in this example is the cumulative normal distribution, and the dashes indicate the point of subjective equality.

JND, is the distance on the x axis corresponding to the 25% and 75% point values on the y axis of the function, divided by 2 (Gescheider, 1997). These two points are selected because they are midpoints between perfect discrimination and random responses.

It is also fundamental to understand that the function drawn in Figure 2.2 is selected for its potential to minimize the deviation between the data points and the function. In the present example, the model selected was based on an assumption often made in psychological science, i.e., the belief that phenomena are distributed according to the properties of the so-called *normal distribution* (or Gaussian function). The function drawn in Figure 2.2 is based on a cumulative normal function. Interestingly, in the field of duration discrimination, researchers frequently use different measures to express the difference threshold. One common way of expressing threshold is to extract the value equivalent to one standard deviation on the psychometric function (Killeen & Weiss, 1987). With such an index, the difference threshold resulting from the example in Figure 2.2 is 17.75 ms.

Note however that other mathematical formulations, like the Weibull and logistic functions (Macmillan & Creelman, 1991), can provide a reasonable description of the psychometric functions on the basis of the same two parameters, the mean and the variance. As well, on the basis of their pseudo-logistic model for accounting for timing data, Killeen, Fetterman and Bizo (1997) recommend the adoption of a pseudo-logistic function to fit parameters of a psychometric function:

$$p = [1 + \exp(\mu - t/0.55\sigma_t)]^{-1} \tag{2.2}$$

where p is the probability of responding that the comparison is longer than the standard and t the value of the comparison intervals. In this equation, μ is the PSE and σ an estimate of sensitivity, i.e., of the difference threshold.

Using psychometric functions is not restricted to cases involving 2AFC tasks (Lapid, Ulrich, & Rammsayer, 2008). There are psychophysical experiments involving no presentation of a standard on each trial, but only the presentation of what is referred to above as the comparison interval. In such a task, an observer is asked to assign the intervals (in the case of time perception tasks) to one of two categories, short or long. Over the course of the trials, the observer develops an implicit standard. This procedure is referred to as the many-to-few method (Allan, 1979; Morgan, Watamaniuk, & McKee, 2000). With such a procedure — which is, strictly speaking, more categorization than discrimination — it is possible to draw psychometric functions like the one in Figure 2.2, and to do the analyses described earlier (see, for instance, Grondin, 2005).

In some studies on duration discrimination, it is not the MCS that is employed, but simply the discrimination between two intervals, one short and one long (see, for instance, Grondin, 1998). Instead of determining the difference threshold, the performance levels are expressed in the terms of the *Signal Detection Theory* (SDT — Bonnet, 1986; Gescheider, 1997; Macmillan & Creelman, 1991). For a given trial in a typical SDT task, an observer is presented, or is not presented, a signal (stimulus) on a background noise, and has to decide if it was only the noise, or the noise plus the signal that was presented. The distributions of the possible internal values of the noise and signal + noise conditions are substituted, in the application to duration discrimination, by the distribution of internal representations of short and long intervals, respectively (Figure 2.3). It is therefore possible to derive from this situation an index of sensitivity and an estimate of response bias. A frequently used index of sensitivity is d' (pronounce d prime), which is based on the assumption that the distributions are normal and have equal variances. The location of a response criterion is often expressed by the index β or c (Macmillan & Creelman, 1991).

2.2.2.1. Structure issue There are different procedures for estimating the capability to discriminate time intervals. One critical issue that will also determine the level of discrimination is the nature of the interval, i.e., the way of marking time. A basic distinction encountered in the literature concerns the structure of the intervals, i.e., filled versus empty (Grondin, 1993; Grondin, Meilleur-Wells, Ouellette, & Macar, 1998; Rammsayer & Lima, 1991). The interval is said to be filled when there is one continuous signal between onset and offset. An observer is asked to judge the duration from the beginning to the end of the signal. An empty interval is the silent period (i.e., involving no stimulation) between two — usually very brief — sensory

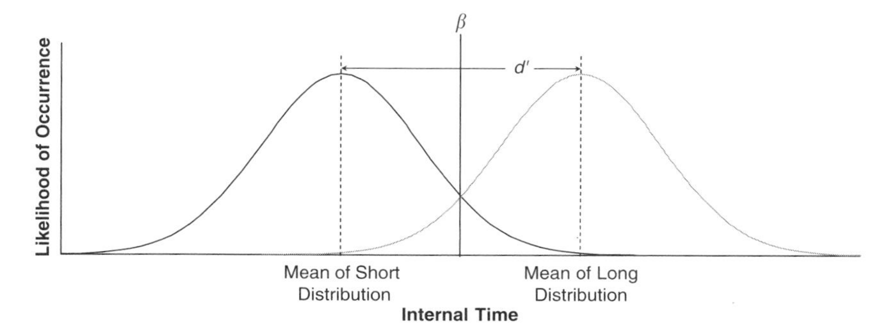

Figure 2.3: Signal detection theory adapted to duration discrimination. The areas related to the short distribution and located to the left and to the right of the response criterion, β, are the proportion of "short" (correct rejection) and "long" (false alarm) responses, respectively; and the areas related to the long distribution and located to the left and to the right of the response criterion, β, are the proportion of "short" (miss) and "long" (hit) responses, respectively.

signals. In other words, two different sensory events mark the beginning and the end of the interval.

Whatever the structure of the interval, filled or empty, other factors determine the level of discrimination. The modality within which the signals are delivered for marking time influences performance. Clearly, discrimination is better when intervals are marked by auditory signals rather than by visual or tactile signals (Grondin, 2003; Grondin & Rousseau, 1991).

For the specific case of empty intervals, the length of the two signals can also be varied, with longer markers resulting in poorer discrimination (Kato & Tsuzaki, 1994; Rammsayer & Leutner, 1996). Moreover, empty intervals are much more difficult to discriminate if the two signals marking time are delivered from two different sensory modes (intermodal conditions: Grondin, Roussel, Gamache, Roy, & Ouellet, 2005; Grondin & Rousseau, 1991; Rousseau, Poirier, & Lemyre, 1983). Finally, signals marking time intervals can be delivered from different sources (auditory or visual) in space, which may result in a kappa effect, i.e., in an impression that duration is longer when there is more space between signals (Grondin & Plourde, 2007a; Jones & Huang, 1982; see Chapters 1 and 5).

2.2.2.2. Rhythmical issue The kappa effect we just referred to is indeed typically observable when a variant of the procedures described earlier is adopted. Instead of judging duration after each presentation of an interval (single stimulus) or after presenting two distinct intervals, multiple consecutive empty intervals are presented, with, for instance, the second marker of the first interval being also the first marker of the second interval. Thus, a series of x brief signals define $x-1$ intervals.

There are indeed numerous experiments involving judgments about the relative duration of intervals conducted in a context involving rhythm or sequences of multiple intervals (Friberg & Sundberg, 1995). In most of these studies, the signals marking a series of intervals are auditory and issued from a single source (or binaurally through earphones). The task of an observer may be to detect the interval in the sequence that is different (briefer or longer) from the others, or to judge whether the last interval of the sequence was shorter or longer than the preceding ones (Grondin, 2001b; ten Hoopen et al., 1995), in which case some distortion of perceived duration may occur (see Chapters 3 and 5). Interestingly, when such a series is delivered, an observer is placed in a position where the next signal can be expected; in other words, instead of judging the duration on the basis of interval measurements, the basis for judging time might be the expectation generated by the regularity of events occurring (Jones & Boltz, 1989; see Chapter 6). In some other experiments, two distinct sequences of intervals are presented. Typically, standard (equal) intervals are presented in the first sequence, followed by the series of equal intervals (comparison) that are shorter or longer than the standards. A typical finding is that increasing the number of intervals presented improves the discrimination of intervals (Drake & Botte, 1993). Interestingly, the manipulation of the duration between the two sequences and the arrangement of blocks of trials within a session generate contexts that affect discrimination level or the perceived duration of some intervals (Jones & McAuley, 2005; McAuley & Jones, 2003; McAuley & Miller, 2007).

2.2.3. *Continuous Tapping*

Although not a psychophysical method *per se*, timing researchers occasionally adopt another classic method besides the discrimination methods briefly presented here to address the issue of variability of time: producing a continuous series of intervals with finger taps on a push-button repetitive tapping; see Chapters 6 and 7). In such a task, an observer is asked to listen to a sequence of brief isochronous stimuli, most often brief auditory sounds, to synchronize their taps with the sounds for a few trials and to pursue the tapping activity at the same pace (i.e., to produce equal intervals) without the external sounds a number of times (often 31 taps marking 30 intervals). This procedure generally leads to the extraction of two dependent variables of interest: the mean (*M*) produced intervals and the variability, expressed by the standard deviation (SD) of the distribution of the produced intervals. From these two dependent variables is derived a third, the coefficient of variation (CV), which is the ratio of SD to *M* (Madison, 2001). By the application of autocorrelation to sequences of intervals, it is possible to identify the portion of the observed variability that can be attributed to the implementation process, i.e., the motor variability, and the portion that is due to a mechanism responsible for keeping track of time (Wing & Kristofferson, 1973).

What is described in the preceding paragraph as a preliminary phase — synchronization — preparing for the production of a series of intervals is indeed, in many studies, the critical issue. Sensorimotor synchronization is, *per se*, an important research field for people interested in music performance, for instance, where excellence relies heavily on the rhythmical coordination of perception and action. The reader will find in Repp (2005) a comprehensive review of the empirical and theoretical issues related to the study of sensorimotor synchronization with tapping.

Whether or not the processing of time intervals is based on the same timing process in perception (discrimination) and motor production (tapping) tasks is an important theoretical issue (Keele et al., 1985; Ivry & Hazeltine, 1995; Repp, 1998). There are indications that interval production can be improved after training for the discrimination of intervals (Meegan, Aslin, & Jacobs, 2000). However, whether the same mechanism is involved in all types of discrimination tasks (Keele, Nicoletti, Ivry, & Pokorny, 1989) or in all types of motor timing tasks (Robertson et al., 1999) remains disputable (see Chapter 7).

It is important to note that the finger-tapping task described here is often referred to as "interval production" or a "production task". Strictly speaking, this may be correct but might lead to some confusion in the time perception literature. As we will see later, in timing and time perception literature, a production task sometimes rather refers to the production (with two finger taps, for instance) of a single interval, where the observer is asked verbally to produce a target interval, in chronometric units (minutes, seconds). Tapping can also be used by an observer to reproduce a single interval just presented by the experimenter.

2.3. Methods From an Animal-Behaviour Perspective

Literature on animal behaviour is filled with examples showing how critical temporal adaptation is. The ecological relevance of a temporal perspective can be observed, for instance, with birds, which can learn not only the frequency of songs but also their durational components (MacDonald & Meck, 2003). As well, animal behaviours like navigation, foraging, reproduction and predator avoidance are somehow linked to time (Hills, 2003).

Indeed, the methods used in the traditional field of animal learning,[1] developed in the first half of the 20th century, provide many examples of the capability of different species to meet the temporal requirements of a task. In his development of operant conditioning, B.F. Skinner used different reinforcement schedules, i.e., different rules governing the conditions under which a reinforcer was delivered (see, for instance,

1. In the traditional field of animal learning, a basic distinction is made between classical (or Pavlovian) conditioning and operant (or Skinnerian) conditioning. The latter is described in the text. The former is the study of the association between an unconditional stimulus (US), which elicits an unconditional response (UR), and a conditional stimulus (CS). Frequent presentations of a US and a CS, either simultaneously or in close succession, eventually lead to the formation of a conditional response (CR) when only the CS is presented. In such experiments, the animal does not have to judge time explicitly, but the integration of the temporal context of events is critical (Gallistel & Gibbon, 2000). The strength of the CR depends on the interval between the presentation of the US and the CS, and on the period elapsed since the last presentation of the US.

Klein, 1991; or Mazur, 1990; or Chapter 10 for a variety of operant-conditioning situations). It should be kept in mind that an animal learns to associate its response (like pecking or tapping) with the arrival of a reinforcer (food). Among these schedules, there is the *fixed interval*. In such a condition, an animal is reinforced, whatever the number of responses it provides in the meantime, only after a fixed amount of time (for instance, 30 s) has elapsed. What is usually observed is an increase in the animal's response rate as it gets closer to the time of reinforcement.[2] Other schedules imply the use of variable periods of time (*variable interval*) before presenting reinforcers, which result in a moderate and steady rate of responding. Even more interesting from a temporal timekeeping perspective is the schedule called *differential reinforcement of low rates* (DRL), a typical case of *temporal differentiation*. With such a schedule, there is a fixed interval (say, 30 s) before the delivery of the reinforcer, but if the animal responds before the end of the interval, the chronometer is set back to zero (the animal has to wait another 30 s). In such a schedule, the animal clearly needs to learn time.

Recent methodological approaches in animal literature were conceived to directly test the mechanisms underlying this ability to keep track of time (Lejeune & Macar, 1994; Lejeune & Wearden, 2006). Some of these methods are interesting in that they can be used to draw psychometric functions comparable to those described earlier. An essential feature of such methods is that the reinforced response is determined by the duration of the stimuli previously presented.

A classical procedure in animal-timing literature is called *bisection*. Typically, the animal first learns, over a series of sessions, to associate a short duration, *S*, with one lever, and a long duration, *L*, with another lever. The duration is marked, for instance, with a visual signal (lit for a period equal to *S* or *L*, the anchors, or referent values). The animal has to tap the appropriate lever to be reinforced (receiving food). Once this discrimination is learned, i.e., when the level of discrimination accuracy is very high, the animal is placed in conditions where interval lengths from *S* to *L* are presented, and the interval presented has to be categorised as *S* or *L*. As was the case for the MCS, it eventually becomes possible to draw a psychometric function where the probability of responding long (i.e., tapping on the lever associated with *L*) on the *y* axis is plotted as a function of time, from *S* to *L*, on the *x* axis. As described earlier, it is possible to extract two important measures, the PSE (or bisection point) and the threshold, i.e., the sensitivity (or the variability of estimates).

A less often used procedure is called *temporal generalization* (Church & Gibbon, 1982; Gibbon, Church, & Meck, 1984). With such a procedure, the animal learns the value of one standard (say, 8-s duration), i.e., the animal is reinforced only when responding after the presentation of an 8-s signal. Once the standard is learned,

2. There are different variants of this fixed interval method, and one that is interesting for animal timing researchers is the *peak procedure* (Catania, 1970; Lejeune, Ferrara, Simons, & Wearden, 1997; Roberts, 1981).

various intervals around (and including) 8 s are presented in a random order. The probability of responding is at its maximum when 8-s signals are presented, and decreases gradually as the distance (shorter or longer) from 8 s increases. The distribution of responses is called the temporal generalization gradient.

With both bisection and temporal generalization procedures, it is possible to test a very important theoretical question in the field of psychological time, that of the scalar variance property. While human timing literature traditionally refers to the Weber's law to describe the relationship between the variability of time and the magnitude of intervals under investigation, scalar timing is the term used in animal-timing literature to describe this property. For instance, the spread of the gradient in a temporal generalization task generally increases as a function of the magnitude of the standard and, consequently, when reported on the same relative scale, the gradients obtained with different standard values are superimposed. As well, in the bisection task, the variability increases as a function of the bisection point. In animal-timing literature, it is most often reported that the scalar property holds for a wide range of intervals (from .1 to 100 s), but not for very short or very long intervals (Lejeune & Wearden, 2006).

It is interesting to note that the bisection method developed in animal timing was largely adopted for the study of scalar timing in humans (Allan, 2002; Allan & Gebhardt, 2001; Allan & Gibbon, 1991; Penney, Allan, Meck, & Gibbon, 1998; Rodriguez-Girones & Kacelnik, 2001; for a review, see Wearden & Lejeune, 2006). Temporal generalization has also been used in humans (Wearden, 1992).

2.4. Methods from a Cognitive Perspective

Beyond time psychophysics and animal-timing literature, there is a huge amount of empirical work published on various psychological time experiments. In most of these studies, the intervals to be judged are relatively long. Indeed, some authors adopt a distinction between time perception and time estimation (Fraisse, 1984). The passage from perception (short intervals) to time estimation (long intervals) is somewhat of a loose concept, as it is usually not based on a firm operational definition or on robust empirical demonstrations. Fraisse reports a transition at some point between 2 and 5 s (see also Michon, 1978), but a distinction based on the Weber fraction (JND/Standard) or the benefit obtained by adopting an explicit counting/segmentation strategy rather points toward a value closer to 1.2–1.5 s (Grondin, 2001a; Grondin, Meilleur-Wells, & Lachance, 1999; Grondin, Ouellet, & Roussel, 2004). Whatever the exact cutoff between perceiving and estimating time, the latter case involves the contribution of cognitive processes; indeed, whether counting is forbidden or permitted is often a methodological issue to be clarified when tasks involve the estimation of long intervals.

Thus, there is a more purely cognitive approach to time. Probably as a consequence of the zeitgeist in psychology in general, such an approach to psychological time was very popular in the late 1960s and the 1970s, and remained an important approach in the 1980s (Block, 1990; Levin & Zakay, 1989). Essentially, although there are multiple methods — as we have seen in the scaling portion of the psychophysics section above — for addressing the question of the perceived or estimated duration of long intervals, in a cognitive perspective three main methods are usually recognized to test the effect of different factors on psychological time.

First, there is a *method of verbal estimation* (VE). After the presentation of a target interval, a participant is asked to provide a verbal estimation of its duration, using temporal units such as seconds or minutes. A second method is called *production* (MP): After the experimenter specifies a target interval in temporal units, a participant produces this interval, for instance, with two verbal "tops", or two finger "taps" marking the beginning and the end or the interval, or by pushing a button for a duration judged equivalent to the target interval. A third method is referred to as *reproduction* (MR). The experimenter somehow presents a target interval (presenting a continuous sound or flash, for instance), and the participant reproduces the length of the interval by some operation. In addition to these three basic methods, some authors report a fourth called the *method of comparison* (Bindra & Waksberg, 1956; Wallace & Rabin, 1960; Zakay, 1990), described in detail in the psychophysical section (discrimination). This method is mostly used for the investigation of the mechanisms involved in the processing of brief temporal intervals.

2.4.1. Main Cognitive Issues

While analysing the variability of estimates has been a central issue in the psychophysical and animal-timing perspectives, most studies conducted with VE, MP or MR focus on perceived duration. In addition to testing the perceived duration of intervals lasting from a few seconds up to a minute in conditions involving sex comparisons, personality issues or abnormal conditions (pathology), a lot of studies conducted in order to understand the effect of attention or the role of memory on time estimates have been based on these three traditional methods. It is not intended to review these effects in this chapter. Block and Zakay (1997) and Roeckelein (2000) provide an overview of the findings in these research areas (see also Chapters 4 and 12).

Nonetheless, it is important to understand the classical methods for investigating the effects of attention on time perception. Research on attention in experimental psychology is a vast world from which time researchers import methods. There are two very important features for describing how attentional mechanisms are studied. One feature — selectivity — is related to the need for selecting specific elements of information in the environment; the other feature is related to the fact that attentional resources are limited. In relation to selectivity, a classical method for investigating the attentional requirement of a cognitive activity is to use a dual-task strategy, where a participant is asked to process two types of information at the same time (Brown, 1997; Brown & Boltz, 2002). Comparing the levels of performance reached in a dual-task situation with the performance in a single-task condition provides an idea of the cost of each of the tasks in terms of resources. In the case of time perception research, a participant is typically asked to concurrently keep track of time and to perform a nontemporal task, sometimes referred to a secondary task, like searching for stimuli on a visual display or completing a simple mathematical calculation. What is usually found is a decrease of the perceived length of an interval as more attention is dedicated to the nontemporal task (Zakay & Block, 1997, 2004). Indeed, with a VE method, the duration is reported to be briefer if less attention is allocated to time. However, with MR, if a nontemporal task is introduced during the reproduction phase, the attention required for performing this task is detracted from the passage of time; consequently, the accumulation of time internally, which was facilitated by attention to time, is disrupted and an additional period (longer time) is required for the person to reach a duration equivalent to the one presented before the reproduction phase. How a secondary, nontemporal, task suffers from attention sharing with a temporal task is discussed further in Chapter 4. Note that there are varieties of dual-task experiments in time research, including performing two temporal tasks concurrently (Brown & West, 1990; Brown, Stubbs, & West, 1992) and specifying in advance, before each trial, the percentage of attention to allocate to each of the two tasks (Casini & Macar, 1997; Grondin & Macar, 1992; Macar, Grondin, & Casini, 1994).

There are other classical methods of investigation in the field of attention that have been used in the context of time perception. For instance, in a typical study on reaction time, a warning signal announces that a target signal will soon be presented. A participant has to react (push a button) as soon as the target is presented. The foreperiod, i.e., the period between the warning and target signals, is varied randomly. Usually, the reaction times get shorter (better performances) as the foreperiod gets longer, which is interpreted as an effect of better attentional preparation as the foreperiod gets older (the occurrence of the target becomes more and more likely). Such a strategy was adopted by Grondin and Rammsayer (2003) for studying time perception: As the foreperiod preceding an interval to be discriminated got older, the duration of the interval to be discriminated was perceived as longer (and often as less variable).

2.4.2. Reliability of the Three Traditional Methods

As noted in the preceding discussion, using different methods leads to different patterns of results, but this is due to the nature of the task. In the example above, the results with VE and MR look opposite but are not conceptually contradictory.

The question that could be raised is whether there is any preferable method to use. Some authors have addressed this question and compared the three methods, VE, MR and MP, sometimes with brief intervals (<1 s, McConchie & Rutschmann, 1971) but usually with long ones (Carlson & Feinberg, 1970; Horstein & Rotter, 1969). While at the term of their literature review Wallace and Rabin (1960) noted a lower degree of accuracy with VE than with MP or MR, Fraisse (1957) found a significant correlation between VE and MP but not between the other methods, and Zakay (1993) observed similar patterns of results with VE and MR.

2.4.3. *Retrospective Timing*

As described in the introduction of this chapter, there is a category of studies in the field of time perception, referred to as *retrospective timing*, which is indeed related to judgments about the duration of past events or of activities in which a participant is involved without knowing that time will have to be estimated (see also Chapters 4 and 12). This type of study is therefore directly related to the memory processes, and it is the remembered duration that is assessed. The most common ways for studying retrospective timing are the MR and VE. Indeed, the choice of method depends on the length of the intervals to be remembered. If intervals are relatively short (say <30 s), then MR is appropriate: In this case, the participant is not informed that the duration of the target interval will have to be reproduced, which avoids the problem of counting that often occurs in the prospective condition when long intervals are under investigation. When intervals are very long, it becomes difficult to use the MR and, consequently, VE is usually preferred. For instance, in a study involving a set of brief (<15 s) melodies to be learned, Boltz (1995; Experiment 1) subsequently asked participants to mentally continue the melody and to indicate with a button press when they reached the end. In the same article (Experiment 2), participants were asked to verbally estimate, to the nearest minute, the duration of films (including commercial breaks) that were very long (up to 57 min).

One problem that can occur with retrospective timing, and that has probably slowed down progress in studying its mechanisms, is the fact that once a trial is completed, the participant is aware that duration is a concern in the experiment. One way to get around this problem is to have a series of activities or tasks performed by the participant and to only inform her/him that the duration of each portion is to be estimated after the tasks/activities have been completed. For instance, in the first study by Boltz (1995), participants learned several melodies before being asked to reproduce their duration (see also Boltz, 2005, for an example with a series of brief videotape sequences). Such a strategy was also adopted by Brown and Stubbs (1988) for judging retrospectively the duration of musical excerpts (from 96 to 570 s), and for judging the length of intervals (from 2 to 8 min) filled with cognitive tasks (Grondin & Plourde, 2007b). The difficulty in studying this range of duration is that it is a bit long for using MR, and also a bit imprecise for VE, where participants might want to round estimates to the nearest minute or half minute. Using multiple tasks or activities before asking for retrospective judgments about time opens the door to the possibility of using different methods, like asking for relative judgments about the duration of these tasks. For instance, a participant can be asked to segment a line, each segment representing the duration of the tasks. Finally, retrospective timing is usually concerned with the accuracy of judgments, and not so much for the variability of estimates. Once again, the perspective of being restricted to a single judgment probably impedes the investigation of the variability issue. One possibility to address the variability issue is to ask participants to estimate the minimum and maximum estimated duration of the tasks, and to operationally define variability as the difference between the maximum and minimum estimates (Grondin & Plourde, 2007b), as some authors have done with prospective timing tasks (see, for instance, Hemmes, Brown, & Kladopoulos, 2004).

2.4.4. Final Comment

In closing this cognitive perspective section, it is important to note that there are psychological time issues related to cognitive processes beyond the research avenues involving explicit judgments about time, whether prospective or retrospective. One such issue involves a much larger temporal scale: How do we organize the chronology of events in our lives? This research avenue is closely related to memory for events that occurred weeks, months, or years ago (Friedman, 1993). Remembering when a past event occurred seems to involve two major processes. One is *location based* and consists of relating events to time patterns, while the other is *distance based* and involves estimating the amount of time between a past event and the present (see Chapters 11 and 12).

2.5. Detecting and Ordering Events

There is a large segment of literature on what is known as "temporal processing" that refers to neither the studies on duration or on explicit judgments about time nor the occurrence of past events as described in the preceding paragraph. This literature rather refers to the temporal integration or segregation of sensory signals or to the order of occurrence in time of brief sensory events. Although many of this book's chapters emphasise the literature on explicit judgments about time, it remains appropriate to briefly inform the reader, in closing this chapter, about the most common methods used in this portion of the temporal processing literature. The reader might want to refer to Hirsh and Sherrick (1961) for their seminal work on the simultaneity versus the successiveness of events, or to Fraisse (1978, 1984) for reviews of early studies.

Generally speaking, a distinction can be made between methods of individuation and methods involving order judgments (Farmer & Klein, 1995). In an individuation task, an observer is asked to determine whether or not only one stimulus is presented. More technically, a researcher might be measuring the threshold to detect a *gap*, i.e., the minimal interval it takes for perceiving a discontinuity in a continuous signal, or a *fusion* threshold, i.e., the minimal duration between two consecutive signals to perceive them as non-simultaneous.

Slightly more complex than the tasks described in the previous paragraph are those related to *temporal order judgments* (TOJ). In addition to the detection of the signals, the TOJ require that these signals be identified and differentiated in order to determine the order of their arrival. Therefore, in such tasks, the signals are different, and the experimenter determines the minimal interval (threshold) between these signals required to perceive their order. Hirsh and Sherrick (1961) reported that the temporal distance required between two signals to perceive their order correctly is much higher than the separation needed to simply determine whether the signals were presented simultaneously or in succession. These authors also noted that the modality of signals is very important when determining the capacity to distinguish simultaneity/successiveness, but this issue is not critical for TOJ.

Different methods and operational definitions can be adopted for measuring thresholds, either in individuation tasks or in TOJ. These technical issues were described in detail above (in the context of the processing of temporal information) and won't be repeated here. The reader should note, however, that there is a large literature on the role of temporal processing, as defined in the present section, in specific language impairments (either related to speech or reading), which offers descriptions of technical issues (Edwards et al., 2004; Farmer & Klein, 1995; Grondin et al., 2007; Tallal, 2003).

Finally, note that the ability to segregate two consecutive stimuli depends partly on the sensory trace left by the first signals. Once again, there is a vast literature on the duration of the stimuli, i.e., on their internal persistence, especially in the visual domain (Di Lollo & Bischoff, 1995; Loftus & Irwin, 1998; Nisly & Wasserman, 1989).

2.6. Conclusions

Understanding research in the field of time perception first requires understanding the nature of the *temporal processing* that is referred to. In the field of specific language impairments, for instance, these terms most often refer to the capability to distinguish whether two sensory events were presented simultaneously or in succession, or which one of two sensory signals occurred first. In the rest of the time perception literature, temporal processing is usually used to refer to the processing of temporal information — this information being the duration itself (a given period or temporal extent).

Another critical issue to take into account when approaching the literature on time perception, especially its cognitive portion, is related to the prospective versus retrospective paradigm. When this issue is left implicit in an article, it is likely that the author is referring to prospective timing, as only a small portion of the writings is concerned with retrospective timing. Special care should also be taken regarding the range of duration that is examined. In animal-timing literature, the same timing process seems to apply to a large range of durations (Lejeune & Wearden, 2006); however, human timing literature shows different sorts of exceptions (Grondin, 2001c) that prevent generalizations about the types of mechanisms involved, and these exceptions are partly due the range of durations scrutinized.

The variability of estimates is an important issue in the study of time. There are several ways of estimating this variability. Interestingly, in both human and animal-timing literature, psychometric functions are used to estimate it, either following classical psychophysical procedures in the former case, or based on bisection or generalization in the latter case. Within a cognitive approach, where the main issue is related to the perceived duration of a time period, three methods (VE, MP and MR) are most often used. It is difficult to say which one is the most reliable, but the length of the time period to be estimated may determine the choice of method.

It is also interesting to note that methods like MR or the comparison of intervals are used not only in behavioural testing but also now in studies on timing addressing the issue of pharmacological effects (Rammsayer, Hennig, Haag, & Lange, 2001; see Chapter 9) or the cerebral bases of temporal processing as investigated with different brain imaging techniques (Pfeuty, Ragot, & Pouthas, 2003a, b; Pouthas, Garnero, Ferrandez, & Renault, 2000; Rao, Mayer, & Harrington, 2001; see Chapter 8). Indeed, it is either the theory or model being tested, the constraints imposed by a special population, or technical issues that guide the experimenter in the choice of an appropriate method of investigation.

Acknowledgements

This research was supported by research grants from the Natural Sciences and Engineering Council of Canada and Social Sciences and Humanities Council of Canada.

References

Allan, L. G. (1979). The perception of time. *Perception and Psychophysics*, *26*, 340–354.

Allan, L. G. (2002). Are the referents remembered in temporal bisection? *Learning and Motivation*, *33*, 10–31.

Allan, L. G., & Gebhardt, K. (2001). Temporal bisection with trial referents. *Perception and Psychophysics*, *63*, 524–540.

Allan, L. G., & Gibbon, J. (1991). Human bisection at the geometric mean. *Learning and Motivation*, *22*, 39–58.

Bindra, D., & Waksberg, H. (1956). Methods and terminology in the studies of time estimation. *Psychological Bulletin*, *53*, 155–159.

Block, R. A. (Ed.) (1990). *Cognitive models of psychological time*. Hillsdale, NJ: Erlbaum.

Block, R. A., & Zakay, D. (1997). Prospective and retrospective duration judgments: A meta-analytic review. *Psychonomic Bulletin & Review*, *4*, 184–197.

Block, R. A., & Zakay, D. (2001). Retrospective and prospective timing: Memory, attention and consciousness. In: C. Hoerl & T. McCormack (Eds), *Time and memory: Issues in philosophy and psychology* (pp. 59–76). Oxford: Clarendon Press.

Boltz, M. G. (1995). Effects of event structure on retrospective duration judgments. *Perception and Psychophysics*, *57*, 1080–1096.

Boltz, M. G. (2005). Duration judgments of naturalistic events in the auditory and visual modalities. *Perception and Psychophysics*, *67*, 1362–1375.

Bonnet, C. (1986). *Manuel pratique de psychophysique*. Paris: Armand Colin.

Brown, S. W. (1985). Time perception and attention: The effects of prospective versus retrospective paradigms and tasks demands on perceived duration. *Perception and Psychophysics*, *38*, 115–124.

Brown, S. W. (1997). Attentional resources in timing: Interference effects in concurrent temporal and nontemporal working memory tasks. *Perception and Psychophysics*, *59*, 1118–1140.

Brown, S. W., & Boltz, M. (2002). Attentional processes in time perception: Effects of mental workload and event structure. *Journal of Experimental Psychology: Human Perception and Performance*, *28*, 600–615.

Brown, S. W., & Stubbs, D. A. (1988). The psychophysics of retrospective and prospective timing. *Perception*, *17*, 297–310.

Brown, S. W., Stubbs, D. A., & West, A. N. (1992). Attention, multiple timing, and psychophysical scaling of temporal judgments. In: F. Macar, V. Pouthas & W. Friedman (Eds), *Time, action, cognition: Towards bridging the gap* (pp. 129–140). Dordrecht, The Netherlands: Kluwer.

Brown, S. W., & West, A. N. (1990). Multiple timing and the allocation of attention. *Acta Psychologica*, *75*, 103–121.

Carlson, V. R., & Feinberg, I. (1970). Time judgment as a function of method, practice, and sex. *Journal of Experimental Psychology*, *85*, 171–180.

Casini, L., & Macar, F. (1997). Effects of attention manipulation on judgments of duration and on intensity in the visual modality. *Memory & Cognition*, *25*, 812–818.

Catania, A. C. (1970). Reinforcement schedules and psychophysical judgments: A study of some temporal properties of behavior. In: W. N. Schoenfeld (Ed.), *The theory of reinforcement schedules* (pp. 1–42). New York: Appleton-Century-Crofts.

Church, R. M., & Gibbon, J. (1982). Temporal generalization. *Journal of Experimental Psychology: Animal Behavior Processes*, *2*, 165–186.

Cornsweet, T. N. (1962). The staircase method in psychophysics. *American Journal of Psychology*, *75*, 485–491.

Di Lollo, V., & Bischoff, W. F. (1995). Inverse-intensity effect in duration of visible persistence. *Psychological Bulletin*, *118*, 223–237.

Drake, C., & Botte, M-C. (1993). Tempo sensitivity in auditory sequences: Evidence for a multiple-look model. *Perception and Psychophysics*, *54*, 277–286.

Edwards, V. T., Giaschi, D. E., Dougherty, R. F., Edgell, D., Bjornson, B. H., Lyons, C., & Douglas, R. M. (2004). Psychophysical indexes of temporal processing abnormalities in children with developmental dyslexia. *Developmental Neuropsychology*, *25*, 321–354.

Eisler, A., Eisler, H., & Montgomery, H. (2004). A quantitative model for retrospective subjective duration. *NeuroQuantology*, *4*, 263–291.

Eisler, H. (1976). Experiments on subjective duration 1878–1975: A collection of power function exponents. *Psychological Bulletin*, *83*, 185–200.

Farmer, M. E., & Klein, R. M. (1995). The evidence for a temporal processing deficit linked to dyslexia. *Psychonomic Bulletin and Review*, *2*, 460–493.

Fechner, G. (1860/1965). *Elements of psychophysics*. New York: Holt, Rinehart and Winston.

Fraisse, P. (1957). *Psychologie du temps* (Psychology of time). Paris: Presses Universitaires de France.

Fraisse, P. (1978). Time and rhythm perception. In: E. Carterette & M. Friedman (Eds), *Handbook of perception* (Vol. VIII, pp. 203–254). New York: Academic Press.
Fraisse, P. (1984). Perecption and estimation of time. *Annual Review of Psychology*, *35*, 1–36.
Friberg, A., & Sundberg, J. (1995). Time discrimination in a monotonic, isochronic sequence. *Journal of Acoustical Society of America*, *98*, 2524–2531.
Friedman, W. J. (1993). Memory for the time of past events. *Psychological Bulletin*, *113*, 44–66.
Gallistel, C. R., & Gibbon, J. (2000). Time, rate and conditioning. *Psychological Review*, *107*, 289–344.
Gescheider, G. A. (1997). *Psychophysics: Method, theory and application*. Hillsdale, NJ: Erlbaum.
Gibbon, J., Church, R. M., & Meck, W. H. (1984). Scalar timing in memory. In: J. Gibbon & L. G. Allan (Eds), *Annals of the New York Academy of Sciences: Vol. 423, timing and time perception* (pp. 52–77). New York: New York Academy of Sciences.
Glicksohn, J., & Myslobodsky, M. S. (2006). *Timing the future: The case for a time-based prospective memory*. London: World Scientific.
Grondin, S. (1993). Duration discrimination of empty and filled intervals marked by auditory and visual signals. *Perception and Psychophysics*, *54*, 383–394.
Grondin, S. (1998). Judgments of the duration of visually marked empty intervals: Linking perceived duration and sensitivity. *Perception and Psychophysics*, *60*, 319–330.
Grondin, S. (2001a). A temporal account of the limited processing capacity. *Behavioral and Brain Sciences*, *24*, 122–123.
Grondin, S. (2001b). Discriminating time intervals presented in sequences marked by visual signals. *Perception and Psychophysics*, *63*, 1214–1228.
Grondin, S. (2001c). From physical time to the first and second moments of psychological time. *Psychological Bulletin*, *127*, 22–44.
Grondin, S. (2003). Sensory modalities and temporal processing. In: H. Helfrich (Ed.), *Time and mind II* (pp. 75–92). Goettingen, Germany: Hogrefe & Huber.
Grondin, S. (2005). Overloading temporal memory. *Journal of Experimental Psychology: Human Perception and Performance*, *31*, 869–879.
Grondin, S., Dionne, G., Malenfant, N., Plourde, M., Cloutier, M., & Jean, C. (2007). Temporal processing skills of children with and without specific language impairment. *Canadian Journal of Speech-Language Pathology and Audiology*, *31*, 38–46.
Grondin, S., & Macar, F. (1992). Dividing attention between temporal and nontemporal tasks: A performance operating characteristic — POC — analysis. In: F. Macar, V. Pouthas & W. Friedman (Eds), *Time, action, cognition: Towards bridging the gap* (pp. 119–128). Dordrecht, The Netherlands: Kluwer.
Grondin, S., Meilleur-Wells, G., & Lachance, R. (1999). When to start explicit counting in time-intervals discrimination task: A critical point in the timing process of humans. *Journal of Experimental Psychology: Human Perception and Performance*, *25*, 993–1004.
Grondin, S., Meilleur-Wells, G., Ouellette, C., & Macar, F. (1998). Sensory effects on judgments of short-time intervals. *Psychological Research*, *61*, 261–268.
Grondin, S., Ouellet, B., & Roussel, M.-È. (2004). Benefits and limits of explicit counting for discriminating temporal intervals. *Canadian Journal of Experimental Psychology*, *58*, 1–12.
Grondin, S., & Plourde, M. (2007a). Discrimination of time intervals presented in sequences: Spatial effects with multiple auditory sources. *Human Movement Science*, *26*, 702–716.
Grondin, S., & Plourde, M. (2007b). Judging multiminute intervals retrospectively. *Quarterly Journal of Experimental Psychology*, *60*, 1303–1312.

Grondin, S., & Rammsayer, T. (2003). Variable foreperiods and duration discrimination. *Quarterly Journal of Experimental Psychology, 56A*, 702–765.
Grondin, S., & Rousseau, R. (1991). Judging the relative duration of multimodal short empty time intervals. *Perception and Psychophysics, 49*, 245–256.
Grondin, S., Roussel, M.-È., Gamache, P.-L., Roy, M., & Ouellet, B. (2005). The structure of sensory events and the accuracy of judgments about time. *Perception, 34*, 45–58.
Helfrich, H. (Ed.) (2003). *Time and mind II: Information processing perspectives*. Seattle, WA: Hogrefe & Huber.
Hemmes, N. S., Brown, B. L., & Kladopoulos, C. N. (2004). Time perception with and without a concurrent nontemporal task. *Perception and Psychophysics, 66*, 328–341.
Hicks, R. E., Miller, G., & Kinsbourne, M. (1976). Prospective and retrospective judgments of time as a function of amount of information processed. *American Journal of Psychology, 89*, 719–730.
Hills, T. T. (2003). Toward a unified theory of animal event timing. In: W. H. Meek (Ed.), *Functional and neural mechanisms of interval timing* (pp. 77–112). Boca Raton, FL: CRC.
Hirsh, I. J., & Sherrick, C. E. (1961). Perceived order in different sense modalities. *Journal of Experimental Psychology, 62*, 423–432.
Horstein, A. D., & Rotter, G. S. (1969). Research methodology in temporal perception. *Journal of Experimental Psychology, 79*, 561–564.
Ivry, R. B., & Hazeltine, R. E. (1995). The perception and production of temporal intervals across a range of durations: Evidence for a common timing mechanism. *Journal of Experimental Psychology: Human Perception and Performance, 21*, 3–18.
Jones, B., & Huang, Y. L. (1982). Space-time dependencies in psychophysical judgment of extent and duration: Algebraic models of tau and kappa effects. *Psychological Bulletin, 91*, 128–142.
Jones, M. R., & Boltz, M. G. (1989). Dynamic attending and responses to time. *Psychological Review, 96*, 459–491.
Jones, M. R., & McAuley, J. D. (2005). Time judgments in global temporal contexts. *Perception and Psychophysics, 67*, 398–417.
Kato, H., & Tsuzaki, M. (1994). Intensity effect on discrimination of auditory duration flanked by preceding and succeeding tones. *Journal of the Acoustical Society of Japan (E), 15*, 349–351.
Kearnbach, C. (1991). Simple adaptive testing with the weighted up-down method. *Perception and Psychophysics, 49*, 227–229.
Keele, S., Pokorny, R., Corcos, D., & Ivry, R. (1985). Do perception and motor production share common timing mechanisms: A correlational analysis. *Acta Psychologica, 60*, 173–191.
Keele, S. W., Nicoletti, R., Ivry, R., & Pokorny, R. A. (1989). Mechanisms of perceptual timing: Beat-based or interval-based judgements? *Psychological Research, 50*, 251–256.
Killeen, P. R., Fetterman, J. G., & Bizo, L. A. (1997). Time's causes. In: C. M. Bradshaw & E. Szabadi (Eds), *Time and behaviour: Psychological and neurobehavioral analyses* (pp. 79–131). Amsterdam: Elsevier Science.
Killeen, P. R., & Weiss, N. A. (1987). Optimal timing and the Weber function. *Psychological Review, 94*, 455–468.
Klein, S. B. (1991). *Learning: Principles and application* (2nd ed.). New York: McGraw-Hill.
Lapid, E., Ulrich, R., & Rammsayer, T. H. (2008). On estimating the difference limen in temporal-discrimination tasks: A comparison of the 2AFC and the reminder tasks. *Perception and Psychophysics, 70*, 291–305.

Lejeune, H., Ferrara, A., Simons, F., & Wearden, J. H. (1997). Adjusting to changes in the time of reinforcement: Peak-interval transitions in rats. *Journal of Experimental Psychology: Animal Behavior Processes*, *23*, 211–231.
Lejeune, H., & Macar, F. (1994). Régulations temporelles. In: J. Requin, M. Richelle & M. Robert (Eds), *Traité de psychologie expérimentale*. Paris: Presses Universitaires de France.
Lejeune, H., & Wearden, J. H. (2006). Scalar properties in animal timing: Conformity and violations. *Quarterly Journal of Experimental Psychology*, *59*, 1875–1908.
Levin, I., & Zakay, D. (Eds). (1989). *Time and human cognition: A life-span perspective*. Amsterdam: North Holland.
Loftus, G. R., & Irwin, D. E. (1998). On the relations among different measures of visible and informational persistence. *Cognitive Psychology*, *35*, 135–199.
Macar, F., Grondin, S., & Casini, L. (1994). Controlled attention sharing time estimation. *Memory & Cognition*, *22*, 673–686.
MacDonald, C. J., & Meck, W. H. (2003). Time flies and may also sing: Cortico-striatal mechanisms of interval timing and birdsong. In: W. H. Meck (Ed.), *Functional and neural mechanisms of interval timing* (pp. 393–418). Boca Raton, FL: CRC.
Macmillan, N. A., & Creelman, C. D. (1991). *Detection theory: A user's guide*. New York: Cambridge University Press.
Madison, G. (2001). Variability of isochronous tapping: Higher order dependencies as a function of intertap interval. *Journal of Experimental Psychology: Human Perception and Performance*, *27*, 411–421.
Mazur, J. E. (1990). *Learning and behavior* (2nd ed.). Englewood Cliffs, NJ: Prentice Hall.
McAuley, D. J., & Jones, M. R. (2003). Modeling effects of rhythmic context on perceived duration: A comparison of interval and entrainment approaches to short-interval timing. *Journal of Experimental Psychology: Human Perception and Performance*, *29*, 1102–1125.
McAuley, J. D., & Miller, N. S. (2007). Picking up the pace: Effects of global temporal context on sensitivity to the tempo of auditory sequences. *Perception and Psychophysics*, 709–718.
McConchie, R. D., & Rutschmann, J. (1971). Human time estimation: On differences between methods. *Perceptual and Motor Skills*, *32*, 319–336.
Meck, W. H. (Ed.) (2003). *Functional and neural mechanisms of interval timing*. Boca Raton, FL: CRC.
Meegan, D. V., Aslin, R. N., & Jacobs, R. A. (2000). Motor timing learned without motor training. *Nature Neuroscience*, *3*, 860–862.
Michon, J. (1978). The making of the present: A tutorial review. In: J. Requin (Ed.), *Attention and performance VII* (pp. 89–111). Hillsdale, NJ: Erlbaum.
Morgan, M. J., Watamaniuk, S. N. J., & McKee, S. P. (2000). The use of an implicit standard for measuring discrimination thresholds. *Vision Research*, *40*, 2341–2349.
Nisly, T. H., & Wasserman, G. S. (1989). Intensity dependence of perceived duration: Data, theories, and neural integration. *Psychological Bulletin*, *106*, 483–486.
Penney, T. B., Allan, L. G., Meck, W. H., & Gibbon, J. (1998). Memory mixing in duration bisection. In: D. A. Rosenbaum & C. E. Collyer (Eds), *Timing of behaviour: Neural, computational, and psychological perspectives* (pp. 165–193). Cambridge, MA: MIT Press.
Pentland, A. (1980). Maximum likelihood estimation: The best PEST. *Perception and Psychophysics*, *28*, 377–379.
Perret-Clermont, A.-N. (Ed.) (2005). *Thinking time: A multidisciplinary perspective on time*. Cambridge, MA: Hogrefe.
Pfeuty, M., Ragot, R., & Pouthas, V. (2003a). Processes involved in tempo perception: A CNV analysis. *Psychophysiology*, *40*, 69–76.

Pfeuty, M., Ragot, R., & Pouthas, V. (2003b). When time is up: CNV time course differentiates the roles of the hemispheres in the discrimination of short tone durations. *Experimental Brain Research*, *151*, 372–379.

Pouthas, V., Garnero, L., Ferrandez, A.-M., & Renault, B. (2000). ERPs and PET analysis of time perception: Spatial and temporal brain mapping during visual discrimination tasks. *Human Brain Mapping*, *10*, 49–60.

Rammsayer, T. H., Hennig, J., Haag, A., & Lange, N. (2001). Effects of noradrenergic activity on temporal information processing in humans. *Quarterly Journal of Experimental Psychology, Section B: Comparative and Physiological Psychology*, *54B*, 247–258.

Rammsayer, T. H., & Leutner, D. (1996). Temporal discriminationas a function of marker duration. *Perception and Psychophysics*, *58*, 1213–1223.

Rammsayer, T. H., & Lima, S. D. (1991). Duration discrimination of filled and empty auditory intervals: Cognitive and perceptual factors. *Perception and Psychophysics*, *50*, 565–574.

Rao, S. M., Mayer, A. R., & Harrington, D. L. (2001). The evolution of brain activation during temporal processing. *Nature Neuroscience*, *4*, 317–323.

Repp, B. H. (1998). Variations on a theme by Chopin: Relations between perception and production of timing in music. *Journal of Experimental Psychology: Human Perception and Performance*, *24*, 791–811.

Repp, B. H. (2005). Sensorimotor senchronization: A review of the tapping literature. *Psychonomic Bulletin and Review*, *12*, 969–992.

Roberts, S. (1981). Isolation of an internal clock. *Journal of Experimental Psychology: Animal Behavior Processes*, *7*, 242–268.

Robertson, S. D., Zelaznik, H. N., Lantero, D. A., Gadacz Bojczyk, K., Spencer, R. M., Doffin, J. G., & Schneidt, T. (1999). Correlations for timing consistency among tapping and drawing tasks: Evidence against a single timing process for motor control. *Journal of Experimental Psychology: Human Perception and Performance*, *25*, 1316–1330.

Rodriguez-Girones, M. A., & Kacelnik, A. (2001). Relative importance of perceptual and mnemonic variance in human temporal bisection. *Quarterly Journal of Experimental Psychology*, *54A*, 527–546.

Roeckelein, J. E. (2000). *The concept of time in psychology (A resource book and annotated bibliography)*. Westport, CT: Greenwood.

Rousseau, R., Poirier, J., & Lemyre, L. (1983). Duration discrimination of empty time intervals marked by intermodal pulses. *Perception and Psychophysics*, *34*, 541–548.

Stevens, S. S. (1975). *Psychophysics: Introduction to its perceptual, neural and social prospects*. New York: Wiley.

Strathman, A., & Joireman, J. (Eds). (2005). *Understanding behavior in the context of time: Theory, research and application*. Mahwah, NJ: Erlbaum.

Tallal, P. (2003). Language learning disabilities: Integrating research approaches. *Current Directions in Psychological Science*, *12*, 206–211.

Tallal, P., Galaburda, A., Llinas, R. R., & von Euler, C. (Eds). (1993). *Annals of the New York Academy of Sciences: Vol. 682. Temporal information processing in the nervous system: Special reference to dyslexia and dysphasia*. New York: New York Academy of Science.

Taylor, M. M., & Creelman, C. D. (1967). PEST: Efficient estimates on probability functions. *Journal of the Acoustical Society of America*, *74*, 1367–1374.

ten Hoopen, G., Hartsuiker, R., Sasaki, T., Nakajima, Y., Tanaka, M., & Tsumura, T. (1995). Auditory isochrony: Time shrinking and temporal patterns. *Perception*, *24*, 577–593.

Vicario, G. B. (2003). Temporal displacement. In: R. Buccheri, M. Saniga & W. M. Stuckey (Eds), *The nature of time: Geometry, physics and perception* (pp. 53–66). Dordretch, The Netherlands: Kluwer.

Wallace, M., & Rabin, A. (1960). Temporal experience. *Psychological Bulletin*, *57*, 213–235.

Wearden, J. H. (1992). Temporal generalization in humans. *Journal of Experimental Psychology: Animal Behavior Processes*, *18*, 134–144.

Wearden, J. H., & Lejeune, H. (2006). Temporal generalization in humans. *Journal of Experimental Psychology: Animal Behavior Processes*, *18*, 134–144.

Wing, A. M., & Kristofferson, A. B. (1973). Response delay and the timing of discrete motor responses. *Perception and Psychophysics*, *14*, 5–12.

Zakay, D. (1990). The evasive art of subjective time measurement: Some methodological dilemmas. In: R. A. Block (Ed.), *Cognitive models of psychological time* (pp. 59–84). Hillsdale, NJ: Lawrence Erlbaum.

Zakay, D. (1993). Time estimation methods: Do they influence prospective duration estimates? *Perception*, *22*, 91–101.

Zakay, D., & Block, R. A. (1997). Temporal cognition. *Current Directions in Psychological Science*, *6*, 12–16.

Zakay, D., & Block, R. A. (2004). Prospective and retrospective duration judgments: An executive-control perspective. *Acta Neurobiologiae Experimentalis*, *64*, 319–328.

Zelaznik, H. N., Spencer, R. M. C., & Ivry, R. B. (2002). Dissociation of explicit and implicit timing in repetitive tapping and drawing movement. *Journal of Experimental Psychology: Human Perception and Performance*, *28*, 575–588.

Chapter 3

Psychophysical Issues in the Study of Time Perception

Hannes Eisler, Anna D. Eisler and Åke Hellström

This chapter on psychophysical issues in the study of time perception is organized around two main research topics: one topic is related to questions concerning the comparison of successive time intervals; and the other topic is related to the psychophysical function for duration.

3.1. Comparison of Successive Time Intervals

This section presents the main laws, concepts, theoretical issues and empirical findings related to the comparison of successive time intervals. In addition to reviewing some of the laws or findings that were briefly referred to in Chapter 1, this section offers some contemporary and quantitative accounts related to interval comparisons, emphasizing (1) a phenomenon called the *time-order error* and (2) Weber's law.

Except for methods where time intervals are directly estimated, methods of investigating temporal sensation usually involve comparisons of two successive time intervals, with or without a pause (interstimulus interval, ISI) in between. Tasks where the participant is required to reproduce a given interval can be seen as a special case. The objective is to study the precision in sensing small differences in duration between the two intervals as well as the systematic errors (under- and overestimation of one interval relative to the other) that occur. Results regarding precision as well as systematic errors have heavy bearing on the mechanisms that underlie time perception.

3.1.1. Weber's and Fechner's Laws

The physiologist Weber (1834, 1996) undertook to investigate human sensitivity to weight differences by determining the smallest difference between a constant

Psychology of Time

DOI:10.1016/B978-0-08046-977-5.00003-X

(standard) weight and a variable weight that could be discriminated. He found that this difference threshold (*difference limen, DL*, also called the *just noticeable difference, JND*) was proportional to the standard weight. In its simplest form, *Weber's law* may be written

$$\Delta\phi = c\phi \tag{3.1}$$

where ϕ = the standard (St) stimulus, $\Delta\phi$ = the DL and c = a constant. The ratio $\Delta\phi/\phi$, which is constant according to the law, is called the *Weber ratio* (WR, or *Weber fraction*).

Gustav Fechner, the founder of psychophysics (*Elemente der Psychophysik*, 1860), performed extensive series of experiments, often with himself as the participant, which served the purpose of determining human ability to discriminate small differences between successively presented stimuli. Fechner devised various experimental and computational methods to be used for this purpose (see Chapter 2). He made the important assumption that two stimuli that differ by one DL have a constant difference in sensation magnitude. Assuming Weber's law (Equation 3.1) to hold, Fechner deduced a logarithmic relation between physical and subjective stimulus magnitudes:

$$\psi = k \log \frac{\phi}{\phi_0} \tag{3.2}$$

where ψ = sensation magnitude, ϕ = stimulus magnitude, ϕ_0 = the absolute threshold (the faintest perceptible stimulus) and k = a constant. This is what we today call *Fechner's law*.

3.1.2. The Time-Order Error (TOE) and the Indifference Intervals

3.1.2.1. Defining TOE Comparison and discrimination of paired stimuli are not as simple and straightforward operations as one might think. In his experiments with comparisons of successively lifted weights using the *method of right and wrong cases* (a forerunner of the *constant method*, see Chapter 2), Fechner noted that the ratio of right to wrong judgments differed according to whether an incremented comparison weight was lifted before or after a standard weight. He termed this phenomenon *Zeitfehler (time-order error, TOE)* and defined it to be positive when it indicated an overestimation of the first stimulus, relative to the second, and negative in the opposite case. The TOE was treated as a factor that had to be eliminated in the determination of the JND. The TOE has since then been demonstrated for practically every modality, interval duration being no exception. General theoretical discussions of the TOE (e.g., Hellström, 1985; Peak, 1940) are at least partly relevant for the duration modality.

3.1.2.2. The indifference interval: definition and facts In 1868, the German physiologist Karl von Vierordt published his book *Der Zeitsinn nach Versuchen*. Vierordt considered the reproduction of a time interval to be a proper measure of its absolute sensation magnitude. Based on this notion, experiments were performed using Fechner's (1860) *method of average error*. Vierordt found that short intervals tended to be reproduced by too long intervals — in Vierordt's view — overestimated; conversely, long durations were underestimated. This has come to be known as *'Vierordt's law'*. For an intermediate interval, the *indifference interval* or, more generally, *indifference point (IP)*, reproduction was correct, which was interpreted to mean that, for this interval, the ratio of experienced time to physical time (the 'relative sensitivity') equaled 1. For a set of intervals from 0.5 to 8.5 s, bounded by metronome beats and reproduced after a brief ISI, Vierordt found an IP of about 3.5 s, and in another set of intervals up to 4 s, the IP was about 1.5 s. Vierordt also extended his idea to duration comparison. In an experiment using the method of right and wrong cases, eight metronome beats with a fixed St interbeat interval were followed by eight beats whose interbeat interval was the comparison (Co) interval. For Sts of 0.31–1.43 s, negative TOEs were found that increased with the St. Thus no IP was found. Vierordt also measured the WR and found it to increase from 1.4 down to 0.3 s. Thus, he found no empirical support for Weber's law.

Why was the the IP so important to Vierordt? According to him, a reproduction was a direct measure of temporal sensation. Therefore, the IP indicated a critical point in the psychophysical function for time: the point where subjective duration equals physical duration. According to newer views of psychophysics, this view is unrealistic. The reproduction of an St interval is just another interval, which under the given circumstances is experienced as equally long as the St interval. The same holds for a duration which yields a TOE of zero in a comparison experiment.

It may be of interest to mention some of the early experiments that set the stage for later thinking and experimentation. Kollert (1883) presented pairs of intervals (St followed by Co), marked by a metronome, between 0.4 and about 1.5 s, with an ISI equal in length to the St. He used a method similar to the method of limits to determine the DL as the duration difference that could just be sensed — where the Co was no more considered 'equal' to the St. This was done separately for the upper and lower limens ('longer' and 'shorter', respectively). The focus was on the systematic error, revealed by the difference Δ between the upper and lower limens, as well as the average value of the limens. Δ can be seen as a measure of the TOE; it was positive for the shortest intervals and negative for longer intervals. Kollert described this relationship between Δ and St by an exponential function, yielding $\Delta = 0$ for $\mathrm{St} = 0.755$ s, which was thus the IP. He noted that the IP was located at a much shorter duration than in Vierordt's reproduction experiments. Estel (1885) continued Kollert's study using intervals from 1.8 to 8 s, with the same method and partly the same participants (but with bell sounds instead of the metronome). Δ was negative for all Sts; it varied as a periodic function superimposed on a decreasing linear function of St and had minima at successive multiples of the individual IP. Estel found the DL to be correlated with Δ and stated that 'the relative DL is, just like the mean error of estimation, a function of the IP; Weber's law has no validity for the time sense' (p. 65).

The evidence for a connection between DL and Δ is weak; their partial correlations in Estel's data, controlling for St, are indeed negative but only barely significant for one participant. Mehner (1885) used the same method as Estel did in an extensive experiment with himself as the observer, using empty intervals bounded by sounds and Sts of 0.7–12.1 s. He found positive TOEs for Sts <0.7 s or >5 s, and negative TOEs in between (cf. Nakajima, 1958). Mehner reported a tendency for the WR to rise and fall periodically, with minima near multiples of the lowest IP, 0.71 s. However, this was true only for the odd multiples up to nine, so it is hardly an evidence for a connection between WR and IP.

Katz (1906) used the method of right and wrong cases with Sts of 0.3–1.8 s bounded by metronome beats and ISIs of 0–108 s. He confirmed the validity of Vierordt's law and noted that its effect was enhanced when the ISI exceeded 1.8 s. Following Martin and Müller (1899; reviewed by Angell, 1899), Katz explained Vierordt's law by an influence of the *absolute impression* of the second (Co) interval, according to its position above or below the observer's indifference range. This range, usually around 0.6 s, would correspond to durations that are experienced as neither long nor short, and that are sensed without effort, one stimulus arriving just when the perception of the previous one is completed.

In line with this, Woodrow (1934), in reproductions of empty intervals of 0.3–4 s, bordered by brief sounds, determined the IP to be 625 ms. Stott (1935), a student of Woodrow, used durations marked by continuous 1000-Hz tones with the *constant method* to determine the IP for a large number of participants and found the values 0.92 s for novices and 1.6–2.0 s for experienced observers. Woodrow (1935) investigated the effects of prolonged experimentation on comparisons of empty intervals of about 1 s. As the experiment proceeded, the IP shifted toward longer intervals, making the TOE generally more positive. Woodrow's explanation for this (cf. Michels & Helson, 1954; Woodrow, 1933) was that 'the second stimulus of a comparison pair is compared, not with the true magnitude of the first, but with a different magnitude called the effective standard' (p. 150). This magnitude was assumed to arise, initially, by the first stimulus' gravitation toward an absolute IP of 0.625 s (cf. Woodrow, 1934), but as more experience is accumulated, the gravitation would increasingly occur toward the mean of the series instead.

3.1.2.3. Alternative interpretations The focus on the IP may be due to a lingering of Vierordt's (1868) notion that there exists a particular interval that is perceived veridically. However, as we have noted, the estimated IP depends on the range of durations used in an experiment. Furthermore, the phenomena that result in IPs occur in other continua as well. Leuba (1892) proposed a general *law of sense memory*: 'There seems to be a natural tendency in us to shift the sensation held in memory toward the middle of the scale of intensities' (p. 382), and 'memories generally tend toward what has been most frequently experienced before' (p. 383). Hollingworth (1909, 1910) instead described a *central tendency of judgment*, which, he underscored, was a principle of judgment, not sense memory: Reproductions obtained for a set of Sts tend to regress toward the center of this set — greater Sts are underestimated and lesser ones overestimated; this creates a relative, not absolute, IP at this center. The phenomenon is not unique to time perception: Woodrow (1933) studied the comparison of weights using the *constant method* with Sts from 110 to 200 g, either fixed or roving. With fixed Sts, TOEs were consistently negative, whereas with roving Sts, they were positive for light and negative for heavy weights, being around zero for Sts of 130 and 140 g, thus indicating an IP in this region. Helson (1964) accounted for such phenomena by his *adaptation-level (AL) theory*: The IP was considered as another instance of the AL, formed by continuous pooling of stimulus information and being the weighted geometric mean of three classes of stimuli: (1) focal stimuli, (2) background or contextual stimuli and (3) residual stimuli.

3.1.2.4. Measuring indifference intervals Although finding the IP (when one exists) is quite straightforward when using temporal reproduction, its determination with the constant method and similar methods presents some methodological pitfalls. Woodrow (1933, 1935) and Stott (1935) calculated a measure for the IP that rested on a variation of the constant method, where St and Co are presented in both temporal orders. Woodrow (1935) defined, for a constant St, the TOE for each Co as the difference between the proportions of 'Co longer' responses for the orders Co–St and St–Co. The IP was calculated as the magnitude Co_0 of Co where the TOE, thus defined, is zero, that is, where the proportion of 'Co longer' responses is the same in the orders St–Co_0 and Co_0–St — for example, 30%. This method was also used to calculate the mean TOE for an St with its set of Co's. The rationale for this procedure was not stated, but it may have been assumed that, in a hypothetical pair Co_0–Co_0, the proportion of judgments 'second longer' and 'first longer' would be equal. This is not generally true, as we shall see later on. Furthermore, Woodrow's calculation of the IP clashes with his own statement (Woodrow, 1935, p. 138) that '...an indifference interval is by definition precisely an interval toward which the first interval of a comparison pair appears to gravitate — upward when the first interval is shorter than the indifference interval and downward when the first interval is longer'. If Co_0 would be equal to the IP, then in the order Co_0–St, no gravitation would occur, but in the order St–Co_0, St would gravitate toward the IP ($= Co_0$) so that the percentages of 'Co longer' would differ between the two orders, except in the case St = IP.

Does the IP exist? Fraisse (1948) showed, in two reproduction experiments, that the IP was highly dependent on the employed range of Sts (1.138 s with 0.2–1.5 s; 3.65 s with 0.3–12 s), supporting Hollingworth's notion of a central tendency; still, he agreed with Woodrow's idea of an absolute IP of about 0.6 s. In fact, Fraisse proposed that only intervals of at least 0.6 s should be called temporal intervals; shorter ones being merely 'collections of sounds'. He suggested that the calculated IPs could be seen as the midpoints of the ranges, disregarding these brief intervals.

Diverging data exist, which may put the status of Vierordt's law into question. Pöppel (1971) took the relativity of the IP to an experimental test by having participants reproduce only one interval, once. With intervals of 0.5–5 s, an IP emerged at 2.0–2.6 s; with intervals of 10.5–15 s, there was no IP, and in about 2/3 of the cases, the reproduction was shorter than the St. Pöppel concluded that the AL account of the IP phenomenon is invalid and that an 'interindividual temporal constant' in fact exists. Pöppel (2004) suggested that this is another manifestation of a '3-s window' within which temporal integration creates a subjective present. Pöppel's (1971) results for long intervals may be explained by the notion that a duration of approximately 3 s acts as an attractor, in the vein of Woodrow (1933, 1935) and Stott (1935) or as a residual stimulus (Helson, 1964).

Results regarding the IP are quite confusing and hard to summarize. It seems that the initial focus on the IP concept was due to an unrealistic conception of time perception. Durations that are easier to perceive accurately than others may exist. Still, the IP may not necessarily mirror such a property; it does not pertain to a single time interval but to a pair of equally long durations, which in a particular stimulus context and under particular conditions yield a subjective difference of zero. As predicted by the AL- and sensation-weighting (SW) accounts (see below), the IP will often fall in the vicinity of the center of the set of durations but may also be influenced by past stimulation. As we shall see, the subjective difference between two temporal intervals, or two stimuli in general, is highly dependent on the stimulus conditions, such as the ISI. Furthermore, in an experiment where paired successive intervals of similar length are compared, the ISI may be kept constant (with zero as a special case), but the *stimulus onset interval* (SOI; the sum of the first stimulus interval and the ISI), which may play a still greater role in the comparison, necessarily lengthens with the compared intervals.

3.1.3. Quantifying TOEs for Duration

Like perceptual illusions for instance, the TOE can be quantified in physical as well as subjective units (see Chapter 5). In most of the earlier investigations, TOEs were only 'measured' on an ordinal quasi-subjective scale in order to determine the IP. The measure used by Woodrow (1933, 1935) and Stott (1935) belongs to this class but is incorrect (see below). In the *constant method* (see Chapter 2), the TOE is defined in physical units as the difference between the *point of subjective equality* (*PSE*, i.e., the magnitude of Co when it is subjectively equal to St) and the magnitude of St: TOE = PSE − St (with time-order St–Co), and TOE = St − PSE (with time-order Co–St). Thus, in accordance with Fechner's (1860) definition, a negative TOE means that the first-presented stimulus is judged equal to a second-presented stimulus of lesser magnitude. The Δ measure of Kollert (1883) and Estel (1885) also defines the TOE as PSE–St, where PSE = the midpoint between the upper and lower limens.

Various methods of estimating the PSE, and thus the TOE, have been devised (e.g., Guilford, 1954). In many experiments, however, it is not possible to determine the PSE. A measure that is frequently used in such cases is the *percent difference,*

$D\%$, defined as the difference between the percentage of judgments that fall into the categories 'Co<St' and 'Co>St', respectively, for the cumulated data from all stimulus pairs (where the Co's are distributed symmetrically around the St):

$$D\% = 100(p_1 - p_2) = 100\frac{n_1 - n_2}{n_1 + n_2}, \tag{3.3}$$

where n_1 and n_2 are the number of judgments of 'first longer' and 'second longer', respectively, and p_1 and p_2 the corresponding proportions.

Allan (1977) used a definition that can be written as

$$\text{TOE} = P(\text{C}|\text{LS}) - P(\text{C}|\text{SL}). \tag{3.4}$$

Equation 3.4 is used in designs where a longer (L) and a shorter (S) duration are presented in a random sequence of the two possible time orders, and the participant is given a two-alternative forced choice (2AFC) of 'second longer' or 'second shorter' (or the equivalent). The TOE is then defined as the difference between the percentages of correct (C) responses in the two stimulus orders LS and SL. We may note that this measure cannot be expected to be invariant with respect to the degree of difficulty of the task; with large C proportions, there will be a ceiling effect. Transforming these proportions into deviates of the cumulative standard normal distribution (z values), their difference will yield a measure of the TOE in units of the distribution of subjective differences.

Using a third category of 'equal' and/or 'doubtful' is usually avoided; if such judgments are permitted, they are ignored, distributed (equally or proportionally) between the remaining categories or added to the denominator. Hellström (2003) and Hellström and Almkvist (1997) used a simplified scaling method for three-category comparisons, coding 'first longer' as +100, 'second longer' as −100 and 'equal' as 0. The obtained average measure, TOE%, is equivalent to $D\%$.

Hellström (1977) discussed the use of three-category comparisons of durations (or other stimuli), assuming a constant subjective width T of the 'equal' category. The number and proportion of 'equal' judgments are $n_=$ and $p_=$, respectively. Hellström worked out four estimates for the mean subjective difference D between the compared stimuli. If the physical magnitudes of two compared successive stimuli are equal, then this difference yields a measure of the TOE in a fixed subjective unit.

The measures derived by Hellström (1977) rest on considering that the difference between two subjective quantities r_1 and r_2 is compared with two criteria, t_1 and t_2. The resulting differences are r_1-r_2-t_1 and r_1-r_2-t_2. Assuming that the momentary values of these quantities are rectangularly distributed with range R_c yields

$$\left(\frac{D}{T}\right)^* = \frac{p_1 - p_2}{p_=}; \tag{3.5}$$

$$\left(\frac{D}{R_c}\right)^* = \frac{p_1 - p_2}{2} = 0.5 \frac{n_1 - n_2}{n_1 + n_2 + n_=}; \tag{3.6}$$

$$\left(\frac{D}{T}\right)^* = \frac{2}{p}. \tag{3.7}$$

With $n_= = 0$, $(D/R_c)^* = D\%/200$. These measures may be used for an approximate estimation of the TOE in a series of Co's symmetrically spaced around an St.

Assuming a common normal distribution of r_1-r_2-t_1 and r_1-r_2-t_2 with mean D and standard deviation σ_c yields

$$\left(\frac{D}{T}\right)^* = \frac{z_2 + z_1}{z_2 - z_1}; \tag{3.8}$$

$$\left(\frac{\sigma_c}{T}\right)^* = \frac{2}{z_2 - z_1}; \tag{3.9}$$

$$\left(\frac{D}{\sigma_c}\right)^* = \frac{z_2 + z_1}{2}, \tag{3.10}$$

where z_1 and z_2 are the standard normal deviates corresponding to the sample proportions of judgments in the category 'first longer' and in categories 'first longer' and 'equal' combined, respectively. These measures were applied by Hellström (1977) to mixed intra- and interindividual data; Hellström (1993) discussed the limited applicability of the normal distribution to such data and showed that a contaminated normal distribution, modeled by a t distribution with 4 *df*, yielded better fits.

3.1.4. *The Nature of TOEs for Duration*

The TOE, first described by Fechner (1860) for lifted weights, has since then been shown to occur for most, if not all, continua studied. Early investigators did not question the perceptual nature of the TOE. However, many contemporary researchers have questioned its perceptual nature and attempted to explain it as the result of some kind of response bias, that is, the participant's tendency to favor one particular response, for example, 'longer' (Allan, 1977). If the response refers to the second stimulus in relation to the first, as is usual, this will then result in a negative TOE.

Many studies (e.g., Fraisse, 1948; Nakajima, 1951; Nakajima, 1958; Stott, 1935; Vierordt, 1868; Woodrow, 1951) have demonstrated TOEs in duration comparison.

In particular, in keeping with Vierordt's law, positive TOEs usually arise for the shorter durations in a series and negative TOEs for the longer durations.

Allan and Kristofferson (1974; Allan, 1977) proposed a categorization model for comparisons of successive intervals. According to this model, the observer bases the response on coding each interval as long (L) or short (S) based on comparison with an internal criterion. When both durations are coded in the same way (SS or LL), the participant has to guess. The participant may then let the second duration's coding have a greater weight in determining the response so that, for an LL pair, the response tends to be 'second longer' and, for an SS pair, 'second shorter'. This would then account for Vierordt's law (Allan, 1977).

The rationale for assuming a greater weight for the second coding was that the participant was asked to judge whether the second stimulus was the longer or the shorter in the pair. A critical test of the model would then be to change the judgment mode. Jamieson and Petrusic (1975b) had their participants compare visual durations of about 0.3 or 5 s. The pertinent judgment mode (select the longer or the shorter) was indicated after the presentation of each pair. Predominantly negative TOEs were obtained, especially for the long durations. The judgment mode had only small effects and never reversed the TOE direction. Further, the negative TOE changed systematically toward zero when the ISI was increased from 0.5 to 8 s. Jamieson and Petrusic concluded that the TOE is a reliable perceptual phenomenon and is not due to either response bias or criterion shift (see below). Also in another study, Jamieson and Petrusic (1975a) found no significant effects of the judgment mode.

Hellström (1977) presented pairs of durations in the form of 1000 Hz tones. Sts of 1 and 2 s alternated, each St being followed, after an ISI of 1.5 s, by a Co tone drawn from a series of 10 durations centered at the respective St. Four groups were instructed differently as to the mode of judging and responding: Was the first (second) tone in the pair the longer or the shorter [1LS (2LS)]? Was the longer (shorter) tone the first or the second [L12 (S12)]? In addition, there were options of *equal* and *completely uncertain*. No feedback was given. The TOE, defined as the mean value of $(D/\sigma_c)^*$ (Equation 3.10), was positive for the 1 s series and negative for the 2 s series, with only small differences between the four groups. The fact that the TOE, as well as its relation to the level of stimulation, was virtually independent from the judgment mode was taken as evidence that the TOE was not due to either response bias in the form of preferences for one or the other judgment or implicit responses to the absolute stimulus level. Therefore, Hellström concluded that the TOE is a perceptual phenomenon.

As was shown by Eisler (1981a), the categorization model gives a fit to the data of Allan (1977) that is greatly inferior to the fit of Hellström's SW models and Eisler's (1975, 198la, b) parallel-clock (PC) model, which are discussed later in this chapter. Allan (1979) proposed a modified categorization model to account for the results of Jamieson and Petrusic (1975b) and Hellström (1977). According to this, it is the within-pair differences that are compared with a criterion value, categorized as short-long or long-short, and translated to a response in the proper category. This was refuted by Hellström (1985) on the account that in all of Hellström's (1977) groups, the TOEs were negative for the 2 s St and positive for the 1 s St, and that

Hellström (1978) obtained analogous results for loudness stimuli. As Hellström (1985) argued, the effect of the stimulus magnitude level on the TOE would be still more difficult to explain with Allan's (1979) theory. This is because one must assume that the criteria are set before the first stimulus in the pair arrives. This is hard to reconcile with Hellström's (1977) data, which would require at least one difference criterion for each St level. To account for Hellström's (2003) duration comparison data, Allan's (1979) model would need one criterion-position parameter for each stimulus pair in each temporal condition. It is more parsimonious to assume that the judgment is based on comparing a *weighted* duration difference with a criterion. As was shown by Jamieson and Petrusic (1975b, 1978), biased criteria, which may mask the TOEs, can result from providing feedback, a practice that these authors therefore do not recommend.

3.1.5. Quantitative TOE Models

Michels and Helson (1954) formulated a quantitative TOE theory, according to which the second stimulus is not compared directly with the first but with the 'comparative AL', a weighted average of the first stimulus and the series AL (substituting the IP for the latter level; this is the same idea as that of Woodrow, 1935). Reasoning that such weighting should occur for both stimuli, Hellström (1977, 1978, 1979, 1985, 2000, 2003) generalized this theory: The basic form of his *SW model* can be written as

$$d = W_1\psi_1 - W_2\psi_2 + U, \tag{3.11}$$

where d is the subjective difference between two compared successive stimuli. To fit this model to data, Hellström assumed a psychophysical power function $\psi = \alpha\phi^{\beta}$. For duration, he has sometimes used a simplified form of Equation 3.4 (e.g., for computerized neuropsychological testing), assuming a linear psychophysical function for duration, $\beta = 1$ (cf. Allan, 1979). Fitting the more elaborated versions of the model is done by analyzing the dependence of U on W_1 and W_2 over conditions (Hellström, 1979). The full SW model (Hellström, 2003) is:

$$d = [s_1\psi_1 + (1 - s_1)\psi_{r_1}] - [s_2\psi_2 + (1 - s_2)\psi_{r_2}] + b, \tag{3.12}$$

where ψ_1 and ψ_2 are the sensation magnitudes of the stimuli, and s_1 and s_2 their weighting coefficients. The b term was introduced (Hellström, 2003) to account for a possible judgment bias. ψ_{r_1} and ψ_{r_2} are reference levels (ReLs) that monitor the current average subjective level of stimulation but may also reflect assimilation effects and other disturbances caused by extraneous stimuli (Hellström, 1985). The notion of two separate ReLs for the two stimuli was introduced by Hellström (1979) to account for the results of a series of experiments with loudness comparisons; this also made it possible to estimate the 'absolute' values of s_1 and s_2.

As was mentioned before, for a pair of *identical stimuli* ($\psi_1 = \psi_2 = \psi$), d measures the TOE in subjective units. For this case, setting $b = 0$, we obtain

$$d = (s_1 - s_2)\psi + (1 - s_1)\psi_{r_1} - (1 - s_2)\psi_{r_2}. \tag{3.13}$$

For $\psi_{r_1} = \psi_{r_2} = \psi_r$, this becomes

$$\text{TOE} = (s_1 - s_2)(\psi - \psi_r). \tag{3.14}$$

Thus, for $\psi = \psi_r$, TOE $= 0$, so that IP $= \psi_r$. For $s_1 < s_2$, d ($=$ TOE in subjective units) will be inversely proportional to $\psi - \psi_r$.

As can be seen in Figure 3 of Schab and Crowder's (1988) study, the IP increases with the ISI; this may be due to an impact of the ISI on ψ_r. According to the SW model, saying that the first stimulus assimilates or gravitates toward a level ψ_x, for instance, an 'absolute IP', is equivalent to saying that ψ_{r_1} changes toward ψ_x and that s_1 decreases (Hellström, 2000; cf. Michels & Helson, 1954). This may be a possible explanation for the phenomenon of *time shrinking* (Nakajima, ten Hoopen, Hilkhuysen, & Sasaki, 1992; Sasaki, Suetomi, Nakajima, & ten Hoopen, 2002; see Chapter 5), where a short empty time interval, preceded by a shorter interval, is underestimated in comparison with a third interval (i.e., a negative TOE; Allan & Gibbon, 1994).

In Hellström's (1977) experiment, a weight ratio (s_1/s_2) of about 0.72 was found when successive 1000-Hz tones around 1 or 2 s were compared for duration. Hellström (2003) obtained $s_1/s_2 \approx 0.86$ for tonal as well as visual duration. Accordingly, the TOE changed from positive to negative with increasing duration level (cf. Stott, 1935).

Curtis and Rule (1977) developed a model that successfully described judged differences between paired durations. Their model is of the SW type (with differential weighting introduced to account for TOEs). It is equivalent to Equation 3.11 except for an exponent applied to the judgment. Similar models with a different composition rule (' + ' instead of ' − ' sign) were found to give excellent descriptions of judgments of total and average durations in a pair.

Descriptively, the SW model with $s_1 < s_2$ can account for effects of the absolute impression of the second interval (Katz, 1906) or an attention that is more focused on the second interval than on the first (Benussi, 1907), factors that would increase s_2. It can also account for the assimilation or gravitation of the first interval toward an IP, creating an 'effective standard' and thus diminishing s_1 (Woodrow, 1935; cf. Michels & Helson, 1954). Assuming a linear and continuous psychophysical function for duration, the SW model can be seen as a special case of Eisler's (1975) PC model, discussed later in this chapter.

3.1.5.1. Assessing Woodrow's IP calculations Using the SW model as a tool, we can now see that the IP calculations of Woodrow (1933, 1935) and Stott (1935) are incorrect. These calculations were based on (1) calculating TOE as the difference between the subjective difference Co–St in the two orders and (2) finding the point Co_0 where TOE = 0. We shall here represent Woodrow's TOE measure, TOE_W, by the mean of d_{StCo_0} and d_{Co_0St}. Using Equation 3.4, assuming a linear psychophysical function, we find

$$d_{StCo} = [s_1 St + (1 - s_1)\phi_{r_1}] - [s_2 Co + (1 - s_2)\phi_{r_2}] + b, \tag{3.15}$$

$$d_{CoSt} = [s_1 Co + (1 - s_1)\phi_{r_1}] - [s_2 St + (1 - s_2)\phi_{r_2}] + b, \tag{3.16}$$

$$TOE_W = \left[s_1 \frac{St + Co}{2} + (1 - s_1)\phi_{r_1}\right] - \left[s_2 \frac{St + Co}{2} + (1 - s_2)\phi_{r_2}\right] + b. \tag{3.17}$$

Setting $\phi_{r_1} = \phi_{r_2} = \phi_r$, $\phi_1 = \phi_2 = \phi$ and $b = 0$, we obtain

$$TOE_W = \left[s_1 \frac{St + Co}{2} + (1 - s_1)\phi_r - s_2 \frac{St + Co}{2}(1 - s_2)\phi_r\right]; \tag{3.18}$$

$$TOE_W = (s_1 - s_2)\left[\frac{St + Co}{2} - \phi_r\right]. \tag{3.19}$$

When the same St and the same set of Co's around it are presented in the orders St–Co and Co–St, Equation 3.19 also holds, entering the mean Co value in place of Co.

For $Co = Co_0$, TOE = 0, and

$$\phi_r = \frac{(St + Co_0)}{2}. \tag{3.20}$$

This means that ϕ_r, the true IP, is halfway between St and the value calculated by Woodrow and Stott; their method thus exaggerates the deviation of IP from St by a factor of 2.

The subjective difference in the hypothetical pair Co_0–Co_0 is

$$d_{Co_0Co_0} = (s_1 - s_2)\,Co_0 + (1 - s_1)\phi_{r_1} - (1 - s_2)\phi_{r_2} + b, \tag{3.21}$$

which generally is not equal to zero.

In the order St–Co, the physical TOE magnitude equals PSE – St, where PSE is the magnitude of Co for which $d = 0$. We obtain (cf. Hellström, 2000)

$$PhysTOE_{StCo} = \left(\frac{s_1}{s_2} - 1\right)(St - \phi_r). \tag{3.22}$$

For the order Co–St, PhysTOE = St – PSE, and

$$PhysTOE_{CoSt} = \left(1 - \frac{s_2}{s_1}\right)(St - \phi_r). \tag{3.23}$$

In both orders, the TOE depends linearly on St $-$ ϕ_r, and

$$\frac{\text{PhysTOE}_{\text{StCo}}}{\text{PhysTOE}_{\text{CoSt}}} = \frac{s_1}{s_2}. \tag{3.24}$$

Thus, generally, the physical TOE depends on the presentation order of St and Co. If a subjective TOE measure is desired, it must be defined as the subjective difference between two physically equal stimuli, as discussed above.

3.1.5.2. Applying sensation weighting to constant position error McGavren (1965) and Van Allen, Benton, and Gordon (1966) found, for brain-damaged as well as control subjects, generally negative TOEs in comparison of successive auditory durations, a standard and a series of comparison stimuli. They also found that more correct judgments were made when the standard was the first in the pair than when it was the second. Similar results were found by Marchman (1969) for auditory and visual durations of about 0.3 s with an ISI of 12 s; for visual durations with an ISI of 3 s, the effect reversed. Rammsayer and Wittkowski (1990), using the *constant method*, had their participants compare the durations of paired successive noise bursts ranging from 30 to 70 ms. They found a negative TOE. There were more correct responses with the presentation order St–Co than Co–St. This was termed a *constant position error* (CPE), where the CPE was defined by

$$\text{CPE} = P(\text{Correct}|\text{St–Co}) - P(\text{Correct}|\text{Co–St}). \tag{3.25}$$

Again, the SW model may be used as an analytical tool. CPEs are predicted to occur whenever $s_1 \neq s_2$: With $s_1 < s_2$ (the most common case), presenting the stimuli in the order Co–St makes d a less steep function of Co than with the usual order St–Co. Therefore, the measured difference threshold will be larger with Co–St than with St–Co, and accordingly, the proportion of correct responses will be lower. Thus the CPE, as defined by Equation 3.25, becomes positive. Conversely, with $s_1 > s_2$, which may have been the case for Marchman's visual durations with a 3-s ISI, the CPE becomes negative.

3.1.6. From Ekman's Law to Weber's

The experiments that led to the formulation of Weber's (1834) law, which in turn inspired Fechner's (1860) pioneer work, were performed using the method of limits, which directly yields a measure of the DL as the smallest discriminable difference (Holway & Pratt, 1936). Early research on duration discrimination was also largely done with this method. Today, the difference threshold — more often called the JND — is usually measured in a more indirect way. Imagine an experiment where two successive intervals are compared, and the participant is to determine which interval is the longer, using the *constant method* (see Chapter 2). A change in the duration of the second interval will then increase the proportion of 'second longer' judgments — this change is described by the *psychometric function*. After a suitable transformation of the cumulative proportion of 'second longer', often using the Gaussian distribution to obtain normal deviates (z values), the psychometric function will be nearly linear, and the inverse of its slope — indicating the change $\Delta\phi$ needed for a change from (usually) 25% to 75% of 'second longer' judgments — becomes a measure of the JND. Various other methods exist, usually likewise employing a 2AFC paradigm and measuring the JND as the duration difference required to yield 75% correct discriminations.

In order to understand the machinery behind discrimination performance and Weber's law, it is helpful to consider another psychophysical generalization: *Ekman's* (1956, 1959) *law*. According to this law, the standard deviation (SD) of the subjective magnitude σ_ψ evoked by a stimulus is proportional to its mean μ_ψ [i.e., its coefficient of variation (CV), SD/mean, is constant over stimulus magnitudes].

The variance of a difference between two variables X and Y, σ^2_{X-Y}, is equal to $\sigma^2_X + \sigma^2_Y - 2\rho_{XY}\sigma_X\sigma_Y$, where ρ_{XY} is the correlation between X and Y. As was assumed in deriving Equations 3.6–3.8 for comparisons of two successive stimuli, the variance corresponding to the *comparatal dispersion* σ_c (Gulliksen, 1958) is the sum of variances and covariances of the compared quantities r_1 and r_2, and of the category border t. This means that, when two similar stimuli are compared, the measured SD of their subjective difference should be approximately linearly related to their mean subjective magnitude if Ekman's law holds.

In some lines of time perception research, *scalar timing* (Gibbon, 1977; Wearden, 1999) is a working hypothesis for the variability of subjective temporal quantities. According to this, the timing mechanism uses a pulse-emitting pacemaker, a counter, an accumulator and, in some models, a memory component. If scalar timing holds, the CV of the number of pulses accumulated during an interval is constant over intervals. Thus, we have a case of Ekman's law.

If a response category is bounded in its both ends and has an invariant category width, that is, a constant distance between its bounds (over the conditions used in an experiment), then we may predict that the proportion of responses falling into this category will decrease as the dispersion of the categorized quantity increases. According to Ekman's law or scalar timing, this proportion will therefore decrease with the stimulus magnitude. In Hellström's (1977) tone duration comparison experiment, the proportion of 'equal' judgments was much greater for compared durations at the 1-s level than at the 2-s level — an important but little-known result that is also obtained when comparison judgments with an 'equal' category are made on other continua (weight: Hellström, 2000; loudness: Koester, 1945; Needham, 1935). Assuming that the 'equal' category had a subjective width T (bounds: $-T/2$ and $+T/2$) that was constant across stimulus pairs, Hellström's (1977) results indicated (using Equation 3.9) that the comparatal dispersion for durations around 2 s was almost twice as large as for those around 1 s. Other accounts of the results being considered unlikely, this was interpreted as evidence in support of Ekman's law for duration, that is, scalar timing in combination with a close-to-linear psychophysical function.

Ekman's law and scalar timing prescribe (disregarding the variance due to categorization) that the subjective dispersion of a duration difference (the comparatal dispersion) is directly proportional to the mean stimulus magnitude ($\sigma_c = c\mu_\psi$). Then the change in μ_ψ, $\Delta\psi$, needed to change the proportion of correct judgments from 50% to 75% is proportional to $\mu_\psi : \Delta\psi = c'\mu_\psi$. The JND, $\Delta\phi$, is the change in ϕ that causes μ_ψ to change by $\Delta\psi$. If the psychophysical function for duration is a power function ($\mu_\psi = \alpha\phi^\beta$), then $\Delta\phi$ as a function of ϕ (the *Weber* function) approximately follows $\Delta\phi = k\phi$ (with $k = c'/\beta$), which is the classical form of Weber's law.

The above is a simplified account that assumes small values of k; the situation may become more complicated. If Ekman's law holds, the psychometric function should be somewhat skewed because the momentary SD of ψ is not fixed for a given ϕ but increases with its momentary mean. One remedy (others exist) could be to assume that this distribution is lognormal, that is, becomes normal when $\log \phi$ is substituted for ϕ. Also, as we shall see, some researchers have found improved fits to their data by modifying Weber's law in various ways.

Teghtsoonian (1971) found that, for a collection of continua (not including duration), there is an inverse relation among the WR, $\Delta\phi/\phi$ and the power function exponent β. He saw this as evidence that Ekman's law holds with an invariant ratio $\Delta\psi/\mu_\psi \approx 0.03$, which should then also be the WR for a continuum with $\beta = 1$. As the power function exponent for duration has generally been found to be slightly below 1 (Allan, 1979; Eisler, 1976), not far from those for line length, we may compare WRs for length, which are about 0.03, with those for duration, which are typically considerably larger. However, the conditions may not be quite comparable (e.g., with simultaneous presentation for line length). Hellström (2003) estimated WRs for simultaneous and successive line length, tone duration and visual duration under similar conditions and obtained average values of, in order, 0.065, 0.10, 0.17 and 0.29. Apparently, more variability enters in the discrimination process for duration than for other continua.

3.1.7. *Weber's Law for Duration*

Weber's law for duration has assumed great theoretical importance: 'Weber's law is actually not a law, nor it is a goal; it is a guide, a principle' (Grondin, 2001b, p. 38). In the early days of psychophysics, it was the basis for Fechner's psychophysical law; more recently, Weber's law, and modifications of it, is used to test theoretical models for timing mechanisms. Therefore, the problem posed by Estel (1885) and Mehner (1885) is still important: *Does Weber's law hold for time?*

There may be *a priori* reasons for doubt: First, in a comparison experiment with loudness, we do not obtain invariant results in comparisons of successive tones whose durations vary from 0.1 to 1 s (Hellström, 1979). For temporal stimuli, physical stimulus magnitude is identical to duration of stimulus presentation and also determines the minimal SOI. Second, although the periodicities found by early researchers are probably quite elusive, newer studies have in fact found what may be described as breaks in the psychophysical function for duration (Eisler, 1975; Richards, 1964). This may be because, as the stimulus duration increases, processing is switched to new measuring ranges (Eisler, 1975) or new processing stages (Killeen & Taylor, 2000; Staddon & Higa, 1997). Nakajima (1958) described qualitative changes in the perceived pattern of a pair of successive tones as their duration (and/or ISI) increases. Third, there are strong reasons to believe that the neural mechanisms underlying the perception of durations below and above about 1/2 s are different (Rammsayer, 1994), and as is discussed below, results of duration comparisons in these ranges differ greatly in terms of discriminability as well as weighting and TOEs (Hellström & Rammsayer, 2004). Fourth, when the compared stimuli are separated by an ISI, this may serve as a third stimulus of the same kind that can interfere with the comparison process by, for instance, assimilation to the first stimulus (Schab & Crowder, 1988).

3.1.7.1. Alternative ways of measuring discrimination Alternative ways of measuring discrimination are also used in research on duration perception. The *constant method* may be generalized to the case of a single stimulus categorized as long or short by comparison with an internal category limit (e.g., Allan & Kristofferson, 1974; Kristofferson, 1980) or a sequence of repeated standards (e.g., Grondin, 2001). Kristofferson (1980) described (using empty intervals of 0.1–1.48 s, bounded by auditory pulses) how the relationship between the duration threshold and the base duration changes, with extensive practice in one experienced observer (himself), from a strict form of Weber's law to a step function, indicating a discrimination based on temporal quanta.

Needless to say, when assessing discrimination of temporal intervals, the TOE must be taken into account (as Fechner, 1860, made very clear). For instance, with a negative TOE, the JND becomes smaller in ascending than in descending pairs (Needham, 1935). Differential stimulus weighting also results in different JNDs and WRs, according to which of the two stimuli is varied and which is kept constant. Stott (1935) found consistently sharper discrimination with the order St–Co than with Co–St; for St = 1 s, the WRs were 0.11 and 0.38, respectively. This is a consequence of the weight relation $s_1 < s_2$; the first duration has a lower impact on the comparative response than the second one. Therefore, varying the first duration (order Co–St) yields a larger JND. Wackerman and Späti (2006), though not using the differential-weighting account of duration comparison, acknowledge this asymmetry of discriminability. They point out that the discrimination function (the probability of responding 'second longer') should be seen as a two-dimensional function of the first and second stimulus durations and argue that, in measuring discrimination, 'the fixed standard strategies are by no means privileged…and in fact, suboptimal….Ideally, differential sensitivity should be measured in the direction of the gradient of the discrimination function…at a given PSE, to ensure the maximal steepness of the [psychometric function]' (p. 252).

Hellström and Rammsayer (2004) had their participants compare successive white-noise durations with Sts of 0.05 and 1 s, with ISIs of 0.1, 0.3, 0.9 or 2.7 s (only one ISI per participant). The stimuli were presented in the order St–Co or Co–St. Using an adaptive method, JNDs (75% difference thresholds) for 'Co longer' and 'Co shorter' judgments were estimated. In Experiment 1, feedback was given;

in Experiment 2, with ISIs of 0.9 and 2.7 s, there was no feedback. For St = 1 s, the JND was generally smaller with the order St–Co than with Co–St; for St = 0.05 s, the JND relation was the opposite (cf. McGavren, 1965). JNDs increased with shorter ISIs. The TOE (the duration difference that yielded $d = 0$) was positive for St = 0.05 s and negative for St = 1 s and approached zero for longer ISIs. Assuming that the JND always corresponded to a common absolute value of the subjective duration difference d, and using Hellström's SW model, the ratio s_1/s_2 of the weights for the first and second durations was estimated; for St = 1 s, s_1/s_2 was <1, but for St = 0.05 s, $s_1/s_2 > 1$. JNDs were smaller with feedback than without.

The results of Hellström and Rammsayer (2004) are in line with the notion of different modes of stimulus processing for short and long durations (Nichelli, 1993; Rammsayer, 1994, 1999; see Chapter 9). They differ from those of Mo (1974), who found, for visually defined intervals around 0.3, 0.5 and 0.7 s and ISIs of 1, 3 and 5 s, a stimulus-level effect in line with Vierordt's law (indicating $s_1 < s_2$) and increasingly negative TOEs with increasing ISI. These effects, however, decreased when each subject received only one duration level and disappeared when, in addition, there was only one ISI per block. Getty (1975) found, for empty intervals bounded by clicks, with only one ISI (2 s) and one St per session, TOEs that were close to zero for St durations up to about 1 s and increasingly negative for longer durations. Jamieson and Petrusic (1975a) found positive TOEs (measured according to Equation 3.4) for durations in a set of 0.3 and 0.375 s but consistently negative TOEs when these were mixed with durations of 5.0 and 5.4 s. They concluded that the extent of the range was an important factor in determining the TOE.

According to the SW model, the categorized quantity may be identified with d in Equation 3.12, and r_1 and r_2 with the modified subjective quantities of the first and second stimuli (see Hellström, 1979). The measured JND becomes proportional to the comparatal dispersion and inversely related to the impact of a change in the respective duration (indicating, e.g., the relative weights s_1 and s_2 for the first and second intervals).

3.1.7.2. Empirical results Although Estel (1885) rejected Weber's law for duration, it can be said to hold to a fair approximation for his three extensively studied observers (disregarding the possible undulations), over the range of 1.5–5.0 s with a mean WR of 0.104 (range 0.092–0.119) and no clear trend over durations.

Small and Campbell's (1962, Figure 4) display of their own sound-duration data and those of Stott (1935) and Henry (1948) indicates reasonably stable WRs near 0.2 for durations in the region of 40 ms–4.0 s, although with a minimum at about 1.0 s. They also used durations of 0.4 and 4 ms for which the WRs were considerably higher; however, for these durations, one may strongly suspect that the discrimination was based on temporal integration of loudness (Algom, Rubin, & Cohen-Raz, 1989) rather than on duration. Grondin, Ouellet, and Roussel (2001) found roughly constant WRs for visual as well as auditory durations over the range 0.50–0.74 s. Grondin (2001a) found, for intervals marked by brief visual signals, that the WR was roughly constant between 0.6 and 0.9 s but increased between 0.9 and 1.2 s.

Jeon and Fricke (1995) found, for durations of 1000-Hz tones, that the WR decreased for durations of 0.025–0.1 s, stayed almost constant from 0.1 to 2 s and increased again from 2 to 8 s. The participants reported that they counted with the longer durations. The authors ascribe the breakpoints, common for all participants, at 0.1 and 2 s to their using an '"energy", "loudness" or "noisiness"' strategy below 0.1 s and a counting strategy above 2 s. Grondin, Meilleur-Wells, and Lachance (1999) found that, for intervals as short as 1.2 s, counting reduces variability in a duration discrimination task.

Nakajima (1958), using the constant method with tone durations and ISIs both varying between 0.15 and 1.6 s, found WRs of 0.118–0.158. There was no significant tendency for the WR to change with either duration or ISI. (However, a plot of the WR against their sum, the SOI, shows an inverse U-shaped trend. A fitted quadratic function explains 20.2% of the variance, and the quadratic term is significant. At an SOI of 1.62 s, the predicted WR reaches a maximum of 0.145). Westheimer (1999), using durations of 0.15–1.5 s with ISI = 0.6 s, found the JNDs for two observers to rise in a fairly linear fashion, over the range of durations with mean WRs of 0.040 and 0.039 for audition (600-Hz tones), 0.048 and 0.059 for vision (bright circles) and 0.042 and 0.072 for touch (upward displacement of a button). Penner (1976) reported data for empty visually bounded durations 0.3 ms–1 s (ISI = 1 s), which show a quite sharp decline of the WR with duration from 3 ms onward.

Hellström's (2003) results for tonal and visual durations were reanalyzed with respect to JNDs (the change in the second duration required to *change the proportion of 'second longer' from 25% to 75%*) and WRs for each level of the first duration (D_1). For both types of stimuli, mean duration levels of 0.4, 0.8, 1.2 and 1.6 s were used with ISIs of 0.5, 1, 2 and 4 s (all conditions randomly mixed within a session). For tone duration (1000 Hz) and visual duration (a luminous square), the mean WR was 0.154 (range 0.104–0.220) and 0.284 (range 0.187–0.486), respectively. For both sets of durations, the WR tended to increase with shorter values of D_1 and longer ISIs. Multiple regressions were computed with WR as the dependent variable and log ISI and D_1 as independent variables. For tone duration, none of the effects reached significance. For visual duration (adjusted $R^2 = 0.641$), the effect of D_1 on the WR was significant ($\beta = -4.93$). The regression of the DL on D_1 (average over ISIs) yielded an adjusted R^2 of 0.660 and the equation $\text{DL} = 101.8 + 0.150 D_1$. The slope was statistically significant as was the constant.

From the empirical evidence, we may conclude, with Allan (1979), that the simple form of Weber's law does not generally hold for duration discrimination. Various models of this process have been suggested, entailing generalizations of Weber's law. Henry (1948) noted, for his loudness data for 0.032–0.48 s (obtained using a modified *constant method*), a decline of the WR for the longer intervals and described this using a power function modification of Weber's law (Guilford, 1932; 1954): $\Delta\phi = k\phi^n$, or $\Delta\phi/\phi = k\phi^{n-1}$. Creelman (1962) used paired 1000 Hz tones mixed with noise, with an ISI of 0.8 s, and studied duration discrimination as a function of base duration (0.02–0.32 s), increment duration and signal voltage. He used the approach of signal-detection theory and employed d' as his discriminability measure.

For Weber's law to hold, d' would be proportional to the ratio of increment duration to base duration, and taking logarithms, for a fixed increment, the result should be a straight line with slope -1. Empirically, the slopes were lower, indicating that discrimination improves somewhat toward longer base durations. Creelman fitted an equation for predicted d' that builds on a model with pulses generated by a Poisson process, partly forgotten, and counted. He concluded: 'It seems clear that no constantly running "clock" will account for the data.... These data suggest that [the Poisson pulse-rate parameter] λ reflects a general level of activation, and the duration counter, if it exists anywhere in the nervous system, can receive counting pulses from many different sources' (p. 593). Getty (1975) tested two models for duration discrimination. One was built on Creelman's counter model, assuming that the total subjective variance consists a component that is proportional to the interval duration T, k_cT, and a residual component that is constant, V_R. This led to the prediction that the WR will be proportional to $(k_c/T + V_R/T^2)^{1/2}$. The other model (a generalization of Weber's law) instead assumed that the first variance component equals $(k_wT)^2$. This leads to the prediction that the WR is proportional to $(k_w + V_R/T^2)^{1/2}$. In the experiment, silent intervals bounded with clicks were compared by two participants in a 2AFC paradigm. There were 15 St durations from 0.05 to 3.2 s, one per session, with an ISI of 2 s. The generalized Weber-law model was clearly superior to the counter model. There was a rapid increase in the WR for durations longer than 2 s, which both models failed to predict.

The model of Killeen and Weiss (1987) assumes that in reaching the estimate τ of an interval t, the latter is divided optimally into n subintervals. This leads to a generalized form of Weber's law: $\sigma_\tau/t = (A + B/t + C/t^2)^{1/2}$. For long intervals, this reduces to the basic version of the law, with WR $= A^{1/2}$. Killeen and Weiss showed that their model provides good fits to the duration discrimination data of Abel (1972), Henry (1948), Kinchla (1972) and Treisman (1963). Grondin (1993) studied the discrimination of intervals between 0.125 and 4 s. These were of four types: auditory, visual, filled and empty. For each of the four participants, WRs decreased with the interval duration. The model of Killeen and Weiss was fitted to Grondin's data with good results.

3.1.8. Conclusion: Why Sensation Weighting?

As we saw earlier, experiments using different judgment modes have indicated that TOEs for duration, as well as for other continua, are of a perceptual nature. As has been shown by Hellström (1977, 1978, 1979, 2003), the outcomes of comparisons of successive stimuli are well described by the SW model. The similarities between duration and other continua (e.g., weight and loudness) regarding the dependence of stimulus weighting and TOEs on factors such as stimulus magnitude and ISI strongly suggest that the same processes are at work. One complication is, as was mentioned previously, that two essential stimulus factors behind the TOEs — duration and magnitude — are necessarily confused for duration stimuli.

Hellström (1989) suggested that the purpose of the differential SW is to adjust the perceived stimulus difference d so as to maximize the signal-to-noise ratio of a change in d caused by changes in magnitude of the compared stimuli — that is (to simplify), minimizing the JND (cf. Killeen & Weiss, 1987). This mechanism would adjust the weight coefficient for each stimulus so that it reflects the amount of momentarily available information about it, as regards the compared attribute. According to this view, the reason for the pattern of results with increasing ISI is likely to be a shift in the balance between the factors affecting the fate of duration (or other stimulus) information: from mutual (but mainly proactive) blocking of processing ($s_1/s_2 > 1$) to dissipation from memory ($s_1/s_2 < 1$). The TOE is seen as a by-product of the differential weighting, in combination with the ReLs, which play the role of Woodrow's (1935) indifference interval. Also, if Hellström's idea is right, the obtained discrimination performance represents a sort of optimal achievement under the prevailing conditions. For instance, a sudden change in a steady rhythm may be important to notice. The drawback is that systematic errors (TOEs) occur as a by-product, but due to rapid adjustment of the ReLs, these are probably not very important outside the laboratory.

Again, duration perception is special: Short durations are thought to be processed at a low neural level, using an internal pacemaker; in contrast, the perception of durations of about 1 s and longer depends mainly on cognitive processing of experienced events (Rammsayer, 1994). For the latter durations (auditory as well as visual), the ratio s_1/s_2 has consistently been found to be < 1. This was interpreted by Hellström (1985) as being due to dissipation of information from memory, during the ISI, about the first duration.

Schab and Crowder (1988) had participants reproduce the first or second duration in a pair and found that the regression of the reproduction on the first duration was much shallower than on the second. They also found that the coefficient of determination decreased with the ISI and proposed that the TOE was a recency effect of memory. This idea is reminiscent of the theory of Köhler (1923), who explained the commonly appearing negative TOEs, for instance, for lifted weights by assuming a stimulus trace in the brain that fades away with time. It does not seem reasonable to think that a weight we have lifted should seem lighter just because we do not remember it clearly. However, if the estimation of a duration depends on how much of its mental content is retained (Frankenhaeuser, 1959), this may make a past duration tend to seem shorter (Wearden & Ferrara, 1993). The possibility that this may contribute to the negative TOEs often reported in duration comparison cannot be dismissed (cf. Hörmann, 1964; Sixtl, 1963, 1964).

3.2. The Psychophysical Function for Duration: A Novel Approach

In the previous section the problem of discrimination and estimation of subjective differences was considered. In the present part we shall deal with the measurement of subjective (psychological) time and particularly with the psychophysical function for duration. A psychophysical function describes how subjective, experienced, psychological magnitude increases with stimulus intensity. The description below should convey the concept of psychological magnitude.

Imagine you are in a dark room. You light one candle, then a second. Are two candles experienced as twice as bright as one?

You are in a quiet room. A musician enters and begins to play a double bass. Then a second musician joins the first, likewise playing a double bass. Are two double basses experienced as twice as loud as one?

You are driving a car at 100 km/h. You slow down to 50 km/h. Do you feel you are going now half as fast as before?

The answer to all three questions is "no." From this we can draw two conclusions: (1) We, as organisms, are able to measure, i.e., to quantify, our sensations, and (2) these measures need not to be veridical, i.e., they need not agree with the corresponding physical measures (H. Eisler & Eisler, 1991, p. 79).

The implication is that the psychophysical functions for brightness, loudness, and speed are not linear. It will be shown below that the psychophysical function for duration (time) is not linear either, though the deviation from linearity is much less than for, e.g., brightness. Besides, instead of the general "stimulus intensity" we can be specific and use "length of duration." This difference is fundamental; other senses like hearing or taste have particular organs with receptors, appurtenant neural wiring and specific brain centers. All this is rather diffuse as to the perception of duration, though the expression "time sense" is used frequently.

Accordingly, the problem is whether the experience — perception — of subjective duration can be described quantitatively, and how it can be compared to other "senses," i.e., other sensations or perceptions.

The construction of a psychophysical function is often called "scaling" and several scaling methods exist. One of the most common is *magnitude estimation* in which the subjects assign a number to a stimulus in relation to a standard (reference) stimulus (see Chapter 2). An example of the instruction to the subject would be "if the heaviness of weight A is 10, then, if weight B feels twice as heavy, it should be estimated as 20." Typically, a plot of estimates against physical values (expressed in physical units) is linear in log–log coordinates (see, e.g., Stevens, 1975). From this it can be deduced that the psychophysical function is a power function.

Another common method is ratio setting. A subject is presented with one stimulus, the standard, say a tone of a certain sound pressure (experienced as loudness) and it is required to adjust the sound pressure so that the new stimulus, the variable, stands in a prescribed numerical relation to the standard. The task may be to adjust the variable so that it is experienced half as loud as the standard. Typically, a linear plot of adjusted sound pressure versus the sound pressure of the standard is obtained. A mathematical proof, based on this linearity, shows again that the psychophysical function is a power function (H. Eisler, 1974).

Almost all "continua" (e.g., brightness, heaviness, loudness, and so forth) feature power functions, duration included. One of the most common criticisms leveled against psychophysical scaling is the "number problem," i.e., whether the "numerals" used by a subject have the properties ascribed to numbers in the arithmetic system.

A unique property of time allows one to circumvent this pitfall. Time does not stop at the end of an interval presented as stimulus to the subject. It just continues. The method of duration reproduction makes use of this property, in conjunction with a process description of the subject's behavior. In the typical experimental situation the subject is presented with a (standard, reference) duration, for example, indicated by noise, followed by a short pause (a silent interval), after which the same noise resumes and is terminated by the subject's pressing a button, when he/she experiences that the sound after the pause (the variable duration) had lasted as long as the sound before the pause (i.e., as long as the reference duration). The typical finding is that the longer reference durations in the experimental set are reproduced shorter than the reference durations, whereas the opposite is the case for short durations, in accordance with Vierordt's law (Vierordt, 1868). The parallel-clock model (H. Eisler, 1975), see below, accounts for the data obtained and allows the computation of the parameter values of the power function for duration.

3.2.1. *The Parallel-Clock Model*

In a duration reproduction task, it is generally taken for granted that the subject stores the standard duration in memory, and compares the variable duration with this memory. The parallel-clock model works differently. It does not need any memory. Instead the subject uses two sensory registers ("clocks"). One of them accumulates subjective time units from the onset of the first duration (the standard) to the offset of the second (the variable), i.e., to the point in time of the button press. The other accumulates subjective time units during the second sound, i.e., during the reproduction. Accordingly the first sensory register contains the *total* subjective duration, i.e., standard + reproduction. The other register contains the subjective reproduction. When the difference between the contents of the first and the second register equals the contents of the second register the subject experiences the two durations as equal and presses the button. At that moment one register contains the subjective counterpart of the total duration (standard + reproduction) and the other the subjective counterpart of the reproduction. Denoting subjective duration by ψ, and reproduction by subscript r and total (reference duration + reproduction) by subscript *tot* we have

$$\psi_{\mathrm{tot}} - \psi_{\mathrm{r}} = \psi_{\mathrm{r}} \tag{3.26}$$

Figure 3.1 shows the two psychophysical functions, subjective duration as a function of clock time, with the point in time when the subject experiences equality between standard and reproduction indicated by the lines with arrows. The total duration is represented by the upper curve and the reproduction by the lower, right-positioned curve. From the subject's point of view the two durations, standard and reproduction, have lasted the same length of time, which s/he indicates by shutting

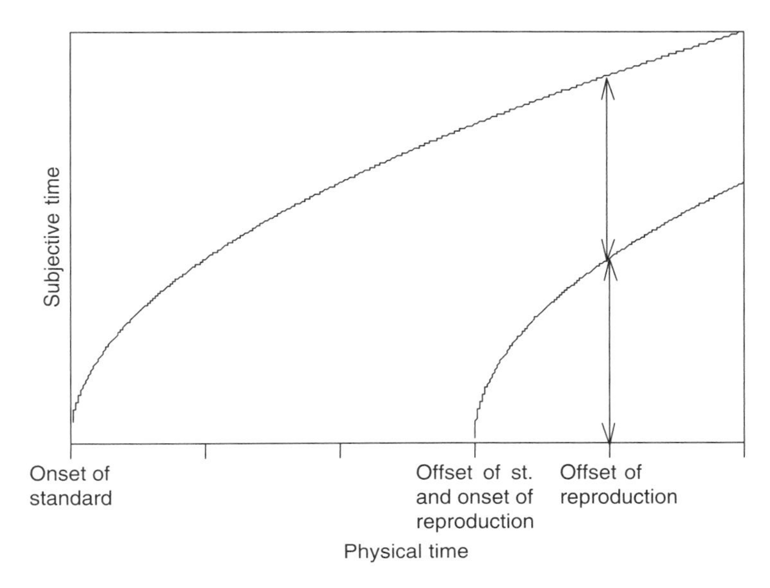

Figure 3.1: The duration reproduction task according to the parallel-clock model. For explanation see text.

off the sound. From the point of view of the researcher this corresponds to the subject's halving the total subjective duration (standard + reproduction), which makes the computation of the parameter values possible. We obtain

$$\psi = \kappa(\phi - \phi_0)^{\beta} \tag{3.27}$$

where ψ denotes subjective and ϕ physical duration, and the exponent β and the subjective zero ϕ_0 are parameters determined from the data, and κ an arbitrary, and thus indeterminable, proportionality constant or subjective unit.

There is, however, a complication. Almost all individual data show a *break* within the experimental range, due to different κ and/or ϕ_0 values of the psychophysical function on both sides of the *break* (see Figure 3.2). The model permits, besides the determination of β (which is the same on both sides of the break), the computation of both ϕ_0 values; furthermore, though each κ value cannot be determined separately, their ratio α can. Although we cannot go through the derivations here, we want to mention that the parameter values are computed from slopes and intercepts like those in the lower panel of Figure 3.2.

What can the parallel-clock model achieve? The parameter values provide a quantitative description of the subject's temporal behavior. Since reproduction is a comparatively simple task, not requiring the cognitive ability to quantify, i.e., for instance, to use numbers, also the psychophysical function for children (see, e.g., A. D. Eisler, 2003), and animals (H. Eisler, 1984a; Zeiler, & Hoyert, 1989) can be determined.

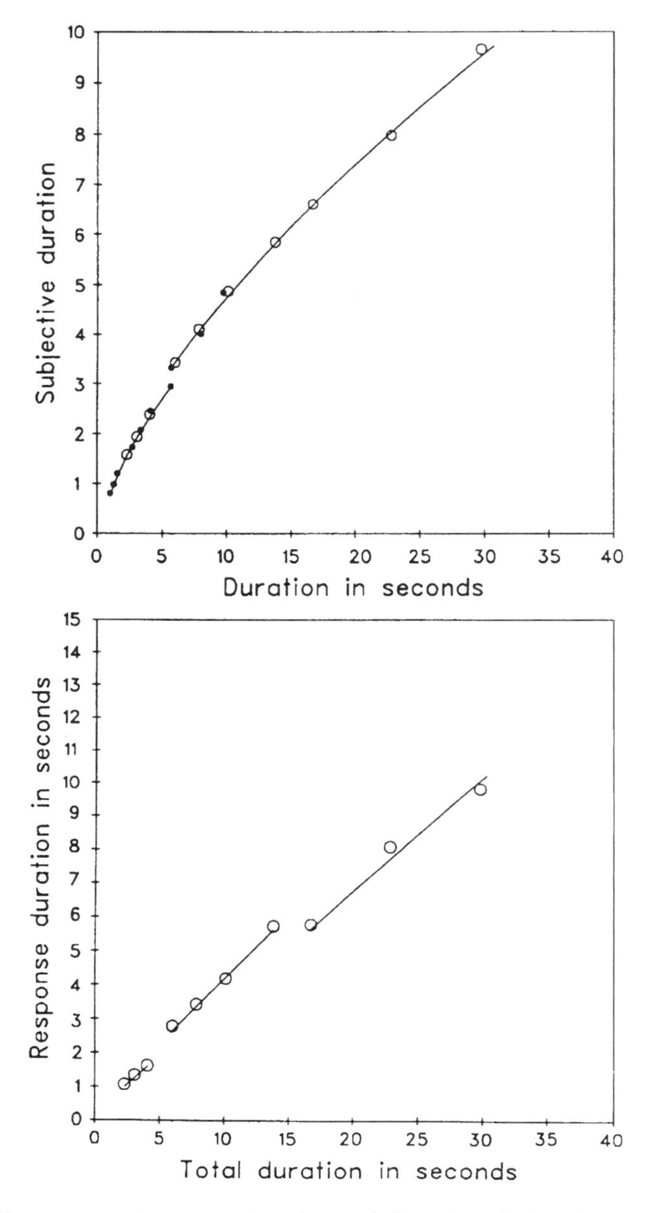

Figure 3.2: Upper panel: the psychophysical function (subjective versus physical duration), with its break, from one subject. ○ denotes total durations and • reproductions. Lower panel: the same subject's raw data (reproductions versus total durations) from which the parameter values of the psychophysical function were computed.

3.2.2. The Psychophysical Function as a Whole

The psychophysical function also deals successfully with certain problems, sometimes in an unexpected way. We shall illustrate with a few examples.

3.2.2.1. Vierordt's law Vierordt's law (1868) connects to the old much-discussed question of the indifference interval (see the previous section, and, e.g., Woodrow, 1951). The indifference interval is the duration for which standard duration and reproduction coincide. Figure 3.3 provides a powerful interpretation of the "indifference interval:" its existence and position is a direct effect of the interaction between the slope and the intercept, which in their turn are determined by the values of β and ϕ_0. In the example given the position can only be inferred because the experimental range does not cover the "indifference interval."

3.2.2.2. Patient with neurological impairment In this part we shall deal with the time perception of the well-known patient H.M. who underwent a bilateral medial temporal lobe resection that included the hippocampus, entailing a severe memory

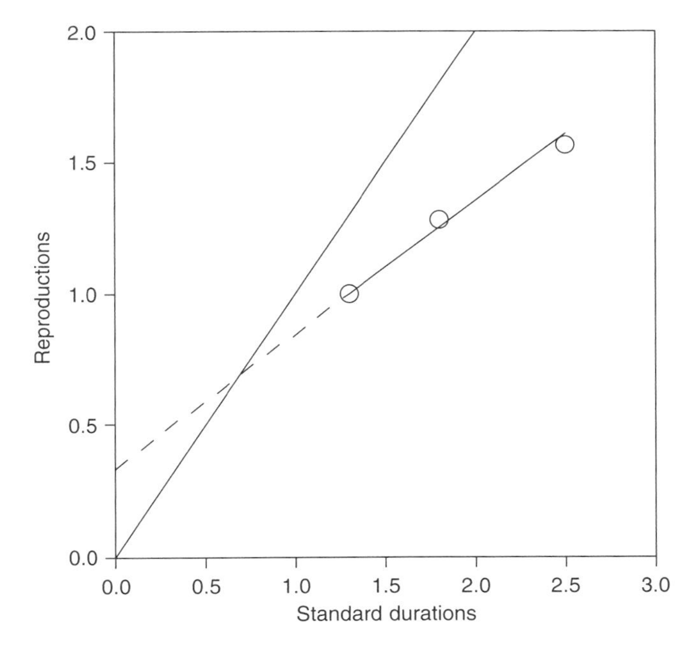

Figure 3.3: Illustration of Vierordt's law. Clipping from the lower panel of Figure 3.2 containing the reproductions of the three shortest durations (here plotted versus standard durations). The intersection of the equality line and the fitted line yields the position of the indifference point. Other subjects with different parameter values could show different positions.

loss (Milner, Corkin, & Teuber, 1968). A detailed treatment of H.M.'s reproduction data (Richards, 1973) using the parallel-clock model showed that H.M.'s divergent duration reproductions were not due to a flaw in his time perception, but that he has difficulty in storing, remembering, and retrieving encoded experience. Our results indicate that H.M. had a tendency to forget more and more what he was supposed to be doing, but is reminded again and again. Our findings favor the view that the damage to the hippocampus affected the permanent encoding and subsequent retrieval of the task given in the instruction (see A. D. Eisler, & Eisler, 2001).

3.2.2.3. Time perception in schizophrenics Schizophrenia is generally regarded as a disorder of cognition (Bleuler, 1911; Spitzer, Endicott, & Rabin, 1978). The research literature on time perception has often suggested that schizophrenics have a disturbed sense of time, and that the schizophrenic's ability to estimate time is disrupted (Davalos, Kisley, & Freedman, 2005; Densen, 1977; Fuchs, 2007; Melges, 1982; Wallace & Rabin, 1960; Wahl & Sieg, 1980).

Minkowski stated as early as 1927 that extreme distortion of subjective time was the central symptom of schizophrenia. Fraisse (1967), on the other hand, pointed out that what seems to be selectively affected in schizophrenics is the feeling of time (Zeitgefühl) and not the biological clock (Zeitsinn) or the notion of time. Therefore, studies on subjective (psychological) time in schizophrenics may lead to better understanding of the cognitive processes and of the vulnerability factors of experiencing time and of time-structuring behavior, which is important knowledge as to how schizophrenic individuals orient themselves in time and space.

A. D. Eisler, Eisler, and Mori (2001) compared time perception of short durations, including intra- and interindividual variability of subjective duration judgments, in schizophrenic and in healthy Japanese males. The psychological methods of reproduction (which is mostly based on biological processes), and of verbal estimation in subjective seconds (which is influenced by cognitive factors), were used. By using these methods for both groups, the intention was to elucidate the relationship between the time distortion and the biological and cognitive factors in the schizophrenic, in comparison with the healthy group.

The values of the parameters of the psychophysical function were computed individually. The results showed that there was no significant difference in the value of the exponent β between the schizophrenic and the healthy group in duration reproduction. In the verbal estimation task, however, the values of the exponent β were significantly different, 0.82 for the schizophrenic and 0.94 for the healthy group (also the schizophrenics' estimates showed an approximately linear function of responses versus reference durations in log–log coordinates). The variability of the estimates between, as well as within, subjects is much greater in the schizophrenics than in the healthy group. Our conclusion is therefore that time sense and ability to perceive subjective duration are *unaffected* in schizophrenics.

Schizophrenics are described in terms of distraction and of chaotic and disorganized behavior. This important aspect of schizophrenic symptomatology typically results in cognitive impairment. The impairment may be at the root of the deviant, though fairly consistent, estimations by the schizophrenic subjects.

This vulnerability entails that the schizophrenics seem to be unable to translate perceived time into numbers (seconds), probably because of their general difficulty to quantify. Taken together, our results *do not support the notion of general distortion* of *time perception* as such in schizophrenia.

3.2.3. Parameter Values as Explanatory Factors

Let's now turn to the parameters of Equation 3.27. Most often in comparisons of different groups (e.g., gender) or experimental conditions (e.g., different loudnesses) the result is simply given as that Group A or subjects under Condition X make longer reproductions, etc., than Group B or subjects under Condition Y. Furthermore, very often the terms over- or underestimation are used without a clear definition. We find this not quite satisfactory. It is also common that only one or very few durations are studied, and it is well known that short durations are reproduced longer and long durations shorter than the corresponding reference durations (Vierordt's law), which makes it difficult to obtain clear conclusions. But knowing the pertinent parameters behind differences opens up the understanding for the processing mechanisms in time perception. But in order to emphasize the explanatory power of the parameters they will be presented systematically one by one together with the group or condition differences they express, mostly based on our experimental data. (cf., H. Eisler, 1995).

3.2.3.1. Variables influenced by the exponent β As will be apparent in the following discussion, the most important parameter is the exponent β. Time perception is rather veridical, so the exponent β is not far from unity, typically about 0.8 – 0.9 (H. Eisler, 1976). As regards experimental conditions, we found that β is a decreasing function of sound intensity (H. Eisler & Eisler, 1992). A serendipitous finding was a lower value of the exponent β for African immigrants living permanently in Sweden, in comparison with native Swedish subjects (A. D. Eisler, 1992, 1995). Young children feature a lower value of the exponent β than adults (see A. D. Eisler, 1976). In a study by A. D. Eisler and Eisler (2006), using duration reproduction, the value of the exponent β was 0.6 for children aged 7–8 years. For children aged 10–14 years, the β value was 0.8, which is about the same as for adult subjects. Thus, our finding contradicts Fraisse, who stated that the abstract quality of the time sense generally does not appear before an age of 15 years (Fraisse, 1967). Finally we wish to point out that results obtained in an experiment with rats showed a value of the exponent β as low as 0.5 (H. Eisler, 1984a; H. Eisler & Eisler, 1991).

3.2.3.2. The subjective unit ratio α As mentioned before, the parallel-clock model does not allow the computation of the proportionality constant (subjective unit) κ. However, almost always does the psychophysical function for duration consist of two segments, which differ as to their κ values. Although these values cannot be determined separately, their ratio $\alpha = \kappa_u / \kappa_l$ can. Differences of both sex and age are expressed in the value of α, which encapsulates the finding that older women reproduce closest to the reference durations (clock time), in contrast to young males who deviate most from the reference durations (A. D. Eisler & Eisler, 1994; H. Eisler & Eisler, 1992). This holds for durations above the break; for shorter durations there is hardly any difference, neither for gender nor age.

The scope of this chapter does not allow interpretations or explanations of the listed findings. They are, however, found in the references given.

3.2.3.3. The subjective zero ϕ_0 The last parameter to deal with is the subjective zero ϕ_0. Our interpretation is that the subject does not register the physical start of the duration correctly, and ϕ_0 indicates the moment of the start as experienced. To be more precise: The value of ϕ_0 denotes the difference between the chronological and the subjective start. This was evidenced in an experimental study by A. D. Eisler, Eisler, and Montgomery (2004) in which prospective and retrospective paradigms were compared. (In a prospective paradigm the subject is informed beforehand that he/she will be requested to make duration judgments. In a retrospective paradigm, on the other hand, the subject is unaware of the fact that s/he will be required to make duration judgments (see Chapters 2 or 4.) The results of this study demonstrate that the difference between prospective and retrospective reproductions lies in a systematic difference in the parameter value of ϕ_0.

3.2.4. Conclusion

The novelty in this research is the application of the parallel-clock model in order to determine parameter values of the psychophysical function for duration. The knowledge of the psychophysical function as a whole as well the knowledge of single parameter values contributes to our understanding of the time perception processing mechanisms, and also elucidates temporal behavior.

Finally, what is probably the most persuasive indication of a biologically based time sense comes from evidence of a completely different kind, namely the previous mentioned ability of animals to judge intervals of time (H. Eisler, 1984a, b, c, 1989, 1990; H. Eisler & Eisler, 1991).

3.2.5. Directions for Future Research

1) Practically all our obtained data (see, for instance, A. D. Eisler & Eisler, 1994; A. D. Eisler et al., 2004) show a break in the psychophysical function for duration, which divides the function into two segments. Therefore, we are inclined to interpret time perception as primarily governed by biological clocks. In particular, the neurophysiological hypothesis of neural loops (see, e.g., A. D. Eisler et al., 2004) deserves attention. It would be interesting to study the neurophysiological processes of timing mechanisms in general within the frame of the parallel-clock model.

This approach could be a further step toward understanding how the brain keeps time.

2) It seems that blind people respond to the same circadian rhythms as sighted people. It is argued that the reason is the social cues following time of day information (Pauley, 1981). Thus, a study of congenitally blind children's subjective time in comparison with sighted children of the same age should provide valuable insights in the biological basis for the human sense of time.

3.3. General Conclusion

The psychology of time is a wide-ranging topic and the pertinent models differ in their orientation, which may be, for instance, psychophysical, cognitive, chronobiological, developmental, social-psychological, or psychoanalytic. Accordingly, the study of time perception benefits from general insights in psychology, particularly perception and psychophysics. Most strikingly, the psychophysical power function, found for almost all sensory continua, applies as well to the experience of duration. Furthermore, this function can be mathematically derived from empirical data (H. Eisler, 1975). Another example is that humans have a tendency to overestimate short intervals of time and underestimate long intervals in relation to physical time. This phenomenon, easily described by the typical parameter values of the psychophysical function for time, is called *Vierordt's law* and has been discussed before in this chapter. Finally, linking the two parts of this chapter, one might consider whether the difference between the subjective κ-units of the two segments of the psychophysical function mirror the same underlying mechanism as the different weights used in the sensation-weighting model.

Much empirical research has been directed toward describing and explaining time perception, a very complex phenomenon indeed. Mach (1865), Meumann (1893), Vierordt (1868), and their followers have provided some insight into three important properties of humans' inner clocks. One is the minimum perceptible interval between two successive excitations (Fraisse, 1963), which seems to be in the order of 10–50 ms. Another is the length of the brief interval of time that can be judged most accurately. This interval lies in the range 0.6–0.8 s (see Fraisse, 1963). The third property is related to the interval of time over which a series of stimuli may extend and yet be experienced as unitary (the subjective present), perhaps a "3-s window" as Pöppel (2004) suggests.

Note

The first part of this chapter on the comparison of successive time intervals was written by Åke Hellström, and the second part on the psychophysical function for duration was written by Hannes Eisler and Anna D. Eisler.

References

Abel, S. M. (1972). Duration discrimination of noise and tone bursts. *Journal of the Acoustical Society of America, 51*, 1219–1223.

Algom, D., Rubin, A., & Cohen-Raz, L. (1989). Binaural and temporal integration of the loudness of tones and noises. *Perception & Psychophysics, 46*, 155–166.

Allan, L. G. (1977). The time-order error in judgments of duration. *Canadian Journal of Psychology, 31*, 24–31.

Allan, L. G. (1979). The perception of time. *Perception & Psychophysics, 26*, 340–354.

Allan, L. G., & Gibbon, J. (1994). A new temporal illusion or the TOE once again? *Perception & Psychophysics, 55*, 227–229.

Allan, L. G., & Kristofferson, A. B. (1974). Psychophysical theories of duration discrimination. *Perception & Psychophysics, 16*, 26–34.

Angell, F. (1899). Review of Martin and Müller's "Zur Analyse der Unterschiedsempfindlichkeit". *American Journal of Psychology, 11*, 266–271.

Benussi, V. (1907). Zur experimentellen analyse des Zeitvergleichs. I. Zeitgrösse und Betonungsgestalt [On the experimental analysis of temporal comparison. I. Temporal magnitude and stress gestalt]. *Archiv für die gesamte Psychologie, 9*, 366–449.

Bleuler, E. (1911). *Dementia praecox or the group of schizophrenias*. New York: International Universities Press.

Creelman, C. D. (1962). Human discrimination of auditory duration. *Journal of the Acoustical Society of America, 34*, 582–693.

Curtis, D. W., & Rule, S. J. (1977). Judgment of duration relations: Simultaneous and successive presentation. *Perception & Psychophysics, 22*, 578–584.

Davalos, D. B., Kisley, M. A., & Freedman, R. (2005). Behavioral and electrophysiological indices of temporal processing dysfunction in schizophrenia. *Journal of Neuropsychiatry and Clinical Neurosciences and Clinical Neurosciences, 17*, 517–525.

Densen, M. E. (1977). Time perception and schizophrenia. *Perceptual and Motor Skills, 44*, 436–438.

Eisler, A. D. (1992). Time perception: Reproduction of duration by two cultural groups. In: S. Iwawaki, Y. Kashima & K. Leung (Eds), *Innovations in cross-cultural psychology* (pp. 304–310). Amsterdam: Swets & Zeitlinger.

Eisler, A. D. (1995). Cross-cultural differences in time perception: Comparison of African immigrants and native Swedes. In: G. Neely (Ed.), *Perception and psychophysics in theory and application* (pp. 137–145). Stockholm: Stockholm University.

Eisler, A. D. (2003). The human sense of time: Biological, cognitive and cultural considerations. In: R. Buccheri, M. Saniga & W. M. Stuckey (Eds), *The nature of time: Geometry, physics and perception* (pp. 5–18). Dordrecht, The Netherlands: Kluwer Academic.

Eisler, A. D., & Eisler, H. (1994). Subjective time scaling: Influence of age, gender, and type A and type B behavior. *Chronobiologia, 21*, 185–200.

Eisler, A. D., & Eisler, H. (2001). Subjective time in a patient with neurological impairment. *Psychologica, 28*, 193–206.

Eisler, A. D., & Eisler, H. (2006). *Subjective time in children in a developmental perspective*. Unpublished manuscript.

Eisler, A. D., Eisler, H., & Montgomery, H. (2004). A quantitative model for retrospective subjective duration. *NeuroQuantology, 2*, 263–291.

Eisler, A. D., Eisler, H., & Mori, S. (2001). Time perception: Comparison of schizophrenic and healthy Japanese males. In: *Abstract book of the VIIth European congress of psychology* (p. 120). London: British Psychological Society.
Eisler, H. (1974). The derivation of Stevens' psychophysical power law. In: H. R. Moskowitz, B. Scharf & J. C. Stevens (Eds), *Sensation and measurement* (pp. 61–64). Dordrecht, Holland: Reidel.
Eisler, H. (1975). Subjective duration and psychophysics. *Psychological Review*, *22*, 429–450.
Eisler, H. (1976). Experiments on subjective duration 1868–1975: A collection of power function exponents. *Psychological Bulletin*, *83*, 1154–1171.
Eisler, H. (1981a). Applicability of the parallel-clock model to duration discrimination. *Perception & Psychophysics*, *29*, 516–520.
Eisler, H. (1981b). The parallel-clock model: Replies to critics and criticism. *Perception & Psychophysics*, *29*, 225–233.
Eisler, H. (1984a). Subjective duration in rats: The psychophysical function. In: J. Gibbon & L. G. Allan (Eds), *Annals of the New York academy of sciences: Vol. 423. Timing and time perception* (pp. 43–51). New York: New York Academy of Sciences.
Eisler, H. (1984b). Knowing before doing: Discrimination by rats of a brief interruption of tine. *Journal of Experimental Analysis of Behavior*, *41*, 329–340.
Eisler, H. (1984c). Comments on Shimp's double dissociation between knowledge and tacit knowledge. *Journal of Experimental Analysis of Behavior*, *41*, 341–344.
Eisler, H. (1989). Serendipity in animal experimentation: Examples from duration scaling in rats. *International Journal of Comparative Psychology*, *3*, 137–149.
Eisler, H. (1990). Breaks in the psychophysical function for duration. In: H.-G. Geissler (Ed.), *Psychophysical explorations of mental structures* (pp. 241–252). Toronto: Hogrefe & Huber.
Eisler, H. (1995). The psychophysical functions for time perception: Interpreting their parameters. In: R. D. Luce, M. D. Zmura, D. D. Hoffman, G. J. Iverson & A. K. Romney (Eds), *Geometric representations of perceptual phenomena: Papers in honor of Tarow Indow on his 70th birthday* (pp. 253–265). Mahwah, NJ: Erlbaum.
Eisler, H., & Eisler, A. D. (1991). A mathematical model for time perception with experimentally obtained subjective time scales for humans and rats. *Chronobiologia*, *18*, 79–88.
Eisler, H., & Eisler, A. D. (1992). Time perception: Effects of sex and sound intensity on scales of subjective duration. *Scandinavian Journal of Psychology*, *33*, 339–358.
Ekman, G. (1956). Discriminal sensitivity on the subjective continuum. *Acta Psychologica*, *12*, 233–243.
Ekman, G. (1959). Weber's law and related functions. *Journal of Psychology*, *47*, 343–352.
Estel, V. (1885). Neue Versuche über den Zeitsinn [New experiments on the time-sense]. *Philosophische Studien (Wundt)*, *2*, 37–65.
Fechner, G. T. (1860). *Elemente der Psychophysik [Elements of psychophysics]*. Leipzig, Germany: Breitkopf & Härtel.
Fraisse, P. (1948). Les erreurs constantes dans la reproduction de courts intervals temporels [The constant errors in the reproduction of short time-intervals]. *Archives de Psychologie*, *32*, 161–176.
Fraisse, P. (1963). *The psychology of time*. New York: Harper & Row.
Fraisse, P. (1967). *Psychologie du temps [Psychology of time]*. Paris: Presses Universitaires de France.
Frankenhaeuser, M. (1959). *Estimation of time*. Stockholm: Almkvist & Wiksell.

Fuchs, T. (2007). The temporal structure of intentionality and its disturbance in schizophrenia. *Psychopathology, 40*, 229–235.

Getty, D. J. (1975). Discrimination of short temporal intervals: A comparison of two models. *Perception & Psychophysics, 18*, 1–8.

Gibbon, J. (1977). Scalar expectancy and Weber's law in animal timing. *Psychological Review, 84*, 279–325.

Grondin, S. (1993). Duration discrimination of empty and filled temporal intervals marked by auditory and visual signals. *Perception & Psychophysics, 54*, 383–394.

Grondin, S. (2001a). Discriminating time intervals presented in sequences marked by visual signals. *Perception & Psychophysics, 63*, 1214–1228.

Grondin, S. (2001b). From physical time to the first and second moments of psychological time. *Psychological Bulletin, 127*, 22–44.

Grondin, S., Meilleur-Wells, G., & Lachance, R. (1999). When to start explicit counting in a time-intervals discrimination task: A critical point in the timing process of humans. *Journal of Experimental Psychology: Human Perception and Performance, 25*, 993–1004.

Grondin, S., Ouellet, B., & Roussel, M.-E. (2001). About optimal timing and stability of Weber fraction for duration discrimination. *Acoustical Science and Technology, 22*, 370–372.

Guilford, J. P. (1932). A generalized psychophysical law. *Psychological Review, 39*, 73–85.

Guilford, J. P. (1954). *Psychometric methods* (2nd ed.). New York: McGraw-Hill.

Gulliksen, H. (1958). Comparatal dispersion, a measure of accuracy of judgment. *Psychometrika, 23*, 137–150.

Hellström, Å. (1977). Time errors are perceptual. An experimental investigation of duration and a quantitative successive-comparison model. *Psychological Research, 39*, 345–388.

Hellström, Å. (1978). Factors producing and factors not producing time errors: An experiment with loudness comparisons. *Perception & Psychophysics, 23*, 433–444.

Hellström, Å. (1979). Time errors and differential sensation weighting. *Journal of Experimental Psychology: Human Perception and Performance, 5*, 460–477.

Hellström, Å. (1985). The time-order error and its relatives: Mirrors of cognitive processes in comparing. *Psychological Bulletin, 97*, 35–61.

Hellström, Å. (1989). What happens when we compare two successive stimuli? In: G. Ljunggren & S. Dornic (Eds), *Psychophysics in action* (pp. 25–39). Berlin: Springer.

Hellström, Å. (1993). The normal distribution in scaling subjective stimulus differences: Less "normal" than we think? *Perception & Psychophysics, 54*, 82–92.

Hellström, Å. (2000). Sensation weighting in comparison and discrimination of heaviness. *Journal of Experimental Psychology: Human Perception and Performance, 26*, 6–17.

Hellström, Å. (2003). Comparison is not just subtraction: Effects of time- and space-order on subjective stimulus difference. *Perception & Psychophysics, 65*, 1161–1177.

Hellström, Å., & Almkvist, O. (1997). Tone duration discrimination in demented, memory impaired, and healthy elderly. *Dementia & Geriatric Cognitive Disorders, 8*, 49–54.

Hellström, Å., & Rammsayer, T. H. (2004). Effects of time-order, interstimulus interval, and feedback in duration discrimination of noise bursts in the 50- and 1000-ms ranges. *Acta Psychologica, 116*, 1–20.

Helson, H. (1964). *Adaptation-level theory*. New York: Harper & Row.

Henry, F. M. (1948). Discrimination of the duration of a sound. *Journal of Experimental Psychology, 38*, 734–743.

Hollingworth, H. L. (1909). The inaccuracy of movement. *Archives of Psychology, 11*, Whole No. 13.

Hollingworth, H. L. (1910). The central tendency of judgment. *Journal of Philosophy, Psychology, and Scientific Methods*, *7*, 461–469.

Holway, A. H., & Pratt, C. C. (1936). The Weber-ratio for intensive discrimination. *Psychological Review*, *43*, 322–340.

Hörmann, H. (1964). Kritische bemerkungen zu einer Untersuchung von F. Sixtl. [Critical remarks on a study by F. Sixtl.]. *Zeitschrift für experimentelle und angewandte Psychologie*, *11*, 667–670.

Jamieson, D. G., & Petrusic, W. M. (1975a). The dependence of time-order direction on stimulus range. *Canadian Journal of Psychology*, *29*, 175–182.

Jamieson, D. G., & Petrusic, W. M. (1975b). Presentation order effects in duration discrimination. *Perception & Psychophysics*, *17*, 197–202.

Jamieson, D. G., & Petrusic, W. M. (1978). Feedback versus an illusion in time. *Perception*, *7*, 91–96.

Jeon, J. Y., & Fricke, F. R. (1995). The effect of frequency on duration judgments. *Acustica*, *81*, 136–144.

Katz, D. (1906). Experimentelle beiträge zur Psychologie des Vergleichs im Gebiete des Zeitsinns. [Experimental contributions to the psychology of comparison in the realm of the time-sense]. *Zeitschrift für Psychologie und Physiologie der Sinnesorgane, Abt. 1*, *42*, 302–340, 414–450.

Killeen, P. R., & Taylor, T. J. (2000). How the propagation of error through stochastic counters affects time discrimination and other psychophysical judgments. *Psychological Review*, *107*, 430–459.

Killeen, P. R., & Weiss, N. A. (1987). Optimal timing and the Weber function. *Psychological Review*, *94*, 455–468.

Kinchla, J. (1972). Duration discrimination of acoustically defined intervals in the 1- to 8-sec range. *Perception & Psychophysics*, *12*, 318–320.

Koester, T. (1945). The time error and sensitivity in pitch and loudness discrimination as a function of time interval and stimulus level. *Archives of Psychology (Columbia University)*, *297*, 1–69.

Kollert, J. (1883). Untersuchungen über den Zeitsinn. [Investigations concerning the time-sense]. *Philosophische Studien (Wundt)*, *1*, 78–89.

Köhler, W. (1923). Zur Theorie des Sukzessivvergleichs und der Zeitfehler. [On the theory of successive comparison and the time-order errors.]. *Psychologische Forschung*, *4*, 115–175.

Kristofferson, A. B. (1980). A quantal step in duration discrimination. *Perception & Psychophysics*, *27*, 300–306.

Leuba, A. (1892). A new instrument for Weber's law; with indications of a law of sense memory. *American Journal of Psychology*, *5*, 370–384.

Mach, E. (1865). Untersuchungen über den Zeitsinn des Ohres. *Sitzungsberichte der Wiener Akademie der Wissenschaften, Kl.*, *51*, 542–548. Wien.

Marchman, J. N. (1969). Discrimination of brief temporal durations. *Psychological Record*, *19*, 83–92.

Martin, L. J., & Müller, G. E. (1899). *Zur Analyse der Unterschiedsempfindlichkeit. [On the analysis of discriminal sensitivity]*. Leipzig, Germany: Barth.

McGavren, M. (1965). Memory of brief auditory durations in comparison discriminations. *Psychological Record*, *15*, 249–260.

Mehner, M. (1885). Zur Lehre vom Zeitsinn. [On the doctrine of the time-sense]. *Philosophische Studien (Wundt)*, *2*, 546–602.

Melges, F. T. (1982). *Time and the inner future: A temporal approach to psychiatric disorders*. New York: Wiley.

Meumann, E. (1893). Beiträge zur Psychologie des Zeitsinns. *Philosophische Studien*, *8*, 431–519.

Michels, W. C., & Helson, H. (1954). A quantitative theory of time-order effects. *American Journal of Psychology*, *67*, 327–334.

Milner, B., Corkin, S., & Teuber, H.-L. (1968). Further analysis of the hippocampal amnesic syndrome: 14-year follow-up study of H. M. *Neuropsychologia*, *6*, 215–234.

Minkowski, D. E. (1927). *La schizophrénie. [Schizophrenia]*. Paris: Payot.

Mo, S. S. (1974). Comparative judgment of temporal duration in conjunction with contextual variability: A test of a memory-storage model of temporal judgment. *Perceptual and Motor Skills*, *38*, 1031–1036.

Nakajima, Sei (1951). On the time-error in the successive comparison of time. *Japanese Journal of Psychology*, *21*, 36–45.

Nakajima, Sh. (1958). The time-error in the successive comparison of tonal durations. *Japanese Journal of Psychology*, *29*, 18–28.

Nakajima, Y., ten Hoopen, G., Hilkhuysen, G., & Sasaki, T. (1992). Time-shrinking: A discontinuity in the perception of auditory temporal patterns. *Perception & Psychophysics*, *51*, 504–507.

Needham, J. G. (1935). The effect of the time-interval upon the time-error at different intensive levels. *Journal of Experimental Psychology*, *18*, 530–543.

Nichelli, P. (1993). The neurophysiology of human temporal processing. In: F. Boller & J. Grafman (Eds), *Handbook of Neuropsychology* (Vol. 8, pp. 339–371). Amsterdam: Elsevier.

Pauley, A. E. (1981). An introduction to chronobiology. In: H. Mayersbach, L. E. Scheving & A. E. Pauley (Eds), *Biological rhythms in structure and function* (pp. 1–21). New York: Alan.

Peak, H. (1940). The time-order error in successive judgments and in reflexes. III. Time-order errors. *Psychological Review*, *47*, 1–20.

Penner, M. J. (1976). The effect of marker variability on the discrimination of temporal intervals. *Perception & Psychophysics*, *19*, 466–469.

Pöppel, E. (1971). Oscillations as possible basis for time perception. *Studium Generale*, *24*, 85–107.

Pöppel, E. (2004). Lost in time: a historical frame, temporal processing units and the 3-second window. *Acta Neurobiologiae Experimentalis*, *64*, 295–301.

Rammsayer, T., & Wittkowski, K. M. (1990). Zeitfehler und Positionseffekt des Standardreizes bei der Diskrimination kurzer Zeitdauern. [Time-order error and position effect of the standard stimulus in the discrimination of short durations]. *Archiv für Psychologie*, *142*, 81–89.

Rammsayer, T. H. (1994). A cognitive-neuroscience approach for elucidation of mechanisms underlying temporal information processing. *International Journal of Neuroscience*, *77*, 61–76.

Rammsayer, T. H. (1999). Neuropharmacological evidence for different timing mechanisms in humans. *Quarterly Journal of Experimental Psychology*, *52B*, 273–286.

Richards, W. (1964). Time estimates measured by reproduction. *Perceptual and Motor Skills*, *18*, 929–943.

Richards, W. (1973). Time reproductions by H.M. *Acta Psychologica*, *37*, 279–282.

Sasaki, T., Suetomi, D., Nakajima, Y., & ten Hoopen, G. (2002). Time-shrinking, its propagation, and Gestalt principles. *Perception & Psychophysics*, *64*, 919–931.

Schab, F. R., & Crowder, R. G. (1988). The role of succession in temporal cognition: Is the time-order error a recency effect of memory? *Perception & Psychophysics*, *44*, 233–242.

Sixtl, F. (1963). Der Zeitfehler (time-order error) beim Schätzen der Reizzeit und als Funktion der Reizlänge, der Intervallzeit und der Versuchswiederholung. [The time-order error in rating of stimulus time and as a function of stimulus duration, interstimulus interval and repetition of the experiment]. *Zeitschrift für experimentelle und angewandte Psychologie*, *10*, 209–225.

Sixtl, F. (1964). Erwiderung und Ergänzung zu Hörmanns Diskussion der Fading-trace-theory. [Rejoinder and elaboration in response to Hörmann's discussion of the fading-trace theory]. *Zeitschrift für experimentelle und angewandte Psychologie*, *11*, 671–678.

Small, A. M., & Campbell, R. A. (1962). Temporal differential sensitivity for auditory stimuli. *American Journal of Psychology*, *75*, 401–410.

Spitzer, R. L., Endicott, J., & Rabin, E. (1978). *Research diagnostic criteria (RDC) for selected groups of functional disorders*. New York: New York State Psychiatric Institute.

Staddon, J., & Higa, J. (1997). Multiple time scales in simple habituation. *Psychological Review*, *103*, 720–733.

Stevens, S. S. (1975). *Psychophysics*. New York: Wiley.

Stott, L. H. (1935). Time-order errors in the discrimination of short tonal durations. *Journal of Experimental Psychology*, *18*, 741–766.

Teghtsoonian, R. (1971). On the exponents in Stevens' law and the constant in Ekman's law. *Psychological Review*, *78*, 71–80.

Treisman, M. (1963). Temporal discrimination and the indifference interval: Implications for a model of the "internal clock". *Psychological Monographs*, *77* (Whole No. 576).

Van Allen, M. W., Benton, A. L., & Gordon, M. C. (1966). Temporal discrimination in brain-damaged patients. *Neuropsychologia*, *4*, 159–167.

Vierordt, K. (1868). *Der Zeitsinn nach Versuchen. [The time-sense according to experiments]*. Tübingen, Germany: Laupp.

Wackerman, J., & Späti, J. (2006). Asymmetry of the discrimination function for temporal duration in human subjects. *Acta Neurobiologiæ Experimentalis*, *66*, 245–254.

Wahl, O. F., & Sieg, D. (1980). Time estimation among schizophrenics. *Perceptual and Motor Skills*, *50*, 535–541.

Wallace, M., & Rabin, A. I. (1960). Temporal experience. *Psychological Bulletin*, *57*, 213–236.

Wearden, J. H. (1999). "Beyond the fields we know...": Exploring and developing scalar timing theory. *Behavioral Processes*, *45*, 3–21.

Wearden, J. H., & Ferrara, A. (1993). Subjective shortening in humans' memory for stimulus duration. *Quarterly Journal of Experimental Psychology. B, Comparative & Physiological Psychology*, *46*, 163–186.

Weber, E. H. (1834). *De pulsu, resorptione, auditu et tactu [On pulse, breathing, hearing, and touch]*. Leipzig: Köhler.

Weber, E. H. (1996). *E. H. Weber on the tactile senses* (2nd ed.). Edited and translated by H. E. Ross & D. J. Murray. Hove: Erlbaum (UK) Taylor & Francis.

Westheimer, G. (1999). Discrimination of short time intervals by the human observer. *Experimental Brain Research*, *129*, 121–126.

Woodrow, H. (1933). Weight-discrimination with a varying standard. *American Journal of Psychology*, *45*, 391–416.

Woodrow, H. (1934). The temporal indifference interval determined by the method of average error. *Journal of Experimental Psychology*, *17*, 167–188.

Woodrow, H. (1935). The effect of practice on time-order errors in the comparison of temporal intervals. *Psychological Review*, *42*, 127–152.

Woodrow, H. (1951). Time perception. In: S. S. Stevens (Ed.), *Handbook of experimental psychology* (pp. 1224–1236). New York: Wiley.

Zeiler, M. D., & Hoyert, M. S. (1989). Temporal reproduction. *Journal of the Experimental Analysis of Behavior*, *52*, 81–95.

Chapter 4

Time and Attention: Review of the Literature

Scott W. Brown

The impact of attention on temporal experience is evident in everyday life. The adage "time flies when you're having fun" succinctly expresses the basic observation that time appears to flow more quickly when one's temporal awareness is minimized. The phrase would be more accurate (but less appealing) if restated as "time flies when you're engaged in some absorbing activity," because the important factor is that attention is distracted from time. When attention *is* focused on time, the opposite effect occurs. In this case, subjective time slows down and "time drags." These familiar experiences form the backdrop for scientific research on the relations between attention and time. The topic has been approached from many different directions, and several reviews relating various aspects of attention and time have appeared previously (Brown, 1997; Glicksohn, 2001; Grondin, 2001; Zakay, 1989). This chapter consists of a broad survey of some of the main ideas and findings in the area.

Research on time and attention covers a wide range of issues because attention itself is a complex topic with many different aspects. One well-known paper (Posner & Boies, 1971) identified alertness, selectivity, and processing capacity as the main components of attention. In a later paper, Posner and Petersen (1990) divided attentional functions into three subsystems — orienting, detecting, and alerting — based on neuroanatomy. Hirst and Kalmar (1987) outlined different metaphors used to describe attentional capacity, including a fuel, a cognitive structure or mechanism, and a skill. Some aspects of attention are relatively unexplored in relation to time perception. For example, studies relating temporal experience to selective attention (Underwood & Swain, 1973) or vigilance (McGrath & O'Hanlon, 1967) have been limited in scope and have failed to attract much research interest. In contrast, focused attention, attentional allocation, and processing resources have generated the most research activity.

Psychology of Time

DOI:10.1016/B978-0-08046-977-5.00004-1

4.1. Attention and Temporal Information Processing

Time perception depends on diverse temporal cues to mark the passage of time. These cues form the basis for a continuously updated temporal record that serves as a framework to organize events and experiences on a subjective timeline. Attention helps determine whether and to what degree these cues are processed, and so plays a critical role in establishing the temporal record. Various theoretical notions concerning the perception and processing of temporal cues are summarized below, with special reference devoted to the influence of attentional processes.

4.1.1. Stimulus Environment

Some theorists have emphasized the role of the stimulus environment in shaping our perception of time. Poynter (1989) described a change/segmentation model in which subjective time is determined by perceived changes and how readily events can be segmented into discrete chunks. The more segments created, the longer the perceived time. Attention affects time insofar as it affects the segmentation process. Attending to the organization of events enhances the coding of segments into easily retrievable chunks. Conversely, the segmentation process is disrupted if attention is distracted away from the structure of events.

Boltz (1992, 1995, 1998; Brown & Boltz, 2002; Jones & Boltz, 1989) offered another view relating the organization of stimulus events to perceived time. This approach emphasizes *event structure*, which ranges from coherent to incoherent. Coherent events are organized, orderly, and predictable. Attentional tracking of these events is aided by their underlying organization, and less effort is needed to process coherent events because their temporal and nontemporal features tend to coincide. Time judgments of such events are relatively accurate. In contrast, incoherent events are disorganized, random, and unpredictable. These events are more difficult to follow, and they require a great deal of attentional effort to process due to their disorganization and disjointedness. In this case, time judgments are more likely to be inaccurate.

4.1.2. Time as Information

In an important paper, Michon (1972) advocated the idea of considering time as information, a concept that has had a major impact on subsequent theorizing. In his *equivalence postulate*, Michon (1972, 1985; Michon & Jackson, 1984) argued that time has the same status as any other stimulus attribute, such as size, loudness, or color. In this view, temporal information (defined as the succession of events) is encoded in a specialized representational system in much the same way that nontemporal information about acoustic or visual properties of a stimulus is encoded. Furthermore, temporal information processing is not a passive process but rather is a deliberate, effortful task that requires attentional capacity (Michon, 1985).

Michon (1972) anticipated later theorists when he stated that due to limits in processing capacity, "…there will be necessarily a trade-off between temporal and nontemporal information…" (p. 242).

These concepts of time as information and the importance of attention in temporal processing appear in an influential mathematical model developed by Thomas and colleagues (Thomas & Brown, 1974; Thomas & Cantor, 1975, 1978; Thomas & Weaver, 1975). The model proposes that perceived time is a weighted average of the output of two independent processors, one of which encodes temporal information and the other encodes nontemporal information. Attention is allocated automatically to the two processors, which operate in parallel. The idea of attention shared between temporal and nontemporal processing in a dual-task situation established a basic framework for researchers studying the effects of resource allocation on time perception.

4.1.3. Internal Clock

The idea of an internal clock mechanism underlying perceived time, first proposed by François (1927) and Hoagland (1933), has been incorporated into many psychophysical models of timing (e.g., Allan, 1992; Church, 1984; Creelman, 1962). Treisman (1963) outlined the basic elements of a clock model. A pacemaker produces a series of neural pulses that enter into a counter/accumulator device. The more pulses accumulated, the longer the perceived time. Studies involving manipulations designed to influence the pulse rate support the model (Burle & Bonnet, 1997; Treisman & Brogan, 1992; Treisman, Cook, Naish, & MacCrone, 1994; Treisman, Faulkner, & Naish, 1992; Treisman, Faulkner, Naish, & Brogan, 1990). For situations in which the length of an interval is to be judged, a comparator (decision-making mechanism) compares the number of accumulated pulses against a standard number associated with the interval stored in memory. The outcome of this comparison determines the subject's judgment.

These basic elements of clock, memory, and decision have been formalized into a highly successful model of animal timing known as the scalar expectancy theory, or SET (Gibbon, 1977; Gibbon, Church, & Meck, 1984). SET is an outgrowth of operant research on timing behavior in rats and pigeons. Several researchers have expanded the scope of SET to include studies of human timing (e.g., Allan & Gibbon, 1991; Malapani & Fairhurst, 2002; Rakitin et al., 1998; Wearden, 1991, 1992; Wearden & McShane, 1988). However, one limitation in the application of SET to human timing is that the model does not adequately address the role of attention in time perception (Block, 1990, 2003; Block & Zakay, 1996; Wearden, 2003). SET is grounded in a behaviorist perspective that deemphasizes cognitive processes such as attention.

4.1.4. Attentional-Gate Model

Zakay and Block (Block & Zakay, 1996; Zakay & Block, 1996, 1997, 1998; Zakay, Block, & Tsal, 1999) developed a timing model that integrates the idea of an internal clock with the notion of attentional resources devoted to temporal information processing. The model is essentially a modified version of SET, in which a new component called the *attentional gate* is situated between the pacemaker and the accumulator mechanism. Pulses pass through the gate before entering the accumulator (or *cognitive counter*). The more attention directed to time, the wider the gate opens, allowing more pulses to enter the counter. The result is a lengthening of perceived time (i.e., longer verbal estimations and reproductions, or shorter temporal productions). Therefore, attention to time is necessary for pulses to be transmitted and counted. If less attention is devoted to time (as in the case of focusing on nontemporal information), then the gate narrows, reducing the number of pulses entering the counter. A lower pulse count shortens perceived time (shorter verbal estimations and reproductions or longer productions). Although the attentional-gate model has been controversial (see Lejeune, 1998, 2000; Zakay, 2000), its main value is that it formally incorporates attention into a pulse-counter timing system.

4.2. Attentiveness to Time

Attention to time involves a heightened consciousness of temporal cues. Stimulus changes, the ordering or succession of events, and the organization of those events all become more salient to the perceiver. The person may engage in some type of timekeeping strategy such as chronometric counting, executing a series of repetitive movements (e.g., rhythmical tapping), or visualizing the sweep of a second hand on a clock face (Brown, Newcomb, & Kahrl, 1995). In this way, attentiveness to time dramatically affects the experience of time.

4.2.1. Prospective versus Retrospective Paradigms

The distinction between prospective and retrospective paradigms relates directly to the issue of attentiveness to time. In the prospective paradigm, subjects are informed that they will be asked to judge the duration of an upcoming interval. These instructions are designed to arouse a "temporal motive" (Doob, 1971) in which one's attention is directed to the passage of time. Most of the studies reported in this paper involve prospective timing. In contrast, subjects tested under the retrospective paradigm are not aware that they will be required to judge time. These subjects are asked for an unexpected time judgment only after the interval has ended. Thus, prospective judgments involve an ongoing attentiveness to time, whereas retrospective judgments rely on incidentally encoded temporal information. Comparisons of the two paradigms are therefore critical in evaluating the role of attention in timing.

Block and Zakay (1997) conducted a meta-analysis of 20 paradigm comparison studies. The major findings were that (a) prospective time judgments were 16%

longer on average compared with retrospective judgments, and (b) retrospective judgments were on average 15% more variable than prospective judgments. These results are consistent with the idea that prospective timing involves a heightened attentiveness to temporal cues. Retrospective judgments, based on fragmentary temporal information, are shorter and less reliable.

A recent study highlights a different aspect of attention as it pertains to the two paradigms. Boltz (2005) had subjects prospectively or retrospectively reproduce the duration of 9.1–11.6 s videotaped scenes that varied in structural coherence. Some scenes depicted coherent events, some depicted incoherent events, and some were intermediate. Prior to the time judgments, each scene was shown on either four or eight occasions, during which subjects rated the scenes on a variety of nontemporal perceptual dimensions. As expected, prospective time judgments were more accurate than retrospective judgments. With more exposures, however, retrospective judgments of the coherent events became as accurate as the prospective judgments. Boltz (2005) argued that the temporal and nontemporal aspects of coherent events are intertwined, and with greater exposure this interrelatedness becomes more prominent. Although attention was directed to nontemporal stimulus features, coherent structure enhanced the incidental processing of temporal information.

4.2.2. The Watched Pot Phenomenon

Numerous writers have observed that attentiveness to the passage of time lengthens temporal perception (e.g., Frankenhaeuser, 1959; James (1890/1950); Sturt, 1925). This state of heightened temporal awareness has been termed "the experience of time-in-passing" (Hicks, Miller, Gaes, & Bierman, 1977), or the "flow" of time (Michon, 1985). Time-in-passing is related to conditions of boredom, impatience, and anticipation (Brown, 1985). As described by Fraisse (1963), attentiveness to time often leads to a familiar temporal illusion: "When a feeling of time arises, our attention turns selectively to the duration and time seems to pass more slowly. 'A watched pot never boils', as the saying goes" (p. 216). A literal watched pot situation was created by Cahoon and Edmonds (1980; see also Block, George, & Reed, 1980). Subjects were individually escorted to a room containing a hot plate and a glass coffee pot filled with water. Subjects in the control condition were informed that there would be a delay in starting the experiment, and that the experimenter would return when everything was ready. Subjects in the experimental condition received identical comments and were further requested to call the experimenter from an adjacent room when the water started to boil. After a 240-s interval, the experimenter returned and asked for an unexpected verbal estimation of the elapsed time. The results supported the watched pot proverb in that the experimental group overestimated the interval compared with the control group. Time for the experimental group appeared to move more slowly.

4.2.3. Expectancy

Expectancy is a condition closely related to the watched pot phenomenon. Expected events give rise to an enhanced temporal awareness as anticipation grows and attention becomes increasingly focused on time. Investigators have approached this topic with a remarkable variety of stimuli, tasks, and methodologies. Some researchers have evaluated the influence of affective factors in which subjects wait for the occurrence of pleasant or unpleasant events. In one study (Edmonds, Cahoon, & Bridges, 1981), subjects overestimated 60 and 240 s intervals spent waiting for a positive event and underestimated the intervals when waiting for a negative event. Other studies have produced mixed results, with some researchers also reporting that waiting for positive events leads to overestimation (Filer & Meals, 1949), but others (Schiff & Thayer, 1968) reporting no differences in the estimated waiting times (48 and 144 s) for positive or negative events. Schiff and Thayer (1968) did find, however, that waiting conditions lengthened time judgments compared with nonwaiting conditions.

Another line of research involves temporal structure in music. Western music consists of an organized set of pitch changes, rhythmical patterns, phrase structures and accents, and temporal hierarchies (Jones & Boltz, 1989). These features provide a rich temporal context that allows the listener to predict when a phrase or melody should end. Jones and Boltz (1989) had subjects compare the duration of pairs of melodies whose lengths ranged from 34 to 37 notes. The structural accents of these stimuli were modified to create the perception of a melody ending earlier or later than expected. For example, a melody ending too early leaves listeners "hanging" at an unresolved point in the sequence. The results showed that melodies that seemed to end too early were judged to be short, whereas melodies that ended too late were judged to be long. This same pattern was obtained in numerous other experiments in which various structural manipulations were used to vary the expected ending points of melodies (e.g., Boltz, 1989; Jones, Boltz, & Klein, 1993; see also Barnes & Jones, 2000, for a related paradigm). Boltz (1993) extended this methodology from musical events to other contexts. In one experiment (Experiment 1), subjects performed a listening task for 36 trials. Then, they were led to believe that they had more, fewer, or the same number of trials remaining in the experiment. The experiment actually concluded after another 36 trials. Subjects expecting fewer trials judged the second half of the experiment to be shorter than the first half, while those expecting more trials judged it to be longer. In Experiment 2, subjects waited for the experiment to begin. Different groups were told that the expected waiting time would be 1, 10, or 20 min. After waiting for 10 min, the subjects were asked to estimate the waiting period. Those waiting for less time than expected underestimated the interval, whereas those waiting for a longer time overestimated it. These results conform to a model emphasizing *temporal contrasts* between observed and expected waiting times (Jones & Boltz, 1989), in which events ending earlier than expected shorten perceived time and those ending later lengthen perceived time.

A different approach to time and expectancy focuses on events preceding the interval to be judged. In a series of psychophysical experiments, Grondin and

Rammsayer (2003) systematically manipulated the duration of the foreperiod, the "empty" interval immediately preceding a brief target interval. The procedure involved first familiarizing subjects with a standard interval (100 or 500 ms, depending on the experiment). Then, a series of comparison intervals of variable durations was presented, and subjects judged whether the comparisons were longer or shorter than the standard. The main focus of the research concerned the foreperiod, which varied from 300–600 ms in some experiments, or 600–1500 ms in others. The results showed that longer foreperiods caused the comparison intervals to be judged longer. The authors argued that as a foreperiod lengthened, there was a growing expectation that the comparison interval would occur, prompting subjects to allocate more attention to time. In terms of a pacemaker-counter perspective, greater attentiveness to time allowed for greater numbers of temporal pulses to be accumulated, thus leading to a lengthening of perceived time.

Fortin and Masse (2000) devised a procedure in which subjects attempted to produce a target interval defined by a tone that was interrupted part way through by a break. In one study (Experiment 1), the target interval was 2 s, and a 3–6 s interruption in the tone occurred either early (500 ms) or late (1500 ms) following tone onset. Subjects were instructed not to include the break duration in producing the interval, but rather to combine the prebreak and postbreak intervals only. The results showed that the later break location was associated with longer temporal productions. Fortin and Masse (2000) explained the results in terms of attentional shifts driven by expectancies: As the prebreak duration increased, more attention was directed to monitoring for the upcoming break and less attention was devoted to time. Attending to the break interfered with the accumulation of temporal pulses, thus lengthening temporal productions. A series of experiments involving a variety of target durations, break durations, number of break locations, cued versus uncued break trials, and empty versus filled breaks showed the same basic pattern of later break locations being associated with longer temporal productions (Fortin & Masse, 2000; Fortin, Bédard, & Champagne, 2005). Tremblay and Fortin (2003) demonstrated the effect in the context of a temporal discrimination task in which subjects classified 2.5–3.5 s intervals as being short or long. Consistent with the previous findings, later break locations were associated with more "short" responses. Macar (2002) reported similar results with temporal reproductions in which subjects timed 2.0–5.8 s intervals while also making brightness or frequency discrimination judgments. Reproductions tended to be shorter when the nontemporal stimuli occurred later rather than earlier in the intervals. Macar (2002) argued that the anticipation of later-occurring nontemporal stimuli caused subjects to divide attention between temporal and nontemporal processing and thus miss temporal cues.

4.2.4. Directed Attention to Time

Several researchers have attempted to manipulate temporal awareness by explicitly directing attention to time. In an early study, Woodrow (1933) had subjects reproduce 0.6–4.0 s intervals demarcated by pairs of tones. Some subjects were instructed to attend only to the two sounds that defined the interval, whereas other subjects were instructed to attend to the interval between the tones. The results indicated that attending to the interval lengthened reproductions relative to attending to the tones. Curton and Lordahl (1974) and McKay (1977) had subjects judge 9–20 s intervals during which they performed tasks designed to focus attention on either the passage of time or the task itself. In both cases, a focus on time served to lengthen perceived time.

Studies of attended versus unattended stimuli have extended these results. In a series of experiments, Mattes and Ulrich (1998) presented brief (70–300 ms) stimuli for time judgments. Prior to stimulus presentation, a cue appeared directing the subjects' attention to a particular stimulus modality or location, depending on the experiment. The results showed that time judgments were longer for attended stimuli (see also Chen & O'Neill, 2001). Similar findings were obtained by Enns, Brehaut, and Shore (1999), who found that 10–150 ms light flashes appearing in attended locations were judged to last longer than those appearing in unattended locations. A different method for directing attention to time was used by Tse, Intriligator, Rivest, and Cavanagh (2004). These investigators employed the *oddball paradigm*, in which a low probability stimulus appears within a sequence of high probability stimuli; because of its novelty, the oddball stimulus prompts greater attentiveness. In a series of experiments involving intervals ranging from 75–4000 ms, the authors showed that oddball stimuli lengthened time judgments. Tse et al. (2004) termed this effect *time's subjective expansion*, and attributed the effect to an "attentional boost" in which attention directed toward a stimulus increases the rate of information processing per unit time.

Ono, Yamada, Chujo, and Kawahara (2007) showed that *selective inattention* to a stimulus affects subsequent judgments of its duration. A pair of stimulus figures, a target and a nontarget, appeared on a screen and subjects judged whether the target was on the left or right. Following this response, a single test stimulus appeared and subjects pressed a button when they judged that it had been displayed for 2 s (i.e., a temporal production task). The test stimulus was the target, the nontarget, or a novel figure. The results showed that nontargets were associated with longer productions (a shortening of perceived time) compared with the other two stimuli. Ono et al. (2007) argued that selectively ignoring the nontargets had decreased their salience, with the result that more attentional resources were required to process these stimuli when they appeared for the time judgment task. Consequently, less attention was devoted to time, which led to longer temporal productions.

4.3. Attentional Resources in Timing

Much of the research on timing centers on attentional resources. The resource theory of attention postulates the existence of a limited pool of attentional capacity (resources) that supports all cognitive processing (Kahneman, 1973; Navon, 1984; Navon & Gopher, 1979; Norman & Bobrow, 1975). Research in this area revolves around topics such as dual-task performance, attentional deployment, interference, and automaticity. These concepts and methods have been very influential in the study of time and attention.

4.3.1. Interference Effect

In an earlier review, Brown (1997) documented an *interference effect* involving temporal/nontemporal dual-task conditions. The interference effect refers to a disruption in timing performance produced by a concurrent distractor task. In a typical study of the interference effect, subjects perform a distractor task and simultaneously attend to the passage of time for an upcoming time judgment. The standard finding is that time judgments under dual-task conditions become shorter, more variable, and/or more inaccurate compared with timing-only, single-task conditions. The literature shows that time judgments are very sensitive to interference, such that distractor tasks with even relatively weak attentional demands can substantially interfere with timing performance.

Since that review, numerous other studies demonstrating the interference effect have appeared. These studies have utilized a broad array of distractor tasks, including perceptual discrimination, mental arithmetic, visual search, target detection, memory, reading, and manual tracking (Baudouin, Vanneste, Pouthas, & Isingrini, 2006; Benuzzi, Basso, & Nichelli, 2005; Brown, 1997, 1998a, b, 2006, 2008; Brown & Bennett, 2002; Brown & Boltz, 2002; Brown & Merchant, 2007; Burle & Casini, 2001; Casini & Ivry, 1999; Casini & Macar, 1997; Coull, Vidal, Nazarian, & Macar, 2004; Franssen & Vandierendonck, 2002; Franssen, Vandierendonck, & Van Hiel, 2006; Gautier & Droit-Volet, 2002; Macar, 2002; Marshall & Wilsoncroft, 1989; Perbal, Couillet, Azouvi, & Pouthas, 2003; Rammsayer & Ulrich, 2005; Shinohara, 1999; Shinohara, Miura, & Usui, 2002; Venneri, Pestell, Gray, Della Sala, & Nichelli, 1998; Venneri, Pestell, & Nichelli, 2003). These studies (combined with those cited in the 1997 review) total 57 articles reporting 77 experiments, all published between 1924 and 2008. Each of these experiments compared time judgment performance under single-task versus dual-task conditions. Of the 77 experiments, 70 (91%) showed the interference effect.

These data establish the interference effect as being the most well-replicated finding in all the time perception literature. In an area often fraught with terminological confusion, contradictory results, and limited conclusions, the interference effect stands out as a phenomenon that transcends differences in methodologies, durations, and task requirements. Consequently, this area has been the focus of an increasing amount of theoretical and experimental work.

4.3.2. Attentional Allocation Model

Research on the interference effect led to the development of an attentional allocation model of timing (Brown, 1985; Brown & West, 1990; Hicks et al., 1977;

Hicks, Miller, & Kinsbourne, 1976; Zakay, 1989, 1993). According to the model, time judgment performance is determined by the amount of attention directed to time. More attention devoted to the flow of temporal events lengthens perceived time, perhaps because more temporal pulses are accumulated into a cognitive counter mechanism or because temporal cues become more salient and are given greater weighting. Under dual-task conditions, resources must be shared between temporal and nontemporal tasks. Less attention to time reduces the amount of temporal information that is encoded and stored. A faulty temporal record of the interval is established, a record that may contain many gaps, omissions, and distortions. The incomplete record leads to greater error in time judgments.

4.3.3. Distractor Task Difficulty

Many researchers have sought to vary the difficulty or complexity of the nontemporal distractor task as a means of exploring interference and resource allocation in timing tasks. The rationale is that the more demanding the distractor task (i.e., the greater the cognitive workload), the more attentional resources it requires, with the result that fewer resources are available for timing. Consequently, timing performance should become increasingly impaired as the distractor task becomes more difficult.

Brown's (1997) review surveyed numerous studies that included two or more levels of concurrent distractor task difficulty. Since that review, at least 18 other articles manipulating task difficulty have appeared (Benuzzi et al., 2005; Brown, 1997, 1998b, 2006, 2008; Brown & Boltz, 2002; Brown & Merchant, 2007; Chastain & Ferraro, 1997; Field & Groeger, 2004; Fink & Neubauer, 2001; Fortin & Couture, 2002; Fortin, Duchet, & Rousseau, 1996; Fortin & Masse, 1999; Fortin & Rousseau, 1998; Kawamura, 2000; Rammsayer & Ulrich, 2005; Zakay, 1998; Zakay & Shub, 1998). Combining these newer papers with those cited in the earlier review yields a total of 49 articles representing 72 individual experiments published between 1938 and 2008. Forty-eight of the 72 experiments (67%) reported that increased distractor task demands led to greater error in time judgment performance. This result supports the idea that timing performance is tied to the availability of resources.

The remaining 24 experiments (33% of the total) either failed to find an effect of task difficulty or reported an anomalous pattern. However, it is important to note that most of these studies did show the classic interference effect when comparing single-task versus dual-task conditions; what they did not show was greater interference with more difficult versions of the concurrent distractor tasks. One explanation to account for this lack of an effect relates to the observation that timing is very sensitive to cognitive workload (Brown, 1997). Because tasks with relatively low workload demands may produce a substantial disruption in timing, tasks with even greater demands may not degrade time judgments beyond an already low level of performance.

4.3.4. Multiple Timing

Brown and West (1990) developed a multiple timing task in which subjects were required to time multiple, overlapping temporal events. In one experiment (Experiment 1), subjects monitored the durations of 1, 2, 3, or 4 concurrent 6–16 s visual temporal targets that had asynchronous onset and offset times. After all the stimulus targets had timed out and disappeared from the screen, subjects reproduced one of those targets selected at random. The results showed a linear increase in absolute error and variability of reproduced durations as a function of the number of temporal targets. Comparable results were obtained in another experiment (Experiment 2) in which subjects had to produce multiple target durations. Similarly, a multiple timing study involving 2 and 5 s temporal productions found an increase in timing variability as the number of temporal targets increased from 1 to 2 (Ambro & Czigler, 1998). All these results are consistent with the idea that the interference effect is related to attentional resource allocation.

Brown, Stubbs, and West (1992) extended the findings to a psychophysical scaling task (see Chapters 2 and 3) in which subjects verbally estimated or reproduced multiple, partially overlapping temporal targets that ranged in duration from 1 to 40 s (Experiment 1) or 6–16 s (Experiment 2). Power functions relating perceived and physical time showed that greater numbers of targets lead to poorer discriminability (i.e., flatter slopes) and increased variability in both experiments. Vanneste and Pouthas (1999) compared younger (M age = 20 years) and older (M age = 65 years) subjects on a multiple timing task involving 6-, 8-, and 10-s overlapping target intervals. Their results indicated that both groups exhibited greater error and variability in reproductions as the number of targets increased from 1 to 3. However, the older subjects showed a greater degree of interference relative to the younger subjects. Vanneste and Pouthas (1999) attributed the greater impairment of the older subjects on the task to age-related reductions in attentional resources and working memory functions.

4.3.5. Attentional Sharing

Attentional sharing is a technique in which subjects are instructed to allocate specified amounts of attention to concurrent tasks. Originally used in studies of visual attention (Kinchla, 1980; Sperling & Melchner, 1978), the method was adapted by Macar and her colleagues to probe the effects of resource allocation on timing. In one study (Grondin & Macar, 1992), subjects judged the duration and/or intensity of a tone. The timing task required subjects to judge whether the tone was short or long (460 ms versus 540 ms in one condition, or 1320 ms versus 1680 ms in another condition); the intensity task was to judge whether the tone was soft or loud. Subjects were assigned to different attentional sharing conditions in which they were instructed to devote relatively greater amounts of attention to one task and correspondingly lesser amounts of attention to the other. The results showed that duration discriminability decreased and intensity discriminability increased as less attention was devoted to time and more was devoted to intensity; an opposite pattern occurred as attention shifted from intensity to time. Numerous studies employing different time judgment methods, durations, and nontemporal tasks have shown the same general result (Casini, Macar, & Grondin, 1992; Coull et al., 2004; Franssen & Vandierendonck, 2002; Macar, Grondin, & Casini, 1994). Typically, the withdrawal of attentional resources from timing yields a graded decrement in time-judgment performance. In some cases, the decrement pertains only to timing, and nontemporal performance remains unaffected (Casini & Macar, 1997; Macar et al., 1994, Experiments 2 and 3). Macar et al. (1994) argued that this difference in interference sensitivity may be due in part to attentional switching between concurrent temporal and nontemporal tasks. Switching attention back and forth may be more detrimental for a timing task than for a nontemporal task.

In a variation of the attentional sharing method, Zakay (1989, 1998) instructed subjects performing concurrent temporal and nontemporal tasks to regard the timing task as either *primary* or *secondary* with respect to the nontemporal task. These instructions produced reliable results showing that both verbal estimations and reproductions were longer when timing was treated as the primary task (see also Kojima & Matsuda, 2000). The results are consistent with a resource model in which more resources devoted to time cause a lengthening of temporal experience.

4.3.6. Attenuation Effect

The attenuation effect refers to a reduction in interference in timing as a result of practice on the distractor task. According to resource theorists, practice on a task reduces the amount of resources the task requires, a phenomenon termed *automaticity* (Brown & Carr, 1989; Logan, 1989; Moors & De Houwer, 2006). Because an automatized task requires fewer resources, it can be performed concurrently with another task with minimal or no interference (Posner & Snyder, 1975; Schneider, 1985). Brown (1998a) reasoned that pairing a timing task with a concurrent well-practiced distractor task should reduce the magnitude of the interference effect.

In a series of experiments (Brown, 1998a; Brown & Bennett, 2002), subjects performed concurrent timing (5-s serial temporal productions) and distractor tasks (either pursuit-rotor tracking or mirror-reversed reading) both before and after receiving extensive practice on the distractor task. Comparisons of pretest (before distractor task practice) and posttest (following practice) measures of timing performance revealed an attenuation effect, in which interference was reduced on the posttest. Practice on the distractor task reduced the amount of resources it required, increasing the availability of resources for timing. Sawyer (1999) obtained similar results in an experiment in which subjects performed a tracing task for an estimated 60-s interval both before and after practice. In another study, Sawyer (2003) showed how variations in workload demands systematically altered timing performance. Subjects performed a card-sorting task for what they judged was a 20-s interval. Relative to a control condition without sorting, temporal productions first increased with the addition of a sorting requirement, then decreased as subjects learned the correct sorting rule, and then increased again when the rule changed.

Brown (1998a) also explored a different practice regime known as *timesharing*. Timesharing refers to rapidly switching attention between concurrent tasks (Abernethy, 1988; Brown, McDonald, Brown, & Carr, 1988). Whereas automaticity involves improving dual-task performance by concentrating practice on a single task to reduce its attentional costs, timesharing involves practice on both tasks together in order to learn how to integrate the tasks and shift focus rapidly and efficiently between them (Brown & Carr, 1989; Wickens, 1992). However, timesharing training was not effective in reducing the interference effect. Brown (1998a) argued that timesharing is an ill-suited strategy for timing tasks because time unfolds on a continuous basis and requires constant monitoring. Attentional switching inevitably misses temporal events (Macar et al., 1994). In contrast, automaticity reduces distraction from time, allowing for continual attentiveness to temporal cues.

In a recent paper, Brown (2008) extended this research by providing subjects with practice on the timing task rather than the distractor task. In one study (Experiment 1), subjects reproduced a series of 6–14 s intervals and received feedback on the accuracy of each time judgment. Subsequent testing under concurrent timing and digit-memory conditions showed that the prior feedback on the timing task reduced dual-task interference relative to a control condition without feedback training. The finding that practice on either the distractor or timing tasks can reduce the resource demand of the task sufficiently to minimize interference highlights the intimate connection between attentional allocation and temporal processing.

4.3.7. Implicit Timing

Temporal information processing is a continuous activity that operates even when attention is directed elsewhere. In everyday experience, we usually have a general idea of how long events have lasted, or whether one interval was longer or shorter than another, even though we were not particularly attentive to time (Brown & Stubbs, 1992). There are also numerous examples of implicit (or incidental) timing in the research literature. One example involves unconscious priming. Ono and Kawahara (2005) had subjects perform a temporal production task in which they allowed complex displays of random-dot patterns to remain on a screen for what they judged to be 2.5 s each. Half the displays were repeated across blocks of trials, and half were unique. The results showed that, although subjects were unaware that some patterns were repeated, temporal productions of the repeated patterns were longer than productions of the unique patterns. Because familiar stimuli are known to shorten perceived time, the results were interpreted as evidence that unconscious priming affected time judgments. Another example involves awakening at predetermined times. Fraisse (1963, pp. 43–47) reviewed a number of early studies on this phenomenon, which suggest that some people are indeed able to awaken at a preselected target time. Tart (1970) asked subjects who slept at home to awaken at specified times and to record the actual times they awoke. Most subjects reported awakening at multiple times throughout the night, although two-thirds of the initial awakenings occurred within ± 1 h of the target time. A more controlled laboratory study (Zung & Wilson, 1971) corroborated the effect, and ruled out the possibility that subjects were relying on environmental cues, as light, sound, and temperature were held constant. Block (1979) noted that these findings "...suggest the operation of subconscious (dissociated) information-processing mechanisms" (p. 200). A final example of implicit timing concerns the psychophysical scaling of retrospective time judgments. Scaling involves the relation between changes in physical time and changes in perceived time. Brown and Stubbs (1988, 1992) presented four different stimulus intervals (ranging from 63 to 570 s, depending on the experiment) to subjects, who then provided retrospective or prospective verbal estimations of each interval. The results showed that, although retrospective judgments were more variable and less accurate than prospective judgments, they did show an approximate correspondence to changes in physical time (see also Grondin & Plourde, 2007). These findings indicate that even when temporal awareness is minimal, some degree of temporal information processing is occurring in an incidental fashion outside conscious awareness.

Does implicit timing require attentional resources? The main evidence concerns comparisons of prospective and retrospective conditions in which subjects perform demanding distractor tasks. Some studies (Block, 1992, Experiment 1; Hicks et al., 1976; Zakay, 1993, Experiment 2) found that workload demands affected prospective, but not retrospective, judgments. These results imply that resources are not important in retrospective timing. However, other studies have shown that workload demands interfered with both types of time judgments (Brown, 1985, Experiments 1 and 2; Brown & Stubbs, 1992; Kurtz & Strube, 2003; Miller, Hicks, & Willette, 1978; Zakay, 1993, Experiment 1), suggesting that both prospective and retrospective timing is dependent upon processing resources. One explanation as to why retrospective judgments may sometimes fail to show interference effects involves distractor task difficulty. Retrospective judgments are uncertain and imprecise to begin with, and so may not show an effect unless the distractor task makes sufficiently strong resource demands. Brown and Stubbs (1992) proposed that temporal processing spans a continuum ranging from *low-resolution timing*, in which temporal information is processed incidentally (as in the case of retrospective conditions), to *high-resolution timing* involving a conscious focus on temporal cues and time-in-passing. In this view, all temporal processing requires resources but the amount of resources mobilized varies with the degree of resolution involved. Fewer resources are devoted to temporal processing in retrospective conditions, and so a distractor task with a relatively strong resource demand may be necessary to produce interference effects.

4.4. Resource Specialization and Time

Most studies of temporal/nontemporal dual-task interference focus exclusively on timing performance. However, performance on the nontemporal distractor task can provide important information as to the nature of the attentional resources that support timing functions.

4.4.1. Bidirectional Interference

An underlying assumption of the attentional allocation model is that concurrent temporal and nontemporal tasks compete for the same resources. Assuming that the two tasks are roughly comparable and have equal priority, each task may receive a less-than-optimal supply of attention. As a result, concurrent timing and distractor tasks should produce a pattern of bidirectional interference in which each task interferes with the other. In the attentional resource literature, this effect is termed a joint *concurrence cost* (Navon & Gopher, 1979). Brown (1997) tested this hypothesis in a series of experiments in which subjects performed timing and distractor tasks both singly and concurrently. The timing task was 2- or 5-s serial temporal production and the distractor tasks were pursuit rotor tracking, visual search, and mental arithmetic. The results showed that the distractor tasks interfered with timing in each case, but the timing task interfered only with mental arithmetic. This pattern suggests that the timing and mental arithmetic tasks rely on common cognitive mechanisms or resources.

A subsequent review of the temporal/nontemporal dual-task literature (Brown, 2006) disclosed only 33 studies that could be evaluated in terms of bidirectional interference. These studies (a) reported performance measures for both timing and distractor tasks and (b) included both single-task and dual-task conditions for each task. Of the 33 studies, 16 showed bidirectional interference, 15 showed interference with the timing task only, and 2 showed interference with the distractor task only. Distractor tasks that interfered with timing generally involved higher level cognitive processes (e.g., mental arithmetic, reading, and attentional tasks), whereas those that did not interfere with timing involved lower level processes (e.g., perceptual judgments, tracking, and pattern detection).

The finding that only some studies report bidirectional interference is not consistent with the standard attentional allocation model, which is predicated on the notion of a single pool of generalized resources (e.g., Kahneman, 1973). Instead, the results are more in line with a multiple resource theory of attention. In this view, there exist several specialized pools of attentional resources (Gopher, Brickner, & Navon, 1982; Wickens, 1980, 1984). These separate resource pools are geared to handle specific types of workload demands, such as visual, auditory, verbal, and spatial processing (Cocchini, Logie, Della Sala, MacPherson, & Baddeley, 2002; Wickens, 1991). According to multiple resource theorists, bidirectional interference occurs when two concurrent tasks utilize resources from the same pool

(Navon & Gopher, 1980; Wickens, 1980). Therefore, the nature of the distractor task is an important issue because some tasks may rely on the same resources used for timing and others may rely on different resources. Bidirectional interference patterns help identify the nature of those resources involved in temporal processing.

4.4.2. *Timing as an Executive Function*

Brown (1997, 2006; Brown & Frieh, 2000) contended that resources specialized for executive control are involved in time perception (see also Fortin, Champagne, & Poirier, 2007; Zakay & Block, 2004). Executive functions (also called *control* functions or *frontal lobe* functions) are those cognitive processes that monitor and regulate thought and behavior. These processes include planning, reasoning, comprehension, and decision making (Baddeley, 1986; Baddeley & Della Sala, 1996). Executive functions play a prominent role in various theories of cognition. One prominent example is the working memory (WM) model, which outlines a multicomponent attentional system emphasizing resource specialization (Baddeley, 1992, 1993; Baddeley & Logie, 1999). The primary component is the *central executive*, which monitors and directs ongoing behavior. It is responsible for all cognitive control functions including integrating information, coordinating dual-task performance, and inhibiting responses to distractions. A related theoretical formulation is the Supervisory Attentional System (SAS), which describes an attentional controller mechanism that integrates multiple inputs, manages dual-task situations, selects responses, and schedules actions (Norman & Shallice, 1986; Shallice & Burgess, 1996).

Several considerations support the hypothesized connection between timing processes and executive functions. The first concerns bidirectional interference effects. Most of the distractor tasks associated with bidirectional interference may be characterized as executive tasks. Mutual interference between timing tasks and executive tasks implies that they rely on a common set of attentional resources. A second line of evidence relating timing and executive function involves neuroanatomy. The frontal lobes have long been associated with executive functioning (e.g., Klingberg, O'Sullivan, & Roland, 1997; Miller & Cohen, 2001; Roberts, Robbins, & Weiskrantz, 1998; Royall & Mahurin, 1996; Stuss & Alexander, 2000), and a substantial literature has implicated the prefrontal cortex in timing processes as well (e.g., Casini & Macar, 1996; Macar, 1998; Macar et al., 2002; Pouthas, Garnero, Ferrandez, & Renault, 2000). These findings suggest that executive processes and timing processes may share related cortical mechanisms. The third consideration is conceptual. Attentiveness to time involves a focus on the succession of events, regulation of self-generated rhythmic responses such as counting or tapping, and continual monitoring and updating of an ongoing temporal record. These processes relate to the executive functions of scheduling, coordination, and integration, functions that are essentially temporal in nature.

Baudouin et al. (2006) reported a link between timing performance and executive functioning in a study comparing young (*M* age = 27.7 years) and elderly (*M* age = 71.7 years) adults. The subjects reproduced 3-, 8-, and 14-s target durations under single-task (timing only) and dual-task (timing plus making odd or even judgments for a series of digits) conditions. They also completed WM tasks designed to measure storage capacity and executive updating functions. Hierarchical regression analyses revealed that the storage task predicted reproduction performance in the single-task condition, whereas the executive task predicted performance in the dual-task condition. Moreover, the older subjects had lower scores on the executive task and showed greater time judgment error in the dual-task condition, compared with the younger subjects. Baudouin et al. (2006) attributed this pattern to an age-related decline in executive functioning, which reduced the ability of the older subjects to divide attention between concurrent temporal and nontemporal processing.

4.4.3. Executive Processing and Interference

Brown (1997, 2006) offered a coordination hypothesis to account for the classic interference effect, in which a distractor task interferes with concurrent timing performance. In this view, the dual-task situation evokes the executive functions of coordination and scheduling. WM researchers have shown that dual-task coordination is itself a resource-demanding executive process (e.g., Baddeley, Logie, Bressi, Della Sala, & Spinnler, 1986; Bourke, Duncan, & Nimmo-Smith, 1996; Logie, Cocchini, Della Sala, & Baddeley, 2004; Logie, Zucco, & Baddeley, 1990; Yee, Laden, & Hunt, 1994). These coordination processes limit the availability of executive resources devoted to timing. Because timing is very sensitive to attentional allocation, the diversion of resources to coordination functions disrupts timing performance.

Dutke (2005) tested the coordination hypothesis in a series of experiments in which subjects attended to time and performed a concurrent counting task. In one experiment (Experiment 1), a series of lists of two-digit numbers was presented for a total duration of 400 s and subjects reproduced the interval. The counting task required that subjects report every third occurrence of a target number. The task was designed so that coordinative (executive resource) and noncoordinative (general resource) demands could be manipulated independently. Coordinative demands were manipulated by having subjects keep track of either a single target or three targets. Noncoordinative demands were manipulated by varying the number of target occurrences (either 14 or 27). Both manipulations increased counting errors, but greater coordinative demands led to a greater underestimation of time whereas greater noncoordinative demands had no effect. Dutke (2005) argued that this pattern supports the coordination hypothesis and points to the involvement of executive resources in timing.

Other research has centered on distractor tasks that produce bidirectional interference with timing. Brown (2006) selected a distractor task specifically for its association with executive processing. WM researchers regard *random number generation* (RNG) as the quintessential experimental task invoking the central executive (Baddeley, 1990, 1993). The task requires that the person produce a string of random digits (or letters). Dual-task experiments confirm that randomization competes for the same resources used by other executive tasks (e.g., Baddeley, Emslie, Kolodny, & Duncan, 1998; Robbins et al., 1996; Teasdale et al., 1995; Towse & Valentine, 1997). In Brown's (2006) study, subjects performed a 5-s serial temporal production task and an RNG task both singly and in combination. The results indicated that temporal productions became longer and more variable under dual-task compared with single-task conditions, which corresponds to the standard interference effect. More critically, four different response measures showed that randomization performance was poorer under dual-task conditions as opposed to single-task conditions. This pattern of bidirectional interference suggests that timing uses the same executive-level resources used by the RNG task.

A recent paper by Brown and Merchant (2007) describes research combining timing and sequencing tasks. The selection of sequencing tasks was based on the notion that sequencing is a fundamental executive function (Royall & Mahurin, 1996). Moreover, sequencing is by nature a temporal task and so may bear a direct relation to time estimation. In one study (Experiment 2), the timing task involved serial temporal productions of 5-s intervals and the sequencing task involved monitoring an alphabetic series of letters for omissions in the sequence. These tasks were performed both separately and concurrently. The results showed performance decrements on both tasks under dual-task conditions. Concurrent sequencing caused temporal productions to become longer and more variable, and concurrent timing lengthened response times and lowered perceptual sensitivity on the sequence task. This pattern of mutual interference supports the idea that timing and sequencing involve common resources.

4.5. Summary and Conclusions

Temporal information in the form of neural pulses, perceived changes, and the organization of events gives rise to one's subjective sense of time. Attention influences the processing and encoding of these temporal cues. As with pain, taste, fatigue, etc., attention to time magnifies the experience. Conditions that direct attention to the flow of time (e.g., instructions, task requirements, or situations designed to promote expectancy or anticipation) act to lengthen perceived time. These findings demonstrate that *focusing on time* is an important attentional process in temporal perception. In contrast, situations that distract attention away from time disrupt temporal processing. Research involving concurrent distractor tasks, variations in distractor task difficulty, and attentional sharing shows that time judgments become shorter, more variable, or more inaccurate when attention is diverted away from timekeeping. These results highlight the critical role of *resource allocation* in temporal perception.

Some findings are not as well established but point to important lines of research. One critical area involves comparisons of prospective and retrospective time judgments. This issue speaks to fundamental questions about time and attention. For example, are the two paradigms governed by similar (Brown & Stubbs, 1988, 1992) or different (Block, 1992) processes? Do experimental manipulations of stimulus complexity, event structure, and resource demands produce the same or different effects in the two paradigms? Mixed results from paradigm comparison studies currently preclude definitive answers to these basic questions. Implicit timing is a related topic. A tentative conclusion is that implicit timing, although not conscious, does use processing resources. This issue is part of a larger debate concerning the involvement of attentional resources in automatized tasks (e.g., Strayer & Kramer, 1990; Hoffman, Nelson, & Houck, 1983; Lajoie, Teasdale, Bard, & Fleury, 1993). Research on the relation between attentional resources and conscious awareness has obvious implications for the study of time. A final issue concerns the role of resource specialization in timing. Interference patterns between concurrent temporal and nontemporal tasks may lead to a better understanding of the cognitive mechanisms involved in timing. Some evidence suggests a connection between time judgments and executive functions such as updating, randomization, and sequencing.

The study of time and attention has advanced our knowledge of psychological time considerably. Perceptual judgments of temporal events are in principle no different from perceptual judgments of nontemporal events. Time is information, and temporal information processing may be described in terms of focusing, mental effort, resource allocation, and other basic attentional phenomena. The challenge ahead is to understand how attention to time regulates the detection, memory, and consciousness of temporal events.

References

Abernethy, B. (1988). Dual-task methodology and motor skills research: Some applications and methodological constraints. *Journal of Human Movement Studies, 14*, 101–132.

Allan, L. G. (1992). The internal clock revisited. In: F. Macar, V. Pouthas & W. J. Friedman (Eds), *Time, action, and cognition: Towards bridging the gap* (pp. 191–202). Dordrecht, The Netherlands: Kluwer Academic Publishers.

Allan, L. G., & Gibbon, J. (1991). Human bisection at the geometric mean. *Learning and Motivation, 22*, 39–58.

Ambro, A., & Czigler, I. (1998). Parallel estimation of short durations in humans. In: V. DeKeyser, G. d'Ydewalle & A. Vandierendonck (Eds), *Time and the dynamic control of behavior* (pp. 143–156). Seattle, WA: Hogrefe & Huber.

Baddeley, A. D. (1986). *Working memory*. New York: Oxford University Press.

Baddeley, A. D. (1990). *Human memory: Theory and practice*. Boston, MA: Allyn & Bacon.

Baddeley, A. D. (1992). Working memory. *Science, 255*, 556–559.

Baddeley, A. D. (1993). Working memory or working attention? In: A. D. Baddeley & L. Weiskrantz (Eds), *Attention: Selection, awareness, and control* (pp. 152–170). New York: Oxford University Press.

Baddeley, A. D., & Della Sala, S. (1996). Working memory and executive control. *Philosophical Transactions of the Royal Society of London, 351B*, 1397–1404.

Baddeley, A. D., Emslie, H., Kolodny, J., & Duncan, J. (1998). Random generation and the executive control of working memory. *Quarterly Journal of Experimental Psychology, 51A*, 819–852.

Baddeley, A. D., & Logie, R. H. (1999). Working memory: The multi-component model. In: A. Miyake & P. Shah (Eds), *Models of working memory: Mechanisms of active maintenance and executive control* (pp. 28–61). New York: Cambridge University Press.

Baddeley, A. D., Logie, R., Bressi, S., Della Sala, S., & Spinnler, H. (1986). Dementia and working memory. *Quarterly Journal of Experimental Psychology, 38A*, 603–618.

Barnes, R., & Jones, M. R. (2000). Expectancy, attention, and time. *Cognitive Psychology, 41*, 254–311.

Baudouin, A., Vanneste, S., Pouthas, V., & Isingrini, M. (2006). Age-related changes in duration reproduction: Involvement of working memory processes. *Brain and Cognition, 62*, 17–23.

Benuzzi, F., Basso, G., & Nichelli, P. (2005). Temporal production and visuospatial processing. *Perceptual and Motor Skills, 101*, 737–758.

Block, R. A. (1979). Time and consciousness. In: G. Underwood & R. Stevens (Eds), *Aspects of consciousness, Vol. 1, Psychological issues* (pp. 179–217). New York: Academic Press.

Block, R. A. (1990). Models of psychological time. In: R. A. Block (Ed.), *Cognitive models of psychological time* (pp. 1–35). Hillsdale, NJ: Lawrence Erlbaum.

Block, R. A. (1992). Prospective and retrospective duration judgment: The role of information processing and memory. In: F. Macar, V. Pouthas & W. J. Friedman (Eds), *Time, action, and cognition: Towards bridging the gap* (pp. 141–152). Dordrecht, The Netherlands: Kluwer Academic Publishers.

Block, R. A. (2003). Psychological timing without a timer: The roles of attention and memory. In: H. Helfrich (Ed.), *Time and mind II: Information processing perspectives* (pp. 41–59). Gottingen, Germany: Hogrefe and Huber.

Block, R. A., George, E. J., & Reed, M. A. (1980). A watched pot sometimes boils: A study of duration experience. *Acta Psychologica, 46*, 81–94.

Block, R. A., & Zakay, D. (1996). Models of psychological time revisited. In: H. Helfrich (Ed.), *Time and mind* (pp. 171–195). Seattle, WA: Hogrefe and Huber.

Block, R. A., & Zakay, D. (1997). Prospective and retrospective duration judgments: A meta-analytic review. *Psychonomic Bulletin and Review, 4*, 184–197.

Boltz, M. (1989). Time judgments of musical endings: Effects of expectancies on the "filled interval effect". *Perception and Psychophysics, 46*, 409–418.

Boltz, M. G. (1992). The incidental learning and remembering of event durations. In: F. Macar, V. Pouthas & W. J. Friedman (Eds), *Time, action, and cognition: Towards bridging the gap* (pp. 153–163). Dordrecht, The Netherlands: Kluwer Academic Publishers.

Boltz, M. G. (1993). Time estimation and expectancies. *Memory and Cognition, 21*, 853–863.

Boltz, M. G. (1995). Effects of event structure on retrospective duration judgments. *Perception and Psychophysics, 57*, 1080–1096.

Boltz, M. G. (1998). The processing of temporal and nontemporal information in the remembering of event durations and musical structure. *Journal of Experimental Psychology: Human Perception and Performance, 24*, 1087–1104.

Boltz, M. G. (2005). Duration judgments of naturalistic events in the auditory and visual modalities. *Perception and Psychophysics, 67*, 1362–1375.

Bourke, P. A., Duncan, J., & Nimmo-Smith, I. (1996). A general factor involved in dual-task performance decrement. *Quarterly Journal of Experimental Psychology*, *49A*, 525–545.

Brown, J. S., McDonald, J. L., Brown, T. L., & Carr, T. H. (1988). Adapting to processing demands in discourse production: The case of handwriting. *Journal of Experimental Psychology: Human Perception and Performance*, *14*, 45–59.

Brown, S. W. (1985). Time perception and attention: The effects of prospective versus retrospective paradigms and task demands on perceived duration. *Perception and Psychophysics*, *38*, 115–124.

Brown, S. W. (1997). Attentional resources in timing: Interference effects in concurrent temporal and nontemporal working memory tasks. *Perception and Psychophysics*, *59*, 1118–1140.

Brown, S. W. (1998a). Automaticity versus timesharing in timing and tracking dual-task performance. *Psychological Research*, *61*, 71–81.

Brown, S. W. (1998b). Influence of individual differences in temporal sensitivity on timing performance. *Perception*, *27*, 609–625.

Brown, S. W. (2006). Timing and executive function: Bidirectional interference between concurrent temporal production and randomization tasks. *Memory and Cognition*, *34*, 1464–1471.

Brown, S. W. (2008). The attenuation effect in timing: Counteracting dual-task interference with time judgment skill training. *Perception*, *37*, 712–724.

Brown, S. W., & Bennett, E. D. (2002). The role of practice and automaticity in temporal and nontemporal dual-task performance. *Psychological Research*, *66*, 80–89.

Brown, S. W., & Boltz, M. G. (2002). Attentional processes in time perception: Effects of mental workload and event structure. *Journal of Experimental Psychology: Human Perception and Performance*, *28*, 600–615.

Brown, S. W., & Frieh, C. T. (2000). Information processing in the central executive: Effects of concurrent temporal production and memory updating tasks. In: P. Desain & L. Windsor (Eds), *Rhythm perception and production* (pp. 193–196). Lisse, The Netherlands: Swets & Zeitlinger.

Brown, S. W., & Merchant, S. M. (2007). Processing resources in timing and sequencing tasks. *Perception and Psychophysics*, *69*, 439–449.

Brown, S. W., Newcomb, D. C., & Kahrl, K. G. (1995). Temporal-signal detection and individual differences in timing. *Perception*, *24*, 525–538.

Brown, S. W., & Stubbs, D. A. (1988). The psychophysics of retrospective and prospective timing. *Perception*, *17*, 297–310.

Brown, S. W., & Stubbs, D. A. (1992). Attention and interference in prospective and retrospective timing. *Perception*, *21*, 545–557.

Brown, S. W., Stubbs, D. A., & West, A. N. (1992). Attention, multiple timing, and psychophysical scaling of temporal judgments. In: F. Macar, V. Pouthas & W. J. Friedman (Eds), *Time, action, and cognition: Towards bridging the gap* (pp. 129–140). Dordrecht, The Netherlands: Kluwer Academic Publishers.

Brown, S. W., & West, A. N. (1990). Multiple timing and the allocation of attention. *Acta Psychologica*, *75*, 103–121.

Brown, T. L., & Carr, T. H. (1989). Automaticity in skill acquisition: Mechanisms for reducing interference in concurrent performance. *Journal of Experimental Psychology: Human Perception and Performance*, *15*, 686–700.

Burle, B., & Bonnet, M. (1997). Further argument for the existence of a pacemaker in the human information processing system. *Acta Psychologica*, *97*, 129–143.

Burle, B., & Casini, L. (2001). Dissociation between activation and attention effects in time estimation: Implications for internal clock models. *Journal of Experimental Psychology: Human Perception and Performance*, *27*, 195–205.
Cahoon, D., & Edmonds, E. M. (1980). The watched pot still won't boil: Expectancy as a variable in estimating the passage of time. *Bulletin of the Psychonomic Society*, *16*, 115–116.
Casini, L., & Ivry, R. B. (1999). Effects of divided attention on temporal processing in patients with lesions of the cerebellum or frontal lobe. *Neuropsychology*, *13*, 10–21.
Casini, L., & Macar, F. (1996). Prefrontal slow potentials in temporal compared to nontemporal tasks. *Journal of Psychophysiology*, *10*, 252–264.
Casini, L., & Macar, F. (1997). Effects of attention manipulation on judgments of duration and of intensity in the visual modality. *Memory and Cognition*, *25*, 812–818.
Casini, L., Macar, F., & Grondin, S. (1992). Time estimation and attentional sharing. In: F. Macar, V. Pouthas & W. J. Friedman (Eds), *Time, action, and cognition: Towards bridging the gap* (pp. 177–180). Dordrecht, The Netherlands: Kluwer Academic Publishers.
Chastain, G., & Ferraro, F. R. (1997). Duration ratings as an index of processing resources required for cognitive tasks. *Journal of General Psychology*, *124*, 49–76.
Chen, Z., & O'Neill, P. (2001). Processing demand modulates the effects of spatial attention on the judged duration of a brief stimulus. *Perception and Psychophysics*, *63*, 1229–1238.
Church, R. M. (1984). Properties of the internal clock. In: J. Gibbon & L. Allan (Eds), *Timing and time perception* (Annals of the New York Academy of Sciences, Vol. 423, pp. 566–582). New York: New York Academy of Sciences.
Cocchini, G., Logie, R. H., Della Sala, S., MacPherson, S. E., & Baddeley, A. D. (2002). Concurrent performance of two memory tasks: Evidence for domain-specific working memory systems. *Memory and Cognition*, *30*, 1086–1095.
Coull, J. T., Vidal, F., Nazarian, B., & Macar, F. (2004). Functional anatomy of the attentional modulation of time estimation. *Science*, *303*, 1506–1508.
Creelman, C. D. (1962). Human discrimination of auditory duration. *Journal of the Acoustical Society of America*, *34*, 582–593.
Curton, E. D., & Lordahl, D. S. (1974). Effects of attentional focus and arousal on time estimation. *Journal of Experimental Psychology*, *103*, 861–867.
Doob, L. W. (1971). *Patterning of time*. New Haven: Yale University Press.
Dutke, S. (2005). Remembered duration: Working memory and the reproduction of intervals. *Perception and Psychophysics*, *67*, 1404–1413.
Edmonds, E. M., Cahoon, D., & Bridges, B. (1981). The estimation of time as a function of positive, neutral, or negative expectancies. *Bulletin of the Psychonomic Society*, *17*, 259–260.
Enns, J. T., Brehaut, J. C., & Shore, D. I. (1999). The duration of a brief event in the mind's eye. *Journal of General Psychology*, *126*, 355–372.
Field, D. T., & Groeger, J. A. (2004). Temporal interval production and short-term memory. *Perception and Psychophysics*, *66*, 808–819.
Filer, R. J., & Meals, D. W. (1949). The effect of motivating conditions on the estimation of time. *Journal of Experimental Psychology*, *39*, 327–331.
Fink, A., & Neubauer, A. C. (2001). Speed of information processing, psychometric intelligence, and time estimation as an index of cognitive load. *Personality and Individual Differences*, *30*, 1009–1021.
Fortin, C., Bédard, M.-C., & Champagne, J. (2005). Timing during interruptions in timing. *Journal of Experimental Psychology: Human Perception and Performance*, *31*, 276–288.
Fortin, C., Champagne, J., & Poirier, M. (2007). Temporal order in memory and interval timing: An interference analysis. *Acta Psychologica*, *126*, 18–33.

Fortin, C., & Couture, E. (2002). Short-term memory and time estimation: Beyond the 2-second "critical" value. *Canadian Journal of Experimental Psychology, 56*, 120–127.

Fortin, C., Duchet, M.-L., & Rousseau, R. (1996). Tapping sensitivity to processing in short-term memory. *Canadian Journal of Experimental Psychology, 50*, 402–407.

Fortin, C., & Masse, N. (1999). Order information in short-term memory and time estimation. *Memory and Cognition, 27*, 54–62.

Fortin, C., & Masse, N. (2000). Expecting a break in time estimation: Attentional time-sharing without concurrent processing. *Journal of Experimental Psychology: Human Perception and Performance, 26*, 1788–1796.

Fortin, C., & Rousseau, R. (1998). Interference from short-term memory processing on encoding and reproducing brief durations. *Psychological Research, 61*, 269–276.

Fraisse, P. (1963). *The psychology of time*. New York: Harper and Row.

François, M. (1927). Contribution a l'étude du sens du temps: la température interne comme facteur de variation de l'appréciation subjective des durées. [Contributions to the study of the sense of time: Internal temperature as a factor in the variation of the subjective appreciation of durations]. *L'Année Psychologique, 28*, 186–204.

Frankenhaeuser, M. (1959). *Estimation of time*. Uppsala, Sweden: Almqvist & Wiksell.

Franssen, V., & Vandierendonck, A. (2002). Time estimation: Does the reference memory mediate the effect of knowledge of results? *Acta Psychologica, 109*, 239–267.

Franssen, V., Vandierendonck, A., & Van Hiel, A. (2006). Duration estimation and the phonological loop: Articulatory suppression and irrelevant sounds. *Psychological Research, 70*, 304–316.

Gautier, T., & Droit-Volet, S. (2002). Attentional distraction and time perception in children. *International Journal of Psychology, 37*, 27–34.

Gibbon, J. (1977). Scalar expectancy theory and Weber's law in animal timing. *Psychological Review, 84*, 279–325.

Gibbon, J., Church, R. M., & Meck, W. H. (1984). Scalar timing in memory. In: J. Gibbon & L. Allan (Eds), *Timing and time perception* (Annals of the New York Academy of Sciences, Vol. 423, pp. 52–77). New York: New York Academy of Sciences.

Glicksohn, J. (2001). Temporal cognition and the phenomenology of time: A multiplicative function for apparent duration. *Consciousness and Cognition, 10*, 1–25.

Gopher, D., Brickner, M., & Navon, D. (1982). Different difficulty manipulations interact differently with task emphasis: Evidence for multiple resources. *Journal of Experimental Psychology: Human Perception and Performance, 8*, 146–157.

Grondin, S. (2001). Time psychophysics and attention. *Psychologica, 28*, 177–191.

Grondin, S., & Macar, F. (1992). Dividing attention between temporal and nontemporal tasks: A performance operating characteristic — POC — analysis. In: F. Macar, V. Pouthas & W. J. Friedman (Eds), *Time, action, and cognition: Towards bridging the gap* (pp. 119–128). Dordrecht, The Netherlands: Kluwer Academic Publishers.

Grondin, S., & Plourde, M. (2007). Judging multi-minute intervals retrospectively. *Quarterly Journal of Experimental Psychology, 60*, 1303–1312.

Grondin, S., & Rammsayer, T. (2003). Variable foreperiods and temporal discrimination. *Quarterly Journal of Experimental Psychology, 56A*, 731–765.

Hicks, R. E., Miller, G. W., Gaes, G., & Bierman, K. (1977). Concurrent processing demands and the experience of time-in-passing. *American Journal of Psychology, 90*, 431–446.

Hicks, R. E., Miller, G. W., & Kinsbourne, M. (1976). Prospective and retrospective judgments of time as a function of amount of information processed. *American Journal of Psychology, 89*, 719–730.

Hirst, W., & Kalmar, D. (1987). Characterizing attentional resources. *Journal of Experimental Psychology: General*, *116*, 68–81.
Hoagland, H. (1933). The physiological control of judgments of duration: Evidence for a chemical clock. *Journal of General Psychology*, *9*, 267–287.
Hoffman, J. E., Nelson, B., & Houck, M. R. (1983). The role of attentional resources in automatic detection. *Cognitive Psychology*, *51*, 379–410.
James, W. (1950). *The principles of psychology, Vol. I* (Original publication date: 1890). New York: Dover.
Jones, M. R., & Boltz, M. (1989). Dynamic attending and responses to time. *Psychological Review*, *96*, 459–491.
Jones, M. R., Boltz, M. G., & Klein, J. M. (1993). Expected endings and judged duration. *Memory and Cognition*, *21*, 646–665.
Kahneman, D. (1973). *Attention and effort*. Englewood Cliffs, NJ: Prentice-Hall.
Kawamura, S. (2000). Effect of phonological processing on temporal processing. *Japanese Psychological Research*, *42*, 178–182.
Kinchla, R. A. (1980). The measurement of attention. In: R. S. Nickerson (Ed.), *Attention and performance VIII* (pp. 213–238). Hillsdale, NJ: Lawrence Erlbaum.
Klingberg, T., O'Sullivan, B. T., & Roland, P. E. (1997). Bilateral activation of fronto-parietal networks by incrementing demand in a working memory task. *Cerebral Cortex*, *7*, 465–471.
Kojima, Y., & Matsuda, F. (2000). Effects of attention and external stimuli on duration estimation under a prospective paradigm. *Japanese Psychological Research*, *42*, 144–154.
Kurtz, R. M., & Strube, M. J. (2003). Hypnosis, attention, and time cognition. *International Journal of Clinical and Experimental Hypnosis*, *51*, 400–413.
Lajoie, Y., Teasdale, N., Bard, C., & Fleury, M. (1993). Attentional demands for static and dynamic equilibrium. *Experimental Brain Research*, *97*, 139–144.
Lejeune, H. (1998). Switching or gating? The attentional challenge in cognitive models of psychological time. *Behavioural Processes*, *44*, 127–145.
Lejeune, H. (2000). Prospective timing, attention and the switch: A response to 'Gating or switching? Gating is a better model of prospective timing' by Zakay. *Behavioural Processes*, *52*, 71–76.
Logan, G. D. (1989). Automaticity and cognitive control. In: J. S. Uleman & J. A. Bargh (Eds), *Unintended thought* (pp. 52–74). New York: Guilford.
Logie, R. H., Cocchini, G., Della Sala, S., & Baddeley, A. D. (2004). Is there a specific executive capacity for dual task coordination? Evidence from Alzheimer's disease. *Neuropsychology*, *18*, 504–513.
Logie, R. H., Zucco, G. M., & Baddeley, A. D. (1990). Interference with visual short-term memory. *Acta Psychologica*, *75*, 55–74.
Macar, F. (1998). Neural bases of interval timers: A brief review. *Cahiers de Psychologie Cognitive/Current Psychology of Cognition*, *17*, 847–865.
Macar, F. (2002). Expectancy, controlled attention and automatic attention in prospective temporal judgments. *Acta Psychologica*, *111*, 243–262.
Macar, F., Grondin, S., & Casini, L. (1994). Controlled attention sharing influences time estimation. *Memory and Cognition*, *22*, 673–686.
Macar, F., Lejeune, H., Bonnet, M., Ferrara, A., Pouthas, V., Vidal, F., & Maquet, P. (2002). Activation of the supplementary motor area and of attentional networks during temporal processing. *Experimental Brain Research*, *142*, 475–485.
Malapani, C., & Fairhurst, S. (2002). Scalar timing in animals and humans. *Learning and Motivation*, *33*, 156–176.

Marshall, M. J., & Wilsoncroft, W. E. (1989). Time perception and the Stroop task. *Perceptual and Motor Skills*, *69*, 1159–1162.
Mattes, S., & Ulrich, R. (1998). Directed attention prolongs the perceived duration of a brief stimulus. *Perception and Psychophysics*, *60*, 1305–1317.
McGrath, J. J., & O'Hanlon, J. (1967). Temporal orientation and vigilance performance. *Acta Psychologica*, *27*, 410–419.
McKay, T. D. (1977). Time estimation: Effects of attentional focus and a comparison of interval conditions. *Perceptual and Motor Skills*, *45*, 584–586.
Michon, J. A. (1972). Processing of temporal information and the cognitive theory of time experience. In: J. T. Frasier, F. C. Haber & G. H. Muller (Eds), *The study of time* (pp. 242–258). New York: Springer-Verlag.
Michon, J. A. (1985). The compleat time experiencer. In: J. A. Michon & J. L. Jackson (Eds), *Time, mind, and behavior* (pp. 20–52). New York: Springer-Verlag.
Michon, J. A., & Jackson, J. L. (1984). Attentional effort and cognitive strategies in the processing of temporal information. In: J. Gibbon & L. Allan (Eds), *Timing and time perception* (Annals of the New York Academy of Sciences, Vol. 423, pp. 298–321). New York: New York Academy of Sciences.
Miller, E. K., & Cohen, J. D. (2001). An integrative theory of prefrontal cortex function. *Annual Review of Neuroscience*, *24*, 167–202.
Miller, G. W., Hicks, R. E., & Willette, M. (1978). Effects of concurrent verbal rehearsal and temporal set upon judgments of temporal duration. *Acta Psychologica*, *42*, 173–179.
Moors, A., & De Houwer, J. (2006). Automaticity: A theoretical and conceptual analysis. *Psychological Bulletin*, *132*, 297–326.
Navon, D. (1984). Resources — A theoretical soup stone? *Psychological Review*, *91*, 216–234.
Navon, D., & Gopher, D. (1979). On the economy of the human-processing system. *Psychological Review*, *86*, 214–253.
Navon, D., & Gopher, D. (1980). Task difficulty, resources, and dual-task performance. In: R. S. Nickerson (Ed.), *Attention and performance VIII* (pp. 297–315). Hillsdale, NJ: Erlbaum.
Norman, D. A., & Bobrow, D. G. (1975). On data-limited and resource-limited processes. *Cognitive Psychology*, *7*, 44–64.
Norman, D. A., & Shallice, T. (1986). Attention to action: Willed and automatic control of behavior. In: R. J. Davidson, G. E. Schwartz & D. Shapiro (Eds), *Consciousness and self-regulation: Advances in research and theory* (Vol. 4, pp. 1–18). New York: Plenum.
Ono, F., & Kawahara, J. (2005). The effect of unconscious priming on temporal production. *Consciousness and Cognition*, *14*, 474–482.
Ono, F., Yamada, K., Chujo, K., & Kawahara, J. (2007). Feature-based attention influences later temporal perception. *Perception and Psychophysics*, *69*, 544–549.
Perbal, S., Couillet, J., Azouvi, P., & Pouthas, V. (2003). Relationships between time estimation, memory, attention, and processing speed in patients with severe traumatic brain injury. *Neuropsychologia*, *41*, 1599–1610.
Posner, M. I., & Boies, S. J. (1971). Components of attention. *Psychological Review*, *78*, 391–408.
Posner, M. I., & Petersen, S. E. (1990). The attention system of the human brain. *Annual Review of Neuroscience*, *13*, 25–42.
Posner, M. I., & Snyder, C. R. R. (1975). Attention and cognitive control. In: R. L. Solso (Ed.), *Information processing and cognition: The Loyola symposium* (pp. 55–85). Hillsdale, NJ: Erlbaum.

Pouthas, V., Garnero, L., Ferrandez, A.-M., & Renault, B. (2000). ERPs and PET analysis of time perception: Spatial and temporal brain mapping during visual discrimination tasks. *Human Brain Mapping*, *10*, 49–60.

Poynter, D. (1989). Judging the duration of time intervals: A process of remembering segments of experience. In: I. Levin & D. Zakay (Eds), *Time and human cognition: A life-span perspective* (pp. 305–321). Amsterdam: Elsevier.

Rakitin, B. C., Gibbon, J., Penney, T. B., Malapani, C., Hinton, S. C., & Meck, W. H. (1998). Scalar expectancy theory and peak-interval timing in humans. *Journal of Experimental Psychology: Animal Behavior Processes*, *24*, 15–33.

Rammsayer, T., & Ulrich, R. (2005). No evidence for qualitative differences in the processing of short and long temporal intervals. *Acta Psychologica*, *120*, 141–171.

Robbins, T. W., Anderson, E. J., Barker, D. R., Bradley, A. C., Fearnyhough, C., Henson, R., Hudson, S. R., & Baddeley, A. D. (1996). Working memory in chess. *Memory and Cognition*, *24*, 83–93.

Roberts, A. C., Robbins, T. W., & Weiskrantz, L. (Eds). (1998). *The prefrontal cortex: Executive and cognitive functions*. New York: Oxford University Press.

Royall, D. R., & Mahurin, R. K. (1996). Neuroanatomy, measurement, and clinical significance of the executive cognitive functions. *American Psychiatric Press Review of Psychiatry*, *15*, 175–204.

Sawyer, T. F. (1999). Allocation of attention and practice in the production of time intervals. *Perceptual and Motor Skills*, *89*, 1047–1051.

Sawyer, T. F. (2003). Allocation of attention and production of time intervals. *Perceptual and Motor Skills*, *96*, 905–908.

Schiff, W., & Thayer, S. (1968). Cognitive and affective factors in temporal experience: Anticipated or experienced pleasant and unpleasant sensory events. *Perceptual and Motor Skills*, *26*, 799–808.

Schneider, W. (1985). Training high-performance skills: Fallacies and guidelines. *Human Factors*, *27*, 285–300.

Shallice, T., & Burgess, P. (1996). The domain of supervisory processes and temporal organization of behavior. *Philosophical Transactions of the Royal Society of London*, *351B*, 1405–1412.

Shinohara, K. (1999). Resource for temporal information processing in interval production. *Perceptual and Motor Skills*, *88*, 917–928.

Shinohara, K., Miura, T., & Usui, S. (2002). Tapping task as an index of mental workload in a time sharing task. *Japanese Psychological Research*, *44*, 144–151.

Sperling, G., & Melchner, M. J. (1978). The attention operating characteristic: Examples from visual search. *Science*, *202*, 315–318.

Strayer, D. L., & Kramer, A. F. (1990). Attentional requirements of automatic and controlled processing. *Journal of Experimental Psychology: Learning, Memory, and Cognition*, *16*, 67–82.

Sturt, M. (1925). *The psychology of time*. New York: Harcourt, Brace, and Company.

Stuss, D. T., & Alexander, M. P. (2000). Executive functions and the frontal lobes: A conceptual view. *Psychological Research*, *63*, 289–298.

Tart, C. T. (1970). Waking from sleep at a preselected time. *Journal of the American Society of Psychosomatic Dentistry and Medicine*, *17*, 3–15.

Teasdale, J. D., Dritschel, B. H., Taylor, M. J., Proctor, L., Lloyd, C. A., Nimmo-Smith, I., & Baddeley, A. D. (1995). Stimulus-independent thought depends on central executive resources. *Memory and Cognition*, *23*, 551–559.

Thomas, E. A. C., & Brown, I. (1974). Time perception and the filled-duration illusion. *Perception and Psychophysics*, *16*, 449–458.
Thomas, E. A. C., & Cantor, N. E. (1975). On the duality of simultaneous time and size perception. *Perception and Psychophysics*, *18*, 44–48.
Thomas, E. A. C., & Cantor, N. E. (1978). Interdependence between the processing of temporal and non-temporal information. In: J. Requin (Ed.), *Attention and performance VII* (pp. 43–62). Hillsdale, NJ: Lawrence Erlbaum.
Thomas, E. A. C., & Weaver, W. B. (1975). Cognitive processing and time perception. *Perception and Psychophysics*, *17*, 363–367.
Towse, J. N., & Valentine, J. D. (1997). Random generation of numbers: A search for underlying processes. *European Journal of Cognitive Psychology*, *9*, 381–400.
Treisman, M. (1963). Temporal discrimination and the indifference interval: Implications for a model of the "internal clock". *Psychological Monographs*, *77*(Whole No. 576), 1–31.
Treisman, M., & Brogan, D. (1992). Time perception and the internal clock: Effects of visual flicker on the temporal oscillator. *European Journal of Cognitive Psychology*, *4*, 41–70.
Treisman, M., Cook, N., Naish, P. L. N., & MacCrone, J. K. (1994). The internal clock: Electroencephalographic evidence for oscillatory processes underlying time perception. *Quarterly Journal of Experimental Psychology*, *47A*, 241–289.
Treisman, M., Faulkner, A., & Naish, P. L. N. (1992). On the relation between time perception and the timing of motor action: Evidence for a temporal oscillator controlling the timing of movement. *Quarterly Journal of Experimental Psychology*, *45A*, 235–263.
Treisman, M., Faulkner, A., Naish, P. L. N., & Brogan, D. (1990). The internal clock: Evidence for a temporal oscillator underlying time perception with some estimates of its characteristic frequency. *Perception*, *19*, 705–743.
Tremblay, S., & Fortin, C. (2003). Break expectancy in duration discrimination. *Journal of Experimental Psychology: Human Perception and Performance*, *29*, 823–831.
Tse, P. U., Intriligator, J., Rivest, J., & Cavanagh, P. (2004). Attention and the subjective expansion of time. *Perception and Psychophysics*, *66*, 1171–1189.
Underwood, G., & Swain, R. A. (1973). Selectivity of attention and the perception of duration. *Perception*, *2*, 101–105.
Vanneste, S., & Pouthas, V. (1999). Timing in aging: The role of attention. *Experimental Aging Research*, *25*, 49–67.
Venneri, A., Pestell, S., Gray, C. D., Della Sala, S., & Nichelli, P. (1998). Memory, attention, and estimation of time. *Brain and Cognition*, *37*, 169–172.
Venneri, A., Pestell, S., & Nichelli, P. (2003). A preliminary study of the cognitive mechanisms supporting time estimation. *Perceptual and Motor Skills*, *96*, 1093–1106.
Wearden, J. H. (1991). Do humans possess an internal clock with scalar timing properties? *Learning and Motivation*, *22*, 59–83.
Wearden, J. H. (1992). Temporal generalization in humans. *Journal of Experimental Psychology: Animal Behavior Processes*, *18*, 134–144.
Wearden, J. H. (2003). Applying the scalar timing model to human time psychology: Progress and challenges. In: H. Helfrich (Ed.), *Time and mind II: Information processing perspectives* (pp. 21–39). Gottingen, Germany: Hogrefe and Huber.
Wearden, J. H., & McShane, B. (1988). Interval production as an analogue of the peak procedure: Evidence for similarity of human and animal timing processes. *Quarterly Journal of Experimental Psychology: Comparative and Physiological Psychology*, *40*, 363–375.

Wickens, C. D. (1980). The structure of attentional resources. In: R. S. Nickerson (Ed.), *Attention and performance VIII* (pp. 239–257). Hillsdale, NJ: Lawrence Erlbaum.

Wickens, C. D. (1984). Processing resources in attention. In: R. Parasuraman & D. R. Davies (Eds), *Varieties of attention* (pp. 63–102). New York: Academic Press.

Wickens, C. D. (1991). Processing resources and attention. In: D. L. Damos (Ed.), *Multiple-task performance* (pp. 3–34). London: Taylor and Francis.

Wickens, C. D. (1992). *Engineering psychology and human performance* (2nd ed.). New York: HarperCollins.

Woodrow, H. (1933). Individual differences in the reproduction of temporal intervals. *American Journal of Psychology*, *45*, 271–281.

Yee, P. L., Laden, B., & Hunt, E. (1994). The coordination of compensatory tracking and anticipatory timing tasks. *Intelligence*, *18*, 259–287.

Zakay, D. (1989). Subjective time and attentional resource allocation: An integrated model of time estimation. In: I. Levin & D. Zakay (Eds), *Time and human cognition: A life-span perspective* (pp. 365–397). Amsterdam: Elsevier.

Zakay, D. (1993). Relative and absolute duration judgments under prospective and retrospective paradigms. *Perception and Psychophysics*, *54*, 656–664.

Zakay, D. (1998). Attention allocation policy influences prospective timing. *Psychonomic Bulletin and Review*, *5*, 114–118.

Zakay, D. (2000). Gating or switching? Gating is a better model of prospective timing (a response to 'switching or gating?' by Lejeune). *Behavioural Processes*, *50*, 1–7.

Zakay, D., & Block, R. A. (1996). The role of attention in time estimation processes. In: M. A. Pastor & J. Artieda (Eds), *Time, internal clocks and movement* (pp. 143–164). Amsterdam: Elsevier.

Zakay, D., & Block, R. A. (1997). Temporal cognition. *Current Directions in Psychological Science*, *6*, 12–16.

Zakay, D., & Block, R. A. (1998). New perspective on prospective time estimation. In: V. DeKeyser, G. d'Ydewalle & A. Vandierendonck (Eds), *Time and the dynamic control of behavior* (pp. 129–141). Seattle, WA: Hogrefe & Huber.

Zakay, D., & Block, R. A. (2004). Prospective and retrospective duration judgments: An executive-control perspective. *Acta Neurobiologiae Experimentalis*, *64*, 319–328.

Zakay, D., Block, R. A., & Tsal, Y. (1999). Prospective duration estimation and performance. In: D. Gopher & A. Koriat (Eds), *Attention and performance XVII: Cognitive regulation of performance — interaction of theory and application* (pp. 557–580). Cambridge, MA: MIT Press.

Zakay, D., & Shub, J. (1998). Concurrent duration production as a workload measure. *Ergonomics*, *41*, 1115–1128.

Zung, W. W. K., & Wilson, W. P. (1971). Time estimation during sleep. *Biological Psychiatry*, *3*, 159–164.

Chapter 5

Time-Based Illusions in the Auditory Mode

Gert ten Hoopen, Ryota Miyauchi and Yoshitaka Nakajima

In this chapter, illusions based on the temporal organization of auditory events are presented. After defining what an illusion is, classical and more recently discovered illusions are described.

5.1. Introduction: Terminology and Examples

5.1.1. The Lemma "Illusion" in Dictionaries and Encyclopedias

It seems sensible to ponder first over the meaning of the word "illusion," which we start doing on the basis of dictionaries and encyclopedias. The *Times English Dictionary* (2000, 2nd ed.) gives: (1) "a false appearance or deceptive impression of reality," (2) "a false or misleading perception or belief; delusion," (3) "*Psychol.* a perception that is not true to reality, having been altered subjectively in some way in the mind of the perceiver." The word illusion stems from the Latin word 'illusio,' meaning deceit or trick, and hence it is not strange to read meaning (4) "a very fine gauze or tulle used for trimmings, veils, etc." It is clear that meaning #3 approximately fits to what psychologists have in mind when thinking of perceptual illusions. Notice that no negative connotations arise from the description in #3, contrary to those in #1 and #2. However, other sources use terms as "incorrect perception" (*Encyclopedia Britannica*) or "wrongly perceived" (*New Oxford Dictionary of English*).

We posit that there is nothing fundamentally wrong or incorrect with perception (except for people with certain kinds of medical treatment, sense organ disturbances, or brain damage) and that the task of the perceptual systems is to provide us with their best possible interpretation of our physical environment. This stance is aptly formulated by Reber (1995) in his dictionary of psychology: "Often one sees illusions characterized as 'mistaken perceptions', a designation that is not really correct and

Psychology of Time

DOI:10.1016/B978-0-08046-977-5.00005-3

misses the point. Mach bands, for example, are illusions but they are not 'mistaken perceptions'. Rather, they are perceptions that result from certain retinal and/or cortical processes that cannot be predicted simply from the stimulus itself. If there is a mistake involved it is on the part of psychologists who don't as yet understand the mechanisms that produce the illusions" (p. 357). That illusions give clues of how perceptual processes operate is expressed by Wikipedia (the free encyclopedia) at June 15, 2007 (the day we finished this chapter) as follows: "An illusion is a distortion of a sensory perception, revealing how the brain normally organizes and interprets sensory stimulation. While illusions distort reality, they are generally shared by most people."

This interpersonal sharing distinguishes illusions from hallucinations, sensory experiences in the absence of stimuli, which are very idiosyncratic. We also exclude abnormal sensory experiences caused, for example, by drug intoxication or sleep deprivation, sometimes called "active illusions" in contrast to "passive illusions." The latter illusions are a result of the functional and structural characteristics of the perceptual system, and are natural and necessary rather than abnormal (Funk & Wagnall's *New Encyclopedia*). We also exclude purely physical phenomena like mirages, refractions, and rainbows, that is, optical effects from the definition of illusions. It is a logical misnomer to use the term "optical illusions" when "visual illusions" is meant. Nonetheless, Googling for "optical illusions" yielded 1,240,000 hits, whereas "visual illusions" yielded only 168,000 hits. In Yahoo, the discrepancy was even larger: 2,490,000 vs. 120,000 hits.

5.1.2. Sensation, Perception, and Illusion

For the sake of simplicity, we confine ourselves to Aristotle's classification of five senses: vision, hearing, touch, taste, and smell. Each of these senses can detect and encode a certain kind of physical or chemical energy stimulating specific receptor cells as a result of which characteristic direct experiences occur, for example, "red," "loud," "itch," "sweet," and "musty," respectively. Stimuli, however, have more physical dimensions. Take, for instance, the case of audition, which is the main focus of this chapter. The vibration of air, for example, has not only a certain intensity, the main determinant of loudness, but also a certain frequency pattern giving rise to perceived pitch and timbre. Moreover, the spatial position of the sound source is the main determinant of its perceived location. Organizing such concomitant dimensions into a coherent phenomenological "whole" is the process of perception. The formation of a percept is not only a bottom-up but also a top–down process, but it is difficult to indicate the border between sensation and perception, especially because the processes can be affected by a gamut of factors such as attention, learning, memory, motivation, and set.

When a percept cannot be easily predicted from an analysis of the physical stimulus array, one speaks of an illusion (Reber, 1995). To set the scene of the study of illusions we discuss two examples: (1) a classic well-known illusion of visual perception, discussed in virtually all introductory textbooks of psychology: the Müller-Lyer illusion; and (2) a recent illusion of auditory perception, the "gap transfer" illusion (Nakajima et al., 2000).

The Müller-Lyer illusion is depicted in Figure 5.1. Two line segments of equal length appear unequal because of arrowheads differently demarcating the line segments. The right line segment between arrowheads pointing toward the line appears longer than the left line segment between arrowheads pointing away from the line. Gregory (1966) offered a plausible explanation: Although the drawings in Figure 5.1 are two-dimensional, the arrows connected to the vertical lines provide depth information (consciously or unconsciously). The left drawing can be interpreted as the nearby outside corner of a building, whereas the right drawing can be interpreted as a faraway inside corner. This three-dimensional interpretation invokes the operation of the size-constancy mechanism that compensates for the apparent distance of objects by increasing the farther corner. However, the retinal images of the lengths of both corners (drawn two-dimensionally) are the same, thus the size-constancy scaling is misapplied, yielding the illusion (see, e.g., Coren, Ward, & Enns, 1999; Dember & Warm, 1979; Schiffman, 1995).

Just like there are optico-geometric illusions, there are illusions in the auditory mode. The *gap transfer* illusion is illustrated in Figure 5.2. The left panel shows the auditory stimulus configuration: A frequency sweep of 2500 ms is interrupted by a silent gap of 100 ms in the middle. A shorter continuous frequency swoop of 500 ms crosses the gap. The right panel shows what most listeners perceive: a continuous frequency sweep and a swoop that is interrupted by a gap. Hence the name *gap transfer*

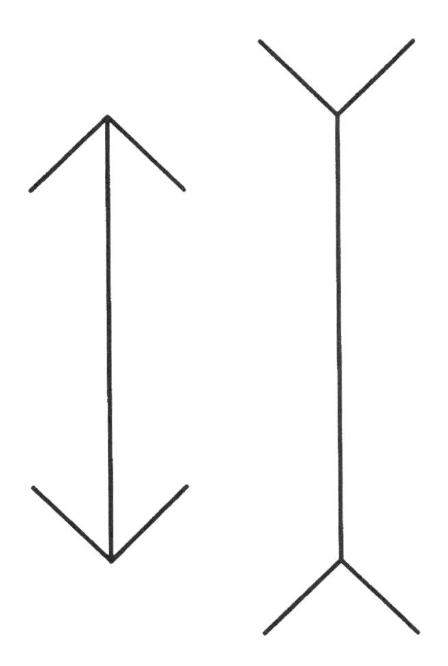

Figure 5.1: The Müller-Lyer illusion.

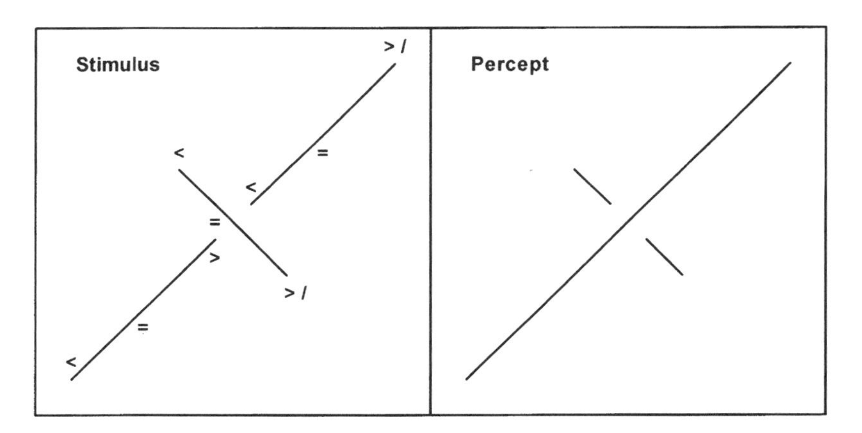

Figure 5.2: The "gap transfer" illusion. See text for explanation.

illusion: Although the physical gap was in the sweep, it is perceived in the swoop. To explain this illusion, Nakajima et al. (2000) proposed an "event construction model," positing that auditory events like frequency glides are decomposed into subevents, individual perceptual elements, that can also be coupled in a nonveridical way as a result of their temporal and frequency proximities. There are four kinds of subevents: (1) onset: a steep rise of sound intensity (denoted by <); (2) termination: a steep fall of sound intensity (denoted by >); (3) filling: a relatively thick distribution of sound energy extending for a certain duration (denoted by =); and (4) silence: a very thin distribution of sound energy for a certain duration (denoted by /). Secondly, the event construction model contains a simple Markov grammar describing which auditory concatenations of the four subevents are grammatical and which ones are ungrammatical. For example, the string < = > / is grammatical, but the string = > / is ungrammatical because an onset (<) is missing.

What happens in the gap transfer illusion (see Figure 5.2, left panel) is that the onset (<) of the swoop and the termination (>) of the first part of the sweep are coupled as a result of their close proximity in the temporal-frequency plane, even though they belong to different sounds physically. Likewise, the onset of the second part of the sweep and the termination of the swoop are coupled. Because the string <> is ungrammatical, and there is sufficient sound energy (filling) from the swoop available, both couplings are made grammatical by insertion of fillings. Consequently, there are two clear auditory events in succession (< = > < = >), which are organized into an auditory stream by the Gestalt principles of proximity and similarity, that is, silences are inserted yielding the string < = > / < = > /, representing the swoop with the perceived gap. The auditory system is left with the remaining subevents from the sweep and the swoop: < = = = > / (first and last filling stem from the sweep and the middle filling from the swoop). Because the auditory system has no indications that these three filling parts belong to different events, the Gestalt principle of good continuation glues them to one filling. Thus, a second auditory stream, comprising an event followed by silence, is constructed by the recoupling process. The listener can direct his selective auditory attention to either the swoop with the gap or the continuous sweep, pushing the other stream in the background (cf., ten Hoopen, 1996 for a detailed account of auditory attention).

We gave two examples of perceptual illusions, one for vision and one for hearing, but illusions have been reported for touch, taste, and smell as well (Cobb, 1999). These five classic senses all have dedicated sense organs, receptor systems, and related brain areas for further processing the sensory information. There is not such a sense organ for time. Time is an attribute of a perceptual configuration, not a sensory experience like "red," "loud," "itch," "sweet," and "musty." Nevertheless, we have a sense of time, but it is misleading to think that the stimulus for perceived time is the passage of physical time (see Chapter 1 for a history of ideas about time in philosophy; and Chapter 13 for ideas about physical time). Of course, physical time is a factor but only one of many. However difficult the concept of time might be, psychologists have to operationalize the sense of time to investigate it in similar ways as they investigate the "easy" senses. As Fraisse (1978) noted: "Time is only a concept that subsumes all the aspects of change in our environment as well as in our life. Changes are incessant. If one wants to analyze them, one has to admit that in change there are events that are like noticeable moments, or to say it differently, that are like figures on a ground. Changes may be characterized by the following two aspects: (a) the succession and order of events; (b) the duration of the event, or the interval between successive events" (p. 203).

In other words, we can use visual, auditory, tactile, or even gustatory and olfactory events to mark time in a relative manner by measuring durations of events, and their stimulus onset asynchrony, by using simple timing devices. In this chapter, we restrict ourselves to time in the auditory modality, that is, durations of and between auditory events, and their temporal patterning. We define a time illusion as a systematic distortion in terms of dilations and/or contractions which cannot easily be predicted from the temporal patterning in physical time. We restrict ourselves to relatively brief temporal extents. Note that several perceptual facts that conform to our definition of "illusion" have been called "effect" or "phenomenon" in the psychological literature. We will use these three words interchangeably.

5.2. Classic Time Illusions

5.2.1. Illusion of a Divided Time Interval

The most classic illusion we know of is the illusion of a divided time interval. A time interval marked by two short sounds is called an empty time interval. If one or more short sounds are inserted between the initial and final marker, it is called a divided time interval. Hall and Jastrow (1886) found that divided time intervals sound longer than empty ones of the same physical duration. This illusion has been investigated by several other researchers (for example, Adams, 1977; Buffardi, 1971; Fraisse, 1961; Israeli, 1930; Nakajima, 1979, 1987; Thomas & Brown, 1974). We discuss Nakajima's work to some extent, because it offers a clear quantification of the illusion. Nakajima's (1979) control condition comprised an empty time interval of fixed duration marked by short sounds (the standard, *S*), preceded or followed by another empty time interval of which the duration can be varied by the listener (the comparison, *C*). The task was to adjust the duration of *C* as many times until satisfied by the match with the *S* duration. Thus, the final adjustment yields the point of subjective equality (PSE) of *S* and the difference between the PSE and the point of objective equality (POE), the duration of *S*, is the constant error (CE). The amount of CE (positive or negative) itself is, of course, not a time illusion, but rather an index of the difference between the physical passage of time and its perception, called protensity by Woodrow (1951). The illusion emerges when inserting a sound in between the initial and final sound markers (experimental condition), and again requiring the listener to adjust the variable — nondivided — *C* to match the (total) *S* duration. When *C* follows the divided *S*, a clear bimodal distribution of overestimations (PSEexperimental – PSEcontrol) was found, one mode at about 100 ms and another one at about 20 ms. Nakajima (1987) argued that the slight overestimations of 20 ms were secondary CEs (we suggest that they may have reflected a time order error (TOE), see Chapter 3), and that the additional overestimations of about 80 ms represented the real illusion. However, when *C* preceded the divided *S* duration, the illusion of overestimation hardly occurred. The distribution was approximately unimodal with a mode of 10 ms, probably also as a cause of a TOE. It seems as if the listeners had been set by the temporal structure of the preceding empty interval *C* (undivided!) to direct their attention only to initial and final markers of the succeeding divided interval, and hence no illusion could emerge. This also sheds light on the fact that, even though *C* came after the divided *S*, still only about half of the adjustments yielded overestimations (mode of 100 ms). The experimental trials, comprising a divided *S* duration followed by an undivided *C*, were interspersed by control trials, comprising an undivided *S* and an undivided *C*. These latter trials probably also created a set to neglect the dividing marker in many cases. A definite answer can only be given by an experiment in which experimental and control trials are not mixed but blocked. Other evidence that attentional set affects the divided time illusion can be found in the study by Adams (1977). In that study, the divided time illusion diminished when the delimiting markers were presented in one ear, and dividing markers in the other ear. The illusion almost disappeared when the delimiting markers were 500 Hz and the dividing marker was 1000 Hz (see ten Hoopen, 1996 for more details).

Given that all markers, delimiting and dividing the empty interval, are processed with the same amount of auditory attention, it is possible to quantify the illusion by applying Nakajima's (1987) model of empty duration perception. In words, the model states that the subjective duration of an empty time interval is directly proportional to its physical duration plus a constant α, thus in formula:

$$\tau(t) = k(t + \alpha) \tag{5.1}$$

in which $\tau(t)$ is the subjective duration as a function of the physical duration t, k is a scaling constant (>0), and α is the so-called supplement constant, the mental time required to process the duration of t. Nakajima (1987) and Nakajima, Nishimura, and Teranishi (1988) showed that α is approximately 80 ms, and for the empty time interval divided by one marker into two physical durations t_1 and t_2 means that the total subjective duration is $k(t_1 + \alpha) + k(t_2 + \alpha) = k(t_1 + t_2 + 2\alpha)$. Because the subjective duration of the corresponding undivided empty interval is $k(t_1 + t_2 + \alpha)$, the overestimation amounts about 80 ms. When straightforwardly deriving from formula (5.1), one can easily extrapolate the amounts of overestimation, which should be about 80 ms for each additional dividing marker.

Nakajima did not do the test, but there are some studies that investigated the effect of the number of dividing markers in an empty time interval on the amount of overestimation (e.g., Buffardi, 1971; Thomas & Brown, 1974). Buffardi varied the number of dividing markers from zero to five (in steps of one) in the auditory, tactile, and visual modalities and the total duration of the interval was 1056 ms. The temporal positions of the dividing markers could be asymmetric, either in the beginning or the end of the total empty interval, or symmetric within the interval. This resulted in 14 different temporal configurations, which were compared in pairs for their duration and scaled by the law of comparative judgment. Disregarding specific temporal position configurations, we averaged the scale values for 0, 1, 2, 3, 4, and 5 dividing markers in the auditory modality (see Buffardi's Table 1, p. 293). The average scale values are .00, .25, .36, .69, .87, and 1.19, which can be linearly fitted very well ($r^2 = .986$). Because we have an interval scale, this means that each extra dividing sound marker adds a constant amount of duration overestimation, supporting the prediction of Nakajima's model. Buffardi's explanation was in terms of the information processing approach to time perception (Ornstein, 1969), in particular in terms of (sub)vocally counting the number of sound markers: More markers take more counting time, causing an increase of overestimation. Such an explanation differs radically from that of Nakajima's. In his model, it is not the processing of the sound markers *per se* but rather that of the interval durations in between them. Establishing an interval duration takes a supplemental amount of time ($\alpha \approx 80$ ms). In other words, it takes time to process an empty duration, and the more intervals are contained in the divided interval, the larger its overestimation, proportional to the number of contained intervals.

Finally, a caveat on nomenclature is in order here. Several researchers confusingly use the expression *filled duration illusion* for what we termed "illusion of a divided time interval." This might cause a misunderstanding, because a filled duration is most often defined as the duration of a homogeneous, continuous stimulus (in this case a sound) in contrast to a duration marked by two brief stimuli, called an empty or unfilled duration (Fraisse, 1978; Grondin, 1993). When not obeying these definitions, one might mistakenly be inclined to think that the filled duration illusion is the fact that a filled interval and an empty interval of equal duration do not sound equally long. Indeed, it is often reported that a filled interval is perceived as being longer than an empty interval of the same duration (see Grondin, 2001, 2003), but this is not what those researchers mean by *filled duration illusion*. Hence we propose that one sticks to "illusion of a divided time interval."

5.2.2. Subjective Rhythm and Illusion of Equal Groups in Isochronous Equitone Sequences

Another well-known classic illusion was reported by Bolton (1894). He developed an accurate device to present sequences of clicks that were of equal spectral composition, intensity, and duration, and the intervals between clicks were equal as well. Although the physical sequence was isochronous (and the clicks identical in all respects), most listeners were able to change their initial percept of a regular beat into a percept of recurring groups of clicks, when required. There were individual preferences for groups of two, three, or four clicks (and for six and eight to a lesser extent), and the first click of each group was heard to be accented. When encouraged, listeners were even able to change the perceived group size but regressed to their preferred group size after listening a while. Subsequent researchers (McDougall, 1903; Stetson, 1905) reported that in addition to subjective accenting, the interval duration between groups tends to be overestimated. Bolton found that when he varied the inter-onset interval (IOI) between the clicks, the number of clicks in the subjective groups changed. There was a preference for group sizes of 2, 3, 4, 6, and 8 when the IOIs were 790, 460, 310, 170, and 140 ms, respectively. Bolton showed that apparent grouping only occurred when the IOI of the isochronous sequence was longer than 115 ms and shorter than 1580 ms. McDougall's (1903) estimate of this latter boundary, beyond which temporal connection of the clicks appears to get lost, was more flexible: 1500–2000 ms. It is interesting and corroborative for these classic estimates of the range of subjective rhythmization, that Repp (2006) concluded from a thorough overview of the literature on rate limits of sensorimotor synchronization, that the upper rate limit for the auditory modality is 100–125 ms and the lower rate limit is 1800 ms.

Subjective rhythm and resonating oscillator. "Subjective rhythm" could be argued to constitute a kind of illusion. As noted by van Noorden and Moelants (1999), subjective rhythm "...is a unique example of how the perception process can subjectively change the appearance of identical elements, ..., the grouping period must be imposed by a periodic fluctuation in the perceptual system" (p. 46). These authors offered an attractive model to explain "subjective rhythm." They hypothesized that the perceptual-motor system is equipped with a resonating harmonic oscillator, having a certain characteristic frequency (f_0) and a certain damping constant (β). The oscillator is driven by the perception of the isochronous sequences, and depending on the sequence tempo, and hence different grouping periods, there is more or less augmentation of the oscillator amplitude beyond its critical damping, called "effective resonance." The authors analyzed three studies in the relevant literature in terms of their resonance model: Parncutt's (1994) study on tapping along with isochronous tone sequences of varying tempi with a speed participants prefer, Handel and Oshinski's (1981) study on tapping along with polyrhythmic sequences, and Vos' (1973) study on perceiving subjective groups in isochronous sequences. Because Vos' study is the least accessible (a Ph.D. study written in Dutch), we will summarize his experiment on subjective rhythm, and van Noorden and Moelants' analysis of it.

Vos (1973) required 15 participants to report the group size which they perceived when isochronous tone sequences of various tempi were presented. Table 5.1 displays the results, which show that group sizes 2, 4, and 8 were predominantly reported. From Vos' data, van Noorden and Moelants (1999) calculated the response probabilities of perceiving the group sizes dependent on the IOI values, by dividing all entries by 15. They reasoned that the theoretical strength of a response is the product of the relative strength of the grouping duration and the relative strength of the group size and fitted their resonance model to the data accordingly. A least-squares solution yielded the two parameters of the resonance curve: $T_0 = 1.100$ ms (the grouping period) and $\beta = 0.22$ (the damping constant) determining the group duration strength, and the other parameters for the group size strength can be read in the last column of Table 5.1. Figure 5.3 shows Vos' observed probabilities (markers are the group size numbers) and the probabilities estimated by the resonance model (curves). The correlation between Vos' data and the model was 0.976 (for the mathematical equation of the model we refer to Equation 3 of the study by van Noorden and Moelants, 1999, p. 46). Also in the tapping data of Parncutt (1994) and Handel and Oshinski (1981), there were specific grouping patterns as a function of tempo which could be fit well by the resonance model. The estimated resonance periods were 550 and 500 ms, respectively, thus approximately half of the period estimated on basis of Vos' (1973) data. For further interesting discussions of the resonance model and related tempo phenomena (preferred tempo, indifference interval, auditory streaming, and musical tempi), one can inspect the study by van Noorden and Moelants (1999).

5.2.2.1. Psychophysiological evidence of subjective rhythm Most of the work on subjective rhythm was done by behavioral methods. Two recent studies offered also psychophysiological evidence. Brochard, Abecasis, Potter, Ragot, and Drake (2003)

Table 5.1: The number of the 15 participants reporting perceived group sizes as a function of the tempo of isochronous sequences (expressed as inter-onset interval) (Vos, 1973).

Perceived group size	**Inter-onset interval (ms)**					
	150	**200**	**300**	**400**	**800**	**Group strength**
2	0	2	1	6	10	.443
3	0	1	0	2	1	.053
4	5	7	12	7	3	.373
5	1	0	1	0	1	.017
6	1	1	1	0	0	.022
7	2	0	0	0	0	.019
8	6	4	0	0	0	.072

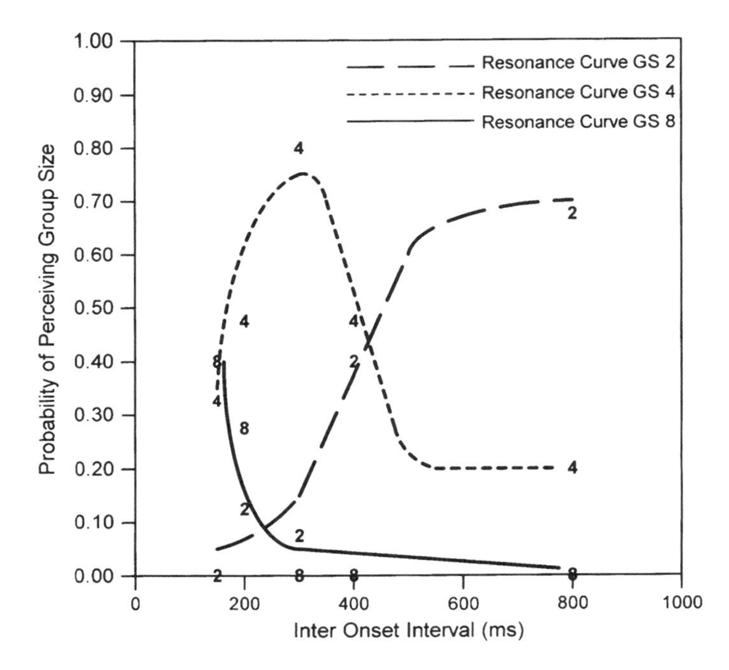

Figure 5.3: van Noorden and Moelants' (1999) analysis of Vos' (1973) data, using resonance curves. Curves represent the model predictions, and the group size probabilities observed by Vos are marked by the corresponding group size numbers. Group size 2: dashed curve; group size 4: dotted curve; group size 8: solid curve.

and Abecasis, Brochard, Granot, and Drake (2005) departed from Jones and Boltz's (1989) dynamic attending theory (see Chapter 6), stating that listeners extract temporal regularities from the beginning of auditory sequences and anticipate those regularities to further unfold in the sequence. The theory postulates that auditory sequences are rhythmically attended to and that accented sounds receive more attention and are processed deeper (see ten Hoopen, 1996, pp. 84–94 for an overview of experimental evidence from speech, musical, and temporal sequences).

Brochard et al. (2003) presented isochronous equitone sequences with a tempo (IOI of 600 ms) giving rise to apparent groups of two and violated the rhythmic expectancies in these so-called "ticktock" sequences. Infrequent deviations (approximately 10%) were imposed either on the 8th, 9th, 10th, or 11th tone in an otherwise isochronous equitone sequence of 13–16 tones by way of a sound intensity decrease of 4 dB SPL. Brochard et al. compared event-related potentials (ERPs) between sound intensity deviated tones 9 and 11 (positions of strong accents) on the one hand, and sound intensity deviated tones 8 and 10 (positions of weak accents) on the other hand (the control was comparing ERPs averaged over deviated tones 8 and 9 with ERPs averaged over deviated tones 10 and 11). There were significant differences between the ERP patterns of the deviated odd-numbered tones and the ERP patterns of the deviated even-numbered tones: the former patterns had larger amplitudes in the late positive parietal component, possibly the so-called P3b component. This means that the violation of the periodic expectancy affected the temporal positions of the strongly accented tones (9 and 11) significantly more than the positions of the even numbered tones. Since the amplitude difference occurred not early but late in the ERP waveform, this suggests an attentional rather than a preattentional process, in line with the theory of rhythmic attending. A subsequent study (Abecasis et al., 2005) offered additional psychophysiological support with special attention to the influence of the metrics of the groupings.

5.2.3. The Tau and Kappa Illusions

Time and space are interdependent not only in physics but also in perception, and with an intricacy as huge as that in physics (Friedman, 1983). Temporal variation of a stimulus sequence can affect the experience of its spatial layout. An example is a tactile situation in which three equidistant spots A, B, and C on the forearm are stimulated successively. Varying the time interval between stimulating loci A and B, and between loci B and C, affects the perceived spatial separation, even though the spots of stimulation are equidistant. If, for instance, the time lapse between stimulating A and B is longer than that between B and C, the perceived distance between A and B is greater than that between B and C (Helson & King, 1931). This is called "tau effect," the name coined by Helson (1930), though the phenomenon was reported decades earlier. Tau effects have been found for other sense modalities as well (see Jones & Huang, 1982 for an overview).

Conversely, spatial variation of a stimulus sequence can affect the experience of its temporal patterning. If, for instance, two successive time intervals (t_1 and t_2) between three visual flashes are equal, that is, the temporal sequence is physically isochronous, the percept of it can become anisochronous if the stimuli are delivered from separate locations. This has been reported long ago by Benussi (1913) and Abe (1935). A bit more recently, Cohen, Hansel, and Sylvester (1953) showed this by systematically varying the spatial distances (d_1 and d_2) between three successive flashes and requiring the observers to adjust the timing of the second flash repeatedly until satisfied by the subjective equality of t_1 and t_2 (a bisecting task). When two consecutive flashes were spaced farther apart, the observer shortened the time interval, and vice versa, when two flashes were spaced closer, the time interval in between was enlarged. Cohen et al. (1953) coined the term "kappa effect" for the phenomenon that spatial structure can affect the perceived temporal pattern. In the penultimate sentence the authors announced their next study (Cohen, Hansel, & Sylvester, 1954): "It may be asked whether the spatial element as such is an essential feature of this type of temporal phenomenon and whether a delimitation of the time intervals by other kinds of nonspatial stimuli such as auditory pitch might produce similar effects" (p. 901).

5.2.3.1. The tau and kappa illusions for pitch distance Cohen et al. (1954) studied the tau and kappa effects in the auditory modality. Their paradigm was the same as in their 1953 study. Three short tones, delimiting two time intervals t_1 and t_2 of which the sum was 1500 ms, were recycled with an intercycle time of 2500 ms. The frequencies of the first and third tones were either 1000 and 3000 Hz (ascending order) or 3000 and 1000 Hz (descending order) (we will not discuss their condition in which these tones were 2000 and 4000 Hz). The task of the observers was to adjust the frequency of the second tone in a series of cycles until they were satisfied that its pitch was halfway the pitches of the first and third tones. The temporal pattern of the cycle could be /500/1000/ ms, /750/750/ ms, and /1000/500/ ms where / denotes the tones. A clear and significant tau illusion was established, as illustrated in Figure 5.4. In the ascending control condition where $t_1 = t_2 = 750$ ms, the adjusted frequency of the middle pitched tone was 1874 Hz. However, in the experimental conditions in which two of the tones (either tones 1 and 2 or tones 2 and 3) were closer in time (500 ms), the frequency was adjusted such that the frequency interval was increased (see Figure 5.4, left panel). Similarly, the frequency intervals between tones closer in time were increased in the descending experimental conditions, where the control middle pitch frequency was 1838 Hz (see Figure 5.4, right panel). Notice by the way that both frequencies of 1874 and 1838 Hz for the halfway pitches between those corresponding to 1000 and 3000 Hz are somewhat higher than the middle pitch to be expected on the basis of perceiving an equal tempered scale, which would have corresponded to 1732 Hz. Nevertheless, we have clear tau effects here, both in the ascending and descending conditions: perceived time and pitch interval are interdependent.

The authors were less lucky in demonstrating a kappa effect when they changed, in a subsequent experiment, the middle pitch adjustment into a middle time adjustment. Observers were required to adjust the temporal position of the second (middle tone) such that t_1 and t_2 were perceived as having equal duration as a function of the three different ratios of frequency intervals installed by the

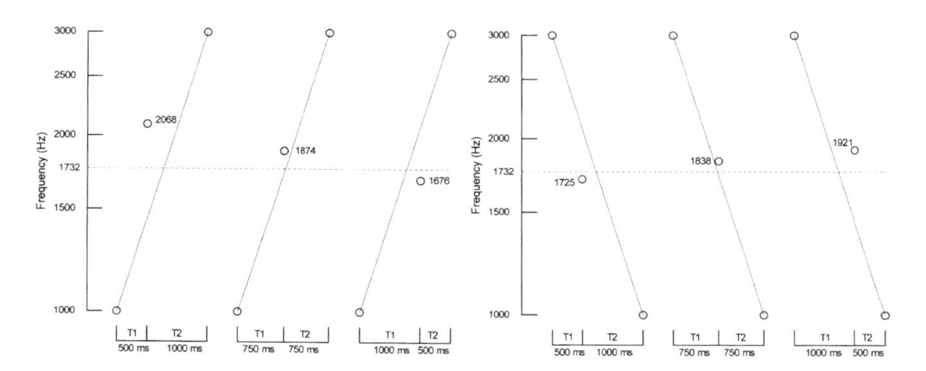

Figure 5.4: Illustrations of the auditory tau effect found by Cohen et al. (1954) in the ascending pitch condition (left panel) and the descending pitch condition (right panel).

experimenter. There was only a slight and statistically not significant influence of frequency intervals on temporal judgments. It is unfortunate that the authors did not report the values of the frequency ratios, nor the values of the adjusted t_1 and t_2, making an analysis of their negative results in view of more recent positive kappa results, to be treated now, impossible.

One of those more recent studies of the tau and kappa illusions has been done by Shigeno (1986), of which we only discuss the latter illusion. She used a psychophysical method different from the method of adjustment applied by Cohen et al. (1954). Ten of her twenty subjects were presented with triplets of pure sine tones (denoted by A, X, and B), each of which lasted 200 ms. The interval between the offset of A and the onset of X was denoted by t_1, and the interval between the offset of X and the onset of B was denoted by t_2. The sum of t_1 and t_2 was always 1 s, and t_1 was varied between 410 and 590 ms in steps of 30 ms, thus t_2 varied complementary from 590 to 410 ms. Thus, it is not exact to report that: "The two times separating these tones were roughly equal…" as Crowder and Neath (1995, p. 380) stated.

The frequencies of the first tone A and the third tone B were fixed at 1000 and 2500 Hz, respectively. The second tone X was varied between 1000, 1350, 1750, 2150, and 2500 Hz. Shigeno employed an AXB task in which subjects were required to judge whether the intermediate tone X was closer in time (not in pitch) to the first tone A or to the third tone B. From these judgments, she calculated the subjective temporal midpoint of the intermediate tones (1000, 1350, 1750, 2150, and 2500 Hz) expressed as t_1 values, which were 514, 508, 497, 483, and 461 ms, respectively. Thus, we see *overestimations* of t_1 (with respect to the objective middle point of 500 ms) by 14 and 8 ms for X-tone frequencies of 1000 and 1350 Hz. This means that t_1 was perceived *shorter* for frequencies lower than the geometric middle pitch of 1581 Hz between 1000 and 2500 Hz. Conversely, we see *underestimations* of t_1 of 3, 17, and 39 ms for X-tone frequencies of 1750, 2150, and 2500 Hz. This means that t_1 was perceived *longer* for frequencies higher than 1581 Hz.

One might criticize that Shigeno did not employ X-tone frequencies that were equally spaced logarithmically between $A = 1000$ Hz and $B = 2500$ Hz. In that case she would probably have observed less unbalance between the amounts of temporal shortening and lengthening of t_1. Nevertheless, her results showed a clear kappa illusion. When the pitch space distance between tones A and X gets smaller, the temporal distance t_1 is perceived to be shorter, and when this pitch space distance gets larger, the temporal distance is perceived to be longer.

A clear kappa illusion was also found with the other 10 subjects who did an AXB task with the synthetic A and B vowels /i/ and /e/, having first formants (F1) of 300 and 520 Hz, and where the F1 value of the intermediate X sound was varied between 300, 350, 410, 470, and 520 Hz. The overestimations of t_1 were 28 and 24 ms when the F1 of middle sound X was 300 and 350 Hz, and the underestimations of t_1 were 24 and 32 ms when the F1 of X was 470 and 520 Hz. When the F1 of sound X was 410 Hz, the CE in time was 0 ms, the subjective temporal position of the synthetic sound equaled its objective position of 500 ms. Because the synthetic sounds ranging between the vowels /i/ and /e/ are not spaced along an equally tempered scale but a linear scale, the F1 of 410 Hz, the physical middle in linear frequency is also the perceptual middle. Hence, the over- and underestimations, i.e., the shortening and lengthening of t_1, were almost perfectly balanced. In conclusion, the kappa illusion was established both in the nonphonetic and phonetic contexts, suggesting that the illusion arises "…at a common stage of auditory information processing before phonetic categorization" (Shigeno, 1986, p. 17).

Jones and Huang (1982) argued that the kappa (and tau) effects are contextual illusions that originate because participants impute a concept of motion from the discontinuous display. The authors followed Anderson's (1974) suggestion that the kappa illusion reflects a linear combination of distance and duration, and that the temporal response is the weighted average of the objective duration (t) and the expected duration, $E(t)$, necessary to cross the distance (d) at imputed constant velocity (v), because $E(t) = d/v$. In a somewhat simplified formula: kappa $(\kappa) = f[wt + (1 - w)E(t)]$. If $w = 1$, the actual duration is used to establish the perceived duration, and no kappa illusion is obtained, but when $0 < w < 1$, the perceived duration is a combination of actual and expected time, and the kappa illusion emerges. The imputed constant velocity idea, first proposed by Price-Williams (1954), is described as follows: In several kappa studies, the display comprised three successive stimulus markers delimiting two distances (d_1 and d_2) and two empty time intervals (t_1 and t_2). Participants somehow grasp the relation between d and t, that is, they impute velocity ($v = d/t$). Although there is no apparent movement (like with stroboscopic movement), the perceptual system seems to notice when there is a change of velocity (when $d_1/t_1 \neq d_2/t_2$) and compensates the value of t_j to restore constant velocity over the whole trajectory as far as possible.

Whereas Jones and Huang (1982) supported their model with data from visual experiments, Henry (2007) applied the model to auditory kappa experiments. In her thesis, she reported two experiments to examine the role of imputed pitch velocity of which we only discuss the first one. Thus, she substituted visual spatial distance by auditory pitch distance on an equal tempered scale, and velocity is expressed as pitch distance traversed in semitones (STs) per time unit. The participants had to judge the *timing* of a target tone X intermediate between tone A (330 Hz = E4) and tone B (523 Hz = C5). Such a tone triplet AXB is called a "kappa cell." The frequency of the target tone X was varied between −3, −1, 0, 1, and 3 semitones (STs) relative to the expected frequency of the target tone if pitch velocity would remain constant from tone A to tone B. Because tones A and B differed by 8 STs, the expected halfway frequency was 415 Hz (G4 sharp). Thus, the levels between which the pitch distance varied can also be expressed as the amount of STs between tone A and tone X (1, 3, 4, 5, and 7 ST). The other variable was context: kappa cell only (context absent) and kappa cell preceded by another three-tone sequence (context present). The kappa-cell only condition is displayed in Figure 5.5. In keeping with previous kappa studies, the frequency and temporal location of the target tone were randomized between trials. The temporal distances between the first tone A and the target tone X were 420, 440, 460, 480, 520, 540, 560, or 580 ms (the isochronous position 500 ms was not used). In the context-absent condition, the task for the participants was to judge whether the second (target) tone X was closer to the first tone A (by responding "short–long") or to the last tone B (by responding "long–short").

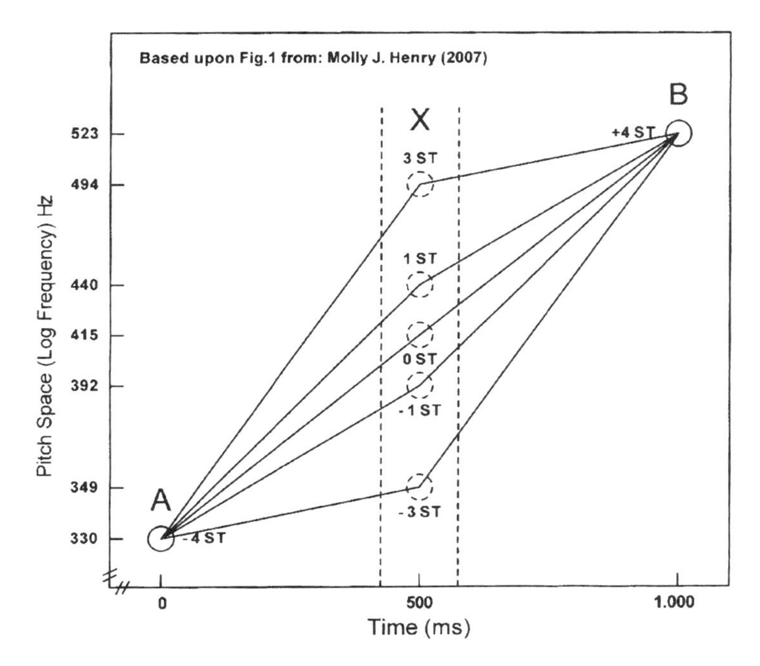

Figure 5.5: The pitch distance conditions used by Henry (2007), expressed as semitone (ST) deviations relative to the expected frequency of the target tone *X* if imputed velocity is constant in the AXB kappa cell. Velocities (in STs per 500 ms) are represented by the inserted solid lines. The temporal positions of the target tone *X* were randomized between 420 and 580 ms, the range indicated by the vertically dotted lines.

For the other group of participants in the "context present" condition, the kappa cell was preceded by another three-tone sequence with IOIs of 500 ms, and the IOI between the third tone and the first tone *A* of the kappa cell was 500 ms as well. The frequencies of the context tones were 165, 208, and 262 Hz, i.e., E3, A3-flat, and C4. Notice that this preceding context sequence has a frequency progression of +4 ST per 500 ms and hence impeccably fits the overall constant velocity of the six tone sequence (except of course for the target tone in the kappa cell). The very plausible idea of Henry (2007) was that supplying extra preceding information of the constant frequency velocity would enable the listener to sharply discriminate velocity distortions due to deviations of the target tone. Hence, a bigger kappa illusion was hypothesized in the "context present" condition. Evidently, the group of participants in this condition was required to give the same judgments (short–long or long–short) about the temporal position of the target tone *X* in the kappa cell, *X* now being the penultimate (fifth) tone in the total sequence of six tones.

The magnitude of the kappa effect was based on the assessment of the relative CEs (see Chapter 2). For the "context absent" condition, Figure 5.6 shows that at the

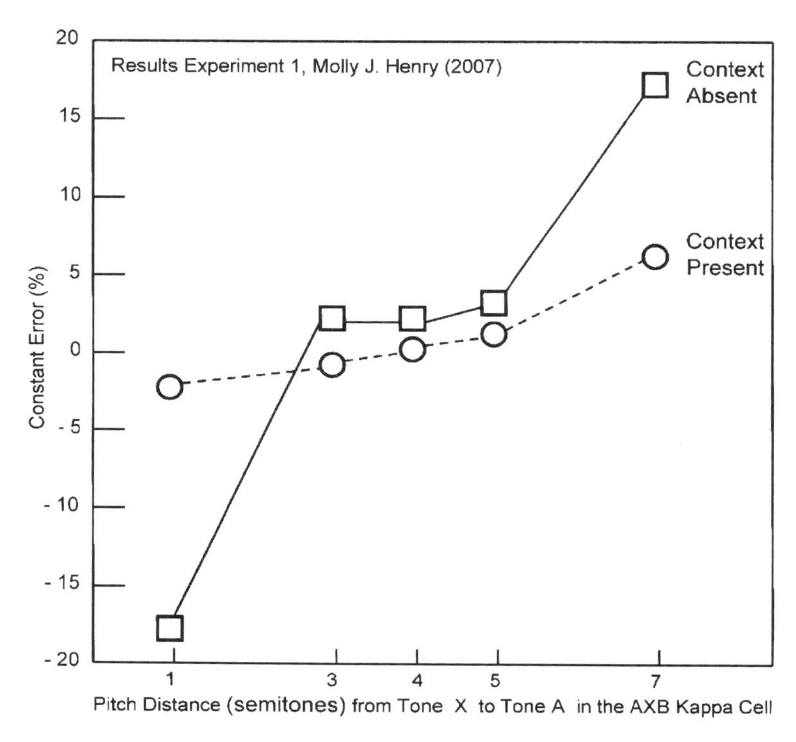

Figure 5.6: Henry's results: the relative constant errors (CE%) as a function of the pitch distance in semitones (ST) between tone *A* and target tone *X* in the context-absent condition (kappa cell only) and the context-present condition.

levels 3, 4, and 5 ST pitch distance between *A* and *X*, there is hardly any kappa effect because the CEs are 0% or close to 0%. At the ST levels of 1 and 7, however, clear kappa effects can be observed. The inserted velocity trajectories in Figure 5.5 illustrate the reason. In the middle trajectory (0 ST) there is no change of velocity by definition, and in the neighboring trajectories (– 1 ST and 1 ST), the velocities in the trajectories before and after tone *X* hardly differ. Therefore, the velocity expectation that has been build up from *A* to *X* is hardly violated by the velocity between *X* and *B*, and hence no compensating temporal shift of tone *X* toward tone *A* or tone *B* is required by the perceptual system. On the other hand, the bottom and top trajectories in Figure 5.5 show big changes of velocity from the AX part to the XB part. Consequently, the perceptual system shifts tone *X* in time toward tone *A* if their pitch distance is only 1 ST (a negative CE of about 18%), but shifts tone *X* in time toward tone *B* if the pitch distance between *A* and *X* is 7 ST (a positive CE of about 18%).

The amounts of the kappa effect in the "context present" condition at pitch distances between *A* and *X* of 1 and 7 STs, though in the same direction, are a lot smaller (CEs of –2.5% and 6%, respectively). As Henry mentions, this result was quite unexpected and contrary to the hypothesis that the kappa illusion would have been boosted by a preceding context that strengthens the velocity trace up till tone *X*. Henry surmised that preceding the kappa cell by another sequence that is isochronous not only reinforces the image of velocity but also shapes a strong isochronous rhythmic grid in which the first and third bounding tones of the kappa cell take part. (Recall that a kappa cell in the "context absent" condition was never isochronous!) She conjectures that such a strong regular rhythm might have segregated the spatial and temporal properties of the kappa cell, as a result of which the kappa illusion is strongly reduced.

There is evidence from visual kappa studies that sequences with a larger velocity produce a stronger kappa illusion (Jones & Huang, 1982). In a follow-up study, the frequency velocity of the auditory kappa cell was varied between 4 ST/800 ms, 4 ST/500 ms, and 4 ST/364 ms (Henry & McAuley, 2007). The authors found that the size of the kappa illusion indeed increased with increasing frequency velocity. Henry and McAuley interpreted this result in the context of the auditory motion hypothesis (MacKenzie, 2007; MacKenzie & Jones, 2005) and we will turn to the work of the latter authors now.

MacKenzie and Jones (2005) proposed the auditory motion (AM) hypothesis, departing from the imputed motion hypothesis (Jones & Huang, 1982). The AM hypothesis claims that the auditory kappa illusion arises as a result of pitch/time expectancies. In a kappa cell, pitch and timing of the three tones convey a rate of change of pitch. The assumption is that the pitch velocity in the first time interval creates an expectancy about the pitch velocity in the second time interval. If this expectancy is violated, that is, $v_2 \neq v_1$, the temporal position of tone *X* is adjusted perceptually to equalize both velocities as far as possible. So far, the AM hypothesis does not differ from the imputed motion hypothesis, however, in addition the AM hypothesis claims that the strength of the illusion is affected by the serial context of the kappa cell.

MacKenzie (2007) reports five experiments. The first one was a baseline study in which monotonic sequences of three and six tones were used to carefully study temporal variations in the absence of pitch variation. The second experiment was an improved replication of Shigeno's 1986 study in which frequency was not varied along a linear scale but along a logarithmic scale (we already stipulated the consequences of linearly spaced frequencies in the kappa cell when discussing Shigeno's study above). The bounding tones *A* and *B* were C5 (523 Hz) and G5 sharp (831 Hz), respectively, in the ascending condition, and G5 sharp and C5 in the descending condition. Thus, tones *A* and *B* were 8 STs apart in frequency. In time, *A* and *B* were separated by an inter-stimulus interval (ISI) of 1.000 ms. The intermediate target tone *X* was varied between C5 sharp, D5 sharp, E5, F5, and G5, thus 1, 3, 4, 5, and 7 ST above tone *A* in the ascending condition, and 7, 5, 4, 3, and 1 ST above tone *A* in the descending condition. Target tone *X* could be presented at eight temporal positions: 430, 450, 470, 490, 510, 530, 550, or 570 ms after tone *A*. Participants in both groups (ascending/descending kappa cell) had to indicate whether they judged tone *X* to be closer in time to tone *A* or tone *B*. At each of the 2 (ascending/descending) × 5 (ST distance) × 8 (temporal position) = 80 levels, the proportion responses "closer in time to tone *B*" [*p*(*B*)] was calculated.

In line with the results of the baseline study, the main effect of temporal position was significant: If tone *X* was objectively closer to tone *B*, participants were more liable to respond "*B*." However, the other significant main effect was the *pitch distance* (ST) between tones *A* and *X*. The closer the pitch of *X* was to that of tone *A*, the smaller the *p*(*B*). Thus, if pitch *X* was closer to pitch *A* or pitch *B*, tone *X* was judged to be closer *in time* to tone *A* or tone *B*. Thus, the classic kappa illusion was obtained (see Figure 5.7).

In Mackenzie's Experiment 3, the ascending kappa cell used in Experiment 2 could be preceded by one of three different serial contexts. All three contexts had the same temporal patterning: tone durations of 200 ms and ISIs of 500 ms, and the ISI between the last tone of the preceding triple and the *A* tone was 500 ms as well. The pitch distances between consecutive tones in the three preceding triplets were 0, 4, and 8 ST (see Figure 5.8). It turned out that the kappa illusion was completely abolished in the 0 ST condition, apparently perceiving no pitch motion at all in the context conflicted with the pitch motion in the kappa cell. Jones (1976) and Jones and Boltz (1989) argued that auditory sequences unfolding in time and pitch according to a regular pattern trajectory facilitate anticipations about future patterning. In the

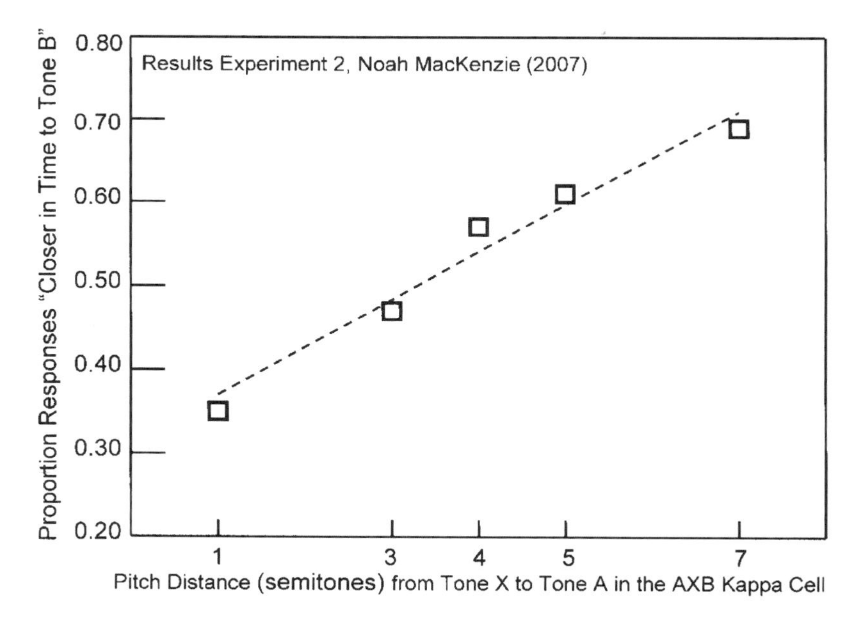

Figure 5.7: Results of MacKenzie's Experiment 2: the proportion of responses "closer to tone *B*" {*p*(*B*)}, the final tone of the kappa cell, as a function of the pitch distance (in semitones, ST) of the middle target tone *X* to the first tone *A* of the kappa cell.

0 ST condition the first three tones build up a temporally expectation of isochrony but not of an increasing pitch. The extrapolation of the 0 ST pitch motion must have interfered with the 4 ST motion. Although the kappa illusion was nullified in the 0 ST condition, it was not strengthened when the preceding three tones unfolded precisely according to the trajectory of the kappa cell (4 ST per tone). This result squares nicely with that of Henry (2007) which we discussed above. Experiment 4 by MacKenzie showed that the kappa illusion in an ascending cell could also be nullified by a preceding descending sequence of three tones.

The stance of AM is that the kappa effect emerges because the perceiver extrapolates the trajectory of imputed auditory motion of the first time interval of the kappa cell and adjusts the second time interval if there is a mismatch of trajectories. The AM hypothesis holds in addition that the kappa effect can be eliminated by a preceding context with a conflicting pitch trajectory. However, it might be that by increasing the speed of the imputed auditory velocity in the kappa cell, the strength of its trajectory can be made more robust, i.e., less susceptible to distortions by the context. Experiment 5 tested this supposition, called the modified auditory motion (MAM) hypothesis. This hypothesis holds that the greater the imputed motion (in the kappa cell), the stronger the kappa illusion is. Like in Experiment 3, there were three preceding tone triples with 0, 4, and 8 ST increase of frequency from tone to

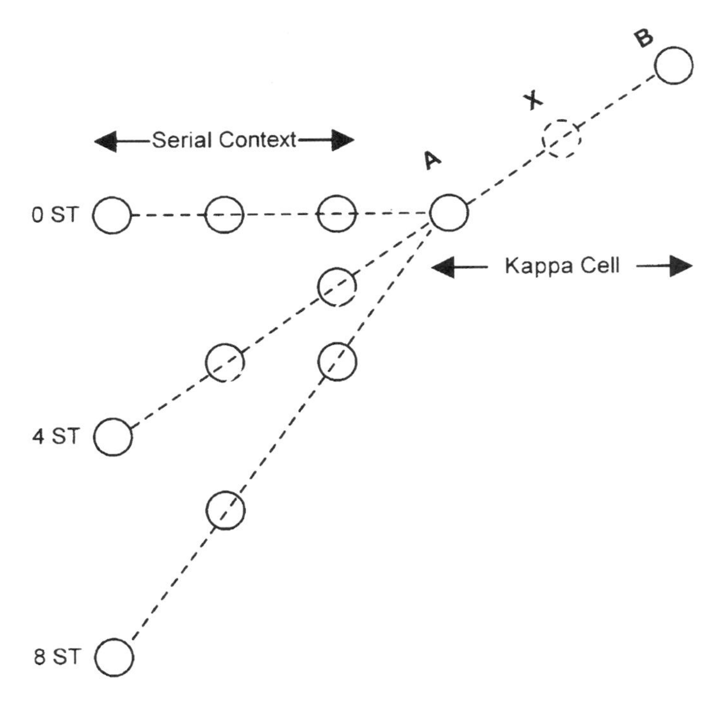

Figure 5.8: Illustration of the stimulus materials that MacKenzie (2007) used in his Experiment 3.

tone, respectively, followed by a kappa cell with the same temporal properties as those in Experiment 3. The only difference was that the frequency increase from tone *A* to tone *B* was not 8 ST but 16 ST (from 523 to 1319 Hz). The procedure was the same as that of Experiment 3. The kappa effect, absent at the 0 ST condition in Experiment 3, was restored. Because the only difference between Experiments 3 and 5 was the pitch velocity 8 and 16 ST, respectively, from *A* to *B* in the kappa cell, the result supports the MAM hypothesis that greater imputed auditory motion produces a stronger, more robust, kappa illusion.

In the experiments we discussed, the stimulus material was very elementary: in several experiments, only the kappa cell was presented, and in other experiments the kappa cell was preceded by a three-tone context. One might wonder whether the kappa illusion can be observed in longer, more meaningful tonal sequences. Boltz (1998) reasoned that a melody, by virtue of its spatiotemporal structure, might be suitable material for experiments to study the imputed velocity hypothesis. She presented her participants with a paired-comparison task and a pair comprised a standard melody and a comparison melody, both of 24 tones. Among other things, the pitch distance between tones was systematically varied. The task was to judge the apparent tempo of the comparison melody with reference to that of the standard melody on a 7-point scale. She found that comparison melodies containing larger pitch skips than the standard were judged to be slower, and conversely, when the comparisons contained smaller pitch skips than the standard they were judged to be faster.

5.2.3.2. The kappa illusion for ambient space distance All studies of the auditory kappa illusion discussed above, implicitly or explicitly took for granted that pitch space in hearing is the equivalent of visual space (cf., the debate between Handel, 1988a, b and Kubovy, 1988). However, auditory motion perception, imputed or real, not only is confined to pitch space but also pertains to ambient auditory space, that is, to our spatial hearing environment, as well. Very probably the perceptual mechanism of perceiving motion of auditory signals through ambient space differs from the mechanism of perceiving motion in pitch space. Thus, it is a legitimate and important question whether the kappa illusion can be found when sounds, demarcating time intervals, differ in location. We know of only one study (Grondin & Plourde, 2007) that examined whether a kappa illusion in ambient auditory space exists, and if so, whether it reduces the occurrence of another illusion, namely time shrinking (TS).

In order to appreciate the elegance of questioning whether two opposing time illusions might compete perceptually, it is necessary at this point to explain TS briefly (but in Section 5.3 we will discuss the TS illusion extensively). If an empty time interval, bounded by short sound markers, is preceded serially by one or more empty time intervals that are shorter, it can be hugely underestimated (shrunk). This has been amply demonstrated by the Nakajima group with several psychophysical methods, among which the method of constant stimuli (see Section 5.3.1, p. 163 for details). In order to grasp Grondin and Plourde's study, in which the constant method was also applied, we describe the temporal pattern and the task. Four short sound markers delimited three empty time intervals, of which the first two empty durations served as the standard (*S*), and the last one as comparison (*C*) duration. The range of *C* values varied in constant small-temporal steps widely enough around the value of *S*, and the participant had to judge whether the randomly presented *C*'s were shorter or longer than *S*. From the psychometric curve, the PSEs were calculated.

One should carefully notice that when *time shrinking* occurs to the last interval of the temporal pattern, this is borne out by a *positive* CE. For if the last time interval in the pattern is shrunk, the PSE yielded by the constant method should be larger than the POE of *S* to obtain perceived isochrony. Conversely, if the kappa illusion *stretches* the last time interval (as a cause of a different spatial location of the last sound marker), this should be borne out by a *negative* CE. For if the last time interval in the pattern is stretched, the PSE yielded by the constant method should be *smaller* than the POE of *S* to obtain perceived isochrony.

Grondin and Plourde (2007, Experiment 2) had three base durations of *S* (75, 150, and 225 ms, and the first three sound markers, delimiting the two *S* intervals were emitted from a loudspeaker left to the median sagittal plane of the participant and the fourth sound marker was emitted from another speaker right of that plane, or vice versa, thus there was a left–right and a right–left presentation. The angular separation between the speakers was varied between approximately 60 and 90°. Still another condition was whether the participants were certain or uncertain. In the certain condition participants knew the sound emitting speaker arrangement for a whole block of trials (either left–right or right–left) but in the uncertain condition left–right and right–left sound emissions were randomized within a block.

The positive or negative CE value (PSE – POE, in ms) indicates the amount of over- or underestimation. Grondin and Plourde reported that they established several negative CEs, especially in the uncertainty conditions, thus evidencing that the kappa illusion overruled the TS illusion. There is, however, a caveat in order here, because the authors did not relate the experimental CEs to the control CEs gathered in their Experiment 1, in which there was a condition where the sound patterns were emitted from one loudspeaker only. Therefore, we subtracted the control CEs at the standard durations of 75, 150, and 225 ms (+8, +6, and +3 ms, respectively) from the corresponding experimental CEs (which is numerically the same as subtracting the control PSEs from the experimental PSEs). Table 5.2 displays this reanalysis of Grondin and Plourde's (2007) data.

It turned out that our reanalysis amplified Grondin and Plourde's conclusion: "...that there are conditions where increasing the spatial distance between sound sources increases the perceived duration of a temporal interval. Moreover, marking the comparison interval with signals delivered from different sources hinders the occurrence of the time shrinking illusion..." (p. 712). As regards the spatial distance between speakers, Table 5.2 shows that the underestimations, indicative for the kappa illusion, are larger when the angular separation is greater but mainly in the certain condition. In the uncertain condition, there was no effect of angular separation. Overall though, the underestimations are larger in the uncertain than in the certain condition. Both in the certain and uncertain conditions, the kappa illusion is much stronger in the left–right condition than in the right–left condition. Although Grondin and Plourde's (2007) study offered evidence for the existence of the kappa

Table 5.2: The differences between the experimental points of subjective equality and the control points of subjective equality (PSEexp − PSEcon in ms) as a function of the level of certainty about emitting loudspeakers (certain, uncertain), the direction of the sound sequence (left–right, right–left), the angular separation of the loudspeakers (60 or 90°), and the standard base duration of the temporal sequence (75, 150, and 225 ms) (Grondin & Plourde, 2007).

		Standard base duration (ms)			
		75	**150**	**225**	**Mean**
Certain	LR 60°	−4	−8	0	−4
	90°	−14	−14	−8	−12
	RL 60°	2	6	4	4
	90°	−1	−2	1	−1
Uncertain	LR 60°	−11	−15	−12	−13
	90°	−16	−14	−12	−14
	RL 60°	−3	−8	−2	−4
	90°	7	−11	−10	−5

Note: LR = left–right condition, RL = right–left condition. All are values rounded to ms.

illusion in ambient auditory space, we agree with the authors that: "This study leaves the door open to multiple research avenues" (p. 714), like investigating the certainty effect, angular separations wider than 60 and 90°, the sound direction effect, and so on. We recommend that researchers tackling these issues, hopefully in the near future, adopt a different psychophysical method. The method of constant stimuli is a rather indirect way to investigate the TS and kappa illusions, and would be better replaced by the more straightforward method of adjustment.

There is a series of studies published in the late 70s and early 80s of the 20th century by one of us (ten Hoopen) that quantified the amount of interaural (ear-alternating) time dilation. In those studies there was no reference to the kappa illusion, nor did any of the reviewers ever suggest that interaural time dilation might be subsumed under the kappa effect. It is by hindsight that we now conclude that the ten Hoopen group quantified a very robust kappa illusion in auditory ambient space. Although this group quantified the illusion, they did not discover it. It was the Axelrod group who published the phenomenon for the first time in 1968. Inspired by studies of human auditory attention in the "Cherry-Broadbent-Moray" tradition, the group started carrying out experiments with animals with systematic brain ablations of the auditory cortex (Axelrod & Diamond, 1965; Kaas, Axelrod, & Diamond, 1967). While monitoring the sounds, the authors haphazardly observed that isochronous click sequences presented to one ear (monaural presentation) had a faster apparent repetition rate than ear-alternating (interaural) sequences. Although the objective rate in both spatial situations was the same, the monaural sequence compellingly slowed down when the clicks were presented one by one alternating between ears, and vice versa, compellingly speeded up when changed from interaural to monaural.

In experiments with human participants, Axelrod and Guzy (1968), Axelrod, Guzy, and Diamond (1968), and Guzy and Axelrod (1972) attempted to quantify the amount of apparent slowing down of interaural click sequences relative to the apparent rate of monaural controls. In their 1972 study, participants had to count the number of clicks in monaural and interaural sequences. The objective rates were 2, 4, 6, and 8 clicks/s, and the number of clicks was varied between 2 and 20. It turned out that, despite equal objective rates, interaural sequences were undercounted more than monaural ones. The authors' explanation was in terms of time-consuming interaural attention switching, a popular concept in those days. In addition, the authors proposed that the mental switching mechanism was fatigable, like a repetitive motor response. However, as ten Hoopen and Vos (1980) demonstrated, this proposal was derived from a faulty analysis of the results. The dependent variable which the authors analyzed was the ratio between the interaural and monaural counts and hence the linear model of analysis of variance was violated. In a following study ten Hoopen, Vos, and Dispa (1982) reanalyzed a previous counting experiment (ten Hoopen & Vos, 1981) and performed a stop-reaction time (stop-RT) experiment in which participants had to react to the unpredictable end of monaural and interaural click sequences, a technique they borrowed from Schaefer (1979). The rationale of the stop-RT task is described by ten Hoopen (1996) and also by ten Hoopen and Akerboom (1983). On basis of the reanalysis and the experiment, the authors concluded that the apparent slowing down of interaural sequences was a perceptual/memory process and not caused by attention switching. ten Hoopen et al. coined the term perceptual onset asynchrony (POA) for the apparent time between successive sounds as the subjective counterpart of stimulus onset asynchrony (SOA) for the physical time between sounds. Figure 5.9 shows that the POA differences between interaural and monaural conditions estimated by the counting task and the stop-RT task converge almost precisely to 25 ms. Special notice should be given to the random and blocked conditions (see Figure 5.9b), which are analogous to the uncertain and certain conditions as described by Grondin and Plourde (2007). Whereas the latter authors found a much smaller kappa effect in the certain (blocked) condition, ten Hoopen et al. (1982) found exactly the same kappa effect in the random (uncertain) and blocked (certain) conditions.

In a subsequent study (Akerboom, ten Hoopen, Olierook, & van der Schaaf, 1983) five stop reaction time experiments were reported that together covered a much wider SOA range than that of 125–250 ms in the study by ten Hoopen et al. (1982), namely from 40 to 2130 ms. The linear fits through the interaural and monaural stop RTs over the whole range yielded the equations: RTint = 235 + 1.12 SOA ms ($r^2 = .99$) and RTmon = 210 + 1.12 SOA ms ($r^2 = .99$). These two regression lines are strictly in parallel, implying that the difference of 235 – 210 = 25 ms between stop-RTs, and thus between interaural and monaural POAs, is not affected at all by the rate of the click sequence. Whether one has 25 clicks per second at the one extreme, or one click at slightly more than 2 s at the other extreme, the interaural time dilation of the interval between successive clicks remains 25 ms. We clearly have a very special

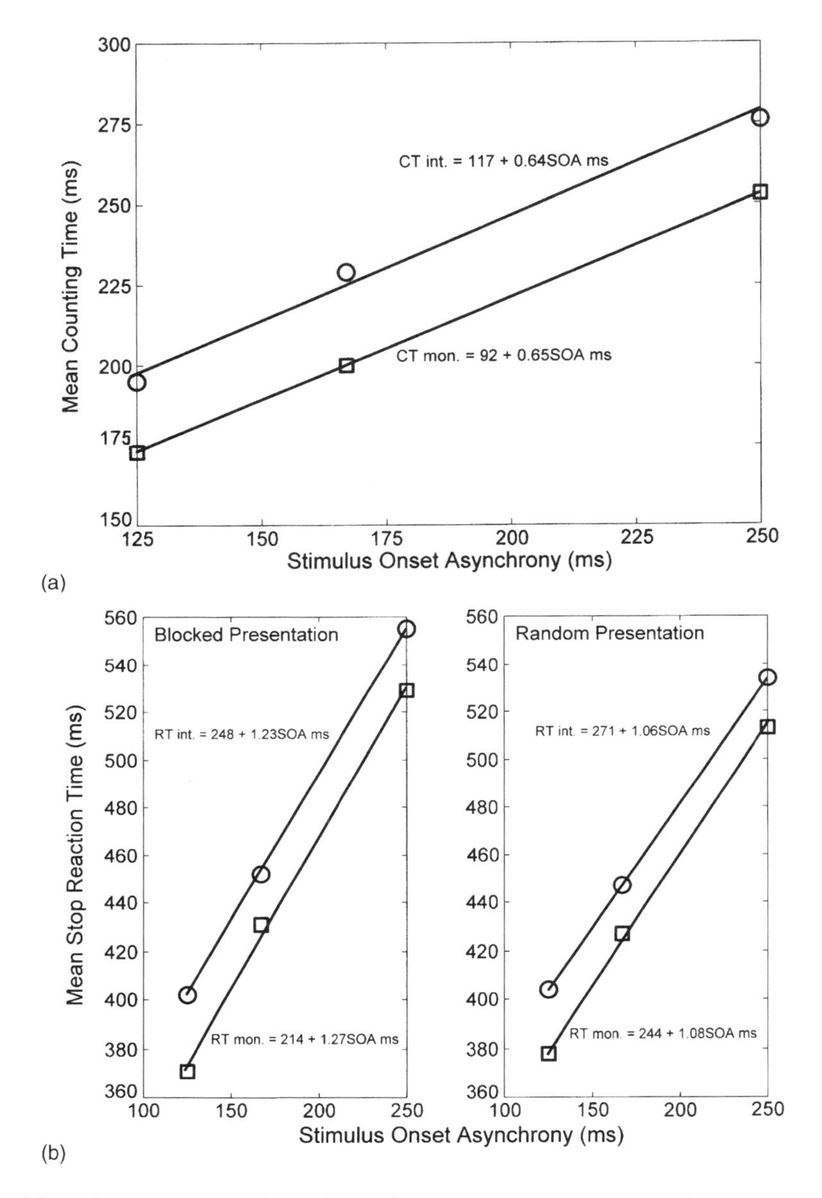

Figure 5.9: (a) Reanalysis of the data of ten Hoopen & Vos (1981). Mean counting times (CT) as a function of tempo, expressed as stimulus onset asynchrony between clicks and presentation mode, monaural (mon) and interaural (int). (b) Mean stop reaction times as a function of tempo, expressed as stimulus onset asynchrony (SOA) between clicks and presentation mode, monaural (mon) and interaural (int). The blocked group received the presentation modes in separate blocks, whereas the random group received the presentation modes randomly mixed within blocks.

kappa illusion here: The magnitude of the illusion is not at all affected by the velocity of the sequence. Note that this result is in strong contrast to what Henry and McAuley (2007) and MacKenzie (2007) observed for pitch space: an increase (strengthening) of the kappa illusion with increasing pitch velocity.

Akerboom et al. (1983) performed a crucial sixth experiment, further investigating Axelrod and Powazek's (1972) finding that the apparent rate of the click sequence depends on the angular separation of the two sound sources. Instead of the method of constant stimuli used by Axelrod and Powazek, Akerboom et al. used the stop-RT task. Clicks in the sequences were presented alternately over loudspeakers and the angular separation between speakers varied from 0 to 180° in steps of 30°. Although the kappa illusion obtained was only 13 ms time dilation when the separation was 180° (compared to 25 ms in the headphones condition), the prediction that the kappa illusion should increase with increasing spatial separation was clearly confirmed. Moreover, the amount of time dilation (apparent slowing down) increased approximately linearly ($r^2 = .86$) with increasing spatial separation between sound locations.

In conclusion, the work by Grondin and Plourde (2007), the Axelrod group, and the ten Hoopen group clearly shows that some form of kappa illusion can operate in auditory ambient space. Extra evidence that the kappa illusion typically arises in spatiotemporal contexts was offered by the Axelrod group that found the same illusion to operate in the tactile modality. Axelrod and Nakao (1974) reported that a sequence of bimanually alternating vibrations had a slower apparent rate than unimanual sequences.

5.3. Modern Time Illusions

The illusion of a divided time interval, subjective rhythm, and the kappa illusion have been reported many decades ago in the time perception literature. More recently, time perception researchers have reported other systematic temporal distortions.

5.3.1. *Time Shrinking*

Time shrinking (TS) is a new illusory phenomenon in auditory time perception that has been first reported by Nakajima and ten Hoopen (1988) in Japanese, and in English by Nakajima, ten Hoopen, and van der Wilk (1991). When three successive short sound bursts mark two neighboring empty durations, the perception of the second duration (t_2) can be affected by the first duration (t_1) under certain time conditions. When t_2 is physically longer than t_1 and the difference between t_2 and t_1 is smaller than about 100 ms, t_2 is often underestimated to a considerable degree. For example, Nakajima et al. (1991) measured points of subjective equality (PSEs) of t_2 in $/t_1/t_2/$ patterns (slashes denote short sound markers delimiting t_1 and t_2) using the method of adjustment. In the experiment, the listeners were instructed to match a comparison time interval (t_c), which was presented a few seconds after the $/t_1/t_2/$ pattern, to the subjective duration of t_2. The results showed that when t_2 was 120 ms and t_1 was 45, 70, and 95 ms, the experimental PSEs of t_2 were significantly smaller than the control PSEs (adjustments of $/t_c/$ to $/t_2/$ presented solely) by about 50, 40, and 20 ms, respectively (see Figure 5.10).

To reliably establish the novelty of this illusory phenomenon, ten Hoopen et al. (1993) conducted three experiments and their results showed that the illusion did not result from (i) a difficulty in resolving the temporal structure, (ii) the misjudgment of the participants that they had adjusted t_c to t_1 instead of t_2, and (iii) a difficulty in detecting the temporal position of the second sound burst caused by forward masking of the first sound burst. These results rejected the alternative explanations for TS based on two types of erroneous judgment and a psychoacoustical argument. Allan and Gibbon (1994) argued that TS could be interpreted as a kind of TOE (see Chapter 3) in the time domain. Sasaki, Suetomi, Nakajima, and ten Hoopen (2002) claimed that even though there are some similarities between TS and TOE, like both being not the result of response bias but rather the cause of perceptual/memory assimilation processes, there are many differences as well. One difference is the robustness of the phenomena. TOEs vary with the psychophysical method used,

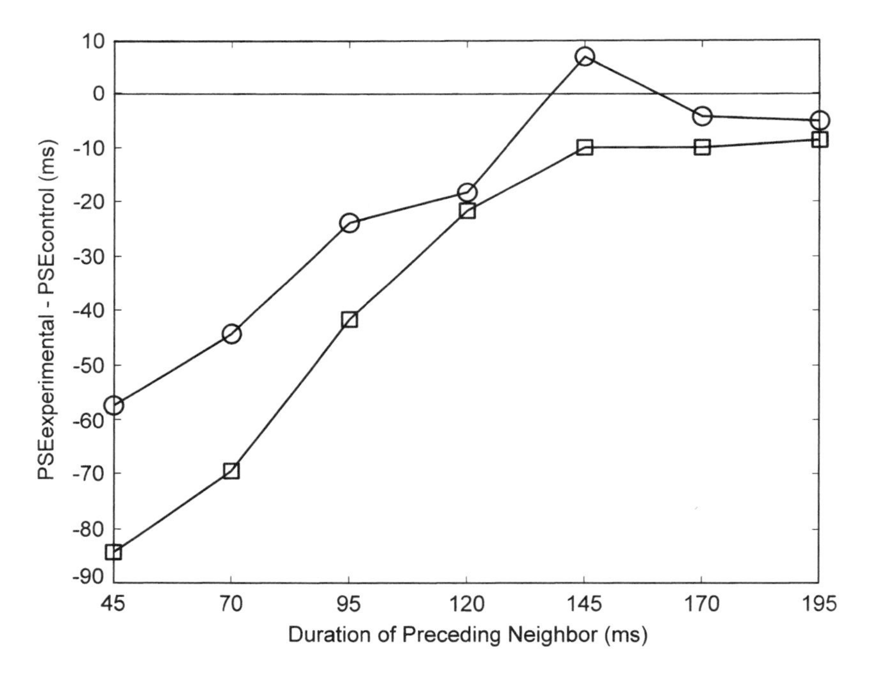

Figure 5.10: Results of Nakajima and ten Hoopen (1988): the mean differences between the experimental and the control points of subjective equality (PSEexperimental – PSEcontrol) of a standard empty time interval (S) of 120 ms as a function of the duration of the immediately preceding empty time interval (P). Square markers are the data of participant GtH and circle markers those of participant YN.

whereas TS appears clearly not only by using the method of adjustment (e.g., Nakajima et al., 1991; Nakajima et al., 2004) but also by using the method of constant stimuli (ten Hoopen et al., 1993), an adaptive method (ten Hoopen et al., 1995; ten Hoopen, Beumer, & Nakajima, 1996), the transformed up–down method (Sasaki, Nakajima, & ten Hoopen, 1998), the method of paired comparisons (ten Hoopen, Boon, Sasaki, & Nakajima, 2006, Miyauchi & Nakajima, 2007), and cross-modal judgments (ten Hoopen et al., 2006). Another difference is that TOE effects are often (but not always) rather small and vary considerably between participants, whereas the TS effects are enormous, and the variability between participants is relatively low (Suetomi & Nakajima, 1998; ten Hoopen et al., 1993; ten Hoopen et al., 2006). The most crucial difference with TOE is that TS takes place only in a narrow time range based on absolute time differences between neighboring durations. When the above considerations are taken into account, TS appears to be a new illusory phenomenon.

To reveal the mechanism of TS, its appearance was systematically investigated by varying the physical time duration of two neighboring time intervals. Nakajima, ten Hoopen, Hilkhuysen, and Sasaki (1992) fixed t_1 at 50 ms, and t_2, of which the duration had to be adjusted by t_c, varied from 40 to 280 ms. The results showed that when the physical duration of t_2 was from 50 to 140 ms, t_2 was significantly underestimated. Beyond 140 ms, the underestimation of t_2 vanished quickly. ten Hoopen et al. (1993) showed this tendency to hold for t_1 values of 40, 80, and 160 ms as well. In addition, when the difference between t_2 and t_1 $(t_2 - t_1)$ was about 80 ms, the amount of TS was maximum regardless of the physical duration of t_1. When $(t_2 - t_1)$ exceeded about 100 ms, TS disappeared suddenly in all t_1 conditions. These results suggested that the absolute difference, not the relative difference, between t_2 and t_1 plays a critical role in the appearance of TS.

Recently, Nakajima et al. (2004) studied the apparent lawfulness of the above tendencies in a more systematic way. They applied a wide range of t_1 from 40 to 480 ms, in steps of 40 ms and varied t_2 from t_1 to $(t_1 + 160)$ ms in steps of 40 ms, that is $(t_2 - t_1)$ was varied from 0 to 160 ms in steps of 40 ms. The results confirmed the following tendencies for the appearance of TS: (i) When $0 \leq t_2 - t_1 \leq 100$ ms, TS takes place, (ii) the amount of TS is maximum when $t_2 - t_1$ is about 80 ms, and (iii) TS decreases rapidly when t_1 exceeds 200 ms (see Figure 5.2). Nakajima et al. (2004) also suggested a model to elucidate the underlying process of TS. The model has two cornerstones: the "processing time hypothesis" (Nakajima, 1987; Nakajima et al., 1988; see Section 5.2.1) and the "concept of assimilation." The authors assumed that the processing time hypothesis holds that the mental time structure of a $/t_1/t_2/$ pattern is $/t_1 + \alpha/t_2 + \alpha/$; however, when t_1 is not too much smaller than t_2, the perceptual system can assimilate the second mental time duration to the first mental time duration by cutting the temporal processing time, α, for the second duration. The temporal processing time for t_2 in which the assimilation takes place is denoted by α' and the value of α' is between 0 and α ms. A quasi-equality between t_1 and t_2 can be detected when $\alpha' = (t_1 + \alpha) - t_2$ ms has passed for the additional processing of t_2. Then, the perceptual system detects the equality $t_1 + \alpha = t_2 + \alpha'$ (see Nakajima et al., 2004 for more details).

TS is not affected by variation of sound marker frequency. Remijn et al. (1999) found that TS clearly appeared even when the sound marker frequencies differed by more than two octaves. Their results suggest that even though the three sound markers may have resided in potentially different streams, TS is not much affected by streaming. On the other hand, the appearance of TS is affected by the sound marker duration. It was found that the amount of TS decreased as the marker duration increased (Yamashita & Nakajima, 1999), and the time condition, in which the amount of the underestimation of t_2 is at maximum, seemed to shift from $t_2 - t_1 = 80$ ms to 60 ms when the marker durations were more than 20 ms (Fujishima & Nakajima, 2006). Yamashita & Nakajima (1999) conducted a supplementary experiment in which one of the three markers in a /160/240/ pattern was varied from 10 to 122 ms and the other two markers were fixed at 10 ms. The results showed that the amount of TS was clearly reduced as a function of the duration of only the final marker. This result demonstrates that when clear enough information of the end of the whole stimulus pattern is not available before the end of the maximum additional processing time for t_2, the detection of the quasi-equality between t_1 and t_2 may be interrupted.

In the above studies, the appearance of TS had been investigated in temporal patterns consisting of two neighboring intervals. To shed light on the appearance of TS in more complex patterns, Remijn et al. (1999) varied the number of preceding intervals between 0 (control condition), 1, 2, 3, 4, and 5 intervals, and measured the PSEs of the consecutive standard interval. When the relationship between the preceding and last intervals satisfied the conditions in which TS takes place, there is no accumulating effect of the number of the preceding intervals. For example, when the preceding neighbors were 50 ms, and the last interval was 100 ms, the PSE of the last interval was around 55 ms regardless of the number of preceding neighbors. Thus, TS is not much affected by the length of the preceding temporal isochronous grid.

In Remijn et al.'s (1999) study, only constant durations within the preceding interval series were applied. To obtain a more detailed view of temporal interactions, Sasaki et al. (2002) investigated whether underestimations of the last interval (t_3) of three successive durations ($/t_1/t_2/t_3/$) would occur by systematically varying the physical durations of t_1, t_2, and t_3. The results showed that t_3 could be affected directly not only by t_2 but also by the relationship between t_1 and t_2, and by the whole time structure, because, even though the relationship between t_2 and t_3 met the conditions necessary for the operation of TS, the perceived duration of t_3 was not shrunk under some time conditions. For example, in the /120/200/ control pattern, the last interval was shrunk to 148 ms. However, when one more preceding interval of 80 ms was added before the /120/200/ pattern (/80/120/200/), the PSE of the last interval became 195 ms. It appeared that t_1 could shrink t_2, and as a result, the subjective duration of t_2 could become inappropriate to shrink t_3. When t_1 was 200 ms (/200/120/200/), TS also disappeared. When there was a similarity between t_1 and t_3, the figural grouping of the first two sound markers and that of the last two sound markers might stand out as a figural Gestalt. As a result, the subjective duration of t_2, residing in the background, might become too weak to shrink t_3. Auditory Gestalt principles of similarity of durations and of temporal proximity could invoke strong figural organizations in these $/t_1/t_2/t_3/$ patterns, which rendered the TS mechanism inoperative. Several auditory demonstrations of the effects discussed above are recorded on the CD accompanying the book by Suetomi, Nakajima, Sasaki, and ten Hoopen (2000).

TS may serve as a tool to further investigate how the auditory and visual modalities process time. Arao, Suetomi, and Nakajima (2000) examined whether a similar kind of TS underestimation would take place with visual temporal patterns comprising three LED flashes, and revealed that underestimation of the last interval also could occur in the visual modality. Their results indicated that the visual system, like the auditory one, needs additional processing time to establish the durations of empty time intervals, and that the visual system also can assimilate the second mental interval to the first one by cutting temporal processing time for the second duration. Simply said, TS could be established, but its temporal lawfulness differed from that in the auditory modality. Whereas TS in the auditory system is most salient when $t_2 - t_1$ is about 80 ms and decreases quickly when $t_2 - t_1$ gets longer, TS for the visual system is most salient when t_2/t_1 is about 1.5 and decreases when it approaches 2.0. In short, for the auditory system the *difference* between t_2 and t_1 has a psychological reality, and in the visual system the *ratio* between t_2 and t_1 has psychological reality.

5.3.2. Bilateral Assimilation and Contrast

The typical classic assimilation hypothesis (cf., Fraisse, 1982) applied to $/t_1/t_2/$ patterns holds that the subjective durations of t_1 and t_2 tend to get closer to each other than one would expect on basis of veridical perception of their physical durations. The assimilation caused by TS appeared only in t_2 and there was no solid evidence from the earlier studies of the Nakajima group that the perception of t_1 was affected by t_2 to a considerable degree. Therefore, TS was called the process of unilateral assimilation (e.g., Nakajima et al., 2004). Already in 1998, however, Sasaki et al. discovered that things were slightly more complicated. In addition to studying $/t_1/t_2/$ patterns typically liable to TS, the authors also studied the mirror patterns. PSEs of t_1 and t_2 were obtained by the method of adjustment. One of the patterns was /75/105/ and as expected, TS was observed: the subjective pattern was /74/79/, thus t_2 shrunk 26 ms. Unexpectedly, the mirror pattern /105/75/ was transformed by the auditory system to /88/82/. Obviously, we have a typical case of classic bilateral assimilation here, in which t_1 approached the value of t_2 and vice versa, though the assimilation was not completely symmetric (assimilations of −17 and +7 ms). But notice that both the unilateral assimilation of TS and the bilateral assimilation yielded the subjective patterns /74/79/ and /88/82/ which are perceived isochronously, given the fact that the 5–6 ms difference between t_1 and t_2 values of about 80 ms is subliminal.

This interesting issue remained dormant in the Nakajima group for several years until Miyauchi and Nakajima (2005) decided to establish the temporal conditions under which bilateral assimilation took place more extensively. They had four total duration conditions $(t_1 + t_2) = 120$, 180, 240, and 360 ms. In the 120 ms condition there were five, and in the other conditions seven different $/t_1/t_2/$ patterns chosen such that t_1 increased in small steps, and t_2 decreased complementary. The experimental PSEs of t_1 and t_2 were established by the method of adjustment and the control PSEs were established by presenting $/t_1/$ and $/t_2/$ solely. As an example the results of the 120 ms condition are portrayed in Figure 5.11. The experimental PSEs of t_1 and t_2 are denoted by triangle markers, whereas the control PSEs of t_1 and t_2 presented singly are denoted by square markers. In the left "t_1-matching task" panel and the right "t_2-matching task" panel, one can see that the control PSEs hardly differ from the point of objective equality (POE). In the right panel, traditional TS can be observed in the patterns /40/80/ and 50/70/: the PSEs of $t_2 = 80$ and 70 ms are 46 and 50 ms, respectively. Notice in the right panel that the complementary t_1 values (40 and 50 ms) show a tendency to be slightly overestimated. Clear bilateral assimilation occurs in the /80/40/ pattern: the PSE of t_1 is 55 ms, and the PSE of t_2 is 46 ms. The overall results of their Experiment 1 showed that unilateral and bilateral assimilation took place when $-80\,\text{ms} \leq (t_1 - t_2) \leq 40\,\text{ms}$ (note that the effect of bilateral assimilation was smaller than that of TS).

In addition, there were some data suggesting that contrast of t_1 also takes place. Miyauchi and Nakajima found that when t_1 was longer than $t_2 + 60$ ms, that is, outside the time range in which assimilation took place, t_1 was overestimated by about 20 ms. This overestimation clearly indicated the existence of contrast. In the studies of TS, the phenomenon of contrast had already been established for the

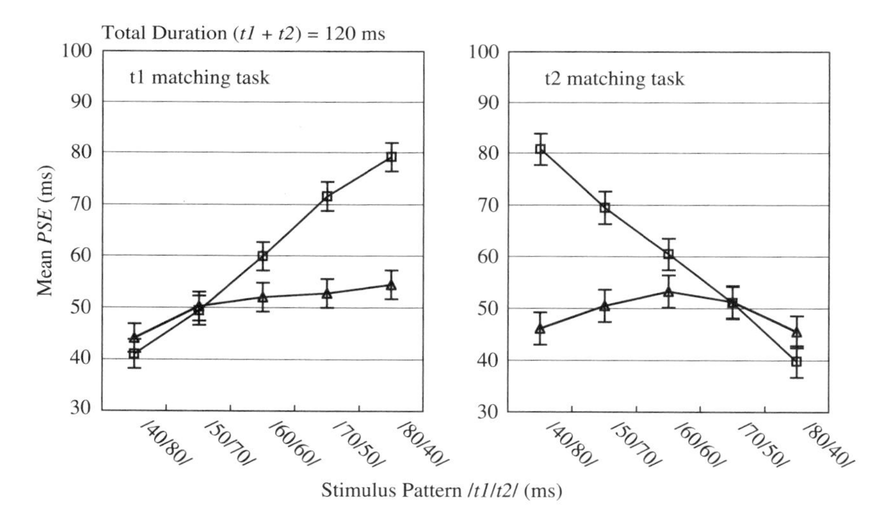

Figure 5.11: Results of Miyauchi and Nakajima (2005): the mean points of subjective equality (PSE) of t_1 and t_2 in the five patterns of which the total duration was 120 ms. The experimental PSEs of t_1 and t_2 are denoted by triangle markers, whereas the control PSEs of t_1 and t_2 presented singly are denoted by square markers.

subjective duration of t_2. When the difference between t_2 and t_1 exceeded 100 ms, TS suddenly disappeared, and many overestimations of t_2 appeared instead. The phenomena of assimilation and contrast of time intervals might be useful for the clarification of the temporal boundaries within which neighboring durations in a sequence are perceived isochronously.

5.3.3. 1:1 Temporal Category

When $-80\,\text{ms} \leq (t_1 - t_2) \leq 40\,\text{ms}$, the perceptual durations of both t_1 and t_2 approach each other due to unilateral (TS) and bilateral assimilation, and the heard impression of the temporal pattern is typically 1:1, that is, a perceived pattern of isochrony. On the other hand, when t_1 and t_2 differ enough, they can be contrasted, that is, the boundary of the 1:1 rhythmic category is perceptually boosted. Thus, both assimilation and contrast cause the constitution of the 1:1 rhythmic category in the temporal domain.

To present evidence that TS gives rise to categorical perception, ten Hoopen et al. (2006) applied the method of paired comparisons and measured the similarity between pairs of $/t_1/t_2/$ patterns having a total duration of 320 ms (Experiments 2 and 3). The results of a cluster analysis and a scaling analysis showed that the patterns /115/205/, /120/200/, /125/195/,..., /160/160/, /165/155/, /170/150/ formed a 1:1 rhythmic category. Notice that this category is very asymmetric as a cause of the TS illusion: nine patterns to the left of the objective 1:1 pattern (/160/ 160/), and only two patterns to the right of pattern /160/160/. These results were substantiated by Experiment 4, in which participants did a cross-modal matching task. Of each of the 57 auditory patterns /20/300/, /25/295/,..., /295/25/, /300/20/, each presented singly in random order, the participants had to visually indicate by proportionally dividing a line length, how they had perceived the heard ratio between t_1 and t_2. A remarkable clear 1:1 category was observed comprising the patterns /120/ 200/, /125/195/,..., /160/160/, /165/155/, /170/150/ (see Figure 5.12). These patterns met the conditions necessary for the appearance of TS and bilateral assimilation.

Miyauchi and Nakajima (2007) estimated the boundaries of the 1:1 categories of $/t_1/t_2/$ patterns having total durations of 180, 360, 540, and 720 ms by requiring same–different judgments between t_1 and t_2 in the $/t_1/t_2/$ patterns. They plotted the percentages of "same" responses as a function of the difference between t_1 and t_2, and fitted sigmoids. The 50% level of the sigmoids determined the boundaries. When the total duration was 180 ms, the $t_1 - t_2$ boundaries embracing the 1:1 category were -75 and 49 ms (rounded), being clearly asymmetric with regard to $t_1 - t_2 = 0$ ms. To compare this result with our previous studies, we also give the 1:1 boundaries in terms of patterns (rounded to 5 ms): /55/125/ and /115/65/. For the total duration of 360 ms, the embracing boundaries were -75 and 52 ms, again asymmetric, and in terms of patterns: /145/215/ and /205/155/. Note that the $(t_2 - t_1)$ differences of the left patterns are 70 ms for both total durations (180 and 360 ms), where we have a typical TS boundary of the 1:1 category. The $t_1 - t_2$ differences of the right patterns

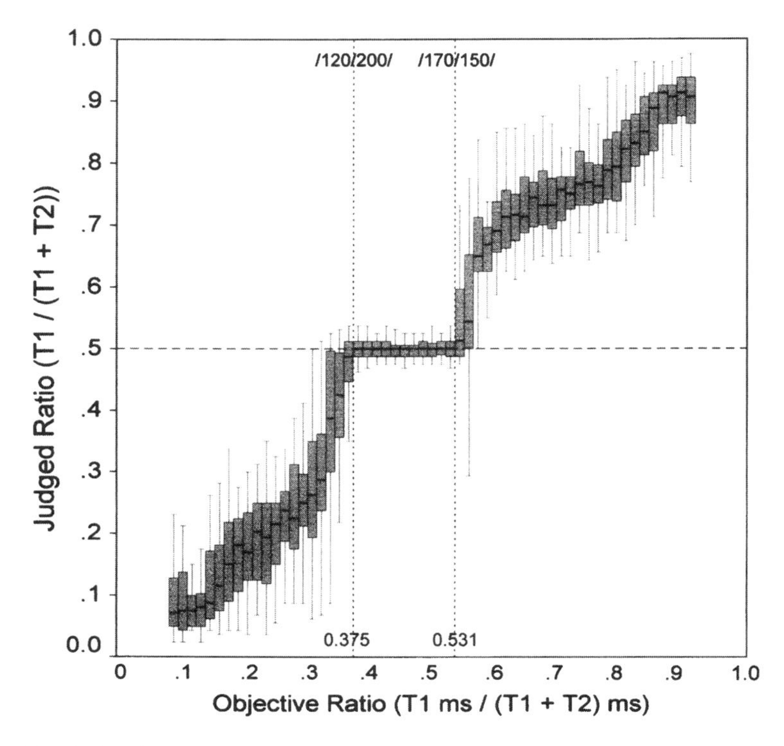

Figure 5.12: Judged temporal ratio in the visual/auditory cross modal matching task (ten Hoopen et al., 2006). Judged $T_1/(T_1 + T_2)$ in percentages as a function of the objective T_1 duration, represented as box and whisker plots of the 32 judgments for each of the 57 auditory temporal patterns from /20/300/ ms to /300/20/ ms. The inserted vertical dotted lines indicate the asymmetric 1:1 category boundaries.

are both 50 ms, where we have a typical boundary of the 1:1 category determined by bilateral assimilation. The fact that this boundary estimate of $t_1 - t_2 = 50$ ms is somewhat larger than the 40 ms found in the study by Miyauchi and Nakajima (2005) might be caused by the different methods applied: the method of adjustment versus the same–different judgments in the study by Miyauchi & Nakajima (2007). When the total duration was 540 ms, the 1:1 category became slightly more symmetric: the $t_1 - t_2$ boundary estimates were −68 and 60 ms, and in terms of patterns: /235/305/ and /300/240/. When the total duration was 720 ms, these figures were −73 and 82 ms, thus slightly asymmetric in the opposite direction, and in terms of patterns, the 1:1 category boundaries were /325/395/ and /400/320/. Whereas the category widths were almost equal when the total duration was 180, 360, and 540 ms (124, 127, and 128 ms, respectively), the category width at 720 ms was larger (155 ms).

In rhythm perception, studies of categorical perception have been performed to establish categorical boundaries between rhythms with simple integral ratios like 2:1 and 1:1 (e.g., Clarke, 1987; Fraisse, 1978, 1982; Povel, 1981, 1984). The boundaries of such rhythmic categories appear to be changed by age, musical experience, and context of temporal pattern (Desain & Honing, 2003; Drake, 1993; Large, 2000, see Chapter 6). In contrast, the asymmetric 1:1 category resulting from unilateral (TS) and bilateral assimilation appears very robust. The emergence of this category was not affected by the way of measurement, the amount of musical training, and cultural (Dutch versus Japanese) difference (ten Hoopen et al., 2006). In addition, the absolute difference between neighboring durations t_1 and t_2 played a critical role in the perceptual construction of the category. Furthermore, in older work by one of us (Nakajima et al., 1988) no evidence of other rhythmic categories of integral ratios appeared by the ratio judgment experiments with two neighboring empty durations. We suspect that the asymmetrical 1:1 category may be first formed in the subjective time dimension before the formation of other rhythmic categories can take place. The time-shrinking illusion, and very probably bilateral assimilation as well, not only produces strong perceptual phenomena but also can affect the temporal patterning of musical performances such that systematic deviations from the score arise (Gabrielsson, 1974; Stobart & Cross, 2000; ten Hoopen et al., 2006).

5.3.4. Time Swelling

The time-swelling illusion was accidentally discovered by Sasaki, Nakajima, & ten Hoopen (1993) who reasoned that because time shrinking (TS) is a central and robust auditory perceptual process, it might operate not only on patterns comprising empty durations but also on patterns comprising filled durations. The authors presented temporal patterns consisting of two contiguous sine tones of 1000 Hz. In order to enable the listener to distinguish between the contiguous filled durations t_1 and t_2, t_1 was 76 dB SPL, and t_2 was 70 dB SPL (see Figure 5.13, bottom). In the same vein as in their previous experiments utilizing empty time intervals (see Figure 5.13, top), the filled duration t_2 had to be matched by a variable comparison filled duration (t_c) to establish the PSE of t_2. Under the hypothesis that TS operates on filled duration

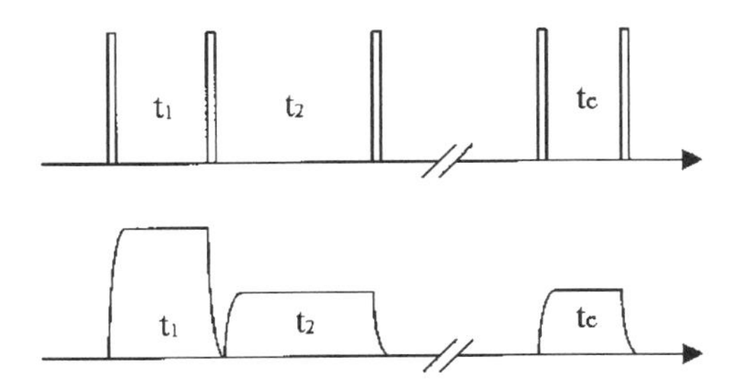

Figure 5.13: Top: typical auditory temporal $/t_1/t_2/$ pattern of empty durations followed by an empty duration comparison interval (t_c), all marked by short sounds, as used in time-shrinking studies. Bottom: analogous pattern of filled durations as used by Sasaki et al. (1993).

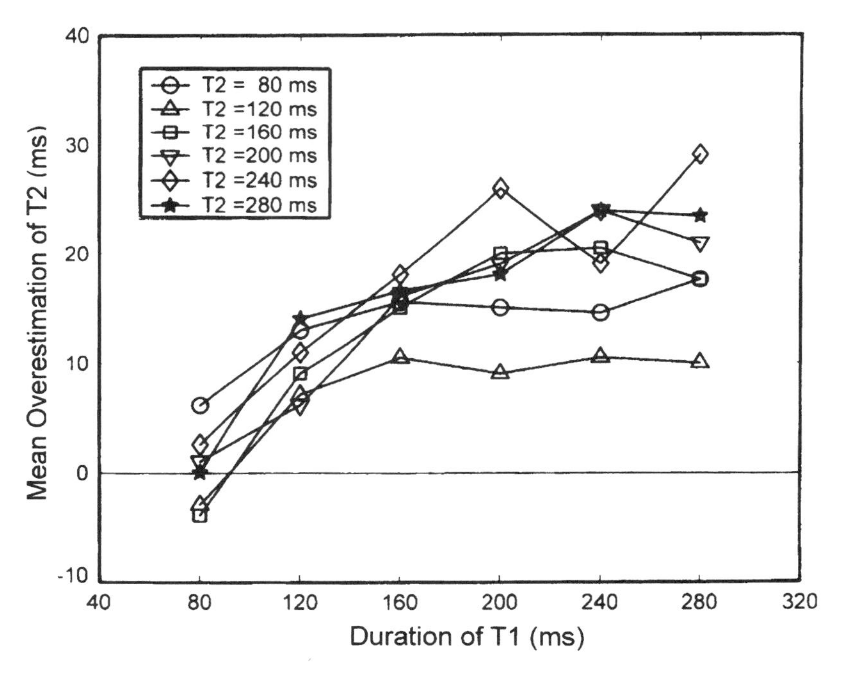

Figure 5.14: Results of Sasaki et al. (1993). Mean overestimations of t_2 as a function of the durations of t_1 and t_2.

patterns too, the expectation was that t_2 should be underestimated in $/t_1/t_2/$ patterns typically liable to TS (see Figure 5.14 for these patterns). However, this was not the case at all, on the contrary, in almost all temporal patterns, *overestimations* of t_2 were established. Because the data were published in Japanese, and may not be so easily accessible, we reproduce Figure 2 of Sasaki et al. (1993) here as Figure 5.14. The authors suspected that the unexpected overestimations of t_2 might be related to auditory continuity effects.

The first study reporting an auditory continuity effect was by Miller and Licklider (1950). If 50 ms bursts of a sine tone and more intense white noise were alternated one by one, the sine tone appeared to continue through the noise. The authors drew an analogy to the visual "picket fence" effect. Thurlow (1957) established a continuity effect by alternating sine tones of different frequencies and called it an auditory figure-ground effect. Vicario (1960), who independently discovered a continuity effect, called it the acoustic tunnel effect. It seems as if the auditory system interprets the more intense sounds, either noises or sine tones, as "figure" and creates connecting fainter sounds in between the actual present ones to form a continuous "background." This interesting continuity effect remained dormant in the literature and it was not until more than two decades later that the Warren group (e.g., Warren, Obusek, & Ackroff, 1972) replicated the continuity effect, renamed it "auditory induction," and formulated their explanation: "If there is contextual evidence that a sound may be present at a given time, and if the peripheral units stimulated by a louder sound include those which would be stimulated by the anticipated fainter sound, then the fainter sound may be heard as present" (p. 1151). At this point, it is important to distinguish between actual and potential simultaneous masking. If, for example, a small part of a speech stream is masked by a loud cough, the auditory system might restore the masked speech sounds, called phonemic restoration (see Samuel, 1996 for a summary of the literature). However, in case of the continuity effect, the fainter sounds are physically absent during the presence of the louder sounds and therefore cannot be restored by definition, but they are induced or synthesized by the perceptual system if there is sufficient contextual information.

The smallest building block of the auditory "picket fence" containing just enough context seems to be: "faint sound–loud sound–faint sound." There are indeed several studies that established the continuity illusion with just one building block (e.g., Bennett, Parasuraman, Howard, & O'Toole, 1984; Kluender & Jenison, 1992), that is, there is no need for repetitive cycling of fainter with louder sounds to obtain the induced perceptual continuity of the faint sound. For clarity of further discussion, we explain some jargon: When the alternating faint and loud sounds have the same spectral compositions (tone–tone or noise–noise), the continuity is called homophonic. When the faint and loud sounds have different spectral compositions (noise–tone), the continuity is called heterophonic. The louder sound is called the inducer and the fainter sound the inducee (cf., Warren, 1999).

The patterns used by Sasaki et al. (1993) did not even consist of the elementary building block: The patterns only comprised a 76 dB sine tone followed by a 70 dB sine tone. The authors proposed that the overestimation of the duration of the trailing fainter sine tone might be caused by incomplete temporal induction. A possible explanation in terms of Warren's rule is that the more intense tone is a potential masker. However, Ueda and Ohtsuki (1996) offered strong evidence against such an explanation. They replicated Sasaki et al.'s (1993) study with an important improvement. They varied the intensity level difference between the leading and the contiguously trailing sine tone of 70 dB. The leading tone could be either 76 or 64 dB. In the pattern 280–240 ms, where Sasaki et al. (1993) found the biggest overestimation of t_2 by about 30 ms, Ueda and Ohtsuki established an overestimation of t_2 by about 30 ms when the t_1 sine tone was 76 dB, but they established also an overestimation of 30 ms when t_1 was 64 dB. Hence, Ueda and Ohtsuki argued that the potential masker rule of Warren et al. could not explain the illusory lengthening of t_2.

A study by Simons (1995), carried out just before Ueda and Ohtsuki's study, supports their results and conclusion. Simons had a heterophonic condition in which a 1/3 octave band noise centered around 1000 Hz and lasting 1 s was immediately followed by a 200 ms sine tone of 1.000 Hz. The intensity level differences with the band noise were +6, 0, and −6 dB. He established an overestimation of 30 ms of the 200 ms tone of 1000 Hz, when the band noise was 6 dB more intense. Note the precise correspondence between this 30 ms overestimation with the overestimations reported by Sasaki et al. (1993) and Ueda and Ohtsuki (1996). When the band noise and sine tone had equal intensity (the 0 dB condition), Simons found a significant overestimation of 20 ms of the 200 ms tone. Even when the sine tone was −6 dB with respect to the band noise intensity level, he found a small but significant overestimation of 5 ms. These data support Ueda and Ohtsuki's results and their rejection of Warren's potential masker explanation.

It is interesting that the Warren group observed incomplete homophonic continuity in their repetitive cycling paradigm. Warren, Bashford, Healy, and Brubaker (1994) reported increases in the apparent duration of the fainter sound (the inducee), which alternated with a sound of higher intensity (the inducer). The inducer was a 70 dB, 1 kHz sine tone, and the inducee was a 66 dB sine tone, varying between nine frequency values, one value also 1 kHz, and the other eight frequencies were 1, 2, 6, and 10 semitones (STs) higher or lower. Both the inducer and the inducee lasted 200 ms. The apparent duration of the inducee was established by the method of adjustment. It was found that the subjective duration of the 1 kHz inducee was 400 ms, implying that the inducee perceptually continued completely through the inducer. Thus, though the POE of the inducee was 200 ms, its PSE was 400 ms. Incomplete continuity was found for the other frequencies, the subjective durations of the inducees were significantly longer than their baseline subjective durations (measured in absence of the inducer), except for frequencies which were 6 and 10 semitones lower than 1kHz. It was found that the closer the frequencies of inducer and inducee were, the larger the overestimation of the inducee became, in particular when the frequency of the inducee was higher than that of the inducer. In sum, in addition to complete induction when the center frequencies of the inducer and inducee were both 1 kHz, we have also examples of incomplete induction in the Warren et al.'s (1994) study.

In the pioneering work of Sasaki et al. (1993), Simons (1995), and Ueda and Ohtsuki (1996), significant overestimations of the filled duration t_2 were established, and Sasaki et al. called this illusion "time swelling." Several follow-up experiments were performed in the laboratory of the present first author (GtH) of which we will summarize the most relevant ones now. Because the pattern durations in the pioneering studies were relatively short, van Buuringen (1997) decided to apply longer durations, and he also varied the intensity level difference between the first and second filled durations (t_1 and t_2). His stimuli were heterophonic: a 1/3 octave noise band around 1000 Hz lasting 1 s was immediately followed by a pure sine tone of 1000 Hz, which could last 200, 400, or 600 ms. Participants were required to adjust the duration of a 1000 Hz comparison sine tone (t_c) presented 2 s after the filled $/t_1/t_2/$ pattern as many times as they wanted until satisfied by the match between t_2 and t_c. The final adjustment was registered as the PSE. There was a control condition in which the sine tones had to be matched when not preceded by the band noise. Table 5.3 gives the differences between the experimental and control PSEs, and shows clearly that t_2 was overestimated at all durations and intensity level differences. The pattern is clear: illusory lengthening increases with increasing t_2 duration and with increasing intensity level difference. Nonetheless, even at the −6 dB level difference the overestimations of the t_2 duration were significant, replicating Simons (1995) and Ueda and Ohtsuki (1996). Hence, van Buuringen's study amplified the doubt about the explanatory value of Warren's rule of potential simultaneous masking for time swelling.

van Bergen et al. (1997) also extended the range of t_2 durations: They used durations from 100 to 800 ms in steps of 100 ms. The intensity level difference between the preceding 1/3 octave band noise of 1 s and the contiguously following sine tone was kept constant at 6 dB, but the center frequency of the band noise was varied between 500, 1000, and 2000 Hz. The sine tone frequency was varied between 500, 1000, and 2000 Hz as well, and all nine frequency combinations of band noise and sine tone were tested. The procedure was the same as that of van Buuringen (1997). The results showed that the overestimations increase with increasing t_2 duration and are larger when the band noise center frequency and the sine tone frequency are equal. Nevertheless, when the sine tone frequency deviated 1 or even 2 octaves from the band noise center frequencies of 500 and 2000 Hz, substantial overestimations were also obtained at the durations from 400 to 800 ms, and curiously enough, the overestimations hardly differed between 1 and 2 octaves deviation between band noise and sine tone. In case the band noise center frequency was 1000 Hz, the overestimations of the 2000 Hz sine tones (1 octave higher) were larger than those of the 500 Hz sine tones (1 octave lower).

Bakker et al. (1998) investigated the effect of the duration t_1 of the *band noise* on the amount of time swelling of t_2. Like in the previous experiments, the band noise was 1/3 octave centered around 1000 Hz. The duration of the band noise could be 50, 100, 150, 200, 300, 400, or 500 ms. Because loudness increases with increasing duration of the noise, Bakker et al. decided to equalize the loudness by increasing the intensity level for each duration relative to the intensity of the longest band noise of 500 ms. To accomplish this iso-loudness criterion, they performed an experiment in which participants had to adjust the intensity of each duration until its loudness was the same as that of the standard 76 dB SPL 500 ms band noise. The resulting dB values ranged rather linearly between 76 dB (500 ms) and 78 dB (50 ms), and these dB values were adopted for the experiment proper. The band noise was immediately followed by a relatively short 1000 Hz sine tone of 300 ms or a relatively long

Table 5.3: Mean experimental points of subjective equality (PSEexp) and control points of subjective equality (PSEcon) as a function of intensity level difference (−6, 0, and +6 dB) and tone duration (200, 400, and 600 ms). All values are in ms (van Buuringen, 1997).

	Intensity level difference								
	−6 dB			**0 dB**			**+6 dB**		
Tone duration (ms)	200	400	600	200	400	600	200	400	600
PSEexp	216	422	635	228	466	684	239	486	692
PSEcon	198	402	600	198	402	600	198	402	600
Overestimations	18	20	35	30	64	84	41	84	92

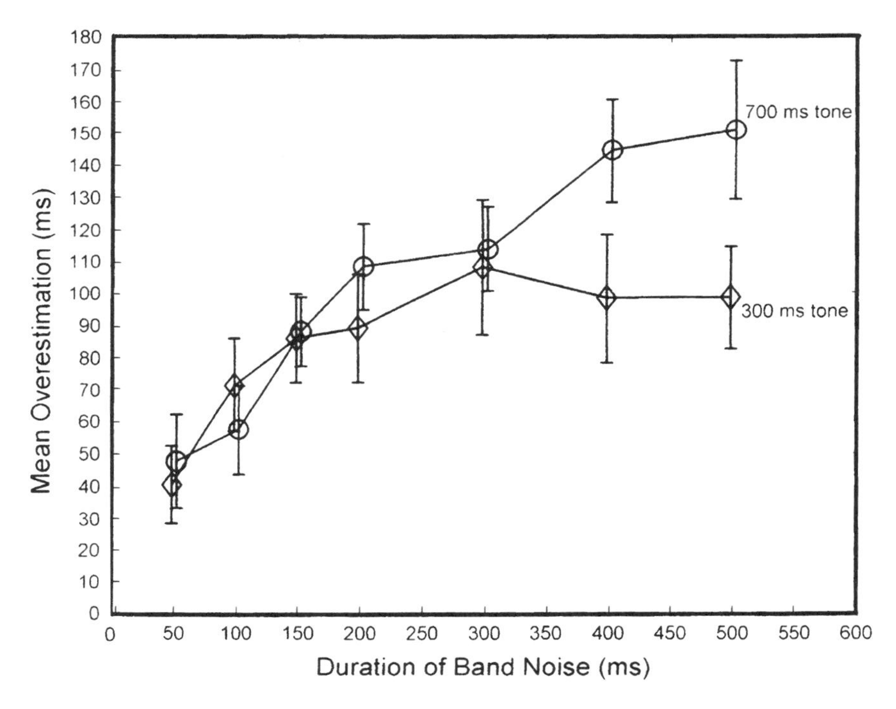

Figure 5.15: Results of Bakker et al. (1998). Mean overestimation of a sine tone of 1000 Hz as a function of its duration (300 or 700 ms), and the duration of the immediately preceding 1/3 octave band noise with center frequency 1000 Hz.

1000 Hz sine tone of 700 ms. The participants had to adjust t_c until it matched the duration of t_2. Figure 5.15 portrays the results. Even when the preceding band noise was only as short as 50 ms, the overestimations of the sine tone durations of 300 and 700 ms were 40–50 ms, and increased to 110 ms when the band noise duration increased to 300 ms. At this value, there was a dissociation of the amount of time swelling: When the band noise duration increased further to 400 and 500 ms, the overestimation of the 300 ms sine tone remained the same, but for the 700 ms tone the overestimation increased to 150 ms. The most salient finding by Bakker et al. was that even a preceding band noise as short as 50 ms already caused huge overestimations of the succeeding sine tone. This fact suggests that with the present stimuli, it might be rather actual forward masking instead of potential simultaneous masking that produces time swelling of the sine tone.

Support for this conviction can be found in the study by Kallman and Morris (1984) who required their participants to judge whether a target sine tone, which had a duration of 38 or 72 ms, was short or long. The target tone was preceded or succeeded by a masking tone of 100 ms. The ISI between masker and target (or target and masker) was varied between 20, 40, 60, 80, 160, 250, and 500 ms. Both the forward and backward masking results showed that the percentage correct judgments of the sine tone duration (short or long) decreased with decreasing ISI, and decreased at a greater rate for the shorter ISIs. At the ISI of 20 ms, duration judgments were worst. The backward masking results replicated a previous study by Massaro and Idson (1976), but the forward masking results could not be predicted by Massaro's interruption theory (e.g., Massaro, 1975). Kallman and Morris stated that: "This finding is problematic to an interruption theory of duration masking and suggests that alternative explanations of auditory duration masking — for example, explanations that incorporate integrative processes — need to be developed" (p. 609).

Massier (1997) tested the conviction that the overestimation of the sine tone might be the result of forward masking by the immediately preceding band noise. Instead of asking for a short–long judgment about the duration of the sine tone, as was done by Kallman and Morris, he required his participants to adjust the duration of t_c to that of the sine tone (t_2). Massier varied the gap size between the band noise and the sine tone from 0 ms (the control) to 50 ms in steps of 10 ms. The band noise was 1/3 octave, centered around 1000 Hz, and the 1000 Hz sine tone duration was varied between 100 and 800 ms in steps of 100 ms. At all eight durations he observed that the overestimations were dramatically reduced by insertion of a 10 ms gap, and were nullified or nearly so when the gap was 20 ms. Figure 5.16 shows the reduction of time swelling as a function of the gap size, averaged over the eight durations.

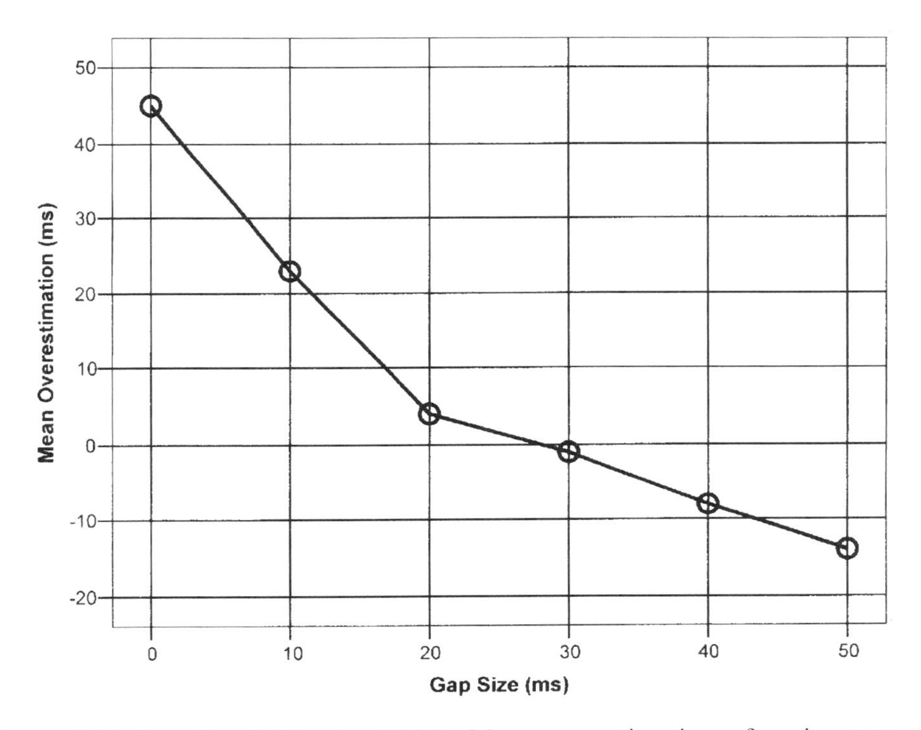

Figure 5.16: Results of Massier (1997). Mean overestimation of a sine tone of 1000 Hz preceded by a 1/3 octave band noise with center frequency 1000 Hz as a function of the gap size between band noise and sine tone.

At this place it seems worthwhile to refer to an interesting series of studies done by Tsuzaki and colleagues. Whereas in the experiments discussed above, the band noise preceded the sound (noise or tone) to be judged for duration, Tsuzaki et al. replaced part of the sound (speech or tone) by noise after it had started. By and large, the duration of the manipulated speech sound or tone shrunk as compared to the perceived duration of the intact sound. Although this duration shrinkage was highly significant, it was moderate as compared to the amounts of time swelling as discussed above. At the present state of our knowledge it is difficult to explain the perceptual processes underpinning of Tsuzaki et al.'s results and hence we refer to the studies by Tsuzaki and Kato (2000), Tsuzaki, Kato, and Tanaka (2003), and Tsuzaki and Kato (2005a, b) for possible explanations. But one thing seems apparent: duration shrinkage in the Tsuzaki's paradigm with continuous sounds differs fundamentally from time shrinking in the Nakajima's paradigm with empty durations as was aptly stated by Tsuzaki and Kato (2005b, p. 41). We now return to the time-swelling illusion to give its explanation in terms of the event construction model.

5.3.4.1. Event construction model Although Sasaki et al. (1993) initially supposed that time swelling might be related to the continuity illusion, there are two arguments against this supposition. Firstly, stimulus patterns comprising a band noise, contiguously followed by a sine tone, cannot by definition give a clue to the perceptual system that a tone might continue through the noise, for the simple reason that there is no tone preceding the noise. Secondly, Ueda and Ohtsuki (1996), Simons (1995), and van Buuringen (1997) convincingly showed that the overestimations could also occur when the leading tone (in tone–tone patterns) or leading band noise (in the band noise–tone patterns) was equally or even less intense than the trailing tone. Thus, an alternative explanation is that the onset of the trailing sine tone is perceptually blurred by actual forward masking (the amount of blurring being determined by the intensity and frequency relations between forward masker and sine tone). According to the auditory grammar of Nakajima, an auditory event should start with an onset (a subevent), and if the onset is masked, it should be perceptually restored. The perceptual act of restoration, however, takes time and this mental processing time adds to the duration of the sine tone. This is an elaboration of Kallman and Morris' (1984) proposal that integrative processes should be incorporated to explain the effect of forward masking on auditory duration, and we will now discuss this elaboration in detail.

As said in the introduction, Nakajima presented an "event construction model" for auditory perceptual organization containing a simple grammar. The key idea of this model is that there are elements smaller than auditory events, so-called subevents: onset, termination, filling, and silence as we discussed in the introduction. The grammar (see Figure 5.17) determines which temporal orders of subevents are grammatical and which ones are not.

Let us now explain the time-swelling illusion in terms of the event construction model. Given that the onset of the tone to be judged for duration is masked by the preceding band noise, the string of subevents representing the pattern is the following

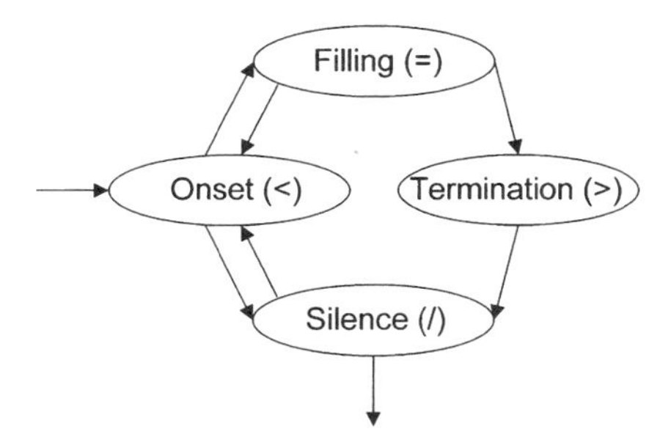

Figure 5.17: Markov process generating grammatical auditory events.

(the subevents are alphabetized for reference purposes):

<	=	>	=	>	/
a	b	c	d	e	f

This string of subevents is not grammatical, however, because the filling of the sine tone (at d) is not preceded immediately by an onset. Still, the listener is required to judge the duration of the tone, and it is evident this cannot been done without clear clues of onset and termination of the tone. The easiest solution is to restore the onset of the sine tone perceptually (denoted by RO for restored onset). Then, the string of subevents would look like:

<	=	>	<	=	>	/
a	b	c	RO	d	e	f

However, the auditory grammar (inspect Figure 5.17) does not allow that an onset (RO) immediately follows a termination (c). The grammatical solution is to insert a silence (denoted by IS for inserted silence) between the termination (at c) and the onset (at RO). The string of subevents would look like:

<	=	>	/	<	=	>	/
a	b	c	IS	RO	d	e	f

Though this string is grammatical, it does not reflect the correct temporal structure of the stimulus pattern, because there was no silence between masker and sine tone. The perceptual solution is to divide the string of subevents into two events (streams). When asked to carefully listen, observers claim that the sine tone already seems to start before the band noise is finished. Thus, it seems as if the tone protrudes backwards into the band noise. This is diagrammed by the temporal overlap between the two events:

<	=	>	/
a	b	c	IS
<	=	>	/
RO	d	e	f

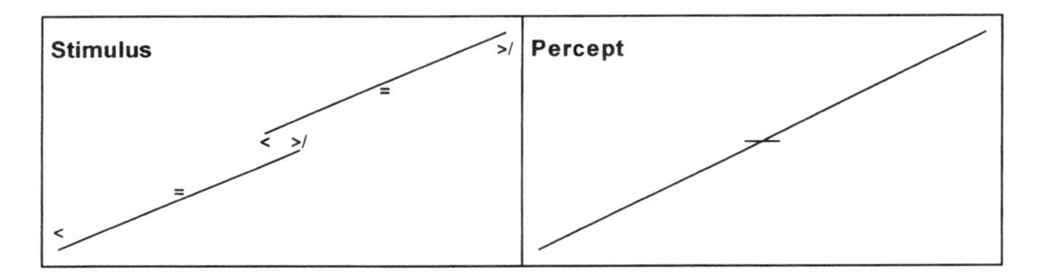

Figure 5.18: Illustration of the "split-off" illusion. See text for explanation.

Nakajima (1996) and Nakajima and Sasaki (1996) described how several other auditory illusions can be satisfactorily explained by the event construction model, like the gap transfer illusion which we discussed in the introduction (see also Nakajima et al., 2000) and the "split-off" illusion (see also Nakajima et al., 2000; Remijn & Nakajima, 2005).

We will finish this section on modern time illusions by describing the latter illusion. The split-off illusion, like the gap transfer illusion, is not a purely temporal illusion but arises by particular combinations of temporal and frequency characteristics of the auditory stimuli. Figure 5.18 (left panel) diagrams such a combination. Two frequency sweeps overlap each other during 200 ms. The first sweep increases from 367 to 966 Hz in 1400 ms. The second sweep starts 200 ms before the end of the first one and increases from 1035 to 2724 Hz in 1400 ms. The right panel of Figure 5.18 shows what listeners report (either verbally or by drawing the perceived pattern): one long sweep accompanied by a short tone in the middle of it. The event construction model explains this illusion as follows: Because the onset of the second sweep and the termination of the first sweep are close enough to each other in time and frequency (proximity principle), they are connected. Such a connection grammatically requires the insertion of a filling between onset and termination (< = >), because the pattern </> is ungrammatical (as can be inspected in Figure 5.17). This filling is possible since there is enough continuous sound energy available during the overlap of the sweeps. As a result of coupling the onset of the second auditory event with the termination of the first auditory event, the two sweeps miss their termination and onset, respectively. The remaining part of sound energy in the middle is used to "glue" the stripped sweeps together to one long sweep, or stated more formally: a short filling (=) connects the longer fillings (═ ═) belonging to the first and second sweep.

5.4. Summary and Conclusions

In the introduction we made a short tour through dictionaries and encyclopedias as regards the lemma "illusion" in order to mark out the concept. Then the importance of the study of illusions for understanding processes of sensation and perception was discussed and this was exemplified by two perceptual illusions: the Müller-Lyer illusion (a classic one) and the gap transfer illusion (a modern one).

In Section 5.2 we restricted ourselves mainly to auditory perception, and discussed "the illusion of a divided time interval," "subjective rhythmization," and "the kappa illusion" for pitch distance and ambient space distance. The old studies were discussed as well as recent replications. In the next section, the following auditory illusions were explained: "time shrinking," "bilateral assimilation and contrast," "1:1 temporal categorical perception," "time swelling," and the "split-off illusion." We elucidated that several of the discussed illusions can be explained by the "event construction model."

Several of the auditory time illusions we discussed are purely temporal. However, the kappa illusion is a consequence of the interdependency of time and space, and the gap transfer and split-off illusions result from special interactions of time and frequency, and time swelling is affected by frequency and intensity relations. There are many more auditory illusions as a result of a peculiar interplay of time, space, frequency, and intensity, which we did not discuss here: for example, "streaming," the "octave illusion," the "scale illusion," the "roll effect," and the "continuity illusion." For excellent descriptions and explanations of these and other illusions we refer to Bregman (1990), Deutsch (1999), Handel (1989), Plomp (2002), and Warren (1999).

Several illusions that we discussed in this chapter can be listened to at: http://www.design.kyushu-u.ac.jp/~ynhome/ENG/Demo/illusions2nd.html.

References

Abe, S. (1935). Experimental study on the co-relation between time and space. *Tohoku Psychologica Folia*, *3*, 53–68.

Abecasis, D., Brochard, R., Granot, R., & Drake, C. (2005). Differential brain response to metrical accents in isochronous auditory sequences. *Music Perception*, *22*, 549–562.

Adams, R. D. (1977). Intervening stimulus effects on category judgments of duration. *Perception and Psychophysics*, *21*, 527–534.

Akerboom, S., ten Hoopen, G., Olierook, P., & van der Schaaf, T. (1983). Auditory spatial alternation transforms auditory time. *Journal of Experimental Psychology: Human Perception and Performance*, *9*, 882–897.

Allan, L. G., & Gibbon, J. (1994). A new temporal illusion or the TOE once again? *Perception and Psychophysics*, *55*, 227–229.

Anderson, N. H. (1974). Algebraic models in perception. In: E. C. Carterette & M. P. Friedman (Eds), *Handbook of perception* (Vol. 2). New York: Academic Press.

Arao, H., Suetomi, D., & Nakajima, Y. (2000). Does time-shrinking take place in visual temporal patterns? *Perception*, *29*, 819–830.

Axelrod, S., & Diamond, I. T. (1965). Effects of auditory cortex ablation on ability to discriminate between stimuli presented to the two ears. *Journal of Comparative Physiological Psychology*, *59*, 79–89.

Axelrod, S., & Guzy, L. T. (1968). Underestimation of dichotic click rates: Results using methods of absolute estimation and constant stimuli. *Psychonomic Science*, *12*, 133–134.

Axelrod, S., Guzy, L. T., & Diamond, I. T. (1968). Perceived rate of monotic and dichotically alternating clicks. *Journal of the Acoustical Society of America*, *43*, 51–55.
Axelrod, S., & Nakao, M. (1974). Apparent slowing of bimanually alternating pulse trains. *Journal of Experimental Psychology*, *102*, 164–166.
Axelrod, S., & Powazek, M. (1972). Dependence of apparent rate of alternating clicks on azimuthal separation between sources. *Psychonomic Science*, *26*, 217–218.
Bakker, F., Boermans, M., Borsboom, J., van Dijk, D., van Emden, R., van der Kooij, J., & van Wely, R. (1998, July). *Auditory continuity: Illusionary lengthening at short bandnoise durations*. Research Report OZP9703 for the Section of Experimental & Theoretical Psychology, Leiden University, The Netherlands.
Bennett, K. B., Parasuraman, R., Howard, J. H., Jr., & O'Toole, A. J. (1984). Auditory induction of discrete tones in signal detection tasks. *Perception and Psychophysics*, *35*, 570–578.
Benussi, V. (1913). *Psychologie der Zeitauffassung*. Heidelberg: Carl Winters Universitäts-buchhandlung.
Bolton, T. L. (1894). Rhythm. *American Journal of Psychology*, *6*, 145–238.
Boltz, M. G. (1998). Tempo discrimination of musical patterns: Effects due to pitch and rhythmic structure. *Perception and Psychophysics*, *60*, 1357–1373.
Bregman, A. S. (1990). *Auditory scene analysis: The perceptual organization of sound*. Cambridge, MA: The MIT Press.
Brochard, R., Abecasis, D., Potter, D., Ragot, R., & Drake, C. (2003). The "ticktock" of our internal clock: Direct brain evidence of subjective accents in isochronous sequences. *Psychological Science*, *14*, 362–366.
Buffardi, L. (1971). Factors affecting the filled-duration illusion in the auditory, tactual, and visual modalities. *Perception and Psychophysics*, *10*, 292–294.
Clarke, E. F. (1987). Categorical rhythm perception: An ecological perspective. In: A. Gabrielsson (Ed.), *Action and perception in rhythm and music* (pp. 19–33). Stockholm: Royal Swedish Academy of Music, No. 55.
Cobb, V. (1999). *How to really fool yourself: Illusions for all your senses*. San Francisco, CA: Jossey-Bass.
Cohen, J., Hansel, C. E. M., & Sylvester, J. D. (1953). A new phenomenon in time judgment. *Nature*, *172*, 901.
Cohen, J., Hansel, C. E. M., & Sylvester, J. D. (1954). Interdependence of temporal and auditory judgments. *Nature*, *174*, 642–644.
Coren, S., Ward, L. M., & Enns, J. T. (1999). *Sensation and Perception* (5th ed.). Fort Worth: Harcourt Brace College Publishers.
Crowder, R. G., & Neath, I. (1995). The influence of pitch on time perception in short melodies. *Music Perception*, *12*, 379–386.
Dember, W. N., & Warm, J. S. (1979). *Psychology of Perception* (2nd ed.). New York: Holt, Rinehart and Winston.
Desain, P., & Honing, H. (2003). The formation of rhythmic categories and metric priming. *Perception*, *32*, 341–365.
Deutsch, D. (Ed.) (1999). *The Psychology of music* (2nd ed.). San Diego, CA: Academic Press.
Drake, C. (1993). Reproduction of musical rhythms by children, adult musicians, and adult nonmusicians. *Perception and Psychophysics*, *53*, 25–33.
Fraisse, P. (1961). Influence de la durée et de la fréquence des changements sur l'estimation du temps. *Année Psychologique*, *61*, 325–339.
Fraisse, P. (1978). Time and rhythm perception. In: E. C. Carterette & M. P. Friedman (Eds), *Handbook of Perception* (Vol. VIII, pp. 203–254). New York: Academic Press.

Fraisse, P. (1982). Rhythm and tempo. In: D. Deutsch (Ed.), *Psychology of music* (pp. 149–180). New York: Academic Press.
Friedman, M. (1983). *Foundations of Space-Time Theories*. Princeton University Press.
Fujishima, Y., & Nakajima, Y. (2006, November). *The effect of marker duration on time shrinking*. Poster session presented at the Fourth Joint Meeting of the Acoustical Society of America and the Acoustical Society of Japan, Honolulu, Hawaii. (*Journal of the Acoustical Society of America, 120*, 3085).
Gabrielsson, A. (1974). Performance of rhythm patterns. *Scandinavian Journal of Psychology, 15*, 63–72.
Gregory, R. L. (1966). *Eye and brain*. New York: World University Library.
Grondin, S. (1993). Duration discrimination of empty and filled intervals marked by auditory and visual signals. *Perception and Psychophysics, 54*, 383–394.
Grondin, S. (2001). From physical time to the first and second moments of psychological time. *Psychological Bulletin, 127*, 22–44.
Grondin, S. (2003). Sensory modalities and temporal processing. In: H. Helfrich (Ed.), *Time and mind II: Information processing perspectives* (pp. 75–92). Goettingen, Germany: Hogrefe & Huber.
Grondin, S., & Plourde, M. (2007). Discrimination of time intervals presented in sequences: Spatial effects with multiple auditory sources. *Human Movement Science, 26*, 702–714.
Guzy, L. T., & Axelrod, S. (1972). Interaural attention shifting as response. *Journal of Experimental Psychology, 95*, 290–294.
Hall, G. S., & Jastrow, J. (1886). Studies of rhythm. *Mind, 11*, 55–62.
Handel, S. (1988a). Space is to time as vision is to audition: Seductive but misleading. *Journal of Experimental Psychology: Human Perception and Performance, 14*, 315–317.
Handel, S. (1988b). No one analogy is sufficient: Rejoinder to Kubovy. *Journal of Experimental Psychology: Human Perception and Performance, 14*, 321.
Handel, S. (1989). *Listening: An introduction to the perception of auditory events*. Cambridge, MA: The MIT Press.
Handel, S., & Oshinski, J. S. (1981). The meter of syncopated auditory polyrhythms. *Perception and Psychophysics, 30*, 1–9.
Helson, H. (1930). The tau effect: An example of psychological relativity. *Science, 71*, 536–537.
Helson, H., & King, S. M. (1931). The tau effect: An example of psychological relativity. *Journal of Experimental Psychology, 14*, 202–217.
Henry, M. J. (2007). *On the role of imputed velocity in the auditory kappa effect*. M.A. thesis, Bowling Green State University.
Henry, M. J., & McAuley, J. D. (2007, March). *The role of imputed velocity in the auditory kappa effect*. Paper presented at the 17th Annual Meeting of the New England Sequencing and Timing Conferences.
Israeli, N. (1930). Illusions in the perception of short time intervals. *Archives of psychology, 19*, number 113.
Jones, B., & Huang, Y. L. (1982). Space-time dependencies in psychophysical judgment of extent and duration: Algebraic models of the tau and kappa effects. *Psychological Bulletin, 91*, 128–142.
Jones, M. R. (1976). Time, our lost dimension: Toward a new theory of perception, attention, and memory. *Psychological Review, 83*, 323–355.
Jones, M. R., & Boltz, M. G. (1989). Dynamic attending and responses to time. *Psychological Review, 96*, 459–491.

Kaas, J. H., Axelrod, S., & Diamond, I. T. (1967). An ablation study of the auditory cortex in cat using binaural tonal patterns. *Journal of Neurophysiology*, *30*, 710–724.

Kallman, H. J., & Morris, M. D. (1984). Duration perception and auditory masking. In: J. Gibbon & L. G. Allan (Eds), *Timing and Time Perception* (Vol. 423, pp. 608–609). New York: Annals of the New York Academy of Sciences.

Kluender, K. R., & Jenison, R. L. (1992). Effects of glide slope, noise intensity, and noise duration on the extrapolation of FM glides through noise. *Perception and Psychophysics*, *51*, 231–238.

Kubovy, M. (1988). Should we resist the seductiveness of the space:time:vision:audition analogy? *Journal of Experimental Psychology: Human Perception and Performance*, *14*, 318–320.

Large, E. W. (2000, August). *Rhythm categorization in context*. Paper presented at the 6th International Conference on Music Perception and Cognition, Keele University, UK.

MacKenzie, N. (2007). *The kappa effect in pitch/time context*. Ph.D. thesis, The Ohio State University.

MacKenzie, N., & Jones, M. R. (2005, November). *The auditory kappa effect revisited*. Paper presented at the 46th annual meeting of the Psychonomic Society, Toronto, Ontario, Canada.

Massaro, D. W. (1975). *Experimental Psychology and Information Processing* (pp. 425–474). Chicago, IL: Rand McNally College Publishing Company.

Massaro, D. W., & Idson, W. L. (1976). Temporal course of perceived auditory duration. *Perception and Psychophysics*, *20*, 331–352.

Massier, E. F. (1997). *Incomplete auditory continuity: Stimulus pattern, order of standard and comparison and connectedness between bandnoise and sine tone*. Master's thesis for the Section of Experimental and Theoretical Psychology, Leiden University, The Netherlands.

McDougall, R. (1903). The structure of simple rhythm forms. *Psychological Monographs*, *4*, 309–416.

Miller, G. A., & Licklider, J. C. R. (1950). The intelligibility of interrupted speech. *Journal of the Acoustical Society of America*, *22*, 167–173.

Miyauchi, R., & Nakajima, Y. (2005). Bilateral assimilation of two neighboring empty time intervals. *Music Perception*, *22*, 411–424.

Miyauchi, R., & Nakajima, Y. (2007). The category of 1:1 ratio caused by assimilation of two neighboring empty time intervals. *Human Movement Science*, *26*, 717–727.

Nakajima, Y. (1979). A psychophysical investigation of divided time intervals shown by sound bursts. *Journal of the Acoustical Society of Japan*, *35*, 145–151 (in Japanese with English summary and English figure captions).

Nakajima, Y. (1987). A model of empty duration perception. *Perception*, *16*, 485–520.

Nakajima, Y. (1996, August). *A simple grammar for auditory organization: Streams, events, and subevents*. Paper for the Symposium "Approaches to Auditory Organization," XXVI International Congress of Psychology, Montreal, Canada.

Nakajima, Y., Nishimura, S., & Teranishi, R. (1988). Ratio judgments of empty durations with numeric scales. *Perception*, *17*, 93–118.

Nakajima, Y., & Sasaki, T. (1996, December). *A simple grammar of auditory stream formation*. Paper for the Third Joint Meeting of the Acoustical Society of America and the Acoustical Society of Japan, Honolulu.

Nakajima, Y., Sasaki, T., Kanafuka, K., Miyamoto, A., Remijn, G., & ten Hoopen, G. (2000). Illusory recouplings of onsets and terminations of glide tone components. *Perception and Psychophysics*, *62*, 1413–1425.

Nakajima, Y., & ten Hoopen, G., (1988). The effect of preceding time intervals on duration perception. *Proceedings of the Acoustical Society of Japan*, Autumn meeting (pp. 381–382).

Nakajima, Y., ten Hoopen, G., Hilkhuysen, G., & Sasaki, T. (1992). Time-shrinking: A discontinuity in the perception of auditory temporal patterns. *Perception and Psychophysics, 51*, 504–507.

Nakajima, Y., ten Hoopen, G., Sasaki, T., Yamamoto, K., Kadota, M., Simons, M., & Suetomi, D. (2004). Time-shrinking: The process of unilateral temporal assimilation. *Perception, 33*, 1061–1079.

Nakajima, Y., ten Hoopen, G., & van der Wilk, R. G. H. (1991). A new illusion of time perception. *Music Perception, 8*, 431–448.

Ornstein, R. E. (1969). *On the experience of time*. Baltimore, MD: Penguin Books.

Parncutt, R. (1994). A perceptual model of pulse salience and metrical accent in musical rhythms. *Music Perception, 11*, 409–464.

Plomp, R. (2002). *The intelligent ear*. Mahwah, NJ: LEA Publishers.

Povel, D. J. (1981). Internal representation of simple temporal patterns. *Journal of Experimental Psychology: Human Perception and Performance, 7*, 3–18.

Povel, D. J. (1984). A theoretical framework for rhythm perception. *Psychological Research, 45*, 15–337.

Price-Williams, D. R. (1954). The kappa effect. *Nature, 173*, 363–364.

Reber, A. S. (1995). *Dictionary of Psychology* (2nd ed.). London: Penguin Books.

Remijn, G., van der Meulen, G., ten Hoopen, G., Nakajima, Y., Komori, Y., & Sasaki, T. (1999). On the robustness of time-shrinking. *Journal of the Acoustical Society of Japan (E), 20*, 365–373.

Remijn, G. B., & Nakajima, Y. (2005). The perceptual integration of auditory stimulus edges: An illusory short tone in stimulus patterns consisting of two partly overlapping glides. *Journal of Experimental Psychology: Human Perception and Performance, 31*, 183–192.

Repp, B. H. (2006). Rate limits of sensorimotor synchronization. *Advances in Cognitive Psychology, 2*, 163–181.

Samuel, A. (1996). Phoneme restoration. *Language and Cognitive Processes, 11*, 647–654.

Sasaki, T., Nakajima, Y., & ten Hoopen, G. (1993, May). *The effect of a preceding neighbor-tone on the perception of filled durations*. Proceedings of the Acoustical Society of Japan, Spring Meeting. (pp. 347–348) (in Japanese with English figure captions).

Sasaki, T., Nakajima, Y., & ten Hoopen, G. (1998). Categorical rhythm perception as a result of unilateral assimilation in time-shrinking. *Music Perception, 16*, 201–222.

Sasaki, T., Suetomi, D., Nakajima, Y., & ten Hoopen, G. (2002). Time-shrinking, its propagation, and Gestalt principles. *Perception and Psychophysics, 64*, 919–931.

Schaefer, F. (1979, April). *Gerichtete und verteilte Aufmerksamkeit bei der Einschatzung richtungsalternierender Clicks*. Paper presented at the 21. Tagung Experimentell arbeitender Psychologen, Heidelberg, Germany.

Schiffman, H. R. (1995). *Sensation and perception* (4th ed.). New York: John Wiley.

Shigeno, S. (1986). The auditory tau and kappa effects for speech and nonspeech stimuli. *Perception and Psychophysics, 40*, 9–19.

Simons, M. (1995). *Time swelling: An incomplete heterophonic induction in a non-repetitive design*. Master's thesis for the Section of Experimental and Theoretical Psychology, Leiden University, The Netherlands.

Stetson, R. H. (1905). A motor theory of rhythm and discrete succession. *Psychological Review, 12*, 250–270, and 292–350.

Stobart, H., & Cross, I. (2000). The Andean anacrusis? Rhythmic structure and perception in Easter songs of Northern Potosi, Bolivia. *British Journal of Ethnomusicology, 9*, 63–94.

Suetomi, D., & Nakajima, Y. (1998). How stable is time-shrinking? *Journal of Music Perception and Cognition*, *4*, 19–25.

Suetomi, D., Nakajima, Y., Sasaki, T., & ten Hoopen, G. (2000). Demonstrations of time-shrinking. In: P. Desain & L. Windsor (Eds), *Rhythm perception and production* (pp. 175–181). Lisse: Swets and Zeitlinger.

ten Hoopen, G. (1996). Auditory attention. In: O. Neumann & A. F. Sanders (Eds), *Handbook of perception and action, Vol. 3: Attention* (pp. 79–112). London: Academic Press.

ten Hoopen, G., & Akerboom, S. (1983). The subjective tempo difference between interaural and monaural sequences as a function of sequence length. *Perception and Psychophysics*, *34*, 465–469.

ten Hoopen, G., Beumer, M., & Nakajima, Y. (1996). What differs between the first and the last interval of a click sequence simulating a mora structure, the DT or the PSE? A replication of Tanaka, Tsuzaki, and Kato (1994). *Journal of the Acoustical Society of Japan (E)*, *17*, 155–158.

ten Hoopen, G., Boon, R., Sasaki, T., & Nakajima, Y. (2006). The counterpart of "time-shrinking" in playing regular sounding triplets of tones on the alto recorder. *Trans Technical Committee Psychological And Physiological Acoustics, The Acoustical Society of Japan*, *36*, 731–736.

ten Hoopen, G., Hartsuiker, R., Sasaki, T., Nakajima, Y., Tanaka, M., & Tsumura, T. (1995). Perception of auditory isochrony: Time-shrinking and temporal patterns. *Perception*, *24*, 577–593.

ten Hoopen, G., Hilkhuysen, G., Vis, G., Nakajima, Y., Yamauchi, F., & Sasaki, T. (1993). A new illusion of time perception-II. *Music Perception*, *11*, 15–38.

ten Hoopen, G., Sasaki, T., Nakajima, Y., Remijn, G., Massier, B., Rhebergen, K., & Holleman, W. (2006). Time-shrinking and categorical temporal ratio perception: Evidence for a 1:1 temporal category. *Music Perception*, *24*, 1–22.

ten Hoopen, G., & Vos, J. (1980). Attention switching is not a fatigable process: Methodological comments on Axelrod & Guzy (1972). *Journal of Experimental Psychology: Human Perception and Performance*, *6*, 180–183.

ten Hoopen, G., & Vos, J. (1981). Attention switching and patterns of sound locations in counting clicks. *Journal of Experimental Psychology: Human Perception and Performance*, *7*, 342–355.

ten Hoopen, G., Vos, J., & Dispa, J. (1982). Interaural and monaural clicks and clocks: Tempo difference versus attention switching. *Journal of Experimental Psychology: Human Perception and Performance*, *8*, 422–434.

Thomas, E. A. C., & Brown, I., Jr. (1974). Time perception and the filled-duration illusion. *Perception and Psychophysics*, *16*, 449–458.

Thurlow, W. R. (1957). An auditory figure-ground effect. *American Journal of Psychology*, *70*, 653–654.

Tsuzaki, M., & Kato, H. (2000). Shrinkage of perceived tonal duration produced by extra sounds: Effects of spectral density, temporal position, and transition direction. *Perception*, *29*, 989–1004.

Tsuzaki, M., & Kato, H. (2005a). Durational shrinking by noise replacement in quasi-isochronous and hyper-isochronous contexts. *Acoustical Science and Technology*, *26*, 27–34.

Tsuzaki, M., & Kato, H. (2005b). Effects of deviation from isochronism on the durational shrinkage by noise replacement. *Acoustical Science and Technology*, *26*, 35–42.

Tsuzaki, M., Kato, H., & Tanaka, M. (2003). Shrinkage in the perceived duration of speech and tone by acoustic replacement. *Japanese Psychological Research*, *45*, 129–139.

Ueda, K., & Ohtsuki, M. (1996). The effect of sound pressure level difference on filled duration extension. *Journal of the Acoustical Society of Japan (E)*, *17*, 159–161.

van Bergen, I., Croes, S., Ferrada, O., Jongsma, H., Klinkenberg, J., Raatgever, B., ten Voorde, H., & van Zetten, I. (1997, June). *Incomplete auditory continuity as a* function *of the frequency* relation *between noise and tone*. Research Report OZP9602 for the Section of Experimental & Theoretical Psychology, Leiden University, The Netherlands.

van Buuringen, E. (1997). *Time swelling: Illusory lengthening of tones, peripheral and central causes*. Master's thesis for the Section of Experimental and Theoretical Psychology, Leiden University, The Netherlands.

van Noorden, L., & Moelants, D. (1999). Resonance in the perception of musical pulse. *Journal of New Music Research*, *28*, 43–66.

Vicario, G. (1960). L'effetto tunnel acustico. *Rivista di Psicologia*, *54*, 41–52.

Vos, P. G. M. M. (1973). *Waarneming van metrische toonreeksen [Perception of metrical tone sequences]*, Ph.D. thesis. Nijmegen University: Stichting Studentenpers.

Warren, R. M. (1999). *Auditory perception: A new analysis and synthesis*. Cambridge: Cambridge University Press.

Warren, R. M., Bashford, J. A., Jr., Healy, E. W., & Brubaker, B. S. (1994). Auditory induction: Reciprocal changes in alternating sounds. *Perception and Psychophysics*, *55*, 313–322.

Warren, R. M., Obusek, C. J., & Ackroff, J. M. (1972). Auditory induction: Perceptual synthesis of absent sounds. *Science*, *176*, 1149–1151.

Woodrow, H. (1951). Time perception. In: S. S. Stevens (Ed.), *Handbook of Experimental Psychology* (pp. 1224–1236). New York: John Wiley.

Yamashita, M., & Nakajima, Y. (1999). The effect of marker duration on time-shrinking. In: S. W. Yi (Ed.), *Music, mind and science* (pp. 211–218). Seoul: Seoul National University Press.

Chapter 6

Resonating to Musical Rhythm: Theory and Experiment

Edward W. Large

6.1. Introduction

> Music is a temporal art ... in the banal sense that its tones are given in temporal succession. ...Music is a temporal art in the more exact sense that, for its ends, it enlists time as force. ...Music is a temporal art in the special sense that in it time reveals itself to experience (Victor Zuckerkandl, 1956, pp. 199–200).

Music is an interactive activity in which dancing, singing, toe tapping, playing an instrument, or even simply listening is temporally coordinated with complex, rhythmically structured acoustic stimulation. Analyses of scores and recordings reveal musical sounds to be intricate dynamic patterns, in which elegant serial structures unfold in elaborate temporal organizations. Thus, when humans "synchronize" musical interactions, we enter into a form of temporal coordination that is among the most elaborate observed in nature. For example, temporal interaction in music contrasts with observations of simple synchronous chorusing in other species. In insects and amphibians, coordination of rhythmic visual or auditory communication signals appears to be limited to synchronization or antisynchronization of periodic events (Buck, 1988; Greenfield, 1994; Klump & Gerhardt, 1992). Moreover, synchronous chorusing has rarely been reported among nonhuman primates (Merker, 2000). It has been argued that the ability to temporally coordinate dynamic patterns with complex auditory stimuli was an important adaptation in the development of human communication (Merker, 2000).

This chapter considers the complexity of human musical rhythm and discusses its implications for the coordination of perception, attention, and behavior. Following

Psychology of Time

DOI:10.1016/B978-0-08046-977-5.00006-5

this introduction, Section 6.2 begins with music analytic perspectives, which address musical complexity and the phenomenology of pulse and meter. With few exceptions, even the most complex rhythmic interactions are organized around a fundamental frequency called a pulse. Pulse is endogenously generated, and it is experienced as varying in strength such that some pulses are felt as strong and others as weak, suggesting a metrical property. When humans organize complex temporal interactions, they synchronize — or more generally, entrain — pulse frequencies. However, investigation of rhythm and rhythmic interactions in humans has, to a large extent, been confined to periodic behavior and synchronization/antisynchronization, and it is from these studies that we have gleaned most of our current knowledge of human rhythmic perception and behavior. Therefore, Section 6.3 offers a brief, historically oriented outline of studies of periodic rhythmic behavior. The goal will be to interpret these results within the context of musical rhythm perception, setting the stage for the remainder of the discussion.

Sections 6.4 and 6.5 constitute the core of the chapter. Section 6.4 introduces a resonance theory of musical rhythm, beginning with a brief tutorial on neural resonance, and moving on to review linear and nonlinear oscillator models of pulse and meter that have been proposed over the past several years. The goal is to show how this approach predicts the main psychological attributes of pulse and meter. Section 6.5 will review the empirical literature on musical pulse and meter, focusing on studies that use music and/or complex rhythms and have explored the theoretical predictions of neural resonance. The chapter closes with a discussion of some of the significant open issues in this area.

6.2. Rhythm, Pulse, and Meter

The sounds that humans use for communication may be conceived as complex, temporally structured sequences of nearly discrete events, such as musical notes and speech syllables. In common musical parlance, meter refers to canonical patterns of timing and accentuation that serve as conventional frameworks for performing music. Similarly, in linguistics, meter refers to the temporal organization of stress patterns in a speech utterance. In music perception and cognition, however, *pulse* and *meter* refer to percepts. They are responses to patterns of timing and (depending on the theorist) stress in the acoustic rhythm. Although responsive to stimulus properties, pulse and meter are not themselves stimulus properties. These terms refer to endogenous dynamic temporal referents that shape experiences of musical rhythms. The rhythms of music, which are temporally complex and richly articulated, are heard in relation to a relatively stable percept of pulse and meter. In this section I focus on the phenomenology of this experience, as related by music theorists.

6.2.1. Musical Rhythm

To illustrate the nature of rhythmic pattern in music, Figure 6.1A shows the sound pressure wave for the beginning of a musical sequence, the first four bars of the Aria

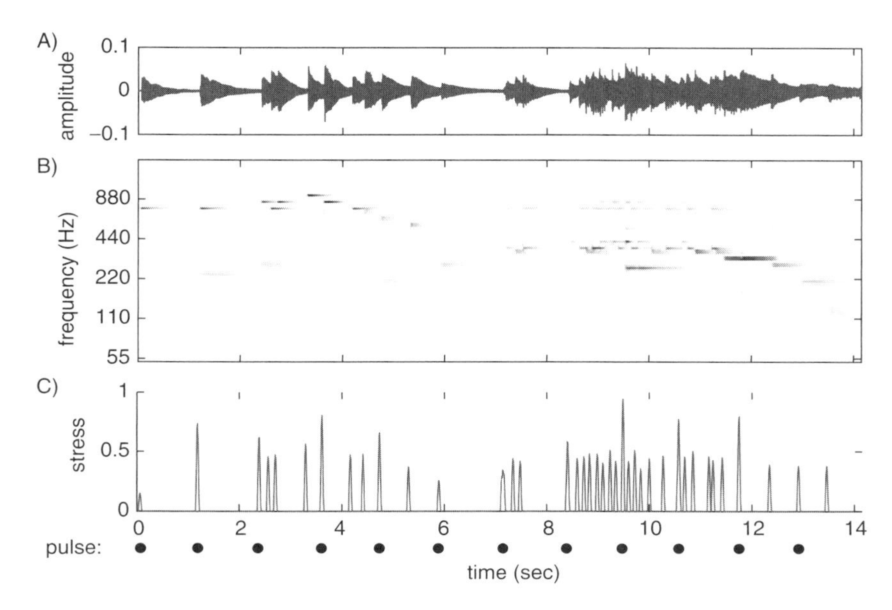

Figure 6.1: The first four bars of the Aria from by J. S. Bach's *Goldberg Variations*, as performed by a student pianist. (A) Acoustic sound pressure; (B) spectrogram; and (C) event onsets and hypothetical pulses.

from J. S. Bach's *Goldberg Variations*, as performed on piano. The subtlety of the temporal organization can be appreciated, in part, by examining the amplitude modulation of the acoustic time series. Each event has a relatively well-defined onset, followed by a gradual decay of amplitude, and often the next event begins before the previous sound has ended. The complexity of the relationships between serial and temporal structures can be further apprehended by observing how the frequency components of individual musical events delineate a potentially endless variety of temporal intervals (see Figure 6.1B).

When I refer to the rhythm of the sequence, I refer to the organization of events in time,[1] and specifically to patterns of onset timing and event stress. Figure 6.1C illustrates these concepts by attempting to isolate the *rhythmic pattern* from other aspects of the musical pattern. It shows impulses marking the onset times of the various events, with differing amounts of stress represented as impulse amplitude.[2]

1. The term *rhythm* is commonly used to refer both to the stimulus and to aspects of its perception (e.g., its perceived grouping, see Lerdahl & Jackendoff, 1983). Throughout this review I use the term to refer to the stimulus structure.

2. Impulse amplitude is a common representation of stress. However, pitch, duration, and other aspects of the acoustic wave – which play significant roles in the perception of stress – are problematic for this simple approach.

The key observation is this: Although we casually discuss musical rhythms as though they were periodic, they almost never are. The onset times of musical events mark a wide variety of temporal intervals. It is likely that we tend to think of musical rhythms as periodic because we tend to feel them as periodic. At the bottom of Figure 6.1C, I have illustrated a hypothetical pulse for this musical performance, with dots drawn near the times at which one might tap along with this rhythm. Pulses correspond to some events but not to others. Sometimes the event coinciding with a pulse has more stress than its immediate neighbors, often it does not. In general, the relationship between timing, stress, and pulse is quite subtle.

6.2.2. *Pulse and Meter*

Pulse, as described by music theorists, is a kind of *endogenous periodicity*, explained by Cooper and Meyer (1960) as "a series of regularly recurring, precisely equivalent" psychological events that arise in response to a musical rhythm. There is wide agreement that pulse, although responsive to a rhythmic stimulus, is not itself a stimulus property (Epstein, 1995; Lerdahl & Jackendoff, 1983; London, 2004; Yeston, 1976; Zuckerkandl, 1956). Rather, pulse provides a stable, dynamic referent with respect to which a complex musical rhythm is experienced. *Stability* is emphasized by Cooper and Meyer (1960), who observe that pulse, "once established, tends to be continued in the mind and musculature of the listener" even after a rhythmic stimulus ceases. *Periodicity* is assumed by most theorists, especially those who are concerned primarily with musicological analysis (for example, Figure 6.2) (Cooper & Meyer, 1960; Lerdahl & Jackendoff, 1983; Yeston, 1976; Zuckerkandl, 1956). Others highlight the significance of tempo change or rubato in music performance. Epstein (1995), for example, emphasized that pulse, as experienced in actual music, is not purely periodic but responds to tempo change in a way that is important in the conveyance of motion and emotion in music. The pulses in Figure 6.1C, for example, are not purely periodic.

Pulse exhibits a *generalized synchrony* with musical rhythm. The term synchrony alone does not suffice, because the complexity of musical rhythm means that not every event onset can coincide with a periodic pulse (Figure 6.1C), and pulses may

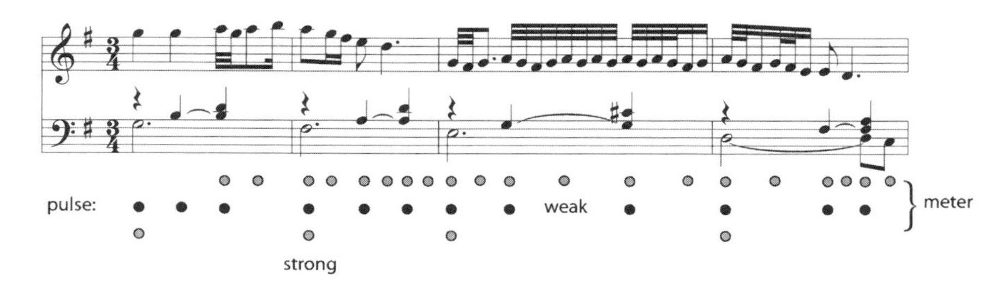

Figure 6.2: Notation and music theoretic metrical structure for the first four bars of the *Goldberg Variations* Aria.

occur in the absence of event onsets, even in analysis of notated rhythms (Figure 6.2) (cf., Lerdahl & Jackendoff, 1983). Yet there is a tendency for pulses to gravitate toward event onsets in a way that produces (approximate) synchrony when a stimulus rhythm is purely periodic. To complicate matters even further, some musical rhythms are syncopated, such that event onsets may regularly fall between experienced pulses, for example. Cooper and Meyer (1960) argue that pulse continues even if musical events "fail for a time to coincide with the previously established pulse," in effect arguing that pulse has a special kind of temporal stability — that pulses need not always gravitate toward event onsets. However, "(syncopated) passages point to the re-establishment of pulse coincidence" so that synchrony is somehow more stable than syncopation. Thus, the term generalized synchrony is more accurate and will be operationalized in subsequent sections.

Individual pulses are usually perceived to possess differing degrees of *metrical accent*. The terms *meter* and *metrical structure* refer to patterns of regularly recurring stronger and weaker pulses (Cooper & Meyer, 1960; Lerdahl & Jackendoff, 1983). Theorists sometimes transcribe metrical structures as in Figure 6.2, using arrangements of dots, called beats, that can be aligned with a musical score (Lerdahl & Jackendoff, 1983; London, 2004; Yeston, 1976). For example, in Lerdahl and Jackendoff's (1983) system, the fundamental pulse periodicity (the rate at which one might spontaneously tap with a musical rhythm) would be notated as a single row of beats, and the pattern of strong and weak pulses as additional rows of beats at related frequencies. The time points at which the beats of more levels coincide denote stronger pulses. This notational convention facilitates the discussion of structural constraints for metrical accent. Lerdahl and Jackendoff (1983) propose two kinds of constraints, one on the relative frequencies and the other on the relative phases, of adjacent beat levels. Western tonal music, they argue, adheres to restrictive constraints. With respect to a particular referent level (e.g., the pulse level in Figure 6.2), the next higher frequency must be either the second or third harmonic (a 2:1 or 3:1 frequency relationship); the next lower frequency must be either the second or third subharmonic (a 1:2 or 1:3 frequency relationship). The relative phases of adjacent levels must be such that the discrete beats come into temporal alignment on each cycle of the slower frequency. Figure 6.2 illustrates three structural levels, the fundamental pulse frequency, its second harmonic (2:1) and its third subharmonic (1:3). More comprehensive structural descriptions, encompassing non-Western musical cultures including those of the Balkans, South Asia, Africa, and Latin America, additionally allow simple integer frequency ratios, such as 3:2, 4:3, 5:2, and so forth (London, 2004; cf., Yeston, 1976).

The process by which pulse and meter emerge is referred to as *induction*. The key questions involve the complex relationship between a stimulus rhythm and an experienced pulse and meter. Onset timing is widely agreed to be critical in the perception of pulse and meter. Somewhat more controversial is the role of stress at the musical surface (Cooper & Meyer, 1960; Lerdahl & Jackendoff, 1983; Zuckerkandl, 1956). Stress arises through complex interactions of loudness, duration, pitch, and harmony (Huron & Royal, 1996; Jones, 2008; Jones & Yee, 1993; Lerdahl & Jackendoff, 1983), and there is no simple calculation to arrive at its quantification. Theorists disagree on the role of stress in determining perceptions of pulse and meter (Jones, 2008). For example, Lerdahl and Jackendoff (1983) describe pulse and meter as perceptual inferences from timing and stress patterns in an acoustic stimulus, while Zuckerkandl (1956) argues that pulse and meter arise solely from the demarcation of time intervals.

As a pattern of metrical accent emerges in response to a rhythmic pattern, it stabilizes, becoming resistant to change (Epstein, 1995; Lerdahl & Jackendoff, 1983; London, 2004; Yeston, 1976; Zuckerkandl, 1956). Once stabilized, a single stressed event at the musical surface cannot change an unaccented pulse into an accented pulse; the pattern can be destabilized only in the face of strongly contradictory evidence (Cooper & Meyer, 1960; Lerdahl & Jackendoff, 1983; Zuckerkandl, 1956). The stability of metrical accent patterns is key to explaining syncopation, a fundamental concept in musical rhythm. "Syncopation takes place where cues are strongly contradictory yet not strong enough or regular enough to override the inferred pattern" (Lerdahl & Jackendoff, 1983, pp. 17–18). Thus, the stability of pulse and meter, and in particular, the response to syncopated rhythms, is of significant interest in the study of rhythm perception. Some theorists highlight the potential multistability of metric structures, the possibility that more than one accent pattern could be perceived (at different times or by different individuals) for a given rhythm (Lerdahl & Jackendoff, 1983; London, 2004).

Not all theorists conceive of meter as a structure of discrete time points. For Zuckerkandl (1956), meter is a series of waves that carry the listener continuously from one downbeat to the next. Time is not considered an "empty vessel, which contains the tones," but it is an active force, experienced as waves of intensification (Zuckerkandl, 1956). A tone acquires its special rhythmic quality from its place in the cycle of the wave, from "the direction of its kinetic impulse." Metric waves are described as a natural consequence of the passage of time, made perceivable by the rhythmic organization of music. Section 6.4 will link concepts of pulse and meter to neural oscillation, and continuous time formalisms will be prominent in that discussion.

6.2.3. Summary

In summary, musical rhythms comprise complex patterns of stress and timing, and are not periodic. Pulse is a nearly periodic experience, while meter corresponds to the percept of alternating strong and weak pulses. Pulse and meter are influenced by patterns of timing, and perhaps stress, in the stimulus. Yet pulse and meter are not stimulus properties, but they are endogenous dynamic structures with reference to which musical patterns are experienced. Pulse is a stable, endogenous periodicity that exhibits a generalized form of synchrony with complex rhythmic patterns. Strong and weak pulses alternate forming stereotypical patterns called metrical structures, which can be described in terms of phase and frequency relationships among multiple frequency components. Frequency relationships among components appear restricted to harmonics (e.g., 1:2, 1:3), subharmonics (e.g., 2:1 and 3:1), and, in general other simple integer ratios (e.g., 3:2, 4:3). The notion of stability is important here, and applies to multiple aspects of pulse and meter. Pulse is stable in the sense that it can continue in the absence of a stimulus, and it possesses a form of temporal, or phase stability such that it normally synchronizes with events, but can persist in the face of rhythmic conflict, or syncopation. Finally, metrical structures are stable in the sense that, once induced, they tend not to change to reflect stimulus accentuation, but provide a temporal referent against which rhythm is experienced.

6.3. Periodic Rhythms

Most of our current knowledge of human rhythmic behavior comes from studies of the perception of periodic acoustic stimuli, the production of periodic behavior, and synchronization or antisynchronization of periodic behavior with periodic stimuli. Because this work has formed the basis for studies that involve complex musical rhythms, I briefly review some of the basic results in this area to set the stage for our discussion of musical pulse and meter.

Stevens (1886) introduced the *synchronize-continue paradigm*, in which participants listened to a periodic sequence, synchronized taps to the sequence, and continued tapping after the stimulus sequence was discontinued. He used a metronome to produce stimulus sequences of various rates, and recorded Morse-key taps on moving paper. He reported that listeners were able to internalize and reproduce, with some variability, the periodicity of the stimulus. The inter-tap intervals (ITIs) observed in such experiments have often been used to test the ability to estimate, remember, and reproduce time (Bartlett & Bartlett, 1959; Wing & Kristofferson, 1973b). However, from a musical perspective, continuation tapping may be considered the simplest demonstration of endogenous periodicity: Pulse is induced in response to a periodic rhythm, it stabilizes, and when the stimulus rhythm ceases it persists, in the form of rhythmic motor behavior.

As measured by continuation tapping, pulse is pseudo-periodic. It includes both short-term fluctuations, which Stevens described as a "constant zigzag," and longer term fluctuations, described as "larger and more primary waves." Two-level timing models (Daffertshofer, 1998; Wing & Kristofferson, 1973a) have been proposed to predict short-term fluctuations as a negative lag one autocorrelation of the ITI sequence, which are often reported in experiments that collect short sequences (tens of taps). Studies that collect hundreds of successive intervals, and apply a spectral analysis to the resultant time series, typically find that the spectrum is characterized by a linear negative slope in log power versus log frequency (Delignières, Lemoine, & Torre, 2004; Gilden, Thornton, & Mallon, 1995; Lemoine, Torre, & Didier, 2006; Yamada, 1996; Madison, 2004). Thus, longer term temporal fluctuations exhibit a $1/f$ structure, a ubiquitous feature in biological systems (West & Shlesinger, 1989, 1990), that has recently been observed in other psychological time series (Gilden, 2001; Van Orden, Holden, & Turvey, 2003).

Pulse also has a characteristic timescale. Fraisse (1978) reported pulse tempi of around 600 ms (1.67 Hz or 100 bpm), based on data from both spontaneous tapping and preferred tempo tasks. The notion of a universal preferred tempo has since given way to the notion of a tempo region that elicits good performance on tasks such as tempo discrimination and perception–action coordination (Drake, Jones, & Baruch, 2000; London, 2004; McAuley, Jones, Holub, Johnston, & Miller, 2006). Drake and Botte (1993) measured tempo discrimination at various rates, reporting adherences to Weber's law (JND ~ 2%) within a limited range from about 200 ms (5 Hz or 300 bpm) to about 1 s (1 Hz or 60 bpm). Repp measured the upper limit of pulse perception using subharmonic synchronization, and while individual differences were large, 100 ms (10 Hz or 600 bpm) represents an extreme limit (Repp, 2003b). A lower limit of pulse perception had been putatively indexed by transition from anticipation to reaction tapping at about 2.4 s (.43 Hz or 25.6 bpm) (Mates, Muller, Radil, & Poppel, 1994), however, a more comprehensive study has found no such clear transition up to inter-onset times of 3.5 s (Repp & Doggett, 2007). Moreover, the notion of fixed limits has been seriously called into question (Drake, 1993; Drake et al., 2000a; Drake & Palmer, 1993; McAuley, Jones, Holub, Johnston, & Miller, 2006). In the most comprehensive set of studies to date participants, aged 4–95, performed both synchronize-continue and tempo judgment tasks. In these studies preferred tempo was found to slow with age, and the width of the entrainment region to widen up to about age 65, when it narrows again.

Research on coordination of motor behavior with periodic auditory stimuli has a long history (Dunlap, 1910; Fraisse, 1978; Michon, 1967; Stevens, 1886; Woodrow, 1932; see Chapter 1), and over the past several years numerous studies have probed the coordination of periodic behavior with periodic auditory sequences (for a recent review, see Repp, 2005). One commonly observes a tendency of taps to precede auditory events, known as the anticipation tendency.[3] Although at one time thought to result from differential delays for auditory stimuli and proprioceptive feedback, this hypothesis has not held up (Aschersleben, 2002; Aschersleben, Gehrke, & Prinz, 2001) and the results to date suggest multiple determinants of this tendency (Repp, 2005). Additionally, fractal or $1/f$ structure has also been reported in coordination with periodic sequences (Chen, Ding, & Kelso, 1997; Pressing & Jolley-Rogers, 1997).

A major issue has been the maintenance of synchrony with temporally fluctuating stimuli, studied using phase and/or tempo perturbations of periodic sequences. Overall, people can track temporally fluctuating sequences, and it has been suggested that phase coupling and tempo adaptation depend upon different mechanisms (Repp, 2001b; Thaut, Miller, & Schauer, 1998a). People respond quickly and automatically to phase perturbations of periodic sequences (Large, Fink, & Kelso, 2002; Repp, 2001a, 2002a, 2003a; Thaut, Tian, & Azimi-Sadjadi, 1998b) and phase correction response profiles are nonlinear (Repp, 2002b). People are also able to adapt to tempo perturbations (Large et al., 2002); however, tempo tracking appears to be a controlled process, requiring active attending (Repp, 2001b; Repp & Keller,

3. An important methodological concern is the amount of delay that is present in tap-time measurements relative to the arrival of sound at the ear. This is not frequently reported in such studies.

2004). A related area is that of antisynchronization, a simple form of syncopation in which listeners are instructed to maintain a 1:1 frequency relationship between repeated motor movements and a series of periodically delivered tones, in an antiphase fashion (see Repp, 2005). Such behavior is stable for lower frequencies; however, increases in stimulus presentation rate induce a spontaneous switch in behavior from syncopation to synchronization (Kelso, DelColle, & Schöner, 1990; Mayville, Bressler, Fuchs, & Kelso, 1999) at about 400 ms (2.5 Hz or 150 bpm).

Interestingly, people report percepts of metrical accent even in unaccented, periodic event sequences. Bolton (1894) asked subjects to listen to an isochronous series of tones of identical frequency and intensity. He found that such sequences are actually heard as accented, such that strong pulses alternate with weak pulses, usually in 1:2 patterns, but sometimes in 1:3 or other patterns. He called this phenomenon subjective rhythmization, although using the current terminology it would be more appropriate to name it *subjective meter*. Notice that according to this astonishing observation, people spontaneously hear subharmonics of the rhythmic frequency that is presented. Vos (1973) investigated this phenomenon in greater detail. He presented isochronous tone sequences at various tempi, and after each presentation listeners reported the size of the groups in which they heard the sequence. The number of responses in each category was found to depend on both the tempo and the group size. Vos found a clear tendency to prefer group sizes 2, 4, and 8, with subharmonics 3, 5, 6, and 7 more rarely reported. Spontaneous perception of structure has also been observed in synchronization tasks. Parncutt (1994) presented isochronous tone sequences with various tempi to participants and asked them to tap along with the sequences in a regular way. He found that for faster sequences, people tended to tap subharmonics of the event frequency that was presented, similar to the reported groupings in perceptual experiments (Vos, 1973). Thus, people perceive and produce metric relationships such as 1:2 and 1:3 spontaneously, in the absence of stressed stimulus events.

6.3.1. Summary

Studies with periodic, unaccented event sequences have confirmed and extended basic predictions of music theorists. In response to periodic sequences, an endogenous periodicity stabilizes, and can then persist after cessation of the stimulus. Pulse is not strictly periodic; however, it has both short-term and longer timescale ($1/f$) structure. Pulse has a characteristic timescale, which changes with age. People can synchronize motor actions with periodic stimuli, and they tend to anticipate stimulus events in periodic sequences. Synchrony is a stable state, resistant to perturbations in phase and tempo. Antisynchrony (syncopation) is also stable at lower frequencies but reverts to synchrony as it loses stability. Finally, people spontaneously perceive metrical accent patterns even in periodic stimuli, in the form of subharmonics of the rhythmic frequency of the stimulus. In the next section, I consider the kinds of neural processes that might exhibit these basic characteristics.

6.4. A Theoretical Framework

To briefly summarize the discussion so far, pulse and meter refer to the experience of a regular temporal structure in a rhythm whose actual temporal structure may be quite complex. Nevertheless, the percept depends upon the multiple periodicities of the stimulus sequence. Therefore, it is not surprising that one of the main frameworks that has emerged for theorizing about musical meter involves resonance (e.g., Large & Kolen, 1994; van Noorden & Moelants, 1999). *Resonance* refers to the response of an oscillation, exposed to a periodic stimulus, whose frequency stands in some particular relationship to the oscillator's natural frequency. In general, both linear and nonlinear oscillators resonate, and both linear and nonlinear resonance models have been proposed to account for perceptions of pulse and meter. However, these exhibit different properties, and therefore make different predictions, as we shall see.

In this section I describe a theory that links the phenomenology of pulse and meter with concepts of neural oscillation, which is a nonlinear phenomenon. The basic idea is that when a network of neural oscillators, spanning a range of natural frequencies, is stimulated with a musical rhythm, a multifrequency pattern of oscillations is established. Endogenous pulse is linked with the concept of spontaneous oscillation, generalized synchrony with entrainment, and metric accent structure with higher order resonances, found in nonlinear oscillators at simple integer ratios. The stability properties of pulse and meter will be thought of as dynamical stability within this framework: amplitude stability in a limit cycle, phase stability in entrainment, and pattern stability in a network of neural oscillators.

6.4.1. *Neural Oscillation*

Interaction of excitatory and inhibitory neural populations can give rise to neural oscillation. This arrangement is illustrated schematically in Figure 6.3A, showing the necessary synaptic connections between excitatory and inhibitory populations (Aronson et al., 1990; Hoppenstaedt & Izhikevich, 1996; Izhikevich, 2007; Wilson & Cowan, 1973). There are many different mathematical models available that can be used to describe nonlinear oscillations, and the principal concern is to choose a level of mathematical abstraction that is appropriate for the type of data that are available and the type of predictions that are desired. Figure 6.3B shows the main possibilities: (1) the biophysical level, where each neuron is modeled by its own set of Hodgkin–Huxley equations (Hodgkin & Huxley, 1952); (2) the oscillator level, where various mathematical simplifications of more detailed models are available; or (3) the canonical level, which results from mathematical analysis of oscillator-level models, given certain assumptions about parameter values (cf., Hoppenstaedt & Izhikevich, 1997). Discrete time models have also been studied, enabling analysis of oscillator behavior under slightly different assumptions than canonical models. Importantly, such analysis has shown that, under certain assumptions, all nonlinear oscillator models share a set of universal properties, independent of many details (Wiggins,

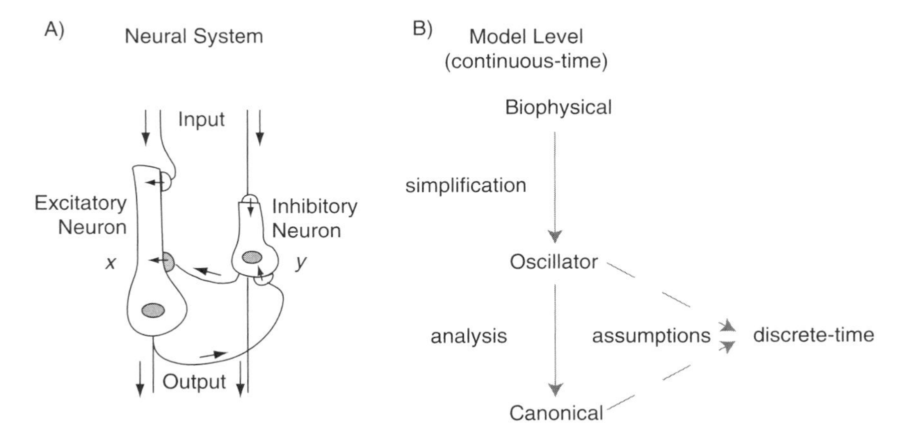

Figure 6.3: Neural oscillation. (A) A neural oscillation can arise from the interaction between excitatory and inhibitory neural populations (adapted from Hoppenstaedt & Izhikevich, 1996). (B) Multiple levels of mathematical abstraction for describing neural oscillation.

1990). This makes such models especially attractive from the point of view of modeling human behavior.

A detailed discussion of neural oscillation is beyond the scope of this chapter; however, I present some of the main ideas and results from this literature to demonstrate the basic predictions of neural resonance, as well as to enable deeper understanding of specific models that have been proposed for pulse and meter. In this section, the reader will encounter a few equations, which should be treated as guideposts, to enable connection of these ideas with the theoretical neuroscience literature. Less mathematically inclined readers can ignore these details, but should read the sections on universal properties of nonlinear oscillation and oscillator models of pulse and meter. The reader who chooses to embrace the details will find a rich research area that has only begun to be explored by theorists. Excellent general introductions to nonlinear dynamics are the books by Strogatz (1994) and Scheinerman (1996); a thorough and readable treatment of nonlinear oscillation with a strong focus on experimentation is the book by Pikovsky, Rosenblum, and Kurths (2001). Two excellent and rigorous, but readable, discussions of neural oscillation are the books by Hoppenstaedt and Izhikevich (1997) and Izhikevich (2007).

6.4.1.1. Biophysical models At the biophysical level, one can construct realistic models of neural oscillation in which each neuron is described by a set of Hodgkin–Huxley equations (Hodgkin & Huxley, 1952). In animals, this approach has enabled understanding of neural pattern generation (Marder, 2000) and neural responses to external sound stimuli (e.g., Large & Crawford, 2002). However, no one has yet ventured a model of human rhythm perception at this level, for two main reasons. First, biophysical models are stated in terms of voltage and conductance, making predictions about variables that are best observed in neurophysiological experiments. Second, the large systems of equations necessary to predict human behavior would be rather intractable, both from the point of view of mathematical analysis and computer simulation (but see Izhikevich & Edelman, 2008).

6.4.1.2. Oscillator models Beginning in the 1960s, theorists such as FitzHugh (1961), Nagumo, Arimoto, & Yoshizawa (1962), Wilson and Cowan (1973), and others applied various simplifying assumptions to produce more tractable mathematical models of neural oscillation. FitzHugh and Nagumo, for example, created a two-dimensional simplification of the four-dimensional Hodgkin–Huxley neuron. The Wilson–Cowan model of neural oscillation (Wilson & Cowan, 1973) can be thought of as describing two neural populations, one excitatory and one inhibitory, as illustrated schematically in Figure 6.3A. Each population is modeled by a single differential equation (Hoppenstaedt & Izhikevich, 1996).

$$\begin{aligned} \frac{dx}{dt} &= -x + S(\rho_x + ax - by + s(t)) \\ \frac{dy}{dt} &= -y + S(\rho_y + cx - dy) \end{aligned} \qquad (6.1)$$

Here x describes the activity of the excitatory population and y describes the activity of the inhibitory population. The parameters a and d capture properties of the excitatory and inhibitory populations, respectively, while b and c capture the interaction of the two populations. The function S is sigmoidal, and ρ_x and ρ_y are parameters that control whether the system oscillates spontaneously or comes to rest. The sigmoid function is a nonlinearity that limits the maximum amplitude of the oscillation, so x and y vary between zero and one. The time-varying input, $s(t)$, represents an input rhythm. It also appears inside the sigmoid function, meaning that coupling to the external input is also nonlinear. In principle, input can affect both populations, but for simplicity I consider only input to the excitatory population. Figure 6.4A shows the time series generated by Equation 6.1, for a stimulus with a frequency (ω_0) that approximates the natural frequency of the oscillator (ω). Figure 6.4B plots x and y against one another, revealing the oscillation as a cycle in the state space trajectory.

Oscillator-level models such as Wilson–Cowan (Hoppenstaedt & Izhikevich, 1996; Wilson & Cowan, 1973) are two-dimensional and in the absence of stimuli they exhibit two stable behaviors: They can oscillate spontaneously (limit cycle) or they relax toward a stable state (fixed point).[4] Below, I will associate the spontaneous oscillation of a stable limit cycle with the endogenous periodicity of musical pulse. The details of oscillator behavior can be diverse, however, making it difficult to

4. Another influential model for human rhythmic behavior is a van der Pol–Rayliegh hybrid model (Haken, Kelso, & Bunz, 1985; Jirsa, Fink, Foo, & Kelso, 2000), which includes nonlinear coupling and exhibits similar properties to neural models.

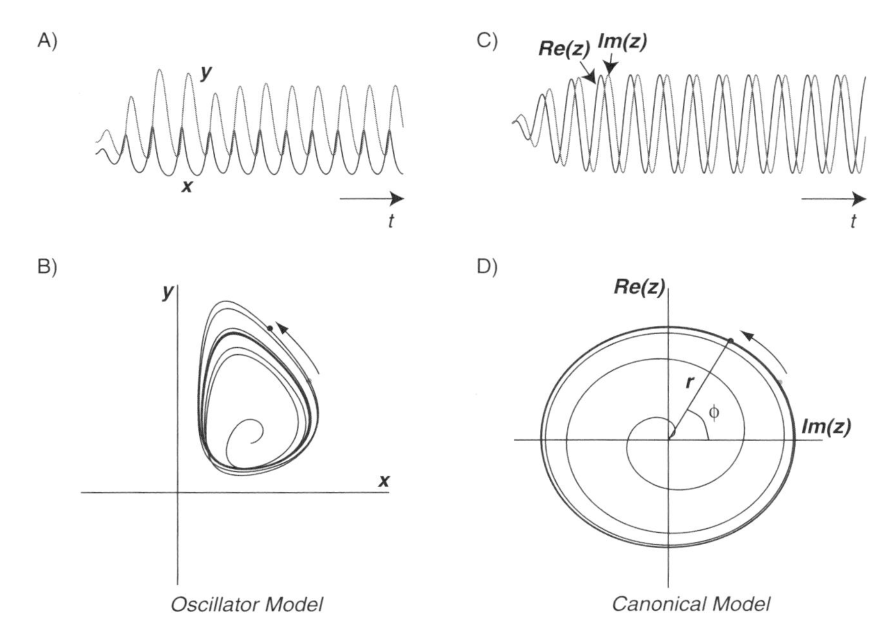

Figure 6.4: Transforming an oscillator-level model to a canonical model. (A) Time series generated by a driven Wilson-Cowan system (Equation 6.1). (B) The time series of (A) projected onto state space (x, y). (C) Time series generated by the equivalent canonical model (Equation 6.2). (D) The time series of (C) projected onto state space ((Re(z), Im(z)), in Cartesian coordinates, or (r, ϕ) in polar coordinates).

compare the predictions of different models at this level of description. Therefore, we employ normal-form analysis (Wiggins, 1990), which involves a coordinate transformation, followed by a Taylor expansion of the nonlinearities, truncating at some point ignoring the *higher order terms* of the expansion (abbreviated as h.o.t in Equation 2). Effectively, this transforms the oscillation in Figure 6.4A and B to the oscillation in Figure 6.4C and D, regularizing the limit cycle and approximating the nonlinearities, producing what is called a canonical model. A canonical model is usually the simplest (in analytical terms) of a class of equivalent dynamical models. More importantly, this transformation works for virtually any model of neural oscillation, under certain assumptions that are generally reasonable for neural systems (Hoppenstaedt & Izhikevich, 1997).

6.4.1.3. The canonical models The canonical model is useful because it reveals significant similarities among the behavior of all neural oscillators, despite potentially important physiological differences. The surprising result is that virtually all neural oscillator models share the same canonical model (Hoppenstaedt & Izhikevich, 1996). Thus, the canonical model uncovers universal properties, making predictions that hold under a rather general set of assumptions (Hoppenstaedt & Izhikevich, 1997). The following is the canonical model for neural oscillation as derived from the Wilson–Cowan model of Equation 6.1 (Aronson et al., 1990; Hoppenstaedt & Izhikevich, 1996).

$$\frac{dz}{dt} = z(\alpha + i\omega + (\beta + i\delta)|z|^2) + cs(t) + \text{h.o.t.} \tag{6.2}$$

This differential equation is two-dimensional, because z is a complex variable, having real (Re(z)) and imaginary (Im(z)) parts. It has both real (α, β) and imaginary (ω, δ) parameters as well, whose meanings will be disclosed momentarily. For simplicity, the connection strength, c, of the time-varying rhythmic stimulus, $s(t)$, is taken to be a real number. This model can be readily analyzed. For example, Equation 6.2 may be rewritten in polar coordinates, by setting $z = re^{i\phi}$, and using Euler's formula $e^{i\phi} = \cos\phi + i\sin\phi$. This transformation reveals the dynamics of amplitude, r, and phase, ϕ, separately and clearly.

$$\begin{aligned} \frac{dr}{dt} &= r(\alpha + \beta r^2) + cs(t)\cos\phi + \text{h.o.t.} \\ \frac{d\phi}{dt} &= \omega + \delta r^2 - c\frac{s(t)}{r}\sin\phi + \text{h.o.t.} \end{aligned} \tag{6.3}$$

The polar formulation makes no assumptions about the canonical equation, and it is not an approximation. It shows how the parameters relate directly to the behavior of the oscillator in terms of changes in amplitude and phase. The parameters are α, the bifurcation parameter, β, the nonlinear saturation parameter, ω, the eigen frequency (natural frequency; $\omega = 2\pi f$, f in Hz), and δ, the frequency detuning parameter. The connection strength, c, represents influences of the stimulus on the oscillator. The canonical model allows one to manipulate properties of the oscillation separately. For example, the bifurcation parameter (α), which determines whether or not the system oscillates spontaneously, can be manipulated independently of frequency (ω). We can also see that when $\delta \neq 0$, the instantaneous frequency of the oscillator depends not only on its natural frequency (ω) but also on its amplitude ($\omega + \delta r^2$). The main properties revealed by this analysis are described next.

6.4.2. Universal Properties of Neural Oscillators

Universal properties of neural oscillation are revealed in the canonical form (Equations 6.2 and 6.3). These properties are generic, and thus expected to be observed in all neural oscillators, despite differences in neurophysiology or network organization. I focus on those predictions that relate to the main phenomenological properties of pulse and meter: endogenous periodicity, generalized synchrony, and metrical accent.

6.4.2.1. Spontaneous oscillation Consider a nonlinear oscillator in the absence of a stimulus (e.g., Equation 6.3, with $s(t) = 0$). In this case the oscillator can display two behaviors depending upon the bifurcation parameter α. As illustrated in Figure 6.5A, when $\alpha < 0$ the system behaves as a damped oscillator, but when $\alpha > 0$ (negative damping) the system generates a spontaneous oscillation. In the latter case, the amplitude of the oscillation stabilizes at $r = \sqrt{\alpha/\beta}$. $\alpha = 0$ is the bifurcation point, the critical value of the parameter at which the behavior changes from damped oscillation to spontaneous oscillation. The bifurcation is called the Andronov-Hopf bifurcation. If one continues the expansion of higher order terms one finds other bifurcations, such as the Bautin bifurcation (Guckenheimer & Kuznetsov, 2007) that also lead to spontaneous oscillation. The capacity for spontaneous oscillation may explain the experience of endogenous periodicity. It predicts the capacity of pulse to continue after a stimulus ceases ($s(t) = 0$), as observed in some experiments.

6.4.2.2. Entrainment When a stimulus is present, spontaneous oscillation continues; however, stimulus coupling affects the oscillation's phase. Figure 6.5B plots coupling as a function of relative phase for two different stimulus frequencies. The two curves depict two different amounts of frequency (mis)match between the stimulus and the oscillation. The point at which each function crosses the horizontal axis with negative slope is a stable state, the relative phase at which the system settles in the long run. The phase coupling described above (Equations 6.2 and 6.3), and depicted in Figure 6.5B, generates 1:1 synchrony, and additionally provides a means of predicting systematic deviations from precise synchrony, such as the anticipation tendency observed in some synchronization experiments. If the frequency of a stimulus (ω_o) is equal to that of the oscillator (ω) the two enter into a state of precise synchrony. If oscillator frequency is greater than that of the stimulus, relative phase will be negative, anticipating the stimulus. The capacity for 1:1 synchrony is observed in both linear and nonlinear models. Entrainment of nonlinear oscillators also predicts a more general form of synchrony (e.g., 1:2, 3:2, 3:1). The terms that describe this behavior, however, are hidden in the higher order terms of Equations 6.2 and 6.3. Higher order terms describe the capacity for antiphase and multifrequency modes of coordination with rhythmic stimuli, described in more detail next.

6.4.2.3. Higher order resonance Figure 6.5C presents the results of three simulations of an array of nonlinear oscillators, based on Equation 6.2. The frequencies of the oscillators in the array vary from 0.5 to 8.0 Hz, along a logarithmic frequency gradient, and the stimulus is a sinusoid with a frequency of 2 Hz (period 500 ms). In these simulations, I included *higher order terms* (abbreviated h.o.t. in Equation 6.2) to illustrate some of the coordination modes possible for neural oscillations. These simulations illustrate a number of important properties of nonlinear resonance. First, nonlinear oscillators have a sort of filtering behavior, responding maximally to stimuli near their own frequency. At low levels, high frequency selectivity is achieved. As stimulus amplitude increases, frequency selectivity deteriorates due to nonlinear compression ($\beta < 0$). Frequency detuning

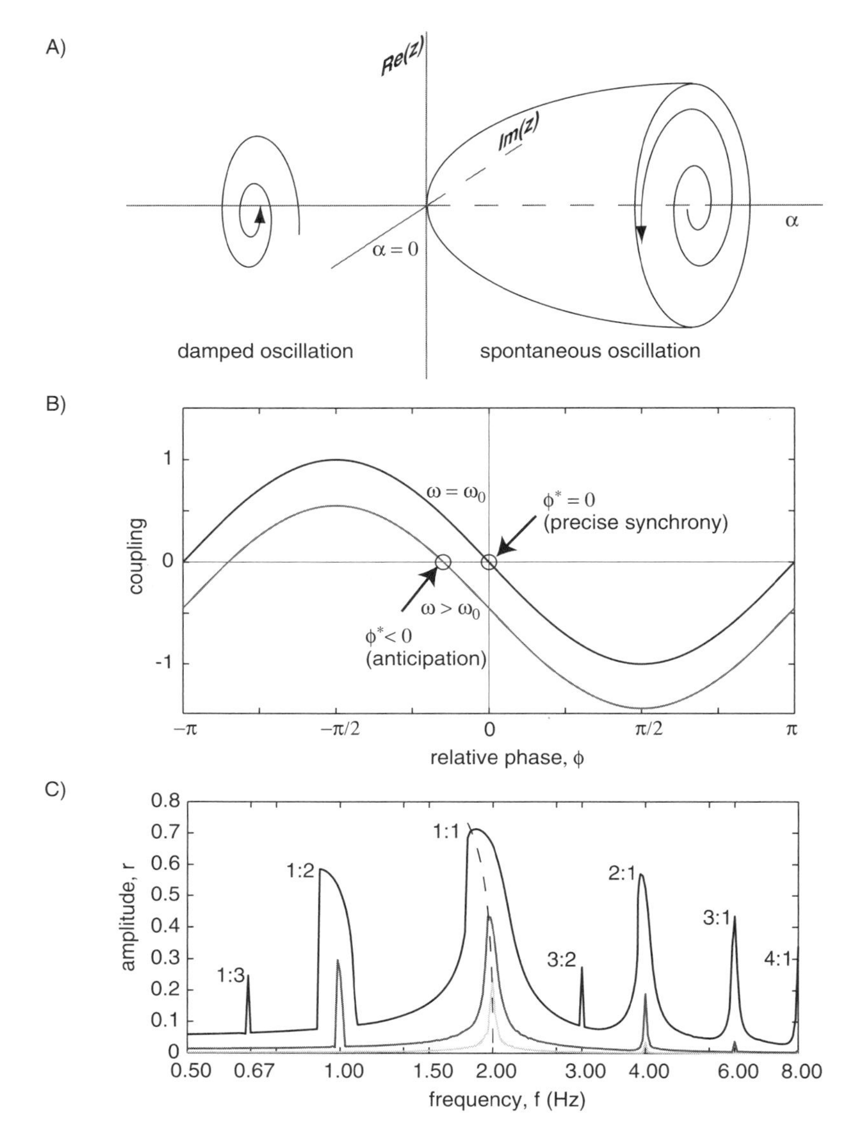

Figure 6.5: Three universal properties of nonlinear oscillation: spontaneous oscillation, entrainment, and higher order resonance. (A) Spontaneous oscillation: When the bifurcation parameter crosses zero, a spontaneous oscillation is generated, as energy is added into the system. (B) Entrainment: Entrainment of phase is brought about by stimulus coupling (see Equation 6.3). (C) Higher order resonance: The amplitude response of a nonlinear oscillator bank (Equation 6.2) stimulated with a sinusoid at 2 Hz, at three different amplitudes.

($\delta \neq 0$) predicts that the peaks in the resonance curve begin to bend as the strength of the stimulus increases. Most importantly, oscillations arise at frequencies that are not present in the stimulus, due to nonlinear stimulus coupling, described in the higher order terms. The strongest response is found at the stimulus frequency, but oscillations are also observed at harmonics (e.g., 2:1 and 3:1), subharmonics (e.g., 1:2 and 1:3), and more complex integer ratios (e.g., 3:2) of the stimulus frequency. At low stimulus intensities, higher order resonances are small; they increase with increasing stimulus intensity. Nonlinear resonance predicts that metrical accent may arise even when no corresponding frequency is present in the stimulus. This could explain the subharmonic accent patterns that have been observed in perception and coordination with periodic sequences (e.g., Parncutt, 1994; Vos, 1973). Moreover, coupling between oscillators in such a network would also exhibit nonlinear resonances, giving rise to stable patterns of metrical accent, and favored frequency ratios including harmonics, and subharmonics, and integer ratios (cf., Large, 2000a). Coupling between oscillators in a multifrequency network (e.g., Large & Palmer, 2002) may also explain the subdivision effects that have been observed in synchronization experiments (Large et al., 2002; Repp, 2008), as described in the next section.

6.4.3. A Discrete Time Model

Before moving on to review particular resonance models of pulse and meter, I briefly describe a related mathematical abstraction that has proven useful for capturing pulse and meter, the discrete time circle map. If we consider an oscillator spontaneously generating an oscillation with a stable limit cycle amplitude, and we further assume that the stimulus is not too strong (Pikovsky et al., 2001) then we can ignore amplitude and work entirely in the phase dimension. Thus, we consider the phase equation of the system above (Equation 6.3, assume $r(t) = 1$) and to further simplify matters, we also ignore frequency detuning ($\delta = 0$) and higher order terms.

$$\frac{\mathrm{d}\phi}{\mathrm{d}t} = \omega - cx(t)\sin\phi \tag{6.4}$$

Next, assume the stimulus to be a periodic series of discrete impulses (arguably a reasonable assumption for rhythmic stimuli), with fixed period, T_0 ($T_0(\mathrm{s}) = 1/f_0$ (Hz); note also, $\omega_0 = 2\pi f_0$). Then the above phase equation can be integrated to create the discrete time (stroboscopic) mapping,

$$\phi_{n+1} = \phi_n + \omega T_0 - c\sin(\phi_n) \tag{6.5}$$

known as a circle map. Formally, one should also apply the operation modulo 2π to the right hand side, but it is omitted here for simplicity of presentation. Once this transformation has been accomplished, the phase variable, ϕ, represents relative phase, the phase of the oscillator when an input event occurs. Importantly, although Equation 6.5 is derived here from the canonical model (cf., Pikovsky et al., 2001), circle maps can be arrived at in several different ways, and are used in the study of relaxation oscillations as well. In this case, Equation 6.5 has been derived using the truncated normal form, thus this coupling term takes on the simplest possible form (a sine function). In the general case the coupling term would be a more complex periodic function.[5] The discrete time model is simple, but powerful. Although it ignores the dynamics of amplitude, it exhibits entrainment and higher order resonance properties that make it useful for describing important aspects of pulse and meter, as discussed below.

To sum up, the hypothesis of neural resonance to rhythmic stimuli makes certain generic predictions about responses to rhythms. It predicts endogenous periodicity as spontaneous oscillation in the neural system. It predicts the generalized synchrony of pulse and meter as entrainment of nonlinear oscillations to an external stimulus. It predicts the perception of metrical accent as higher order resonances in nonlinear oscillators. It is crucial to realize that neural resonance is not a computational model that adds mechanisms for entrainment and multifrequency resonance to an underlying clock mechanism. The predictions arise from the intrinsic physics of neural oscillation, as revealed by mathematical analysis. The next section reviews how mathematical models, at various levels of abstraction, have been used to create specific computational simulations of pulse and meter.

6.4.4. Models of Pulse and Meter

Historically, the study of neural oscillation has followed the path from most detailed to most abstract, from Hodgkin-Huxley (1952) through the oscillator-level models of FitzHugh (1961), Nagumo et al. (1962), Wilson and Cowan (1973), and others, to canonical models of Aronson et al. (1990) and Hoppenstaedt and Izhikevich (1996). Resonance models of pulse and meter perception have so far followed the opposite course, from most abstract to least abstract, beginning with discrete time models (Large & Kolen, 1994; McAuley, 1995) through linear resonance models (Scheirer, 1998; Todd, O'Boyle, & Lee, 1999) and the canonical nonlinear model of Large (2000a), to the oscillator-level model of Eck (2002).

6.4.4.1. Discrete time models The first nonlinear resonance models of pulse and meter were the discrete time models of Large and Kolen (1994) and McAuley (1995), which were soon followed by the more refined approaches of Toiviainen (1998), Large and Jones (1999), Large and Palmer (2002), and others. All adopted the most abstract mathematical model of nonlinear oscillation, the circle map, and therefore make quite general predictions. Furthermore, all share the basic goal of modeling

5. In the continuous time canonical model (Equations 6.2 and 6.3), this coupling term captures only 1:1 coupling, higher order terms are required to produce the higher order resonances. However, owing to the differences between the continuous time and discrete time formulations, in this map, the coupling term produces the full variety of higher order resonances pictured in Figure 6C.

perception and attention in a temporally flexible way that could deal with the naturally variable tempi of music performance (see Palmer, 1997).

To create a model of phase entrainment to musical rhythm, it is first assumed that a musical rhythm (Figure 6.6A) may be adequately described as temporally discrete impulses (Figure 6.6B). Such data is readily collected in the laboratory in the form of MIDI recordings of musical performances, and retains the most basic information about event timing. The key insight is to replace the fixed period, T_0, of a discrete

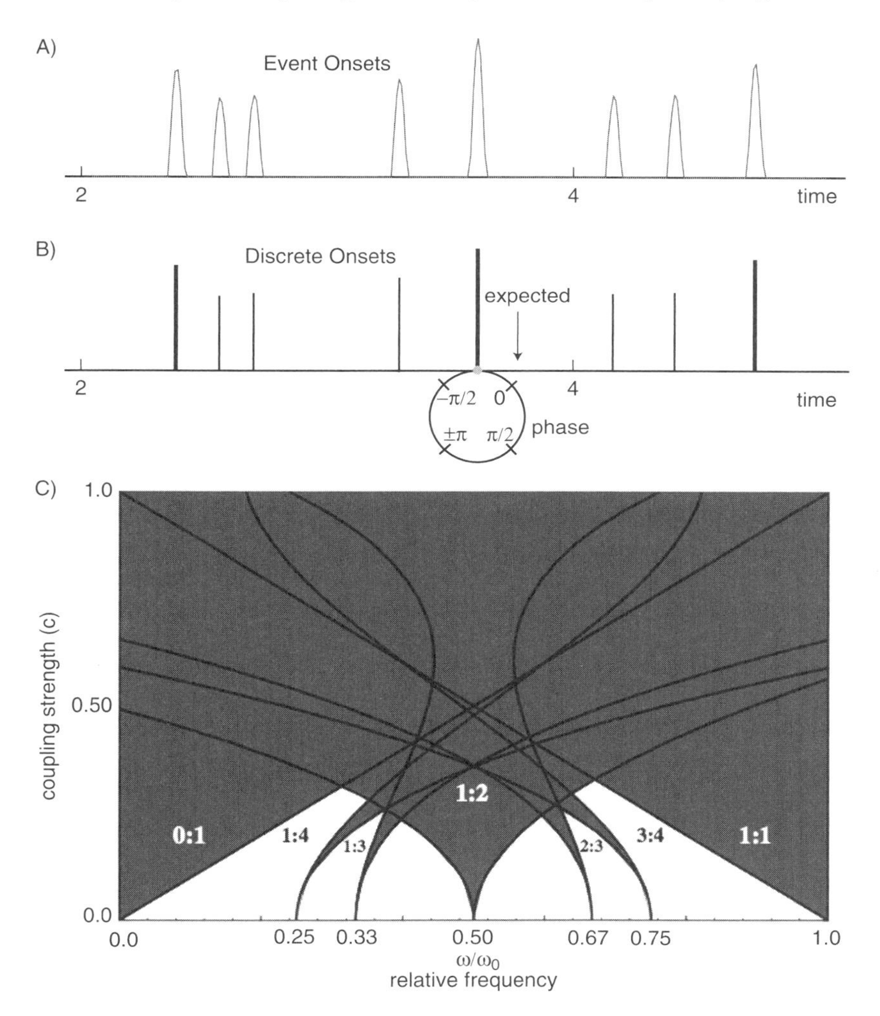

Figure 6.6: Discrete time models of pulse. (A) Continuous time series of event onsets from the *Goldberg Variations*. (B) Discrete time representations of the same onsets. Onsets coinciding with the basic pulse are shown as heavy lines. Time is transformed into relative phase *via* Equation 6.6. (C) Resonance regions in a discrete time model (adapted from Large & Kolen, 1994).

map with the succession of IOIs recorded in a music performance.[6]

$$\phi_{n+1} = \phi_n + \omega(t_{n+1} - t_n) - cF(\phi_n) \tag{6.6}$$

This formulation was conceived as a model of temporal expectation by Large and Kolen (1994), who linked this approach to Meyer's theory of musical emotion. The idea is that a specific point in the limit cycle, $\phi = 0$, corresponds to the times at which musical events are expected, illustrated in Figure 6.6B. According to McAuley (1995), the basic theoretical insight is to model the perception of time as phase. The models implicitly assume a stable limit cycle, or endogenous oscillation, although they are silent on the issue of how such an oscillation might arise.

One of the most interesting aspects of the behavior of a simple discrete time model is the nonlinear resonances that arise in the system. These were studied through analysis as well as numerical simulation of the basic phase equation (Large & Kolen, 1994; McAuley, 1995). Figure 6.6C shows the results of one such analysis, illustrating that a neural oscillator responds both to its own frequency and to frequencies that approximate integer ratios of its frequency. In the figure, only a few of the largest regions are shown. The resonance regions of Figure 6.6C are generic. In biophysical and oscillator-level models, the same resonances are observed; however, the regions they occupy in parameter space may appear transformed.

In early models, generally one or a few oscillators were considered, and the focus was on tracking changes in performance tempo. It was noted at that time that phase entrainment alone would not provide sufficient flexibility to follow large tempo changes (Large & Kolen, 1994; McAuley, 1995). Thus, a model of tempo adaptation was added as a parameter dynamics, and such models became known as adaptive oscillator models (McAuley, 1995). Finally, all that is required of the phase-coupling function, F, is that it be periodic. $F = \sin$ is the simplest choice; however, for tracking very complex rhythms, a modification can be used. The modification was to limit the extent of phase adaptation to a critical region, or temporal receptive field, within which the oscillator will adapt to tempo change (Large & Kolen, 1994; Large & Palmer, 2002). Outside this region, events will have little phase-resetting effect. As pointed out by Eck (2002), the effect of this choice of F was for the model to behave more like a relaxation oscillator. Large and Jones (1999) conceptualized this window as an expectancy region, termed an attentional pulse, within which events were expected. We discuss a conceptualization of oscillator dynamics as attentional dynamics in the next section.

6.4.4.2. Canonical models Owing to the special relationship between linear resonance models and the canonical form of Equation 6.2, I consider linear models as a special case of canonical models.[7] In linear models of rhythm perception,

6. It should also be noted that phase varied from 0 to 1, whereas the equations here work in radians, and $\omega = 2\pi/T$, because of the way they have been derived.

7. Equation 6.2 can be used to create a linear resonance model that is directly comparable to the nonlinear model. To do this, one chooses the coefficients of the nonlinear terms (β and δ) to be zero, and one also ignores higher order terms (because there are none).

bandpass or comb filters (Oppenheim & Schafer, 1975) are arranged in an array by center frequency, from lowest to highest, and stimulated with a continuous time representation of a rhythmic stimulus (e.g., Figure 6.1C). Scheirer (1998) constructed a gradient-frequency bank of comb filters, similar to pitch tracking models, but presented a continuous time rhythmic signal, creating a continuous time model for pulse and meter (see also Klapuri, Eronen, & Astola, 2006). Todd et al. (1999) proposed a similar model, using bandpass filters. In such a model, a linear filter bank extracts the amplitude and phase of the frequency components of a rhythmic stimulus, and the output with the highest amplitude can be used to drive a motor output, providing a model of synchronization behavior (Todd, O'Boyle, & Lee, 1999). Bandpass filter models predict 1:1 phase synchrony of resonators with stimulus frequencies, and capture metrical accent to the extent that a metrical stress pattern is physically present in the stimulus time series. Simple linear resonators do not exhibit spontaneous oscillations or higher order resonances. Interestingly, comb filters are sensitive to multiple frequencies (comparable to higher order resonances) but at the expense of temporal delays on a rhythmic timescale (100 ms to several seconds). However, even comb filters do not possess stability properties that enable resistance to change in the face of syncopation (cf., Large, 2000a). Nevertheless, various linear models have had success in identifying tempo, beat, and meter in digital audio recordings, especially for certain musical styles (Eck, 2006; Klapuri et al., 2006; Scheirer, 1998).

Large (2000a) used a canonical model of nonlinear resonance to model meter perception. The model was a network of nonlinear oscillators, arranged along a frequency gradient, quite similar in concept to an array of linear filters (cf., Scheirer, 1998; Todd et al., 1999). Large's model was essentially the truncated normal form of Equation 6.2, and ignored higher order terms, and thus did not include higher order resonances. Instead, the focus of this model was to show how network interactions could give rise to stable oscillations and multifrequency patterns of oscillation. Rhythmic input drove the system through bifurcations, giving rise to self-sustained oscillations at several frequencies. The resulting patterns dynamically embodied beat and meter; they were stable and persistent in the face of rhythmic conflict. The performance of the model was compared with the results of a pulse induction study (Snyder & Krumhansl, 2001, described in further detail below) in which musicians tapped along with musical rhythms. The network matched human performance for natural musical signals and showed a similar pattern of breakdowns as the input degraded.

6.4.4.3. Oscillator-level models Eck (2002) used the FitzHugh–Nagumo model (FitzHugh, 1961; Nagumo et al., 1962) to simulate neural synchronization to music-like rhythms. FitzHugh–Nagumo model is a two-variable simplification of the Hodgkin–Huxley model, and Eck chose the parameters of his model such that the oscillators operated in relaxation mode, meaning that the pair of differential equations exhibited both a fast and a slow timescale, which provided certain advantages in modeling responses to musical rhythms. First, the model displays a sort of phase-dependent input filter, responding strongly to events that happen near phase zero (where the oscillator "expects" events to occur) and relatively less to events at other points in the cycle. Second, the model exhibits stable synchronization in large groups, enabling potentially large networks of oscillators to contribute to an emergent percept of meter. Finally, such oscillators display asymmetrical responses to early versus late events, as humans sometimes do (e.g., Jones, Moynihan, MacKenzie, & Puente, 2002; Zanto, Large, Fuchs, & Kelso, 2005). Eck tested the ability of the oscillator model to determine downbeats in the patterns of Essens and Povel (1985), and the model simulated human responses well.

6.4.5. Summary

The neural resonance theory of pulse and meter holds that listeners experience dynamic temporal patterns, and hear musical events in relation to these patterns, because they are intrinsic to the physics of the neural systems involved in perceiving, attending, and responding to auditory stimuli. Nonlinear oscillations are ubiquitous in brain dynamics, and the theory merely asserts that some neural oscillations — perhaps in distributed cortical and subcortical areas — entrain to the rhythms of auditory sequences. The generic predictions of the theory arise from mathematical analysis of neural oscillation. This is not a computational theory in the sense that pulse and meter are computed by special purpose mechanisms. However, computer models of pulse and meter can be created based on the general theory. These should be treated as simulations of a physical phenomenon based on mathematical models that make necessary simplifying assumptions about neural oscillations. As such, not every model makes predictions about every aspect of pulse and meter. Models formulated at different levels of abstraction may make qualitatively different kinds of predictions. Moreover, models may be constructed to isolate certain aspects while ignoring others. Thus, different models should be evaluated in their respective contexts. The computational models that have been proposed to date have explored a relatively small area of the space of possibilities afforded by neural oscillation. Additional possibilities are suggested by the empirical findings discussed next.

6.5. Nonperiodic Rhythms and Musical Stimuli

One point that arises from the preceding theoretical discussion is that it is important to distinguish between the type of physical system hypothesized by resonance theory, and individual computational models, which may simulate the system at different levels of abstraction. Experiments address different levels of abstraction as well. Some address canonical predictions — spontaneous oscillation, entrainment, and higher order resonance. Some reveal details of the phenomena, such as asymmetries in attending or synchronizing, or the relative prominence of higher order resonances. Others address implicit predictions such as neural correlates or development. Exploration of different tasks and constraints has uncovered resonance-like effects in perception, attention, and motor coordination. In this section, I consider how various empirical studies, conducted with musical stimuli and other nonperiodic rhythms, bear upon the predictions of neural resonance. The discussion is organized according to the theoretical issues, although the fit is rarely neat and tidy, because individual studies may addresses multiple concerns.

6.5.1. ***Spontaneous Oscillation***

The first prediction of neural resonance is spontaneous oscillation, i.e., pulse is an endogenous periodicity that can exist outside the influence of a rhythmic stimulus. Palmer and Krumhansl (1990) demonstrated endogenous pulse in a perceptual task by using goodness-of-fit judgments for events presented in *imagined* metrical contexts. Low-pitched sounds represented the first event in a measure, and listeners were instructed to think of these as the first of 2, 3, 4, or 6 intervening pulses. After several beats, a probe tone was presented at one of the imagined pulse times. The results implied that participants successfully imagined a pulse, and their ratings further revealed differential accent strengths that conformed to metrical patterns. The authors interpreted this to imply abstract knowledge of metrical structure internalized through musical experience. But this result can also be considered from the point of view of neural resonance. On the basis of this interpretation, they found not only support for a stable endogenous pulse but also that the complex response pattern observed was consistent with higher order resonance. In principle, this technique could be used to ask more specific questions about pulse stability.

The next question that arises is that of periodicity versus pseudo-periodicity. Empirical research on music performance has clearly demonstrated that pulse in musical performance is not periodic, and has revealed important relationships between musical structure and patterns of temporal fluctuation (for a review, see Palmer, 1997). For example, rubato is used to mark group boundaries, especially phrases, with decreases in tempo and dynamics, and amount of slowing at a boundary reflecting the depth of embedding (Henderson, 1936; Shaffer & Todd, 1987; Todd, 1985). Patterns of temporal fluctuation have further been shown to reflect the metrical structure of the music (Henderson, 1936; Palmer & Kelly, 1992; Sloboda, 1985). Thus, as Epstein (1995) emphasizes, pulse in music is not rigidly periodic, and in musical interactions, pulse must coordinate in a temporally flexible way. It has not yet been established whether pulse in music performance exhibits $1/f$ structure, nor have any studies used musical patterns as stimuli for continuation tapping of sufficient length to gauge long-term structure. Given the structure observed in continuation from simple periodic sequences, such studies might provide valuable insight into the nature of musical pulse.

Resonance theory implies that biologically preferred periods should exist (McAuley, 1995), and studies with periodic stimuli and behavior support this prediction (Fraisse, 1978; McAuley et al., 2006; Parncutt, 1994; Vos, 1973). van Noorden and Moelants (1999) extended such studies to musical stimuli, by asking listeners to tap along with a wide variety of musical excerpts. They determined the distribution of perceived pulse tempi for musical pieces heard on radio and in recordings of several styles, and fit the distributions with linear resonance curves, showing that over a wide variety of musical rhythms, resonance peaks varied from about 300 ms (3.3 Hz or 200 bpm) to about 600 ms (1.7 Hz or 100 bpm), and depended on musical style. Thus, pulse in music can vary over a wide tempo range that depends on many factors. They used the same technique to fit tempi of perceived pulse in the subjective meter study of Vos (1973), the pulse tapping study of Parncutt (1994), and a study in which listeners tapped the pulse of polyrhythms (Handel & Oshinsky, 1981). They were able to characterize the latter three datasets (Handel & Oshinsky, 1981; Parncutt, 1994; Vos, 1973) with a resonance period of 500–550 ms (about 2 Hz or 120 bpm) and a width at half height of about 400–800 ms (2.5 Hz or 150 bpm to 1.25 Hz or 75 bpm). It is critical to remember, however, that in the experiments of Vos and Parncutt people responded at pulse frequencies that were not present in the stimuli, but at subharmonics of stimulus frequencies.[8] Thus, although linear resonance curves can fit the tempo distributions, they cannot *explain* subharmonic synchronization behavior (cf., McKinney & Moelants, 2006). On the other hand, nonlinear resonance curves as shown in Figure 6.5C, with peaks at a preferred frequency and also at harmonics and subharmonics, can explain such behavior.

Other studies have considered the process of pulse induction in mechanical performances of composed music (e.g., Snyder & Krumhansl, 2001; Toiviainen & Snyder, 2003). These measured the number of beats required for participants to start tapping, which can be taken as an index of the amount of time to reach a stable limit cycle (the so-called relaxation time; Large, 2000a). They varied the amount of musical information (i.e., pitch), level of syncopation, and level of musical training. Both amount of musical information and level of syncopation affected relaxation time, which varied between about 3 and 12 beats on average over different conditions. Moreover, timing information was more important than pitch information in determining the number of beats required to hear a pulse. For highly syncopated sequences, a greater instance of unsuccessful synchronization was also observed, and this has been replicated for more carefully controlled rhythmic patterns (Patel, Iversen, Chen, & Repp, 2005). In addition to synchronization at the frequency of the notated beat (about 600 ms or 100 bpm), participants also often synchronized at harmonics and subharmonics of this frequency, frequencies that were also usually present in the rhythms, and so were not necessarily indicative of higher order resonance. One resonance model of pulse and meter has replicated these results in some detail (Large, 2000a).

6.5.2. *Entrainment*

Many studies have also examined ongoing entrainment with complex and musical rhythms. One recurrent finding is that the anticipation tendency is generally not

8. In Handel and Oshinsky's experiment listeners generally tapped at frequencies that were present in the polyrhythms, and the same would likely be true for most of the musical rhythms.

observed in synchronization with musical stimuli (Snyder & Krumhansl, 2001; Toiviainen & Snyder, 2003). This may be significant because the anticipation tendency is reliably observed in synchronization with periodic stimuli, and it has been suggested to imply the ability to predict upcoming events, and thus is sometimes considered the signature of an endogenous rhythmic process (Engstrom, Kelso, & Holroyd, 1996; Mates et al., 1994). Importantly, however, even randomly timed "raindrops" interspersed amongst periodic events appear to defeat the anticipation tendency (Wohlschlager & Koch, 2000), indicating that spectro-temporal complexity itself somehow is responsible for the elimination of this effect. From the point of view of resonance, early tapping indicates a rhythmic process whose period is shorter than that of the stimulus sequence, leading Wohlschlager and Koch (2000) to suggest that empty time intervals are perceptually underestimated. However, direct tests of this hypothesis have not yielded strong support (Flach, 2005; Repp, in press). One possibility is that this is a dynamical effect arising from the frequency detuning that occurs in nonlinear resonance (i.e., the bend in the resonance curve of Figure 6.5C).

A few studies have quantified stability in the face of rhythmic conflict, by comparing phase entrainment to periodic versus metrically structured versus more syncopated rhythms (Patel et al., 2005; Snyder & Krumhansl, 2001; Toiviainen & Snyder, 2003). Compared with synchronization to periodic rhythms of the same pulse frequency, metrical structuring does not improve overall synchronization accuracy (Patel et al., 2005). Listeners are generally able to synchronize with syncopated patterns as well; however, level of syncopation is a good predictor of pulse-finding difficulty (Patel et al., 2005; Snyder & Krumhansl, 2001). Moreover, metrical position of the first note of excerpts biases participants to tap with the corresponding phase (Snyder & Krumhansl, 2001; Toiviainen & Snyder, 2003). Syncopation causes more off-beat taps, more switches between on-beat and off-beat tapping, higher variability of the inter-tap interval, and larger deviations from the beat, findings that are predicted by Large's (2000a) nonlinear resonance model. Thus, stability in the face of rhythmic conflict is not absolute, both humans and nonlinear oscillators tend to fare more poorly as rhythms become more complex.

Using a rhythm reproduction task, Essens and Povel (1985) provided evidence that metric rhythms are easier to remember and reproduce than rhythms. They explained this as a memory effect, although Large and Jones (1999) argued that maintenance of attentional coordination was the primary difficulty, an argument that is supported in a general way by findings of motor coordination difficulty. However, Fitch and Rosenfeld (2007) used a recognition memory task to assess the immediate and longer term perceptual salience and memorability of rhythm patterns as a function of amount of syncopation. They found that for highly syncopated rhythms, listeners tended to reset the phase of the pulse (in memory), often pursuing a strategy of reinterpreting the rhythm as more standard or canonical. Thus, rhythmic complexities such as syncopation have implications for real time coordination as well as for memory.

Only a few studies have addressed responses to phase perturbations in complex rhythms, and because these have specific relevance to higher order resonance, I discuss these in the next section. Here I focus on the issue of following tempo fluctuations in musical sequences, an issue that has been of primary concern in the development of resonance-based approaches (Large & Jones, 1999; Large & Kolen, 1994; Large & Palmer, 2002; McAuley, 1995). Drake, Penel, and Bigand (2000) asked listeners to tap the pulse of musical excerpts in varied Western tonal styles, each presented mechanically synthesized, mechanically accented, or expressively performed by a concert pianist. Results confirmed that musicians and nonmusicians are readily able to coordinate with temporally fluctuating musical performances. Entrainment with expressive versions occurred at slower frequencies, within a narrower range of synchronization levels, and corresponded more frequently to the theoretically correct metrical hierarchy. Repp (2002c) showed that synchronization with expressively timed music was better than synchronization with a sequence of identical tones that mimicked the expressive timing pattern, or with music that followed a structurally inappropriate (phase-shifted) expressive timing pattern, emphasizing the importance of musical information beyond onset timing.

Dixon, Goebl, and Cambouropoulos (2006) asked listeners to rate the correspondence of click tracks to musical excerpts and, on different trials, to tap along with the excerpts. Their data suggested that in rubato performances, perceived pulses did not coincide precisely with sounded events, instead listeners heard smooth tempo changes, such that some events were early and others late with respect to perceived pulse. This observation is consistent with tempo-tracking dynamics that have been proposed for nonlinear oscillators (e.g., Large & Kolen, 1994). Honing (2005, 2006) has provided an analysis that suggests that perceptual limitations on tracking ability may be taken into account as performers shape temporal fluctuations. Large and Palmer (2002) showed that nonlinear oscillators can track tempo changes successfully, and they showed how deviations from temporal expectancies (embodied in the oscillations) could be successfully used to discern the structural interpretations (phrase and melody) intended by the performers. Overall, the available evidence suggests that listeners smoothly track tempo fluctuations, nonlinear oscillators can track tempo fluctuations of complex rhythms, and deviations from temporal expectancies may provide a means of perceiving structural intentions of performers. Interestingly, the study of musical entrainment has almost exclusively focused on tapping with recorded music; the issue of real time musical interactions between people has so far received far less attention (Repp, 2005).

6.5.3. Higher Order Resonance

Resonance theory predicts spontaneous harmonic and subharmonic resonance (see Figure 6.5C), and experiments with periodic stimuli have borne out some of these predictions (Vos, 1973; Parncutt, 1994). A further hypothesis suggests that multiple endogenous frequencies would couple internally to instantiate dynamic metrical patterns (Large & Jones, 1999; Large, 2000a; Jones, 2008). Moreover, Large and Palmer (2002) demonstrated that, when stimulated with temporally fluctuating rhythms, internally coupled oscillations (with metrically related frequencies) are more resilient than individual oscillators in tracking temporal fluctuations, such as rubato. Such predictions have recently been evaluated with musical stimuli and more complex rhythms.

Repp (1999, 2002c) considered both perception of timing and synchronization of taps with a mechanical excerpt of Chopin's *Etude in E major, Op.10, No.3.*, sequenced on a computer with precise note durations and a steady tempo, creating an isochronous excerpt. In perception experiments, accuracy of time-change detection exhibited a consistent pattern when averaged across trials and participants, even though the music was in strict time. In synchronization experiments, accuracy also exhibited a consistent pattern across trials and participants; moreover, synchronization accuracy profiles correlated strongly with detection accuracy profiles. Listeners' endogenous temporal fluctuations reflected mainly the metrical structure of the music (Repp, 2005). Musical structure and/or spontaneous higher order resonance may have influenced both perception of sequence timing and timing of coordinated movement. This finding is consistent with the hypothesis of a network of oscillators of different frequencies, coupled together in the perception of a complex rhythm (Large & Jones, 1999; Large, 2000a; Large & Palmer, 2002).

Two recent studies (Large et al., 2002; Repp, 2008) have implicated higher order resonances and internal coupling of endogenous oscillations in coordination of motor behavior with complex rhythms. Large et al. (2002) explicitly instructed participants to synchronize at different metrical levels on different trials, with complex rhythms that contained embedded phase and tempo perturbations. They observed that adaptation to perturbations at each tapping frequency reflected information from other metrical levels. In Repp's study, participants tapped on target tones ("beats") of isochronous tone sequences consisting of beats and subdivisions (1:*n* tapping). Phase perturbations at subdivisions perturbed tapping responses, despite the fact that both task instructions and stimulus design encouraged listeners to ignore the perturbations. Moreover, responses were observed both when subdivisions were present throughout the sequence and when they were introduced only in the cycle containing the perturbation. These results show that synchronization to complex rhythms is not merely a process of error correction; rather listeners covertly monitor multiple levels of temporal structure. This provides evidence for spontaneous resonance at harmonics (subdivisions) and internal coupling among multiple endogenous frequencies. To date such observations have been limited to complex rhythms, and it will be important to extend these experiments to musical excerpts.

A number of studies have shown perceptual categorization of time intervals, and demonstrated that metric context modulates categorization (Clarke, 1987; Desain & Honing, 2003; Essens, 1986; Large, 2000b; Povel, 1981; Schulze, 1989). With brief rhythms, Nakajima and colleagues report an intriguing phenomenon, called time shrinking (ten Hoopen et al., 2006; see Chapter 5). When a short time interval is followed by a long one, listeners underestimate the latter, revealing gravitation to a preferred interval ratio of 1:1. Using three-element rhythmic figures, expressed as serial interval ratios, Desain and Honing (2003) notated patterns along the perimeter of an equilateral triangle to assess combined weights of different ratios, finding systematic distortions of rhythms favoring simple temporal ratios. Moreover, listeners perceive both rhythmic categories and temporal deviations from categorical durations, where duration categories appear determined by metrical context (Clarke, 1987; Desain & Honing, 2003; Large, 2000b). Further support for the preferential stability of integer-ratio frequency relationships in meter comes from studies of North American adults asked to synchronize and then continue tapping to complex (additive) meter patterns (Snyder, Hannon, Large, & Christiansen, 2006) (serial interval ratios of 2 + 2 + 3 or 3 + 2 + 2). During synchronization participants produced long:short serial ratios that were between the target ratio of 3:2 and a simple-meter ratio of 2:1, and during continuation the ratios were stretched even more toward 2:1. Thus, people raised in North America (at least) find it difficult to produce additive accent patterns.

6.5.4. Dynamic Attending

Dynamic attending theory (DAT) addresses 'in-the-moment' expectancies that occur during listening (Jones, 1976; Jones & Boltz, 1989). Large and Jones (1999) theorized that active *attending rhythms* synchronize with temporally structured sequences, generating temporal expectancies for future events, thus linking dynamic attention with the concepts of nonlinear resonance (Large, 2000a; Large & Kolen, 1994; McAuley & Jones, 2003). Large and Jones (1999) proposed that endogenous oscillations focus pulses of attending energy toward expected points in time, enabling attentional tracking of complex rhythmic sequences, and online temporal anticipation of individual events. This notion of attentional energy goes beyond the mere existence of neural resonance, to address the issue of how resonance may be exploited by an organism to enable attentional coordination with the dynamic external world (for a review, see Jones, 2008). By virtue of the close link between DAT and neural resonance, much of the empirical research presented in the general context of resonance is directly relevant to DAT. Here I point out the empirical findings that relate specifically to the issue of focusing attentional energy toward individual events as rhythmic sequences unfold in time.

Evidence for the temporal targeting of attentional energy comes from time discrimination, pitch discrimination, and phoneme monitoring tasks, using both sensitivity (*percent correct* or d') and reaction time measures (Barnes & Jones, 2000; Jones & McAuley, 2005; Jones & Yee, 1997; Jones et al., 2002; Large & Jones, 1999; McAuley & Kidd, 1995; Quene & Port, 2005). For example, time and pitch discrimination judgments are thwarted when made in the context of metrically irregular sequences. Jones and Yee (1997) found that when musicians and nonmusicians had to determine "when" a slightly asynchronous tone occurred in metrically regular versus irregular patterns, metrically regular sequences supported time-change detection, while irregular sequences did not, even when metrically regular and irregular sequences were controlled for statistical regularity. Moreover, global context effects of timing and tempo change disrupted time-change detection as predicted by resonance models of meter perception (Jones & McAuley, 2005; Large & Jones, 1999). Temporal regularity has also been found to affect the accuracy and speed of pitch judgments in rhythmic sequences. In one recent study, participants listened for a target's pitch change within recurrent nine-tone patterns having largely isochronous rhythms. Sensitivity to pitch changes (d') was enhanced for probes that occurred at expected, versus unexpected times. Moreover, attentional focus was temporally asymmetric (cf., Eck, 2002), such that disruption of pitch change was greater for tones that occurred early versus those that occurred late (Jones et al., 2006). In a phoneme monitoring experiment, regular versus irregular timing of stressed vowels facilitated reaction times (Quene & Port, 2005), providing support for a domain-general dynamic attentional mechanism. Theoretically, Large and Jones (1999) linked the notion of entrainment *via* phase coupling to attentional capture in the time domain; faster reaction times and higher false alarm rates for temporally unexpected events support the notion of attentional capture (Penel & Jones, 2005).

6.5.5. Development

In part because coordination with music is observed in all known cultures, and because neural resonance provides a potentially universal explanatory mechanism, pulse and meter have been hypothesized to constitute a universal aspect of musical perception and behavior (Trehub & Hannon, 2006). Thus, it is logical to ask whether infants perceive meter. In one study, Bergeson and Trehub (2006) found that 9-month-old infants detected a change in the context of strong metric sequences but not in the context of sequences that induce a metric framework only weakly or not at all. This observation is consistent with adult findings (e.g., Yee, Holleran, & Jones, 1994), thus supporting dynamic attending in infants. Two additional experiments by Bergeson and Trehub (2006) found that infants were able to detect changes in duple meter but not in triple meter patterns. Another study, found that 7-month-old infants discriminated both duple and triple classes of rhythm on the basis of implied meter, despite occasional ambiguities and conflicting grouping structure (Hannon & Johnson, 2005). Additionally, infants categorized melodies on the basis of contingencies between metrical position and tonal prominence.

The above findings are consistent with predispositions for auditory sequences that induce a metric percept, and provide evidence for a preference for 1:2 over 1:3 temporal organization, as predicted by higher order resonance in nonlinear systems (see Figure 6.5C). However, 6-month-old infants were able to perceive rhythmic distinctions within the context of additive stress patterns (aka complex meters), but 12-month-old infants were not (Hannon & Trehub, 2005). Brief exposure to foreign music enabled 12-month-olds, but not adults, to perceive rhythmic distinctions in this foreign musical context. This finding raises some questions related to the universality of structural relationships in meter, a question to which I return below.

Finally, a fundamental sound-movement interaction in the perception of rhythm has been demonstrated in infants. Phillips-Silver and Trainor (2005) showed that bouncing 7-month-old infants on every second versus every third beat of an ambiguous auditory rhythmic pattern influences whether that pattern is perceived in duple (1:2) or in triple (1:3) form. Moreover, visual information was not necessary for this effect, indicating a strong, early developing interaction between auditory and vestibular information in the human nervous system. This early cross-modal interaction between body movement and perception of musical rhythm persists into adulthood as well (Phillips-Silver & Trainor, 2007). Parallel results from adults and infants suggest that the movement-sound interaction develops early and is fundamental to music processing throughout life.

6.5.6. Neural Correlates

Resonance theory predicts that listeners experience temporally patterned metrical structures, and hear musical events in relation to these patterns, because they would be intrinsic to the physics of oscillatory neural systems driven by rhythmic stimuli. The generic predictions of the theory—spontaneous oscillation, entrainment and higher order resonance—arise from mathematical analysis of neural oscillation. To close the loop, then, it makes sense to attempt to identify neural activity that anticipates events within a sequence, persists in the absence of acoustic events, demonstrates phase stability, and is sensitive to metrical structures. Electroencephalography (EEG) and magnetoencephalography (MEG) are the two main techniques for studying the temporal dynamics of auditory processing in the human brain, and this section will concentrate on this literature. Studies of music utilizing functional imaging techniques and brain lesion data have been ably reviewed elsewhere (Peretz & Zatorre, 2005), although at the end of the section, we will touch upon the results of a few recent studies that are of greatest relevance to issues that have been raised in the current review.

Long-latency auditory event-related potentials (ERPs) have been studied extensively but typically with stimulus repetition rates slower than rhythmic tempos, in part because the responses diminish in amplitude at fast tempos and because responses from adjacent tone onsets begin to overlap at IOIs around 500 ms (Carver, Fuchs, Jantzen, & Kelso, 2002). However, using rhythmic stimuli, a number of authors have observed emitted potentials (or omitted stimulus potentials), which display an early modality-specific negative component (Simson, Vaughan, & Ritter, 1976) with topography and latency similar to the N100, a negative deflection 100 ms after tone onset (Janata, 2001). This earlier component of the emitted potential may reflect mental imagery, rather than a violation of expectation (Janata, 1995, 2001), as with later components. Emitted potentials are also observed as a positive peak around 300 ms after the omitted event, and have been equated with the P300, which occurs following an oddball event (see, e.g., Besson, Faita, Czternasty, & Kutas, 1997). Brochard, Abecasis, Potter, Ragot, and Drake (2003) utilized an oddball methodology to study subjective meter (Bolton, 1894; Vos, 1973). Tones were decremented in intensity at odd (hypothetically strong) or even (hypothetically weak) metrical positions, and P300 responses to omitted tones were observed. Differences in the P300 to odd and even tones provided evidence of subharmonic neural responses indicative of subjective metrical accent. Another study using probe beats in different metrical patterns observed that the P300 plays a role in metrical processing for musicians (Jongsma, Desain, & Honing, 2004).

Snyder and Large (2005) observed that peaks in the power of induced beta- and gamma-band activity (GBA), anticipated tone onset (average ~0 ms latency), were sensitive to intensity accents, and persisted when expected tones were omitted, as if an event actually appeared. By contrast, evoked activity occurred in response to tone onsets (~50 ms latency) and was strongly diminished during tone omissions. Thus, the features of induced and evoked activity matched the main predictions for pulse and meter. Zanto et al. (2005) tested the synchrony of GBA, using phase perturbations of a periodic stimulus. Sequence periodicity was violated every 6–10 tones with an early or late tone onset. After both types of perturbation, the latency of the induced activity relaxed to baseline in a fashion similar to what has been observed in motor synchronization studies (e.g., Large et al., 2002; Repp, 2002a). Additionally, asymmetric responses were observed to early versus late tones (cf., Eck, 2002; Jones et al., 2002). A recent MEG study found subharmonic rhythmic responses in the beta band when subjects were instructed to impose a subjective meter on a periodic stimulus (Iverson, Repp, & Patel, 2006), and Fujioka, Large, Trainor, and Ross (2008) reported anticipatory beta-band responses for periodic sequences, and metrical sequences, but not randomly timed sequences. Thus, beta- and gamma-band responses to auditory rhythms in EEG and MEG correlate with predictions of neural resonance.

Finally, functional imaging studies strongly support the notion that rhythmic information is represented across broad cortical and subcortical networks, in a manner that is dependent upon task and level of syncopation (Chen, Penhune, & Zatorre, 2008; Grahn & Brett, 2007; Jantzen, Oullier, Marshall, Steinberg, & Kelso, 2007; Sakai et al., 1999). It is known that metrical rhythms are easier to remember and reproduce than more syncopated rhythms (Essens & Povel, 1985; Fitch & Rosenfeld, 2007), and recently it has been observed that metrical rhythms result in characteristic patterns of functional brain activation (Sakai et al., 1999). Grahn and Brett (2007) observed improved reproductions for metric rhythms, and observed that these rhythms also elicited higher activity in the basal ganglia and SMA, suggesting that these motor areas play a role in mediating pulse and meter perception. Musicians show additional activation unrelated to rhythm type in premotor cortex, cerebellum, pre-SMA, and SMA. Chen et al. (2008) investigated how performance and neural activity were modulated as musicians and nonmusicians tapped in synchrony with progressively more syncopated auditory rhythms. A functionally connected network was implicated, with secondary motor regions recruited in musicians and nonmusicians, while musicians recruited the prefrontal cortex to a greater degree than nonmusicians. The dorsal premotor cortex appeared to mediate auditory–motor interactions. Finally, when subjects *continued* synchronized versus antisynchronized rhythmic movements, different patterns of functional brain activation were observed, despite the fact that the rhythmic stimulus had ceased and the movement itself was identical under the two different conditions (Jantzen et al., 2007).

6.5.7. *Summary*

Experiments with musical rhythms and other nonperiodic laboratory rhythms have turned up findings that are broadly consistent with fundamental predictions of neural resonance: spontaneous oscillation, entrainment, and higher order resonance. The relevant timescales of the phenomena have been identified, and a number of important details of temporal engagements with music have been cataloged. Signatures of nonlinear oscillation have been reported across a range of tasks involving perception, attention, categorization, memory, and performance. Infants as young as seven months show effects of higher order resonance in discrimination and categorization. Potential physiological correlates of neural resonance have been identified. Engagement in rhythmic tasks has been shown to activate broad cortical and subcortical networks. An increasing number of studies are directly evaluating the predictions of nonlinear resonance, yet a surprising number of areas remain largely untouched.

6.6. The Future

6.6.1. *Neural Theories of Pulse and Meter Perception*

A careful reader will have noticed that, to date, computational simulations of pulse and meter have been derived from mathematical models of single-neuron action potentials or from models of alternating excitatory and inhibitory activity. As observed by Eck (2002), the timescale of such neural processes may not provide a good match to the timescale of musical pulse and meter (Parncutt, 1994; van Noorden & Moelants, 1999; Vos, 1973). Therefore, it is fair to ask whether neural resonance really is a plausible theory of pulse and meter. A clue to the answer may come from the experiment of Snyder and Large (2005), who observed bursts of cortical beta- and gamma-band activity to have properties associated with pulse and meter. Bursting is a dynamic state where a neuron repeatedly fires discrete groups, or *bursts* of action potentials, and each burst is followed by a period of quiescence before the next occurs. Inter-burst periods, the time interval between one burst and the next, would be generally consistent with timescales of musical pulse and meter.

Burst oscillation is not yet as well understood as simpler forms of neural oscillation. For example, a complete classification of electrophysiological types of bursters is not currently available. Nevertheless, burst oscillation is currently receiving a great deal of attention in the computational neuroscience literature, and mathematical analyses (Coombes & Bressloff, 2005; Izhikevich, 2007) have shown that bursters display key properties we have relied upon to predict pulse and meter. Moreover, burst oscillation displays both fast and slow timescales (Izhikevich, 2007) as do relaxation oscillations. Figure 6.7 shows a computational simulation of burst oscillation (Izhikevich, 2000) responding to a simple rhythm, displaying both entrainment to the sequence and persistence in the absence of a stimulus event. Neuronal bursting is thought to play an important role in communication between

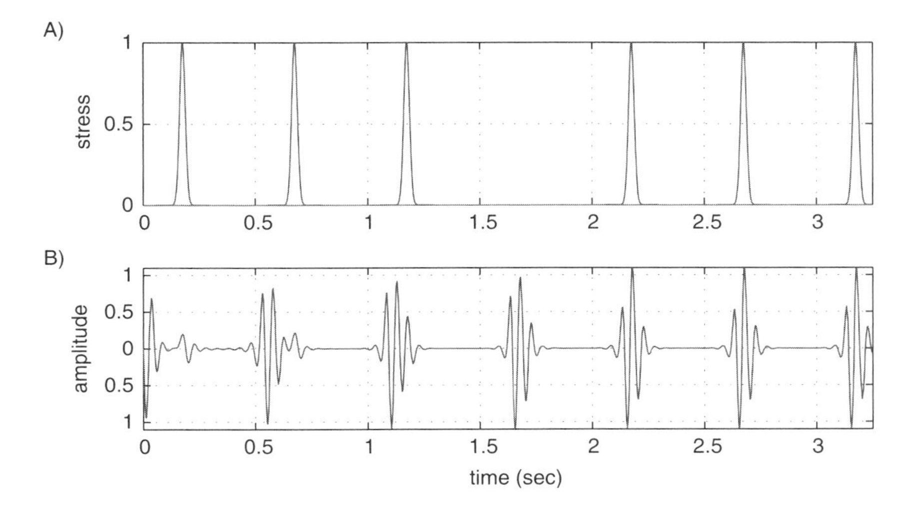

Figure 6.7: Response of a burst oscillator (Izhikevich, 2000) to a rhythmic pattern. (A) Continuous time series representation of event onsets. (B) Bursts of activity entrain to the stimulus and are observed in the absence of a stimulus event.

neurons, and neural bursting figures prominently in motor pattern generation and neural synchronization. The picture that emerges is one of rhythmic communication, *via* neural bursting, between different neural areas as they resonate to musical rhythms. Bursting may also provide additional properties and degrees of freedom that would expand the explanatory potential of neural oscillation with regard to musical rhythm and in relation to other musical dimensions.

6.6.2. Meter or Rhythm?

An interesting issue that is sometimes posed as a challenge to nonlinear resonance is that of the complex meters found in some musical cultures of the Balkans, South Asia, Africa, and Latin America (London, 1995). Complex meters typically contain three beat levels: a slow isochronous level corresponding to the measure, a fast isochronous level that subdivides the measure (into 5, 7, 11, or 13 beats, for example), and an intermediate beat level that groups the faster beats in an uneven fashion, thus creating a nonisochronous pulse. The nonisochronous pulse falls within the typical pulse timescale (van Noorden & Moelants, 1999), and serves as the framework for drumming and dancing that accompanies the music.

In contemplating this issue, there are several questions to consider. First, it is imperative to ask whether "complex meters"—accentuation patterns used as conventional frameworks for making music—are meters in the sense that has been discussed here. An alternative would be that complex stress patterns are compelling specifically because they thwart an intrinsic expectation of periodicity. This begs the hefty theoretical question of how can we establish whether any given pattern of stress qualifies as a pulse or a meter. Unfortunately, the field currently lacks an empirical, operational definition. If it turns out that complex meters meet whatever definition the field can muster, then we must ask whether the spontaneous generation of these particular nonisochonous patterns can be explained within the framework of neural oscillation. Moreover, irrespective of how these questions are answered, the larger question—spontaneous generation of musical rhythm, in all its temporally fluctuating, syncopated, and nonperiodic complexity—remains. As far as I can tell, this is a question that has been almost completely ignored. Here I merely observe that significant theoretical possibilities, such as chaotic oscillation and burst oscillation, remain unexplored. Thus, in terms of music making, the relationship between complex (nonperiodic) musical rhythms, pulse, and meter remains a mystery.

6.6.3. Pitch and Rhythm

In the above discussion, we said next to nothing about the musical content of the stimulus, beyond its temporal structure. At the surface, it is rather surprising that resonance models of pulse and meter have been as successful as they have, while almost totally ignoring intensity, pitch, harmony, and other important musical dimensions. However, in many cases, rhythmic information seems to be significantly more important than melodic accents in predicting listeners' perception of meter (Hannon, Snyder, Eerola, & Krumhansl, 2004; Snyder & Krumhansl, 2001). Huron and Royal (1996) have questioned the effectiveness of melodic accents for marking meter, suggesting that melody and meter are perceptually independent. However, is it really appropriate to ignore other kinds of musical salience, such as *pitch accents* (Jones, 2008)? Jones' joint accent structure hypothesis suggests that temporal, melodic, harmonic, and other factors interact to provide periodicity information. Indeed, it appears that melodic patterns can contribute to a listener's sense of meter and that listeners also respond differentially to various combinations of melodic and temporal accents (Hannon, Snyder, Eerola, & Krumhansl, 2004; Jones & Pfordresher, 1997), especially if the relative salience of different accent types are well calibrated (Ellis & Jones, 2008; Windsor, 1993).

If we accept that melodic and other musical accents can affect meter, then the significant theoretical question arises of how such information couples into a resonant system. Is it sufficient to consider accents arising from different features (intensity, duration, pitch, harmony, and timbre) as combining into a single a scalar value that determines the strength of each stimulus event? Probably not. The flip side of this coin is the effect of pulse and meter on the perception of individual musical events. Recall Zuckerkandl's (1956) view of meter as a series of waves, away from one downbeat and toward the next. As such, meter is an active force; each tone is imbued with a special rhythmic quality from its place in the cycle of the wave, from "the direction of its kinetic impulse." It is, perhaps, a start to show that attention is differently allocated in time; however, it seems clear that future work must consider these issues. Perhaps, if high-frequency neural oscillations are important in binding acoustic features (Wang & Chang, 2008), and if bursts of high-frequency oscillation are operative in resonance to rhythm, this will provide a theoretical vehicle for a future understanding of the relationship between rhythm and melody.

6.6.4. Emotional Responses

According to Meyer, composers and performers set up expectancies in listeners, which they skillfully manipulate, fulfilling some and thwarting others, and it is through expectancy violations that listeners come to experience affective responses to music. Meyer's theory is wonderfully dynamic and seems to explain a great deal about human responses to music (Huron, 2006; Juslin & Sloboda, 2001; Meyer, 1956). However, Meyer dealt mainly with melody and harmony; rhythm is scarcely mentioned. Large and Kolen (1994) explicitly linked resonance to temporal expectancy and to Meyer's theory of musical affect, arguing that the expectancy theory should also extend into the temporal domain; dynamic attending theory is also deeply concerned with temporal expectancy (Jones, 1976). Such considerations imply that violations of temporal expectancies should give rise to affective responses. After all, global rhythm characteristics, such as tempo and articulation, have already been linked to communication of basic emotions through music. Do temporal expectancy violations, such as syncopations or tempo fluctuations, give rise to affective responses? In one study, in which listeners rated the moment-to-moment level of perceived emotionality while listening to musical performances, a systematic relationship between emotionality ratings, timing, and loudness was observed (Sloboda & Lehmann, 2001). This type of study has the potential to link violations of temporal expectancy, which can be measured and modeled in great detail for specific pieces of music, with dynamical musical affect, which is still not well understood. Thus, this area also seems a promising one for future research.

6.7. Concluding Remarks

I have argued that universal properties of nonlinear resonance predict the fundamental features of pulse and meter. The approach derives its predictions from a simple physical hypothesis that pulse and meter arise when nonlinear neural oscillations are driven by musical rhythms. The predictions themselves derive from analyses of neural oscillation. Thus, pulse and meter are seen not as computational "problems" to be solved by the brain; they are simply what happens when nonlinear resonators, operating at the proper timescale, are stimulated by music. To suggest that pulse and meter are therefore "innate" does not really hit the mark; it would be more apt to claim that they are intrinsic to the physics of neural oscillation. All that is then required is coupling to a rhythmic stimulus. A great deal of evidence now supports these predictions, and numerous questions remain open for future investigation.

Acknowledgements

I gratefully acknowledge the support of the NSF (BCS-0094229), the AFOSR (FA9550-07-C0095), and the J. William Fulbright Foreign Scholarship Board. I also wish to thank Mari Reiss Jones, Joel Snyder, Felix Almonte, and Reyna Gordon for helpful comments on an earlier draft of this manuscript. Thanks also to Summer Rankin for her invaluable assistance.

References

Aronson, D. G., Ermentrout, G. B., & Kopell, N. (1990). Amplitude response of coupled oscillators. *Physica D: Nonlinear Phenomena*, *41*(3), 403–449.

Aschersleben, G. (2002). Temporal control of movements in sensorimotor synchronization. *Brain and Cognition*, *48*, 66–79.

Aschersleben, G., Gehrke, J., & Prinz, W. (2001). Tapping with peripheral nerve block. *Experimental Brain research*, *136*(3), 331–339.

Barnes, R., & Jones, M. R. (2000). Expectancy, attention, and time. *Cognitive Psychology*, *41*(3), 254–311.

Bartlett, N. R., & Bartlett, S. C. (1959). Synchronization of a motor response with an anticipated sensory event. *Psychological Review*, *66*, 203–218.

Bergeson, T. R., & Trehub, S. E. (2006). Infants' perception of rhythmic patterns. *Music Perception*, *23*(4), 345–360.

Besson, M., Faita, F., Czternasty, C., & Kutas, M. (1997). What's in a pause: Event-related potential analysis of temporal disruptions in written and spoken sentences. *Biological Psychology*, *46*(1), 3–23.

Bolton, T. L. (1894). Rhythm. *American Journal of Psychology*, *6*(2), 145–238.

Brochard, R., Abecasis, D., Potter, D., Ragot, R., & Drake, C. (2003). The "tick-tock" of our internal clock: Direct brain evidence of subjective accents in isochronous sequences. *Psychological Science*, *14*(4), 362–366.

Buck, J. (1988). Synchronous rhythmic flashing of fireflies. II. *The Quarterly Review of Biology*, *63*(3), 265–289.

Carver, F. W., Fuchs, A., Jantzen, K. J., & Kelso, J. A. (2002). Spatiotemporal analysis of the neuromagnetic response to rhythmic auditory stimulation: Rate dependence and transient to steady-state transition. *Clinical Neurophysiology*, *113*(12), 1921–1931.

Chen, J. L., Penhune, V. B., & Zatorre, R. J. (2008). Moving on time: Brain network for auditory motor synchronization is modulated by rhythm complexity and musical training. *Journal of Cognitive Neuroscience*, *20*(2), 226–239.

Chen, Y., Ding, M., & Kelso, J. A. S. (1997). Long memory processes ($1/f^{\alpha}$ type) in human coordination. *Physical Review Letters*, *79*(22), 4501–4504.

Clarke, E. F. (1987). Categorical rhythm perception: An ecological perspective. In: A. Gabrielsson (Ed.), *Action and perception in rhythm and music* (pp. 19–33). The Royal Swedish Academy of Music.

Coombes, S., & Bressloff, P. C. (Eds). (2005). *Bursting: The genesis of rhythm in the nervous system*. World Scientific Press.

Cooper, G., & Meyer, L. B. (1960). *The rhythmic structure of music*. Chicago, IL: University of Chicago Press.

Daffertshofer, A. (1998). Effects of noise on the phase dynamics of nonlinear oscillators. *Physical Review E*, *58*(1), 327.

Delignières, D., Lemoine, L., & Torre, K. (2004). Time intervals production in tapping and oscillatory motion. *Human Movement Science*, *23*, 87–103.

Desain, P., & Honing, H. (2003). The formation of rhythmic categories and metric priming. *Perception*, *32*(3), 341–365.

Dixon, S., Goebl, W., & Cambouropoulos, E. (2006). Perceptual smoothness of tempo in expressively performed music. *Music Perception*, *23*(3), 195–214.

Drake, C. (1993). Reproduction of musical rhythms by children, adult musicians and adult nonmusicians. *Perception and Psychophysics*, *53*, 25–33.

Drake, C., & Botte, M. (1993). Tempo sensitivity in auditory sequences: Evidence for a multiple-look model. *Perception and Psychophysics*, *54*, 277–286.

Drake, C., Jones, M. R., & Baruch, C. (2000). The development of rhythmic attending in auditory sequences: Attunement, referent period, focal attending. *Cognition*, *77*, 251–288.

Drake, C., & Palmer, C. (1993). Accent structures in music performance. *Music Perception*, *10*, 343–378.

Drake, C., Penel, A., & Bigand, E. (2000). Tapping in time with mechanically and expressively performed music. *Music Perception*, *18*, 1–24.

Dunlap, K. (1910). Reactions to rhythmic stimuli, with attempt to synchronize. *Psychological Review*, *17*, 399–416.

Eck, D. (2002). Finding downbeats with a relaxation oscillator. *Psychological Research*, *66*(1), 18–25.

Eck, D. (2006). Identifying metrical and temporal structure with an autocorrelation phase matrix. *Music Perception*, *24*(2), 167–176.

Ellis, R., & Jones, M. R. (2008). The role of accent salience and joint accent structure in meter perception. *Journal of Experimental Psychology: Human Perception and Performance*, in press.

Engstrom, D. A., Kelso, J. A. S., & Holroyd, T. (1996). Reaction-anticipation transitions in human perception-action patterns. *Human Movement Science*, *15*(6), 809–832.

Epstein, D. (1995). *Shaping time: Music, the brain, and performance*. London: Schirmer Books.

Essens, P. J. (1986). Hierarchical organization of temporal patterns. *Perception and Psychophysics*, *40*, 69–73.

Essens, P. J., & Povel, D. (1985). Metrical and nonmetrical representation of temporal patterns. *Perception and Psychophysics*, *37*, 1–7.

Fitch, W. T., & Rosenfeld, A. J. (2007). Perception and production of syncopated rhythms. *Music Perception*, *25*(1), 43–58.

FitzHugh, R. (1961). Impulses and physiological states in theoretical models of nerve membrane. *Biophysical Journal*, *1*(6), 445–466.

Flach, R. (2005). The transition from synchronization to continuation tapping. *Human Movement Science*, *24*(4), 465–483.

Fraisse, P. (1978). Time and rhythm perception. In: E. C. Carterette & M. P. Friedman (Eds), *Handbook of perception*. New York: Academic.

Fujioka, T., Large, E. W., Trainor, L. J., & Ross, B. (2008). Time courses of cortical beta and gamma-band activity during listening to metronome sounds in different tempo, *10th International Conference on Music Perception and Cognition*. Sapporo, Japan.

Gilden, D. L. (2001). Cognitive emissions of 1/f noise. *Psychological Review*, *108*, 33–56.

Gilden, D. L., Thornton, T., & Mallon, M. W. (1995). 1/f noise in human cognition. *Science*, *267*, 1837–1839.

Grahn, J. A., & Brett, M. (2007). Rhythm and beat perception in motor areas of the brain. *Journal of Cognitive Neuroscience*, *19*(5), 893–906.

Greenfield, M. D. (1994). Synchronous and alternating choruses in insects and anurans: Common mechanisms and diverse functions. *American Zoologist*, *34*(6), 605–615.

Guckenheimer, J., & Kuznetsov, Y. A. (2007). Bautin bifurcation. *Scholarpedia*, *2*, 1853.

Haken, H., Kelso, J. A. S., & Bunz, H. (1985). A theoretical model of phase transitions in human hand movements. *Biological Cybernetics*, *51*, 347–356.

Handel, S., & Oshinsky, J. S. (1981). The meter of syncopated auditory polyrhythms. *Perception and Psychophysics*, *30*(1), 1–9.

Hannon, E. E., & Johnson, S. P. (2005). Infants use meter to categorize rhythms and melodies: Implications for musical structure learning. *Cognitive Psychology*, *50*(4), 354–377.

Hannon, E. E., Snyder, J. S., Eerola, T., & Krumhansl, C. L. (2004). The role of melodic and temporal cues in perceiving musical meter. *Journal of Experimental Psychology: Human Perception and Performance*, *30*(5), 956–974.

Hannon, E. E., & Trehub, S. E. (2005). Tuning in to musical rhythms: Infants learn more readily than adults. *Proceedings of the National Academy of Sciences*, *102*, 12289–12290.

Henderson, M. T. (1936). Rhythmic organization in artistic piano performance. In: C. E. Seashore (Ed.), *Objective analysis of musical performance, University of Iowa studies in the psychology of music IV* (pp. 281–305). Iowa City: University of Iowa Press.

Hodgkin, A., & Huxley, A. (1952). A quantitative description of membrane current and its application to conduction and excitation in nerve. *Journal of Physiology*, *117*, 500–544.

Honing, H. (2005). Is there a perception-based alternative to kinematic models of tempo rubato? *Music Perception*, *23*(1), 79–85.

Honing, H. (2006). Computational modeling of music cognition: A case study on model selection. *Music Perception*, *23*(5), 365–376.

Hoppenstaedt, F. C., & Izhikevich, E. M. (1996). Synaptic organizations and dynamical properties of weakly connected neural oscillators: I: Analysis of a canonical model. *Biological Cybernetics*, *75*, 117–127.

Hoppenstaedt, F. C., & Izhikevich, E. M. (1997). *Weakly connected neural networks*. New York: Springer.

Huron, D. (2006). *Sweet anticipation: Music and the psychology of expectation*. Cambridge, MA: MIT Press.

Huron, D., & Royal, M. (1996). What is melodic accent? Converging evidence from musical practice. *Music Perception*, *13*(4), 489–516.

Iverson, J. R., Repp, B. H., & Patel, A. D. (2006). *Metrical interpretation modulates brain responses to rhythmic sequences*. San Diego, CA: The Neuroscience Institute.

Izhikevich, E. M. (2000). Subcritical elliptic bursting of bautin type. *Society for Industrial and Applied Mathematics*, *60*, 503–535.

Izhikevich, E. M. (2007). *Dynamical systems in neuroscience: The geometry of excitability and bursting*. Cambridge, MA: MIT Press.

Izhikevich, E. M., & Edelman, G. M. (2008). Large-scale model of mammalian thalamocortical systems. *Proceedings of the National Academy of Sciences of the United States of America*, *105*(9), 3593–3598.

Janata, P. (1995). ERP measures assay the degree of expectancy violation of harmonic contexts in music. *Journal of Cognitive Neuroscience*, *7*(2), 153–164.

Janata, P. (2001). Brain electrical activity evoked by mental formation of auditory expectations and images. *Brain Topography*, *13*(3), 169–193.

Jantzen, K. J., Oullier, O., Marshall, M., Steinberg, F. L., & Kelso, J. A. S. (2007). A parametric fMRI investigation of context effects in sensorimotor timing and coordination. *Neuropsychologia*, *45*, 673–684.

Jirsa, V. K., Fink, P., Foo, P., & Kelso, J. A. S. (2000). Parametric stabilization of biological coordination: A theoretical model. *Journal of Biological Physics*, *26*(2), 85–112.

Jones, M. R. (1976). Time, our lost dimension: Toward a new theory of perception, attention, and memory. *Psychological Review*, *83*, 323–335.

Jones, M. R. (2008). Musical time. In: S. Hallam, I. Cross & M. Thaut (Eds), *Oxford handbook of music psychology*. Oxford: Oxford University Press.

Jones, M. R., & Boltz, M. (1989). Dynamic attending and responses to time. *Psychological Review*, *96*, 459–491.

Jones, M. R., & McAuley, J. D. (2005). Time judgments in global temporal contexts. *Perception and Psychophysics*, *67*(3), 398–417.

Jones, M. R., Johnston, H. M., & Puente, J. (2006). Effects of auditory pattern structure on anticipatory and reactive attending. *Cognitive Psychology*, *53*(1), 59–96.

Jones, M. R., Moynihan, H., MacKenzie, N., & Puente, J. (2002). Temporal aspects of stimulus-driven attending in dynamic arrays. *Psychological Science*, *13*, 313–319.

Jones, M. R., & Pfordresher, P. Q. (1997). Tracking musical patterns using joint accent structure. *Canadian Journal of Experimental Psychology*, *51*(4), 271–290.

Jones, M. R., & Yee, W. (1993). Attending to auditory events: The role of temporal organization. In: S. McAdams & E. Bigand (Eds), *Thinking about sound: The cognitive psychology of human audition*. Oxford: Clarendon Press.

Jones, M. R., & Yee, W. (1997). Sensitivity to time change: The role of context and skill. *Journal of Experimental Psychology: Human Perception and Performance*, *23*, 693–709.

Jongsma, M. L. A., Desain, P., & Honing, H. (2004). Rhythmic context influences the auditory evoked potentials of musicians and nonmusicians. *Biological Psychology*, *66*(2), 129–152.

Juslin, P. N., & Sloboda, J. (2001). Psychological perspectives on music and emotion. In: P. N. Juslin & J. Sloboda (Eds), *Music and emotion: Theory and research*. New York: Oxford University Press.

Kelso, J. A. S., DelColle, J. D., & Schöner, G. (1990). Action perception as a pattern formation process. In: *Attention and performance xiii* (pp. 139–169). Hilldale, NJ: Erlbaum.

Klapuri, A. P., Eronen, A. J., & Astola, J. T. (2006). Analysis of the meter of acoustic musical signals. *IEEE Transactions on Audio, Speech, and Language Processing*, *14*(1), 342–355.

Klump, G. M., & Gerhardt, H. C. (1992). Mechanisms and function of call timing in male-male interactions in frogs. In: P. K. McGregor (Ed.), *Playback and studies of animal communication* (pp. 153–174). New York: Plenum Press.

Large, E. W. (2000a). On synchronizing movements to music. *Human Movement Science*, *19*, 527–566.

Large, E. W. (2000b). *Rhythm categorization in context*. Paper presented at the Proceedings of the International Conference on Music Perception and Cognition.

Large, E. W., & Crawford, J. D. (2002). Auditory temporal computation: Interval selectivity based on post-inhibitory rebound. *Journal of Computational Neuroscience*, *13*, 125–142.
Large, E. W., Fink, P., & Kelso, J. A. S. (2002). Tracking simple and complex sequences. *Psychological Research*, *66*, 3–17.
Large, E. W., & Jones, M. R. (1999). The dynamics of attending: How we track time varying events. *Psychological Review*, *106*(1), 119–159.
Large, E. W., & Kolen, J. F. (1994). Resonance and the perception of musical meter. *Connection Science*, *6*, 177–208.
Large, E. W., & Palmer, C. (2002). Perceiving temporal regularity in music. *Cognitive Science*, *26*, 1–37.
Lemoine, L., Torre, K., & Didier, D. (2006). Testing for the presence of 1/f noise in continuation tapping data. *Canadian Journal of Experimental Psychology*, *60*, 247–257.
Lerdahl, F., & Jackendoff, R. (1983). *A generative theory of tonal music*. Cambridge, MA: MIT Press.
London, J. (1995). Some examples of complex meter and their implications for models of metric perception. *Music Perception*, *13*, 59–78.
London, J. (2004). *Hearing in time: Psychological aspects of musical meter*. Oxford: Oxford University Press.
Madison, G. (2004). Fractal modeling of human isochronous serial interval production. *Biological Cybernetics*, *90*(2), 105–112.
Marder, E. (2000). Motor pattern generation. *Current Opinion in Neurobiology*, *10*(6), 691–698.
Mates, J., Muller, U., Radil, T., & Poppel, E. (1994). Temporal integration in sensorimotor synchronization. *Journal of Cognitive Neuroscience*, *6*(4), 332–340.
Mayville, J. M., Bressler, S. L., Fuchs, A., & Kelso, J. A. (1999). Spatiotemporal reorganization of electrical activity in the human brain associated with a timing transition in rhythmic auditory-motor coordination. *Experimental Brain Research*, *127*(4), 371–381.
McAuley, J. D. (1995). Perception of time as phase: Toward an adaptive-oscillator model of rhythmic pattern processing. *Unpublished doctoral dissertation, Indiana University Bloomington*.
McAuley, J. D., & Jones, M. R. (2003). Modeling effects of rhythmic context on perceived duration: A comparison of interval and entrainment approaches to short-interval timing. *Annual Meeting of the Psychonomic Society, November 1998, Dallas, TX, USA*, *29*(6), 1102–1125.
McAuley, J. D., Jones, M. R., Holub, S., Johnston, H. M., & Miller, N. S. (2006). The time of our lives: Life span development of timing and event tracking. *Journal of Experimental Psychology: General*, *135*(3), 348–367.
McAuley, J. D., & Kidd, G. R. (1995). Temporally directed attending in the discrimination of tempo: Further evidence for an entrainment model. *Journal of Acoustical Society of America*, *97*(5), 3278.
McKinney, M. F., & Moelants, D. (2006). Ambiguity in tempo perception: What draws listeners to different metrical levels? *Music Perception*, *24*(2), 155–166.
Merker, B. (2000). Synchronous chorusing and human origins. In: N. L. Wallin, B. Merker & S. Brown (Eds), *The origins of music*. Cambridge, MA: MIT Press.
Meyer, L. B. (1956). *Emotion and meaning in music*. Chicago, IL: University of Chicago Press.
Michon, J. A. (1967). *Timing in temporal tracking*. Assen, NL: van Gorcum.
Nagumo, J., Arimoto, S., & Yoshizawa, S. (1962). An active pulse transmission line simulating nerve axon. *Proceedings of the IRE*, *50*(10), 2061–2070.

Oppenheim, A. V., & Schafer, R. W. (1975). *Digital signal processing*. Englewood Cliffs, NJ: Prentice Hall.
Palmer, C. (1997). Music performance. *Annual Review of Psychology*, *48*, 115–138.
Palmer, C., & Kelly, M. H. (1992). Linguistic prosody and musical meter in song. *Journal of Memory and Language*, *31*(4), 525–542.
Palmer, C., & Krumhansl, C. L. (1990). Mental representations for musical meter. *Journal of Experimental Psychology: Human Perception and Performance*, *16*(4), 728–741.
Parncutt, R. (1994). A perceptual model of pulse salience and metrical accent in musical rhythms. *Music Perception*, *11*, 409–464.
Patel, A. D., Iversen, J. R., Chen, Y., & Repp, B. H. (2005). The influence of metricality and modality on synchronization with a beat. *Experimental Brain Research*, *163*(2), 226–238.
Penel, A., & Jones, M. R. (2005). Speeded detection of a tone embedded in a quasi-isochronous sequence: Effects of a task-irrelevant temporal irregularity. *Music Perception*, *22*(3), 371–388.
Peretz, I., & Zatorre, R. (2005). Brain organization for music processing. *Annual Review of Psychology*, *56*, 89–114.
Phillips-Silver, J., & Trainor, L. J. (2005). Feeling the beat: Movement influences infant rhythm perception. *Science*, *308*(5727), 1430.
Phillips-Silver, J., & Trainor, L. J. (2007). Hearing what the body feels: Auditory encoding of rhythmic movement. *Cognition*, *105*(3), 533–546.
Pikovsky, A., Rosenblum, M., & Kurths, J. (2001). *Synchronization: A universal concept in nonlinear sciences*. Cambridge: Cambridge University Press.
Povel, J. D. (1981). Internal representations of simple temporal patterns. *Journal of Experimental Psychology: Human Perception and Performance*, *7*, 3–18.
Pressing, J., & Jolley-Rogers, G. (1997). Spectral properties of human cognition and skill. *Biological Cybernetics*, *76*(5), 339–347.
Quene, H., & Port, R. F. (2005). Effects of timing regularity and metrical expectancy on spoken-word perception. *Phonetica*, *62*(1), 1–13.
Repp, B. H. (1999). Relationships between performance timing, perception of timing perturbations, and perceptual-motor synchronization in two chopin preludes. *Journal of Australian Psychology*, *51*, 188–203.
Repp, B. H. (2001a). Phase correction, phase resetting, and phase shifts after subliminal timing perturbations in sensorimotor synchronization. *Journal of Experimental Psychology: Human Perception and Performance*, *27*(3), 600–621.
Repp, B. H. (2001b). Processes underlying adaptation to tempo changes in sensorimotor synchronization. *Human Movement Science*, *20*(3), 277–312.
Repp, B. H. (2002a). Phase correction following a perturbation in sensorimotor synchronization depends on sensory information. *Journal of Motor Behavior*, *34*(3), 291–298.
Repp, B. H. (2002b). Phase correction in sensorimotor synchronization: Nonlinearities in voluntary and involuntary responses to perturbations. *Human Movement Science*, *21*(1), 1–37.
Repp, B. H. (2002c). The embodiment of musical structure: Effects of musical context on sensorimotor synchronization with complex timing patterns. In: *Common mechanisms in perception and action* (pp. 245–265). Oxford: Oxford University Press.
Repp, B. H. (2003a). Phase attraction in sensorimotor synchronization with auditory sequences: Effects of single and periodic distractors on synchronization accuracy. *Journal of Experimental Psychology: Human Perception and Performance*, *29*(2), 290–309.

Repp, B. H. (2003b). Rate limits in sensorimotor synchronization with auditory and visual sequences: The synchronization threshold and the benefits and costs of interval subdivision. *Journal of Motor Behavior*, *35*(4), 355–370.
Repp, B. H. (2005). Sensorimotor synchronization: A review of the tapping literature. *Psychonomic Bulletin and Review*, *12*(6), 969–992.
Repp, B. H. (in press). Metrical subdivision results in subjective slowing of the beat. *Music Perception*.
Repp, B. H. (2008). Multiple temporal references in sensorimotor synchronization with metrical auditory sequences. *Psychological Research*, *72*(1), 79–98.
Repp, B. H., & Doggett, R. (2007). Tapping to a very slow beat: A comparison of musicians and nonmusicians. *Music Perception*, *24*(4), 367–376.
Repp, B. H., & Keller, P. E. (2004). Adaptation to tempo changes in sensorimotor synchronization: Effects of intention, attention, and awareness. *Quarterly Journal of Experimental Psychology*, *57*(3), 499–521.
Sakai, K., Hikosaka, O., Miyauchi, S., Takino, R., Tamada, T., Iwata, N. K. et al. (1999). Neural representation of a rhythm depends on its interval ratio. *Journal of Neuroscience*, *19*(22), 10074–10081.
Scheinerman, E. R. (1996). *Invitation to dynamical systems*. Prentice Hall.
Scheirer, E. D. (1998). Tempo and beat analysis of acoustic musical signals. *Journal of the Acoustical Society of America*, *103*, 588–601.
Schulze, H. H. (1989). Categorical perception of rhythmic patterns. *Psychological Research*, *51*, 10–15.
Shaffer, L. H., & Todd, N. P. M. (1987). The interpretive component in musical time. In: A. Gabrielsson (Ed.), *Action and perception in rhythm and music* (pp. 139–152). Stockholm: The Royal Swedish Academy of Music.
Simson, R., Vaughan, H. G., & Ritter, W. (1976). The scalp topography of potentials associated with missing visual or auditory stimuli. *Electroencephalography and Clinical Neurophysiology*, *40*(1), 33–42.
Sloboda, J. A. (1985). Expressive skill in two pianists-metrical communication in real and simulated performances. *Canadian Journal of Psychology*, *39*(2), 273–293.
Sloboda, J. A., & Lehmann, A. C. (2001). Tracking performance correlates of changes in perceived intensity of emotion during different interpretations of a chopin piano prelude. *Music Perception*, *19*(1), 87–120.
Snyder, J. S., Hannon, E. E., Large, E. W., & Christiansen, M. H. (2006). Synchronization and continuation tapping to complex meters. *Music Perception*, *24*(2), 135–145.
Snyder, J. S., & Krumhansl, C. L. (2001). Tapping to ragtime: Cues to pulse finding. *Music Perception*, *18*, 455–489.
Snyder, J. S., & Large, E. W. (2005). Gamma-band activity reflects the metric structure of rhythmic tone sequences. *Cognitive Brain Research*, *24*(1), 117–126.
Stevens, L. T. (1886). On the time sense. *Mind*, *11*, 393–404.
Strogatz, S. H. (1994). *Nonlinear dynamics and chaos: With applications to physics, biology, chemistry and engineering*. Cambridge, MA: Perseus Books.
ten Hoopen, G., Nakajima, Y., Remijn, G., Massier, B., Rhebergen, K., & Holleman, W. (2006). Time-shrinking and categorical temporal ratio perception: Evidence for a 1:1 temporal category. *Music Perception*, *24*, 1–22.
Thaut, M. H., Miller, R. A., & Schauer, L. M. (1998a). Multiple synchronization strategies in rhythmic sensorimotor tasks: Phase vs. period correction. *Biological Cybernetics*, *79*(3), 241–250.

Thaut, M. H., Tian, B., & Azimi-Sadjadi, M. R. (1998b). Rhythmic finger tapping to cosine-wave modulated motronome sequences: Evidence of subliminal entrainment. *Human Movement Science*, *17*, 839–863.

Todd, N. P. M. (1985). A model of expressive timing in tonal music. *Music Perception*, *3*, 33–59.

Todd, N. P. M., O'Boyle, D. J., & Lee, C. S. (1999). A sensory-motor theory of rhythm, time perception, and beat induction. *Journal of New Music Research*, *28*, 5–28.

Toiviainen, P. (1998). An interactive midi accompanist. *Computer Music Journal*, *22*, 63–75.

Toiviainen, P., & Snyder, J. S. (2003). Tapping to bach: Resonance-based modeling of pulse. *Music Perception*, *21*(1), 43–80.

Trehub, S. E., & Hannon, E. E. (2006). Infant music perception: Domain-general or domain-specific mechanisms? *Cognition*, *100*(1), 73–99.

van Noorden, L., & Moelants, D. (1999). Resonance in the perception of musical pulse. *Journal of New Music Research*, *28*, 43–66.

Van Orden, G. C., Holden, J. C., & Turvey, M. T. (2003). Self-organization of cognitive performance. *Journal of Experimental Psychology: General*, *132*, 331–350.

Vos, P. G. (1973). *Waarneming van metrische toonreeksen*. Nikmegen: Stichting Studentenpers.

Wang, D. L., & Chang, P. S. (2008). An oscillatory correlation model of auditory streaming. *Cognitive Neurodynamics*, 2, 7–19.

West, B. J., & Shlesinger, M. F. (1989). On the unbiquity of 1/f noise. *International Journal of Modern Physics B*, *3*, 795–819.

West, B. J., & Shlesinger, M. F. (1990). The noise in natural phenomena. *American Scientist*, *78*, 40–45.

Wiggins, S. (1990). *Introduction to applied nonlinear dynamical systems and chaos*. New York: Springer-Verlag.

Wilson, H. R., & Cowan, J. D. (1973). A mathematical theory of the functional dynamics of cortical and thalamic nervous tissue. *Kybernetik*, *13*, 55–80.

Windsor, L. (1993). Dynamic accents and categorical perception of metre. *Psychology of Music*, *21*, 127–140.

Wing, A. M., & Kristofferson, A. B. (1973a). Response delays and the timing of discrete motor responses. *Perception and Psychophysics*, *14*(1), 5–12.

Wing, A. M., & Kristofferson, A. B. (1973b). Timing of interresponse intervals. *Perception and Psychophysics*, *13*(3), 455–460.

Wohlschlager, A., & Koch, R. (2000). Synchronization error: An error in time perception. In: P. Desian & L. Windsor (Eds), *Rhythm perception and production* (pp. 115–127). Lisse, The Netherlands: Swets & Zeitlinger.

Woodrow, H. (1932). The effects of rate of sequences upon the accuracy of synchronization. *Journal of Experimental Psychology*, *15*, 357–379.

Yamada, M. (1996). Temporal control mechanism in equaled interval tapping. *Applied Human Science*, *15*, 105–110.

Yee, W., Holleran, S., & Jones, M. R. (1994). Sensitivity to event timing in regular and irregular sequences: Influences of musical skill. *Perception and Psychophysics*, *56*(4), 461–471.

Yeston, M. (1976). *The stratification of musical rhythm*. New Haven: Yale University Press.

Zanto, T. P., Large, E. W., Fuchs, A., & Kelso, J. A. S. (2005). Gamma-band responses to perturbed auditory sequences: Evidence for synchronization of perceptual processes. *Music Perception*, *22*(3), 531–547.

Zuckerkandl, V. (1956). *Sound and symbol: Music and the external world*. (W. R. Trask, Trans). Princeton, NJ: Princeton University Press.

Chapter 7

Behavioral Analysis of Human Movement Timing

Howard N. Zelaznik, Rebecca M. C. Spencer and Richard B. Ivry

Human beings behave as though time is important. People wear watches or use cell phones to keep on time. Our digital video recorders get set to capture our favorite television shows, alarm clocks go off, classes are scheduled to start and stop on time, and hence forth. Even the family dog gently nudges her owner's face at 4:28 P.M., reminding him that it is 2 min away from dinner time. Obviously, the dog cannot tell time from a clock, even a digital one, but somehow behaves as though she can tell time (see Chapter 10).

The literature contains many demonstrations of how skilled movements involve amazingly precise "timing." Bootsma and van Wieringen (1990) studied international caliber table tennis players. For these performers the temporal window for a good hit was on the order of 4 ms. In baseball, a batter has less than 600 ms to "see" a pitch, organize a swing, and get the bat in the right place at the right time. Because we are amazed at these levels of timing skill we tend to infer that people possess an internal timekeeper, some sort of clock-like process that is capable of metering out time. Furthermore, because of our dependence upon clocks for our social, play, and work life, and due to the exquisite timing behavior associated with skilled activity, it is easy to conclude that human beings have developed special-purpose timekeepers, or perhaps one timekeeper to perform the hypothesized clock function in many, if not all of these tasks.

On the other hand, there is growing concern over the clock metaphor, both in how it applies to the performance of human skills and also in research on animal learning. Zeiler (1998, 1999) eloquently argues that just because we behave in temporal coordination with our world, does not mean that we have an internal timer within our brain. Moreover, there is a need to define what is meant by the statement "internal timing." Zeiler (1998) describes an internal clock as a device that can time arbitrary intervals. If such an internal clock exists, then the principles of timing across many arbitrarily defined timing tasks must share common principles of

Psychology of Time

DOI:10.1016/B978-0-08046-977-5.00007-7

behavior. Specifically, Zeiler states that: "Consistency across different situations would be compelling evidence for a universal time processing system driven by an internal clock for dealing with arbitrary time intervals" (Zeiler, 1998, p. 91). This quote reflects the theoretical background of this chapter and leads to this critical question: What do empirical investigations reveal concerning the consistency of performances across various timing tasks and situations?

Several examples over the past three decades serve to highlight the notion that skill in timing does not have to require a clock. Staddon and Higa (1999) have shown how much of the work on how animals learn to produce well-timed behavior can be explained by normal memory decay processes instead of positing an internal timekeeper. In the human motor control arena, Kugler and Turvey (1987; see also, Kugler, Kelso, & Turvey, 1980) have argued that temporal regularities may be emergent properties of a self-organizing system such as the motor control system. As such, these models do not require a timekeeper process and indeed, they have provided many examples in which behavior can be modeled by the dynamical systems in which time is not explicitly controlled.

A hybrid position is that the timing-with-a-timer versus timing-without-a-timer distinction may capture a basic feature of timing. Some tasks may involve the utilization of an internal process that operates as a form of timing mechanism, specifying when certain events or actions should occur. For other tasks, temporal features may be emergent and not involve the operation of an internal timing mechanism. This chapter will describe our collaborative work over the past eight years that has championed this hybrid position. Specifically, we will outline and synthesize the behavioral and neuroscientific evidence that supports a distinction we make between event and emergent timing. We attempt to meet Zeiler's challenge by showing how timing can exhibit both generality and specificity.

The approach taken in this review is on the behavioral level of analyses (Keele, 1981), although we will highlight some neurophysiological evidence that supports the behavioral work. The extension of cognitive psychology into motor control in the 1970s resulted in extensive research programs asking how simple movements were timed, both in terms of performance and learning. These studies can be classified into two basic types. One is the timing of a movement interval, in which the movement itself is the timed goal. These tasks used to be called rapid-timing tasks (see Schmidt & White, 1972). The second set of studies examines the timing of a performer's movement relative to some experimenter-determined standard, for example, produce tapping movements at a rate defined by a metronome. This latter type of task involves some sort of anticipatory action and usually places more emphasis on coincident accuracy rather than accuracy in the duration of a subject's movement. We began the chapter with a review of this work, revisiting it in the light of recent theorizing.

7.1. Types of Timing Tasks

Timing discrimination refers to the capability to judge one time interval to be the same or different from another time interval. Oftentimes this task is presented in a two-choice forced alternative task. The subject is presented with a standard time interval, either defined by the duration of a tone or light (filled interval), or by two brief tones or light flashes that define the temporal interval (empty interval). A comparison interval is then presented in the same fashion as the standard. The subject judges whether the comparison is shorter or longer in duration than the standard (e.g., Ivry & Hazeltine, 1995; see Chapters 2, 3, and 5).

Movement duration timing refers to tasks in which the goal is to produce a movement of a particular duration. This duration can be specified in real units of time such as milliseconds (ms), or the duration is judged as long or short by an arbitrary unit (Newell & Chew, 1974). In the 1970s the rapid-timing task was the archetypal movement duration-timing task. The subject moved a handle, usually along a relatively frictionless track, to cross a finish line within a temporal goal (see Schmidt & White, 1972; Zelaznik, Shapiro, & Newell, 1978; Zelaznik & Spring, 1976 for examples). The goal was to learn to produce movements with a duration as close to the temporal goal as possible.

Interval production refers to a timing task in which the interval between experimenter-defined events within a movement series needs to be controlled (Michon, 1967; Wing & Kristofferson, 1973a, b). A popular interval-production task is repetitive tapping. Figure 7.1 depicts the tapping-timing task as well as the circle-drawing task used in our research (Robertson et al., 1999). In tapping, the duration of each tap downward and tap upward is not the goal of the task, but rather the interval of time between touchdowns is specified, usually by a pacing signal system such as a metronome (Billon & Semjen, 1995). In circle drawing, depicted on the right-hand panel, the movement duration goal, and the interval goal are isomorphic due to the continuous nature of the circle-drawing task. Zelaznik, Spencer, and Ivry (2002) developed an intermittent circle-drawing task in which there are two temporal goals. The first being the duration of the circle movement, and the second being the interval of time from the completion of circle n to the initiation of circle $n + 1$. In the continuous task, the latter interval, of course, is zero. In the intermittent case, the pause duration also can be manipulated by an experimenter.

Finally, there are timing tasks in which the goal or one of the goals is to coordinate a movement to be coincident with an external event. Such tasks are sometimes referred to as coincident timing. In the United States, the archetypal coincident-timing task is batting when playing baseball; in the British Commonwealth, it is batting when playing cricket. In these two tasks, there are two temporal goals. The first goal is to move the bat with the proper speed and/or timing. The second goal is to get the bat to the right place "on time," i.e., when the ball is there. Poulton (1957) distinguished between two types of visual processing to allow subjects to be coincident with an external event. When the performer can see the moving object, timing can be accomplished *via* receptor anticipation. Information from the changing environment is used during the unfolding action to anticipate the time of interception and this estimate can be continually adjusted. In other words, in receptor anticipation there is full preview of the moving environment that requires interception. In contrast, when the performer has limited input, the situation is referred to as perceptual anticipation. For example, the moving object may be view

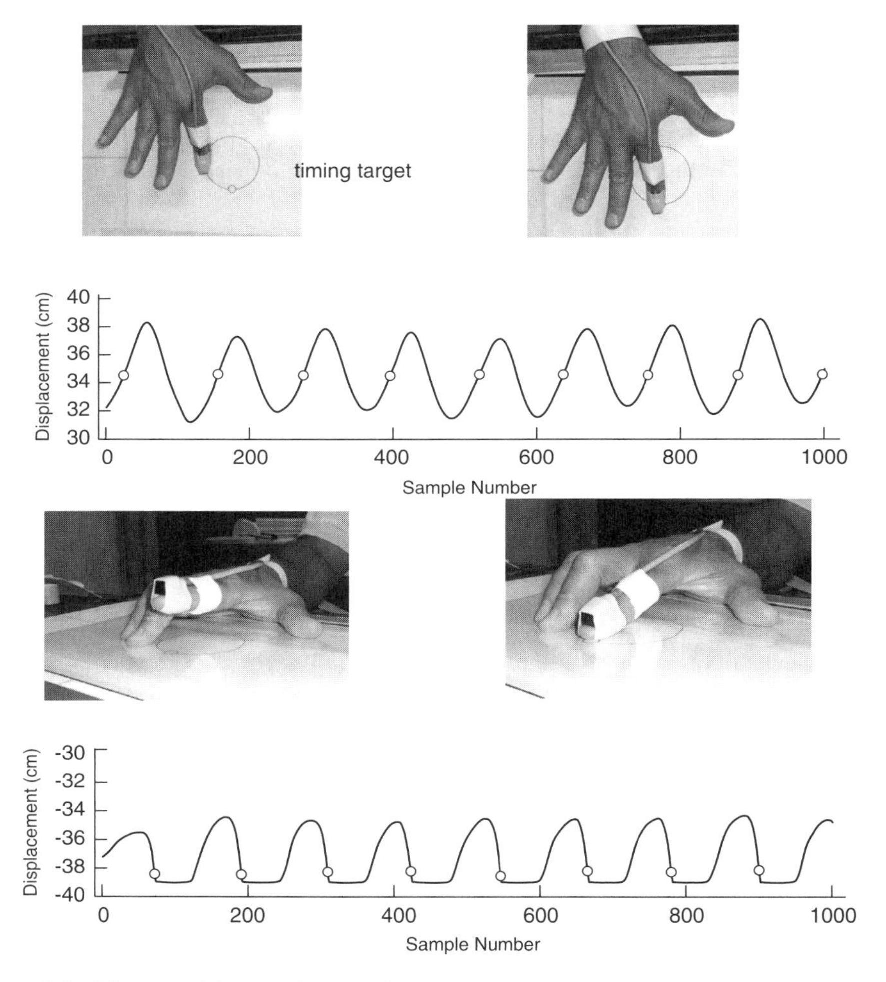

Figure 7.1: Picture of first author performing a circle-drawing timing task (top row), and the medial–lateral trajectory (*X* dimension) of eight cycles of a 2 Hz (500-ms period) task. The open circles represent when the index finger crossed the center of the small timing target circle. The bottom half of the figure depicts the tapping task. The index finger touching down defines the end of one cycle and the beginning of the next. The superior–inferior trajectory (*Z* dimension) for seven intervals at a 2 Hz rate is depicted. Open circles depict when our algorithm determined the definition of a cycle.

and then become obscured, perhaps because the performer has moved in a manner that obstructs the view. An example in baseball is when a fly ball is hit over the head of an outfielder. The fielder cannot continuously look at the moving ball, but instead must base his/her movements on the anticipated location of the ball. At some critical period, he/she will attempt to relocate the ball and make the catch. A cricket fielder has a similar situation as a baseball outfielder.

Poulton (1957) also described the knowledge of the performer in terms of the duration required for the movement, or what is referred to as effector anticipation. In order for the baseball batter to get the bat to the proper place at the proper time, the batter needs to have knowledge about the duration of the bat swing in order to know when to initiate the swing. Effector anticipation, at least in large part, is assumed in many skills to be open loop. At some point, the athlete is committed to a particular swing without being able to adjust the trajectory or speed in anticipation of some future event (McLeod, 1987; Watts & Bahill, 2000).

7.2. Duration Timing

The timing of movement duration can be distinctly different from the timing of intervals. As noted above, the goal in repetitive tapping is not the duration of the finger movement, but rather the interval of time between a common landmark across successive cycles of the finger trajectory. In contrast, the duration of the movement trajectory is the goal of the task in duration-timing tasks. Work on duration timing blossomed in the 1970s primarily due to the emergence of research on the motor program (Keele, 1968) and generalized motor program (Pew, 1974; Schmidt, 1975). Both of these ideas led researchers to ask questions about duration timing, and in particular how temporal information was represented. In duration timing in discrete tasks, the performer moves an upper limb from point A to point B, or through point B. The goal of the task is to cover the specified distance in the prescribed movement time. Given that these movements have a distinct start and end, they are classified as discrete (Hogan & Sternad, 2007). In the former task of stopping at point B, these movements usually are considered aimed hand movements, whereas tasks requiring timed movement through a finish line have been called rapid timing (Schmidt, Zelaznik, Hawkins, Frank, & Quinn, 1979).

Schmidt et al. (1979) posited that to control movement time, the duration and amplitude of the muscular forces are controlled. When movement time increases the performer scales, the duration of the agonist and antagonist muscular forces with movement time. Corcos, Gottlieb, and Agarwal (1989), on the other hand, envision a strategy in which these open-loop ballistic movements can be timed by controlling the amplitude of a step-pulse force signal to the muscles. According to impulse-timing theory (Schmidt et al., 1979), the duration of EMG activity for the agonist and antagonist muscular forces are scaled with movement duration. So, a 500-ms movement will have an agonist duration twice that of a 250-ms movement. This behavior presumably is derived from the generalized motor program that is stretching or compressing the entire muscular-force-time pattern proportional to movement duration. The amplitude of the impulse is scaled to peak velocity. For rapid discrete movements, Corcos et al. (1989) observed that changes in angular excursion with a fixed duration are accomplished by changing the amplitude of the force impulse. Alternatively, when duration is changed, the duration of the force impulse scales to duration. These results also are consistent with the idea of impulse timing. It would be reasonable to assume that a central time-keeping process is used to control the duration of these muscular forces.

How is duration learned in these tasks? On the first trial, subjects exhibit a large amount of error. With knowledge of results, they are able to quickly learn to become temporally accurate and consistent. One idea is that the subject evaluates the feedback to learn the appropriate motor commands to control the duration of the movement on the next trial. Through a series of trials a motor program is developed in which the durations of the agonist and antagonist muscular activities are specified and controlled. But this leads to the question, how is duration represented? Is the duration of a task an integral part of the movement trajectory that cannot be trained separately? Alternatively, duration might be represented in a manner independent from the movement trajectory.

Three studies demonstrate that active movement practice is not essential for learning movement timing (Newell, 1976; Zelaznik & Spring, 1976; Zelaznik et al., 1978). These experiments are important because they also bear on the notion of amodal timing — the idea that timekeeping and control can be invested in a modular process that is shareable across a variety of motor tasks (Keele & Ivry, 1987). The three sets of studies all used the same procedure. Prior to performing a rapid-timing task (i.e., target move times between 130 and 250 ms), the subject hears the sound that would be produced when someone performs the movement. This presentation was either live or presented *via* audiotape. Importantly, the subject never viewed the movement apparatus, nor was he/she provided with a visual demonstration of the task.

Following a phase of listening practice, the subject was required to perform the rapid-timing task. There were two surprising results. Subjects who were given auditory exposure performed better than control subjects, and this advantage was present from the first trial. Second, these subjects were also able to reduce error during the production trials, even when they were not given specific information about the duration of their movements. Furthermore, Zelaznik et al. (1978) showed that subjects need not hear the actually correct movement duration, but that experiencing a range of durations, and never the correct one, resulted in the best learning and performance of the timing task.

Although these studies were conducted to test basic ideas of motor learning (Adams, 1971; Schmidt, 1975), they are instructive in showing the commonality between perceptual temporal judgments and the motoric control of movement duration. If motor timing were specific to an output modality, it would be hard to explain how auditory-only practice led to better initial performance. In contrast, this improvement follows from the assumption that the auditory training allowed subjects to compare the quality of auditory feedback obtained when they actually produced the movement to that expected based on the initial training (see Adams, 1971 or Schmidt, 1975). These studies thus support the idea of common timing processes for perception and production, and furthermore demonstrate the value of nonmovement practice in skill development.

7.3. Timing in Open Skills

Open skills are those in which the relevant environment is in motion and thus the performer must match his/her movements to that environment. Hitting a pitched baseball is a classic example of an open skill. In contrast, closed skills refer to actions where the relevant environment is stationary, for example, driving a golf ball. In open skills (Gentile, 1972; Poulton, 1957), the performer must coordinate movement to the ever-changing environment. Thus, in order to overcome inherent reaction-time delays in responding to stimuli, the individual must anticipate and initiate and/or modify actions to be coincident with the environment at some time in the future. Baseball and cricket batting, as mentioned earlier, are the archetypal tasks in this domain. Furthermore, open skills oftentimes require the performer to adjust the duration and/or speed of their movement. It is possible that open skills possess two timing tasks, coincident anticipation plus duration timing of the movement.

According to the above-described notion, the performer, *via* effector anticipation, knows the duration of his/her movement. To make the action coincident with some desired event, the performer needs to determine when the object will be at the coincident point, and then initiate the movement when the time before the coincident point equals the movement duration. How can the performer determine the time remaining before the object gets to the hitting point?

David Lee (Lee & Reddish, 1981) discovered a very elegant solution that does not appear to require the animal to conduct a lot of computations. As an object approaches, the retinal projection of the object increases in size, and the rate of change also increases. The latter is called the rate of dilation. Lee and Reddish showed that the ratio of size to the rate of dilation provides direct information on time to contact. While this model is based upon a nonaccelerating object (not typical of any ball in flight), they showed that this simplification is not a problem for most interception problems. Lee, Davies, Green, and Van Der Weel (1993) call the time-to-contact parameter the tau margin.[1] In this type of model, the performer knows the critical value of tau margin required to successfully "trigger" the planned action.

Schmidt (1972) developed a measure to determine how well a triggering model describes anticipation timing behavior. Imagine that the performer has completely programmed the movement to intercept a target. If he/she initiates the movement 1 ms too late, then the movement will arrive 1 ms too late. When considered over the range of possible timing errors, the prediction is that there should be a perfect correlation between initiation time and the signed errors in timing. Schmidt called this measure IP, the index of preprogramming.

Bootsma and van Wieringen (1990) have shown that variability in paddle angle at the moment of contact in nationally ranked table tennis players is less than the variability at the initiation of the movement. If in fact the movement were triggered

1. The tau parameter in the time-to-contact studies described here is totally different and independent from the tau effect referred to in Chapter 5, and which designated the effect of duration on perceived space.

in a preprogrammed fashion, variability at the start would be equal to variability at the finish. On the other hand, Bootsma and van Wieringen (1990) argue that the performers match their movement with the changing tau margin. In this manner, they do not need to use a preprogrammed strategy, but rather can use a prospective strategy, so variability at the finish is less than variability at the start. This latter prediction was upheld. Le Runigo, Benguigui, and Bardy (2005) went on to show that nationally ranked French table tennis players use this type of strategy more effectively than novices.

Montagne, Laurent, Durey, and Bootsma (1999) tested a counter-intuitive prediction of this model. The task involved a ball that moved along a straight line and had to be intercepted. In one condition, the ball moved exactly in line with the subject's hand. As such, the subject just has to wait for the object to arrive. In another conditions, the ball moved along a diagonal path, thus reaching the same point of interception obliquely. Surprisingly, in both conditions, the hand moved back and forth during the approach of the target. Montagne et al. (1999) interpret these velocity reversals as the result of the subject matching the changing tau margin as the ball approaches, and thus evidence for the prospective strategy.

Craig, Pepping and Grealy (2005) showed how "time to contact" specified in optical tau (a spatially derived variable) can be coupled with an internal timekeeper tau gap (time remaining before coincident point) to be able to time repetitive movements as well as aiming movements. In this model the spatial tau is coupled to the tau gap by a proportionality constant, and the trajectory is constantly being updated to keep the movement on a path to be coincident with the value of tau being equal to zero. In other words, there are two gaps that the person must coordinate. There is the spatial gap between the finger and the spatial target that needs to be "hit" coincident with the temporal interval being over. This latter interval is the temporal gap. Craig et al. (2005) ask whether there is a need for internally generated temporal information to solve this task. Rather, they suggest that time is the result of the way the spatial gap is changing over time. In other words, time is derived from the changing spatial event structure. The work of Craig et al., and that of Bootsma, is related to a very nagging, albeit old question in the teaching of motor skills.

Gentile (1972, 1998) proposed that principles needed to learn and teach skills are specific to the nature of the skill. The major distinction used by Gentile (1972), following the lead of Poulton (1957), is the open versus closed skill distinction. Whereas closed skills require specificity of a movement pattern, open skills demand matching the movement to the environment. Gentile thought that these two classifications had serious ramifications for the teaching of open skills, because the coordination with the changing environment means that a fixed-action motor program is not functional. On the other hand, Schmidt (1975) views the open skill as a closed skill with a variable temporal trigger. This idea is closer to the triggering notion of open, ballistic skills. Gentile (1972) infers that the open tasks are radically different from the closed ones and that teaching these two types of timing skills is very different.

The resolution of the best way to teach interception skills leads to some very interesting predictions and hopefully some enlightenment of the issue raised above.

Table 7.1: Transfer of training design to assess how to teach an open skill.

Acquisition practice conditions	Transfer
1. Practice movement alone	Practice the interception task combined
2. Practice perception alone	Practice the interception task combined
3. Practice movement alone and then practice perception alone	Practice the interception task combined
4. Control	Practice the interception task combined

Let us lay out a possible study (Table 7.1). Imagine a task similar to the baseball-batting task developed by Schmidt and Sherwood (1982) in which a participant executes a backswing–foreswing movement attempting to intercept a moving target. The instructions further require that the target should be contacted at the point of maximum movement velocity and that timing error should be minimized. Four groups of subjects are tested. One group practices just a coincident task in which they press a button coincident with the moving object reaching the target. A second group practices the movement task only, maximizing consistency in achieving maximum velocity at the impact point; the target remains at the impact point. A third group practices each component separately. Each of these three groups is then tested on the perception–action task. Finally, a control group only practices the combined perception–action task. If the Bootsma notion is correct, there will be little benefit of the perceptual or motor practice on the performance of the combined task. In other words, the performance of the two groups on the perception–action task should not be better than the initial performance of the group that only practices this task. If Schmidt (1975) is correct then there should be ample transfer from the movement-only condition to the interception task.

7.4. Interval Timing

In most studies of repetitive timing, the actual timing of the duration of each response is secondary to the timing of intervals between landmarks in the movement trajectory. Figure 7.1 depicts this issue in a schematized version of the most well-known and studied interval-timing task, tapping. The circles along the trajectory of the finger denote the end of one interval and the initiation of the subsequent time interval. What you see in this figure is the actual time course of the finger trajectory and is not considered as part of the "timing" task. A slow movement initiated early can be on time, as can a fast movement initiated later in time. In fact, Billon, Semjen, and Stelmach (1996) showed that in tapping, temporal variability was minimized at the point of contact (the timing criterion), whereas timing variability to an arbitrarily picked location on the trajectory exhibited greater variability. Balasubramaniam, Wing, and Daffertshofer (2004) have shown that finger trajectories that are less symmetrical improve timing accuracy in synchronization. What is clear from these studies is that movement trajectory is just a vehicle to time particular events. The work by Balasubramaniam can also be seen as a manifestation of controlling the tau gap. The overall goal is not to produce a particular trajectory with a particular duration, but rather to achieve the coincident point on time. Craig et al. (2005) make a similar point in their work. The subject coordinates spatial gap to a temporal gap. This coupling might in fact specify an event.

In repetitive tapping, there is usually no coordination with the environment (other than to initially synchronize to a metronome), no auditory output goal, nor any goal to communicate a signal from these movements. Nonetheless, this impoverished timing task has been widely adopted. In practical terms, performance reaches near-asymptotic levels with minimal practice. Theoretically, researchers have turned to this task based on the assumption that performance is guided by some sort of internal clock that provides a central representation of time used to control interval production. Indeed, as we will discuss later, this same mechanism is thought to be involved in interval perception. An inference from this approach is that timing in interval production is amodal.

Keele and colleagues (Keele & Hawkins, 1982; Keele & Ivry, 1987; Keele, Pokorny, Corcos, & Ivry 1985) promoted the idea that human performance can be conceptualized as being comprised of a collection of elementary computations. Building on this framework, they hypothesized that one such computation might be timing, and that this computation could be used across a range of task domains. As such, these computations are not linked to a particular effector system, nor to a particular skill.

The initial evidence for this hypothesis came from individual difference studies. If there is some sort of amodal timing mechanism, then one should observe correlated individual differences between different tasks that draw upon this computation. Keele and Hawkins (1982) observed significant correlations in timing variability between finger tapping, elbow flexion-extension timing, and foot tapping. In other words, an individual who could consistently produce well-timed movements in one of these timing tasks would tend to be consistent in the other tasks. Keele, Ivry, and Pokorny (1985) argued that such computations were not limited to the motor system. Individual differences in a perception task, duration discrimination, were correlated with individual differences in a production task, repetitive tapping. These initial studies provided strong support for the notion that timing was an encapsulated computation that could be applied to a variety of tasks.

Franz, Zelaznik, and Smith (1992) extended these findings by showing links between movements with distal and proximal effectors. Subjects produced repetitive movements (2.5 Hz) in one of four different modes: finger tapping, arm tapping, jaw opening and closing, and oral vocalization (repeat the syllable "pa"). The major dependent variable was the coefficient of variation, defined as the within-trial standard deviation divided by the mean-produced interval (see Chapter 2). There were significant, although modest (around .40), correlations for the coefficient of variation for the four tasks. More importantly, using Wing and Kristofferson's (1973a, b; see Chapter 2) model, Franz et al. found that estimates of the component of variability associated with a central timekeeper were correlated, but estimates of the component of variability associated with motor implementation were only correlated for movements produced by a similar effector system (proximal versus distal). The finger and arm task showed correlated individual differences in implementation variance as did speech and nonspeech jaw movements. In contrast, the correlation between speech and limb tasks for implementation variance was not reliable. The authors argued that the clock variance results were capturing the shared amodal timing process, whereas implementation variance was effector specific.

Ivry, Keele, and Diener (1988) provided neuropsychological evidence in support of the idea that timing can be viewed as an amodal computation. Individuals with unilateral lesions of the cerebellum were tested on the repetitive-tapping task. As would be expected, these individuals exhibited larger timing variability when tapping with the ipsilesional effector (the side affected by the cerebellar lesion) compared to the contralesional effector. Of greater interest was the observation that individuals with lateral lesions exhibited an elevated clock variance. In contrast, individuals with medial lesions showed the reverse pattern; they exhibited increased implementation variance. In another study, patients with cerebellar pathology were found to be also impaired on a duration-discrimination task (Ivry & Keele, 1989). To capture this dual pattern of deficits, as well as related findings across a range of tasks, Ivry and Keele (1989) proposed that a primary role for the cerebellum is to provide a representation of the precise timing between salient events. These events might correspond to the successive taps during repetitive tapping or the onset/offset of stimuli that mark the duration of intervals for perceptual analysis. More generally, the cerebellar timing hypothesis provided a parsimonious account of cerebellar involvement in a wide range of tasks such as eye blink conditioning and speech perception and production (see Ivry, Spencer, Zelaznik, & Diedrichsen, 2002).

A limitation of this perspective was revealed by Robertson et al. (1999). In this work the correlation between continuous timing in circle drawing and tapping were examined. The circle-drawing timing task had not been used in studies of motor timing; rather, variants of it had been used in studies of bimanual coordination. As can be seen in Figure 7.1, during circle drawing, subjects traced a large circle, attempting to enter the small circle (12 o'clock) coincident with the "beep" of the metronome. The subjects were told not to be concerned with tracing a perfect circle, but rather should just use the circle as a guide for the overall path. The instructions emphasized that the movements should be made continuously and smoothly.

The task is, at least superficially, similar to repetitive tapping. A metronome is used to establish the movement rate and is then disengaged. The subject attempts to move as accurately and as precisely as possible matching their self-paced rate with that of the just-heard metronome rate. When performed with the dominant hand, performance reaches asymptote after a trial or two (Zelaznik & Spencer, unpublished experiment) and the standard deviation is about 4% of the goal interval, similar to that observed in repetitive tapping. The data can also be analyzed in the same manner. Trials are detrended to remove any overall drift, and the main measure of variability is the coefficient of variation in timing. This measure is then converted to a percentage.

It was assumed that variability on these two tasks would be correlated across individuals, similar to what had been found in the studies described above. However, to our surprise, timing variability in the tapping task was not correlated with timing variability in the circle-drawing task (Robertson et al., 1999, Experiment 1). A second experiment indicated specificity within the circle-drawing task. Circle diameter varied from 2.5 to 20 cm, with each diameter step a doubling of the previous. Significant correlations within the circle-drawing timing tasks were limited to adjacent diameters, and only when the cycle duration was relatively short (550 ms). If the duration was longer (800 ms), performance was not correlated in a consistent manner across the different amplitude conditions. Thus, timing in circle drawing seems to be very specific, related to movement size and movement period. More importantly, the results suggest that distinct processes underlie the temporal regularities observe in tapping and circle drawing.

In a third experiment, Robertson et al. provided converging evidence that timing processes in tapping and circle drawing are separable. An estimate of timing variability is given by the slope of the function relating variance to duration squared, a form of Weber's law (Getty, 1975; Ivry & Corcos, 1993; Ivry & Hazeltine, 1995). Across tasks, similar slope values have been found between motor and perceptual timing (Ivry & Hazeltine, 1995) as well as between tapping and eye-blink conditioning (Green, Ivry, & Woodruff-Pak (1999)). However, Robertson et al. (1999) found that the Weber slope for circle drawing was much shallower than that found for tapping, providing further evidence that tapping and circle drawing do not share a common timing process.

The work of Robertson et al. (1999) suggested that tapping and circle drawing did not draw on a common timing process. This led us to consider why and how these tasks might differ. There are at least two possible reasons why timing variability in tapping and continuous circle-drawing timing were unrelated. One hypothesis is derived from the observation that the spatial demands and degrees of freedom are different for the two tasks. Commonalities between these two tasks in terms of temporal control may be masked by these additional sources of variability.

A second hypothesis can be derived by considering the trajectories of the movements produced during tapping or circle drawing. Tapping involves a series of salient events that define the successive intervals. As such, the performer could use a representation that allows the interval between these events to be timed. During circle drawing, the trajectories are, by definition, continuous. There is no singularity (or set of singularities) that appear to be more salient than other points in the trajectory. We hypothesized that timing under such conditions might be emergent.

To contrast these two hypotheses, we developed a variant of the circle-drawing task (Zelaznik et al., 2002). Our goal was to have people draw circles, matching the spatial properties of normal circle drawing, but introduce an event structure. To this end, participants were trained to produce intermittent circles. In this task, the subject is instructed to alternate between a movement phase in which they produce a circle and a pause phase in which they stop prior to the onset of the next cycle. In this manner, a discontinuity is imposed on each cycle. By varying the duration of the movement and pause phases, the overall cycle duration can be specified.

Timing variability on the intermittent circle-drawing task and tapping were found to be correlated with one another, but neither was reliably correlated with variability on the continuous circle-drawing task. Moreover, the two event-based tasks, tapping and intermittent circle drawing were positively correlated with performance on a duration-discrimination task. That is, people who were better in perceiving temporal differences were also more consistent in producing regularly timed taps or intermittent circles. The continuous circling task did not correlate with the perception task.

Taken together, the papers by Robertson et al. (1999) and Zelaznik et al. (2002) led to the inference that amodal timing was not the only type of motor timing. At the very least, the results suggested two forms of temporal control, forms we have come to refer to as event and emergent timing. In the former, we assume that time is an explicit part of the goal representation in the sense that this representation can control when salient events should be produced (e.g., contact the table surface in tapping, initiate each circle in intermittent circle drawing), judge the duration of perceptual events, or provide the coupling between action and perception (e.g., synchronize movements with a metronome). In contrast, when the action lacks a salient event structure, timing may be emergent. Temporal regularities may reflect the operation of some other control process, for example, maintaining a constant angular velocity would result in perfectly timed continuous circles. Such a control process would be difficult to employ for tasks with discontinuities.

As described above, the cerebellum has been hypothesized to provide the neural computations required for temporal control. While this hypothesis did not make a distinction between event and emergent timing, the types of tasks used to assess the hypothesis generally involved discontinuities, or an event structure. This led us to ask if the cerebellum would be differentially involved in event-based and emergent-based timings (Spencer, Zelaznik, Diedrichsen, & Ivry, 2003). In particular, would this structure be disproportionately involved in the former? To test this, patients with unilateral cerebellar lesions were required to make repetitive movements, either by producing continuous circles, intermittent circles, or by finger tapping (in different blocks). For all three conditions, the target cycle duration was 800 ms. Consistent with prior studies (e.g., Ivry et al., 1988), the coefficient of variation for tapping with the ipsilesional hand was greater than that for the contralesional hand. This same pattern was observed for the intermittent circle-drawing task. Of course these patients have ataxia and, thus, an increase in variability is not surprising. However, the patients did not show any impairment on the continuous circle-drawing task. That is, they were no more variable when using their ipsilesional, impaired arm compared to when using their contralesional, unimpaired arm. Indeed, their performance on this task was similar to that observed in college-aged subjects.

Although this result was consistent with the event-emergent distinction, there were other differences between the two tasks. For example, by definition, higher movement velocities are required for intermittent circle drawing compared to continuous circle drawing. Thus, the lack of cerebellar effect on continuous circle might be due to the fact that these movements are produced more slowly (a comparison of velocity between tapping and circle drawing is not meaningful given the differences in effectors).

In a final experiment we manipulated movement speed in a continuous movement task involving finger flexion/extension performed in midair (Spencer et al., 2003, Experiment 3). The subjects performed four finger-timing tasks. The first was the traditional table-top tapping with a period of 1000 ms. The second task involved the same 1000-ms period, but now the subjects tapped without touching the table top, but were instructed to pause at the peak extension, so a pause was inserted in the movement. The final two conditions required the subjects to tap smoothly, without table contact at each of two periods, 500 and 1000 ms. The 500-ms period condition produced movements with the same peak velocity as the table tapping and intermittent tapping conditions. Similar to the first two experiments, we showed that the two intermitted tasks, table-top tapping and intermittent tapping showed decrements when performed by subjects with compromised cerebellar processes, whereas the continuous tasks were spared any performance decrements. Thus, the final experiment by Spencer et al. (2003) demonstrated that the timing decrements observed for intermittent (discrete-like) movements was not due to a confounding of movement speed with intermittency.

Spencer, Ivry, and Zelaznik (2005) examined whether it is the timing component in tapping that requires cerebellar processing, or just the discrete nature of the tapping task. Participants with cerebellar lesions and age-matched controls were tested on three conditions. In a no-timing condition, the participant was required to press and release a response key. In the short-timing condition, they were required to press the key, hold it in a depressed position for less than 400 ms, and then release the key. The long-timing condition was the same, but now the hold period was extended to 350–950 ms. The third condition was to produce a flexion-extension finger movement with no pause at all. Thus, the short and the long conditions required the same basic movements (flexion, then extension), but introduced a temporal goal. Individuals with bilateral cerebellar lesions were impaired on the short- and long-press tasks relative to controls, but were equal to controls on the "no timing just press and release" task. Unexpectedly, the individuals with unilateral lesions did not show a lateralized effect; performance with their unimpaired limb was equivalent to the impaired limb. However, overall performance was much poorer compared to previous work, perhaps because the timing conditions varied from trial to trial and thus required a constant shift in attention. To address this possibility, we repeated the experiment, but now blocked the three conditions. Now performance with the impaired limb was compromised on the short- and long-duration tasks, but not on the no-timing task.

This study provides an important piece of support for the event-emergent distinction. It is possible that the dissociations observed in the study by Spencer et al. (2003) were related to the fact that tapping and intermittent circle drawing reflect problems that patients with cerebellar damage have in initiating or terminating movement. In our 2005 study, the three conditions have the same movement requirements in the sense that each response involves a single flexion and extension phase. If the impairments associated with cerebellar damage are related to problems with initiating and terminating movements, then the impairment should have been either similar across all three conditions, or perhaps more pronounced in the no timing condition (since the transition between flexion and extension is fastest). However, the opposite was true: The patients were most impaired when required to *time* the interval between two events. This result supports the idea that it is the timing of events that requires specialized cerebellar timing processes.

Further evidence of a role of the cerebellum in event-based timing comes from a recent fMRI study (Spencer, Verstynen, Brett, & Ivry, 2007). Participants were trained to perform a fast or a slow flexion-extension set of finger movements at two rates (550- or 950-ms period) and to make these movements either smoothly or by briefly pausing prior to each flexion phase. Following training, each of these four tasks was performed in the scanner. Two important findings emerged from this study. First, no cerebellar regions showed greater activation during continuous movements compared to the discontinuous conditions. Second, a small region in lobule V/VI was significantly more active for the discontinuous movements than for the continuous case. The medial locus of this difference was surprising given the earlier work of Ivry et al. (1988; but see Harrington, Lee, Boyd, Rapcsak, & Knight, 2004). Nonetheless, of the regions sampled (including motor, premotor, and SMA), the cerebellum was the only region to show a difference between the continuous and discontinuous conditions. Activation in other areas varied with movement speed.

7.5. Event–Emergent Timing Distinction

To summarize, we have proposed a fundamental distinction between two ways in which timing regularities may be controlled. Event timing involves an explicit representation of time. By explicit we do not mean conscious; rather, we mean that there is some type of signal that specifies the timing of salient events and thus can define the task goal in terms of its temporal structure. This type of computation should show correlated individual differences with other timing tasks that require event timing, such as eye-blink conditioning, speech perception, and temporal discrimination (Ivry et al., 2002).

Emergent "timing" is indirect. For movements, temporal regularities can result from the control of movement dynamics. This notion borrows its intellectual currency from the dynamical systems view (see Turvey, 1977), in the claim that time is not inherent in any representation of movement and/or control. As noted above, for circle drawing, controlling a dynamic variable like angular velocity could serve as a mediator of emergent timing (Spencer et al., 2003).

We admit that the term "emergent timing" is a bit awkward. Given that we actually mean that time is not controlled, to then state that the movement is emergently timed invokes a notion of timing control. We do not consider this process to be a clock-like process. Thus, when we state that circle drawing is emergently timed, that does not mean that all circle-drawing timing tasks use the same "timer." It means that the timing properties of emergently timed movements are highly specific to the context of the task, because there is no explicit representation of time. Thus, we observe correlations between temporal variability in drawing 2.5-cm diameter circles and 5-cm circles, but not between 2.5-cm circles and 10- or 20-cm circles. This is the case because the dynamics of the small 2.5-cm circles are different enough from the 10- and 20-cm circles. Similarly, Robertson et al. (1999) did not find significant correlations for timing variability between continuous circle drawing and line drawing. We note that the angular velocity account might lead one to expect correlated individual differences among all circle-drawing tasks. However, even if a common strategy is used across different amplitudes, the implementation may be highly specific. This interesting question has not received sufficient experimental attention.

The distinction between event and emergent timing appears to be entwined to a great extent with the cerebellar timing hypothesis (Ivry & Keele, 1989; Ivry & Spencer, 2004). Indeed, the event-emergent distinction provides an important constraint on the domain of cerebellar timing, suggesting that the representational capabilities of this structure may be limited to event-based timing. The dissociation of the role of the cerebellum in timing in tapping and circle drawing supports the event-emergent timing distinction, but is not crucial to the idea. It may well be that the cerebellum contributes to both event- and emergent-related processes, although the contribution may not be symmetric (Schlerf, Spencer, Zelaznik, & Ivry, 2007). Alternatively, the cerebellum may not contribute to timing in the sense we've suggested for both event-based and emergent-based tasks (see Diedrichsen, Criscimagna-Hemminger, & Shadmehr, 2007; Harrington et al., 2004). Nonetheless, from the perspective taken in this chapter, the event-emergent distinction provides a parsimonious account of a number of surprising behavioral dissociations. Whether there is a "seat" for event timing is an important question, but one that is independent from the psychological question. The event-emerging timing distinction rests upon the evidence there is a behavioral dissociation between different types of timing tasks and/or different independent variables affect timing differentially (Zeiler, 1999). Whether or not the importance of the cerebellum parallels the behavioral dissociations is a different matter.

7.6. Kinematics and Timing Processes

We have hypothesized that a temporal representation is required when there are salient events that act as anchors for interval-timing control; the representation of the task goal specifies the timing of these events. This form of explicit timing is hypothesized to be absent in tasks in which timing is emergent. The consequences of this representational distinction can be observed behaviorally. For example, Spencer and Zelaznik (2003) showed that in tapping, temporal precision is greatest, as reflected by the lowest coefficient of variation, when timing was measured at the touchdown point of the tap (see also Billon & Semjen, 1995). However, in circle drawing, timing precision is equivalent when measured at any point along the circle trajectory.

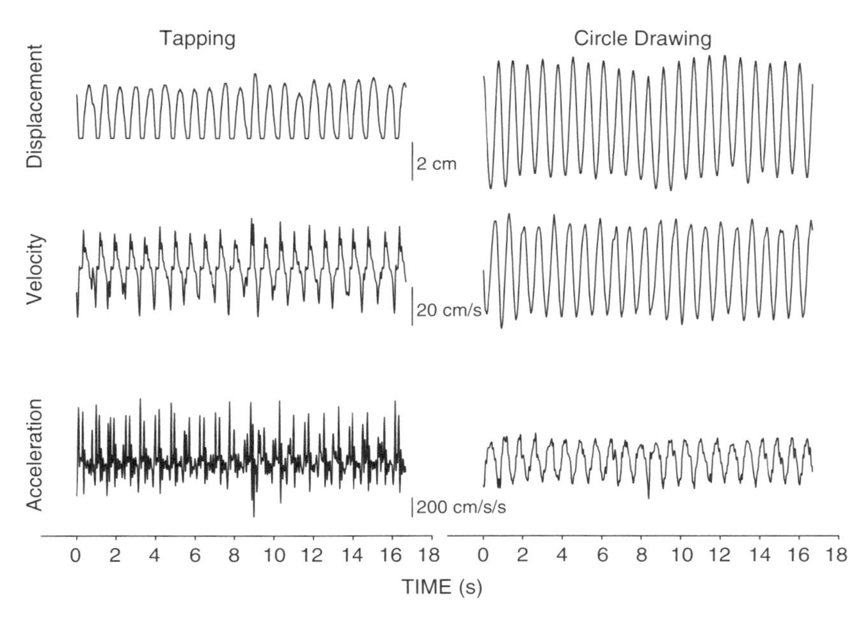

Figure 7.2: Kinematic comparisons of tapping and circle drawing. Again a randomly selected 2 Hz (500-ms period) condition was selected for each task.

These differences are also evident in the trajectories (Figure 7.2). One of the reasons for the differences between repetitive tapping and continuous circle drawing is that circle drawing is a very smooth movement with no discernable anchor points in the movement trajectory. In Figure 7.2, a typical tapping-kinematic record is displayed in the left panel, and a typical circle-drawing record is displayed on the right. The superior–inferior movement of the finger in tapping and the anterior–posterior movement of the finger in circle drawing are presented. The acceleration pattern is sinusoidal in circle drawing. In contrast, tapping exhibits a much more jittery acceleration pattern clearly possessing some additional higher frequency components related to the periods of little movement (pauses) in tapping that are not present in circle drawing. These aspects of the changes in acceleration are captured by the derivative of acceleration, known as jerk. In fact, jerk has been hypothesized as a kinematic quantity minimized in motor control strategies (Flash & Hogan, 1985). Perhaps high levels of jerk produce psychologically salient events that invoke event-timing processes, or the salience of a psychological event results in a decrease in movement smoothness. Smooth continuous movements exhibit low levels of jerk and cannot then provide events for timing, and timing is emergent.

Rheaume, Lemoine, Balasubramaniam, and Zelaznik (in preparation) examined whether variation in jerk is associated with signatures of event and emergent timing. Twelve subjects performed the continuation-timing task by table tapping, circle drawing, and in a third condition, tapping without contact (in midair). For each condition, participants produced a long series of 600 consecutive intervals, with the first 16 paced by a metronome at 2 Hz. Our analysis focused on the middle 512 intervals, with the lag one covariance serving as our marker of event timing. As alluded to above, the study by Wing and Kristofferson model (1973b) assumes that movements controlled by central (event) timing will result in a negative lag one covariance. This assumption is routinely supported in tapping, but rarely if ever reliably observed in circle drawing (Robertson et al., 1999), another behavioral indicator in support of the event/emergent distinction. In Rheaume et al.'s study, we were most interested in what would happen when people tapped without contact. It is hard to produce these movements smoothly over 600 intervals and there is considerable variability across individuals in terms of the kinematics in this condition. There were a total of 36 conditions (12 subjects by 3 tasks). We divided these conditions into low, moderate, and high normalized mean-squared jerk, and then computed the average lag one covariance for these 3 sets of 12. Figure 7.3 shows the relation between normalized mean-squared jerk (Teulings, Contreras-Vidal, Stelmach, & Adler, 1997) and lag one covariance, as a function of whether jerk is high, medium, or low. One can clearly see the monotonically decreasing relation. It also is instructive to view this relation across the range of lag one covariance values, and with each task. These results are depicted in Figure 7.4.

As can be seen in Figure 7.4, there was a clear monotonic relation between normalized mean-squared jerk and lag one covariance. When jerk values are small, the lag one covariance is positive. When jerk values are large, the lag one covariance is negative. The correlation coefficient is −.61. What is also seen in this figure is that

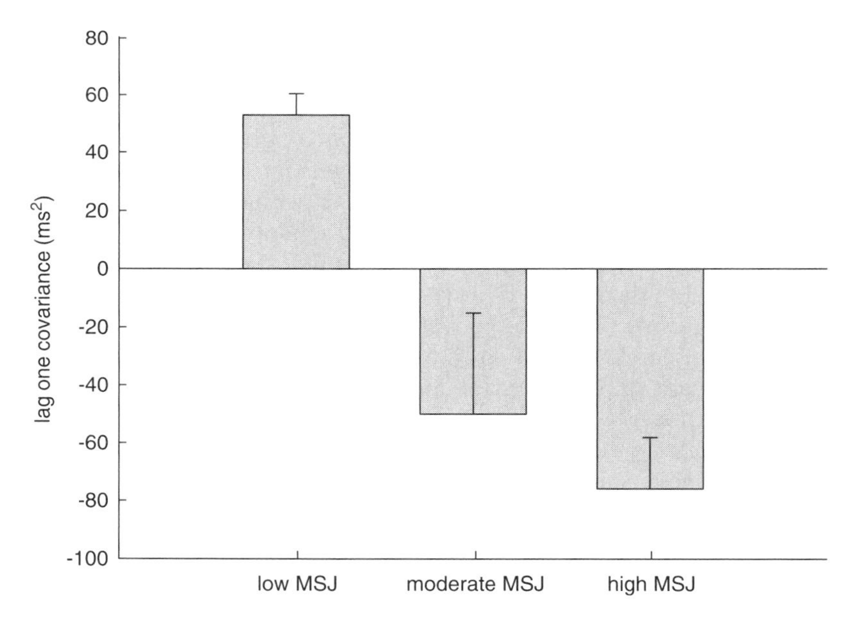

Figure 7.3: Lag one covariance and mean-squared jerk (MSJ) relation (from Rheaume et al., in preparation).

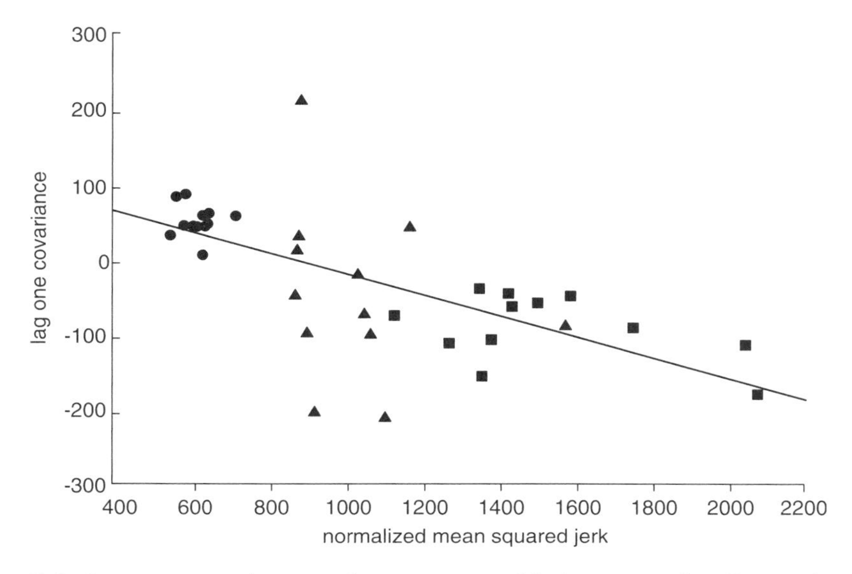

Figure 7.4: Lag one covariance and mean-squared jerk scatter plot (from Rheaume et al., in preparation).

within the tapping task (the square symbols) there is a clear linear relation between the lag one covariance and normalized mean-squared jerk ($r = .43$). To our knowledge this is the first direct evidence that movement smoothness, as indicated by normalized mean-squared jerk, is related to the movement timing precision. For circle drawing, jerk is not only positive but also is not related to the lag one covariance. This is because the lag one covariance–jerk relation is capturing event timing, and not emergent timing.

7.7. Instantiating Timed Behavior

How does a subject instantiate a timed movement? In tapping, the metronome establishes the temporal goal and then an internal timing mechanism is engaged to define the timing of salient events such as the onset of each tap or time of contact from one cycle to the next. With emergent timing, we propose that there is no representation of the temporal goal, at least in terms of controlling the movements across cycles. But people do match their movement rate to that defined by the metronome when circle drawing. How might this be done? Obviously, people can set a movement period to match an external timekeeper. They must do this in circle drawing as well as in tapping. Zelaznik et al. (2005) proposed that event timing is involved in establishing the initial movement rate or interval for circle drawing, and then there is a transformation to emergent timing. The latter becomes possible as the participant matches dynamic properties (e.g., velocity, stiffness) to the desired movement frequency.

To test the transformation hypothesis, subjects listened to a metronome producing four intervals. They did not produce movements in synchrony with the tones. Rather, the subject attempted to learn the prescribed interval from listening. After a brief pause, the subject produced four continuous circles in the circle-drawing timing task, or four tapping intervals (five taps) in the tapping-timing task.

Timing variability was computed differently than in our previous work. Rather than calculate within-trial variability across successive cycles, we calculated variability separately for each ordinal position of the four-interval trial. That is, variability was calculated for each interval between trials (e.g., variability for interval *n* across 70 trials). For circle drawing, interval one and interval four of circle drawing had elevated variability compared to the second and third intervals. For tapping, the four intervals were equally precise. In addition, we asked whether individual differences in timing variability were correlated for tapping and circle drawing with respect to each interval. Most interesting, timing variability for the first interval of circle drawing was correlated with each and every tapping interval. The correlations between tapping and circle drawing were absent for intervals 2, 3, and 4.

We interpreted these results as indicating that the initiation of repetitive movements in circle-drawing timing requires event timing, with a gradual transformation to emergent timing. This transformation comes about as the dynamics of control are instantiated (Zelaznik et al., 2005). The increased variability to stop a cyclical movement does not at this point seem to require event timing, given that the variability in interval four was not related to circle drawing. In a study of cyclical movements, similar to circle drawing in properties, van Mourik and Beek (2004) show that the first hemi-cycle of a cyclical bout is markedly different than the subsequent hemi-cycles. This result is consistent with the transformation hypothesis.

Schlerf et al. (2007) examined the transformation hypothesis in a neuropsychological study. The key question here was whether the patients would show a disproportionate increase in variability on the first interval during circle drawing. In terms of a replication of the study by Spencer et al. (2003), the patients were more impaired on tapping than circle drawing, although in this study they also showed a smaller but reliable impairment on circle drawing. However, we found no evidence that the initial interval in circle drawing exhibited elevated temporal variability, a result that is at odds with the transformation hypothesis.

It remains unclear what to make of this result. It may be that a between-trial analysis is noisy because there is fluctuation in movement rate from one trial to the next. Participants were also given feedback about movement rate at the end of each trial. There may be considerable variability in how the participants use this information to adjust their performance from one trial to the next, adding further sources of variability to the task.

7.8. Higher Order Goals and Timing Control

Many movement scientists tend to concentrate on the relation between dynamics and control. The influential Haken, Kelso, and Bunz (1985) model of bimanual coordination posits that simultaneously activating homologous muscles on each limb is more stable than activating nonhomologous muscles. Normally, homologous muscle activation produces what is known as in-phase coordination, and the nonhomologous case produces antiphase coordination. When movement frequency is increased, antiphase coordination will abruptly shift to in-phase coordination (Kelso, 1995).

While this effect is nicely described by dynamic systems models, the source of constraint has been the subject of considerable debate, especially in light of recent demonstrations of the influence of representational factors (Mechsner, Kerzel, Knoblich, & Prinz, 2001; Semjen & Ivry, 2001; Spencer, Semjen, Yang, & Ivry, 2006). For example, Spencer et al. (2006) showed that a crucial difference between anti- and in-phase coordination pertains to how people spontaneously represent the event structure of each cycle in these two conditions. For antiphase movements, people represent the cycle as composed of two events (e.g., flexion phase for each hand); for in-phase movements, there may be only a single event per cycle. By this view, as frequency is ramped up, the maintenance of a more complex two-event structure cannot be sustained and a phase transition occurs to a simpler single-event structure. Thus, Spencer et al. (2006) demonstrate that coordination is not determined solely by the relationship of the effectors in a spatial reference frame, or a muscle reference frame. Rather, perceptual events are also crucial in determining modes of coordination.

Another example of the importance of goal representation comes from the work of Franz, Zelaznik, Swinnen, and Walter (2001). Subjects were required to produce rhythmical semicircles, one with each upper limb. As shown in Figure 7.5, only the bottom–top condition produced a breakdown in coordination. The reason was

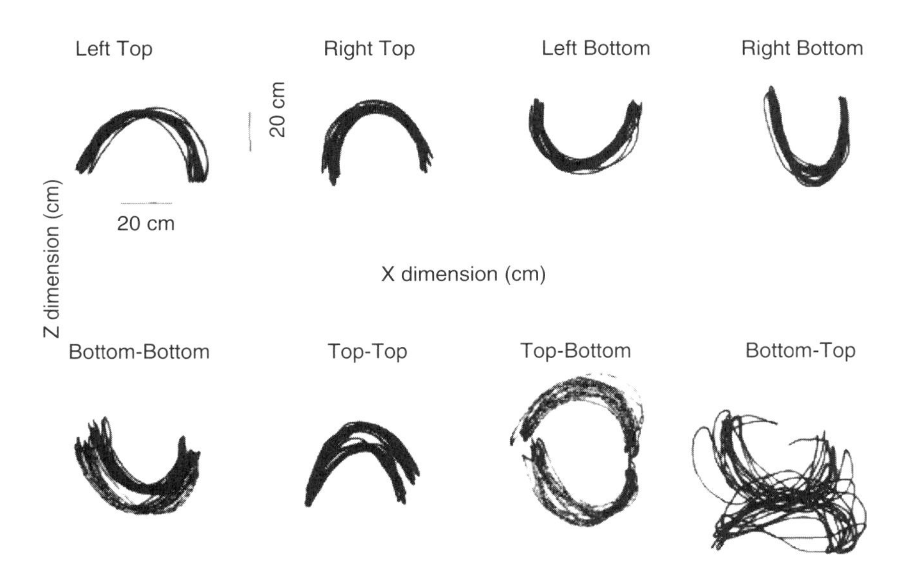

Figure 7.5: Coordination tasks used in the study by Franz et al. (2001).

that in the other three bimanual cases the task produced a clear whole perception, a gestalt, and the gestures were guided by that gestalt. Mechsner et al. (2001) demonstrated this notion in a dramatic manner by showing that subjects could produce a 4:3 bimanual cycling task, if the consequences of these actions resulted in percept that maintained a 1:1 ratio (see also, Rosenbaum, Dawson, & Challis, 2006).

Zelaznik and Rosenbaum (in preparation) were interested in whether events for timing reside only in the kinematic level or whether perceptual demands of timing might determine whether events become salient. The perceptual goals for tapping and circle drawing may differ. Although the same set of instructions are given — that the participant should be as accurate and consistent as possible in maintaining the movement rate established during the synchronization phase — goal representations might be different between the two tasks. Thus, it is possible that timing differences in circle drawing are not due to its kinematic nature compared to tapping, but due to differences in goal demands and representation.

This leads to the prediction that if provided with an appropriate goal when circle drawing, one which invokes an event structure, then the processes involved in circle drawing and tapping should become more similar. To begin to explore this issue, Zelaznik and Rosenbaum devised a new version of continuation-timing task. In the first experiment, subjects listened to the metronome producing 15 intervals (i.e., 16 beats). Following the metronome presentation of the temporal interval, the participant either tapped or drew circles. When the subject touched the table top during tapping or completed a cycle in circle drawing, a sound was produced. The subjects were instructed to produce a series of beeps (for a total of 31 intervals) that were identical to the series that they just listened to. There were two target durations, 500 and 800 ms periods. The participants were also tested on a duration-discrimination task (Zelaznik et al., 2002).

The production tasks now have identical behavioral goals. These are to produce a series of tones that match the tones just heard. Thus, we consider these tasks as having the same event structure, from the auditory level. First, we found that participants did not have difficulty performing this new timing task. The average duration was virtually identical to the goal duration, and the coefficient of variation in timing was 4% or less. Indeed, under these new conditions, tapping and circle drawing have equivalent values of the coefficient of variation. In all of our previous work with the continuation paradigm, tapping was always more variable temporally than circle drawing. In this modified task, tapping has become more consistent. Second, the effect of duration squared on detrended variance was the same for tapping and circle drawing. In other words, the Weber slopes were equivalent.

What is extremely interesting is that the lag covariance structure (lag 1 to 3) was similar for the four production tasks (Figure 7.6). This is the first time we have consistently observed a negative lag one covariance for circle drawing. Furthermore, the size of the lag one covariance is about the same as in tapping. Thus, it seems as though by creating a similar goal for tapping and circle drawing, the control processes have become identical. In particular, the auditory feedback has created an event structure for circle drawing.

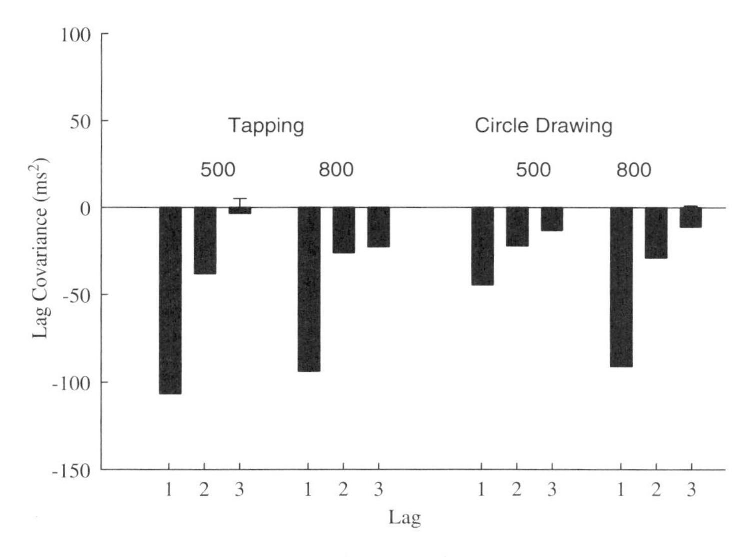

Figure 7.6: Lag covariance structure of timing for sound (Zelaznik & Rosenbaum, in preparation) study.

Table 7.2: Correlations of coefficient of variation and temporal discrimination sensitivity for Zelaznik and Rosenbaum (in preparation). Significant correlations ($p < .05$) are in boldface.

	Tapping 800	Circle 500	Circle 800	Time P500	Time P800
Tapping 500	**.73**	**.35**	**.40**	.24	**.44**
Tapping 800		**.34**	**.37**	.10	.29
Circle 500			**.64**	.15	.12
Circle 800				.27	**.39**
Time P500					**.73**

Evidence in support of the above inference is drawn from the individual difference correlations (Table 7.2). First, timing precision in the two tapping tasks and in the two circle-drawing tasks were correlated. Second, and most importantly, timing precision in tapping was correlated with timing precision in circle drawing. Although these across-task correlations are not high, they are reliable. This latter result is theoretically important because it allows us to infer that the differences and/or similarities in timing processes between tasks cannot just be due to local differences in movement kinematics.

Individual differences in duration discrimination were not correlated with timing variability in the production tasks, contrary to results of Zelaznik et al. (2002) and Ivry and Hazeltine (1995). This problematic result does not have a simple explanation. First, it could be the case that the correlations across production tasks reflect the sharing of an additional process, which is not event timing. Perhaps we are capturing the individual differences in feedback utilization to produce the metronome, and as such we would then not expect these process to exhibit a consistent relation with temporal discrimination. However, we do not want to let these issues distract us from the important finding that the basic difference between repetitive tapping and circle drawing can reside at a goal level rather than at a kinematic level.

This experiment is important relative to the overall framework on event and emergent timing. The bulk of our work beginning in the Robertson et al.'s (1999) paper showed differences between timing in tapping and drawing from an individual difference perspective, Weber slope approach, and a striking dissociation in our neurophysiological data. A nagging doubt behind the corpus of this work is that there are many differences between tapping and circle drawing, and it is these differences which make it difficult to isolate shared forms of temporal control. However, our motivation in this new study (Zelaznik & Rosenbaum, in preparation) was that by producing salient events (i.e., the tones), people would rely on a common timing strategy, one that involves event timing. These salient events do not have to be kinematic.

7.9. Summary and Conclusions

We have provided several lines of evidence that lead to the inference that a single, amodal timing process cannot account for performance in all rhythmic movement tasks. In other words, people do not possess a single timing ability, or module, that provides the computation necessary and sufficient to produce temporal regularities for all motor-timing tasks. Tasks that possess salient events, which then determine the goal representation of the task, rely upon event timing. Seen in this light, event timing is the timing computation module envisioned by Keele and Ivry (1987). However, if the goal leads to a kinematic control strategy, such as moving smoothly and not controlling a temporal event, emergent timing is observed. This initial taxonomy has seen a wide degree of behavioral support *via* the dissociations between timing in tapping and circle drawing described in this chapter. If we are able to show how goal representations determine timing strategies, then kinematic models of timing control will have to be joined with issues of goal representation (Spencer & Ivry, 2007).

References

Adams, J. A. (1971). A closed loop theory of motor learning. *Journal of Motor Behavior*, *3*, 111–150.

Balasubramaniam, R., Wing, A. M., & Daffertshofer, A. (2004). Keeping with the beat: Movement trajectories contribute to movement timing. *Experimental Brain Research*, *159*, 129–134.

Billon, M., & Semjen, A. (1995). The timing effects of accent production in synchronization and continuation tasks performed by musicians and nonmusicians. *Psychological Research, 58*, 206–217.
Billon, M., Semjen, A., & Stelmach, G. E. (1996). The timing effects of accent production in periodic finger-tapping sequences. *Journal of Motor Behavior, 28*, 198–210.
Bootsma, R. J., & van Wieringen, P. C. W. (1990). Timing an attacking forehand drive in table tennis. *Journal of Experimental Psychology: Human Perception and Performance, 16*, 21–29.
Corcos, D. M., Gottlieb, G. L., & Agarwal, G. C. (1989). Organizing principles for single-joint movements II. A speed-sensitive strategy. *Journal of Neurophysiology, 62*, 358–368.
Craig, C., Pepping, G. J., & Grealy, M. (2005). Intercepting beats in predesignated target zones. *Experimental Brain Research, 165*, 490–504.
Diedrichsen, J., Criscimagna-Hemminger, S. E., & Shadmehr, R. (2007). Dissociating timing and coordination as functions of the cerebellum. *Journal of Neuroscience, 27*, 6291–6301.
Flash, T., & Hogan, N. (1985). The coordination of arm movements: An experimentally confirmed mathematical model. *The Journal of Neuroscience, 5*, 1688–1703.
Franz, E. A., Zelaznik, H. N., & Smith, A. (1992). Evidence of common timing processes in the control of manual, orofacial, and speech movements. *Journal of Motor Behavior, 24*, 281–287.
Franz, E. A., Zelaznik, H. N., Swinnen, S., & Walter, C. (2001). Spatial conceptual influences on the coordination of bimanual actions: When a dual task becomes a single task. *Journal of Motor Behavior, 33*, 103–112.
Gentile, A. (1972). A working model of skill acquisition with application to teaching. *Quest, 17*, 3–23.
Gentile, A. (1998). Implicit and explicit processes during acquisition of functional skills. *Scandinavian Journal of Occupational Therapy, 5*, 7–16.
Getty, D. J. (1975). Discrimination of short temporal intervals — Comparison of 2 models. *Perception and Psychophysics, 18*, 1–8.
Green, J. T., Ivry, R. B., & Woodruff-Pak, D. S. (1999). Timing in eyeblink classical conditioning and timed-interval tapping. *Psychological Science, 10*, 19–23.
Haken, H., Kelso, J. A. S., & Bunz, H. (1985). A theoretical model of phase transitions in human hand movements. *Biological Cybernetics, 51*, 347–356.
Harrington, D. L., Lee, R. R., Boyd, L. A., Rapcsak, S. Z., & Knight, R. T. (2004). Does the representation of time depend on the cerebellum? Effect of cerebellar stroke. *Brain, 127*, 561–574.
Hogan, N., & Sternad, D. (2007). On rhythmic and discrete movements: Reflections, definitions and implications for motor control. *Experimental Brain Research, 181*, 13–30.
Ivry, R., Spencer, R. M., Zelaznik, H. N., & Diedrichsen, J. (2002). The cerebellum and event timing. In: S. M. Highstein & W. T. Thach (Eds), *The cerebellum: Recent developments in cerebellar research* (Vol. 978, pp. 302–317). New York: New York Academy of Sciences.
Ivry, R. B., & Corcos, D. M. (1993). Slicing the variability pie: Component analysis of coordination and motor dysfunction. In: K. M. Newell & D. M. Corcos (Eds), *Variability and motor control* (pp. 415–447). Urbana, IL: Human Kinetics.
Ivry, R. B., & Hazeltine, R. E. (1995). Perception and production of temporal intervals across a range of durations: Evidence for a common timing mechanism. *Journal of Experimental Psychology: Human Perception and Performance, 21*, 3–18.

Ivry, R. B., & Keele, S. W. (1989). Timing functions of the cerebellum. *Journal of Cognitive Neuroscience*, *1*, 136–152.
Ivry, R. B., Keele, S. W., & Diener, H. C. (1988). Dissociation of the lateral and medial cerebellum in movement timing and movement execution. *Experimental Brain Research*, *73*, 167–180.
Ivry, R. B., & Spencer, R. M. C. (2004). The neural representation of time. *Current Opinion in Neurobiology*, *14*, 225–232.
Keele, S. W. (1968). Movement control in skilled motor performance. *Psychological Bulletin*, *70*, 387–403.
Keele, S. W. (1981). Behavioral analysis of movement. In: J. M. Brookhart & V. B. Mountcastle (Eds.), *The Nervous System* (pp. 1391–1414). Bethesda, MD.
Keele, S. W., & Hawkins, H. L. (1982). Explorations of individual differences relevant to high level skill. *Journal of Motor Behavior*, *14*, 3–23.
Keele, S. W., Ivry, R., & Pokorny, R. (1985). On the nature of the clock underlying perception and movement. *Bulletin of the Psychonomic Society*, *23*, 273.
Keele, S. W., & Ivry, R. B. (1987). Modular Analysis of timing in motor skill. In: G. H. Bower (Ed.), *The psychology of learning and motivation* (Vol. 21, pp. 183–228). New York: Academic Press.
Keele, S. W., Pokorny, R. A., Corcos, D. M., & Ivry, R. (1985). Do perception and motor production share common timing mechanisms: A correlational analysis. *Acta Psychologica*, *60*, 173–191.
Kelso, J. A. S. (1995). *Dynamic patterns*. Cambridge, MA: MIT Press.
Kugler, P. N., Kelso, J. A. S., & Turvey, M. T. (1980). On the concept of coordinative structures as dissipative structures I. Theoretical lines of convergence. In: G. E. Stelmach & J. Requin (Eds), *Tutorials in motor behavior* (pp. 3–47). Amsterdam: North Holland.
Kugler, P. N., & Turvey, M. T. (1987). *Information, natural law, and the self-assembly of rhythmic movement*. Hillsdale, NJ: Lawrence Erlbaum Associates.
Le Runigo, C., Benguigui, N., & Bardy, B. G. (2005). Perception-action coupling and expertise in interceptive actions. *Human Movement Science*, *24*, 429–445.
Lee, D. N., Davies, M. N. O., Green, P. R., & Van Der Weel, F. R. (1993). Visual control of velocity of approach by pigeons when landing. *Journal of Experimental Biology*, *180*, 85–104.
Lee, D. N., & Reddish, P. E. (1981). Plummeting gannets: A paradigm of ecological optics. *Nature*, *293*, 293–294.
McLeod, P. (1987). Visual reaction time and high-speed ball games. *Perception*, *16*, 49–59.
Mechsner, F., Kerzel, D., Knoblich, G., & Prinz, W. (2001). Perceptual basis of bimanual coordination. *Nature*, *414*, 69–73.
Michon, J. A. (1967). *Timing in temporal tracking*. Soesterberg, The Netherlands: Institute for Perception-TNO.
Montagne, G., Laurent, M., Durey, A., & Bootsma, R. (1999). Movement reversals in ball catching. *Experimental Brain Research*, *129*, 87–92.
Newell, K. M. (1976). Motor learning without knowledge of results through the development of a response recognition mechanism. *Journal of Motor Behavior*, *8*, 209–217.
Newell, K. M., & Chew, R. A. (1974). Recall and recognition in motor learning. *Journal of Motor Behavior*, *6*, 245–253.
Pew, R. W. (1974). Human-perceptual motor performance. In: I. B. H. Kantowitz (Ed.), *Tutorials in performance and cognition* (pp. 1–39). Hillsdale, NJ: Lawrence Erlbaum.
Poulton, E. C. (1957). On prediction in skilled movements. *Psychological Bulletin*, *54*, 467–478.

Rheaume, N. R., Lemoine, L., Balasubramaniam, R., & Zelaznik, H. N. (in preparation). One over f behavior of tapping and circle drawing timing tasks.

Robertson, S., Zelaznik, H., Lantero, D., Gadacz, K., Spencer, R., Doffin, J. et al. (1999). Correlations for timing consistency among tapping and drawing tasks: Evidence against a single timing process for motor control. *Journal of Experimental Psychology: Human Perception and Performance*, *25*, 1316–1330.

Rosenbaum, D. A., Dawson, A. M., & Challis, J. H. (2006). Haptic tracking permits bimanual independence. *Journal of Experimental Psychology: Human Perception and Performance*, *32*, 1266–1275.

Schlerf, J. E., Spencer, R. M. C., Zelaznik, H. N., & Ivry, R. B. (2007). Timing of rhythmic movements in patients with cerebellar degeneration [Electronic Version]. *Cerebellum* from http://dx.doi.org/10.1080/14734220701370643.

Schmidt, R. A. (1972). Index of preprogramming (IP): Statistical method for evaluating role of feedback in simple movements. *Psychonomic Science*, *27*, 83–87.

Schmidt, R. A. (1975). A schema theory of discrete motor skill learning. *Psychological Review*, *82*, 225–260.

Schmidt, R. A., & Sherwood, D. E. (1982). An inverted-u relation between spatial error and force requirements in rapid limb movements-Further evidence for the impulse-variability model. *Journal of Experimental Psychology-Human Perception and Performance*, *8*, 158–170.

Schmidt, R. A., & White, J. L. (1972). Evidence for an error detection mechanism in motor skills: A test of Adams' closed-loop theory. *Journal of Motor Behavior*, *4*, 143–154.

Schmidt, R. A., Zelaznik, H. N., Hawkins, B., Frank, J. S., & Quinn, J. T., Jr. (1979). Motor-output variability: A theory for the accuracy of rapid motor acts. *Psychological Review*, *86*, 415–451.

Semjen, A., & Ivry, R. B. (2001). The coupled oscillator model of between-hand coordination in alternate-hand tapping: A reappraisal. *Journal of Experimental Psychology: Human Perception and Performance*, *27*, 251–265.

Spencer, R. M., Ivry, R. B., & Zelaznik, H. N. (2005). Role of the cerebellum in movements: Control of timing or movement transitions? *Experimental Brain Research*, *161*, 383–396.

Spencer, R. M. C., & Ivry, R. B. (2007). The temporal representation of in-phase and anti-phase movements. *Human Movement Science*, *26*, 226–243.

Spencer, R. M. C., Semjen, A., Yang, S., & Ivry, R. B. (2006). An event-based account of coordination stability. *Psychonomic Bulletin and Review*, *13*, 702–710.

Spencer, R. M. C., Verstynen, T., Brett, M., & Ivry, R. (2007). Cerebellar activation during discrete and not continuous timed movements: An fMRI study. *Neuroimage*, *36*, 378–387.

Spencer, R. M. C., & Zelaznik, H. N. (2003). Weber (slope) analyses of timing variability in tapping and drawing tasks. *Journal of Motor Behavior*, *35*, 371–382.

Spencer, R. M. C., Zelaznik, H. N., Diedrichsen, J., & Ivry, R. B. (2003). Disrupted timing of discontinuous but not continuous movements by cerebellar lesions. *Science*, *300*, 1437–1439.

Staddon, J. E. R., & Higa, J. J. (1999). Time and memory: Towards a pacemaker-free theory of interval timing. *Journal of the Experimental Analysis of Behavior*, *71*, 215–251.

Teulings, H. L., Contreras-Vidal, J. L., Stelmach, G. E., & Adler, C. H. (1997). Parkinsonism reduces coordination of fingers, wrist, and arm in fine motor control. *Experimental Neurology*, *146*, 159–170.

Turvey, M. T. (1977). Preliminaries to a theory of action with reference to vision. In: R. E. Shaw & J. Bransford (Eds), *Perceiving, acting and knowing* (pp. 211–265). Hillsdale, NJ: Lawrence Erlbaum.

van Mourik, A. M., & Beek, P. J. (2004). Discrete and cyclical movements: Unified dynamics or separate control? *Acta Psychologica, 117*, 121–138.

Watts, R. G., & Bahill, A. T. (2000). *Keep your eye on the ball: Curveballs, knuckleballs, and fallacies of baseball, revised and updated.* New York: Freeman.

Wing, A. M., & Kristofferson, A. B. (1973a). Response delays and the timing of discrete motor responses. *Perception and Psychophysics, 14*, 5–12.

Wing, A. M., & Kristofferson, A. B. (1973b). The timing of interresponse intervals. *Perception and Psychophysics, 13*, 455–460.

Zeiler, M. D. (1999). Time without clocks. *Journal of the Experimental Analysis of Behavior, 71*, 288–291.

Zeiler, M. D. D. (1998). On sundials, springs, and atoms. *Behavioural Processes, 44*, 89–99.

Zelaznik, H. N., Shapiro, D. C., & Newell, K. M. (1978). On the structure of motor recognition memory. *Journal of Motor Behavior, 10*, 313–323.

Zelaznik, H. N., Spencer, R. M. C., & Ivry, R. B. (2002). Dissociation of explicit and implicit timing in repetitive tapping and drawing movements. *Journal of Experimental Psychology: Human Perception and Performance, 28*, 575–588.

Zelaznik, H. N., Spencer, R. M. C., Ivry, R. B., Baria, A., Bloom, M., Dolansky, L. et al. (2005). Timing variability in circle drawing and tapping: Probing the relationship between event and emergent timing. *Journal of Motor Behavior, 37*, 395–404.

Zelaznik, H. N., & Spring, J. (1976). Feedback in response recognition and production. *Journal of Motor Behavior, 8*, 309–312.

Zelaznik, H. N., & Rosenbaum, D. A. (in preparation). Goals determine timing individual differences.

Zelaznik, H. N., & Spencer, R. M. C. (unpublished experiment). Lack of practice effects in timing in circle drawing.

Chapter 8

Imaging Time

Trevor B. Penney and Latha Vaitilingam

Much of the early research on time perception focused on establishing the psychophysical laws that govern it (see Chapter 3 — Grondin, 2003). For example, Vierordt (1868) noted that short time intervals tend to be overestimated whereas long time intervals tend to be underestimated (Vierordt's law — see Chapters 1 and 3). This search for the laws underlying temporal behavior has continued into modern times, but it has also been complemented by a quest to determine the neural underpinnings and brain structures responsible for our sense of time. This is not to say, however, that the desire to understand how the brain senses, represents, manipulates, and makes decisions about time is new (see Chapter 1). Indeed, many researchers over the past century have posed variants of the question: "To what cerebral process is the sense of time due?" (James, 1890, p. 632) However, James and his contemporaries were at a disadvantage in that they did not have an arsenal of neuroimaging techniques that permit observation of the functioning human brain. Indeed, the ability to measure the brain activity underlying human cognition has been generally available, in various forms, within the past 40 years only.

Typically, the term neuroimaging refers to measurement methods that provide anatomical localization of neural activity. In the human domain, the noninvasive versions of these techniques include positron emission tomography (PET), functional magnetic resonance imaging (fMRI), and functional near-infrared spectroscopy (fNIRS), with fMRI currently being far more common than either PET or fNIRS. However, a broader definition of neuroimaging would include measures of brain activity that are not necessarily directed toward the question of spatial localization of function, such as electroencephalography (EEG), magneto-encephalography (MEG) and the event-related potential (ERP) and event-related field (ERF) measures that are derived from EEG and MEG, respectively. A broad definition of neuroimaging is useful because contributions to our understanding of time perception have been made by online high-temporal resolution measures of information processing, contributions that could not have been made using PET, fMRI, or fNIRS.

Psychology of Time

DOI:10.1016/B978-0-08046-977-5.00008-9

Moreover, an adequate answer to James' original question about the cerebral processes underlying timing will eventually require the establishment of clear correspondences between spatial localization of various timing and timing-related cognitive functions and high temporal resolution measures of those functions. Although ERP and ERF studies have much to offer (Pouthas, 2003), particularly when source analyses are conducted in conjunction with PET or fMRI studies using the same task (e.g., Pouthas, Garnero, Ferrandez, & Renault, 2000), here we focus on spatial localization of interval-timing function and limit discussion to the extant fMRI and PET studies of interval timing only. First, however, the chapter begins with a description of brain imaging.

8.1. Neuroimaging Techniques

Prior to discussing what neuroimaging reveals about interval-timing function, it is necessary to briefly describe the basis of each of the neuroimaging techniques used in the studies of human interval timing discussed here. These techniques include fMRI, PET, fNIRS, and the event-related optical signal (EROS). In general, neuroimaging techniques provide quite different views of the neural and cognitive substrates of time perception because they rely on different measures of brain activity. In some cases, the measures directly reflect neural activity whereas in others the measure is more indirect. One consequence of this is that certain techniques currently provide excellent spatial resolution and relatively poor temporal resolution (e.g., fMRI — see Hinton, 2003), whereas others offer relatively poor spatial resolution and excellent temporal resolution (e.g., EEG). In addition, there are techniques that provide a reasonable compromise between spatial and temporal resolution (e.g., EROS).

8.1.1. fMRI

Blood oxygen level dependent (BOLD) fMRI relies on detection of changes in the concentration of deoxygenated hemoglobin within specific areas of brain tissue as a marker for brain activity. Although somewhat counterintuitive, levels of deoxygenated blood are lower in the immediate vicinity of active tissue as compared to inactive tissue. This is because the vascular system provides active tissue with excess oxygenated blood, thereby flushing the deoxygenated hemoglobin from the vicinity of the active tissue. Consequently, fMRI is an indirect measure of neural activity. Although the spatial resolution is excellent, depending on recording parameters on the order of a few millimeters, its temporal resolution, as generally used in cognitive neuroscience, is relatively poor. This is because there is a lag of several seconds between neural activity and the hemodynamic response to that activity. However, with accurate modeling of the hemodynamic response, in conjunction with proper experimental and imaging sequence design, the temporal resolution of fMRI can be in the low hundreds of milliseconds. One disadvantage of fMRI for studying interval timing, however, is that the recording situation is noisy due to the sounds induced when the magnetic gradients are turned on and off during scanning. This can make use of auditory timing signals quite difficult, and the researcher must also be concerned about the possibility that the scanner noise acts as a metronome when using seconds-range stimuli. Nonetheless, sparse imaging sequences permit one to do gradient switches less frequently, which in turn allows auditory stimuli to be presented in the absence of scanner noise (e.g., Hall et al., 1999; Zaehle et al., 2007).

In spite of the difficulties in applying the fMRI technique to questions about interval timing, it remains the gold standard in human functional brain imaging because the entire brain can be imaged noninvasively in a relatively short period of time. Moreover, the ability to detect activity in subcortical structures is critical for a complete understanding of the brain areas involved in time perception, as will become clear below.

8.1.2. PET

PET also relies on blood flow changes to determine which areas of the brain are active during a particular cognitive function. However, with this technique, participants have a short-lived radioactive substance (e.g., radioactive glucose) injected into the bloodstream. Given that more blood flows to active regions of the brain, there is greater radioactivity in those areas. PET offers good spatial resolution because the 3D reconstruction of radioactive sources can be co-registered with an anatomical MRI of the participant's brain. The spatial resolution does not quite match that of fMRI, however, and the temporal resolution is limited by blood flow changes and the specific details of the radioactive substance (e.g., its half-life).

Limitations of this technique include the need to inject radioactive material into the participant and the impact of a tracer's half-life on its usefulness for answering questions about cognitive function. That said, the ability to custom-design-specific agents to target particular brain receptors or neurotransmitter systems makes PET a powerful tool for investigating the brain basis of cognitive function, although to date there have been relatively few studies of interval timing using PET.

8.1.3. Optical Imaging

There are several approaches available for taking advantage of changes in the optical properties of brain tissue that reflect, either directly or indirectly, changes in neural activity. fNIRS relies on the impact of blood oxygenation on light absorption. It is possible to measure whether or not a particular area of brain tissue is active by measuring changes in the absorption of near-infrared light traveling between a light source and light detector placed on the participant's head. Of course, as a blood-flow-based measure of brain activity, this technique has similar limitations on temporal resolution as does fMRI. Moreover, it is not currently possible to noninvasively image subcortical structures with this technique.

An alternative optical imaging approach is to use frequency-modulated light sources and to measure changes in photon flight time between a light source and a light detector (the event-related optical signal — EROS, see Gratton & Fabiani, 2001 for review). The light-scattering properties of neurons change with activity such that inactive tissue scatters more light and photon flight time is shorter as compared to that of photons passing through active tissue. These changes in scattering occur with changes in the electrical state of neurons and therefore they are a more direct measure of neural activity than are hemodynamic-based measures. This approach offers good temporal resolution, on the order of tens of milliseconds depending on the recording montage. However, the limitations include an inability to image deep brain structures and trade-offs between the number of source-detector bundles used and temporal resolution. To the best of our knowledge, the only studies to date that have used optical imaging in a paradigm that required processing of temporal information were experiments examining preattentive change detection (Sable et al., 2007; Tse, Tien, & Penney, 2006; Tse & Penney, 2007). Given the passive nature of the processing in these experiments, which are not reviewed here, however we expect increased use of this technique to address basic questions about interval-timing function in the future.

8.2. Timing Tasks and Imaging the Internal Clock

The types of interval-timing tasks used in the laboratory are usually prospective, meaning that participants are told in advance that they will be asked to make an explicit duration judgment (Graf & Grondin, 2006). For example, they could have to make a comparison between two or more intervals (duration discrimination) and categorize them in some way (same versus different; short versus long; etc.), to make a response when a duration equivalent to an earlier presented duration has elapsed (reproduction, e.g., peak interval procedure), to produce a duration that corresponds to some verbal label for a quantity of time such as 5 s (production), or to provide a verbal label for the amount of time demarcated by some stimulus (verbal estimation, see Chapter 2). Alternatively, a participant may be informed that a duration judgment is required after the stimulus or event has elapsed (retrospective timing: see Chapters 2, 4, and 12). One could frame a retrospective time-judgment task in many different ways (e.g., provide a verbal label for the duration or reproduce the duration), but ultimately such tasks are limited to a single trial because once asked for a duration judgment retrospectively, the participant will likely expect to be asked again in future, thereby eliminating the true retrospective nature of the task on subsequent trials. One consequence of this constraint on number of trials is that all of the neuroimaging studies described in this chapter used prospective-timing paradigms and explicit-duration judgments. The participants were aware that the critical task information was duration and they could therefore bring their complete, consciously controlled, information-processing machinery to bear on the task (see Lewis & Miall, 2003a, for a discussion of automatic and controlled timing).

A fundamental question in the study of interval timing concerns the existence of a dedicated internal clock (see also Chapters 7 and 9). Much of the early research to isolate the structural and functional components of the putative internal clock was completed using nonhuman animals (see Gibbon, Malapani, Dale, & Gallistel, 1997; Meck, 1996, 2005, 2006; Buhusi & Meck, 2005 for reviews). This work included pharmacological and brain lesion studies in rats and revealed the basal ganglia and frontal cortex as significant players in the perception, representation, and decision processes surrounding interval timing. Modern neuroimaging techniques such as PET and fMRI allow the question of the internal clock to be examined in normal, i.e., nonpatient, human populations.

However, many of the first neuroimaging studies of human timing behavior were strongly influenced by prior studies of patient populations, which guided both the selection of tasks used to examine timing, and the control conditions used for comparison of activation patterns. One reason for this is that the fMRI and PET techniques are a particularly good match for researchers who come from the neuropsychological tradition of approaching brain function from the perspective of localization of function, i.e., identifying particular brain structures with specific sensory or cognitive functions. Therefore, it is not surprising that in light of the extensive use of tapping and rhythm-detection paradigms in various patient populations, these paradigms were then among the first to be examined with fMRI and PET (e.g., Lejeune et al., 1997; Penhune, Zatorre, & Evans (1998); Rao, Harrington, Haaland, Bobhoby, Cox, & Binder, 1997; Schubert, von Cramon, Niendorf, Pollman, & Bublak, 1998), with a particular focus on examining the brain structures governing motor control and motor timing.

The emphasis in this chapter, however, is on studies of interval timing that have a more cognitive focus (e.g., duration discrimination, production, and reproduction), and less of a motor component as compared to tapping and rhythm reproduction. We take this approach for three reasons. First, there is now a reasonable body of neuroimaging studies that have investigated timing using duration discrimination, production, and reproduction (i.e., cognitive timing) to make a restricted review viable. Second, most of the literature on tapping and rhythm reproduction has been covered in earlier reviews that discussed motor timing and/or offered broad reviews of the then available timing literature (e.g., Lewis & Miall, 2003a; see Chapters 6 and 7). Third, we were interested in examining the extent to which different research groups report activity in the same structures and posit the same or different functional roles for those structures.

It is important to note that even within the limited set of interval-timing tasks discussed here, there is much variety in the specific details of the tasks, the durations examined, and the control or baseline conditions used to isolate the brain structures active during interval timing. In some cases, the control condition was a simple rest task, in other cases a passive viewing task intended to control for stimulus processing only, and in yet other cases, a sensorimotor task intended to control for both basic sensory and motor processes. The rationale behind these subtraction approaches is that any activation that is greater in the timing task than in the control task should be part of an information-processing network involved in interval timing. Indeed, the simplest approach to uncovering the network underlying time perception is to compare brain activity in a timing task against activity in a rest or passive viewing condition. If one assumes that no cognitive processes specific to the function of interest (e.g., interval timing) occur during passive viewing, then using this as a control condition permits the researcher to remove the influence of basic sensory processing on the brain activity pattern and increases the likelihood that this activation pattern reflects the cognitive function of interest. Of course, the assumption that participants empty their minds in a passive viewing condition and merely absorb the sensory information is tenuous, but these comparisons do provide hints about the brain structures that underlie interval timing. These initial models of the timing network can then be refined in light of further comparisons with the activation patterns elicited by other tasks.

It is also clear that many cognitive processes involved in interval timing are not unique to it. For example, working memory, attention allocation, and decision processes are part and parcel of many other cognitive operations. Consequently, researchers often use the same or a highly similar paradigm and stimulus sequence to compare the brain activation patterns elicited when a participant is asked to make decisions based on the duration information present in the stimulus stream as compared to some other characteristic of the stimulus stream (e.g., pitch). In its purest form, the rationale is that these comparisons permit isolation of mechanisms that are specific to interval timing rather than more general information-processing mechanisms. In practice, it is necessary to be cautious in drawing such conclusions because a particular process may be recruited to varying degrees in both the timing and the control task with the result that the difference in activation levels is quantitative rather than qualitative.

Finally, a significant point of discussion in the timing literature concerns whether sub- and suprasecond durations are timed by the same or different neural circuits (see Gibbon et al., 1997; Lewis & Miall, 2003a; Chapter 9). Given this possibility, our approach here is to follow the lead of Lewis and Miall (2003a) in grouping the sub- and suprasecond imaging studies separately. In the following sections, we outline the similarities and differences in brain activation across tasks, comparison conditions, and durations. We do not discuss functional interpretations in the sections describing activation patterns, but rather delay that discussion until the final section where a general overview is possible. Activation data from the sub- (Tables 8.1 and 8.2) and suprasecond studies (Tables 8.3 and 8.4) reviewed here are also presented below. The tables present the complete record of brain-activation increases in interval timing relative to control conditions within the studies, whereas in the text below we generally restrict discussion to salient similarities (e.g., activations common across two or more studies) and differences (unexpected or absence of expected activations) between studies. Moreover, in most cases the anatomical descriptions of activation locations present in the tables are those used by the study authors. Generally, if the authors provided a more specific location description, then we report the more specific location in the table (e.g., frontal operculum versus inferior frontal gyrus). However, where authors reported activation locations as Brodmann areas in the absence of structural labels, we

Table 8.1: Summary of findings involving cortical structures with subsecond timing tasks.

Task	Contrast	Study	Modality		Prefrontal/ frontal cortex	Pre-SMA/ SMA	Premotor/ motor cortex	Temporal lobe	Parietal lobe	Medial occipital cortex	Insula	Cingulate
DD	T > Rest	Belin et al. (2002) (PET)	Aud		$R_{orbitoPFC}$, R_{IFO}, R_{IFG}, R_{MFG}			R_{MTG}	R_{Inf}			
		Jueptner et al. (1995) (PET)	Aud		B_{DLPFC}			$B_{MTG/STG}$				$B_{Ant.}$
		Reiterer et al. (2005)	Aud		L_{IFG}	B_{SMA}		L_{PAC}, $B_{Pos.STG}$, $L_{Pos.v.STG}$, L_{MTG}, B_{STS}			L	
	T > Cont	Jueptner et al. (1995) (PET)	Aud									$B_{v.Ant.}$
		Pouthas et al. (2005)	Vis	S&L	R_{DLPFC}, B_{VLPFC}	Pre	$B_{Lat.PMC}$		R_{IPS}		$B_{Ant.}$	Ant.
		Tregellas et al. (2006)	Aud	E	$^{\#}_{DLPFC}$, $^{\#}_{FO}$	$^{\#}_{SMA}$	$^{\#}_{PMC}$	B_{STG}		L	#	
				D	B_{DLPFC}, B_{FO}	SMA	B_{dPMC}, B_{vPMC}	B_{STG}		L	B	
				D > E	B_{DLPFC}, B_{FO}	SMA					B	
	T > Oth.	Lewis and Miall (2003b)	Vis	.6s	B_{DLPFC}, R_{VLPFC}, L_{FO}, B_{FP}	B_{pre}	R_{dPMC}, B_{vPMC}	L_{STG}	$B_{Inf.}$, R_{IPS}		$B_{Ant.}$	
				.6 > 3s	B_{VLPFC}, R_{FO}			L_{STG}, R_{MTG}, R_{STS}			L	
		Reiterer et al. (2005)	Aud									

Table 8.1: (*Continued*)

Task	Contrast	Study	Modality		Prefrontal/ frontal cortex	Pre-SMA/ SMA	Premotor/ motor cortex	Temporal lobe	Parietal lobe	Medial occipital cortex	Insula	Cingulate
TG	T > Cont	Ferrandez et al. (2003)	Vis		$B_{pars.O}$, R_{FC}, B_{GF}, R_{DLPFC}		L_{AGF}	B_{STG}	$B_{Inf.}$		$B_{Ant.}$	$L_{Ant.}$
		Maquet et al. (1996) (PET)	Vis		R_{PFC}			$L_{fusi.g}$	$R_{Inf.}$			d.Ant.
	T > Oth.	Ferrandez et al. (2003)	Vis		$L_{pars.O}$, $B_{pars.T/OBFC}$	B_{SMA}	$L_{AF/M1}$	B_{STG}	$B_{Inf.}$		R	
		Maquet et al. (1996) (PET)	Vis									
DRP	T > Cont	Jahanshahi et al. (2006)	Aud	S&L S>L	B_{SFG}, L_{MFG}, $R_{sup-mesial\ FG}$		$L_{Lat.PMC}$	L_{STG}, L_{MTG}				$L_{Ant.}$

DD: duration discrimination; DRP: duration reproduction; TG: temporal generalization; T: timing; Oth.: other (intensity — Ferrandez et al., 2003, Maquet et al., 1996 (PET); length — Lewis and Miall, 2003b; pitch — Reiterer et al., 2005), cont.: control (lift finger in alternation after cue — Jueptner et al., 1995 (PET), press response button after stimuli (no timing involved) — Ferrandez et al., 2003, Jahanshahi et al., 2006, Maquet et al., 1996 (PET), Pouthas et al., 2005).

E: easy condition, D: difficult condition, D > E: difficult > easy comparison, S&L: short, long > control comparison, S > L: short >long comparison.B: bilateral activation; L: activation in the left hemisphere; R: activation in the right hemisphere; ant.: anterior; d: dorsal; inf.: inferior; lat.: lateral; pos.: posterior; sup: superior; sup-mesial: superior mesial; v: ventral.

AG: angular gyrus; AGF: agranular frontal area; DLPFC: dorsolateral prefrontal cortex; dPMC: dorsal premotor cortex; FC: frontal cortex; FG: frontal gyrus; FO: frontal operculum; FP: frontal pole; fusi.: fusiform; fusi.g: fusiform gyrus; GF: granular frontal area; IFG: inferior frontal gyrus; IFO: inferior frontal operulum; IPS: intraparietal sulcus; M1: primary motor cortex; MFG: middle frontal gyrus; MFTG: middle frontal temporal gyrus; MTG: middle temporal gyrus; OBFC: orbitofrontal cortex; PAC: primary auditory cortex; pars.O.: pars opercularis; pars.T.:pars triangularis; PFC: prefrontal cortex; PMC: premotor cortex; SFG: superior frontal gyrus; SMA: supplementary motor area; SMG: supramarginal gyrus; STG: superior temporal gyrus; STS: superior temporal sulcus; sul.: sulcus; VLPFC: ventrolateral prefrontal cortex; vPMC: ventral premotor cortex.

Note: #less conservative threshold.

Table 8.2: Summary of findings involving subcortical structures with subsecond timing tasks (cen.: central, ver.:vermis. Other abbreviations as in Table 8.1).

Task	Contrast	Study	Modality		Basal ganglia	Lentiform N.	Putamen	Caudate nucleus	Thalamus	Substantia niagra	Red nucleus	Cerebellum
DD	T > Rest	Belin et al. (2002) (PET)	Aud				R	R	$R_{dmedial}$, $R_{Pos.}$			$B_{Lat.}$, $L_{Pos.}$, $L_{Cen.}$, $L_{Ant.}$
		Jueptner et al. (1995) (PET)	Aud									
		Reiterer et al. (2005)	Aud									B
	T > Cont	Jueptner et al. (1995) (PET)	Aud			B		R	B			B, $B_{ver.}$
		Pouthas et al. (2005)	Vis					R				
		Tregellas et al. (2006) (easy:E; difficult:D)	Aud	E	#				#			$B_{ver.}$
				D			B	R	B			$B_{ver.}$
				D>E			B					
	T > Oth.	Lewis and Miall (2003b)	Vis	.6s								L
				.6>3s								L
		Reiterer et al. (2005)	Aud									
TG	T > Cont	Ferrandez et al. (2003)	Vis				B_{Ant}	R	R			$B_{ver.}$
		Maquet et al. (1996) (PET)	Vis									$B_{ver.}$, L
	T > Oth.	Ferrandez et al. (2003)	Vis				L					
		Maquet et al. (1996) (PET)	Vis									
DRP	T > Cont	Jahanshahi et al. (2006)	Aud	S&L						L	L	
				S>L				L				R

Table 8.3: Summary of findings involving cortical structures with suprasecond timing tasks.

Task	Contrast	Study	Modality		Prefrontal/frontal cortex	Pre-SMA/ SMA	Premotor/ motor cortex	Temporal lobe	Parietal lobe	Precuneus	Occipital lobe	Cuneus	Insula	Cingulate
DD	T > Rest	Harrington et al. (2004a)	Aud	Enc.	$R_{medial\ FC}$, $R_{Inf.FC.}$,			B_{Sup}	$B_{Inf.}$, L_{Sup}, L_{AG}	R	$R_{ling.gy}$			$L_{Ant.}$, $R_{Pos.}$
		Nenadic et al. (2003)	Aud		$R_{medial\ FC}$, $R_{IFG.}$, R_{MFG}, $R_{Inf.FC}$			$R_{Sup\ MTG}$, $B_{Sup/tra\ TG}$					L, R_{Ant}	$L_{Ant./sul.}$
		Volz et al. (2001)	Aud		$R_{medial-SFG,\ IFG,\ MFG}$			Sup, middle						
	T > Cont	Pouthas et al. (2005)	Vis	S&L	R_{DLPFC}, B_{VLPFC}	Pre	$B_{Lat.PMC}$		R_{IPS}				B_{Ant}	Ant.
				L > S	R_{IFG}	Pre	$B_{Lat.PMC}$							Ant.
		Rao et al. (2001)	Vis	Early	B_{FO}	L_{pre}, L_{SMA}	B_{dPMC}, B_{vPMC}	$R_{Sup.}$, L_{Middle}	$R_{IPS/AG}$, $R_{Sup.}$	R			$B_{Ant.}$	$L_{Ant.}$
				Late	B_{DLPFC}, B_{FO}, B_{IFG}	L_{pre}, L_{SMA}	R_{dPMC}		$B_{IPS/AG}$, $L_{Sup.}$	L			B_{Ant}	$L_{Ant.}$
	T > Oth.	Coull et al. (2004)	Vis		R_{DLPFC}, L_{VLPFC}, R_{FO}	Pre	R_{dPMC}	$R_{Sup.}$, $R_{Middle.}$, $R_{Inf.}$	$B_{Inf.}$					
		Lewis and Miall (2003b)	Vis	3s	B_{DLPFC}, L_{vFO},	R_{pre}			$R_{Inf.}$				B_{Ant}	
				3 > .6s	R_{FP}, L_{VLPFC}				$L_{Inf.}$					$L_{Pos.sul}$
		Livesey et al.(2007)	Vis	C.eas	B_{PFC}, B_{IFG}		B_{pre}		$R_{Inf.}$				*B*	
				C.diff	B_{IFG}				L_{SMG}				*B*	
		Nenadic et al. (2003)	Aud											
		Rao et al. (2001)	Vis	Early	R_{FO}								R	
				Late	R_{DLPFC}									
		Smith et al. (2003)	Vis		R_{DLPFC}, R_{IFG}, R_{MFG}	B_{SMA}								
		Volz et al. (2001)	Aud		R_{SFG}									

DP	T > Rest	Tracy et al. (2000)						R_{ITG},						
	T > Oth.	Lewis and Miall (2002)	Vis	Motor	$B_{DLPFC/VLPFC}$, L_{DLPFC}, R_{VLPFC}	B_{pre}, B_{SMA}	B_{pre}, L_{M1}		B_{IPS}, $B_{Sup.}$, $R_{postcent.gy}$, R_{Sup}, $R_{Inf.}$				B	$R_{Ant.}$
				Press.	R_{DLPFC}	R_{pre}, SMA	R_{pre}		R_{IPS}, $R_{Inf.}$				R	$R_{Ant.}$
DRP	T > Rest	Hinton et al. (2004)	Vis			SMA/CMA					B_{V1}		B	
	T > Cont	Hinton and Meck (2004)	Aud Vis		B_{DLPFC}, B_{PFC}			STG						Ant.
		Jahanshahi et al. (2006)	Aud	S&L			L_{LPMC}							
				L > S	R_{DLPFC}	R_{SMA}	B_{LPMC}, R_{PMC}		$R_{IPS/AG}$, R_{Sup}			R	R_{border}	
		Kudo et al. (2004)	Vis		R_{IFG}, L_{SFG},	L_{SMA}	L_{dPMC}		L_{SM1}	L	$L_{ling.gy.}$			L_{Ant}
		Macar et al. (2002)	Tact	S&L	B_{DLPFC}	R_{SMA}	$L_{precent.\ gy}$		$R_{Inf.}$					$R_{Ant.}$
				Short	#B_{DLPFC}	SMA, #R_{SMA}	#$L_{precent.\ gy}$							#$R_{Ant.}$
				Long	R_{DLPFC}, #L_{DLPFC}	R_{SMA}	#$L_{precent.\ gy}$		$R_{Inf.}$					$R_{Ant.}$
	T > Oth.	Hinton et al. (2004)	Vis											

DP: duration production; oth.: other (colour discrimination — Coull et al., 2004, Livesey et al., 2007, length — Lewis & Miall, 2003b, pitch discrimination — Nenadic et al., 2003, Rao et al., 2001, Volz et al., 2001, order judgment — Smith et al., 2003, counting — Hinton et al., 2004, motor and pressure — Lewis & Miall, 2002); cont.: control (passively view stimulus — Hinton & Meck, 2004, Kudo et al., 2004, press response button after stimuli (no timing involved) — Jahanshahi et al., 2006, Macar et al., 2002, Pouthas et al., 2005, Rao et al., 2001). C.eas: colour discrimination easier than timing task; C.diff: colour discrimination more difficult than timing task; early: early imaging epochs (emphasizing encoding of temporal information); enc.: encoding condition; S&L: short, long > control comparison; short: short duration condition; L > S: long > short comparison; late: later imaging epochs (emphasizing decision and response selection components of the tasks); long: long duration condition; motor: motor condition; press.: pressure condition.

Ant./sul.: anterior/sulcus; medial-Sup.: medial superior; sup/tra: superior/traverse.

A1: primary auditory cortex; CMA: cingulated motor area; IFS: inferior frontal sulcus; IPG: intraparietal gyrus; ITG: inferior temporal gyrus; ling.Gy: lingual gyrus; LPMC: lateral premotor cortex; nuc.: nucleus; postcent.gy: postcentral gyrus; postcent.sul: postcentral sulcus; precent.gy: precentral gyrus; SFS: superior frontal sulcus; SM1: primary sensorimotor cortex; SPG: superior parietal gyrus; TG: temporal gyrus; V1: primary visual cortex. Other abbreviations as in Table 8.1.

Table 8.4: Summary of findings involving subcortical structures with suprasecond timing tasks.

Task	Contrast	Study	Modality		Globus pallidus	Putamen	Caudate nucleus	Thalamus	Substantia niagra	Red nucleus	Cerebellum	Brainstem
DD	T > Rest	Harrington et al. (2004a)	Aud	Enc.		L	R_{Body}, L_{Tail}, L_{Body}				$B_{Decl.}$, $L_{Pyr.}$, $L_{Tub.}$	
		Nenadic et al. (2003)	Aud			B	R	$R_{Ant\ /med.d.}$				
		Volz et al. (2001)	Aud			$R_{Pos.}$	B	R_{Ant}				
	T > Cont.	Pouthas et al. (2005)	Vis	S&L			R					
				L > S			R					
		Rao et al. (2001)	Vis	Early		R	$B_{medial\ head}$	$R_{cent.med}$ $R_{v.Ant.}$				
				Late		B	$B_{medial\ head}$, $R_{lat.body}$	$R_{cent.med}$ $R_{v.Ant.}$			B_{ver}	
	T > Oth.	Coull et al. (2004)	Vis			L_{Ant}						
		Lewis and Miall (2003b)	Vis	3s								
				3s > .6s								
		Livesey et al. (2007)	Vis	C.easy		B					$L_{Sup.}$	
				C.diff		L						
		Nenadic et al. (2003)	Aud			$^{\#}R$						
		Rao et al. (2001)	Vis	Early		R	R					
				Late								

		Smith et al. (2003)	Vis								L	
		Volz et al. (2001)	Aud			$R_{Pos.}$		R				
DP	T > Rest	Tracy et al. (2000)									$R_{lat-medial\ gy.}$	
	T > Oth.	Lewis and Miall (2002)	Vis	Motor Press.		R	L				L	
DRP	T > Rest	Hinton et al. (2004)	Vis									
	T > Cont.	Hinton and Meck (2004)	Aud, Vis			B	L	R				
		Jahanshahi et al. (2006)	Aud	S&L					L	L		
				L > S		R					R	
		Kudo et al. (2004)	Vis		R						$B_{Pos.}$, $R_{Ant.}$, $R_{nuc.}$, $R/L_{ver.}$	L/R
		Macar et al. (2002)	Tact	S&L								
				Short		#L						
				Long								
	T > Oth.	Hinton et al. (2004)	Vis									

Cent.med: central medial; decl.: declive; med.d.: medial dorsal; pyr: pyramis; tub: tuber; ver.: vermis (other abbreviations as in Table 8.3).

provide structural labels in the table instead (Ferrandez et al., 2003; Jueptner et al., 1995).

8.3. Subsecond Timing

Several research groups have used subsecond duration-discrimination tasks in which participants compared a probe interval to a standard interval (Belin et al., 2002; Jueptner et al., 1995; Lewis & Miall, 2003b; Pouthas et al., 2005; Reiterer et al., 2005; Tregellas, Davalos, & Rojas, 2006) in conjunction with fMRI or PET measures of brain activity. Of the six studies cited above, four used auditory stimuli and two (Lewis & Miall, 2003b; Pouthas et al., 2005) used visual stimuli. Three auditory and one visual study used filled intervals (Belin et al., 2002; Lewis & Miall, 2003b; Reiterer et al., 2005; Tregellas et al., 2006), whereas one auditory study and the remaining visual study used empty intervals demarcated by brief tones (Jueptner et al., 1995) or LED flashes (Pouthas et al., 2005; see Chapter 2 for the methodological description of filled and empty intervals). All of the auditory studies used standard and probe stimuli that were less than 600 ms, whereas both visual studies used both sub- and suprasecond durations, but we limit discussion to the subsecond data in this section. Moreover, the task demands and comparison conditions differed across experiments. Several studies required participants to indicate whether the second interval was longer or shorter than the first (Jueptner et al., 1995; Pouthas et al., 2005; Reiterer et al., 2005; Tregellas et al., 2006), one required comparison to a previously learned standard (Lewis & Miall, 2003b), and Belin et al. (2002) required participants to detect and respond to a deviant stimulus presented among a train of standard stimuli. Some groups manipulated task difficulty across the experimental run (Belin et al., 2002; Reiterer et al., 2005; Tregellas et al., 2006) and treated task difficulty as an analysis factor, whereas others did not. Finally, some groups compared timing to passive rest (e.g., absence of stimulation; Jueptner et al., 1995; Reiterer et al., 2005), stimulus presentation in the absence of a motor response (Belin et al., 2002), simple control conditions such as responding to the second of two intervals or stimuli presented (Jueptner et al., 1995; Pouthas et al., 2005; Tregellas et al., 2006), or a more demanding control task (Lewis & Miall, 2003b; Reiterer et al., 2005).

It is clear from the above summary that even when different research groups use what may be fairly labeled as the same class of task, e.g., duration discrimination, the differences in timing tasks and analytical approaches may be substantial with consequences for the patterns of brain activation obtained and conclusions drawn from those activation patterns. Indeed, it is possible that the disparity in task details would translate into minimal consistency of activation across labs and experiments. Alternatively, consistent activation obtained across a disparate group of timing tasks and comparison control tasks permits a stronger claim that the activation pattern truly reflects the brain structures that are involved in interval timing. Therefore, a critical question is whether or not there are consistent patterns of activation across interval-timing tasks.

As described above, three auditory modality experiments compared a duration-discrimination timing condition to a rest condition. All of these studies reported activations in the frontal cortex, but the details of these activations differ. For example, bilateral dorsal prefrontal cortex (DLPFC) was explicitly reported in one of the three studies (Jueptner et al., 1995) only, although Belin et al. (2002) also reported right prefrontal cortex and right middle frontal gyrus activity. Belin et al. (2002) and Reiterer et al. (2005) reported inferior frontal gyrus activation, but this was limited to the right side, including the frontal operculum, in the former, whereas it was on the left side in the latter. All three studies also reported activity in the temporal lobe. Common to all studies was activation in the middle temporal gyrus (MTG), however in one study MTG activation was on the right (Belin et al., 2002), in one it was on the left and accompanied by bilateral superior temporal sulcus (STS) activity (Reiterer et al., 2005), and in the third the MTG activity was bilateral and also accompanied by bilateral superior temporal gyrus (STG) activation (Jueptner et al., 1995). The cerebellum was active bilaterally in two studies (Belin et al., 2002; Reiterer et al., 2005). Finally, only Reiterer et al. (2005) reported activity in the left insula and only Belin et al. (2002) reported activation in the right inferior parietal lobule and the basal ganglia, specifically the right putamen, right caudate, and right thalamus.

Looking across these studies, which used highly similar tasks, we see a pattern of activation that includes frontal cortex and superior and middle temporal cortex but is perhaps slightly less consistent than one would have expected given the task similarities. Of course, activation differences are likely related to the different imaging methodologies used (PET — Jueptner et al., 1995; Belin et al., 2002 versus fMRI — Reiterer et al., 2005) and the methodological state of the art at the time the experiment was conducted (e.g., blocked versus event-related designs).

For the three studies that compared timing to simple control tasks such as responding to a stimulus in the absence of timing, the DLPFC and the frontal operculum were active bilaterally in one study (Tregellas et al., 2006), whereas the right DLPFC and bilateral VLPFC were active in another (Pouthas et al., 2005). Both Jueptner et al. (1995) and Pouthas et al. (2005) reported anterior cingulate activation, although this was the only significant cortical activation reported by the former group for the timing versus control task. Tregellas et al. (2006) and Pouthas et al. (2005) both reported bilateral activations in the premotor cortex and insula, with the former also reporting SMA and bilateral STG activity and the latter reporting pre-SMA activity and right intraparietal sulcus activity. Subcortically, the right caudate nucleus was active in all three studies, whereas the putamen, thalamus, and cerebellum were bilaterally active only in the studies by Jueptner et al. (1995) and Tregellas et al. (2006).

Lewis and Miall (2003b) used the same visual stimulus, a white line, for four different conditions: time, length, side, and rest. The condition in effect on a particular trial was indicated by a cue word presented prior to the trial start. In the time and length conditions, participants were required to attend to stimulus duration and length, respectively, and categorize the stimulus as "more" or "less" than the appropriate dimension of a standard stimulus. The authors attempted to control for attention processes by contrasting the time and length conditions. For the 600-ms stimuli, the time condition elicited greater activation than the length condition in the bilateral DLPFC, right VLPFC, left frontal operculum, bilateral frontal pole-MFG, pre-SMA, right PMC, left STG, right intraparietal sulcus, bilateral inferior parietal lobe, anterior insula, and left cerebellum.

Finally, Reiterer et al. (2005) compared timing to a pitch-discrimination task but failed to obtain any significant activation differences, an outcome that calls into question the interval-timing specificity of the activations obtained in their timing versus resting baseline comparison.

In contrast to discrimination tasks in which the standard is presented on every trial, temporal generalization places much greater demand on the participant's ability to maintain a representation of the standard duration throughout the test session. Pouthas and her colleagues have conducted both a PET (Maquet, Lejeune, Pouthas, et al., 1996) and an fMRI study (Ferrandez et al., 2003) of temporal generalization using essentially the same task in both experiments. In the original PET study, participants experienced six examples of a 700-ms visual (LED illumination) standard stimulus at the beginning of the experiment and subsequently judged whether comparison stimuli (490, 595, 700, 805, and 910 ms) were the same or different from the standard. In the control task, a 700-ms stimulus (LED illumination) was presented 100 times and the participants had to respond at random on one of two buttons after each LED offset. Participants also completed an intensity generalization task in which they indicated whether comparison intensities were the same or different from the previously learned standard intensity. For the intensity task, all stimuli were presented for 700 ms. The only difference between the paradigms used in the PET and the fMRI studies was the interstimulus interval (ISI). In the former case the ISI ranged from 1500 to 2300 ms (1900 ms average), whereas in the latter case it ranged from 2200 to 3200 ms (2700 ms average).

In the PET experiment (Maquet et al., 1996), relative to the control task, the duration-generalization task elicited activation of the right prefrontal cortex, the left fusiform gyrus, the right inferior parietal lobule, the anterior cingulate, the cerebellar vermis bilaterally, and the left cerebellar hemisphere. Some of the same areas, as well as others, were activated in the fMRI experiment (Ferrandez et al., 2003) — specifically, the right dorsolateral prefrontal cortex, bilateral pars opercularis, right frontal cortex including the frontal eye fields, bilateral granular frontal area, left agranular frontal area, bilateral anterior insula, left anterior cingulate, bilateral superior temporal gyrus, and bilateral inferior parietal lobule. Subcortically, the anterior putamen bilaterally, right caudate nucleus, right thalamus, and the bilateral cerebellar vermis were active.

Interestingly, in the PET study, comparison of the duration-generalization task with the intensity task failed to reveal any differences in brain activity. However, the same comparison for the fMRI study revealed activity in the left pars opercularis, bilateral par triangularis/orbitofrontal cortex, right insula, bilateral SMA, left premotor area and motor area, bilateral inferior parietal lobule, and bilateral superior temporal gyri. Subcortically, the left putamen was the only differentially active structure.

The final study of interest for this section is that of Jahanshahi, Jones, Dirnberger, & Frith (2006), who used a duration reproduction task, which is not a common task choice for subsecond range timing. These authors asked participants to reproduce short and long intervals (500 and 2000 ms, respectively) demarcated by two 50-ms tones. In the control task, participants merely pressed the response button as soon as a tone was presented. The authors did not separately compare the 500- and 2000-ms conditions with the control task, but rather examined the combination of the 500- and 2000-ms conditions against the control. This comparison revealed greater activation in the left lateral premotor cortex, the left substantia nigra, and the left red nucleus only.

Across the nine subsecond interval-timing studies discussed above, a total of 14 activation comparisons were described. Several cortical areas were active across four or more comparison conditions; these areas were the cerebellum (nine reports), the DLPFC (including reports of MFG activity), IFG and STG (eight reports each), PMC and insula (seven reports each), the cingulate (six reports), the pre-SMA (six reports), SMA and inferior parietal lobule (five reports each). Subcortically, common areas of activation included the cerebellum (nine reports), the caudate (six reports), and thalamus and putamen (five reports each).

8.4. Suprasecond Timing

Numerous authors have examined interval timing using durations greater than 1000 ms. These studies included duration-discrimination tasks similar to those used in the subsecond-discrimination experiments described above (Coull, Vidal, Nazarian, & Macar, 2004; Harrington et al., 2004a; Livesey, Wall, & Smith, 2007; Nenadic et al., 2003; Pouthas et al., 2005; Rao, Mayer, & Harrington, 2001; Smith, Taylor, Lidzba, & Rubia, 2003; Volz et al., 2001), as well as duration production and reproduction tasks (Hinton & Meck, 2004; Kudo et al., 2004; Lewis & Miall, 2002; Macar et al., 2002; Tracy, Faro, Mohamed, Pinsk, & Pinus, 2000).

8.4.1. Duration Discrimination

Of the nine duration-discrimination studies, two used filled auditory intervals (Nenadic et al., 2003; Volz et al., 2001), two used empty auditory intervals (Harrington et al., 2004a; Rao et al., 2001), four used filled visual intervals (Coull et al., 2004; Lewis & Miall, 2003b; Livesey et al., 2007; Smith et al., 2003), and one used empty visual intervals (Pouthas et al., 2005). All studies used durations greater than 1 s only, with the exception of the studies by Lewis and Miall (2003b) and Pouthas et al., which, as noted above, included a subsecond timing condition and the Coull et al.'s (2004) study that included a 540-ms duration along with 1080- and 1620-ms durations. On most trials in the Coull et al.'s experiment the participants experienced at least one, if not two, suprasecond stimuli. Consequently, we have included this experiment in the suprasecond section of the article only. We present the suprasecond data from Lewis and Miall (2003b) and Pouthas et al. (2005) here also.

As was the case for the subsecond experiments, there is some variability in task demands and comparison conditions across the eight suprasecond experiments. The studies required participants to judge whether the first or second stimulus was of longer duration (Livesey et al., 2007; Nenadic et al., 2003; Smith et al., 2003; Volz et al., 2001), whether the second stimulus was the same as or different from the first (Coull et al., 2004; Pouthas et al., 2005), and whether the second stimulus was longer or shorter than the first (standard) stimulus (Harrington et al., 2004a; Rao et al., 2001). Some researchers manipulated task difficulty (Harrington et al., 2004a; Nenadic et al., 2003; Volz et al., 2001) or attention allocation (Coull et al., 2004) across the experimental run or between experiments (Livesey et al., 2007). Finally, researchers compared timing to rest (Harrington et al., 2004a; Nenadic et al., 2003; Volz et al., 2001), a simple control condition such as responding to one of the stimuli presented (Pouthas et al., 2005; Rao et al., 2001), or a more demanding pitch discrimination (Nenadic et al., 2003; Volz et al., 2001), color discrimination (Coull et al., 2004; Livesey et al., 2007), or temporal-order discrimination (Smith et al., 2003) control task. Note that although Volz et al. (2001) compared the performance and brain-activation patterns of patients with schizophrenia and control participants, our interest here is limited to the data from the control participants only. In addition, the analyses presented by Rao et al. (2001) were designed to tease apart encoding and decision processes involved in interval timing by categorizing activations as occurring early or late in an analysis epoch. In the following, we refer to their early and late epoch categorizations in reporting the results of their analyses.

Relative to rest, several frontal regions were reported as active in suprasecond timing. These include the IFG (right hemisphere — Nenadic et al., 2003; hemisphere not specified — Volz, 2001), the right inferior frontal cortex (Harrington et al., 2004a; Nenadic et al., 2003), the right medial frontal cortex (Harrington et al., 2004a; Nenadic et al., 2003), the right medial superior frontal gyrus (Volz et al., 2001), and the middle frontal gyrus (right hemisphere — Nenadic et al., 2003; hemisphere not specified — Volz et al., 2001). Moreover, the left anterior and right posterior cingulate (Harrington et al., 2004a), and the left anterior cingulate/cingulate sulcus (Nenadic et al., 2003), were also active during timing as compared to rest. The common activation areas in the temporal lobe were the superior temporal cortex (bilateral — Harrington et al., 2004a; hemisphere not specified — Volz et al., 2001), middle temporal cortex (hemisphere not specified — Volz et al., 2001), right superior MTG (Nenadic et al., 2003), and bilateral superior/transverse temporal gyrus (Nenadic et al., 2003). The insula was active bilaterally in one study (Nenadic et al., 2003). Subcortically, there was common activation in the putamen (left hemisphere — Harrrington et al., 2004; bilateral — Nenadic et al., 2003; right hemisphere — Volz et al., 2001), and the caudate (bilateral — Harrington et al., 2004a and Volz et al., 2001; right hemisphere — Nenadic et al., 2003).

Relative to a control condition of responding to one of the presented stimuli (Pouthas et al., 2005; Rao et al., 2001) duration discrimination revealed common areas of activation in the DLPFC (right hemisphere — Pouthas et al., 2005; bilateral — Rao et al., 2001 — late epoch), VLPFC/IFG (right hemisphere — Pouthas et al., 2005; bilateral — Rao et al., 2001 — early and late epoch), and motor areas (pre-SMA hemisphere not specified — Pouthas et al., 2005; left pre-SMA and left SMA — Rao et al., 2001 early and late epochs; bilateral premotor cortex — Pouthas et al., 2005; Rao et al., 2001 early epoch; right premotor cortex — Rao et al., 2001 late epoch). The anterior cingulate (hemisphere not specified — Pouthas et al., 2005; left — Rao et al., 2001 early and late epochs), the intra parietal sulcus (right — Rao et al., 2001 early epoch; Pouthas et al., 2005; bilateral — Rao et al. 2001 late epoch), and bilateral anterior insula (Pouthas et al., 2005; Rao et al., 2001 early and late epochs) were also active across experiments. Subcortically, Pouthas et al. (2005) showed activation in the right caudate nucleus only, whereas Rao et al. (2001) showed activation in the caudate bilaterally (early and late epochs), the right putamen in the early epoch and bilateral putamen in the late epoch, and the right thalamus (early and late epochs).

The control tasks used in the above studies, however, do not control for the degree of perceptual monitoring, memory demands, and decision processes that are brought to bear in an interval-timing task. Relative to temporal order discrimination, duration discrimination elicited activation in the right DLPFC, right IFG, and the right MFG, as well as the bilateral SMA (Smith et al., 2003). A comparison of timing with pitch discrimination revealed activity in the right superior frontal gyrus, right putamen, and right thalamus (Volz et al., 2001), but a subsequent study from the same group showed an activity increase in the right putamen only, and even then only at a reduced significance threshold (Nenadic et al., 2003). Of the two experiments that used color discrimination as a control task, the common areas of activation included the prefrontal cortex (right DLPFC, left VLPFC, right IFG — Coull et al., 2004; bilateral PFC and bilateral IFG — Livesey et al., 2007), the inferior parietal lobule (bilateral — Coull et al., 2004; right in the easy condition, left in difficult condition — Livesey et al., 2007). Finally, in the duration discrimination versus line length discrimination comparison by Lewis and Miall (2003b), the 3-s stimuli in the time condition elicited greater activation than the length condition in the bilateral DLPFC, left VLPFC, left ventral frontal operculum, right frontal pole, right pre-SMA, right inferior parietal lobe, and bilateral anterior insula.

Across the nine suprasecond duration-discrimination studies described above, a total of fifteen activation comparisons were described. Several cortical areas were active across four or more comparison conditions: the VLPFC/IFG (12 reports); DLPFC/SFG/MFG (9 reports); insula (8 reports); SMG (7 reports); STG, PMC, and cingulate (6 reports each); pre-SMA (5 reports); and MTG (4 reports). Subcortically, common areas of activation included the putamen (11 reports), caudate (7 reports), and thalamus (5 reports).

For similar cognitive timing tasks (duration discrimination and temporal generalization) it is clear that many brain areas are activated by both sub- and suprasecond durations, and the proportion of studies within a duration category showing activation in these areas was similar across the two duration ranges. These areas include the DLPFC, IFG, cingulate, PMC, pre-SMA, STG, insula, caudate, putamen, and thalamus. Given these broad commonalities in activation, it would seem that, at least within the domain of cognitive timing, milliseconds and seconds range timing likely share common timing components, if not the entire network.

8.4.2. Duration Production and Reproduction

Several groups have examined brain activity in duration production and reproduction tasks. Typically, these studies use much longer durations than those used in a same–different temporal discrimination experiment and there is greater variation across task types as compared to the duration discrimination and temporal generalization tasks described above. Hence, in the following discussion we describe each of the experimental approaches and the activation patterns reported for those individual experiments, rather than the common areas across one or more experiments. At the end of the section we summarize the regions that are consistently activated across the various duration production and reproduction tasks.

Tracy et al. (2000) used a duration production task in which participants raised their dominant hand when the target interval, ranging from 12 to 24 s, had elapsed. In a forward counting control task, participants silently counted up from the number given, ranging from 6 to 20, until they were told to stop. In a backward counting control task, participants counted backwards by sevens from the number given, ranging from 67 to 100, until they were told to stop. In the dual task, participants were asked to estimate a given interval, ranging from 11 to 22 s, while they counted backwards by sevens. According to Tracy et al. (2000), the data analyses in their experiment were designed to reveal activity unique to time estimation, activity related to timing accuracy, and the relationship of activation magnitude to the magnitude of the duration being timed. Within the framework of these analyses the following were found: activity unique to time estimation occurred in the right inferior temporal gyrus and the right lateral area of the medial cerebellar gyrus; activity related to time estimation accuracy was present in the right middle frontal gyrus, the left posterior parietal cortex, and the right lateral cerebellum; and activity in the right hemisphere middle, superior and inferior frontal gyri, and the inferior temporal cortex reflected the relationship between the size of the estimated interval and the actual time interval. Clearly, many of these areas correspond to areas that were activated in the experiments described above.

In contrast to the study by Tracy et al. (2000), Lewis and Miall (2002) asked participants to produce a 3-s interval on the first trial and on each subsequent trial they were cued to produce a duration that they thought was either just noticeably longer or just noticeably shorter than the duration they had produced on the previous trial. Pressure, motor, and rest conditions were also included in the experiment. Similar to the timing task, in the pressure condition participants were asked to modify the force of their button press from trial to trial, but the first button press was at a pretrained force level. In the motor condition participants merely responded to a cue and in the rest condition they were asked to remain still and to visually fixate on a single point.

The areas of activity reported by Tracy et al. (2000) were very sparse compared to the range of areas reported by Lewis and Miall (2002). Relative to the motor task, the timing task elicited activity bilaterally in the DLPFC, VLPFC, bilateral pre-SMA, bilateral SMA, bilateral pre motor cortex, left primary motor cortex, right anterior cingulate, bilateral insula, bilateral intraparietal sulcus, bilateral superior and right inferior parietal lobule, left cerebellar hemisphere, and the left caudate and right putamen. Relative to the pressure task, the timing task elicited activation in a subset of the areas that were active relative to the motor task. These were the right DLPFC, right premotor cortex, right pre-SMA, SMA, right intraparietal areas, right inferior parietal lobule, and the right anterior cingulate gyrus.

Several authors have used duration-reproduction tasks in which interval timing is compared to a rest or baseline state (Hinton, Harrington, Binder, Durgerian, & Rao, 2004), a control condition in which the timing stimulus is passively viewed (Hinton & Meck, 2004; Kudo et al., 2004), or a control condition in which the timing stimulus is presented, but participants merely press a button after stimulus presentation (Jahanshahi et al., 2006; Macar et al., 2002) rather than time the stimulus. Comparisons with cognitively demanding tasks, such as counting (Hinton et al., 2004), have also been made. Finally, the stimulus modality of the sample duration has also varied across duration reproduction experiments. Visual (Hinton & Meck, 2004; Hinton et al., 2004; Kudo et al. 2004), auditory (Hinton & Meck, 2004; Jahanshahi et al., 2006), and tactile (Macar et al., 2002) stimuli have all been used.

Relative to baseline, Hinton et al. (2004) found that timing increased activation bilaterally in the SMA, cingulate motor area, bilateral insula, and bilateral primary visual cortex (V1). The pattern of activity reported by Hinton et al. (2004) is somewhat different from that reported using a very similar version of the peak-interval duration reproduction task (Hinton & Meck, 2004), but with comparisons against a passive viewing control condition. On timing + motor test trials, the stimulus was presented and the participant responded by squeezing a response bulb. Stimulus presentation was identical in the control task, but participants did not have to time the signal or make a motor response. In the motor-alone task, participants had to make a response when a cue was presented, but did not have to time the stimuli. Finally, in the timing-alone task, participants were asked to time the signal, but they did not make a motor response. In the timing + motor task (not shown in the tables), cortical regions of activation included the primary and secondary visual cortices, primary and secondary auditory cortices, prefrontal cortex including the superior and middle frontal gyri, the orbitofrontal cortex, and the left DLPFC. Subcortical structures included the caudate bilaterally, the putamen bilaterally, and the thalamus bilaterally. The timing task elicited activity in the bilateral PFC, including DLPFC, superior temporal gyrus, anterior cingulate cortex, left caudate, bilateral putamen, and right thalamus. The motor task elicited activity in the primary motor cortex and the thalamus only. The peak-interval task as implemented in Hinton and Meck (2004) elicited a much wider set of brain activations as compared to that of Hinton et al. (2004). Moreover, the activated areas in the former experiment correspond reasonably well with areas reported in other reproduction tasks.

For example, relative to a control condition in which participants felt a tactile timing stimulus, but did not respond until cued to do so, a low seconds (2.2, 2.7, and 3.2 s) and high seconds (9, 11, and 13 s) duration reproduction task elicited activity in a similar set of brain structures (Macar et al., 2002). An analysis combining the short and long conditions versus control revealed activity in the bilateral DLPFC, the right SMA, the left PMC, the right anterior cingulate cortex, and the right inferior parietal lobule. Analysis of the long-duration condition versus the long control condition revealed activation in the right DLPFC, the right SMA, the right anterior cingulate cortex, and the right inferior parietal cortex. At a lower activation threshold, the left DLPFC and the left PMC were also activated. Analysis of the short-duration condition versus the short control condition revealed activation in the SMA, and at a lower threshold, activation in the bilateral DLPFC, the right SMA, the left PMC, the right anterior cingulate cortex, and the left putamen.

As noted above, Jahanshahi et al. (2006) also used a reproduction task with a relatively short suprasecond reproduction duration (2000 ms) as well as a subsecond reproduction duration (500 ms). Relative to the control task, the 500 and 2000 ms reproductions elicited greater activation in the left lateral premotor cortex, the left substantia nigra, and the left red nucleus.

The final duration reproduction data set to consider is that of Kudo et al. (2004). These authors examined a duration-reproduction task in relation to a passive viewing control task. In the timing task, the participants were asked to respond in anticipation of the final flash in a sequence of eight LED flashes, which occurred at a delay of 1.5–2.5 s after the penultimate flash. Therefore, to perform well in the timing task, participants had to time the delay between flashes and respond appropriately. Relative to the passive viewing control condition, the timing condition elicited significant activation in the right IFG, left SFG, the left SMA, the left dorsal premotor cortex, the left primary sensorimotor area, the left anterior cingulate cortex, the left precuneus, the left lingual gyrus, the right globus pallidus, the bilateral cerebellum, and the brainstem.

Across the seven suprasecond duration production and reproduction studies discussed above, a total of 10 activation comparisons were described. Several cortical areas were active across three or more comparison conditions. These include the DLPFC/MFG/SFG (nine reports), SMA (eight reports), cingulate cortex (seven reports), inferior parietal lobule (six reports), insula (four reports), inferior parietal sulcus and IFG/VLPFC (three reports each). Subcortically, common areas of activation included the putamen (three reports) and cerebellum (four reports).

8.5. Explicit Comparison of Sub- and Suprasecond Durations

Three neuroimaging studies of interval timing have explicitly compared timing a duration greater than 1000 ms with timing a duration less than 1000 ms. As noted above, Lewis and Miall (2003b) used the same visual stimulus, a white line, for four different conditions, (time, length, side, and rest) and the condition in effect on a particular trial was indicated by a cue word presented prior to trial start. Comparison of the 600-ms and 3-s time conditions revealed greater activation for the 600-ms condition in the bilateral VLPFC and STG, bilateral frontal operculum, right MTG, right STS, left insula, and left cerebellum. However, the left posterior cingulate sulcus and the inferior parietal lobule were more active in the 3-s condition as compared to the 600-ms condition. The main goal of the study was to examine putative differences in the neural structures underlying duration processing in the seconds and milliseconds range. Although both interval ranges activated a set of common brain areas, there were also regions that showed differential activation for different durations, which the authors took as evidence for distinct systems underlying milliseconds and seconds range processing of duration.

Pouthas et al. (2005) also compared stimuli greater and less than 1000 ms within the same experiment. They found that relative to the short-duration condition, the long-duration condition elicited increased activation in the right IFG, pre-SMA, bilateral premotor cortex, the anterior cingulate cortex, and the right caudate nucleus. Finally, in the study of duration reproduction by Jahanshahi et al. (2006), described above, the subsecond reproduction condition elicited greater activation than the suprasecond reproduction condition in the bilateral superior frontal gyrus, left middle frontal gyrus, the left superior temporal gyrus, left middle temporal gyrus, and the left anterior cingulate. Greater activation for the short condition was also present in the left caudate nucleus and in the right cerebellar hemisphere. In contrast, greater activation was observed for suprasecond reproduction as compared to subsecond reproduction in the right DLPFC, right SMA, bilateral premotor cortex, right superior parietal cortex, right inferior parietal sulcus, inferior parietal lobule, right cuneus, right insula, right putamen, and the right cerebellum.

Taken together the comparison of timing tasks and ranges both across studies and within studies appears to suggest that differences in activation patterns are more quantitative rather than qualitative. Consequently, in the following discussion of the relationship between brain structure and function we do not distinguish between sub- and suprasecond interval-timing studies or the various timing tasks.

8.6. From Structure to Function

Demonstration that particular brain structures are consistently active when participants perform interval-timing tasks is a first step toward confirming that these structures are part of a timing network. The preceding survey of the literature showed many common areas of activation across a wide range of timing tasks and stimulus durations. Consequently, a strong case can be made for the involvement of regions within the frontal, temporal, and parietal cortices as well as basal ganglia structures in tasks that require participants to time a stimulus. However, a list of structures activated in timing tasks does not demonstrate that these areas are exclusively, or even primarily, engaged in timing behavior or that, taken together, they form an *internal clock*.

8.6.1. Information Processing Model

The critical next step is to attempt to place the obtained brain activation patterns within an interpretive framework of perceptual and cognitive function. Many timing theorists include attention, memory, and decision functions as critical components of the internal clock in addition to what may be thought of as a timer component (i.e., a pacemaker–accumulator mechanism; see Chapters 3 and 9 — Meck, 1984; Penney, Allan, Meck, & Gibbon, 1998). The information-processing (IP) model of interval timing developed by Gibbon, Church, and Meck (1984) to accompany the scalar expectancy theory mathematical model of timing has played a prominent role in human and animal studies of interval timing over the past two decades and has been regularly featured in interpretations of neuroimaging data. Many of the authors of the studies summarized above attributed activity in particular brain structures with specific perceptual and/or cognitive aspects of the scalar timing IP model.

The model comprises clock, memory, and decision stages, with attention allocation impacting the function of the clock stage. Given that attention, memory, and decision processes are involved in most cognitive functions, however, one might ask whether the memory and decision functions implicated in interval timing are timing specific or are more general memory and decision mechanisms that receive input from the clock mechanism and do computations on that input. Moreover, it is possible that interval-timing-specific memory or decision mechanisms would be spatially co-localized with memory and decision mechanisms that receive and operate on other forms of information. Fortunately, demonstrations of spatially dissociable brain areas for memory representation of different information categories based on fMRI data suggest that it is possible to dissect co-localized regions of brain tissue that perform similar, yet distinct, computational or representational functions (e.g., Haxby et al., 2001). In the following sections we briefly highlight the associations various research groups have drawn between components or processes of the IP model of interval timing and the specific brain regions activated in their interval-timing studies.

8.6.1.1. Clock and attention In the IP account of interval timing, the clock stage comprises a pacemaker, switch, and an accumulator. The pacemaker is typically conceptualized as a pulse generator that sends pulses to the accumulator. Whether pulses are accumulated depends on the state of the switch and switch closure is in turn influenced by allocation of attention (Meck, 1984). The basal ganglia have been implicated in interval-timing function by both human-patient studies and nonhuman animal research (Gibbon et al., 1997; Ivry & Spencer, 2004; Meck, 1996; Meck & Benson, 2002; Pastor, Artieda, Jahanshahi, & Obeso, 1992), and the posited functional role of the basal ganglia in such studies has often been that of a pacemaker–accumulator mechanism.

Recent neuroimaging studies provide increased evidence for a central role of the basal ganglia in human interval timing (e.g., Coull et al., 2004; Ferrandez et al., 2003; Hinton & Meck, 2004; Jahanshahi et al., 2006; Livesey et al., 2007; Pouthas et al., 2005; Rao et al., 2001; Stevens, Kiehl, Pearlson, & Calhoun, 2007; Tregellas et al.,

2006). Some authors have implicated the basal ganglia in clock function without necessarily specifying the nature of the clock function involved (e.g., pacemaker, accumulator, or switch) or a specific basal ganglia structure, whereas others have made quite specific claims about structure, function, or both.

Ferrandez et al. (2003) described the basal ganglia and in particular the left putamen as serving as a clock mechanism that internally represents time. However, these authors included the bilateral SMA as a part of this clock mechanism. Pouthas et al. (2005) suggested that the pre-SMA may serve as a clock mechanism in its own right, or receive output from a clock mechanism located in the striatum. Livesey et al. (2007) also associated the clock mechanism with the putamen, but Nenadic et al. (2003) stressed that the right putamen activation they obtained was not necessarily a direct correlate of the internal clock. Finally, Harrington et al. (2004a) associated clock function with the right caudate.

Other researchers have been more specific in their allocation of particular timing functions, such as temporal encoding and accumulator to basal ganglia structures. For example, Belin et al. (2002) suggested that the basal ganglia encode time intervals. Two groups have associated the caudate nucleus with encoding (Pouthas et al., 2005; Rao et al., 2001), although Rao and colleagues have also included the putamen as part of the encoding mechanism (Harrington et al., 2004a; Rao et al., 2001). Tregellas et al. (2006) interpreted their basal ganglia activation pattern as consistent with this encoding interpretation.

Several authors have explicitly attributed accumulator function to particular structures. For example, Macar et al. (2002) suggested that the SMA acts as a temporal accumulator for temporal information, whereas Smith et al. (2003) associated the right MFG with the accumulator. Finally, Lewis and Miall (2002) suggested that the premotor region serves as the accumulator, but this was framed as a function of build-up cells, which the authors view as being parallel to the notion of a temporal accumulator.

The concept of attention has been invoked at several levels within the interval-timing literature. One idea ties attention closely to the clock stage of the IP model because, as noted above, attention determines switch closure and maintenance in the closed state. Indeed, Rao and colleagues suggested that the right inferior parietal cortex modulates attention during interval encoding and may regulate the start and stop of accumulation (Harrington et al., 2004a; Rao et al., 2001).

Coull et al. (2004) suggested that several brain areas are responsible for allocating attention to time. These regions include the pre-SMA, SMA, right premotor, right prefrontal, and right temporal cortices, bilateral intraparietal sulcus, as well as the putamen. One source of support for this timing-specific view is that the sustained attention demands and task difficulty were equal for the time and color discrimination tasks in their study, which counters an interpretation of prefrontal activity as simply reflecting to attentional load. In contrast, Tregellas et al. (2006) suggested that operculum activity reflects attending to order in time, whereas STG activity reflects attentional modulation of primary sensory areas (Tregellas et al., 2006). However, other authors posit a nontiming-specific attentional role for brain areas such as the inferior parietal cortex (Belin et al., 2002; Lewis & Miall, 2002,

2003b; Pouthas et al., 2005), frontal cortex including prefrontal cortex and premotor areas (Belin et al., 2002; Lewis & Miall, 2002; Volz et al., 2001), the cingulate cortex (Lewis & Miall, 2002; Maquet et al., 1996; Pouthas et al., 2005), and the left cerebellum (Belin et al., 2002).

Although researchers are to be commended for attempting to attribute activation in particular brain structures to specific aspects of a theoretical model, it is often difficult to determine whether a structure plays a role that should be attributed to a clock function such as encoding/temporal accumulation, or whether the role is that of a memory function that should be considered under the memory or decision stage of the IP model of timing. We return to this issue below.

8.6.1.2. Memory stage Memory functions, such as maintaining and updating temporal representations have been attributed to the frontal cortex by many authors (e.g., Tracy et al., 2000; Volz et al., 2001). For example, several authors have suggested that the premotor cortex may be responsible for the storage and maintenance of temporal information (Ferrandez et al., 2003; Jahanshahi et al., 2006; Pouthas et al., 2005; Rao et al., 2001). However, this is not to imply that this is a role exclusively played by the premotor cortex. For example, Ferrandez et al. (2003) claimed that the right VLPFC, the left premotor areas, as well as the parietal cortex, maintain temporal information in working memory. Maquet et al. (1996) have also suggested involvement of inferior frontal cortex and inferior parietal cortex in visuospatial working memory for time, but they also noted that it is difficult to distinguish memory load from attention. Several groups (Hinton & Meck, 2004; Jahanshahi et al., 2006; Nenadic et al., 2003), have included the DLPFC as part of the working-memory circuit involved in interval timing.

In contrast, the pre-SMA may be involved in working-memory processes that are not specific to interval timing (Ferrandez et al., 2003; Livesey et al., 2007; Nenadic et al., 2003; Rao et al., 2001). So, although regions of frontal cortex have been implicated in working-memory functions across a broad array of stimulus types, specific structures unique to working memory for time have not yet been isolated using brain imaging methods. Indeed, Livesey et al. (2007) found that prefrontal activity was largely absent when the control task was more difficult than the timing task.

Additional structures associated with memory rehearsal networks for time include the right parahippocampus, hippocampus, right inferior frontal, and superior temporal cortex, which may form a rehearsal network (Harrington et al., 2004a). Other authors have suggested that the temporal cortex represents duration (Ferrandez et al., 2003) is involved in auditory imagery (Lewis & Miall, 2003b), or governs strategies related to auditory imagery (Coull et al., 2004).

8.6.1.3. Decision and response processes Given decision and memory are interdependent (Harrington et al., 2004a), it is difficult to tease apart brain structures supporting memory and decision functions. As a result, many of the brain areas associated with memory representations have also been implicated in decision and response processes such as comparing two intervals and selecting a response.

In the studies reviewed here, decision and response processes have been associated with a wide range of structures including the anterior cingulate cortex (Hinton & Meck, 2004; Kudo et al., 2004; Macar et al., 2002; Nenadic et al., 2003), which may play a role in attention related to response selection (Pouthas et al., 2005), various aspects of the frontal cortex (Belin et al., 2002), such as the SMA (Jahanshahi et al., 2006; Kudo et al., 2004; Tregellas et al., 2006), and the DLPFC (Ferrandez et al., 2003; Harrington et al., 2004a; Macar et al., 2002; Nenadic et al., 2003; Rao et al., 2001; Tregellas et al., 2006). Although Tregellas et al. (2006) suggest that the DLPFC plays a specific role in temporal processing rather than a general working-memory role, Ferrandez et al. (2003) claim that the role of the DLPFC in making comparison and maintaining information is not timing specific. Other structures implicated in decision and responses processes include the insula (Tregellas et al., 2006), the temporal cortex (superior — Harrington et al., 2004a; inferior — Tracy et al., 2000), the parietal cortex and parahippocampus (Harrington et al., 2004a), and the putamen (Harrington et al., 2004a; Tregellas et al., 2006).

8.6.1.4. Other timing-related functions Many studies demonstrated cerebellar activation in timing tasks (Belin et al., 2002; Jueptner et al., 1995; Rao et al., 2001; Smith et al., 2003; Tregellas et al., 2006). However, whether this activation reflects an operation that is specific to timing or is a more general function, possibly related to motor control or the detection of stimulus onsets and/or offsets, is unresolved. For example, Lewis and Miall (2003b) found greater cerebellum activity in the 600-ms condition as compared to the 3-s condition even though the task was nonmotor timing in both cases, although in an earlier paper (Lewis & Miall, 2002) these authors claimed that the cerebellum is not involved in temporal-specific processing. Moreover, although Harrington et al., (2004a) attributed a temporal processing role to the cerebellum because it was active during the encoding phase of their task, they also pointed out that the cerebellum is known to participate in many sensory and cognitive functions and therefore the activation pattern may merely have reflected sensory input monitoring and optimization with respect to memory representations during the encoding phase of the task (Harrington, Lee, Boyd, Rapcsak, & Knight, 2004b). Consistent with a nontiming-specific view, Maquet et al. (1996) found cerebellar activation for both timing and intensity discriminations and concluded the activation may relate to discrimination tasks in general and not timing in particular. Pouthas et al. (2005), Jahanshahi et al. (2006), and Rao et al. (2001) hold a similar position, but see Ivry and Spencer (2004) and Lee et al. (2007) for an alternative view of the timing functions of the cerebellum.

Attribution of specific timing functions to specific brain structures based on fMRI data, at least with respect to the most prevalent IP pacemaker–accumulator model is difficult. Although the IP model distinguishes between the three stages of pacemaker–accumulator, memory, and decision processes, we see that in terms of the theoretical interpretations of activation patterns offered by a range of authors, the boundaries are less well defined. For example, using fMRI to discriminate a working memory representation of a temporal variable from that held in a putatively distinct accumulator module and a decision module is difficult given decision or comparison processes also require access to or activation of memory representations of currently unfolding time interval (accumulated value) and a remembered representation of a target time. Consequently, it may be difficult to isolate a single brain structure as responsible for decision.

Finally, and perhaps more importantly, it is possible that interval timing is a more distributed function or capacity than has previously been suggested by proponents of IP pacemaker–accumulator models of interval timing. One such distributed timing model is the striatal beat frequency (SBF) model proposed by Matell.

8.6.2. Striatal Beat Frequency Model

Although the standard IP pacemaker–accumulator model is able to account for a large body of behavioral and physiological data, and has been used effectively to make testable predictions about the interval-timing system, there are challenges to its validity on both theoretical and empirical grounds. Theoretically, for example, it is difficult to conceptualize a single, physiologically sound, accumulator mechanism that would be capable of operating across the range of durations that have been employed in interval-timing paradigms (i.e., several orders of magnitude). More importantly, there are empirical data that challenge some of the basic assumptions of the pacemaker–accumulator model (see Buhusi & Meck, 2005 and Meck & Malapani, 2004 for discussion). For example, although the role of the pacemaker has often been attributed to substantia nigra dopaminergic function, recent studies suggest that the relationship is not straightforward. If dopaminergic connections between the substantia nigra and the striatum determine the rate of the pacemaker, then the relationship between absolute levels of dopamine in particular brain structures (e.g., substantia nigra) and behavior would be expected to have a different pattern from what is empirically observed. For example, large changes in striatal dopamine release result in rather small changes in interval-timing behavior in nonhuman animals (Matell, King, & Meck, 2004). In addition, the behavioral changes shown by humans with Parkinson's disease who are tested on and off dopamine medication do not correspond to simple changes in the speed of an internal clock. Rather, when PD patients are asked to learn two target durations, the memory of the larger and smaller durations are distorted toward each other (i.e., memory migration) when participants are off medication (Malapani et al., 1998).

The SBF model provides an alternative account of the neural basis of timing behavior (Matell & Meck, 2000). Within this framework, interval timing emerges from activity in thalamo-cortical-striatal loops. Specifically, medium spiny neurons in the basal ganglia receive input from cortical neural oscillators and are able to detect specific patterns of cortical activation that correspond to arrival of reward or feedback. The role of the substantia nigra pars compacta is to synchronize the cortical oscillations via a burst of activity at timing signal onset, maintain attentional activation of thalamo-cortical-striatal circuits via sustained activity, and finally update cortico-striatal transmission by a burst of activity at the expected target time. The cortical inputs in such thalamo-cortical-striatal loops originate from a wide area of cortex including supplementary motor area, prefrontal cortex, and the posterior parietal cortex and that activity in these circuits has been related to processes such as integration of a particular stimulus dimension over time and event counting (see Buhusi & Meck, 2005 for a review of the SBF model).

Several authors have interpreted at least part of their interval-timing neuroimaging results within the SBF framework (Coull et al., 2004; Jahanshahi et al., 2006; Stevens et al., 2007). For example, Jahanshahi et al. (2006) claimed that the substantia nigra activation in their study reflected a reinforcement signal and reset mechanism consistent with the SBF model and Coull et al. (2004) suggested that frontal structures invoke a "time scale or time line" and that the putamen then "detects the target duration within the invoked time scale." The relationship of the Stevens et al.'s (2007) study to the SBF framework is described in the following section.

8.6.3. The Way Forward

Given the possibility of a distributed timing network (e.g., SBF model) with different thalamo-cortical-striatal circuits playing different roles in various aspects of timing behavior, what research directions are most likely to improve our understanding of the neural basis of interval timing using non-invasive neuroimaging in human participants? There are several promising studies in the literature that suggest a clear way forward. In the following we describe two examples.

First, Stevens et al. (2007) used spatial independent component analysis (ICA) to examine functional connectivity within fronto-striatal circuits. This study was not reviewed above because the tasks used (e.g., synchronization and syncopation tapping) were outside the purview of the present chapter. However, the analytic approach these authors used for the fMRI data is quite promising and may be key to future efforts directed toward unlocking the functional roles of brain circuits involved in timing. Specifically, the spatial ICA allows one to determine whether spatially distinct brain activations share similar hemodynamic changes over time. Shared changes over time can be taken as evidence that those spatially distinct areas form a functional circuit. Indeed, Stevens et al. (2007) isolated one such circuit that showed activation across all of the timing tasks. The active brain areas included the right middle frontal gyrus, left cingulate, SMA (superior frontal gyrus), right MTG and right SMG, bilateral insula, bilateral caudate, bilateral putamen, bilateral globus pallidus, and bilateral thalamus. The authors noted that this functional network was engaged both when the timing task had explicit motor demands and when it did not. The authors noted this activation pattern is consistent with the SBF model described above. Of particular relevance here is that most of these areas were consistently reported as active in the nontapping interval-timing studies reviewed above.

Although performance in interval-timing tasks is associated with a range of brain structures and determining the functional role of each structure is a difficult problem, progress in addressing this problem can be made by taking advantage of the fundamental psychophysical properties of interval timing revealed in the behavioral-timing literature and using these properties to refine the analysis of neuroimaging data. For example, an important feature of interval timing is time-scale invariance (aka the scalar property). That is to say, timing variability increases in proportion to the duration being timed. As Meck and Malapani (2004) have pointed out, if specific brain structures are responsible for interval timing, then one or more structures should show evidence that the variation in brain activity is proportional to the duration being timed. Indeed, demonstrating that a particular brain structure shows a time scale invariant change in activation intensity would be strong evidence that the structure plays a specific role in interval timing rather than merely reflecting a more general memory or decision process that is present in many cognitive tasks. Meck and Malapani (2004) reanalyzed fMRI data from Hinton (2003) to determine whether the variation in right putamen activation (%hemodynamic signal change) as a function of target duration would show evidence for the scalar property. Hinton had tested participants with 11- and 17-s target intervals in an interval-timing condition and a motor-timing condition. The reanalysis by Meck and Malapani (2004) revealed that the interval-timing condition showed evidence for scalar variance in activation, i.e., normalized hemodynamic response functions superimposed in relative time, whereas in the motor-timing condition the right putamen activation did not show evidence of scalar variance. This finding is important because it further illustrates the idea that although determining the brain areas that are active in interval-timing tasks is an important first step toward establishing how the brain times, isolation of particular psychological processes to subcomponents of that network will require careful examination of brain activation patterns that correspond to the psychophysical characteristics of interval timing.

8.7. Conclusion

The preceding review of the extant interval-timing brain imaging literature suggests that although a picture of the structures apparently involved in interval timing is slowly emerging from the fMRI and PET literature, it is not yet a high-definition image. The exact nature of the duration-discrimination network, both in terms of the brain structures involved, the processes they contribute, and whether these processes are "timing unique" or more general information-processing abilities, remains to be determined (e.g., Buonomano, 2007; Eagleman, in press). The fine tuning of this image, as researchers in the field readily admit, requires advances in fMRI data analysis as well as input from studies of patient populations, nonhuman animals, and methodologies, such as event-related potentials, that provide a higher temporal resolution picture of the processes involved in interval timing.

Acknowledgments

The authors would like to express their gratitude to Warren Meck and Annett Schirmer for comments on an earlier version of this manuscript. Preparation of this manuscript was partially supported by grant R581000060112/133 from the National University of Singapore.

References

Belin, P., McAdams, S., Thivard, L., Smith, B., Savel, S., Zilbovicius, M., Samson, S., & Samson, Y. (2002). The neuroanatomical substrate of sound duration discrimination. *Neuropsychologia*, *40*, 1956–1964.

Buhusi, C. V., & Meck, W. H. (2005). What makes us tick? Functional and neural mechanisms of interval timing. *Nature Reviews Neuroscience*, *6*, 755–765.

Buonomano, D. V. (2007). The biology of time across different scales. *Nature Chemical Biology*, *3*, 594–597.

Coull, J. T., Vidal, F., Nazarian, B., & Macar, F. (2004). Functional anatomy of the attentional modulation of time estimation. *Science*, *303*, 1506–1508.

Eagleman, D. M. (in press). How does the timing of neural signals map onto the timing of perception? In: R. Nijhawan (Ed.), *Problems of space and time in perception and action.* Cambridge: Cambridge University Press.

Ferrandez, A. M., Hugueville, L., Lehericy, S., Poline, J. B., Marsault, C., & Pouthas, V. (2003). Basal ganglia and supplementary motor area subtend duration perception: An fMRI study. *NeuroImage*, *19*, 1532–1544.

Gibbon, J., Church, R. M., & Meck, W. H. (1984). Scalar timing in memory. *Annals of The New York Academy of Sciences*, *423*, 52–77.

Gibbon, J., Malapani, C., Dale, C., & Gallistel, C. R. (1997). Toward a neurobiology of temporal cognition: Advances and challenges. *Current Opinion in Neurobiology*, *7*, 170–179.

Graf, P., & Grondin, S. (2006). Time perception in time-based prospective memory. In: J. Glicksohn & M. S. Myslobodsky (Eds), *Timing the future: The case for a time-based prospective memory* (pp. 1–24). World Scientific Publishing.

Gratton, G., & Fabiani, M. (2001). Shedding light on the event-related optical signal. *Trends in Cognitive Sciences*, *5*, 357–363.

Grondin, S. (2003). Studying psychological time with Weber's law. In: R. Buccheri, M. Saniga & M. Stuckey (Eds), *The nature of time: Geometry, physics and perception* (pp. 33–41). Dordretch, The Netherlands: Kluwer.

Hall, D. A., Haggard, M. P., Akeroyd, M. A., Palmer, A. R., Summerfield, A. Q., Elliot, M. R., Gurney, E. M., & Bowtell, R. W. (1999). "Sparse" temporal sampling in auditory fMRI. *Human Brain Mapping*, *7*, 213–223.

Harrington, D. L., Boyd, L. A., Mayer, A. R., Sheltraw, D. M., Lee, R. R., Huang, M., & Rao, S. M. (2004a). Neural representation of interval encoding and decision making. *Cognitive Brain Research 21*, 193–205.

Harrington, D. L., Lee, R. R., Boyd, L. A., Rapcsak, S. Z., & Knight, R. T. (2004b). Does the representation of time depend on the cerebellum? *Brain*, *127*, 1–14.

Haxby, J. V., Gobbini, M. I., Furey, M. L., Ishai, A., Schouten, J. L., & Pietrini, P. (2001). Distributed and overlapping representations of faces and objects in ventral temporal cortex. *Science*, *293*, 2425–2430.

Hinton, S. C. (2003). Neuroimaging approaches to the study of interval timing. In: W. H. Meck (Ed.), *Functional and neural mechanisms of interval timing* (pp. 419–438). Boca Raton, FL: CRC Press.

Hinton, S. C., Harrington, D. L., Binder, J. R., Durgerian, S., & Rao, S. M. (2004). Neural systems supporting timing and chronometric counting: An fMRI study. *Cognitive Brain Research*, *21*, 183–192.

Hinton, S. C., & Meck, W. H. (2004). Frontal–striatal circuitry activated by human peak-interval timing in the supra-seconds range. *Cognitive Brain Research*, *21*, 171–182.

Ivry, R. B., & Spencer, R. M. C. (2004). The neural representation of time. *Current Opinion in Neurobiology*, *14*, 225–232.

Jahanshahi, M., Jones, C. R. G., Dirnberger, G., & Frith, C. D. (2006). The substantia nigra pars compacta and temporal processing. *Journal of Neuroscience*, *26*, 12266–12273.

James, W. (1890). *The principles of psychology*, Vol. 1. http://psychclassics.yorku.ca/James/Principles/prin15.htm

Jueptner, M., Rijntjes, M., Weiller, C., Faiss, J. H., Timmann, D., Mueller, S. P., & Diener, H. C. (1995). Localization of a cerebellar timing process using PET. *Neurology*, *45*, 1540–1545.

Kudo, K., Miyazaki, M., Kimura, T., Yamanaka, K., Kadota, H., Hirashima, M. et al. (2004). Selective activation and deactivation of the human brain structures between speeded and precisely timed tapping responses to identical visual stimulus: An fMRI study. *NeuroImage*, *22*, 1291–1301.

Lee, K-H., Egleston, P. N., Brown, W. H., Gregory, A. N., Barker, A. T., & Woodruff, P. W. R. (2007). The role of the cerebellum in subsecond time perception: Evidence from repetitive transcranial magnetic stimulation. *Journal of Cognitive Neuroscience*, *19*, 147–157.

Lejeune, H., Maquet, P., Bonnet, M., Casini, L., Ferrara, A., & Macar, F. (1997). The basic pattern of activation in motor and sensory temporal tasks: Positron emission tomography data. *Neuroscience Letters*, *235*, 21–24.

Lewis, P. A., & Miall, R. C. (2002). Brain activity during non-automatic motor production of discrete multi-second intervals. *Neuroreport*, *13*, 1731–1735.

Lewis, P. A., & Miall, R. C. (2003a). Distinct systems for automatic and cognitively controlled time measurement: Evidence from neuroimaging. *Current Opinion in Neurobiology*, *13*, 250–255.

Lewis, P. A., & Miall, R. C. (2003b). Brain activation patterns during measurement of sub- and supra-second intervals. *Neuropsychologia*, *41*, 1583–1592.

Livesey, A. C., Wall, M. B., & Smith, A. T. (2007). Time perception: Manipulation of task difficulty dissociates clock functions from other cognitive demands. *Neuropsychologia*, *45*, 321–331.

Macar, F., Lejeune, H., Bonnet, M., Ferrara, A., Pouthas, V., Vidal, F. et al. (2002). Activation of the supplementary motor area and of attentional networks during temporal processing. *Experimental Brain Research*, *142*, 475–485.

Malapani, C., Rakitin, B., Levy, R., Meck, W. H., Deweer, B., Dubois, B., & Gibbon, J. (1998). Coupled temporal memories in Parkinson's disease: A dopamine-related dysfunction. *Journal of Cognitive Neuroscience*, *10*, 316–331.

Maquet, P., Lejeune, H., Pouthas, V., Bonnet, M., Casini, L., Macar, F. et al. (1996). Brain activation induced by estimation of duration: A PET study. *NeuroImage*, *3*, 119–126.

Matell, M. S., King, G. R., & Meck, W. H. (2004). Differential modulation of clock speed by the administration of intermittent versus continuous cocaine. *Behavioral Neuroscience*, *118*, 150–156.
Matell, M. S., & Meck, W. H. (2000). Neuropsychological mechanisms of interval timing behavior. *BioEssays*, *22*, 94–103.
Meck, W. H. (1984). Attentional bias between modalities: Effect on the internal clock, memory, and decision stages used in animal time discrimination. *Annals of The New York Academy of Sciences*, *423*, 528–541.
Meck, W. H. (1996). Neuropharmacology of timing and time perception. *Cognitive Brain Research*, *3*, 227–242.
Meck, W. H. (2005). Neuropsychology of timing and time perception. *Brain and Cognition*, *58*, 1–8.
Meck, W. H. (2006). Neuroanatomical localization of an internal clock: A functional link between mesolimbic, nigrostriatal, and mesocortical dopaminergic systems. *Brain Research*, *1109*, 93–107.
Meck, W. H., & Benson, A. M. (2002). Dissecting the brain's internal clock: How frontal–striatal circuitry keeps time and shifts attention. *Brain and Cognition*, *48*, 195–211.
Meck, W. H., & Malapani, C. (2004). Neuroimaging of interval timing. *Cognitive Brain Research*, *21*, 133–137.
Nenadic, I., Gaser, C., Volz, H. P., Rammsayer, T., Hager, F., & Sauer, H. (2003). Processing of temporal information and the basal ganglia: New evidence from fMRI. *Experimental Brain Research*, *148*, 238–246.
Pastor, M. A., Artieda, J., Jahanshahi, M., & Obeso, J. A. (1992). Time estimation and reproduction is abnormal in Parkinson's disease. *Brain*, *115*, 211–225.
Penhune, V. B., Zatorre, R. J., & Evans, A. C. (1998). Cerebellar contributions to motor timing: A PET study of auditory and visual rhythm reproduction. *Journal of Cognitive Neuroscience*, *10*, 752–765.
Penney, T. B., Allan, L. G., Meck, W. H., & Gibbon, J. (1998). Memory mixing in duration bisection. In: D. A. Rosenbaum & C. E. Collyer (Eds), *Timing of behavior: Neural, psychological and computational perspectives* (pp. 165–193). Cambridge, MA: MIT Press.
Pouthas, V. (2003). Electrophysiological evidence for specific processing of temporal information in humans. In: W. H. Meck (Ed.), *Functional and neural mechanisms of interval timing* (pp. 439–456). Boca Raton, FL: CRC Press.
Pouthas, V., Garnero, L., Ferrandez, A. M., & Renault, B. (2000). ERPs and PET analysis of time perception: Spatial and temporal brain mapping during visual discrimination tasks. *Human Brain Mapping*, *10*, 49–60.
Pouthas, V., George, N., Poline, J. B., Pfeuty, M., VandeMoorteele, P. F., Hugueville, L. et al. (2005). Neural network involved in time perception: An fMRI study comparing long and short interval estimation. *Human Brain Mapping*, *25*, 433–441.
Rao, S., Harrington, D., Haaland, K., Bobholz, J., Cox, R., & Binder, J. (1997). Distributed neural systems underlying the timing of movements. *Journal of Neuroscience*, *17*, 5528–5535.
Rao, S. M., Mayer, A. R., & Harrington, D. L. (2001). The evolution of brain activation during temporal processing. *Nature Neuroscience*, *4*, 317–323.
Reiterer, S. M., Erb, M., Droll, C. D., Anders, S., Ethofer, T., Grodd, W., & Wildgruber, D. (2005). Impact of task difficulty on lateralization of pitch and duration discrimination. *Neuroreport 16*, 239–242.
Sable, J. J., Low, K. A., Whalen, C. J., Maclin, E. L., Fabiani, M., & Gratton, G. (2007). Optical imaging of temporal integration in the human auditory cortex. *European Journal of Neuroscience*, *25*, 298–306.

Schubert, T., von Cramon, D. Y., Niendorf, T., Pollman, S., & Bublak, P. (1998). Cortical areas and the control of self-determined finger movements: An fMRI study. *Neuroreport*, *9*, 3171–3176.

Smith, A., Taylor, E., Lidzba, K., & Rubia, K. (2003). A right hemispheric frontocerebellar network for time discrimination of several hundreds of milliseconds. *NeuroImage*, *20*, 344–350.

Stevens, M. C., Kiehl, K. A., Pearlson, G., & Calhoun, V. D. (2007). Functional neural circuits for mental timekeeping. *Human Brain Mapping*, *28*, 394–408.

Tracy, J. I., Faro, S. H., Mohamed, F. B., Pinsk, M., & Pinus, A. (2000). Functional localization of a "Time Keeper" function separate from attentional resources and task strategy. *NeuroImage*, *11*, 228–242.

Tregellas, J. R., Davalos, D. B., & Rojas, D. C. (2006). Effect of task difficulty on the functional anatomy of temporal processing. *NeuroImage*, *32*, 307–315.

Tse, C. Y., & Penney, T. B. (2007). Optical imaging of cortical activity elicited by unattended temporal deviants. *IEEE Engineering in Medicine and Biology Magazine*, *26*, 52–58.

Tse, C. Y., Tien, K. R., & Penney, T. B. (2006). Event-related optical imaging reveals the temporal dynamics of right temporal and frontal cortex activation in pre-attentive change detection. *NeuroImage*, *29*, 314–320.

Vierordt, K. (1868). *Der Zeitsinn nach Versuchen*. Tübingen, Germany: H. Laupp'schen Buchhandlung.

Volz, H.–P., Nenadic, I., Gaser, C., Rammsayer, T., Hager, F., & Sauer, H. (2001). Time estimation in schizophrenia: An fMRI study at adjusted levels of difficulty. *Neuroreport*, *12*, 313–316.

Zaehle, T., Schmidt, C. F., Meyer, M., Baumann, S., Baltes, C., Boesiger, P., & Jancke, L. (2007). Comparison of "silent" clustered and sparse temporal fMRI acquisitions in tonal and speech perception tasks. *NeuroImage*, *37*, 1195–1204.

Chapter 9

Neuropharmacological Approaches to Human Timing

Thomas H. Rammsayer

After presenting a brief history of neuropharmacological approaches to human timing, this chapter briefly describes the general model systems approach for studying specific brain-behavior relationships, two theoretical perspectives for studying human timing, and the major methods for assessing timing performances. These issues are followed by a detailed description of the main pharmacological sources for modulating human timing, namely the dopaminergic, glutamatergic, noradrenergic, and GABAergic ones.

9.1. A Brief History of Neuropharmacological Approaches to Human Timing

According to Fraisse (1963), the first scientific report of pharmacologically induced effects on the experience of time came from Moreau de Tours (1845). He described that, under the influence of cannabis, time seems to drag unbearably in a way that minutes become hours and hours feel like days. As early as 1892, the German psychiatrist Emil Kraepelin systematically examined drug effects on the reproduction of a 30-s time interval. While a dose of 30 g of alcohol produced considerable over-reproduction, an infusion of 5 g of "yellow tea" resulted in under-reproduction of the 30-s target interval. Subsequent studies with stimulants, such as amphetamines (Dews & Morse, 1958; Frankenhaeuser, 1959; Goldstone, Boardman, & Lhamon, 1958), caffeine (Frankenhaeuser, 1959; Joerger, 1960), marihuana (Bromberg, 1934), mescaline (Pick, 1919; Šerko, 1913), thyroxine (Sterzinger, 1935, 1938), and depressant drugs, such as alcohol (Joerger, 1960), barbiturates (Frankenhaeuser, 1959; Rutschman & Rubinstein, 1966), chloroform (Jones, 1909), nitrous oxide (Frankenhaeuser, 1959; Steinberg, 1955), and scopolamine (Heimann, 1952), led to

Psychology of Time

DOI:10.1016/B978-0-08046-977-5.00009-0

the conclusion that pharmacological agents that cause neural excitation tend to accelerate the time sense, whereas depressant drugs produce the reverse effect (Fischer, 1966; Fraisse, 1963). This oversimplifying generalization, however, was challenged by a large number of negative or inconclusive results (cf., Doob, 1971; Orme, 1969).

Nevertheless, the finding that drugs may affect human timing performance could imply the existence of a basic physiological process underlying temporal information processing — an idea already introduced by Piéron (1923). Such a conception of a biological internal clock did not become popular until 1933, when Hudson Hoagland, a professor of general physiology, put forward the notion that human time experience is governed by a biochemical clock in the brain (Hoagland, 1933); see also Hoagland, 1966). He observed in two subjects with fever caused by influenza and in one subject with experimentally induced hyperthermia, that their speed of counting at what they believed to be a rate of 1 per second was faster than with normal body temperature. Based on these results, he proposed the model of an internal clock controlled by a temperature-dependent chemical pacemaker underlying temporal information processing. According to his model, subjective time is determined by the velocity of chemical processes in the brain. Since heat speeds up chemical reactions, he concluded that the speed of counting as well as time judgments is temperature dependent. This hypothesis, claiming that an increase in body temperature is associated with an increase in internal clock speed, was in agreement with the outcome of a preceding study by François (1927). François found that his subjects, when asked to tap at a certain rate, showed consistently an increase in tapping speed when their body temperature was elevated. Although several studies were performed to further explore Hoagland's biochemical-clock hypothesis, available data appear to be highly inconsistent (cf., Rammsayer, 1997a)

9.2. The Model Systems Approach for Studying Specific Brain-Behavior Relationships

Increasing evidence for the neurochemical coding of behavior points to the significance of pharmacopsychological or neuropharmacological approaches within the field of cognitive neurosciences (Russel, 1987). From this perspective, the ultimate aim of neuropharmacological approaches is to discover neurochemical brain systems, characterized by specific neurotransmitters, that are mediating specific human behavior. This can be achieved by utilizing the specific pharmacologic actions and action mechanisms of drugs for a better understanding of the neurobiological basis of behavioral processes (Janke, 1983).

Drugs can act at several places within a neuron where they can exert the so-called agonistic or antagonistic actions. Drugs that bind to physiological receptors and mimic the effects of the endogenous regulatory compounds or neurotransmitters are termed *receptor agonists*. Drugs can also act as precursors, resulting in increased amounts of the natural neurotransmitter, while others act by releasing more of the neurotransmitter into the synaptic cleft or by blocking the reuptake of the neurotransmitter into the presynaptic neurons. These latter drugs are called *indirect agonists* since their agonistic effects are not brought about directly at the receptor site. Similarly, drugs that interfere with or prevent the action of a specific neurotransmitter at the respective receptors are termed *receptor antagonists*, whereas *indirect antagonists*, for example, inhibit the synthesis of a neurotransmitter or interfere with storage of the neurotransmitter which, in turn, results in depletion of the neuron. Thus, with regard to human timing, present neuropharmacological approaches use agonistic and antagonistic drugs as research tools for elucidation of brain mechanisms underlying temporal information processing.

When studying brain-behavior relationships, the researcher will be faced with the general problem that manipulation of a single neurotransmitter system may also cause significant changes in the levels of activity of other neurotransmitter systems. Since it does not seem possible to experimentally manipulate a single neurotransmitter system without affecting other ones, the so-called single-transmitter-multiple-behavior strategies do not appear to be appropriate for elucidation of brain-behavior relationships. Furthermore, a given neurotransmitter can produce different behavioral effects depending upon where it acts in the brain. Thus, with several neurotransmitters, each having multiple sites of action, it becomes important to avoid a "new phrenology" of sorts that assigns each possible site of action to a single category of behaviors (Solomon, 1986).

Unlike single-transmitter-multiple-behavior strategies, the model systems approach (Kandel, 1976; Thompson, 1976) represents a more suitable strategy for studying specific brain-behavior relationships. The model systems approach can be described best as a single-behavior-multiple-brain-systems strategy that originates with a well-characterized behavior. By attempting to discover how different neurotransmitter systems in the brain contribute to the specific behavior under investigation, the single-behavior-multiple-brain-systems strategy facilitates inferences from a single behavior to underlying neurobiological processes. At the same time, the potential traps of assigning a single neurotransmitter system or brain structure to a single behavior may be minimized by this approach (Solomon, 1986).

Within the framework of the models system approach, this book chapter will present findings from neuropharmacological studies on human interval timing. Since preliminary evidence suggests that temporal information processing in humans is less likely to be affected by the neurotransmitters serotonin and acetylcholine (Rammsayer, 1989, 1999), the major focus of the studies discussed in the following is on the involvement of the dopaminergic, glutamatergic, noradrenergic, and GABAergic neurotransmitter systems in human interval timing.

Based on these considerations, the model systems approach provides a promising neuropharmacological strategy to elucidate the neurobiological basis of temporal information processing in humans. Furthermore, this approach may also help to provide some converging evidence for the assumption of distinct-timing mechanisms underlying temporal information processing in the range of seconds and milliseconds. Such evidence could be obtained if it can be shown that a pharmacological agent effectively influences one range of durations whereas the other remains unaffected.

9.3. Distinct-Timing Hypothesis versus Single-Clock Model

The central nervous system processes temporal information over a wide range of durations, from microseconds to circannual rhythms (Block, 1990; Carr, 1993; Mauk & Buonomano, 2004; Rammsayer, 1992). Therefore, it is not surprising that early theoretical accounts of interval timing already put forward the idea of distinct mechanisms underlying temporal processing of durations in the subsecond and suprasecond ranges (Klien, 1919; Lehmann, 1912; Münsterberg, 1889; Wundt, 1903). More recently, in the field of human timing and temporal information processing, a distinction has been made between *perception* of time and *estimation* of time (Fraisse, 1984; Rammsayer, 1992). Estimation of time refers to processing of time intervals in the range of seconds, minutes, or more, whereas perception of time refers to temporal processing of extremely brief durations in the range of milliseconds. There may also be differences in the mechanisms underlying time estimation and time perception. Research suggests that temporal processing of brief durations below approximately 500 ms appears to be beyond cognitive control, based on processes that are automatic, and, most likely, located at a subcortical level (Lewis & Miall, 2003a; Michon, 1985; Mitrani, Shekerdjiiski, Gourevitch, & Yanev, 1977; Rammsayer & Lima, 1991). Unlike temporal processing of time intervals in the range of milliseconds, temporal processing of longer intervals is cognitively mediated (Michon, 1985; Zakay, 1990). Converging evidence for two qualitatively different timing mechanisms involved in temporal processing of extremely brief intervals shorter than approximately 300–500 ms, on the one hand, and longer intervals, on the other hand, has been provided by neurocomputational approaches to human timing (Buonomano & Merzenich, 1995; Karmarkar & Buonomano, 2007; Mauk & Buonomano, 2004). Based on these considerations, the notion of two distinct mechanisms underlying temporal processing of intervals below and above approximately 500 ms has been referred to as the *distinct-timing hypothesis*.

Eventually, there is some evidence that temporal processing of durations not exceeding the psychological present may be based on mechanisms different from those involved in the timing of longer intervals (Block, 1990; Cohen, 1966; Elbert, Ulrich, Rockstroh, & Lutzenberger, 1991; Fraisse, 1984; Michon, 1978; Pöppel, 1978, 1997). The psychological present, which is said to have an upper limit of approximately 3–5 s (Block, 1979; Fraisse, 1984; Pöppel, 1972, 1997), is defined as the period of time during which an interval can be perceived as a single unit.

Despite this functional distinction between *time perception* and *time estimation*, to date, internal clock models based on neural counting provide a useful heuristic and conceptual framework for explaining animal timing as well as human performance on temporal information processing in the subsecond and second ranges (e.g., Church, 1984; Grondin, 2001; Rammsayer & Ulrich, 2001). The central features of such an internal clock are a pacemaker and an accumulator. The pacemaker generates pulses, and the number of pulses relating to a physical time interval is recorded by the accumulator. Thus, the number of pulses counted during a given time interval is the internal representation of the interval. Hence, the higher the clock rate, the finer the temporal resolution of the internal clock will be, which is equivalent to greater timing accuracy. More or less explicitly, two additional stages of temporal information processing have been assumed to translate clock readings into behavior (e.g., Creelman, 1962; Gibbon, Church, & Meck, 1984; Treisman, 1963). A memory stage enables storage of the outcome from the accumulator. Eventually, at the decision stage, the remembered duration, previously stored in memory, is compared with the current perceived duration. This final decision process results in the identification of an appropriate behavioral response, for example, "first interval longer" when two temporal intervals have to be compared.

More recently, Zakay and Block emphasized the role of attention in temporal processing by proposing a so-called attentional-gate model (Zakay, 2000; Zakay & Block, 1996, 1997). This model integrates concepts derived from traditional internal-clock models (e.g., Allan & Kristofferson, 1974; Creelman, 1962; Rammsayer & Ulrich, 2001; Treisman, 1963; Treisman, Faulkner, Naish, & Brogan, 1990) and cognitive models of timing (e.g., Brown, 1997; Gibbon & Church, 1984). Basically, the attentional-gate model also proposes a pacemaker-counter system. On their way to the counter, however, all pulses must pass through a cognitive gate, which is controlled by the amount of attentional resources allocated to temporal information processing. The gate opens more widely or more frequently as more attention is paid to time, and, thus, more pulses are transferred to the cognitive counter. Since the number of pulses counted during a given time interval is the internal temporal representation of this interval, timing accuracy is effectively mediated by the attentional gate. Thus, simultaneous switching of attention between temporal and nontemporal information processing should result in a decreased number of pulses arriving at the accumulator and, thus, increased timing variability. As a consequence, timing performance should become poorer with decreasing attentional resources allocated to temporal information.

9.4. Assessment of Interval Timing

Many authors report that there are four major experimental tasks for assessing accuracy of temporal information processing in humans (Bindra & Waksberg, 1956; Doob, 1971; Hicks, Miller, & Kinsbourne, 1976; Wallace & Rabin, 1960; Zakay, 1990). (1) *Verbal estimation*: The duration of a presented target interval is estimated verbally in terms of conventional temporal units such as seconds or minutes. (2) *Temporal production*: An interval is produced equal to a duration that is verbally indicated by the experimenter. (3) *Temporal reproduction*: After the presentation of a target interval, the participant is required to reproduce an interval of equal duration by means of some operation. (4) *Comparison*: After the presentation of two intervals, the participant has to decide which one appeared to be longer (see Chapter 2).

For investigating temporal processing of very brief intervals in the range of milliseconds, the method of comparison proved to be much more appropriate than the former three methods. This is because verbal estimations and temporal productions use a translation of duration into socially learnt time units and, thus, depend on the relation of subjective time to clock time (Block, 1989; Clausen, 1950). No such translations, however, are learnt for durations in the range of milliseconds. Furthermore, with reproduction as well as production methods, the participant activates and stops some measurement device. While this appears to be an appropriate procedure for estimation of longer intervals, motor response latencies are much too long for reliable assessment of timing of extremely brief intervals in the range of milliseconds. Therefore, when directly contrasting timing performance in the second- and subsecond ranges, the method of comparison should be applied.

Several other timing tasks, such as temporal generalization, temporal bisection, or peak interval procedures, developed originally as methods for studying timing in animals (e.g., Church & Deluty, 1977; Church & Gibbon, 1982; Meck & Church, 1984), have also been applied to investigate interval timing in humans (e.g., McCormack, Brown, Maylor, Darby, & Green, 1999; Penney, Gibbon, & Meck, 2000; Wearden, 1991; see Chapters 2 and 8). To date, however, these procedures have almost never been employed in neuropharmacological studies with healthy human subjects.

9.5. Neuropharmacological Modulation of Human Timing

9.5.1. *Dopaminergic Modulation*

Neuropharmacological studies in animals support the notion that pacemaker speed of the hypothesized internal clock used for the timing of intervals is positively related to the effective level of brain dopamine (DA). An acceleration of pacemaker speed is suggested by numerous studies in rats using the indirect DA agonist methamphetamine (e.g., Buhusi & Meck, 2002; Çevik, 2003; Maricq & Church, 1983; Maricq, Roberts, & Church, 1981; Matell, Bateson, & Meck, 2006; Meck, 1983, 1996). On the other hand, the DA receptor antagonist haloperidol has been shown to produce a deceleration in pacemaker speed (e.g., Buhusi & Meck, 2002; MacDonald & Meck, 2005; Maricq & Church, 1983; Meck, 1983, 1996). Furthermore, observations that the effect of haloperidol on clock speed is eliminated after lesions to the prefrontal cortex (Matell & Meck, 2004; Meck, 1996) may point to the involvement of DA-related higher cortical functions in the processing of temporal information in the suprasecond range.

There are two distinct classes of DA receptors, referred to as D1 and D2 receptor families. The D1 receptor family comprises the so-called D1 and D5 receptor subtypes, whereas the D2 receptor family can be subdivided into D2, D3, and D4 receptor subtypes (Andersen et al., 1990; Civelli, Bunzow, Grandy, Zhou, & van Tol, 1991). Unlike DA receptors of the D2 receptor family, which are either negatively coupled or not coupled to adenyl cyclase at all, D1-like receptors are positively coupled to adenyl cyclase under most conditions (Seeman & Grigoriadis, 1987). As suggested by animal studies, the ability of a pharmacological agent to reduce pacemaker speed is positively correlated with the drug's D2-binding affinity (Meck,

1986). Eventually, the striatal beat-frequency model of interval timing in animals proposes that striatal neurons perform a coincidence-detection function that is modulated by dopaminergic inputs from the substantia nigra pars compacta (Buhusi & Meck, 2005; Matell & Meck, 2004; Meck, 2006). These findings from animal studies may be indicative of a crucial role of the neurotransmitter DA for human interval timing. It is important to note that all these animal studies employed timing tasks in the suprasecond range.

There is also some indirect evidence from clinical studies pointing to the detrimental effect of haloperidol on interval timing in humans. These clinical studies on haloperidol have found significant impairment in performance in tests of duration discrimination with base durations in the range of seconds both in schizophrenic patients and patients with Tourette's syndrome relative to untreated patients (Goldstone & Lhamon, 1976; Goldstone, Nurnberg, & Lhamon, 1979). These latter findings, however, are difficult to interpret since schizophrenia is known to be related to dysfunctional dopaminergic neurotransmission in the brain (cf., Davis, Kahn, Ko, & Davidson, 1991). Numerous clinical studies indicated that schizophrenic patients exhibit severe temporal distortions when judging the duration of intervals (Carlson & Feinberg, 1968; Davalos, Kisley, & Ross, 2003; Densen, 1977; Elvevåg et al., 2003; Tysk, 1983; Wahl & Sieg, 1980). These timing deficits in schizophrenic patients have been attributed to deviations from the physiological level of dopaminergic activity in the brain (Rammsayer, 1990; Yang et al., 2004). From this point of view, these clinical studies endorse the view that the neurotransmitter DA is somehow involved in the modulation of interval timing in humans. Nevertheless, in order to further elucidate the crucial role of DA for human interval timing, the effect of DA should be investigated in healthy volunteers that do not suffer from psychiatric disorders, such as schizophrenia or Tourette's syndrome, which are believed to be associated with dysfunctional dopaminergic activity in the brain. These considerations necessitate application of the neuropharmacological model systems approach in healthy human subjects.

In a first series of neuropharmacological experiments, Rammsayer (1989) studied the effects of a single dose of 3 mg of the D2 receptor antagonist haloperidol and 100 mg of the DA precursor L-dopa on temporal discrimination of brief auditory intervals ranging from 20 to 80 ms. Interval timing was reliably impaired under haloperidol, supporting the notion that the DA-antagonistic influence of haloperidol caused a decrease in pacemaker speed. No change in the performance on interval timing, however, could be revealed for L-dopa as compared with placebo. This failure to replicate the effects of the indirect DA agonist methamphetamine on pacemaker speed, as had been demonstrated in the above mentioned animal studies, may be due to different pharmacological properties of methamphetamine and L-dopa. While L-dopa is a precursor of DA, methamphetamine stimulates the release of newly synthesized DA and blocks the active reuptake process in the nerve terminals (Carboni, Imperato, Perezzani, & DiChiara, 1989; Hurd & Ungerstedt, 1989). Furthermore, in a subsequent study, Rammsayer and Vogel (1992) evaluated the effect of the indirect DA antagonist alpha-methyl-*p*-tyrosine (AMPT), an inhibitor of tyrosine hydroxylase on interval timing. Although AMPT treatment resulted in a pronounced reduction of more than 50% for DA and more than 60% for its metabolites DOPAC and HVA, performance on interval timing was affected neither in the subsecond nor in the second range as compared with a placebo group.

At first sight, these findings seem to be at variance with the general assumption that interval timing in humans is positively related to the effective level of brain DA. It should be noted, however, that, unlike the D2 receptor antagonist haloperidol, AMPT exerts its DA antagonistic effect by blocking the hydroxylation of tyrosine to L-dopa (DeQuattro & Sjoerdsma, 1968). Inhibition of this first and rate-limiting step of DA synthesis results in a significant reduction of endogenous levels of catecholamines and their metabolites (Carlsson, Roos, Wålinder, & Skott, 1973). Similarly, L-dopa and amphetamine are not directly active on DA receptors (Laverty, 1978; Moore, 1977). In this respect, the lack of effect on interval timing observed under L-dopa and AMPT may suggest the following alternative interpretation of the pharmacological properties of the internal-clock mechanism: Changes in pacemaker speed are more likely to depend on specific changes in D2 receptor activity rather than on other intraneuronal processes such as changes in the rate of synthesis or release of DA.

Proceeding from this assumption, in two double-blind studies investigating temporal processing of both extremely brief intervals below 500 ms and intervals longer than 500 ms, either 3 mg of haloperidol, 150 mg of remoxipride, or placebo was administered in a single oral dose (Rammsayer, 1993, 1997b). These two D2 receptor blockers were chosen due to their different pharmacological properties on the two major DA brain systems, the mesostriatal and the mesolimbocortical DA system. The mesostriatal DA system consists of dopaminergic neurons projecting from the substantia nigra to the striatal complex, while the neurons of the mesolimbocortical DA system originate in the ventral tegmental area and the medial substantia nigra. Unlike neurons of the mesostriatal DA system, neurons of the mesolimbocortical DA system primarily project to limbic, allocortical, and neocortical areas (Björklund & Lindvall, 1986). There are also functional differences between both these major DA systems. Mesolimbocortical DA neurons play a crucial role in working-memory processes, associative learning, locomotor activity, active avoidance, and incentive-reward motivation. The mesostriatal DA system, on the other hand, is primarily involved in motor response activation, execution of learned motor programs, and sequencing of behavior. It is important to note that remoxipride primarily blocks D2 receptors of mesolimbocortical DA neurons (Gerlach & Casey, 1990), while haloperidol blocks D2 receptors in all DA brain systems.

In both these studies (Rammsayer, 1993, 1997b), contrasting the effects of haloperidol and remoxipride on interval timing in the subsecond and second ranges, interval timing in the second range was significantly impaired by both drugs as compared with placebo. On the other hand, only haloperidol, but not remoxipride, produced a reliable decrease in the performance on interval timing in the subsecond range. The differential effects of haloperidol and remoxipride on the timing of very brief intervals in the range of milliseconds may reflect the different pattern of the pharmacological action of both drugs. Haloperidol, like most traditional neuroleptics, typically causes unwanted motor side effects, while the pharmacological profile of remoxipride is that of a so-called "atypical" antipsychotic drug with a low potential for extrapyramidal side effects. An explanation for this relatively low potential for motor side effects seen with remoxipride may be its much more pronounced action on D2 receptors located in the mesolimbocortical areas of the brain rather than on those in the striatum (Ögren et al., 1984; Seeman, 1990). While the antipsychotic effect of neuroleptics, whether typical or atypical with respect to motor side effects, appears to depend on their common ability to block D2 receptors in mesolimbocortical areas (e.g., Crow, Deakin, & Longden, 1977; Seeman, 1987), the differential effects on interval timing in the subsecond range observed with haloperidol and remoxipride suggest that the pharmacological property to effectively modulate timing performance is likely to depend on D2 receptor antagonistic effects in the basal ganglia. If mesolimbocortical DA activity were involved in temporal processing of very brief intervals, then performance should have been affected by both the typical (haloperidol) as well as the atypical (remoxipride) antipsychotic drug. As this was not found in both studies, the pronounced deteriorating effect of haloperidol on timing of intervals in the subsecond range as compared with placebo and remoxipride indicates that the timing mechanism underlying temporal processing of intervals in the range of milliseconds depends on D2 receptor activity in the basal ganglia. Taken together, the observed differential effect is consistent with the assumption of two distinct-timing mechanisms underlying temporal processing of extremely brief and longer intervals.

Numerous behavioral and pharmacopsychological studies show that working-memory processes are modulated by dopaminergic mesolimbocortical projections to the prefrontal cortex (e.g., Brozoski, Brown, Rosvold, & Goldman, 1979; Goldman-Rakic, 1996; Kimberg, D'Esposito, & Farah, 1997; Luciana, Depue, Arbisi, & Leon, 1992; Müller, von Cramon, & Pollmann, 1998; Park & Holzman, 1993; Sawaguchi, Matsumura, & Kubota, 1990). Thus, within the framework of the distinct-timing hypothesis, the deteriorating effects of haloperidol and remoxipride on the timing of intervals in the second range may have been caused by drug-induced impairment of memory processes. Such an interpretation is supported by the finding that haloperidol as well as remoxipride adversely affected memory processes in healthy volunteers. For example, 100 mg of remoxipride caused a decrease in performance in memory tasks (Mattila, Mattila, Konno, & Saarialho-Kere, 1988) and, similarly, 3 mg of haloperidol caused pronounced deficits in cognitive functioning in healthy human subjects (King, 1993; McClelland, Cooper, & Pilgrim, 1990; Squitieri, Cervone, & Agnoli, 1977). Thus, from a neuropharmacological point of view, there is converging evidence for the assumption that the impairing effect of haloperidol and remoxipride on interval timing in the second range is likely brought about by blockade of D2 receptors in the mesolimbocortical DA system. This is because both the typical neuroleptic haloperidol and the atypical neuroleptic remoxipride exert DA antagonistic effects in this region of the brain.

Taken together, although the involvement of the basal ganglia in motor activity is by far the most striking of their functions, the outcome of both studies (Rammsayer, 1993, 1997b) suggests that the basal ganglia also play an important role in human timing of intervals in the subsecond range. Furthermore, timing of intervals in the second range seems to be dependent on cognitive functioning and, therefore, pharmacological treatment with D2 receptor blockers may produce deficits in timing performance due to impairment of working-memory functions mediated by the mesolimbocortical DA system.

9.5.1.1. Evidence from studies on Parkinson's disease Additional converging evidence for the involvement of dopaminergic mechanisms within the basal ganglia in human timing is provided by clinical studies on Parkinson's disease (PD). PD is caused by selective loss of dopaminergic neurons within the substantia nigra pars compacta leading to a reduced availability of the neurotransmitter DA in the striatum. Thus, patients suffering from PD are characterized by extremely low levels of DA activity in the basal ganglia (Agid et al., 1989; Dauer & Przedborski, 2003; Hornykiewicz, 1972; Kaasinen & Rinne, 2002).

To our knowledge, no studies on temporal discrimination of extremely brief intervals in the range of milliseconds seem to exist that compared unmedicated PD patients with healthy controls. In one of the first studies comparing medicated PD patients with age-matched healthy controls, Artieda, Pastor, Lacruz, and Obeso (1992) found that temporal discrimination in the range of milliseconds was significantly impaired in the former group. Similar results for medicated PD patients were reported by subsequent studies (Harrington, Haaland, & Hermanowicz, 1998; Rammsayer & Classen, 1997; Riesen & Schnider, 2001). Furthermore, accuracy and precision of timing of self-paced movement in Parkinson patients has been shown to vary as a function of DA activity in the basal ganglia (Harrington et al., 1998; O'Boyle, Freeman, & Cody, 1996; Pastor, Jahanshahi, Artieda, & Obeso, 1992b). Thus, deficits in temporal processing of durations in the range of milliseconds may represent a function highly sensitive for degeneration of DA-containing neurons in the basal ganglia. The lack of a functional relationship between performance on temporal processing of extremely brief durations and motor symptoms (Rammsayer & Classen, 1997) suggests that these timing deficits observed in PD patients should be considered a trait marker of vulnerability to decreasing levels of dopaminergic activity rather than a state-dependent indicator of the acute clinical symptomatology. In addition, these findings support the hypothesis that the integrity of dopaminergic neurotransmission in the basal ganglia is crucial for faultless and unimpaired processing of temporal information in the range of milliseconds.

When comparing timing performance of longer intervals in the suprasecond range, several studies also reported changes in timing performance consistent with the notion of a PD-related decrease in pacemaker speed (e.g., Malapani, Deweer, & Gibbon, 2002; Malapani et al., 1998; Perbal et al., 2005; Pastor et al., 1992b), whereas others failed to detect differences in temporal accuracy between medicated PD patients and healthy controls (e.g., Lange, Tucha, Steup, Gsell, & Naumann, 1995; Riesen & Schnider, 2001). In one study, medicated PD patients' temporal productions were even significantly shorter than those of the control group. Within the framework of the general DA hypothesis of human timing, the lack of a difference in temporal accuracy between medicated PD patients and controls may be indicative of effective pharmacological treatment that compensated for the

PD-related hypodopaminergic state, whereas the latter observation suggests that (overdosed?) dopaminergic anti-Parkinsonian medication could have abnormally accelerated pacemaker speed in PD patients. Such a conclusion is consistent with the finding that withdrawal of dopaminergic medication results in shorter verbal estimations (Lange et al., 1995; Pastor, Artieda, Jahanshahi, & Obeso, 1992a) and longer time productions (Lange et al., 1995) in PD patients compared with healthy controls. It is conceivable that PD-related DA deficit in the basal ganglia could have slowed down pacemaker speed. As a consequence, PD patients' verbal estimates of a presented time interval will be reduced and the operative production of a duration given in conventional time units will be increased relative to healthy controls.

It should be noted, however, that, unlike temporal processing of intervals in the range of milliseconds (Rammsayer & Classen, 1997), performance on temporal processing of longer intervals seems to be positively related to disease severity (Pastor et al., 1992a; Perbal et al., 2005). Thus, timing performance of longer intervals seems to reflect hypodopaminergic states associated with PD. An alternative hypothesis has been put forward by Chara Malapani and colleagues (Malapani et al., 1998, 2002; Malapani & Rakitin, 2003). In their studies, PD patients on and off L-dopa medication were compared with healthy controls by applying a peak-interval procedure. With their task, duration of two standard intervals (8 and 21 s) had to be memorized during a training session. Then, during a subsequent testing session, the participant was required to reproduce the two memorized durations. In line with previous studies, reproductions of medicated PD patients did not differ from healthy controls. On the other hand, however, when PD patients off medication were asked to reproduce the two intervals in separate blocks within one testing session, they over-reproduced the short and under-reproduced the long target duration. This so-called "migration effect" was no longer observed when the patients were instructed to reproduce only one of the two target durations in a testing session. Therefore, the DA-dependent migration effect has been attributed to dysfunction in temporal memory encoding and retrieval (Malapani & Rakitin, 2003; Malapani et al., 2002).

9.5.2. Glutamatergic Modulation

Although there is converging pharmacopsychological evidence for dopaminergic modulation of human interval timing, it remains unclear whether the mechanism underlying interval timing in the subsecond range depends on the general integrity of the basal ganglia, irrespective of the neurotransmitter system involved, or whether it can be considered a highly specific function of the effective level of dopaminergic activity in this brain system. Therefore, as suggested by the model systems approach, the effect of another neurotransmitter predominant in the basal ganglia on interval-timing performance would be highly desirable to become investigated. Since glutamate receptors play a major role in neurotransmission within the basal ganglia and are present in all nuclei of the basal ganglia with the highest density being present in the striatum (Hallett & Standaert, 2004; Ravenscroft & Brotchie, 2000), the glutamatergic neurotransmitter system represents the most promising candidate for a single-behavior-multiple-brain-systems strategy. Glutamate is the primary excitatory amino neurotransmitter in the mammalian brain. In the adult human brain, glutamatergic *N*-methyl-D-aspartate (NMDA) subreceptors are most densely located in the hippocampus, cerebral cortex, and the basal ganglia. If it could be shown that timing of very brief intervals in the subsecond range is not influenced by NMDA receptor antagonistic pharmacological treatment, this would provide converging evidence for the notion that timing of such brief intervals is mediated by specific dopaminergic mechanisms.

In addition, several lines of evidence suggest that NMDA receptors play an important role in memory and cognition. For example, it has been shown that NMDA receptor antagonists induce deficits in episodic and semantic memory performance in healthy volunteers (Adler, Goldberg, Malhotra, Pickar, & Breier, 1998; Hetem, Danion, Diemunsch, & Brandt, 2000; Krystal et al., 1994; Morgan, Mofeez, Brandner, Bromley, & Curran, 2004; Rammsayer, 2001; Rockstroh, Emre, Tarral, & Pokorny, 1996). Similarly, several human studies revealed that NMDA receptor antagonists, such as ketamine, produce a reliable deteriorating effect on prefrontal executive and working-memory functions (e.g., Adler et al., 1998; Krystal et al., 1994, 1999; Morgan et al., 2004; Rockstroh et al., 1996). In the light of these results and given the notion that interval timing of longer intervals in the second- and suprasecond ranges relies mainly upon working-memory processes, NMDA receptor antagonistic pharmacological treatment could also be expected to result in impaired performance on time estimation.

In a recent study on glutamatergic modulation of interval timing in humans (Rammsayer, 2006), the NMDA receptor antagonist memantine caused a reliable performance decrement in temporal processing of intervals in the range of seconds, while timing of intervals in the subsecond range remained unaffected. Such a pattern of results is consistent with the notion of two distinct processing systems for automatic and cognitively controlled timing, respectively (Lewis & Miall, 2003b; Rammsayer, 1999). The automatic system measures time without attentional or cognitive modulation, and is primarily involved in timing of intervals in the subsecond range. Although glutamate receptors play a major role in neurotransmission within the basal ganglia, the outcome of the present experiment suggests that temporal processing of extremely brief intervals in the range of milliseconds is not affected by a pharmacologically induced decrease in NMDA receptor activity. This finding supports the notion that timing of very brief intervals is rather selectively influenced by dopaminergic activity in the basal ganglia. Cognitively controlled timing, on the other hand, has been assumed to be based on higher level cognitive mechanisms which fulfill attentional and memory requirements associated with temporal processing of longer intervals (Brown, 1985, 1997; Fortin & Breton, 1995; Fortin & Rousseau, 1987; Grondin & Macar, 1992; Rammsayer & Lima, 1991; Zakay, 1998). Thus, the deleterious effect of the NMDA receptor antagonist memantine on temporal processing of intervals in the range of seconds may have been caused by drug-induced impairment of working-memory capacity. From this perspective, the outcome of the present study provided additional converging evidence for the notion that temporal processing of longer intervals is cognitively mediated.

As already mentioned, working-memory processes seem to be effectively modulated by dopaminergic activity (e.g., Brozoski et al., 1979; Goldman-Rakic, 1996; Müller et al., 1998). More specifically, animal and human studies provided convincing evidence for the notion that substantial deviations from the physiological level of prefrontal DA activity, resulting in either hypo- or hyperdopaminergic states, produce severe cognitive impairment (Arnsten, 1998; Barch, 2004; Castner, Goldman-Rakic, & Williams, 2004; Cools, 2006; Robbins, 2000). In the light of these results, the impaired timing of intervals in the second range after treatment with the NMDA receptor antagonist memantine (Rammsayer, 2006) may also be indicative of the notion that some aspect of timing of longer intervals depends on dopaminergic neurotransmission. For example, a large number of studies showed that systemic administration of NMDA receptor antagonists increase dopaminergic activity in the prefrontal cortex of both animal (e.g., Deutsch, Tam, Freeman, Bowers, & Roth, 1987; Verma & Moghaddam, 1996) and human subjects (e.g., Breier et al., 1998; Smith et al., 1998). In Rammsayer's (2006) study, this well-established interaction between NMDA receptor activity and dopamine release in the prefrontal cortex may have induced a hyperdopaminergic state that caused deterioration of cognitive mechanisms involved in temporal processing of intervals in the second range.

All in all, the deleterious effect of the NMDA receptor antagonist memantine on interval timing in the second range may have been caused by drug-induced impairment of working-memory functions and, thus, provides converging evidence for the notion that temporal processing of longer intervals in the range of seconds is cognitively mediated. Timing of intervals in the subsecond range, on the other hand, was not found to be susceptible to a pharmacologically induced decrease in NMDA receptor activity and, thus, appeared to be selectively dependent on dopaminergic mechanisms within the basal ganglia.

9.5.3. Noradrenergic Modulation

The noradrenergic neurotransmitter system has been shown to be strongly involved in the neuronal modulation of attention (Berridge, Arnsten, & Foote, 1993; Coull, 1998; Coull, Frith, Dolan, Frackowiak, & Grasby, 1997). Therefore, studying the effects of noradrenergic activity in the brain on interval timing appears to be a worthwhile effort in order to further explore the differential significance of attentional processes for temporal processing of intervals in the subsecond and second ranges. Therefore, Rammsayer, Hennig, Haag, and Lange (2001) investigated the effects of the specific noradrenaline reuptake inhibitor reboxetine on interval timing in humans. In this study, interval timing in the second range was significantly improved by a single oral dose of 2 mg of reboxetine as compared with placebo. There was, however, no effect of enhanced noradrenergic activity on interval timing in the subsecond range.

Cognitive timing of differences between two intervals requires a subject to divide attention between temporal and nontemporal information processing (Thomas & Weaver, 1975; Zakay & Block, 1996, 1997). To be more specific, any sensory stimulus consists of nontemporal information presented for a given duration. Therefore, when performing an interval-timing task, processing of nontemporal information interferes with processing of temporal information and, thus, may decrease task accuracy (see Chapter 4). In this sense, nontemporal information represents a distracting stimulus during temporal processing. Under this condition, pharmacologically enhanced noradrenergic activity may have enabled subjects to better focus their attention on task-relevant *temporal* information attenuating the influence of distracting *nontemporal* information. Such an interpretation is supported by animal studies showing that noradrenergic activation helps to focus attention on task-relevant information by attenuating the influence of distracting stimuli (Robbins, 1984), whereas noradrenaline depletion in rodents causes increased distractibility (Carli, Robbins, Evenden, & Everitt, 1983; Roberts, Price, & Fibiger, 1976). Furthermore, in nonhuman primates, noradrenergic alpha-2-receptor agonists, such as clonidine or guanfacine, improved working-memory performance (Arnsten & Goldman-Rakic, 1985; Cai, Ma, Xu, & Hu, 1993; Schneider & Kovelowski, 1990). Similarly, in human patients suffering from dementia of the frontal type or attention-deficit hyperactivity disorders, alpha-2-receptor agonists appear to remediate specific attentional functions *via* frontal cortex (Arnsten, Steere, & Hunt, 1996; Coull, Hodges, & Sahakian, 1996). Based on these findings, the performance-enhancing effect of the noradrenaline reuptake inhibitor reboxetine on timing of intervals in the second range may be due to its beneficial effect on prefrontal cortex functions such as maintaining working-memory performance under distracting conditions.

Unlike interval timing in the range of seconds, timing of intervals in the subsecond range appears to be rather independent of attentional processes. Mattes and Ulrich (1998) showed that timing of intervals up to 300 ms was not influenced by changes in directed attention. Furthermore, their data suggested that attention does not affect the internal-clock mechanism *per se*. These findings may account for the differential effects of reboxetine on interval timing in the subsecond and second ranges: While timing of longer intervals can, at least partly, be considered a function of directed attention as, for instance, suggested by the attentional-gate model, timing of extremely brief intervals seems to be less sensitive to pharmacologically induced changes in directed attention. These findings provide additional converging evidence for the notion that temporal processing of intervals in the range of seconds is based on working-memory processes including aspects of directed attention. Processing of intervals in the range of milliseconds, on the other hand, appears to be mediated by subcortical processes beyond cognitive control and not responsive to changes in noradrenergic activity.

9.5.4. GABAergic Modulation

Gamma-aminobutyric acid (GABA) is one of the major inhibitory neurotransmitters that is present in about 40% of the synapses in the brain (Rosenzweig, Leiman, & Breedlove, 1999). The few neuropharmacological studies on GABAergic modulation of interval timing in humans used the benzodiazepine midazolam to pharmacologically influence GABAergic activity. Benzodiazepines bind strongly to specific receptors of the so-called GABA receptor complex and, thus, enhance GABAergic neurotransmission in the brain.

The original objective of neuropharmacological experiments using benzodiazepines was to provide some additional evidence for the notion of two distinct-timing mechanisms underlying the timing of intervals in the subsecond and second ranges, respectively. With this end in view, the effect of benzodiazepine-induced memory impairment on interval timing was assessed. As a research tool to investigate the effects of pharmacologically induced memory impairment on temporal information processing, the benzodiazepine midazolam was used. Midazolam is a short-acting benzodiazepine that possesses marked memory-impairing effects (File, Skelly, & Girdler, 1992; Rammsayer, Rodewald, & Groh, 2000). Based on previous findings from experimental (e.g., Brown, 1985, 1997; Fortin & Breton, 1995; Fortin & Rousseau, 1987; Rammsayer & Lima, 1991; Zakay, 1998) and neuropharmacological (e.g., Rammsayer, 1993, 1997b, 2006; Rammsayer et al., 2001) studies suggesting that timing of intervals in the second range is cognitively mediated and appears to be dependent on working-memory processes, one would predict interval timing in the second range to be also adversely affected by memory-impairing midazolam treatment. Unlike interval timing in the second range, interval timing in the subsecond range should not be expected to deteriorate because temporal processing of intervals in the range of milliseconds does not involve memory processes.

In two double-blind placebo-controlled experiments, either 15 mg (Rammsayer, 1994) or 11 mg (Rammsayer, 1999) of midazolam was administered in a single oral dose. In both studies, timing of intervals in the second range was markedly impaired under midazolam as compared with placebo, while timing of intervals in the subsecond range was affected by neither 15 nor 11 mg of midazolam. Since benzodiazepines are known to directly affect memory functions, the observed midazolam-induced decrease in performance on interval timing in the second range may be due to midazolam's impairing effect on memory processes associated with temporal information processing. In this respect, reduced timing performance can be considered a consequence of pharmacologically induced deterioration of memory functions that result in a more variable cognitive representation of the durations to be compared and, thus, considerably decreasing task accuracy. On the other hand, the lack of a midazolam-induced effect on interval timing in the subsecond range is consistent with the assumption that temporal processing of extremely brief intervals in the range of milliseconds is beyond cognitive control and independent of memory processes. The overall pattern of results on midazolam-induced changes in performance on interval timing supports the general notion of two distinct-timing mechanisms underlying temporal processing of intervals in the second and subsecond ranges, respectively.

9.6. Conclusions

The outcome of the neuropharmacological studies on interval timing in humans suggests that temporal processing of intervals in the range of seconds is based on working-memory processes including aspects of directed attention. Accordingly, any pharmacological treatment that interferes with maintaining the activation of memory units or attentional processes in working memory appears to interfere with temporal processing of longer intervals. This interpretation is corroborated by a large number of dual-task studies (see Chapter 4). All these neuropharmacological and experimental findings are consistent with the general notion that any treatment, that either directly affects or effectively interferes with active information processing in working memory, results in impaired timing of intervals in the second range. Unlike timing of longer intervals, temporal processing of extremely brief intervals in the range of milliseconds appears to be beyond cognitive control, highly sensory in nature, and primarily modulated by DA activity in the basal ganglia.

This neuropharmacological evidence for two distinct-timing mechanisms underlying temporal processing of intervals in the second and subsecond ranges is at variance with the popular notion of single internal clock based on a pacemaker-counter mechanism. Although the pacemaker-counter model has proven effective in providing a conceptual framework for much of the psychophysical data relating to temporal processing, there is increasing evidence that pacemaker-counter models cannot account for all of the available experimental data (Karmarkar & Buonomano, 2007; Mauk & Buonomano, 2004). Therefore, Karmarkar and Buonomano (2007) put forward the distinct-timing hypothesis by introducing a state-dependent network model for timing of intervals in the subsecond range. Rather than relying on a pacemaker-counter mechanism or a linear metric of time, according to their model, time is implicitly encoded in the state of a neural network. First data reported by Karmarkar and Buonomano (2007) are consistent with the notion that, for intervals in the subsecond range, there is a no-linear metric of time, whereas timing of intervals lasting a second or longer is mediated by mechanisms that generate a linear metric of time. Although the state-dependent network model seems to be limited to intervals below approximately 500 ms, the mechanisms for subsecond and second temporal processing are considered highly overlapping (Karmarkar & Buonomano, 2007), i.e., timing in intermediary ranges (e.g., intervals ranging from 400 to 800 ms) may be accurately performed by either of the two mechanisms.

Similarly, a reanalysis of some of the neuropharmacological studies on human interval timing, described in this book chapter, also suggests that the existence of two distinct-timing mechanisms underlying temporal processing of intervals in the subsecond and second ranges, respectively (Hellström & Rammsayer, 2002). These two timing mechanisms, however, are assumed not to be completely independent of each other. The subcortical, automatic or sensory, timing mechanism which is associated with the timing of very brief intervals in the subsecond range, also assists the cognitive timing mechanism for processing of longer intervals in the second or suprasecond range. Thus, Hellström and Rammsayer (2002) proposed a preliminary model of interval timing with two qualitatively different mechanisms for temporal information processing, one for brief and long intervals, and one for longer intervals only. For the longer intervals, the readings of the two timing mechanisms are weighted together in such manner as to improve interval timing by minimizing error variance. Unquestionably, additional neuropharmacological studies are needed to further elaborate this model and to assess in more detail differential effects of various pharmacological substances on human timing of intervals in the subsecond and second ranges, respectively.

References

Adler, C. M., Goldberg, T. E., Malhotra, A. K., Pickar, D., & Breier, A. (1998). Effects of ketamine on thought disorder, working memory, and semantic memory in healthy volunteers. *Biological Psychiatry*, *43*, 811–816.

Agid, Y., Cervera, P., Hirsch, E., Javoy-Agid, F., Lehericy, S., Raisman, R., & Ruberg, M. (1989). Biochemistry of Parkinson's disease: 28 years later: A critical review. *Movement Disorders*, *4*, S126–S144.

Allan, L. G., & Kristofferson, A. B. (1974). Psychophysical theories of duration discrimination. *Perception and Psychophysics*, *16*, 26–34.

Andersen, P. H., Gingrich, J. A., Bates, M. D., Dearry, A., Falardeau, P., Senogles, S. E., & Caron, M. G. (1990). Dopamine receptor subtypes: Beyond D1/D2 classification. *Trends in Psychopharmacological Sciences*, *11*, 231–236.

Arnsten, A. F. T. (1998). Catecholamine modulation of prefrontal cortical cognitive function. *Trends in Cognitive Sciences*, *2*, 436–447.

Arnsten, A. F. T., & Goldman-Rakic, P. S. (1985). Alpha-2 adrenergic mechanisms in prefrontal cortex associated with cognitive decline in aged nonhuman primates. *Science*, *230*, 1273–1276.

Arnsten, A. F. T., Steere, J. C., & Hunt, R. D. (1996). The contribution of alpha2-noradrenergic mechanisms to prefrontal cortical cognitive function. *Archives of General Psychiatry*, *53*, 448–455.

Artieda, J., Pastor, M. A., Lacruz, F., & Obeso, J. A. (1992). Temporal discrimination is abnormal in Parkinson's disease. *Brain*, *115*, 199–210.

Barch, D. M. (2004). Pharmacological manipulation of human working memory. *Psychopharmacology*, *174*, 126–135.

Berridge, C. W., Arnsten, A. F. T., & Foote, S. L. (1993). Noradrenergic modulation of cognitive function: Clinical implications of anatomical, electrophysiological and behavioural studies in animal models. *Psychological Medicine*, *23*, 557–564.

Bindra, D., & Waksberg, H. (1956). Methods and terminology in the studies of time estimation. *Psychological Bulletin*, *53*, 155–159.

Björklund, A., & Lindvall, O. (1986). Catecholaminergic brain stem regulatory systems. In: American Physiological Society (Ed.), *Handbook of physiology. Section 1. The nervous system. Vol. IV. Intrinsic regulatory systems of the brain* (pp. 155–235). Bethesda, MD: American Physiological Society.

Block, R. A. (1979). Time and consciousness. In: G. Underwood & R. Stevens (Eds), *Aspects of consciousness* (Vol. 1, pp. 179–217). London: Academic Press.

Block, R. A. (1989). Experiencing and remembering time: Affordances, context, and cognition. In: I. Levin & D. Zakay (Eds), *Time and human cognition: A life span perspective* (pp. 333–363). Amsterdam, The Netherlands: North-Holland.

Block, R. A. (1990). Models of psychological time. In: R. A. Block (Ed.), *Cognitive models of psychological time* (pp. 1–35). Hillsdale, NJ: Lawrence Erlbaum.

Breier, A., Adler, C. M., Weisenfeld, N., Su, T. P., Elman, I., Picken, I., Malhotra, A. K., & Pickar, D. (1998). Effects of NMDA antagonism on striatal dopamine release in healthy subjects: Application of a novel PET approach. *Synapse*, *29*, 142–147.

Bromberg, W. (1934). Marihuana intoxication. A clinical study of *cannabis sativa* intoxication. *American Journal of Psychiatry*, *91*, 303–330.

Brown, S. W. (1985). Time perception and attention: The effects of prospective versus retrospective paradigms and task demands on perceived duration. *Perception and Psychophysics*, *38*, 115–124.

Brown, S. W. (1997). Attentional resources in timing: Interference effects in concurrent temporal and nontemporal working memory tasks. *Perception and Psychophysics*, *59*, 1118–1140.

Brozoski, T. J., Brown, R. M., Rosvold, H. E., & Goldman, P. S. (1979). Cognitive deficit caused by regional depletion of dopamine in prefrontal cortex of rhesus monkey. *Science*, *205*, 929–932.

Buhusi, C. V., & Meck, W. H. (2002). Differential effects of methamphetamine and haloperidol on the control of an internal clock. *Behavioral Neurosciences*, *116*, 291–297.

Buhusi, C. V., & Meck, W. H. (2005). What makes us tick? Functional and neural mechanisms of interval timing. *Nature Reviews Neuroscience*, *6*, 755–765.

Buonomano, D. V., & Merzenich, M. M. (1995). Temporal information transformed into a spatial code by a neural network with realistic properties. *Science*, *267*, 1028–1030.

Cai, J. X., Ma, Y., Xu, L., & Hu, X. (1993). Reserpine impairs spatial working memory performance in monkeys: Reversal by the alpha2-adrenergic agonist clonidine. *Brain Research*, *614*, 191–196.

Carboni, E., Imperato, A., Perezzani, L., & DiChiara, G. (1989). Amphetamine, cocaine, phencyclidine and nomifensine increase extracellular dopamine concentrations preferentially in the nucleus accumbens of freely moving rats. *Neuroscience*, *28*, 653–661.

Carli, M., Robbins, T. W., Evenden, J. L., & Everitt, B. J. (1983). Effect of lesions to ascending noradrenergic neurons on performance of a 5-choice serial reaction task in rats: Implications for theories of dorsal noradrenergic bundle function based on selective attention and arousal. *Behaviour and Brain Research*, *9*, 361–380.

Carlson, V., & Feinberg, I. (1968). Individual variations in time judgment and the concept of an internal clock. *Journal of Experimental Psychology*, *77*, 631–640.

Carlsson, A., Roos, B. E., Wålinder, J., & Skott, A. (1973). Further studies on the mechanism on antipsychotic action: Potentiation by α-methyltyrosine of thioridazine effects in chronic schizophrenics. *Journal of Neural Transmission*, *34*, 125–132.

Carr, C. E. (1993). Processing of temporal information in the brain. *Annual Review of Neuroscience*, *16*, 223–243.

Castner, S. A., Goldman-Rakic, P. S., & Williams, G. V. (2004). Animal models of working memory: Insights for targeting cognitive dysfunction in schizophrenia. *Psychopharmacology*, *174*, 111–125.

Çevik, M.Ö. (2003). Effects of methamphetamine on duration discrimination. *Behavioral Neurosciences*, *117*, 774–784.

Church, R. M. (1984). Properties of the internal clock. In: J. Gibbon & L. G. Allan (Eds), *Timing and Time Perception* (pp. 566–582). New York: New York Academy of Sciences.

Church, R. M., & Deluty, M. Z. (1977). Bisection of temporal intervals. *Journal of Experimental Psychology: Animal Behavior Processes*, *3*, 216–228.

Church, R. M., & Gibbon, J. (1982). Temporal generalization. *Journal of Experimental Psychology: Animal Behavior Processes*, *8*, 165–186.

Civelli, O., Bunzow, J. R., Grandy, D. K., Zhou, Q. Y., & van Tol, H. H. (1991). Molecular biology of the dopamine receptors. *European Journal of Pharmacology, 207*, 277–286.

Clausen, J. (1950). An evaluation of experimental methods of time judgment. *Journal of Experimental Psychology, 40*, 756–761.

Cohen, J. (1966). Subjective time. In: J. T. Fraser (Ed.), *The voices of time* (pp. 257–275). New York: George Braziller.

Cools, R. (2006). Dopaminergic modulation of cognitive function-implications for L-DOPA treatment in Parkinson's disease. *Neuroscience and Biobehavioral Reviews, 30*, 1–23.

Coull, J. T. (1998). Neural correlates of attention and arousal: insights from electrophysiology, functional neuroimaging and psychopharmacology. *Progress in Neurobiology, 55*, 343–361.

Coull, J. T., Frith, C. D., Dolan, R. J., Frackowiak, R. S. J., & Grasby, P. M. (1997). The neural correlates of the noradrenergic modulation of human attention, arousal and learning. *European Journal of Neuroscience, 9*, 589–598.

Coull, J. T., Hodges, J. R., & Sahakian, B. J. (1996). The alpha2 antagonist idazoxan remediates certain attentional and executive dysfunction in patients with dementia of frontal type. *Psychopharmacology, 123*, 239–249.

Creelman, C. D. (1962). Human discrimination of auditory duration. *Journal of the Acoustical Society of America, 34*, 582–593.

Crow, T. J., Deakin, J. F. W., & Longden, A. (1977). The nucleus accumbens — Possible site of antipsychotic action of neuroleptic drugs? *Psychological Medicine, 7*, 213–221.

Dauer, W., & Przedborski, S. (2003). Parkinson's disease: Mechanisms and models. *Neuron, 39*, 89–909.

Davalos, D. B., Kisley, M. A., & Ross, R. G. (2003). Effects of interval duration on temporal processing in schizophrenia. *Brain and Cognition, 52*, 295–301.

Davis, K. L., Kahn, R. S., Ko, G., & Davidson, M. (1991). Dopamine in schizophrenia: A review and reconceptualization. *American Journal of Psychiatry, 148*, 1474–1486.

Densen, M. E. (1977). Time perception and schizophrenia. *Perceptual and Motor Skills, 44*, 436–438.

DeQuattro, V., & Sjoerdsma, A. (1968). Catecholamine turnover in normotensive and hypertensive man: Effects of antiadrenergic drugs. *Journal of Clinical Investigation, 47*, 2359–2373.

Deutsch, A. Y., Tam, S.-Y., Freeman, A. S., Bowers, M. B. J., & Roth, R. H. (1987). Mesolimbic and mesocortical dopamine activation induced by phencyclidine: Contrasting patterns to striatal response. *European Journal of Pharmacology, 134*, 257–264.

Dews, P. B., & Morse, W. H. (1958). Some observations on an operant in human subjects and its modification by dextro amphetamine. *Journal of the Experimental Analysis of Behavior, 1*, 359–364.

Doob, L. W. (1971). *Patterning of time*. New Haven, CT: Yale University Press.

Elbert, T., Ulrich, R., Rockstroh, B., & Lutzenberger, W. (1991). The processing of temporal intervals reflected by CNV-like brain potentials. *Psychophysiology, 28*, 648–655.

Elvevåg, B., McCormack, T., Gilbert, A., Brown, G. D., Weinberger, D. R., & Goldberg, T. E. (2003). Duration judgements in patients with schizophrenia. *Psychological Medicine, 33*, 1249–1261.

File, S. E., Skelly, A. M., & Girdler, N. M. (1992). Midazolam-induced retrieval impairments revealed by the use of flumenazil: A study in surgical dental patients. *Journal of Psychopharmacology, 6*, 81–87.

Fischer, R. (1966). Biological time. In: J. T. Fraser (Ed.), *The voices of time* (pp. 357–382). New York: George Braziller.

Fortin, C., & Breton, R. (1995). Temporal interval production and processing in working memory. *Perception and Psychophysics*, *57*, 203–215.
Fortin, C., & Rousseau, R. (1987). Time estimation as an index of processing demand in memory search. *Perception and Psychophysics*, *42*, 377–382.
Fraisse, P. (1963). *The psychology of time*. London: Harper and Row.
Fraisse, P. (1984). Perception and estimation of time. *Annual Review of Psychology*, *35*, 1–36.
François, M. (1927). Contribution a l'étude du sens du temps. La temperature interne, comme facteur de variation de l'appréciation subjective des durées. *Année Psychologique*, *28*, 186–204.
Frankenhaeuser, M. (1959). *Estimation of time*. Uppsala: Almqvist and Wiksells.
Gerlach, J., & Casey, D. E. (1990). Remoxipride, a new selective D2 antagonist, and haloperidol in cebus monkeys. *Progress in Neuropsychopharmacology and Biological Psychiatry*, *14*, 103–112.
Gibbon, J., & Church, R. M. (1984). Sources of variance in an information processing theory of timing. In: H. L. Roitblat, T. G. Bever & H. S. Terrace (Eds), *Animal cognition* (pp. 465–488). Hillsdale, NJ: Lawrence Erlbaum Associates.
Gibbon, J., Church, R. M., & Meck, W. H. (1984). Scalar timing in memory. In: J. Gibbon & L. G. Allan (Eds), *Timing and time perception* (pp. 52–77). New York: New York Academy of Sciences.
Goldman-Rakic, P. S. (1996). Regional and cellular fractionation of working memory. *Proceedings of the National Academy of Sciences of the United States of America*, *93*, 13473–13480.
Goldstone, S., Boardman, W. K., & Lhamon, W. T. (1958). Effect of quinal barbitone, dextro-amphetamine, and placebo on apparent time. *British Journal of Psychology*, *49*, 324–328.
Goldstone, S., & Lhamon, W. T. (1976). The effects of haloperidol upon temporal information processing by patients with Tourette's syndrome. *Psychopharmacology*, *50*, 7–10.
Goldstone, S., Nurnberg, H. G., & Lhamon, W. T. (1979). Effects of trifluoperazine, chlorpromazine and haloperidol upon temporal information processing by schizophrenic patients. *Psychopharmacology*, *65*, 119–124.
Grondin, S. (2001). From physical time to the first and second moments of psychological time. *Psychological Bulletin*, *127*, 22–44.
Grondin, S., & Macar, F. (1992). Dividing attention between temporal and nontemporal tasks: A performance operating characteristic-POC-analysis. In: F. Macar, V. Pouthas & W. Friedman (Eds), *Time, action, cognition: Towards bridging the gap* (pp. 119–128). Dordrecht, The Netherlands: Kluwer.
Hallett, P. J., & Standaert, D. G. (2004). Rationale for and use of NMDA receptor antagonists in Parkinson's disease. *Pharmacology and Therapeutics*, *102*, 155–174.
Harrington, D. L., Haaland, K. Y., & Hermanowicz, N. (1998). Temporal processing in the baal ganglia. *Neuropsychology*, *12*, 3–12.
Heimann, H. (1952). *Die Scopolaminwirkung*. Basel: Karger.
Hellström, Å., & Rammsayer, T. (2002). Mechanisms behind discrimination of short and long auditory durations. In: J. A. da Silva, E. H. Matsushima & N. P. Ribeiro-Filho (Eds), *Annual meeting of the international society for psychophysics* (pp. 110–115). Rio de Janeiro, Brazil: The International Society for Psychophysics.
Hetem, L. A. B., Danion, J. M., Diemunsch, P., & Brandt, C. (2000). Effect of a subanesthetic dose of ketamine on memory and conscious awareness in healthy volunteers. *Psychopharmacology*, *152*, 283–288.

Hicks, R. E., Miller, G. W., & Kinsbourne, M. (1976). Prospective and retrospective judgements of time as a function of the amount of information processed. *American Journal of Psychology*, *89*, 719–730.

Hoagland, H. (1933). The physiological control of judgments of duration: Evidence for a chemical clock. *Journal of General Psychology*, *9*, 267–287.

Hoagland, H. (1966). Some biochemical considerations of time. In: J. T. Fraser (Ed.), *The voices of time* (pp. 312–329). New York: George Braziller.

Hornykiewicz, O. (1972). Neurochemistry of parkinsonism. In: A. Lajtha (Ed.), *Handbook of neurochemistry* (Vol. 7, pp. 465–501). New York: Plenum.

Hurd, Y. L., & Ungerstedt, U. (1989). Ca^{2+} dependence of the amphetamine, nomifensine, and Lu 19-005 effect on in vivo dopamine transmission. *European Journal of Pharmacology*, *166*, 261–269.

Janke, W. (1983). *Response variability to psychotropic drugs*. Oxford: Pergamon Press.

Joerger, K. (1960). Das Erleben der Zeit und seine Veränderung durch Alkoholeinfluss. *Zeitschrift für Experimentelle und Angewandte Psychologie*, *7*, 126–161.

Jones, E. E. (1909). The waning of consciousness under chloroform. *Psychological Review*, *16*, 48–54.

Kaasinen, V., & Rinne, J. O. (2002). Functional imaging studies of dopamine system and cognition in normal aging and Parkinson's disease. *Neuroscience and Biobehavioral Reviews*, *26*, 785–793.

Kandel, E. R. (1976). *The cellular basis of behavior*. New York: Freeman.

Karmarkar, U. R., & Buonomano, D. V. (2007). Timing in the absence of clocks: Encoding time in neural network states. *Neuron*, *53*, 1–12.

Kimberg, D. Y., D'Esposito, M., & Farah, M. J. (1997). Effects of bromocriptine on human subjects depend on working memory capacity. *Neuroreport*, *8*, 3581–3585.

King, D. J. (1993). Measures of neuroleptic effects on cognition and psychomotor performance in healthy volunteers. In: I. Hindmarch & P. D. Stonier (Eds), *Human psychopharmacology* (Vol. 4, pp. 195–209). Chichester: John Wiley.

Klien, H. (1919). Beitrag zur Psychopathologie und Psychologie des Zeitsinns. *Zeitschrift für Pathopsychologie*, *3*, 307–362.

Krystal, J. H., D'Souza, D. C., Karper, L. P., Bennett, A., Abi-Dargham, A., Abi-Saab, D., Cassello, K., Bowers, M. B., Vegso, S., Heninger, G. R., & Charney, D. S. (1999). Interactive effects of subanesthetic ketamine and haloperidol in healthy humans. *Psychopharmacology*, *145*, 193–204.

Krystal, J. H., Karper, L. P., Seibyl, J. P., Freeman, G. K., Delaney, R., Bremner, J. D., Heninger, G. R., Bowers, M. B., & Charney, D. S. (1994). Subanesthetic effects of the noncompetitive NMDA antagonist, ketamine, in humans. *Archives of General Psychiatry*, *51*, 199–214.

Lange, K. W., Tucha, O., Steup, A., Gsell, W., & Naumann, M. (1995). Subjective time estimation in Parkinson's disease. *Journal of Neural Transmission*, *46*(Suppl.), 433–438.

Laverty, R. (1978). Catecholamines: Roles in health and disease. *Drugs*, *16*, 418–440.

Lehmann, A. (1912). *Grundzüge der Psychophysiologie*. Leipzig, Germany: Reisland.

Lewis, P. A., & Miall, R. C. (2003a). Distinct systems for automatic and cognitively controlled time measurement: Evidence from neuroimaging. *Current Opinion in Neurobiology*, *13*, 1–6.

Lewis, P. A., & Miall, R. C. (2003b). Brain activation patterns during measurement of sub- and supra-second intervals. *Neuropsychologia*, *41*, 1583–1592.

Luciana, M., Depue, R. A., Arbisi, P., & Leon, A. (1992). Facilitation of working memory in humans by a D2 dopamine receptor agonist. *Journal of Cognitive Neuroscience*, *4*, 58–68.

MacDonald, C. J., & Meck, W. H. (2005). Differential effects of clozapine and haloperidol on interval timing in the supraseconds range. *Psychopharmacology*, *182*, 232–244.

Malapani, C., Deweer, B., & Gibbon, J. (2002). Separating storage from retrieval dysfunction of temporal memory in Parkinson's disease. *Journal of Cognitive Neuroscience*, *14*, 311–322.

Malapani, C., & Rakitin, B. C. (2003). Interval timing in the dopamine-depleted basal ganglia: From empirical data to timing theory. In: W. H. Meck (Ed.), *Functional and neural mechanisms of interval timing* (pp. 485–514). Boca Raton, FL: CRC Press.

Malapani, C., Rakitin, B. C., Levy, R., Meck, W. H., Deweer, B., Dubois, B., & Gibbon, J. (1998). Coupled temporal memories in Parkinson's disease: A dopamine-related dysfunction. *Journal of Cognitive Neuroscience*, *10*, 316–331.

Maricq, A. V., & Church, R. M. (1983). The differential effects of haloperidol and methamphetamine on time estimation in the rat. *Psychopharmacology*, *79*, 10–15.

Maricq, A. V., Roberts, S., & Church, R. M. (1981). Methamphetamine and time estimation. *Journal of Experimental Psychology: Animal Behavior Processes*, *7*, 18–30.

Matell, M. S., Bateson, M., & Meck, W. H. (2006). Single-trials analyses demonstrate that increases in clock speed contribute to the methamphetamine-induced horizontal shifts in peak-interval timing functions. *Psychopharmacology*, *188*, 201–212.

Matell, M. S., & Meck, W. H. (2004). Cortico-striatal circuits and interval timing: Coincidence detection of oscillatory processes. *Cognitive Brain Research*, *21*, 139–170.

Mattes, S., & Ulrich, R. (1998). Directed attention prolongs the perceived duration of a brief stimulus. *Perception and Psychophysics*, *60*, 1305–1317.

Mattila, M. J., Mattila, M. E., Konno, K., & Saarialho-Kere, U. (1988). Objective and subjective effects of remoxipride, alone and in combination with ethanol or diazepam, on performance in healthy subjects. *Journal of Psychopharmacology*, *2*, 138–149.

Mauk, M. D., & Buonomano, D. V. (2004). The neural basis of temporal processing. *Annual Review of Neuroscience*, *27*, 304–340.

McClelland, G. R., Cooper, S. M., & Pilgrim, A. J. (1990). A comparison of the central nervous system effects of haloperidol, chlorpromazine and sulpiride in normal volunteers. *British Journal of Clinical Pharmacology*, *30*, 795–803.

McCormack, T., Brown, G. D. A., Maylor, E. A., Darby, R. J., & Green, D. (1999). Developmental changes in time estimation: Comparing childhood and old age. *Developmental Psychology*, *35*, 1143–1155.

Meck, W. H. (1983). Selective adjustment of the speed of internal clock and memory processes. *Journal of Experimental Psychology: Animal Behavior Processes*, *9*, 171–201.

Meck, W. H. (1986). Affinity for the dopamine D2 receptor predicts neuroleptic potency in decreasing the speed of an internal clock. *Pharmacology, Biochemistry and Behavior*, *25*, 1185–1189.

Meck, W. H. (1996). Neuropharmacology of timing and time perception. *Cognitive Brain Research*, *3*, 227–242.

Meck, W. H. (2006). Neuroanatomical localization of an internal clock: A functional link between mesolimbic, nigrostriatal, and mesocortical dopaminergic systems. *Brain Research*, *1109*, 93–107.

Meck, W. H., & Church, R. M. (1984). Simultaneous temporal processing. *Journal of Experimental Psychology: Animal Behavior Processes*, *10*, 1–29.

Michon, J. A. (1978). The making of the present: A tutorial review. In: J. Requin (Ed.), *Attention and performance VII* (pp. 89–111). Hillsdale, NJ: Lawrence Erlbaum Associates.

Michon, J. A. (1985). The compleat time experiencer. In: J. A. Michon & J. L. Jackson (Eds), *Time, mind, and behaviour* (pp. 21–52). Berlin, Germany: Springer.

Mitrani, L., Shekerdjiiski, S., Gourevitch, A., & Yanev, S. (1977). Identification of short time intervals under LSD_{25} and mescaline. *Activas Nervosa Superior*, *19*, 103–104.

Moore, K. E. (1977). The actions of amphetamine on neurotransmitters: A brief review. *Biological Psychiatry*, *12*, 451–462.

Moreau de Tours, J. (1845). *Du haschisch et de l'aliénation mentale*. Paris: Fortin, Masson.

Morgan, C. J. A., Mofeez, A., Brandner, B., Bromley, L., & Curran, H. V. (2004). Acute effects of ketamine on memory systems and psychotic symptoms in healthy volunteers. *Neuropsychopharmacology*, *29*, 208–218.

Müller, U., von Cramon, D. Y., & Pollmann, S. (1998). D1- versus D2-receptor modulation of visuospatial working memory in humans. *Journal of Neuroscience*, *18*, 2720–2728.

Münsterberg, H. (1889). *Beiträge zur experimentellen Psychologie*, Heft 2. Freiburg, Germany: Akademische Verlagsbuchhandlung von J. C. B. Mohr.

O'Boyle, D. J., Freeman, J. S., & Cody, F. W. (1996). The accuracy and precision of self-paced, repetitive movements in subjects with Parkinson's disease. *Brain*, *119*, 51–70.

Ögren, S.-O., Hall, H., Köhler, C., Magnusson, O., Lindbom, L. O., Ängeby, K., & Florvall, L. (1984). Remoxipride, a new potential antipsychotic compound with selective antidopaminergic actions in the brain. *European Journal of Pharmacology*, *102*, 459–474.

Orme, J. E. (1969). *Time, experience, and behaviour*. New York: American Elsevier Publishing Company.

Park, S., & Holzman, P. S. (1993). Association of working memory deficit and eye tracking dysfunction in schizophrenia. *Schizophrenia Research*, *11*, 55–61.

Pastor, M. A., Artieda, J., Jahanshahi, M., & Obeso, J. A. (1992a). Time estimation and reproduction is abnormal in Parkinson's disease. *Brain*, *115*, 211–225.

Pastor, M. A., Jahanshahi, M., Artieda, J., & Obeso, J. A. (1992b). Performance of repetitive wrist movements in Parkinson's disease. *Brain*, *115*, 875–891.

Penney, T. B., Gibbon, J., & Meck, W. H. (2000). Differential effects of auditory and visual signals on clock speed and temporal memory. *Journal of Experimental Psychology: Human Perception and Performance*, *26*, 1770–1787.

Perbal, S., Deweer, B., Pillon, B., Vidailhet, M., Dubois, B., & Pouthas, V. (2005). Effects of internal clock and memory disorders on duration reproductions and duration productions in patients with Parkinson's disease. *Brain and Cognition*, *58*, 35–48.

Pick, A. (1919). Zur Psychopathologie des Zeitsinns. *Zeitschrift für Pathopsychologie*, *3*, 430–441.

Piéron, H. (1923). Les problèmes psychophysiologiques de la perception du temps. *Année Psychologique*, *24*, 1–25.

Pöppel, E. (1972). Oscillations as possible basis for time perception. In: J. T. Fraser, F. C. Haber & G. H. Müller (Eds), *The study of time* (pp. 219–241). Berlin, Germany: Springer.

Pöppel, E. (1978). Time perception. In: R. Held, H. W. Leibowitz & H.-L. Teuber (Eds), *Handbook of sensory physiology* (Vol. 8, pp. 713–729). Berlin, Germany: Springer.

Pöppel, E. (1997). A hierarchical model of temporal perception. In: A. Preis & T. Hornowski (Eds), *Fechner Day '97: Proceedings of the 13th annual meeting of the international society for psychophysics* (pp. 15–20). Poznan, Poland: Wydawnictwo Poznanske.

Rammsayer, T., & Classen, W. (1997). Impaired temporal discrimination in Parkinson's disease: temporal processing of brief durations as an indicator of degeneration of dopaminergic neurons in the basal ganglia. *International Journal of Neuroscience*, *91*, 45–55.

Rammsayer, T., & Ulrich, R. (2001). Counting models of temporal discrimination. *Psychonomic Bulletin and Review*, *8*, 270–277.

Rammsayer, T. H. (1989). Dopaminergic and serotoninergic influence on duration discrimination and vigilance. *Pharmacopsychiatry*, *22*(Suppl.), 39–43.

Rammsayer, T. H. (1990). Temporal discrimination in schizophrenic and affective disorders: Evidence for a dopamine-dependent internal clock. *International Journal of Neuroscience*, *53*, 111–120.

Rammsayer, T. H. (1992). *Die Wahrnehmung kurzer Zeitdauern*. Münster, Germany: Waxmann.

Rammsayer, T. H. (1993). On dopaminergic modulation of temporal information processing. *Biological Psychology*, *36*, 209–222.

Rammsayer, T. H. (1994). Temporal information processing and memory. In: L. M. Ward (Ed.), *Fechner day '94. Proceedings of the tenth annual meeting of the international society for psychophysics* (pp. 48–53). Vancouver, Canada: The International Society for Psychophysics.

Rammsayer, T. H. (1997a). Effects of body core temperature and brain dopamine activity on timing processes in humans. *Biological Psychology*, *46*, 169–192.

Rammsayer, T. H. (1997b). Are there dissociable roles of the mesostriatal and mesolimbocortical dopamine systems on temporal information processing in humans? *Neuropsychobiology*, *35*, 36–45.

Rammsayer, T. H. (1999). Neuropharmacological evidence for different timing mechanisms in humans. *Quarterly Journal of Experimental Psychology, Section B: Comparative and Physiological Psychology*, *52*, 273–286.

Rammsayer, T. H. (2001). Effects of pharmacologically induced changes in NMDA-receptor activity on long-term memory in humans. *Learning and Memory*, *8*, 20–25.

Rammsayer, T. H. (2006). Effects of pharmacologically induced changes in NMDA receptor activity on human timing and sensorimotor performance. *Brain Research*, *1073–1074*, 407–416.

Rammsayer, T. H., Hennig, J., Haag, A., & Lange, N. (2001). Effects of noradrenergic activity on temporal information processing in humans. *Quarterly Journal of Experimental Psychology, Section B: Comparative and Physiological Psychology*, *54B*, 247–258.

Rammsayer, T. H., & Lima, S. D. (1991). Duration discrimination of filled and empty auditory intervals: Cognitive and perceptual factors. *Perception and Psychophysics*, *50*, 565–574.

Rammsayer, T. H., Rodewald, S., & Groh, D. (2000). Dopamine-antagonistic, anticholinergic, and GABAergic effects on declarative and procedural memory functions. *Cognitive Brain Research*, *9*, 61–71.

Rammsayer, T. H., & Vogel, W. H. (1992). Pharmacologic properties of the internal clock underlying time perception in humans. *Neuropsychobiology*, *26*, 71–80.

Ravenscroft, P., & Brotchie, J. (2000). NMDA receptors in the basal ganglia. *Journal of Anatomy*, *196*, 577–585.

Riesen, J. M., & Schnider, A. (2001). Time estimation in Parkinson's disease: Normal long duration estimation despite impaired short duration discrimination. *Journal of Neurology*, *248*, 27–35.

Robbins, T. W. (1984). Cortical noradrenaline, attention and arousal. *Psychological Medicine*, *14*, 13–21.

Robbins, T. W. (2000). Chemical neuromodulation of frontal-executive functions in humans and other animals. *Experimental Brain Research*, *133*, 130–138.

Roberts, D. C. S., Price, M. T. C., & Fibiger, H. C. (1976). The dorsal tegmental noradrenergic projection: An analysis of its role in maze learning. *Journal of Comparative Physiology and Psychology*, *90*, 363–372.

Rockstroh, S., Emre, M., Tarral, A., & Pokorny, R. (1996). Effects of the novel NMDA-receptor antagonist SDZ EAA 494 on memory and attention in humans. *Psychopharmacology*, *124*, 261–266.

Rosenzweig, M. R., Leiman, A. L., & Breedlove, S. M. (1999). *Biological psychology*. Sunderland, MA: Sinauer Associates.

Russel, R. W. (1987). Drugs as tools for research in neuropsychobiology: A historical perspective. *Neuropsychobiology*, *18*, 134–143.

Rutschman, J., & Rubinstein, L. (1966). Time estimation, knowledge of results, and drug effects. *Journal of Psychiatric Research*, *4*, 107–114.

Sawaguchi, T., Matsumura, M., & Kubota, K. (1990). Effects of dopamine antagonists on neuronal activity related to a delayed response task in monkey prefrontal cortex. *Journal of Neurophysiology*, *63*, 1401–1412.

Schneider, J. S., & Kovelowski, C. J. (1990). Chronic exposure to low doses of MPTP. I. Cognitive deficits in motor asymptomatic monkeys. *Brain Research*, *519*, 122–128.

Seeman, P. (1987). Dopamine receptors and the dopamine hypothesis of schizophrenia. *Synapse*, *1*, 133–152.

Seeman, P. (1990). Atypical neuroleptics: Role of multiple receptors, endogenous dopamine, and receptor linkage. *Acta Psychiatrica Scandinavica*, *82*(Suppl.), 14–20.

Seeman, P., & Grigoriadis, D. (1987). Dopamine receptors in brain and periphery. *Neurochemistry International*, *10*, 1–25.

Šerko, A. (1913). Im Mescalinrausch. *Jahrbücher für Psychiatrie und Neurologie*, *34*, 355–366.

Smith, G. S., Schloesser, R., Brodie, J. D., Dewey, S. L., Logan, L., Vitkun, S. A., Simkowitz, P., Hurley, A., Cooper, T., Volkow, N. D., & Cancro, R. (1998). Glutamate modulation of dopamine measured in vivo with positron emission tomography (PET) and ^{11}C-raclopride in normal human subjects. *Neuropsychopharmacology*, *18*, 18–25.

Solomon, P. R. (1986). Strategies for studying brain-behavior relationships. *Behavioral and Brain Sciences*, *9*, 344–345.

Squitieri, G., Cervone, A., & Agnoli, A. (1977). A study on short-term memory in man. Interactions with nooanaleptic and nootropic drugs. In: F. Antonelli (Ed.), *Proceedings of the 3rd congress of the international college of psychosomatic medicine* (pp. 742–751). Rome: Pozzi.

Steinberg, H. (1955). Changes in time perception induced by an anaesthetic drug. *British Journal of Psychology*, *46*, 273–279.

Sterzinger, O. (1935). Chemopsychologische Untersuchungen über den Zeitsinn. *Zeitschrift für Psychologie*, *134*, 100–131.

Sterzinger, O. (1938). Neue chemopsychologische Untersuchungen über den menschlichen Zeitsinn. *Zeitschrift für Psychologie*, *143*, 391–406.

Thomas, E. A. C., & Weaver, W. B. (1975). Cognitive processing and time perception. *Perception and Psychophysics*, *17*, 363–367.

Thompson, R. F. (1976). The search for the engram. *American Psychologist*, *31*, 209–227.

Treisman, M. (1963). Temporal discrimination and the indifference interval: implications for a model of the "internal clock". *Psychological Monographs*, *77*, 1–31.

Treisman, M., Faulkner, A., Naish, P. L. N., & Brogan, D. (1990). The internal clock: Evidence for a temporal oscillator underlying time perception with some estimates of its characteristic frequency. *Perception*, *19*, 705–743.

Tysk, L. (1983). Estimation of time and the subclassification of schizophrenic disorders. *Perceptual and Motor Skills*, *57*, 911–918.

Verma, A., & Moghaddam, B. (1996). NMDA receptor antagonists impair prefrontal cortex function as assessed via spatial delayed alternation performance in rats: Modulation by dopamine. *Journal of Neuroscience*, *16*, 373–379.
Wahl, O. F., & Sieg, D. (1980). Time estimation among schizophrenics. *Perceptual and Motor Skills*, *50*, 535–541.
Wallace, M., & Rabin, A. (1960). Temporal experience. *Psychological Bulletin*, *57*, 213–235.
Wearden, J. H. (1991). Do humans possess an internal clock with scalar timing properties? *Learning and Motivation*, *22*, 59–83.
Wundt, W. (1903). *Grundzüge der physiologischen Psychologie*. Leipzig, Germany: Engelmann.
Yang, Y. K., Yeh, T. L., Chiu, N. T., Lee, I. H., Chen, P. S., Lee, L. C., & Jeffries, K. J. (2004). Association between cognitive performance and striatal dopamine binding is higher in timing and motor tasks in patients with schizophrenia. *Psychiatry Research*, *131*, 209–216.
Zakay, D. (1990). The evasive art of subjective time measurement: Some methodological dilemmas. In: R. A. Block (Ed.), *Cognitive models of psychological time* (pp. 59–84). Hillsdale, NJ: Lawrence Erlbaum Associates.
Zakay, D. (1998). Attention allocation policy influences prospective timing. *Psychonomic Bulletin and Review*, *5*, 114–118.
Zakay, D. (2000). Gating or switching? Gating is a better model of prospective timing (a response to 'switching or gating?' by Lejeune). *Behavioural Processes*, *50*, 1–7.
Zakay, D., & Block, R. A. (1996). The role of attention in time estimation processes. In: M. A. Pastor & J. Artieda (Eds), *Time, internal clocks and movement* (pp. 143–164). Amsterdam, The Netherlands: Elsevier.
Zakay, D., & Block, R. A. (1997). Temporal cognition. *Current Directions in Psychological Science*, *6*, 12–16.

Chapter 10

Can Animals Cognitively Travel to the Past and Future?

Bill Roberts

Observations of animal behavior might lead the casual observer to conclude that animals can remember the past and anticipate the future. Many laboratory experiments have shown that animals can learn and remember that a conditioned stimulus is followed by an unconditioned stimulus or that pressing a bar or running a path in a maze will lead to food reward. Pet owners know that their dog or cat learns and remembers places in the home where it can eat, hide, or seek attention. With respect to anticipation of the future, animals hoard food or fly toward the equator in apparent anticipation of winter.

The problem with these examples is that the behavior involved does not require memory for or anticipation of specific events in the past or future. Thus, an animal may freeze when it hears a tone because it has learned that shock follows tone, and it may press a bar because it has learned that a bar press is followed by food delivery. Although it has a general representation of these contingencies, it may not remember any specific instance in the past when a tone was followed by shock or a bar press was followed by food. The distinction that is being made here is between semantic memory and episodic memory. Tulving (1972, 1983, 1985) defined semantic memory in humans as memory for general information, such as the months of the year or capital cities of the world. Although most people remember these pieces of information, they do not remember when they learned them. Episodic memory, on the other hand, was defined as memory for specific past events that contained information about where and when they happened. Furthermore, episodic memory was associated with autonoetic consciousness, a feeling that these memories are part of one's personal past or autobiographic memory. Tulving (1983) specifically stated that episodic memory is uniquely human and would not be found in animals. Thus, an animal responding to a conditioned stimulus or pressing a bar for reward bases its behavior on semantic memory and not episodic memory. The animal has learned general rules that the unconditioned stimulus follows the conditioned stimulus and

Psychology of Time

DOI:10.1016/B978-0-08046-977-5.00010-7

pressing the bar yields food, but it does not remember specific trials on which these events occurred.

Behavior which suggests that animals are planning for the future also may be accounted for by alternate mechanisms. Thus, birds flying toward the equator or squirrels burying nuts as winter approaches may arise from innate behavioral predispositions to respond to changes in light and temperature cues at certain times of year and not to a cognitive anticipation of the onset of winter. One way to test these alternative possibilities is to program negative consequences for these adaptive behaviors and see if the behaviors are affected. For example, Baker and Anderson (1995) with black-capped chickadees and Lucas and Zielinski (1998) with Carolina chickadees allowed birds to cache food in different locations and then pilfered the cached food before birds were released to recover it. Although birds repeatedly found their caches missing, they continued to cache food at the same rate as they did before their food was pilfered.

Rats also hoard food. McKenzie, Bird, and Roberts (2005) allowed rats to hoard food items on an 8-arm radial maze. The radial maze contains a circular central platform with arms radiating out from it in a spoke-like fashion. Rats carried pieces of food from the center of the maze to enclosed boxes at the ends of the arms. While rats were removed from the maze for 45 min, the experimenter pilfered all of the food items that had been cached on one side of the maze but not the other. Thus, when rats were returned to the maze to recover their caches, those on one side of the maze were missing. During as many as 25 daily trials of this procedure, rats continued to cache food items equally on both sides of the maze. In other words, pilfering cached food had no impact on subsequent caching, suggesting that caching behavior was modular or an innate predisposition unaffected by its consequences.

Findings of this nature then lead us to question whether animals can anticipate and plan for the future. Several authors have boldly concluded that animals cannot peer into the future. Gilbert (2006) discusses the mechanisms involved in humans' imagination of the future and how these mechanisms lead us to distort or overlook future problems. He also states that "The human being is the only animal that thinks about the future" (p. 4). Based on their observations of monkeys and apes, Bischof (1978, 1985) and Bischof-Kohler (1985) argued that to the extent that these animals behaved as if they were preparing to take action in the future, such behavior was limited to actions that would lead to the satisfaction of a motivational state currently experienced. The Bischof-Kohler hypothesis suggests that chimpanzees may prepare sticks to dip into termite mounds or to carry stones to a nut-cracking site only because they are hungry for termites or nuts at the time these behaviors are performed. Unlike a human, a chimpanzee would not prepare a tool or store food for a need it would only experience hours later.

Earlier reviews of the possibility of mental time travel in animals largely echoed these comments. Suddendorf and Corballis (1997) and Roberts (2002) examined the behavioral evidence for episodic memory and future planning in animals and found little evidence to support either possibility. I summarized this position as the *stuck-in-time hypothesis*. Borrowed from Vonnegut's (1969) novel, *Slaughterhouse-Five*, the hypothesis suggests that humans are mentally unstuck in time and can readily construct a personal past and anticipate a personal future. Time extending into a past and future from the present moment is a human abstraction that does not exist in animals. Animals may live in a permanent present. Their use of past experiences may be limited to semantic memory, and their anticipation of the future may be limited to what Gilbert (2006) calls *nextism*. That is, an animal can anticipate the very next thing that will follow a current event, such as a shock will follow the sound of a tone or a food pellet dropping into a feeder will follow a bar press. However, animals cannot anticipate an event that may occur at the *n*th position in a sequence of events or that will only occur many minutes or hours in the future.

The stuck-in-time hypothesis was intended to be largely propaedeutic. Its purpose was to spur further research on the question of mental time travel in animals to find out if the hypothesis held or perhaps was incorrect. This purpose has largely been realized, as a number of studies have since been performed, which now suggest the possibility that animals may have something like episodic memory and may be able to anticipate the future. This new evidence will be reviewed and discussed.

10.1. Can Animals View the Future?

10.1.1. Self-Control

The issue of whether an animal can expect some event in the extended future typically has been addressed by allowing it to make choices, which lead to different immediate and delayed outcomes. In research on what has been called self-control in animals, an animal chooses between two alternative responses, one of which leads to an immediate small reward and the other to a delayed large reward. Several species have been tested in operant chambers where one choice leads to 2-s access to food 0.1 s later, but the other choice leads to 6-s access to food 6 s later (Logue, 1988; Mazur & Logue, 1978; Tobin, Chelonis, & Logue, 1993). Rats and pigeons tested with this procedure typically show a strong preference for the immediate smaller reward. In keeping with the idea of nextism, Logue (1988) suggested that an animal's time window into the future may be very short and that, functionally, the animal's choice may be between the immediate reward and nothing at all because it cannot anticipate an event 6 s into the future.

Other earlier findings with a somewhat different procedure did support the idea that rats could look further into the future than just the next event. Flaherty and Checke (1982) examined how much effort rats would spend working for a mediocre reward when a more valued reward would become available some time in the future. Rats were given the opportunity to drink water containing 0.15% saccharin for 3 min at the beginning of a session, but an opportunity to drink preferred water containing 32% sucrose would arise in the future. In three different groups of rats, the water containing sucrose was made available 1, 5, or 30 min after the opportunity to drink saccharin water. If rats could anticipate the arrival of sucrose water, presumably they would be less inclined to drink saccharin water. This was indeed the case, but the inhibitory effects of delayed sucrose water on saccharin water consumption declined over 30 min. Timberlake, Gawley, and Lucas (1987) examined the time horizon in rats in a similar but somewhat different fashion. Rats were trained to press a lever for food reward on a progressive ratio schedule that increased the number of presses required for a food pellet by one each time the lever was pressed. This schedule was designed to mimic searching in a patch for food where an animal would have to work harder by traveling farther to find food as the patch depleted. In different groups of rats, a lever that delivered food for every press (continuous reinforcement: CRF) was made available 4, 8, 16, 64, or 120 min after the start of a session. Thus, if a rat could inhibit responding on the initial progressive ratio schedule, it would gain more food for less work when the future CRF bar became available. Although rats did not totally inhibit responding on the progressive ratio lever, they did respond more slowly than control rats that were given no access to a CRF bar. This effect lasted up to the 16-min interval but disappeared when the CRF bar was delayed for 32 min. Rats then showed some anticipation of a future improved foraging situation that would not occur for as much as 16 min into the future.

10.1.2. Temporal Myopia

Silberberg, Widholm, Bresler, Fujita, and Anderson (1998) reported yet another phenomenon that suggested a limited future time window in animals. Two species of macaque monkeys (*Macaca fascicularis* and *M. fuscata*) and a chimpanzee (*Pan troglodytes*) were offered the choice between two quantities of a favored food; although the ratio between the two quantities was held constant, the absolute amounts varied between trials. For example, the chimpanzee was offered a choice between 1 and 2 peanuts and preferred 2 peanuts on about 75% of the trials. When offered a choice between 4 and 8 peanuts, however, the chimpanzee showed indifference by choosing each quantity on about 50% of the trials. Why did this striking change in preference occur as the amount of food increased? Silberberg et al. suggested that these nonhuman primates were showing *temporal myopia*. That is, they could only focus on their current need and could not anticipate a future need. If the chimpanzee's current hunger for peanuts met or exceeded 2 peanuts, then it chose 2 over 1. With a choice between 4 and 8 peanuts, its hunger may have been satisfied by 4 peanuts. The chimpanzee could not anticipate that if it took 8 and ate 4 of them, it would have 4 left for a later time when it would become hungry for peanuts again. Without this foresight, 4 and 8 peanuts equally satisfied its current need, and thus it did not prefer one quantity over the other.

In studies designed to study temporal myopia in New World monkeys, two squirrel monkeys (*Saimiri sciureus*), Jake and Elwood, were offered a choice between different numbers of peanuts (McKenzie, Cherman, Bird, Naqshbandi, & Roberts, 2004). Surprisingly, these monkeys showed no sign of the temporal myopia effect and chose the larger quantity regardless of the number of peanuts. When offered a choice between 2 and 4 peanuts or between 10 and 20 peanuts, Jake and Elwood both chose the larger quantity on about 80% of the trials. Further measurements of consumption showed that it took the monkeys about 2 h to eat 20 peanuts, with intervals during the 2 h when no peanuts were eaten. Taking 20 peanuts then provided for a future need.

It may be argued that taking the larger quantity of food may simply represent an evolved foraging tendency in squirrel monkeys and not anticipation of future need. In order to further explore the issue of future planning in squirrel monkeys, two experiments were carried out to see if the monkey's preference for the larger quantity could be reversed if choice of the smaller amount led to a future advantage. Selective pilfering was used in the first study. After a clear preference for 20 over 10 peanuts was established, the monkeys were tested over an experimental phase during which the experimenter returned to the monkey's cage 15 min after its initial choice and pilfered all of the remaining peanuts if the monkey had chosen 20 peanuts but not if it had chosen 10 peanuts. Since monkeys typically ate 6–8 peanuts in 15 min, they would gain more peanuts in the long run by choosing 10 than by choosing 20. Figure 10.1 shows the results of this study for initial and final baseline (no pilfering) phases and for the intermediate pilfering phase. Both monkeys chose 20 peanuts on about 80% of the initial and final baseline phases, levels that significantly exceeded the chance level of 50%. During the pilfer phase, choice of the larger quantity dropped and did not differ significantly from chance. A further observation to suggest that monkeys were anticipating that their peanuts would be pilfered was that

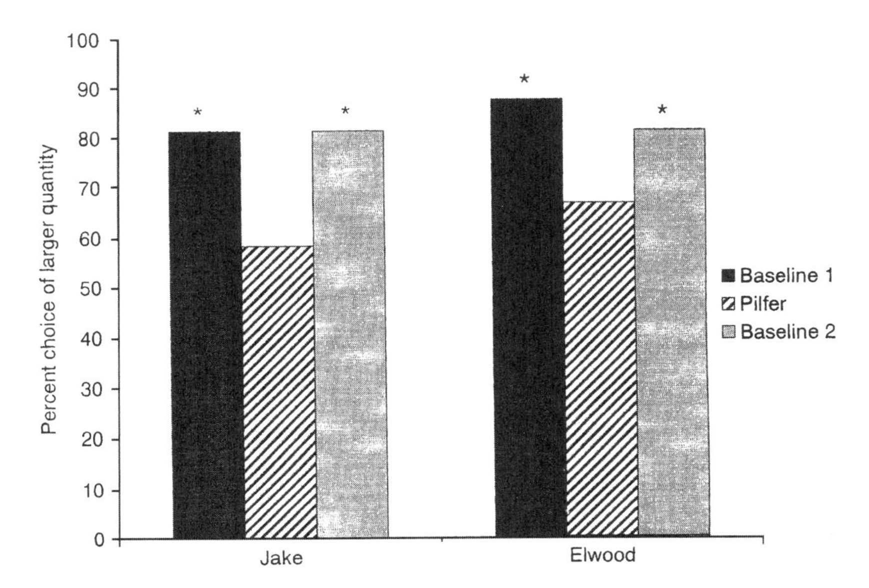

Figure 10.1: Percentage of trials on which each monkey chose the larger quantity (20 peanuts) during baseline sessions and during experimental sessions when choice of the larger quantity led to pilfering 15 min later. (Reprinted with permission from McKenzie et al. (2004). Copyright 2004 by the Psychonomic Society.)

on some trials, they took peanuts from the food trays and hid them on the floors of their cages before the experimenter returned to remove them.

In a second experiment, McKenzie et al. (2004) used a replenishment instead of a pilfering manipulation, and the difference in the number of peanuts that could be obtained by anticipating the future outcome of a trial was increased. Jake and Elwood now chose between 2 and 4 peanuts and again showed a significant preference for 4 peanuts on baseline sessions. During an experimental phase, choice of 2 peanuts, but not 4 peanuts, led to replenishment of the food tray; the experimenter returned after 15 min and put 10 more peanuts in the tray. By choosing 2 peanuts initially, the monkey could obtain $2 + 10 = 12$ peanuts in total, 8 more peanuts than it would obtain if it initially chose 4 peanuts. Figure 10.2 shows that both monkeys chose 4 peanuts on 80% or more of the trials during baseline 1 and 2 testing, but choice of 4 peanuts dropped to around 30% on replenishment trials. It appears that both monkeys anticipated replenishment and made the choice that yielded the largest net outcome.

10.1.3. Caching and its Consequences

Although the studies described earlier failed to find an impact of selective pilfering on caching behavior in chickadees and rats, a more recent study by Clayton, Dally, Gilbert, and Dickinson (2005) reveals that caching behavior is substantially modified

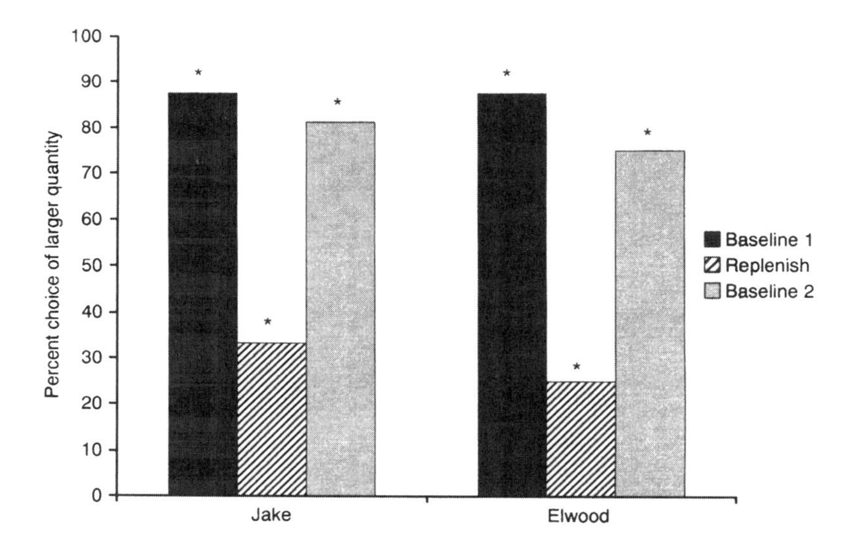

Figure 10.2: Percentage of trials on which each monkey chose the larger quantity (4 peanuts) during baseline sessions and during experimental sessions when choice of the smaller quantity led to replenishment 15 min later. (Reprinted with permission from McKenzie et al. (2004). Copyright 2004 by the Psychonomic Society.)

by its consequences in scrub jays. Different groups of birds cached worms in trays in the laboratory. When jays were returned to the trays to recover their caches after a retention interval, the worms were replenished with fresh, degraded, or pilfered worms. When given repeated trials with these consequences in place, jays in the pilfer and degrade groups stopped caching worms, while jays in the replenish group continued to cache worms. It was concluded that jays are highly sensitive to the consequences of caching and do not continue to cache food when it is degraded or stolen.

Emery and Clayton (2001) examined the effects of an observer on caching behavior in scrub jays. When a jay could see another jay watching while it cached food items, it later re-cached the originally cached items to new locations. This finding suggests that scrub jays anticipated possible thievery of their food caches by another bird and thus hid food in new safer locations. An additional interesting outcome of this experiment was that only scrub jays that themselves had previously pilfered food from other jays' caches showed a tendency to re-cache food after being observed caching. This finding seems to support the old adage that "it takes one to know one."

10.1.4. The Bischof-Kohler Hypothesis

The Bischof-Kohler hypothesis presents a potential fly in the ointment for these demonstrations of future planning in animals. It may be argued that rats, squirrel monkeys, and scrub jays all were hungry for the food they ultimately attained when they inhibited bar pressing, chose the smaller number of peanuts, or re-cached worms. Recall that the Bischof-Kohler hypothesis argues that an animal cannot plan for a future need that it does not currently experience. Very recent experiments now challenge even this position. In these experiments, the motivational state of an animal is precisely controlled to guarantee that "planning behavior" is carried out while the animal experiences no need for the incentive it will ultimately attain. Through experience, however, the animals can learn to anticipate that a need not currently experienced will arise in the future.

One such experiment was arranged by Naqshbandi and Roberts (2006), again using the squirrel monkeys Jake and Elwood. In this experiment, the food offered to the monkeys was dates. An important effect of date consumption was that it made the monkeys thirsty. Thus, clear increases in water intake above baseline levels were noted after Jake and Elwood consumed dates. Both monkeys were given repeated trials during initial and final baseline phases in which they chose between 1 and 4 dates. Four dates were chosen on 80% or more of these baseline trials, and water was constantly available throughout testing. During the experimental phase that intervened between baseline phases, the monkeys were also offered a choice between 1 and 4 dates. Just before making this choice, the experimenter removed the monkey's water bottle. Since the monkey had unlimited water up to the time of the choice, it was not thirsty when it chose between 1 and 4 dates. The choice of each quantity of dates had different consequences. If only 1 date was taken, the monkey's water bottle was returned 30 min later, but, if it chose 4 dates, return of the water bottle was delayed for 3 h.

The effects of these contingencies are illustrated in Figure 10.3. High levels of choice of the larger amount (4 dates) is found on initial baseline and final baseline trials. During experimental (E) trials, however, choice of 4 dates dropped progressively down to 20% on Blocks E3 and E5 and reached zero on Block E4. The monkeys clearly reversed their preference for 4 dates between baseline and experimental trials. The important point of the experiment is that this reversal of preference for number of dates occurred while the monkeys were not thirsty for water but affected the readiness with which a thirst they would experience in the future would be reduced. Thus, the monkeys planned for a future need they did not currently experience.

Experiments that involve similar types of manipulations of motivational state have very recently been reported with scrub jays. Raby, Alexis, Dickinson, and Clayton (2007) designed experiments in which scrub jays planned their own breakfast on the preceding evening. Jays initially were placed in one of two compartments, A or C, on several successive mornings. In Compartment A, they always were fed powdered pine nuts, but in mornings when they were placed in Compartment C, they

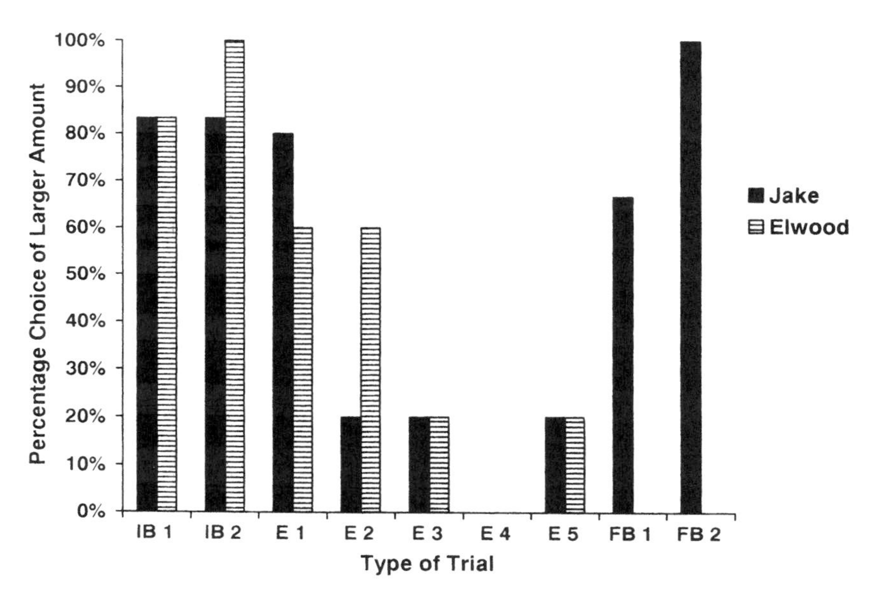

Figure 10.3: Percentage of trials on which each monkey chose the larger quantity (4 dates) during initial baseline (IB) sessions, final baseline (FB) sessions, and experimental (E) sessions when choice of the smaller quantity led to return of the water bottle sooner than choice of the larger quantity. (Reprinted with permission from Naqshbandi and Roberts (2006). Copyright 2006 by the American Psychological Association.)

received no food. Two hours before darkness in the evening of each day, they were placed in a third compartment, B, and allowed to eat powdered pine nuts. On a test evening, after eating powdered pine nuts, the jays were given whole pine nuts and could freely cache them in sand placed in the cells of ice cube trays found in Compartments A and C. The experimenters found that jays cached three times more pine nuts in Compartment C than in Compartment A. Why? By provisioning Compartment C with pine nuts, the jays ensured that they would have pine nuts for breakfast the next morning regardless of which compartment they were placed in, either in Compartment A (provided by the experimenter) or in Compartment C (cached by the jay itself). Importantly, this strategic provisioning of pine nuts the evening before occurred while jays were satiated on pine nuts.

In a second experiment, Raby et al. (2007) gave scrub jays different breakfast foods in Compartments A and C. For example, jays were given peanuts in Compartment A on some mornings and dog kibble in Compartment C on other mornings. In the evenings, scrub jays ate powdered peanuts and dog kibble in Compartment B. After eating meals of powdered peanuts and dog kibble on the test evening, birds were given whole peanuts and pieces of dog kibble that they could freely cache in trays in Compartments A and C. Jays showed a clear preference for caching peanuts in Compartment C and dog kibble in Compartment A. This behavior ensured that both compartment would contain peanuts and dog kibble for breakfast. Thus, scrub jays planned a variety menu for breakfast while not hungry for either breakfast item during the caching phase the prior evening.

In an impressive further demonstration of future planning in scrub jays, Correia, Dickinson, and Clayton (2007) initially demonstrated that prefeeding controls birds' hunger for specific foods. Jays were prefed meals of either pine seeds or dog kibble to repletion and then were given an opportunity to eat and cache both foods. Birds strongly preferred to eat and cache the food they had not been prefed. Two groups of scrub jays then were given 3 days of testing, each of which consisted of four phases. In the first phase, they were prefed one food, say pine seeds, for 3 h. In Phase 2, birds were given an opportunity to cache either pine seeds or dog kibble. In the third phase, the two groups were treated differently. Group Different was prefed dog kibble, different from the pine seeds it was prefed in Phase 1, and Group Same was prefed pine seeds, the same food it has been prefed in Phase 1. In Phase 4, birds from both groups were allowed to recover the food they cached in Phase 2. The caching activity in Phase 2 is the important dependent variable in this experiment. On the first day of testing, birds in both groups cached more dog kibble, the food not prefed in Phase 1. However, on Days 2 and 3, the two groups cached different foods. Group Different predominantly cached pine seeds, but Group Same predominantly cached dog kibble. This difference in caching behavior corresponds to the needs each group of birds would experience at the end of Phase 3. Based on their experience on Day 1, jays could anticipate on Days 2 and 3 that they would be either satiated on kibble and hungry for pine seeds (Group Different) or would be satiated on pine seeds and hungry for kibble (Group Same). Thus, Group Different cached pine seeds, and Group Same cached kibble. Note that Group Different preferentially cached pine seeds, even though they had just ingested a large meal of pine seeds. Birds anticipated the food they would be prefed in Phase 3, based on Day 1 experience, and thus cached the food they would be hungry for during the Phase 4 recovery.

The monkey and scrub jay findings appear to mount a strong challenge to the Bischof-Kohler hypothesis. These animals did appear to plan for a future need clearly not experienced at the time they made choices or cached food items to satisfy that future need. As one further demonstration of future planning in animals, recall the point that chimpanzees preparing termite mound probes or carrying rocks for cracking nuts might only be preparing to satisfy a current need a short time into the future. Mulcahy and Call (2006) arranged a long-term tool selection test for bonobos (*P. paniscus*) and orangutans (*Pongo pygmaeus*). These nonhuman primates learned to use several tools in order to solve different problems that led to food reward. On critical tests, animals were shown the problem but not allowed to work at its solution for delays as long as 14 h. The critical aspect of these experiments was that animals were allowed to select a tool that could be used to solve the problem in the future. Both bonobos and orangutans significantly preferred to take the tool that would be appropriate for the solution of a problem they would not encounter until 14 h later. Although need states were not specifically manipulated in these experiments, they clearly suggest that apes made long-term plans.

10.2. The Question of Episodic Memory

Although the studies just discussed suggest that some animals are able to anticipate the future, they do not indicate whether animals can anticipate specific times in the future. One concern with the breakfast experiments of Raby et al. (2007) is that scrub jays might have been storing food in novel locations without anticipating its consumption for breakfast. That is, having found pine seeds in Compartment A and not in Compartment C, jays may have cached most seeds in Compartment C in the evening because they have an innate predisposition to distribute types of food between different locations. Such a strategy may lower the probability of that food type being wiped out by a predator. To find out if jays provisioned Compartment C in anticipation of breakfast, in a further experiment, jays might be given pine seeds in Compartment A in the morning and nothing in Compartment A at noon. In Compartment C, they would receive nothing in the morning and pine seeds at noon. If birds still cached most seeds in Compartment C on the evening test, it would suggest that they are planning for breakfast, a specific time in the future, and not lunch. Equal caching in Compartments A and C, on the other hand, would indicate that jays did not anticipate morning instead of noon.

10.2.1. Episodic-Like Memory in Scrub Jays

By contrast, studies of episodic memory have focused specifically on the question of when or how long ago an event occurred in the past, as well as what that event was and where it occurred. A key discovery here was the finding that scrub jays remember what, where, and when information about hoarded food (Clayton & Dickinson, 1998, 1999). Birds were given two types of food to cache in different trays, preferred wax worms and less preferred peanuts. Opportunities to recover these caches occurred 4 h or 5 days later. As would be the case in nature, the worms became degraded over the 5-day period but not over the 4-h period. Peanuts remained fresh at both intervals. After experiencing these outcomes on several trials, the jays were given test trials in which cached foods were removed from the trays and not replaced to control for odor cues. Scrub jays went directly to the worm locations when tested at 4 h but reversed this preference and made initial visits to peanut locations when tested at 5 days. Clayton and Dickinson argued that birds not only remembered what foods they had cached and where they had cached them, but also when in past time they had cached them.

How precise is scrub jays' ability to remember when they cached a particular type of food? Is it limited to the fairly large difference between 4 h and 5 days? To examine this question, Clayton, Yu, and Dickinson (2001) had scrub jays cache three different foods, worms, crickets, and peanuts, in different tray locations. On different trials, worms and peanuts were cached or crickets and peanuts were cached. Recovery tests were given at three intervals after caching, 4, 28, and 100 h, with fresh peanuts always placed at peanut cache sites at every interval. Crickets remained fresh after 4- and 28-h intervals but were degraded after 100 h, and worms were degraded after both 28 and 100 h. After some experience with these temporally based outcomes, the jays searched for their caches accordingly on test trials. Thus, they searched first for worms at 4 h, first for crickets at 28 h, and first for peanuts at 100 h. The birds appeared to be quite sensitive to the state of their hoards after different time intervals, suggesting that memory for when different foods were hoarded was quite precise.

Although scrub jays clearly showed memory for what, where, and when in these food-caching experiments, Tulving had additionally defined episodic memory as a type of memory based on autonoetic consciousness (Tulving, 1985) or a feeling that memories belonged to one's personal past. Because we obviously cannot tap the consciousness of a scrub jay (if it has one), Clayton and Dickinson (1998, 1999; Griffiths, Dickinson, & Clayton, 1999) described the scrub jay's memory as *episodic-like memory*. Episodic-like memory then has the behavioral characteristics of human episodic memory (what-where-when) but not the introspective characteristics.

10.2.2. Failure to Find Episodic-Like Memory in Other Species

The discovery of episodic-like memory in scrub jays prompted other investigators to look for this phenomenon in other species of animals. In my laboratory, we undertook a series of experiments with rats to provide a paradigm similar to that used by Clayton and Dickinson with scrub jays. Rats are known to hoard food and other items, and we undertook to study memory in rats for cached food on the radial maze (Bird, Roberts, Abroms, Kit, & Crupi, 2003). The radial maze used consisted of a circular central platform from which eight arms radiated outward and each ended in an enclosed compartment. The maze was elevated about 60 cm off the floor. Pieces of food were placed on the central platform, and rats carried these food items to the compartments at the ends of the arms of the maze. Rats were removed from the compartments, with the food item left in the compartment. After a rat had cached four food items, it was taken off the maze and returned to its home cage for 45 min. It was then returned to the center of the maze and allowed to forage freely among the eight arms, with food found only in compartments at the end of arms where the rat had previously cached food. The progress of this memory testing is shown in Figure 10.4. The figure plots accuracy of choice behavior (corrected for chance performance) against trials for two groups of rats, one that cached pieces of cheese freely on any four of the eight arms and one in which rats were forced to cache pieces of cheese on four randomly chosen arms. The figure shows that rats learned to return accurately to their caches and that whether the rat chose the arms to cache in or they were chosen randomly made no difference. In a further experiment, we offered rats two foods to cache, cubes of cheese and pieces of pretzel. A consumption test showed

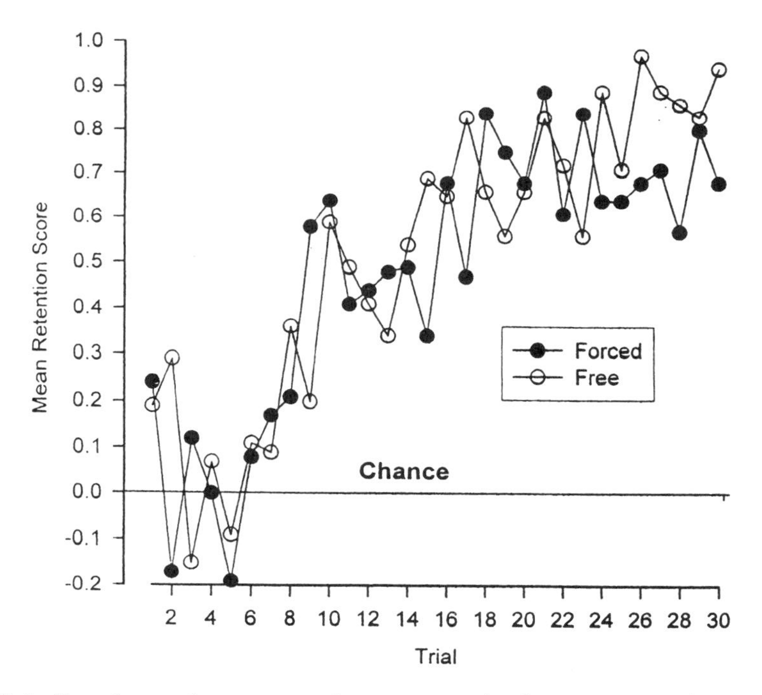

Figure 10.4: Rats learned to accurately return to the four arms on the radial maze where they cached food items. One group was forced to cache on arms chosen by the experimenter, and another group freely chose the arms on which they cached food. (Reprinted with permission from Bird et al. (2003). Copyright 2003 by the American Psychological Association.)

that rats strongly preferred cheese over pretzel, and this preference appeared in caching and recovery behavior. Rats again cached and recovered accurately, but they regularly cached cheese before pretzels and recovered cheese caches before pretzel caches.

Given that we had established preferential caching and recovery behavior for different foods in the rat, we were now in a position to test for episodic-like memory. Bird et al. (2003, Experiment 6) trained two groups of rats to cache pieces of cheese and pretzel and then tested their ability to recover these items 1 or 25 h later. As in the Clayton and Dickinson experiments, the preferred food was degraded and made inedible at one retention interval but not the other. Cheese was soaked in a bitter quinine solution, and rats refused to eat it after this degradation. One group of rats, the 1-h Degrade Group, always found their cached cheese had degraded after 1 h, and the other group of rats, the 25-h Degrade Group, always found that their cached cheese had degraded after 25 h. At the alternate recovery interval, fresh cheese was available at the cache sites; fresh pretzels were available at their cache sites on all tests. The experiment was designed to see if rats, like scrub jays, would come to visit cheese caches first at the nondegrade interval but visit pretzel caches first at the degrade interval. Figure 10.5 shows the results of this experiment plotted over blocks of four trials. The dependent variable plotted is mean rank of entry into the arms

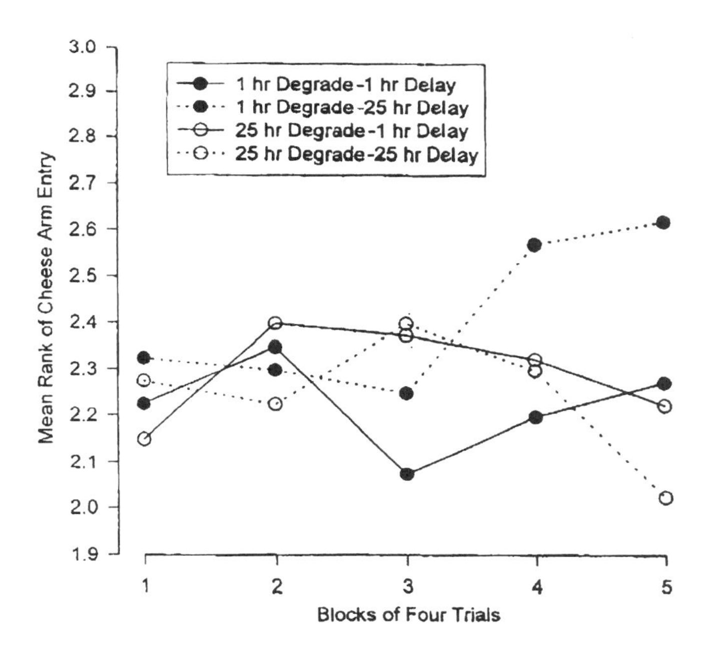

Figure 10.5: Mean rank of entry into arms containing cheese plotted over blocks of four trials for 1- and 25-h degrade groups each tested on different trials after 1- and 25-h delays. (Reprinted with permission from Bird et al. (2003). Copyright 2003 by the American Psychological Association.)

where cheese had been cached. Although the rats were trained for 20 trials at each interval, there is no suggestion of episodic-like memory. This evidence would have appeared as higher ranks at intervals when the cheese was degraded than at intervals when the cheese was fresh, and no such trends appeared.

Roberts and Roberts (2002) also looked for episodic-like memory in rats on a radial maze using a different procedure. Rats were placed on an eight-arm maze and allowed to enter arms freely with one food item found on each new arm visited. Rats normally visit different arms on the maze with repeat visits made to arms only after visits to a number of other arms have been made. Two groups of rats were trained. An Experimental Group of rats was trained under an unusual contingency. If a rat revisited the first arm it had entered on the maze, it received a large reward of 10 food items. In the Control Group, revisiting the initial arm entered yielded no more reward than entering any other arm. Thus, if a rat could remember the first place it visited (where and when episodic-like memory) and could learn that revisiting that place yielded a 10-fold reward, it should revisit that arm early in its sequence of arm entries. The results (shown in Figure 10.6) again yielded no evidence of episodic-like memory. The mean arms entered before revisiting the initial arm entered did not differ between experimental and control groups over 30 daily trials. Rats in the

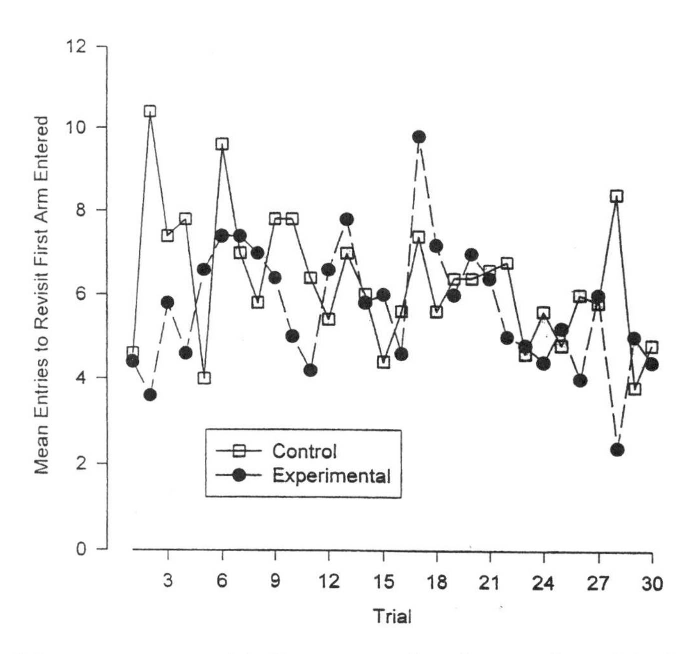

Figure 10.6: Mean arms entered before re-entering the arm first visited plotted over 30 trials. The Experimental Group received 10 pellets for re-entering the initial arm, but the Control Group received only 1 pellet. (Reprinted with permission from Roberts and Roberts (2002). Copyright 2002 by the Helen Dwight Reid Educational Foundation.)

Experimental Group did not return to the initial arm visited any sooner than rats in the Control Group.

Failure to find episodic-like memory in new species was not limited to rats. Hampton, Hampstead, and Murray (2005) had rhesus monkeys search three foraging sites in a testing room and find preferred and nonpreferred foods at two of those sites. The monkeys were allowed to search the sites once again after 1 or 25 h. After 1 h, the same foods as found an hour earlier were present and edible at their respective sites. After 25 h, however, the preferred food was degraded and inedible. Would monkeys preferentially visit the preferred food first after 1 h but the nonpreferred food first after 25 h? They did not, as the monkeys tended to visit the site of the preferred food after both 1 and 25 h.

10.2.3. Evidence from Different Experimental Paradigms

Some other researchers have reported finding evidence of episodic-like memory in species other than scrub jays using different memory paradigms and perhaps definitions of episodic-like memory. Zentall has taken the position that episodic memory is demonstrated only when a subject remembers an episode it did not anticipate having to remember (Zentall, 2005; Zentall, Clement, Bhatt, & Allen, 2001). He suggests that once an animal has experienced a learning trial and then been tested for memory of what was learned, the animal may anticipate a future test after the next trial and thus rehearse the learned information into semantic memory.

In order to examine memory on an unexpected test, Zentall et al. (2001) trained pigeons to peck a center key in an operant conditioning chamber when the key contained a pattern of vertical lines (for food reward) and to inhibit pecking when the key contained a pattern of horizontal lines (no food reward). Once this go-no-go discrimination was established, red and green lights appeared on side keys to the left and right of the center key after the pigeon had pecked or not pecked the center key. If it had pecked vertical lines on the center key, it now had to peck the red key for reward, but if it had inhibited pecking horizontal lines on the center key, it had to peck the green key for reward. The pigeons had been trained to perform symbolic delayed matching-to-sample, in which response to red or green keys was arbitrarily (symbolically) matched to the pattern on the center key and to the pigeon's own behavior (pecking or not pecking). In the second phase of the experiment, the same pigeons were trained by an autoshaping procedure to peck the center key when it was yellow but not when it was blue. The stage was now set for a surprise test of memory in Phase 3 of the experiment. During the presentation of the yellow and blue stimuli, a peck or nonpeck to the center key was followed by the presentation of red and green side keys. Would pigeons show memory for having pecked the center key by choosing red and for not having pecked the center key by choosing green? They did indeed choose the correct red and green keys on 72% of the trials, which was significantly higher than the chance level of 50%. Pigeons then reported correctly on their own most recent behavior when they did not anticipate and thus prepare for the test.

In experiments that involved memory for odors, rats were trained to dig for a reward in cups that contained scented sand (Fortin, Wright, & Eichenbaum, 2004; Eichenbaum, Fortin, Ergorul, Wright, & Agster, 2005). Rats dug in cups A, B, C, and D, each of which contained a different odor. The rats then were given a memory test in which they chose between two odors from the list, with the cup sampled earlier in the list containing reward and the cup sampled later in the list containing no reward. Thus, rats might have been tested with combinations such as A + D or B + C. These were working-memory tests because the odors used changed from one trial to next. Rats learned to choose the earlier odor on probe tests quite significantly above chance. Of further importance, they did so even when the spatial positions of the cups presented were different from their original positions. Thus, rats could use only memory for what the odors were and when in the order they occurred to identify which one was presented first. Eichenbaum et al. (2005) argued that these experiments showed episodic-like memory in rats because rats could only have performed accurately if they remembered when each odor was encountered in the lists.

10.2.4. The Babb and Crystal Experiments

A critic might argue that the studies by Zentall et al. (2001) and Eichenbaum et al. (2005) involved immediate memory for very recently performed behaviors or stimuli experienced and do not capture the scope of time involved in the Clayton and Dickinson's (1998, 1999) studies of episodic-like memory in scrub jays. Recall that scrub jays remembered when different foods were cached over as long a period as 5 days. Fortunately, in recent studies with rats, Babb and Crystal (2005, 2006a, 2006b) have developed a paradigm similar to that used by Clayton and Dickinson in which long-term episodic-like memory is revealed.

In Babb and Crystal's experiments, rats were placed on an eight-arm radial maze for two phases on each trial, an initial study phase and a subsequent test phase. In the initial study phase, rats were allowed to enter only four randomly chosen arms that each contained food. Three of the arms contained standard reward pellets, but the fourth arm contained the strongly preferred reward of chocolate. After rats entered the four arms and consumed their contents, they were returned to their home cages for a retention interval. When rats were returned to the maze after the retention interval for the test phase, all of the arms on the maze were open, with the four arms that were closed in the study phase now containing the standard reward pellets. The experimental manipulation of primary interest was the replenishment of chocolate on the arm where it was found in the study phase at selected retention intervals. On some trials, the retention interval was 30 min, and, on other trials, it was 4 h. At the 30-min interval, the arm that previously contained chocolate was empty, as were the arms that contained pellets in the study phase. At the 4-h interval, however, chocolate was replenished on the arm where it had been found in the study phase. The experiment then contained the three components of episodic-like memory, what, where, and when. To obtain the preferred chocolate reward (what), rats had to remember where it had been found and when it had been found. If it had been found 30 min earlier, then return to the chocolate arm was futile, but if it had been found 4 h earlier, return to the chocolate arm yielded more chocolate.

Babb and Crystal's (2005) experiment showed that rats remembered what, where, and when. When the study phase occurred at 9 a.m. and the test was carried out at 9:30 a.m. or 1 p.m., rats made more early visits to the chocolate arm at 1 p.m. than at 9:30 a.m. Thus, rats used memory for how long ago the chocolate had been found to cue a return to the chocolate arm. One criticism of this procedure was that rats might be using the time of day when the test took place to cue early or late return to the chocolate arm encountered in the study phase. That is, cues available at 1 p.m. might tell the rat to return sooner than cues provided at 9:30 a.m. To control for this possibility, Babb and Crystal (2006a) gave rats the study phase at 9 a.m. and then tested rat's memory at 10 a.m. either on the same day or on the next day. The retention interval then was 1 or 25 h, and chocolate was replenished only after 25 h. Because rats were always tested at 10 a.m., time of day could not be a cue for whether or not to return to the chocolate arm. Under these conditions, rats still made early returns to the chocolate arm after 25 h but not after 1 h.

The reliability of Babb and Crystal's findings was strengthened by their replication in our laboratory (Naqshbandi, Feeney, McKenzie, & Roberts, 2007). Rats were given a study phase in which they found food pellets on three arms of an eight-arm radial maze and chocolate on a fourth arm. Memory was tested after 30 min or 4 h, as in the Babb and Crystal (2005) study, but our experiment involved two manipulations different from their study. We also controlled for the time of day at testing as a cue for chocolate replenishment or nonreplenishment by always testing rats' memory at 1 p.m. Thus, when the retention interval was 4 h, the study phase was given at 9 a.m., but when the retention interval was 30 min, the study phase was given at 12:30 p.m. The second new manipulation was to examine memory for when chocolate was found using both short and long retention intervals. Two groups of rats were used, with chocolate replenished after 30 min but not after 4 h in one group and chocolate replenished after 4 h but not after 30 min in the other group.

The results of this experiment are shown in Figure 10.7 as the proportion of trials on which rats entered the arm that contained chocolate in the first four arms entered on the retention test. Episodic-like memory is shown by a higher proportion at the retention interval when chocolate was replenished than when it was not replenished. It can be seen that this pattern appeared both when chocolate was replenished after 30 min and after 4 h. Tests at short and long retention intervals were randomly mixed over daily trials, and performance is shown for the first half of the experiment (Trials 1–14) and the second half of the experiment (Trials 15–28). Notice that the difference in the heights of the bars increased over trials. Rats learned to use retention interval as a cue, and statistical analysis showed that they discriminated equally well when chocolate was replenished at 30 min and 4 h.

Additional variations in the procedure were introduced in a second experiment. Instead of using chocolate as the preferred food, cheese, another highly preferred food, was used. Two groups again were used, but, in contrast to the first experiment,

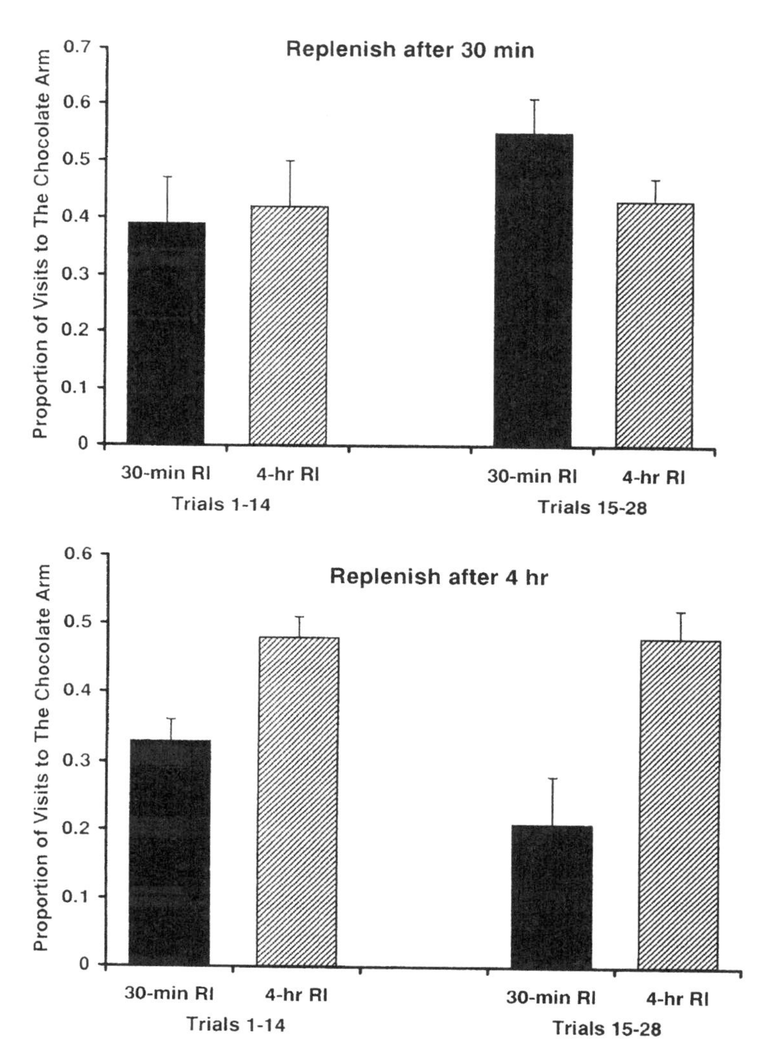

Figure 10.7: Proportion of trials on which rats re-visited the chocolate arm within the first four arm entries at retention intervals (RI) of 30 min and 4 h. Chocolate was replenished after 30 min for the group shown in the upper panel and after 4 h for the group shown in the lower panel. (Reprinted with permission from Naqshbandi et al. (2007). Copyright 2007 by Elsevier Science.)

cheese was placed on the arm where it was found in the study phase after both 30 min and 4 h. The cheese that was found on the arm varied with retention interval. In one group, fresh cheese was found after 30 min and degraded cheese was found after 4 h; in the other group, fresh cheese was found after 4 h and degraded cheese was found after 30 min. The experiment then was designed to see if the episodic-like memory effect would be found in rats with degraded food, as it was found by Clayton and Dickinson (1998, 1999) with scrub jays but not by Bird et al. (2003) with rats.

Figure 10.8 shows the results of this experiment for the initial and final 10 trials of testing in each group. The results are very similar to those of the first experiment.

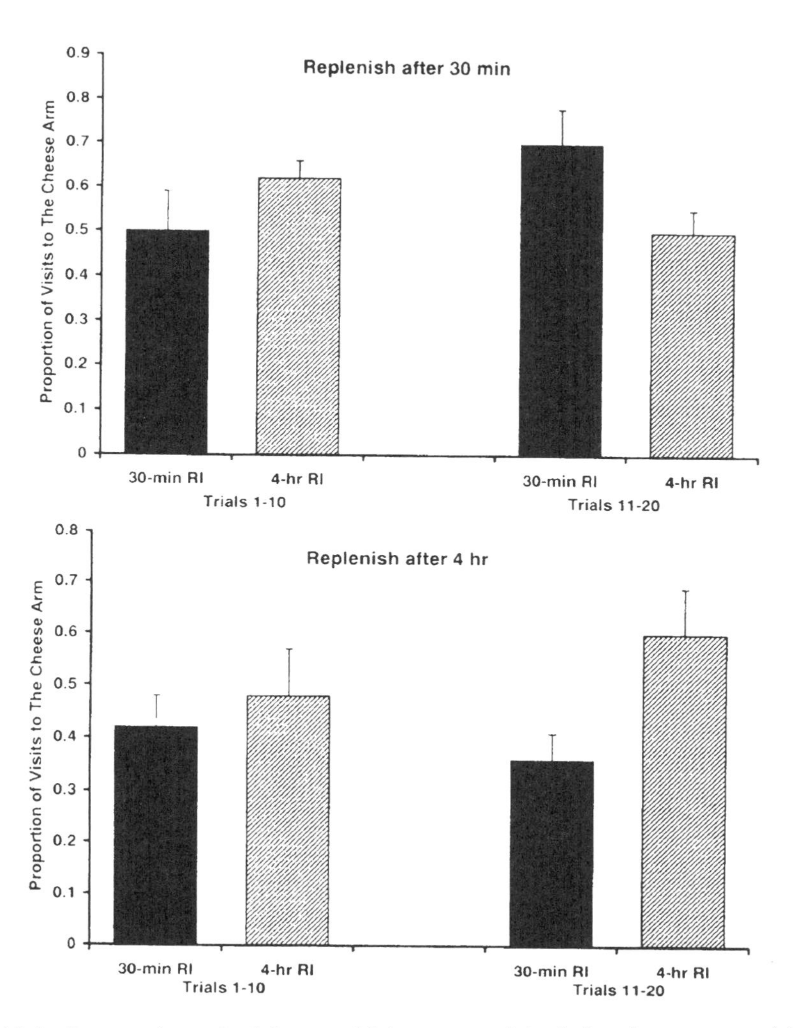

Figure 10.8: Proportion of trials on which rats re-visited the cheese arm within the first four arm entries at retention intervals (RI) of 30 min and 4 h. Cheese was replenished after 30 min and degraded after 4 h for the group shown in the upper panel and was replenished after 4 h and degraded after 30 min for the group shown in the lower panel. (Reprinted with permission from Naqshbandi et al. (2007). Copyright by Elsevier Science.)

Rats entered the arm containing cheese sooner at the interval when fresh cheese was replenished than at the interval when degraded cheese was placed on the arm. This effect became magnified over trials and was equally strong when fresh cheese was replenished at 30 min and 4 h. It appears that the episodic-like memory effect in rats is robust under a variety of experimental conditions.

It is often suggested that episodic memory is flexible in the sense that many personal episodes can be remembered and the significance of these episodes might change in light of new information. Episodic-like memory in rats appears to have some of these characteristics. Memory for many episodes is shown by the fact that the tests-given rats involve working memory, or memory for a different arm containing the preferred reward on each trial. In addition, Babb and Crystal (2005, 2006a) have shown that the significance of an episodic-like memory can be changed. After rats had found chocolate on one of the four arms visited in the study phase, they were given chocolate in their home cage and then were made ill by injection of lithium chloride. Taste-aversion experiments have shown that this procedure creates an aversion to the taste of the substance ingested and followed by illness. When now placed back on the maze at the long retention interval (when chocolate was replenished), rats now avoided the arm where they had found chocolate during the study phase. Thus, the significance of memory for a food was changed from preferred to nonpreferred.

The significance of preferred foods found on the radial maze can be temporarily altered by prefeeding (Babb & Crystal, 2006b). Rats found preferred grape and raspberry pellets on different arms of the maze in the study phase. They normally went to both of these arms early in their arm visits because both flavored pellets were replenished at a long retention interval. If rats were prefed one type of flavored pellet (either grape or raspberry) during the retention interval, however, they would then enter the arm containing the pellets not prefed and avoid the arm containing the pellets prefed.

As one last demonstration of memory flexibility, rats that had been trained for a number of trials to return to the arm that contained chocolate in the study phase now encountered grape pellets on one arm of the maze during a study phase. They returned to the grape arm early at the 25-h retention interval but not the 1-h retention interval, just as they had when chocolate was on the arm (Babb & Crystal, 2006b). The significance of foods that have equal hedonic value appears to be interchangeable in the rat's episodic-like memory.

10.3. Concluding Comments

Reviews that largely concluded that animals were stuck in time or could not mentally time travel (Suddendorf & Corballis, 1997, 2007; Roberts, 2002) may have to be amended in light of the spate of new research that has addressed this question. Scrub jays refuse to cache food when they find their caches pilfered or degraded, and they recache food when they discover another scrub jay has been watching them. Rats reduce their efforts to obtain a costly food when an opportunity for less costly food is a few minutes in the offing. Squirrel monkeys reverse their normal preference for a larger amount of food when choice of a smaller amount will yield a delayed replenishment that provides more food in the long run. All of these findings suggest that animals have some ability to anticipate the future consequences of their actions. They appear able to project the future results of their behaviors beyond a nextism principle (Gilbert, 2006).

But just how far can they anticipate a future event? The Bischof-Kohler hypothesis suggested not very far and not at all if the later event involved a need different from an animal's present motivational state. Some recent experiments appear to contradict the Bischof-Kohler hypothesis (Correia et al., 2007; Mulcahy & Call, 2006; Naqshbandi & Roberts, 2006; Raby et al., 2007). When need state is precisely controlled, squirrel monkeys make food choices that anticipate a state of thirst that is not experienced at the time of choice. Scrub jays cache foods they have no hunger for at the moment so that they will be available for breakfast the next morning when they will be hungry for them. Bonobos and orangutans choose an appropriate tool they will need to obtain food 14 h later.

All of these findings suggest that we have underestimated animals' ability to anticipate and plan for future needs or happenings in their environment. Yet, we may only be beginning to understand the nature of future time travel in animals. How far into the future can animals of different species plan? Can animals plan for when different events may occur at different times in the future? Suppose bonobos and orangutans were trained to expect two problems in the future, one sooner and the other later, and these problems required different tools. Suppose further that these tools had to be placed in locations of different accessibility. Would an ape place the tool for the sooner problem in the more accessible location, showing anticipation of the order in which these tools would be needed?

When retrospection in animals is considered, we now have solid evidence that a bird and a mammal show long-term episodic-like memory. Scrub jays selectively prefer to revisit cache sites of preferred worms at a retention interval when the worms remain fresh but prefer to revisit cache sites of less-preferred peanuts at a retention interval when the worms have degraded. Similarly, rats make early revisits to the arm of a radial maze that contained a favored food (chocolate or cheese) at a retention interval when the food replenishes but delay visiting the arm at a retention interval when the food is pilfered or degraded. These behavioral experiments indicate that both scrub jays and rats can form integrated and flexible memories that contain the components of what, where, and when (Babb & Crystal, 2006b; Griffiths et al., 1999; Roberts, 2006).

What research initiatives might be next for the study of episodic-like memory in animals? The search for episodic-like memory should be extended to other species. Although no clear demonstration of long-term episodic-like memory has been shown in nonhuman primates, we surely expect to find it. How far back in time can animals remember when an event occurred? Although scrub jays remembered caching worms 5 days before, could an animal remember a particular event as having occurred a month or more ago? Do some species have longer episodic time windows than others? A major issue that needs to be addressed is the timing mechanism of episodic-like memory. When a scrub jay remembers caching worms or a rat remembers eating chocolate on an arm of a radial maze, does the animal remember when this happened within a larger temporal framework, as humans do? Human episodic memory involves placing past events into a mental calendar of years, months, days, and hours. Do animals have any such calendar-like concept of time within which events can be placed? If they do, what is the basis of such a calendar? Perhaps they keep track of dark–light cycles or internal circadian cycles and use the number of these to remember a point in past time. The other alternative is that animals remember how long ago an event occurred. The amount of time that has elapsed since caching a worm or finding chocolate on an arm may tell an animal whether to revisit or avoid a particular location. Theories of interval timing that have been proposed suggest several mechanisms, including accumulators (Church, Meck, & Gibbon, 1994), behavioral states (Killeen & Fetterman, 1993), fading memory traces (Staddon, Higa, & Chelaru, 1999), and resetting oscillators (Church & Broadbent, 1990). If animals are using interval timing to remember the status of food in different locations, timing studies that indicate which of these mechanisms is the basis of interval timing will be of considerable importance for an understanding of episodic-like memory. Such a finding also would suggest that the temporal basis of episodic memory in people and episodic-like memory in animals may be quite different. These are some of the theoretical research challenges that face this new field of investigation. I look forward to the discovery of exciting and surprising new findings.

References

Babb, S. J., & Crystal, J. D. (2005). Discrimination of what, when, and where: Implications for episodic-like memory in rats. *Learning and Motivation*, *36*, 177–189.

Babb, S. J., & Crystal, J. D. (2006a). Discrimination of what, when, and where is not based on time of day. *Learning and Behavior*, *34*, 124–130.

Babb, S. J., & Crystal, J. D. (2006b). Episodic-like memory in the rat. *Current Biology*, *16*, 1317–1321.

Baker, M. C., & Anderson, P. (1995). Once-pilfered cache sites not avoided by black-capped chickadees. *Animal Behavior*, *49*, 1599–1602.

Bird, L. R., Roberts, W. A., Abroms, B., Kit, K. A., & Crupi, C. (2003). Spatial memory for hidden food by rats (*Rattus norvegicus*) on the radial maze: Studies of memory for where, what, and when. *Journal of Comparative Psychology*, *117*, 176–187.

Bischof, N. (1978). On the phylogeny of human morality. In: G. Stent (Ed.), *Morality as a biological phenomenon*. Berlin, Germany: Abakon.

Bischof, N. (1985). *Das Rutzel Odipus*. Munich, Germany: Piper.

Bischof-Kohler, D. (1985). Zur phyogenese menschlicher motivation. In: L. H. Eckensberger & E. D. Lantermann (Eds), *Emotion und reflexivitut*. Vienna: Urban and Schwarzenberg.

Church, R. M., & Broadbent, H. A. (1990). Alternative representations of time, number, and rate. *Cognition*, *37*, 55–81.

Church, R. M., Meck, W. H., & Gibbon, J. (1994). Application of scalar timing theory to individual trials. *Journal of Experimental Psychology: Animal Behavior Processes*, *20*, 135–155.

Clayton, N. S., Dally, J., Gilbert, J., & Dickinson, A. (2005). Food caching by western scrub-jays (*Aphelocoma californica*) is sensitive to the conditions at recovery. *Journal of Experimental Psychology: Animal Behavior Processes*, *31*, 115–124.

Clayton, N. S., & Dickinson, A. (1998). What, where, and when: Episodic-like memory during cache recovery by scrub jays. *Nature*, *395*, 272–274.

Clayton, N. S., & Dickinson, A. (1999). Scrub jays (*Aphelocoma coerulescens*) remember the relative time of caching as well as the location and content of their caches. *Journal of Comparative Psychology*, *113*, 403–416.

Clayton, N. S., Yu, K. S., & Dickinson, A. (2001). Scrub jays (*Aphelocoma coerulescens*) form integrated memories of the multiple features of caching episodes. *Journal of Experimental Psychology: Animal Behavior Processes*, *27*, 17–29.

Correia, S. P. C., Dickinson, A., & Clayton, N. S. (2007). Western scrub-jays (*Aphelocoma californica*) anticipate future needs independently of their current motivational. *Current Biology*, *17*, 856–861.

Eichenbaum, H., Fortin, N. J., Ergorul, C., Wright, S. P., & Agster, K. L. (2005). Episodic recollection in animals: "If it walks like a duck and quacks like a duck...". *Learning and Motivation*, *36*, 190–207.

Emery, N. J., & Clayton, N. S. (2001). Effects of experience and social context on prospective caching strategies by scrub jays. *Nature*, *414*, 443–446.

Flaherty, C. F., & Checke, S. (1982). Anticipation of incentive gain. *Animal Learning and Behavior*, *10*, 177–182.

Fortin, N. J., Wright, S. P., & Eichenbaum, H. (2004). Recollection-like memory retrieval in rats is dependent on the hippocampus. *Nature*, *431*, 188–191.

Gilbert, D. (2006). *Stumbling on Happiness*. New York, NY: Knopf.

Griffiths, D., Dickinson, A., & Clayton, N. (1999). Episodic memory: What can animals remember about their past? *Trends in Cognitive Sciences*, *3*, 74–80.

Hampton, R. R., Hampstead, B. M., & Murray, E. A. (2005). Rhesus monkeys (*Macaca mulatta*) demonstrate robust memory for what and where, but not when, in an open-field test of memory. *Learning and Motivation*, *36*, 245–259.

Killeen, P. R., & Fetterman, J. G. (1993). A behavioral theory of timing. *Psychological Review*, *95*, 274–295.

Logue, A. W. (1988). Research on self-control: An integrating framework. *Behavioral and Brain Sciences*, *11*, 665–709.

Lucas, J. R., & Zielinski, D. L. (1998). Seasonal variation in the effect of cache pilferage on cache and body mass regulation in Carolina chickadees: What are the trade-offs? *Behavioral Ecology*, *9*, 193–200.

Mazur, J. E., & Logue, A. W. (1978). Choice in a "self-control" paradigm: Effects of a fading procedure. *Journal of Experimental Analysis of Behavior*, *30*, 11–17.

McKenzie, T., Cherman, T., Bird, L. R., Naqshbandi, M., & Roberts, W. A. (2004). Can squirrel monkeys (*Saimiri sciureus*) plan for the future? Studies of temporal myopia in food choice. *Learning and Behavior*, *32*, 377–390.

McKenzie, T. L. B., Bird, L. R., & Roberts, W. A. (2005). The effects of cache modification on food caching and retrieval by rats. *Learning and Motivation*, *36*, 260–278.

Mulcahy, N. J., & Call, J. (2006). Apes save tools for future use. *Science*, *312*, 1038–1040.

Naqshbandi, M., Feeney, M. C., McKenzie, T. L. B., & Roberts, W. A. (2007). Testing for episodic-like memory in rats in the absence of time of day cues: Replication of Babb and Crystal. *Behavioural Processes*, *74*, 217–225.

Naqshbandi, M., & Roberts, W. A. (2006). Anticipation of future events in squirrel monkeys (*Saimiri sciureus*) and rats (*Rattus norvegicus*): Tests of the Bischof-Kohler hypothesis. *Journal of Comparative Psychology*, *120*, 345–357.

Raby, C. R., Alexis, D. M., Dickinson, A., & Clayton, N. S. (2007). Planning for the future western scrub-jays. *Nature*, *445*, 919–921.

Roberts, W. A. (2002). Are animals stuck in time? *Psychological Bulletin*, *128*, 473–489.

Roberts, W. A. (2006). Animal memory: Episodic-like memory in rats. *Current Biology*, *16*, R601–R603.

Roberts, W. A., & Roberts, S. (2002). Two tests of the stuck-in-time hypothesis. *Journal of General Psychology*, *129*, 415–429.

Silberberg, A., Widholm, J. J., Bresler, D., Fujita, K., & Anderson, J. R. (1998). Natural choice in nonhuman primates. *Journal of Experimental Psychology: Animal Behavior Processes*, *24*, 215–228.

Staddon, J. E. R., Higa, J. J., & Chelaru, I. M. (1999). Time and memory: Towards a pacemaker-free theory of interval timing. *Journal of Experimental Analysis of Behavior*, *71*, 215–251.

Suddendorf, T., & Corballis, M. C. (1997). Mental time travel and the evolution of the human mind. *Genetic, Social, and General Psychology*, *123*, 133–167.

Suddendorf, T., & Corballis, M. C. (2007). The evolution of foresight: What is mental time travel and is it unique to humans? *Behavioral and Brain Sciences*, *30*, 299–313.

Timberlake, W., Gawley, D. J., & Lucas, G. A. (1987). Time horizons in rats foraging for food in temporally separated patches. *Journal of Experimental Psychology: Animal Behavior Processes*, *13*, 302–309.

Tobin, H., Chelonis, J. J., & Logue, A. W. (1993). Choice in self-control paradigms using rats. *The Psychological Record*, *43*, 441–454.

Tulving, E. (1972). Episodic and semantic memory. In: E. Tulving & W. Donaldson (Eds), *Organization of Memory*. San Diego, CA: Academic Press.

Tulving, E. (1983). *Elements of Episodic Memory*. Oxford, England: Clarendon Press.

Tulving, E. (1985). How many memory systems are there? *American Psychologist*, *40*, 385–398.

Vonnegut, K. (1969). *Slaughter-House Five*. New York, NY: Dell.

Zentall, T. R. (2005). Animals may not be stuck in time. *Learning and Motivation*, *36*, 208–225.

Zentall, T. R., Clement, T. S., Bhatt, R. S., & Allen, J. (2001). Episodic-like memory in pigeons. *Psychological Bulletin and Review*, *8*, 685–690.

Chapter 11

Developmental Perspectives on the Psychology of Time

William J. Friedman

> "What then is time? I know well enough what it is provided nobody asks me; but if I am asked and try to explain, I am baffled." (St. Augustine, 1961, p. 264)

St. Augustine's dilemma, familiar to anyone beginning to consider the nature of time, is rooted in large measure in the fact that a single word refers to may different things, including natural periodicities, temporal–causal relations, and the distinction between the past, present, and future. Even within psychology, the term *time perception* is often used to describe all of the perceptual and cognitive processes that contribute to our experience of time. But the experience of time is multifaceted, depending on many different processes to adapt to different temporal features of the environment. The multiplicity of temporal experience is perhaps most evident when one examines the development of children's adaptation to time. Different abilities emerge in early infancy, during childhood, during adolescence, and even later, making clear that our experience of time has many different parts.

This chapter was written to illustrate the diversity of humans' experience of time by providing examples of its components and the different ages at which they are found. It is also intended to provide a summary of the main findings from many of the approaches that developmental psychologists have taken. It is not a comprehensive review; the literature is too extensive in some areas for this to be practical in a single chapter. But many of the references can help the interested reader find additional sources in a particular area. In addition to summarizing findings, the concluding section provides some ideas about the reasons behind the developmental pattern.

The general perspective offered here is that the natural and social environments are rich in temporal information of various sorts and that the process of development is a matter of adapting to much of this information. Children experience a physical

Psychology of Time

DOI:10.1016/B978-0-08046-977-5.00011-9

world that includes temporal–causal relations, coincidences of sounds and sights, natural periodicities, and many other kinds of temporal information. The sociocultural environment is also replete with temporal information: names for particular times, cultural tools for measuring time and representing natural and conventional patterns, tense and other ways of representing times relative to the present, schedules and routines, and others. Indeed, an important part of socialization is training children to conform to the temporal expectations of their culture. Children must learn to internalize schedules, coordinate their activities with others, and prepare for events that will occur at specific times in the future. The distinction between time in nature and conventional time is of little importance to children. What does matter is their ability to adapt to these different types of information, thereby allowing them to function effectively in their environment.

11.1. Review of the Development of Temporal Abilities

11.1.1. Perception in Infancy

Children begin the task of adapting to time with a biological head-start: mechanisms that allow them to attend to some kinds of temporal information and retain this information for at least brief periods of time. Even in the first months of life, infants are sensitive to the temporal structure of the auditory and visual stimuli that they experience (Lewkowitz, 1989, 2000). For example, infants of less than 6 months of age can discriminate between different temporal groupings of tones and pauses — what adults would experience as different rhythmic patterns (e.g., Demany, McKenzie, & Vurpillot (1977); Morrongiello, 1984). Researchers have also studied the ability to remember the sequence in which discrete events occur. Gulya, Galluccio, Wilk, and Rovee-Collier (2001) found that 3- and 6-month-old infants can remember something about the sequence in which they had interacted with particular mobiles a day earlier: A mobile was more likely to be recognized if they received its predecessor as a reminder. Lewkowitz (2004) demonstrated that 4- and 8-month-old infants who were habituated to the sight and sound of three different objects falling and striking a surface (e.g., in the order ABC) subsequently looked longer at displays in which the order had been changed (CAB). Even younger infants are sensitive to the order in which words are spoken in a sentence: 2-month-olds discriminate the sound of "cats would jump benches" from "cats jump wood benches" (Mandel, Nelson, & Jusczyk, 1996). Another kind of temporal information to which young infants are sensitive is the synchrony of sensations. Lewkowitz (2000) reviewed evidence demonstrating that this sensitivity is present from the first months of life, and he discussed the role that it might play in infants learning to make connections between different sensory modalities, such as vision and audition.

There is also evidence concerning infants' sensitivity to another kind of temporal regularity, one that adults usually take for granted. Many of the events that we witness day to day, such as an object falling or a cookie being broken into pieces, are temporally unidirectional. (Films of these events would seem anomalous if played in reverse.) These examples of perceptual "arrows of time" (Friedman, 2002a, 2003a) show that adults have mental representations of a variety of temporal–causal regularities. Studies of infants' looking times to videotapes of such events indicate that they respond differently to forward and backward versions of a number of gravity events by 8 months of age. Sensitivity to the temporal–causal information in separation events such as a breaking cookie apparently emerges at some as-yet-unknown time between 12 months and 3(1/2) years (Friedman, 2003a, c). It appears that humans only gradually learn about the temporal structure in the world, even on the very brief time scale of a few seconds.

Other evidence bearing on humans' sensitivity to temporal information is found in the literature on causal perception (Cohen & Oakes, 1993; Leslie, 1984; Leslie & Keeble, 1987; Oakes, 1994; Oakes & Cohen, 1990, 1995). For example, Leslie (1984; Leslie & Keeble, 1987) showed infants of about 6–8 months of age films of simple causal and noncausal events (such as a moving square that appeared to collide with and "launch" another square, on the one hand, or launching taking place without collision, on the other). After the infants habituated to one of the films, they were shown the same film in reverse. Leslie found greater recovery from habituation when the reversal was of a direct launch than when it was of a delayed launch. The results of studies like this one show the early ability to discriminate between dynamic stimuli that differ in how they unfold over time.

11.1.2. The Perception and Measurement of Duration

11.1.2.1. Time perception From early infancy humans are also sensitive to the durations of events (at least when those durations are about 5 s or less), showing the presence of biological mechanisms that permit measurement of durations on these scales. Colombo and Richman (2002) presented 4-month-olds with eight alternating periods of light and dark visual fields. The light fields were 2 s in duration, and the dark fields were 3 s for some infants and 5 s for others. On the ninth trial, the light field did not come on. Measurements of the infants' heart rate revealed that they noticed the "missing" field within about one-half second; their heart rates began decelerating just after 3 or 5 s of the dark field. This allowed the researchers to conclude that the infants had developed rather precise temporally based expectations.

The presence of the early ability to form temporally based expectations should not be surprising in light of an extensive literature showing that animals can measure the lengths of intervals (see, e.g., Meck, 2003). The well-developed theories and techniques in the animal literature have provided the framework for some of the most sensitive tests of humans' capacity to measure amounts of time in early childhood and later. One of the techniques, called temporal bisection (see Chapter 2), involves training children to press one button for the briefer of two stimuli (e.g., 1 s) and another for the longer of the two (e.g., 4 s). During the test phase, they are presented with the durations on which they were trained and a number of durations in between (e.g., 1.5, 2, 2.5, 3, and 3.5 s) and asked to make the same long-or-short choice. Using this method, children as young as 3- to 5-year-olds have proved able to make the discrimination and to produce data roughly similar to those obtained in studies of animals and adult humans: The number of "long" responses increases systematically as test durations grow longer (Droit-Volet, 2003; McCormack, Brown, Maylor, Darby, & Green, 1999). Young children's judgments are not as differentiated as those of 8- or 10-year-olds', apparently because younger children produce more random responses and they have greater difficulty remembering the standard durations (Droit-Volet, 2003). However, despite their lower levels of sensitivity, young children's performance can be well described by the same theoretical models that successfully explain the performance of animals and adults, models that assume the existence of biological clocks.

In addition to the presence of biological clocks, developmental studies show that children experience some of the same illusions of time perception as adults do. For example, when we are engrossed in a task, a given interval of time seems to pass more rapidly than when we have little to do or to think about. By about 8 years of age, children are susceptible to some of the same illusions (Arlin, 1986; Zakay, 1992, 1993). In one of these studies, children who were asked to fill in dotted lines that make up geometric figures produced shorter estimates of 30- and 120-s intervals than those who had no task to perform (Zakay, 1993). Expecting a prize at the end of 30- and 120-s intervals makes them seem longer than if no prize is expected (Zakay, 1993), whereas distraction leads to shorter judgments of 3- to 10-s intervals (Zakay, 1992).

These findings can all be explained by attentional models of time perception (e.g., Zakay, 1989), which assume the division of attention between temporally related information (e.g., number of thoughts or external events or the output of an internal timer) and nontemporal information (e.g., the shapes of the geometric figures). When considerable attention is devoted to the nontemporal information, less is devoted to correlates of the passage of time, resulting in shorter time judgments (see Chapters 4 and 12). Clearly, cognitive factors, in addition to biological timekeepers, influence children's (and adults') experience of duration. The biological timers may be especially important when repeated events have a clear onset and end and are of a constant duration. In other situations, cognitive processes may be more important in determining our impressions of amounts of time.

Although it has not been studied, other cognitive factors probably make young children's temporal experience quite different from adults'. Adults' ability to cope with a boring or unpleasant situation depends in part on their understanding of what is happening and the amount of time they will probably have to wait until it is over. Young children who do not understand what is happening or the reasons for the wait — and who lack an understanding of time measurement, the next topic — are likely to experience the same interval as being interminable.

Studies of time perception in children involve the perception of brief intervals, typically 10 s or less. But there is evidence that children learn and remember information about the durations of much longer events in their everyday lives. In one study (Friedman, 1990), children were taught to use a drawing (a line with a small sandglass at one end and a large one at the other) to indicate different amounts of time. The tester used labels such a "very short" and "very long" to label points on the continuum and then asked the children to use the representation to judge the durations of a number of familiar activities. By 4 years of age, mean judgments were perfectly rank-ordered according to the true durations of the five events. For example, 4-year-old and older children judged drinking a glass of milk as taking less time than watching a cartoon show and a cartoon show as taking less time than sleeping at night. These results indicate that young children have formed mental representations of familiar events that contain information about their durations.

11.1.2.2. Measurement Whenever measurement of time is possible, adults subordinate their impressions of an interval of time to its measured length (for which reason they are prevented from consulting watches or clocks in studies of time perception). Piaget (1969) found that this is not true of children younger than about 7 or 8 years, who believe that the lengths of two intervals that are shown to be equal (e.g., by measuring them with a stopwatch) differ if one is filled with actions performed at a rapid pace and the other with slower actions (see Levin, 1992, for a discussion of this and related research). In addition, few children younger than about 7 or 8 years spontaneously count in order to measure durations in time-perception tasks (Espinoza-Fernádez, Vacas, García-Viedma, García-Gutiérez, & Colmenero, 2004; Wilkening, Levin, & Druyan, 1987). But children as young as 5-year-olds will count in these tasks if a metronome is provided (Wilkening et al., 1987) or if they are instructed to count (Clément & Droit-Volet, 2006). It appears that the basic idea that time is measurable develops before children understand that measurement supersedes other sources of information about the interval (such as the number of events that occurred).

11.1.3. Event Representations

We saw earlier that young infants detect a change in the order in which three objects appear to drop onto a surface and make a sound. Researchers have used another method, imitation of actions, to study the development of memory for the temporal sequence of more complex events — and over longer retention intervals — during infancy and early childhood (e.g., Barr & Hayne, 1996; Bauer & Mandler, 1989, 1992; Bauer & Thal, 1990). In this method, infants and young children are shown demonstrations ranging from two to eight actions in a particular order. For example, they might witness the unfamiliar sequence of an adult putting a crosspiece on a supporting stand, hanging a piece of metal from the crosspiece, and hitting the metal with a mallet. The ability to reproduce acts in the modeled order has been assessed after various retention intervals. In a summary of her research using this method, Bauer (1996) concluded that 11-month-olds are very accurate in their immediate imitation of two-event sequences, and progressively longer sequences can be reproduced through 30 months of age. By 13 months of age, infants show impressive recall over very long retention intervals: 13-month-olds who have seen event sequences modeled twice in 2 weeks show significant recall of the order of the events 8 months later. These studies show that by about 1 year of age, infants have the ability to form representations of brief, novel events — representations that incorporate much of the temporal information in the events and that are preserved over long periods of time.

By 3 years of age, and probably earlier, children can use these abilities to learn about the order of events that unfold over even longer periods of time. Nelson and her colleagues (1986, and see Hudson, Fivush, & Kuebli, 1992) have interviewed young children about familiar events, such as having lunch, baking cookies, or eating in a restaurant. Using prompts such as "What happens when…?" they have found that even 3- and 4-year-olds can describe these events in ways that preserve much of the true order of their constituents. For example, many 4-year-olds can explain what happens when you make cookies (e.g., you put chocolate chips in the dough, place the cookies in the oven, take them out, put the cookies on the table, and then eat them). Young children's descriptions show that they possess representations of familiar events that preserve much of the temporal order of the events. The fact that they describe the events using the timeless present (e.g., "You put them in the oven…") shows that they are referring to general events, not a specific occurrence.

11.1.4. The Representation of Transformations in Early Childhood

Children's knowledge about the temporal organization of familiar events continues to develop in the years after infancy. By 3 to 4 years of age, they are aware of what happens when a variety of familiar transformations (including wetting, melting, breaking, and cutting) take place (Das Gupta & Bryant, 1989; Gelman, Bullock, & Meck, 1980; Goswami and Brown, 1989). For example, when shown an initial state (e.g., a whole apple) and a mediator (a knife), they can select a picture representing the correct end-state (a cut apple) from a number of alternatives (Gelman et al., 1980). Another study focused on sensitivity to a particular subset of arrows of time, ones involving increases in entropy (Friedman, 2001). Three- through eleven-year-old children were asked to judge whether randomizing forces, such as the wind blowing on plastic utensils and paper plates, could make a neat set disordered or, on other problems, a disordered set neat. By 4 to 5 years of age, children showed an awareness that increasing disorder is more likely than increasing order in the face of such forces. Finally, research indicates that young children understand that physical causes precede their effects (Bullock, Gelman, & Baillargeon, 1982; Shultz, 1982).

Another set of studies, on children's biological concepts, shows that by early childhood there is an understanding that growth is progressive and that this property is specific to living things (e.g., Inagaki & Hatano, 1996; Rosengren, Gelman, Kalish, & McCormick, 1991). Young children also know that animals grow larger but not smaller (Rosengren, Kalish, Hickling, & Gelman, 1994). In both cases children reveal knowledge about processes that occur on very long time scales, ones that cannot be continuously observed. (See Montangero & Pownall, 1996, for research on older children's conceptualizations of changes on long time scales.)

11.1.5. The Past and the Future

Adults have a compelling sense of where they are in time and of when particular past and future events have occurred or are expected to occur. Although the past–present–future distinction appears to most adults to be a basic feature of the real world, Nelson (1996) has argued that it is a social construction, one which children must learn. Developmental research shows that the distinction takes years to master, supporting her view (Friedman, 2003b, 2005).

Language measures. One approach to studying children's acquisition of the past–present–future distinction is to examine their production and comprehension of words referring to these categories. Studies of children's spontaneous productions indicate that by the second or third year of life, they refer to events that actually occurred in the past or will occur in the future (Harner, 1982a; Nelson, 1996; Sachs, 1983; Weist, 1989). Two- and three-year-old children begin marking these temporal categories through the use of tense and later use temporal adverbs, such as *yesterday*, *last night*, or *this afternoon*. However, when children of this age first produce these forms, they are seldom used correctly, and errors may persist for several years (Nelson, 2001).

In other studies children's competence was assessed by directing children's attention to past and future events (e.g., some actions that were completed and others that were impending) and eliciting descriptions from the children. Depending on the particular language, correct tense use has been found in many or most children by 2(1/2) to 3(1/2) years of age (Harner, 1981; Weist, Wysocka, Witkowska-Stadnik, Buczowska, & Konieczna, 1984). These studies show that children of these ages can distinguish actions that have just occurred from ones that are expected to occur in the immediate future.

A third method involves measuring children's comprehension of words that refer to past and future times (Harner, 1975, 1976, 1980, 1982b; Weist, 1983), using the terms *before* and *after*, and *yesterday* and *tomorrow*. These studies show that 3-year-olds' performance sometimes exceeds levels that would be expected by chance, and 4-year-olds are very accurate. When future forms are used to refer to the immediate future, they are understood at earlier ages than when the forms refer to the next day. However, past forms are about equally well understood when referring to the immediate past and the preceding day.

Together, the studies using language measures show that young children link linguistic markers of pastness and futurity to times that adults consider to be past and future. But the use of very supportive contexts and brief time scales in these studies means that we cannot generalize the findings to children's ability to discriminate the past–future status of everyday events (Friedman, 2003b).

Differentiation within the past. Other researchers have been interested in children's ability to differentiate the times of events within the past and within the future (Friedman, 2003b). When adults try to remember when past events occurred, they rely on several kinds of information, including when in some time pattern the event occurred (called *location* information) and how long ago the event occurred (called *distance* information) (Friedman, 1993, 1996, 2001b). Research suggests that the main way of remembering locations is to reconstruct when the event must have occurred by relating what is remembered about it to general knowledge of personal, natural, and conventional time patterns. To a more limited extent, adults are also able to use direct impressions of the ages of memories (distance information) to discriminate their times.

Children as young as 4 years of age can link past events to temporal locations, but this does not imply that they share adults' understanding of when the locations occurred. In one study children from 4 to 9 years of age were asked to report something that happened yesterday, last weekend, last summer, and on a number of holidays from the past year (Friedman, 1992). The results showed that even 4- and 5-year-olds could retrieve memories of events that had taken place at many of these temporal locations, often recounting content that was specific to the most recent occurrence of a given time. However, throughout the age range, children had difficulty judging which of a pair of times (e.g., their birthday or Easter) was a longer time ago. It appears that locations are initially like "islands of time" and that only at later ages are children able to use representations of annual time patterns to relate the times of events on such long time scales.

But 4-year-olds are able to use their general knowledge of parts of the day to reconstruct when a particular event must have happened. In one study (Friedman, 1991), 4- to 8-year-olds were asked to remember the time of an event that had happened 7 weeks earlier. They responded by pointing to positions in a row of cards representing the seasons and a row representing the daily activities: waking, eating lunch, eating dinner, and going to bed. Only older children were accurate on the season scale, but 95% of 4-year-olds indicated that the event had happened in the morning (the time that their nursery class met). The ability to reconstruct locations appears to be limited by semantic knowledge about time patterns, knowledge that changes substantially from early to middle childhood.

Other findings show that children as young as 4-year-olds are able to use impressions of the ages of memories (a kind of distance information) to judge the times of past events with some accuracy. Children of this age can judge which of two distinctive events was more recent, one that had occurred 1 week before testing or one that had occurred 7 weeks before the test session (Friedman, 1991). In another study (Friedman, Garner, & Zubin, 1995; and see Friedman & Kemp, 1998), children from 3 to 12 years of age were asked to compare the recency of their birthday and Christmas. This problem is trivially easy for adults, who can use their mental representations of the months of the year (see Section 11.1.7). In contrast, errors were common in children as old as 9-year-olds, again demonstrating that the ability to use representations of annual time patterns to relate the times of events develops in late middle childhood. However, even children less than 6 years of age could answer correctly when one of the events had occurred within the preceding few months and the other had happened much longer ago. Under limited circumstances (when the temporal distance of the nearer of two events to be compared is a small ratio of the distance of the farther event), preschool-age children can use distance information to differentiate the times of past events.

Differentiation of the times of future events. A number of researchers have investigated young children's ability to delay gratification or to plan future activities (e.g., Hudson, Shapiro, & Sosa, 1995; Thompson, Barresi, & Moore, 1997), but little is known about children's understanding of the times of future events beyond the next day or so. A series of studies using spatial representation of the future provides information about the development of a differentiated sense of the future on longer time scales. In these studies children judged the future distances of events by pointing to places on a picture of a road that begins near the viewer and recedes towards distant mountains. In one study 4-, 7-, and 10-year-old children judged the future distances of a daily event, a day of the week, and several annual events by pointing to a spot on the road and by responding to questions such as "How long is it until...?" (Friedman, 2000). The results showed that 4-year-olds produced largely undifferentiated judgments on both the road task and on the verbal tasks. However, about half of 4-year-olds correctly responded that a holiday was coming soon if it actually was within about the next 2 months, and many children of this age correctly judged that other events would not happen for a long time. Probably these young children are retrieving from memory propositions that they have heard from parents and teachers that some events are near and some are distant. Seven-year-olds showed some ability to differentiate future distances of this set of events, apparently by distinguishing two categories of near and far events. Ten-year-olds produced very accurate judgments throughout the range of times, and they used conventional units in answering the verbal questions. A follow-up study of judgments of annual events showed changes within the 4- to 6-year age range: 4-year-olds again failed to distinguish the future distances, 5-year-olds distinguished two categories of near and far events, and 6-year-olds distinguished three categories.

Although one might think that a differentiated sense of the future is a monolithic achievement, findings show that children learn to differentiate future times separately for the parts of the day, days of the week, and parts of the year and that different processes are used for different contents. In the previous study, many 7-year-olds had only a few future-distance categories on the scale of the year but could tell the exact number of days until the weekend. This shows that representations of days of the week could be used before representations of the months. In another set of studies (Friedman, 2002b, 2003b), children judged the future distances of daily events, such as lunch and going to bed. It was found that many 4- and 5-year-olds can differentiate future distances within the day. Interestingly, two problems are common in this age range but diminish over the next several years. First, many children have difficulty adopting the present, rather than the start of the day, as the reference point. Second, many judge the immediately preceding event, breakfast to lie in the near future. Another study showed that those 6- to 8-year-olds who adopted the present as their reference point for judging parts of the day made more differentiated judgments on this time scale than in judging the future distances of annual events. From about 4 to 8 years of age, children appear to judge the future times of the daily events using mental representations of times within the day, whereas they rely on propositions (e.g., "soon," "not for a long time") to distinguish the future distances of annual events.

Past–future confusion. The tendency that many 4-year-olds show to judge a recent event, breakfast, as coming soon is similar to an error that appears when young children judge the past or future distance of annual events (Friedman, 2003b). For example, many children less than 6 years of age responded that their birthday was more recent than Christmas when it was actually longer ago than the holiday but would happen within the next few months (Friedman et al., 1995). Similarly, many 5-year-olds judged Valentine's Day to be coming soon when they were tested shortly after the holiday (Friedman, 2000). Confusion regarding the past–future status of events has also been found when children are given a clear choice between the two. In several studies (Friedman, 2003b), children of about 4 to 5 years of age were shown a horizontal road, with a car half way across it and trained to point to the side behind the car for past times such as *yesterday* and to point ahead of the car for times such as *tomorrow*. When tested about a week before Valentine's Day, 80% correctly pointed to the side representing the future. But about a week after the holiday, only 60% pointed to the side representing the past. In the morning at school, children also had difficulty judging the past–future status of the daily activity breakfast, although they were quite accurate in assigning lunch to the future.

These examples of past–future confusion could stem from the fact that with cyclic content, where events belong to both the past and the future, both answers are actually correct. In another study 4- and 6-year-olds made the same type of judgment for a series of noncyclic events: unusual or unique events that their parents had said had occurred at each of several distances in the past or would occur at each of those distances in the future (Friedman, 2003b). Even the 4-year-olds performed at levels beyond chance expectations, but their accuracy was rather poor: 0.64 correct for the past events and 0.67 correct for the future events. (The values for 6-year-olds were 0.88 and 0.84.) There is some evidence that the changes that take place between 4 and 6 years are related to a growing conceptual understanding of the ways that the past and future relate to the present (Friedman, 2003b). Progress in overcoming past–future confusion also probably follows from the development of increasingly flexible representations of time patterns, such as the parts of the day and times of the year (see Section 11.1.7).

11.1.6. Reasoning about Succession, Simultaneity, and Duration

Other important developmental achievements concern children's ability to draw logical conclusions from information about the order and durations of events. Studies have shown that children understand terms expressing succession and simultaneity by about 4 years of age (Blewitt, 1982), suggesting that these are salient concepts by early childhood. We have also seen that 3-year-olds can discriminate brief durations, and 4-year-olds are aware that different events take different amounts of time. A considerable body of research, much of it inspired by Piaget's (1969) work on the topic, has focused on the development of the ability to reason about these types of information.

Drawing conclusions from the order of two past events. Evidence reviewed in an earlier section shows that even young children represent the order of some causal transformations and are aware that an event can be the consequence of something that happened before but not after it. But some researchers have questioned whether young children have a similar understanding that the order of past events can tell us what information is likely to be current (McCormack & Hoerl, 2005; Povinelli, Landry, Theall, Clark, & Castille, 1999). For example, if an object was recently placed in location A and then moved to location B, it is more likely to be in location B now. When they directly observe such events, very young children can solve this sort of problem by successively updating their knowledge of the location of the object. But if the order information is presented in a more abstract way (e.g., *telling* children the order in which things took place), children in the early preschool years are unable to reason from this information. Using quite different methods, Povinelli et al. (1999) and McCormack and Hoerl (2005) found that children younger than 5 years were unable to reason about the relation between the order in which recent events took place and what the current state must be. Five-year-olds are able to solve such problems.

Reasoning about the relations between duration and succession, distance, and speed. If two runners begin a race at the same time, and one crosses the finish line before the other, adults can infer that the one who came in second ran for more time and ran at a slower speed. The development of the ability to make such inferences was investigated in an ingenious series of studies by Piaget (1969). Most of his methods involved presenting preschool and school-age children with two toys that moved at different speeds and asking them to make temporal comparisons between the events. Piaget found that prior to about 7 years of age children asked to judge the successions and durations of events were usually misled by distance and/or speed information. For example, if shown two toy snails that started and stopped at the same time but moved at different speeds, young children often concluded that the one that went faster (and covered more distance and ended up farther along the table) also moved for a greater amount of time. From these studies Piaget (1969) concluded that young children's understanding of time differs from adults' in a number of respects. First, young children fail to understand that time passes uniformly in different places (and for successive motions; see Section 11.1.2). Second, they are unable to use the logical relations between succession and duration that allow adults to solve the problem of the two runners. Third, they fail to properly separate temporal information (about succession and duration) from information about space and speed. Piaget believed that all of these limitations are overcome as children progress into his stage of concrete operations, at about 7 or 8 years.

Researchers who have used other methods have been able to provide a detailed description of many of the component abilities (see Levin, 1992, for a review).

They have also found that some important abilities are present by early childhood but that others are not predominant until adolescence, if ever. The relevant developments have come to appear more gradual and piecemeal than Piaget theorized them to be.

By 5 years of age, children can correctly compare two durations using information about succession *if* they do not have to deal with differences in spatial displacements of the two objects. Levin (1977) presented children with tasks involving the durations that two dolls slept. The dolls went to bed and woke up at the same time, went to bed simultaneously but woke successively, or went to bed successively and woke up simultaneously. She also presented logically identical problems involving two moving objects (as in Piaget's tasks). Levin found that the youngest children, 5-year-olds, were accurate in comparing durations in the sleeping-doll task, but they failed the task with moving objects. In fact, even at third grade, most children thought that a car that travels farther takes more time, even when information about succession and simultaneity leads to a different conclusion. Another type of integration of succession and duration remains difficult until about seventh grade: If object A begins and stops moving before object B by the same amount of time, the durations are equal (Levin, 1992).

Many of the errors that Piaget and later researchers found stem from confusing temporal information (such as start and stop times or duration) with spatial information (such as the locations where an object started and stopped or the distance it traversed) or from confusing duration with speed (Levin, 1992). A number of researchers have systematically investigated the development of children's understanding of the relations between duration, distance, and speed, (see Levin, 1992, for a review). This development can be illustrated by a study by Matsuda (2001). In her study children from about 4 to 11 years of age were asked to predict the duration, speed, or distance that a train would move when provided with information about a second dimension (and told that the third dimension is held constant). There were three distances, three speeds, and three amounts of time the train could move. To illustrate one of the six problem types, children were told which of the three speeds the train would move and then asked which of three buttons, each producing a different duration of motion (and a whistle blowing for the corresponding duration), should be pressed to get the train to the farthest station. This method allowed Matsuda to assess children's understanding of the physical relations between the three dimensions: (1) when speed is held constant, greater duration is associated with greater distance (as in the example), (2) when duration is held constant, greater speed is associated with greater distance, and (3) when distance is held constant, greater speed is associated with a shorter duration. The first two relations are direct and the third is an inverse one, and this distinction was important in understanding the results.

Matsuda (2001) found that children as young as 4-year-olds make judgments concordant with the first two direct relations (between duration and distance and between distance and speed). Four-year-olds' success with these two relations may stem from a general tendency to link more of any one dimension with more of any other: Children of this age also think that longer durations are associated with more sounds or pictures in an interval or brighter or larger light bulbs (Levin, 1992).

But this "more-is-more" tendency leads to problems with the inverse relation: 4- and 5-year-olds in Matsuda's study incorrectly linked longer durations with faster speeds when distance was held constant. In the following years, between 5 and 8, she found large gains in children's application of the inverse relation between duration and speed. Interestingly, it was not until about 11 years that about half of children referred to the third dimension (the one that was held constant) in explaining their answers to particular problems, leading Matsuda to conclude that it is not until this age (or later) that an integrated understanding of the relations between the three dimensions is achieved. Other studies, using more complex displays with pairs of motions (as in Piaget's tasks), have found confusion between duration and spatial cues well into adolescence, and they have revealed that a quantitative understanding of the relation between duration, distance and speed (e.g., speed = distance/time) eludes even most adolescents (Levin, 1992).

It is apparent from these findings that children's understanding of the relations between duration and succession and between duration, speed, and distance develop over a considerable period of time. By 4 years of age, children correctly expect longer durations to be associated with more distance covered. By 5 years they are able to correctly compare the durations of nonspatial events (such as dolls going to bed and waking) using information about the succession or simultaneity of the starts and endings of the modeled actions. But young children's duration judgments are incorrectly influenced by spatial information (e.g., endpoint or distance covered) and by speed and other quantities. Although considerable progress is seen from early to middle childhood in understanding the relation between speed and duration in relatively simple problems (e.g., Matsuda, 2001), the fragility of these concepts through adolescence is shown by the fact that duration judgments are often swamped by endpoints and speed in more complex displays involving two motions.

11.1.7. Representations of Time Patterns

We have seen that by 3 years of age, children possess representations of familiar activities, such as baking cookies, which incorporate information about the order in which the component actions unfold. Adults, of course, know about much longer time patterns, from daily to annual cycles and even longer temporal regularities. Developing representations of such patterns, which far exceed spans of time that allow continuous attending, would seem to present a formidable challenge, and indeed the development extends from early childhood through adolescence (Friedman, 2005).

The pattern of daily activities and the clock. By 4 to 5 years of age, children not only know about the order of events that transpire over several hours at nursery school (Friedman & Brudos, 1988) but are able to place in order a set of cards representing main events from the waking day (e.g., waking, lunch, dinner, and going to bed at night) (Friedman, 1977, 1990). By 6 years children possess sufficiently flexible representations of the pattern of daily activities that they are able to think about the *backward* order of these events (e.g., if it's dinner time, which was more recent, lunch or waking?) (Friedman, 1990). These representations probably develop at such an early age because 4-year-olds are likely to have thought about where they are within the day hundreds of times.

Although discussions with parents and teachers about past and upcoming activities must also play a role in the development of representations of daily activities, children do not need formal tuition to learn about the order of daily activities. In contrast, conventional time patterns require systematic instruction (Nelson, 1996). Learning about one such cultural tool, the clock, is a protracted process. Seven-year-olds bring to the task some knowledge of the times at which particular activities usually take place, but it is only in the following years that children learn to read the full range of times on analog clocks, and performing some operations (e.g., adding 30 min to the time 4:23) remains difficult through 11 years of age (Friedman & Laycock, 1989).

Longer time patterns. During the elementary-school years, adults also expect children to learn about the days of the week, seasons, and months of the year. Most 6- and 7-year-olds in the populations that have been studied can correctly order a set of cards representing the seasons (Friedman, 1977), and 7- and 8-year-olds, respectively, can recite the days of the week and months in order (Friedman, 1986). But the ability to recite the days and months does not mean that children are able to think flexibly about relative times of occurrence within the week and the year. Only in mid-adolescence does it become possible to solve backward-order problems similar to those that 6-year-olds can solve for daily activities (e.g., "If it's Saturday and you go backward in time, which will you come to first, Thursday or Tuesday?"). A number of findings indicate that adolescents develop mental images of the days of the week and months of the year that allow them greater flexibility in detecting relations between the days or months than the verbal-list representations they initially acquire (Friedman, 1986).

The developmental pattern is different when children learn calendar systems that number the days and months instead of assigning them nonnumerical names. In China, the names of the days of the week (except Sunday) include numbers, as do the names of the months. Kelly, Miller, Feng, and Feng (1999) conducted a study with Chinese and American second and fourth graders and adults to determine whether the presence of numbers in names for times leads to the use of different strategies than that were found in Friedman's (1986) study. Participants were asked to name the day or month that is a particular number of units before or after a stimulus day or month. The results showed that although some Chinese second and fourth graders used the verbal-list process that predominates at these ages in American children — activating and counting each intervening day or month — most used calculation strategies. For example, if the task was to find the month that is seven months after January, they would add seven to one to arrive at month eight as the answer. The availability of numerical names led to faster and more accurate responses by the Chinese than the American children. These findings show that the tools a culture provides to structure time have a strong influence on the representations and processes that children use to adapt to these time patterns.

In addition to mastering the main features of the calendar, adolescents also understand the ages at which some major life events usually take place (Nurmi, 1989, 1991; Nurmi, Poole, & Kalakoski, 1994). For example, when asked to report their hopes and dreams and then to judge the ages at which they expected them to be realized, adolescents chose ages in their 20s that reflected the normative sequence of finishing one's education, getting a job, and getting married. (Interestingly, hardly any adolescents expressed hopes that they expected to attain after age 30.) Although we do not know the nature of the underlying representations, it is clear that adolescents are able to think about times of life over about the next decade.

11.2. Understanding the Developmental Pattern

The variety of topics discussed in this chapter shows that children's adaptation to time involves a wide range of abilities, from perception of the durations and order of very brief events to the representation of annual cycles and even the lifespan. St. Augustine's question cannot be answered in a simple way, because time never becomes an integrated concept. From a psychological point of view, time is many different things: sequences of events; natural and conventional time patterns; the distinction between the past, present, and future; and relations between duration and succession, speed, and distance; to name only a few (see Chapter 1). We have also seen that the process of adaptation to temporal features of the natural and cultural environments is a protracted one, with some abilities present in early infancy and others emerging in adolescence or later.

Despite the paucity of relevant evidence, it may be worth sketching some ideas about why particular temporal abilities appear when they do. I will propose a distinction between psychological mechanisms that have been shaped by evolution to process temporal information and other more general-purpose cognitive processes that children learn to apply to time.

11.2.1. Biologically Based Temporal Abilities

A number of the temporal abilities that appear early in human development are also found in other species, and they probably depend on specific biological mechanisms. One is the ability to develop expectations about the lengths of brief, repeated durations. In the section on time perception, we saw that infants and young children form representations of durations on the order of several seconds, representations that influence infants' visual expectancies and that young children can use to make explicit judgments. It was also noted that there is an extensive literature showing similar timing abilities in other animals. In the animal literature, these abilities have been attributed to special biological mechanisms that measure intervals and retain the measurements. It seems very likely that the same mechanisms are operational early in human development.

We also saw that infants and young children attend to the order of brief events, such as sequences of words, audiovisual displays of objects falling, and sequences of modeled actions. Recent research has shown that rats are also to remember the order of brief experiences, in their case the sequence of a series of odors (Eichenbaum, Fortin, Ergorul, Wright, & Agster, 2005). Humans' sensitivity to the order of auditory stimuli may be rooted in mechanisms adapted to the processing of linguistic input, but the capacity to represent the sequences of actions and other visual events may rely on separate order-encoding mechanisms, perhaps ones related to those that allows rats to remember the order of a sequence of odors.

A third ability, found at least by early childhood, was described in the section on children's differentiation of the past: the capacity to discriminate the ages of events on the order of days to months in the past (called distance information). Studies with a bird species, scrub jays (e.g., Clayton & Dickinson, 1998; De Kort, Dickinson, & Clayton, 2005), have revealed what may be a related ability. Clayton and her colleagues have found that jays can discriminate between different ages of events (e.g., ones that happened 4 h versus 5 days earlier), the hiding of particular foods. It seems unlikely that humans' and jays' abilities to discriminate ages on these long time scales depend on the same interval-timing mechanisms that underlie perception of durations on the order of seconds. We do not yet know what brain processes create information about the ages of memories, but it may be that humans' and jays' discriminations on these long time scales rely on similar neural mechanisms (Friedman, 2007).

11.2.2. General Cognitive Mechanisms Applied to Time

11.2.2.1. Representations and processes Nontemporal cognition depends on a rich array of cognitive, linguistic and other processes, and many of these same processes are used to adapt to temporal features of the environment. Included in this category are the representation of word meanings (and semantic memory in general), episodic memory, and imagery. The ages at which these processes are applied to time probably depend on the intrinsic development of the processes themselves, social influences, and individuals' histories of temporal problem solving.

By early childhood linguistic and semantic-memory processes enable children to begin to acquire temporal adverbs (e.g., *tomorrow*, *last night*) and to learn basic facts about time (e.g., that summer is hot). Young children also can retain for days or weeks adults' statements about which events are coming soon and which will not occur for a long time (e.g., that their birthday is coming soon, or that Christmas is not for a long time), contributing to an early, partially differentiated sense of the future. Of course, these same representations and processes underlie the acquisition of new information throughout later development (e.g., the number of months in the year, the meaning of *Daylight Savings Time*). Furthermore, the meanings of particular words change over time: They become freed from the particular contexts in which they were first acquired and often become linked to representations of time patterns. A child might learn early that Sunday is pancake day but only later develop representations of the days of the week that allow her or him to understand when Sunday occurs relative to other days.

A different language-related ability is also applied to different contents at different ages. Through repeated practice humans can memorize long word sequences. When parents and teachers encourage such practice, even young children learn ordered strings of many words, such as counting numbers and letters of the alphabet. Although the same basic abilities apply, children in Western societies do not usually learn the order of the days of the week and months of the year until middle childhood. The capacity is present by early childhood, but the timing of direct teaching determines the ages at which these verbal-list processes are applied to particular temporal contents.

Another basic cognitive process is mental imagery. As we have seen, children appear to use imagery to represent the relative times of occurrence of main daily activities by about 5 years. But it is not until about 15 years of age that we find evidence for the use of images of the relative times of the days of the week and of the months of the year. Here, there is no reason to think that direct teaching is responsible for the developmental pattern, because most children are probably not taught to represent the parts of a day, days of the week, and months in this way. The ages at which imagery emerges for these contents may be better explained by individual children's history of mental operations and the form of mental representation — imagery — that best captures the structure of the content (Friedman, 1986, 1989, 1990). As noted earlier, temporal orientation within the day probably occurs hundreds of times in early childhood. In contrast, it is not until much later that a similar number of instances of orientation within the week and year are likely to have been accumulated. Adults' repeated requests that children recite the days of the week and months may even delay the development of more flexible, image representations. Imagery may eventually prevail for many kinds of temporal problem solving because of its advantage in capturing information about the relative times of occurrence of the elements of temporal patterns. In general, individuals' representations and processes seem to develop towards forms that are effective in solving repeatedly encountered problems.

A variety of general attentional and memory processes also contribute to humans' adaptation to time (see Chapters 4 and 12). Impressions of amounts of time are available to children by early childhood, as seen in 4-year-olds' ability to judge the duration of familiar events. Studies of duration perception show that at least by 8 years of age, impressions of durations are influenced by manipulations that affect attention, supporting the conclusion that attention to internal and external changes provides children with information about amounts of time. Another example is that the processes underlying episodic memory provide children, like adults, with some of the raw materials they need to reconstruct the times of remembered events. Children as young as 4-year-olds can begin to use their memories of the contents of events (e.g., where they occurred) to infer in what part of the day they happened, and older children can use memory for context to reconstruct times on longer time scales. Here, the developmental timing seems to be influenced by age changes in children's semantic knowledge about time (Friedman & Lyon, 2005).

11.2.2.2. The gradual development of concepts Although we would like to be able to answer questions about when children acquire a particular concept with a single age, developmental research shows that most important concepts develop over many years (Siegler, 1991). In the case of time, there are numerous examples of concepts that children begin to acquire in early childhood but that are substantially enriched over the succeeding years. Children begin to recognize the past–present–future distinction in early childhood, but a conceptual understanding does not appear until at least 6 years, and differentiation of the times of past and future events continues well into middle childhood. By 5 years children can compare two durations using start and stop times in simple situations, but it is not until middle childhood or later that they recognize these as the crucial items of information when there are conflicting spatial cues.

What is responsible for the protracted development of such concepts? In some cases one temporal concept cannot develop fully until children possess adequate representations of time patterns. This is true for children's differentiation of the past and the future, where learning about long conventional time patterns provides a framework for structuring a child's own past and future. We have also seen how a child's history of mental operations can influence developmental timing: It may take many years of thinking about given types of problems for concepts to attain forms that are flexible, free of internal contradictions, and applicable to a broad range of contexts. It is very likely that a third factor, the complexity of the concepts and their interaction with age-related limits in children's brain development and information-processing capacity, also contributes to the ages at which children understand particular aspects of time. Such changes might explain why children grasp the direct relations between duration and distance and between distance and speed before they can systematically relate all three dimensions. In any case it is clear that children do not wait until they have the capacity to understand all of the complexities of the temporal environment before they begin to learn about them. From infancy onward, the social and physical environments are rich sources of temporal information, and children attempt to adapt to them.

Acknowledgments

This paper is based upon work supported by the National Science Foundation under Grant No. 0241558. Any opinions, findings, and conclusions or recommendations expressed in this material are those of the author and do not necessarily reflect the views of the National Science Foundation. This work was also made possible by the awards of Research Status from Oberlin College and a William Evans Fellowship from the University of Otago.

References

Arlin, M. (1986). The effects of quantity and depth of processing on children's time perception. *Journal of Experimental Child Psychology*, *42*, 84–98.

Barr, R., & Hayne, H. (1996). The effect of event structure on imitation in infancy: Practice makes perfect? *Infant Behavior and Development*, *19*, 253–257.

Bauer, P. J. (1996). What do infants recall of their lives? Memory for specific events by one- to two-year-olds. *American Psychologist*, *51*, 29–41.

Bauer, P. J., & Mandler, J. M. (1989). One thing follows another: Effects of temporal structure on 1- to 2-year-olds' recall of events. *Developmental Psychology*, *25*, 197–206.

Bauer, P. J., & Mandler, J. M. (1992). Putting the horse before the cart: The use of temporal order in recall of events by one-year-old children. *Developmental Psychology*, *28*, 441–452.

Bauer, P. J., & Thal, D. J. (1990). Scripts or scraps: Reconsidering the development of sequential understanding. *Journal of Experimental Child Psychology*, *50*, 287–304.

Blewitt, P. (1982). Word meaning acquisition in young children: A review of research and theory. In: H. W. Reese (Ed.), *Advances in child development and behavior* (pp. 139–195). New York: Academic Press.

Bullock, M., Gelman, R., & Baillargeon, R. (1982). The development of causal reasoning. In: W. J. Friedman (Ed.), *The developmental psychology of time* (pp. 209–254). New York: Academic Press.

Clayton, N. S., & Dickinson, A. (1998). What, where and when: Evidence for episodic-like memory during cache recovery in scrub jays. *Nature*, *395*, 272–273.

Clément, A., & Droit-Volet, S. (2006). Counting in a time discrimination task in children and adults. *Behavioural Processes*, *71*, 164–171.

Cohen, L. B., & Oakes, L. M. (1993). How infants perceive a simple causal event. *Developmental Psychology*, *29*, 421–433.

Colombo, J., & Richman, W. A. (2002). Infant timekeeping: Attention and temporal estimation in 4 month-olds. *Psychological Science*, *13*, 475–479.

Das Gupta, P., & Bryant, P. E. (1989). Young children's causal inferences. *Child Development*, *60*, 1138–1146.

De Kort, S. R., Dickinson, A., & Clayton, N. S. (2005). Retrospective cognition by food-caching western scrub-jays. *Learning and Motivation*, *36*, 159–176.

Demany, L., McKenzie, B., & Vurpillot, E. (1977). Rhythm perception in early infancy. *Nature*, *266*, 718–719.

Droit-Volet, S. (2003). Temporal experience and timing in children. In: W. H. Meck (Ed.), *Functional and neural mechanisms of interval timing*. Boca Raton, FL: CRC Press.

Eichenbaum, H., Fortin, N. J., Ergorul, C., Wright, S. P., & Agster, K. L. (2005). Episodic recollection in animals: "If it walks like a duck and quacks like a duck...". *Learning and Motivation*, *36*, 190–207.

Espinoza-Fernádez, L., Vacas, L. de la T., García-Viedma, M. del R., García-Gutiérez, A., & Colmenero, C. J. T. (2004). Temporal performance in 4–8 year old children. The effect of chronometric information in task execution. *Acta Psychologica*, *117*, 295–312.

Friedman, W. J. (1977). The development of children's understanding of cyclic aspects of time. *Child Development*, *48*, 1593–1599.

Friedman, W. J. (1986). The development of children's knowledge of temporal structure. *Child Development*, *57*, 1386–1400.

Friedman, W. J. (1989). The representation of time structures in children, adolescents and adults. In: I. Levin & D. Zakay (Eds), *Psychological time: A life span perspective* (pp. 259–304). Amsterdam: North Holland.

Friedman, W. J. (1990). Children's representations of the pattern of daily activities. *Child Development*, *61*, 1399–1412.

Friedman, W. J. (1991). The development of children's memory for the time of past events. *Child Development*, *62*, 139–155.

Friedman, W. J. (1992). Children's time memory: The development of a differentiated past. *Cognitive Development*, *7*, 171–187.

Friedman, W. J. (1993). Memory for the time of past events. *Psychological Bulletin, 113*, 44–66.
Friedman, W. J. (1996). Distance and location processes in memory for the times of past events. In: D. L. Medin (Ed.), *The psychology of learning and motivation* (Vol. 35, pp. 1–41). Orlando, FL: Academic Press.
Friedman, W. J. (2000). The development of children's knowledge of the times of future events. *Child Development, 71*, 913–932.
Friedman, W. J. (2001). The development of an intuitive understanding of entropy. *Child Development, 72*, 460–473.
Friedman, W. J. (2002a). Arrows of time in infancy: The representation of temporal-causal invariances. *Cognitive Psychology, 44*, 252–296.
Friedman, W. J. (2002b). Children's knowledge of the future distances of daily activities and annual events. *Journal of Cognition and Development, 3*, 333–356.
Friedman, W. J. (2003a). Infants' perception of arrows of time. In: H. Hayne & J. W. Fagen (Eds), *Progress in infancy research* (Vol. 3, pp. 55–94). Mahwah, NJ: Erlbaum.
Friedman, W. J. (2003b). The development of a differentiated sense of the past and the future. In: R. Kail (Ed.), *Advances in child development and behavior* (Vol. 31, pp. 229–269). San Diego, CA: Academic Press.
Friedman, W. J. (2003c). Arrows of time in early childhood. *Child Development, 74*, 155–167.
Friedman, W. J. (2005). Developmental and cognitive perspectives on humans' sense of the times of past and future events. *Learning and Motivation, 36*, 145–158.
Friedman, W. J. (2007). Comment on "Potential role for adult neurogenesis in the encoding of time in new memories". *Hippocampus, 17*, 503–504.
Friedman, W. J., & Brudos, S. L. (1988). On routes and routines: The early development of spatial and temporal representations. *Cognitive Development, 3*, 167–182.
Friedman, W. J., Gardner, A. G., & Zubin, N. R. E. (1995). Children's comparisons of the recency of two events from the past year. *Child Development, 66*, 44–66.
Friedman, W. J., & Kemp, S. (1998). The effects of elapsed time and retrieval on young children's judgments of the temporal distances of past events. *Cognitive Development, 13*, 335–367.
Friedman, W. J., & Laycock, F. (1989). Children's analog and digital clock knowledge. *Child Development, 60*, 357–371.
Friedman, W. J., & Lyon, T. D. (2005). Development of temporal-reconstructive abilities. *Child Development, 76*, 1202–1216.
Gelman, R., Bullock, M., & Meck, E. (1980). Preschoolers' understanding of simple object transformations. *Child Development, 51*, 691–699.
Goswami, U., & Brown, A. L. (1989). Melting chocolate and melting snowmen: Analogical reasoning and causal relations. *Cognition, 35*, 69–95.
Gulya, M., Gallucio, L., Wilk, A., & Rovee-Collier, C. (2001). Infants' long-term memory for a serial list: Recognition and reactivation. *Developmental Psychobiology, 38*, 174–185.
Harner, L. (1975). Yesterday and tomorrow: Development of early understanding of the terms. *Developmental Psychology, 11*, 864–865.
Harner, L. (1976). Children's understanding of linguistic reference to past and future. *Journal of Psycholinguistic Research, 5*, 65–84.
Harner, L. (1980). Comprehension of past and future reference revisited. *Journal of Experimental Child Psychology, 29*, 170–182.
Harner, L. (1981). Children talk about the time and aspects of actions. *Child Development, 52*, 498–506.
Harner, L. (1982a). Talking about the past and the future. In: W. J. Friedman (Ed.), *The developmental psychology of time* (pp. 141–169). New York: Academic Press.

Harner, L. (1982b). Immediacy and certainty: Factors in understanding future reference. *Journal of Child Language*, *9*, 115–124.

Hudson, J. A., Fivush, R., & Kuebli, J. (1992). Scripts and episodes: The development of event memory. *Applied Cognitive Psychology*, *6*, 483–505.

Hudson, J. A., Shapiro, L. R., & Sosa, B. S. (1995). Planning in the real world: Preschool children's scripts and plans for familiar events. *Child Development*, *66*, 984–998.

Inagaki, K., & Hatano, G. (1996). Young children's recognition of commonalities between plants and animals. *Child Development*, *67*, 2823–2840.

Kelly, M. K., Miller, K. F., Feng, G., & Feng, G. (1999). When days are numbered: Calendar structure and the development of calendar processing in English and Chinese. *Journal of Experimental Child Psychology*, *73*, 289–314.

Leslie, A. M. (1984). Spatiotemporal continuity and the perception of causality in infants. *Perception*, *13*, 287–305.

Leslie, A. M., & Keeble, S. (1987). Do six-month-old infants perceive causality? *Cognition*, *25*, 265–288.

Levin, I. (1977). The development of time concepts in young children: Reasoning about duration. *Child Development*, *48*, 435–444.

Levin, I. (1992). The development of the concept of time in children: An integrative model. In: F. Macar, V. Pouthas & W. Friedman (Eds), *Time, action and cognition* (pp. 13–32). Dordrecht, The Netherlands: Kluwer.

Lewkowitz, D. J. (1989). The role of temporal factors in infant behaviour and development. In: I. Levin & D. Zakay (Eds), *Time and human cognition: A life-span perspective* (pp. 9–62). Amsterdam, The Netherlands: North-Holland.

Lewkowitz, D. J. (2000). The development of intersensory temporal perception: An epigenetic systems/limitations view. *Psychological Bulletin*, *126*, 281–308.

Lewkowitz, D. J. (2004). Perception of serial order in infants. *Developmental Science*, *7*, 175–184.

Mandel, D. R., Nelson, D. G. K., & Jusczyk, P. W. (1996). Infants remember the order of words in a spoken sentence. *Cognitive Development*, *11*, 181–196.

Matsuda, F. (2001). Development of concepts of interrelationships among duration, distance, and speed. *International Journal of Behavioural Development*, *25*, 466–480.

McCormack, T., Brown, G. D. A., Maylor, E. A., Darby, R. J., & Green, D. (1999). Developmental changes in time estimation: Comparing childhood and old age. *Developmental Psychology*, *35*, 1143–1155.

McCormack, T., & Hoerl, C. (2005). Children's reasoning about the causal significance of the temporal order of events. *Developmental Psychology*, *41*, 54–63.

Meck, W. H. (Ed.) (2003). *Functional and neural mechanisms of interval timing*. Boca Raton, FL: CRC Press.

Montangero, J., & Pownall, T. (1996). *Understanding changes in time: The development of diachronic thinking in 7- to 12-year-old children*. Philadelphia, PA: Taylor & Francis.

Morrongiello, B. A. (1984). Auditory temporal pattern perception in 6- and 12 month-old infants. *Developmental Psychology*, *20*, 441–448.

Nelson, K. (1986). *Event knowledge: Structure and function in development*. Hillsdale, NJ: Erlbaum.

Nelson, K. (1996). *Language in cognitive development: Emergence of the mediated mind*. Cambridge: Cambridge University Press.

Nelson, K. (2001). Language and the self: From the "experiencing I" to the "continuing me". In: C. Moore & K. Lemmon (Eds), *The self in time: Developmental perspectives* (pp. 15–33). Mahwah, NJ: Erlbaum.

Nurmi, J.-E. (1989). Development of orientation to the future during early adolescence: A four-year longitudinal study and two cross-sectional comparisons. *International Journal of Psychology*, *24*, 195–214.
Nurmi, J.-E. (1991). How do adolescents see their future? A review of the development of future orientation and planning. *Developmental Review*, *11*, 1–59.
Nurmi, J.-E., Poole, M. E., & Kalakoski, V. (1994). Age differences in adolescent future-oriented goals, concerns, and related temporal extension in different sociocultural contexts. *Journal of Youth and Adolescence*, *23*, 471–487.
Oakes, L. M. (1994). Development of infants' use of continuity cues in their perception of causality. *Developmental Psychology*, *30*, 869–879.
Oakes, L. M., & Cohen, L. B. (1990). Infant perception of a causal event. *Cognitive Development*, *5*, 193–207.
Oakes, L. M., & Cohen, L. B. (1995). Infant causal perception. In: C. Rovee-Collier & L. P. Lipsitt (Eds), *Advances in infancy research* (Vol. 9, pp. 1–54). Norwood, NJ: Ablex.
Piaget, J. (1969). *The child's conception of time*. London: Routledge & Kegan Paul.
Povinelli, D. J., Landry, A. M., Theall, L. A., Clark, B. R., & Castille, C. M. (1999). Development of young children's understanding that the recent past is causally bound to the present. *Developmental Psychology*, *35*, 1426–1439.
Rosengren, K. S., Gelman, S. A., Kalish, C. W., & McCormick, M. (1991). As time goes by: Children's early understanding of growth in animals. *Child Development*, *62*, 1302–1320.
Rosengren, K. S., Kalish, C. W., Hickling, A. K., & Gelman, S. A. (1994). Exploring the relation between preschool children's magical beliefs and causal thinking. *British Journal of Developmental Psychology*, *12*, 69–82.
Sachs, J. (1983). Talking about the there and then: The emergence of displaced reference in parent-child discourse. In: K. E. Nelson (Ed.), *Children's language* (Vol. 4, pp. 3–28). Hillsdale, NJ: Erlbaum.
Shultz, T. R. (1982). Rules of causal attribution. *Monographs of the Society for Research in Child Development*, *47*, (1, Serial No. 194).
Siegler, R. S. (1991). *Children's thinking* (2nd ed.). Upper Saddle River, NJ: Prentice-Hall, Inc.
St. Augustine (1961). *Confessions*. London: Penguin.
Thompson, C., Barresi, J., & Moore, C. (1997). The development of future-oriented prudence and altruism in preschoolers. *Cognitive Development*, *12*, 199–212.
Weist, R. M. (1983). Prefix and suffix information processing in the comprehension of tense and aspect. *Journal of Child Language*, *10*, 85–96.
Weist, R. M. (1989). Time concepts in language and thought: Filling the Piagetian void between two to five years. In: I. Levin & D. Zakay (Eds), *Time and human cognitition: A life-span perspective* (pp. 63–118). Amsterdam, The Netherlands: North-Holland.
Weist, R. M., Wysocka, H., Witkowska-Stadnik, K., Buczowska, E., & Konieczna, E. (1984). The defective tense hypothesis: On the emergence of tense and aspect in child Polish. *Journal of Child Language*, *11*, 347–374.
Wilkening, F., Levin, I., & Druyan, S. (1987). Children's counting strategies for time quantification and integration. *Developmental Psychology*, *23*, 823–831.
Zakay, D. (1989). Subjective time and attentional resource allocation: As integrated model of time estimation. In: I. Levin & D. Zakay (Eds), *Time and human cognition: A life-span perspective*. Amsterdam, The Netherlands: North-Holland.
Zakay, D. (1992). The role of attention in children's time perception. *Journal of Experimental Child Psychology*, *54*, 355–371.
Zakay, D. (1993). The roles of non-temporal information processing load and temporal expectations in children's prospective time estimation. *Acta Psychologica*, *84*, 271–280.

Chapter 12

Timing and Remembering the Past, the Present, and the Future

Richard A. Block and Dan Zakay

> "Only those animals which perceive time remember, and the organ whereby they perceive time is also that whereby they remember."
> Aristotle (McKeon, 1941, pp. 607–608)

Although Aristotle scoffed at the idea that the brain carried out faculties such as timing and remembering (Williams, 2004), his statement is prescient. Modern researchers in the multidisciplinary field of cognitive science have revealed some of the processes by which humans and other animals remember events and represent time, including various time-related aspects of remembered events and episodes in their lives. Timing and remembering are two crucial functions without which animals would not be optimally adapted to changing environmental conditions. Specifically, encoding and remembering temporal information enable animals optimally to time actions in response to environmental events. They encode and remember the temporal order of events and the duration of episodes, including approximately when a past event occurred and how long a past episode lasted. Remembering the approximate recency of past events and the approximate duration of past and ongoing episodes helps guide future actions, which include the execution of plans for previously formed intentions.

In humans the interplay between timing and remembering is reflected in various ways. In some cases, timing plays the major role, and remembering is a necessary supportive system. In other cases, remembering plays the major role, and timing is a necessary supportive system. In all cases, however, adequate remembering is a necessary, although not a sufficient condition, for optimal performance. Timing as the main process with remembering as a supportive process is exemplified by autobiographical memory for past events and also by retrospective duration

Psychology of Time

DOI:10.1016/B978-0-08046-977-5.00012-0

judgments. In these two examples, the goal is to remember when a past event occurred or how long an episode took to occur, and in both cases these tasks cannot be accomplished without the use of memory systems.

Evidence that people can remember the approximate duration of an episode (series of related events) comes from two kinds of paradigms. These reveal effects of different variables and seem to require different models (Block, 1990; Block & Zakay, 1997). One is prospective duration timing, which may be called *experienced duration*; and the other is retrospective duration timing, which may be called *remembered duration*. In prospective timing, a person is aware during a duration that he or she must estimate it. This may result from an experimenter's instructions or from everyday relevance and importance of timing. Prospective timing mainly depends on variables that influence the amount of attention a person devotes to time itself (see Block, 2003, for a recent review). On the other hand, in retrospective timing, a person is aware only after a target duration has ended that he or she must estimate it (see also Chapters 2 and 4).

In this chapter, we focus on research and theories concerning the major ways in which timing is linked with remembering: (a) timing the past, focusing on how people estimate the temporal location, or recency, of a past event, and how they estimate the duration of an episode retrospectively; (b) timing the present, focusing on how people estimate the duration of an episode prospectively (while it is in progress); and (c) timing the future, or how people execute a plan to perform an action at a specific future time.

We begin, however, by reviewing some historical and current models that may suggest similarities in the processes underlying timing the past, timing the present, and timing the future.

12.1. Historical and Current Models

Theorists have proposed various models concerning the encoding and remembering of temporal information. We critically and selectively review several important models, using a historical (chronological) organization. We begin with the older, simpler models in order to illustrate the evidence for which they can and cannot easily account.

12.1.1. Hooke's Model

Robert Hooke was a professor of geometry at Gresham College (England). He presented his model in lectures to the Royal Society of London in 1682, which were published 2 years after his death (Hooke, 1705/1969). Hooke proposed a geometric model of memory in which there is an account of time in the brain. According to Hooke's model (Hintzman, 2003b), each memory is formed at the soul's point of

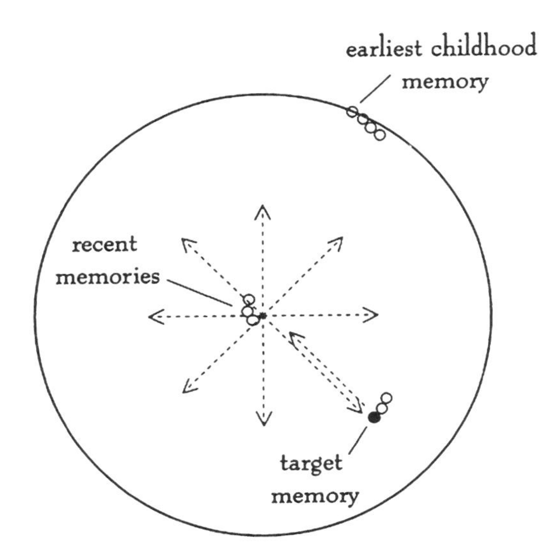

Figure 12.1: Hooke's model of memory. See text for explanation. (Reprinted with permission from Hintzman (2003b). Copyright 2003 by The Psychonomic Society).

interaction, and pressure from newly formed memories displace each memory outward, in an ever-growing sphere, shown in a cross-sectional view in Figure 12.1. Hooke (1705/1969) proposed that there is:

> a continued Chain of Ideas coyled up in the Repository of the Brain, the first end of which is farthest removed from the Center or Seat of the Soul where the Ideas are formed; and the other End is always at the Center, being the last Idea formed, which is always the Moment present when considered: And therefore according as there are a greater number of these Ideas between the present Sensation of Thought in the Center, and any other, the more is the Soul apprehensive of the Time interposed (p. 140).

Hooke said that therefore "the Notion of Time is the Apprehension of the Distance of Ideas from the Center or present Moment. And so Time comes to be apprehended as a Quantity" (p. 140). One problem is that Hooke's model predicts that the apparent recency of a past event is a power function of actual recency, with an exponent of exactly 1/3 (Hintzman, 2003b). Actually, a logarithmic function fits recency judgments better than a power function does (Hinrichs & Buschke, 1968; Hintzman, 2000). Hooke's model is an interesting contribution, even if only for historical reasons.

12.1.2. Bartlett's Contribution

Bartlett (1932/1997) reported a series of influential studies of human remembering. Although he did not focus on time *per se*, Bartlett's book, *Remembering: A Study in Experimental and Social Psychology*, had a large impact on memory research and theories. In his studies, people heard stories or saw drawings. Up to many years later, they were asked to reconstruct (tell or draw) them. Their reproductions were simpler and more regular than the original. Bartlett proposed that people had used schemas (structures containing related information about a concept) in order to encode and remember information. People also used inferences about what must have happened in the story or what must have been seen in the drawing. Bartlett proposed that remembering involves a *reconstruction* of what a person experienced.

Bartlett's view fits nicely with recent findings that contextual information is involved in event dating and duration timing. When people date an event or remember the duration of an episode that they experienced, they make inferences. In the case of event memory, people date an event based on inferences involving other facts (i.e., semantic memory information) that may help them remember the approximate date. In the case of remembered duration, people estimate a duration based on comparisons to other, similar durations, as well as facts about time. Bartlett also emphasized that the term *remembering* is more appropriate than the term *memory*, because the underlying processes involve dynamic acts of reconstruction, not static retrievals of fixed memory traces. His discovery is partly what led us to emphasize the terms *remembering* and *timing* instead of the terms *time* and *memory* in this chapter.[1]

12.1.3. Murdock's Conveyor-Belt Model

Murdock (1972, 1974) proposed a model in which each memory is put on a metaphorical conveyor belt and recedes into the distance over time. Thus, relative recency judgments become less accurate as events age. In this analogy, judging relative recency of events is like judging the relative distance of objects. It is relatively easy for a person to judge that an object 1 m distant is closer than an object 11 m distant, but it is more difficult for a person to judge that an object 101 m distant is closer than an object 111 m distant, even though the two objects are separated by 10 m in both cases. Like all unitary memory-strength models, this model cannot explain the many findings that contextual associations are important in recency judgments. However, it can perhaps explain some of the recent findings that

1. The differences between the words *time* and *timing* and the words *memory* and *remembering* are important. Although the words *time* and *memory* are nouns in their usual usage, the concepts denoted are not things, but actions. Thus, the words *timing* and *remembering* (verb forms) are appropriate. We mainly use them in this chapter (for reasons that will become clear), except when the historical context suggests the use of the words *time* and *memory* (nouns).

remembering may involve the impressionistic retrieval of age-related information from memory traces (see later).

12.1.4. Contextual-Change Model

Fraisse (1957/1963) reviewed empirical findings on various kinds of temporal judgments, including duration judgments, and he proposed that "the length of a duration depends on the number of changes we perceive in it" (p. 218). Subsequently, Block (1990, 1992; Block & Reed, 1978) proposed a contextual-change model, in which a person makes a retrospective duration judgment by assessing the amount of change in cognitive context that occurred during the duration. The term *cognitive context* refers to the circumstances surrounding the occurrence of an event. Wickens (1987) said that context is the "environmental surround [that] is essentially irrelevant to the central task, whose demand characteristics remain the same regardless of the context" (pp. 138 – 139). Viewed in this way, contextual information may involve a person's emotions, the surrounding physical environment, and other such factors (Block, 1992). We discuss contextual information in more detail later in this chapter.

The contextual-change model assumes these memory-encoding processes: (a) During the duration, the person encodes events into memory; (b) Contextual associations are automatically encoded along with each event; and (c) Contextual elements change continually during the duration, although these changes may vary from relatively slow to relatively fast. The contextual-change model also assumes these memory-retrieval processes: (a) At the time a retrospective duration judgment is made, the person assesses the availability of events tagged with the relevant context; (b) Other contextual associations are also automatically retrieved; and (c) The person bases a retrospective duration judgment on the number of different contextual associations that are retrieved, perhaps in a sampling process relying on the availability of varied contextual associations.

12.1.5. Attentional-Gate Model

Most models of timing the present — prospective duration-judgment processes — are based on attentional processes, but still, those judgments rely on both working- and long-term memory functions. An example is the attentional-gate model (Block & Zakay, 1996; Zakay & Block, 1996, 1997). This model is an elaboration of the scalar-timing model (for a review, see Church, 1978; see also Chapters 3 and 9), which was designed to account for animals' timing behavior. The main difference between the attentional-gate model and previous scalar-timing models is that an attentional gate is interposed between the pacemaker and the accumulator. The attentional gate is needed to explain the impact on timing of the amount of attentional resources allocated for timing in a given situation. The attentional gate allows pulses generated by the pacemaker to accumulate only when the gate is opened, which requires attentional resources. Although Lejeune (1998) questioned the need to propose both a switch and a gate in the timekeeping process, separating these components is the best way to account for two different functions: attending to a duration-onset signal and attending to time during a duration (Zakay, 2000). In the scalar-timing model, the switch was required to serve these two very different functions.

According to the attentional-gate model, prospective timing involves the following component processes (see Figure 12.2):

1. A pacemaker emits pulses at a fairly constant rate, although that rate may be affected by arousal level.
2. The flow of pulses reaches an attentional gate. If more attentional resources are allocated for timing, the gate allows more pulses to pass through a switch to an accumulator.
3. The meaning assigned to a situation (a signal) influences a switch. The switch allows pulses to accumulate when a target interval starts, and it stops pulses from accumulating when the target interval ends (or if there is an interruption in it). Thus, the switch is responsible for monitoring a correspondence between the

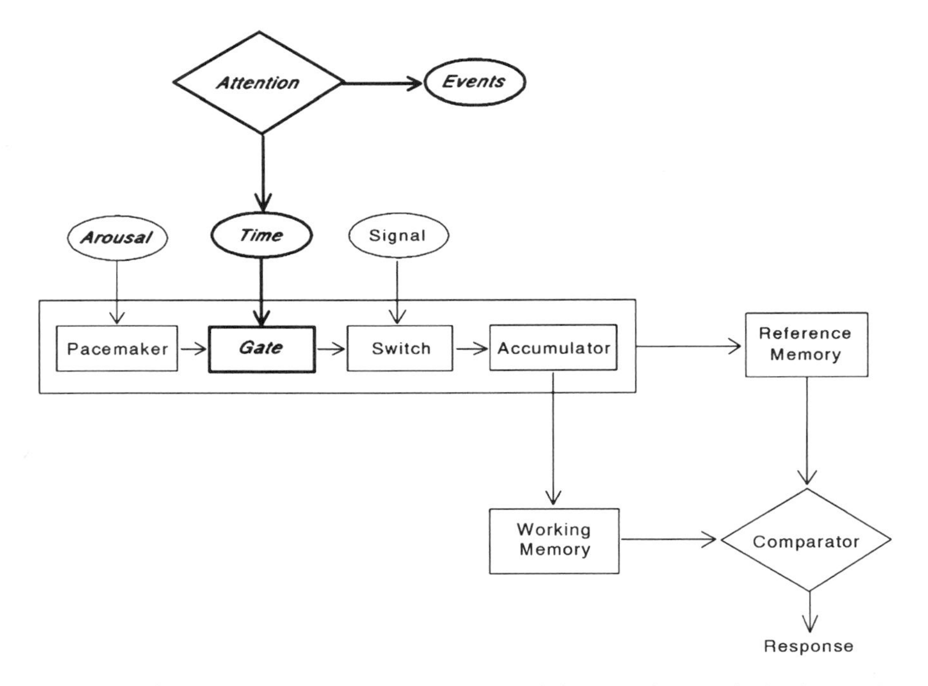

Figure 12.2: The attentional-gate model, adapted from Zakay and Block (1996) and Block (2003). See text for explanation. (Adapted with permission from Block (2003). Copyright 2003 by Hogrefe & Huber Publishers).

number of pulses that are allowed to pass through to the accumulator and the duration of a meaningful target interval.

4. The accumulator counts the number of pulses that were transmitted to it. This count depends on both the attentional gate and the switch. The count is a representation of the duration of an interval under specific conditions.
5. If a target interval must be reproduced, decision processes are employed. The number of ongoing pulses that are counted in the accumulator is constantly being compared with the previous number of pulse counts stored in reference memory and working memory. When a match is obtained, the reproduction is terminated (a response is made). If a target interval has to be produced, a representation of that interval is retrieved from long-term (reference) memory. The rest of the process is the same as in duration reproduction.

The analysis of the process outlined by attentional-gate model clearly indicates that the dependency on memory systems is high because working memory and reference memory are compared on a regular basis, and that comparison results in a decision concerning a response. (For additional discussion of the crucial role of decision processes in prospective timing, see Wearden, 2004). Working memory is therefore the bottleneck in the timing process in that it consumes many of the attentional resources demanded by prospective duration judgment (e.g., Brown, 1997; Fortin & Breton, 1995).

12.1.6. Temporal Context Model

Howard and Kahana (2002) recently proposed a formal model of the encoding of temporal information, which they called the *temporal context model*. As the name of the model implies, it focuses on contextual associations, and it has little to say about time-related processes *per se*. Figure 12.3 (upper panel) shows an earlier model, which Howard and Kahana called the *random context model*. In this model, the current temporal context (T) is associated with the current input event (F), but only random noise influences inputs (t^{IN}) to T. Figure 12.3 (lower panel) shows Howard and Kahana's temporal context model. It assumes that rather than being driven by random contextual fluctuations, retrieval of prior contextual states drives contextual change, or what they called *drift*. In this model, the item-to-context associative matrix (M^{TF} and M^{FT}) produces a tight coupling between the current input event and the temporal context. The temporal context model makes many of the same assumptions about contextual encoding and contextual change as earlier proposals concerning temporal dating of autobiographical events (Friedman, 1993, 2001), as well as concerning the role of contextual changes in duration timing (Block, 1990; Block & Reed, 1978). The temporal context model represents a preliminary step to integrating models of event dating and duration timing in a contextual framework. Additional formal modeling of this kind may be productive.

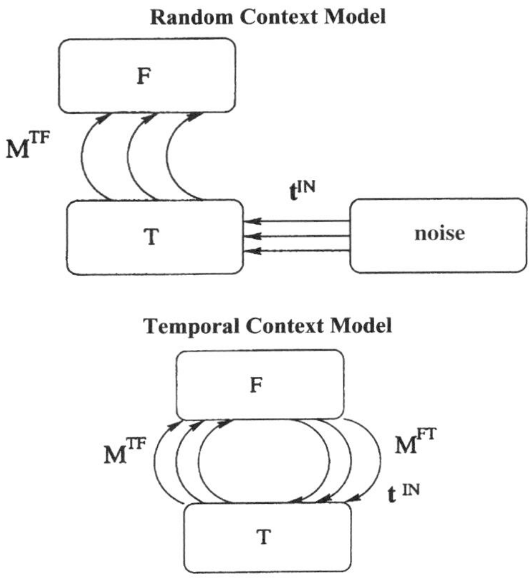

Figure 12.3: The random context model and the temporal context model, from Howard and Kahana (2002). See text for explanation. (Reprinted with permission from Howard and Kahana (2002). Copyright 2001 by Elsevier Science (USA)).

12.2. Timing the Past: Evidence

When people make temporal judgments about past events and episodes, sometimes the judgments concern their temporal location or recency (usually with an autobiographical reference), and sometimes the judgments concern their duration. These two kinds of judgments may involve some similar processes of remembering.

Research on event dating has a relatively long history. We first review some laboratory studies in which people experienced events and subsequently (usually within a few seconds or minutes) were asked to estimate the temporal position or recency of target (test) events. Then we review some nonlaboratory studies in which people experienced everyday events and subsequently (usually weeks, months, or years later) were asked to make temporal memory judgments on target (test) events. Evidence from laboratory and everyday-memory studies converges, suggesting that two major kinds of processes are involved: People may make event-dating judgments by relying on contextual information, by relying on a time-related property of the memory trace itself, or by relying on both.

12.2.1. Laboratory Studies of Past Event Dating

In an early experiment (Hintzman & Block, 1971, Experiment 1), people viewed a series of 50 words, one at a time, under incidental-memory conditions, at least as far as temporal information was concerned: They were told to pay attention to the words for a subsequent memory test, the nature of which was not specified. Thus, they were not forewarned that the test would require event dating. After the series was presented, people were shown the words in random order and were asked to judge the approximate temporal position of each of them in the previous series. Although their performance was far from perfect, they were able to make these judgments with some accuracy. One major finding was particularly interesting: Temporal position judgments for events that had occurred near the start of the series of events were relatively more sensitive to changes in actual temporal position than were temporal position judgments for events that had occurred during the middle or near the end of the series. This is the opposite of what is predicted if temporal position judgments are based on the decaying strength or other similar attributes of memory traces, which would make older events less discriminable than more recent events (cf., Brown, Neath, & Chater, 2007). Additionally, people apparently encode and remember temporal position information even under incidental-memory conditions, and the encoding of this information seems therefore to occur in a relatively automatic way.

Subsequent experiments clarified and extended this finding. In one of them (Hintzman, Block, & Summers, 1973), people viewed two separate series of words. Afterwards, they were unexpectedly asked to judge whether each word had occurred in the first series or the second series, and then to judge whether it had occurred near the beginning, middle, or end of the series. Although their judgments were far from perfect, people were able to make these judgments with some accuracy: They were only about 43–62% correct in dating a word to the actual series of words; they were about 60% correct in dating a word to the actual third of the episode. The kinds of errors that they made were especially revealing. If a person incorrectly judged that a word had occurred in a particular series, he or she nevertheless tended to judge that it had occurred in the correct part of the series. Thus, incorrect event dating was not strictly along a unitary temporal dimension. This finding suggests that people based their position judgments at least partly on incidentally encoded contextual information instead of on a continuous scale of absolute time.

Two kinds of findings suggest that contextual information is automatically encoded (although it is not necessarily, and probably not, automatically retrieved). First, people can make reasonably accurate event-dating judgments even under incidental-memory conditions (e.g., Hintzman & Block, 1971). Second, accuracy of event-dating judgments is little or no better under intentional-memory conditions than under incidental-memory conditions (e.g., Auday, Sullivan, & Cross, 1988). Thus, people automatically encode contextual information when they experience events.[2] When people later need to make an event-dating judgment, they can use contextual information (along with logical inferences based on it) to remember the approximate time at which an event occurred.

---

2. This process, which underlies event dating, is apparently not limited to humans. Scrub jays are able to remember how long ago they cached food items (Clayton & Dickinson, 1998, 1999).

In one of the earliest systematic studies of recency discrimination (Yntema & Trask, 1963, Experiment 2), people saw a long series of words (under intentional-memory conditions). Occasionally, a pair of words appeared, and the person was asked to judge which of the words had appeared more recently. The number of other words that had intervened since each of the target words had appeared was systematically varied over a wide range. The ability to judge recency was a function of the relative recency of the two words. Recency discrimination improved to the extent that the more recent word had occurred recently and that the spacing between the two words had been large. Yntema and Trask (1963) raised the question: "May items in memory be assumed to carry time-tags?" (p. 73). Interestingly, their data are well fit by a logarithmic function (Hintzman, 2000), although Yntema and Trask did not make particular note of this finding.

Hintzman (2003a) conducted three experiments in which he showed people a very long series of words, one at a time, with some of them repeated. The use of a relatively long series creates a so-called *steady-state* condition, which is characterized by few, if any, changes in cognitive context. Each item served as a presented item and as a test item. Subjects were asked to make a recognition-memory (*new/old*) judgment, then a recency judgment if they recognized an item as being *old* (presented earlier in the series). In the first two experiments, Hintzman varied word attributes (orthographic frequency and word concreteness) so that some words would be more memorable than others. He found that recency judgments depended only slightly on the inherent strength, or memorability, of the words; recently judgments did, however, reflect actual recency. In a third experiment, subjects made only recognition memory judgments (specifically, confidence that they had earlier seen a word). The relative effect of actual recency on recognition confidence was much smaller than the effect of actual recency had been in the first two experiments, which suggests that recognition memory and recency judgments are based on different memory properties. Thus, a relatively time-based process was dissociated from recognition memory processes *per se*.

More recently, Hintzman (2004b) also showed people a very long series of items (nouns or first names), one at a time. The rate of presentation of each item was subtly varied such that there were periods of relatively fast presentation rate and periods of relatively slow presentation rate. People did not notice these changes in presentation rate, and there is no evidence that they used them to make recency judgments. He found that recency judgments were directly related to the amount of time that had elapsed since the target word had occurred, and that they were not a function of the number of intervening items. In a follow-up experiment, Hintzman (2005) presented items (first names and pictures), using a methodology similar to that used in his earlier experiments (i.e., Hintzman, 2003a). Once again, recency judgments were "especially sensitive to some unknown, time-specific cue" (p. 862).

Along with Yntema and Trask's (1963) findings, these findings suggest that under conditions in which people are not able to remember any useful contextual information, they can nevertheless remember the approximate recency of an event by relying on some aspect of the memory trace that may serve as a time-specific cue. Thus, recency judgments may be based on an age-related property or properties of a memory trace. Converging evidence comes from studies of everyday memory, which we now consider.

12.2.2. Everyday-Memory Studies of Past Event Dating

Important evidence on how people date past events comes from so-called *everyday-memory* or *autobiographical-memory* studies. In these studies, people typically are asked to record everyday events in writing, such as in a diary, and to include the exact date and time of the event. Many weeks, months, or years later, they are given their own description of some of these events and are asked to make a judgment about when each event occurred. People can make these judgments with some accuracy. However, their judgments reveal systematic biases, called *scale effects*: People may show relatively good accuracy in remembering that an event occurred during a particular time of day but show relatively poor accuracy in remembering the day, month, or year during which the event occurred (Friedman & Wilkins, 1985). Thus, people may remember fine-grained temporal information better than they remember coarse-grained temporal information. This finding rejects the view that memory for recency is based solely on information that relates to time *per se*, such as time tags that are monotonically related to the passing of time. Friedman (1993, 2001; see also Shum, 1998) suggested that people may also rely on a so-called *location-based process*, which involves judging the recency of an event by remembering relevant contextual associations. The caveat is that distinctive contextual associations must have been encoded, which they were apparently not in some of Hintzman's (2003a, 2004b, 2005) laboratory studies.

Most evidence on everyday, autobiographical memories seems to require an explanation in terms of remembering contextual associations. However, some recent evidence requires an explanation in terms of remembering temporal information *per se*, or a so-called *distance-based process*. For example, Friedman (1991) found that 4- to 8-year-old children can often accurately remember the relative recency of two events, one they had experienced 1 week earlier and another they had experienced 7 weeks earlier. This was the case even though the children could not remember the day, month, or season during which each event had occurred. Apparently the children were not relying on contextual associations to landmark events, such as a birthday party, a summer vacation, or a religious holiday (see Chapter 11). Friedman (2001) proposed that the children based their memory for the recency of a past event on a subjective impression of the age of the memory trace, not on a process of remembering the location of the event in a contextualized pattern of events. Importantly, Friedman and Kemp (1998) found that this impressionistic information is a monotonically decelerating function of the actual age of the event: Changes in event dating are more rapid at first (i.e., during the preceding few months); after that, changes in event dating are more gradual. Figure 12.4 shows their findings from an experiment in which young children judged the recency of their latest birthday. The children seemed to be relying on a "direct impression of the ages of events" (Friedman & Kemp, 1998, p. 155). As shown in Figure 12.4, the children's estimates can be fit by either a power function

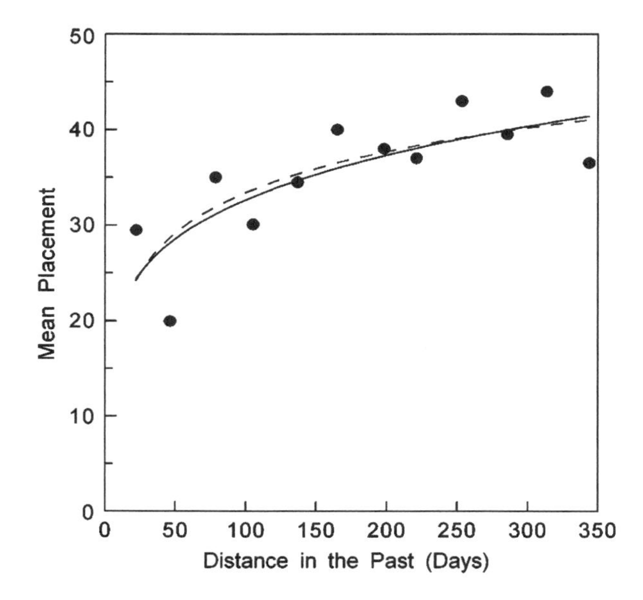

Figure 12.4: Event dating estimates by 3 – 6-year-old children, from Friedman and Kemp (1998, Study 3). Mean placement (estimate) of recency of latest birthday is shown as a function of its actual recency (in days). The best-fitting power function (solid line) and the best-fitting logarithmic function (dashed line) are shown. (Adapted with permission from Friedman and Kemp (1998). Copyright 1998 by Elsevier Publishing).

or a logarithmic function, which are extremely similar. The data are obviously too noisy to decide between the two functions.[3]

12.2.3. Past Event Dating: A Two-Process Model

Findings of both laboratory and everyday-memory studies support a two-process model of event dating. A person may remember the approximate date of a past event by retrieving either (a) contextual associations, along with inferences based on them, or (b) some age-related property or properties of the memory trace that does not involve contextual associations. The former implicates a *location-based* process and the latter implicates a *distance-based* process. Although a location-based process may

3. It is unclear which of the two functions best fits recency and other temporal judgments. The properties of a power function are better than those of a logarithmic function in modeling the forgetting of item information (Wixted & Carpenter, 2007), and it remains to be discovered why the same would not also hold for temporal memory judgments.

yield accurate information in many situations (and may therefore be more frequently used in autobiographical event dating), in other situations a person may have to rely on the more impressionistic information provided by a distance-based process.

12.2.4. Laboratory Studies of Past Duration Timing

The present chapter focuses on remembering, and retrospective duration timing is especially relevant. Because no unique sensory organ or perceptual system subserves timing (Gibson, 1975), most theorists emphasize relatively high-level processes involving memory. Studying how humans and other animals make duration judgments reveals and clarifies these processes (Block & Zakay, 1996; Zakay & Block, 1997).

One fairly general finding on retrospective timing, or remembered duration, is that if a person remembers a greater number of events from the time period, he or she tends to estimate the duration as being longer (Ornstein, 1969). Even if people estimate duration by remembering events, they undoubtedly do not try to retrieve all available memories of events from the time period. Instead, they probably rely on an availability heuristic, in which they remember a duration as being longer to the extent that they can easily, quickly, and vividly remember some events that occurred during the time period.

Remembered duration is not simply based on the availability of individual events; other factors are involved (Block, 1974; Block & Reed, 1978). Changes in cognitive context lengthen remembered duration more than do increases in the number of stimulus events encoded and retrieved. Remembered duration lengthens if people perform different kinds of information-processing tasks during a duration instead of a single task (Block, 1992; Block & Reed, 1978). This is attributed to changes in an aspect of cognitive context called *process context*. In addition, if there are more changes in environmental context, or in the encoding of environmental stimuli, during a time period, the remembered duration of it lengthens (Block, 1982, 1986). Other evidence also suggests that changes in emotions during a time period lengthen remembered duration (e.g., Block, 1982). In short, evidence reveals that the remembered duration of an episode is influenced by changes in cognitive context, including (but not limited to) process-context, environmental-context, and emotional-context changes.

12.2.5. Everyday-Memory Studies of Past Duration Timing

Very few researchers have studied retrospective timing, or remembered duration, under everyday-memory conditions.[4] Consider, however, a monumental study in which 1015 people were each unexpectedly asked to make one retrospective verbal

4. The main reason is that a person can usually provide only one judgment in the retrospective paradigm, because after a person is asked for a duration judgment, he or she is aware that duration timing is relevant and necessary, which is the definition of the prospective paradigm.

estimate (in seconds, or minutes and seconds) of the duration of an activity in which they had just engaged (Yarmey, 2000). A unique method was used, an "opportunity sampling procedure," in which people "were [unobtrusively] timed with a stopwatch while they participated in some specific event" (p. 48). The events, or activities, were either called *invariant* or *variant*, depending on the number of changes during a given activity. An example of an invariant activity is "one cycle of fitness training circuit" (780 s), and an example of a variant activity is "eating in a restaurant" (also 780 s). The duration of each activity ranged from 4 to 5008 s (83 min and 28 s), an unusually wide range of durations.[5]

We adapted these data (Yarmey, 2000, Table 1) and created Figure 12.5. Panel A shows that mean duration judgments were relatively accurate, which contrasts with Yarmey's (2000) description of the duration estimates as being "relatively imperfect" (p. 52). However, people showed the typical tendency to overestimate shorter durations and to slightly underestimate longer durations. These data are well fit by straight lines, which on log–log coordinates reflects the typical finding that duration estimates are a power function of actual duration, with an exponent slightly less than 1 (Eisler, 1976). A somewhat clearer picture emerges when the duration judgments are expressed in terms of a commonly used measure, the duration-judgment ratio — the ratio of estimated duration to actual duration (see Figure 12.5, Panel B). These data show more clearly that people overestimated the relatively short-duration events. Note that the duration-judgment ratio is relatively large for short-duration events compared to long-duration events. They also clearly show their other finding: The duration-judgment ratio is significantly larger for variant events than for invariant events. Although this finding may be interpreted in several ways, it seems to support the hypothesis that retrospective duration judgments lengthen as the degree of segmentation of the episode increases (Poynter, 1983, 1989) or as the number of contextual changes during the episode increases (Block, 1978). This interaction between event duration and type of activity (invariant versus variant) is consistent with other evidence suggesting that changes in cognitive context are less rapid as a duration lengthens (e.g., Hintzman & Block, 1971). Thus, these findings support the hypothesis that changes in cognitive context (in the case of variant events in contrast to the case of invariant events) lengthen remembered duration.

12.2.6. Evidence on Duration Neglect

A general rule of perception is that the overall strength of a percept is a function of the physical intensity of the stimulus that evokes the percept multiplied by its exposure duration (so-called *Bloch's Law*). Bloch's Law holds for ongoing

5. The difference between a variant event and an invariant event may not be the same for short- and long-duration events, because short- and long-duration events may differ on other dimensions. However, Yarmey used an unusually wide range of examples of relatively short-duration and relatively long-duration events, which may reduce the importance of any such confounding.

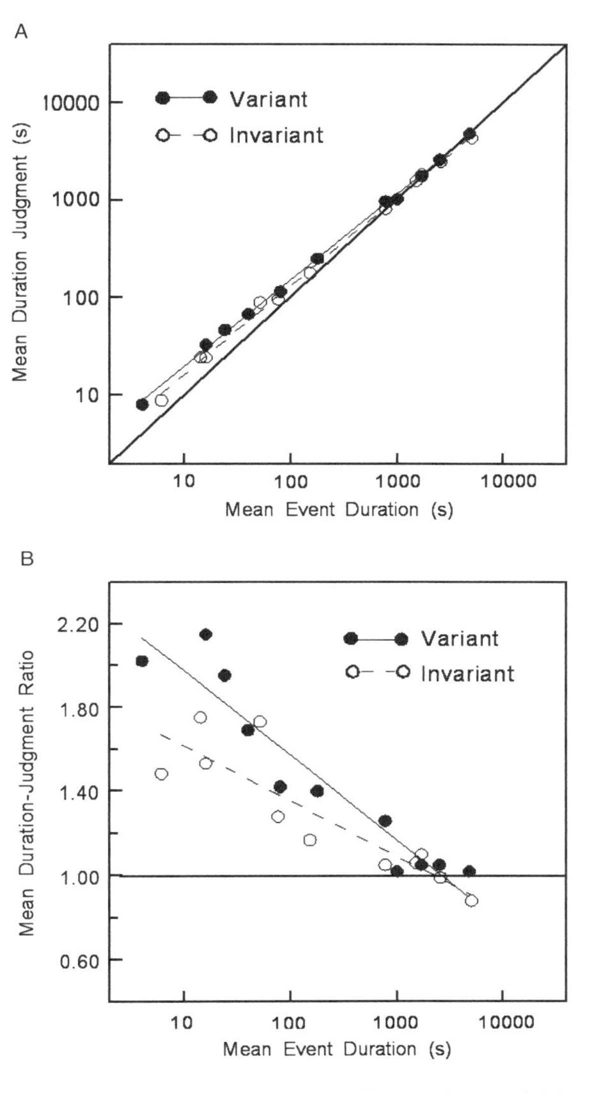

Figure 12.5: Retrospective duration judgment of everyday activities, adapted from Yarmey's (2000) data reported in his Table 1. Panel A shows mean duration judgment (in seconds) on a logarithmic scale as a function of mean event duration (in seconds) on a logarithmic scale for invariant events and variant events; the best linear fit, reflecting a power function, is shown for each type of event. Panel B shows mean duration-judgment ratio (the ratio of estimated event duration to actual event duration) as a function of mean event duration (in seconds) on a logarithmic scale for invariant events and variant events; the best linear fit is shown for each type of event. (Adapted with permission from Yarmey (2000). Copyright 2000 by Wiley InterScience).

stimulation and for brief durations (mainly those under 100 ms). Still, it is of interest to study the role of duration when people are making retrospective evaluations of temporally extended streams of hedonic experiences like pain or pleasure. Fredrickson and Kahneman (1993) found that in such cases people exhibit what they called *duration neglect*, which is a systematic bias towards ignoring the duration of a past experience. Research in various domains revealed that people were utilizing a heuristic called the *peak-and-end rule*, according to which retrospective global evaluations of hedonic sequences were mainly based on the peak level of the experience (i.e., the maximum level of pain or pleasure) and on the respective level at the end of the sequence. It appears that Gestalt characteristics of a sequence, such as its trend and rate of change in addition to the momentary experiences at the most intense and final moments, dominate the overall retrospective evaluation (for a summary, see Ariely & Zakay, 2001).

The consequences of the peak-and-end heuristic imply violations of temporal monotonicity. For example, longer episodes with same average level of pain or pleasure might be evaluated as less aversive or more attractive, respectively, than shorter episodes with same average levels of pain or pleasure (Langer, Sarin, & Weber, 2005). In addition, increasing sequences are evaluated as more attractive than decreasing ones (Loewenstein & Prelec, 1993). If a short interval with a moderate level of pleasure is added to an episode characterized by a high level of pleasure at its end, the overall retrospective hedonic value of the sequence can be lower than that of the original episode. An opposite result is obtained with discomfort (Redelmeier & Kahneman, 1996). These findings hold for various stimulus types such as pain (e.g., Ariely & Carmon, 2000) and positive affect (Fredrickson & Kahneman, 1993).

The tendency of people to underweight the duration of an experience when they retrospectively evaluate its overall hedonic value was empirically confirmed in several studies (e.g., Redelmeier & Kahneman, 1996). Rode, Rozin, and Durlach (2007) found duration neglect when people were asked to rate the hedonic value of meals composed of several dishes, but there was no evidence for peak, primacy, or recency effects in terms of attractiveness of meals.

The duration-neglect phenomenon contradicts not only Bloch's Law but also the discounted utility model. The discounted utility model predicts that people should consider the duration of an experience while evaluating its utility. This model also predicts that people should not consider features of an experience such as improvement or deterioration over time and certainly not for peak and end levels (Ariely & Loewenstein, 2000).

Hsee, Abelson, and Salovey (1991) introduced the term *evaluability effect*. Their argument is that when evaluating items separately or one at a time, attributes that are not easily judged independently are given little weight. However, when the same items are evaluated in an environment that facilitates comparison to other items, respondents place much greater weight on the same attributes. Note that in almost all the studies in which duration neglect was found, sequences were evaluated separately or one at a time. Another important issue that should be noted is that hedonic evaluations were always done retrospectively and therefore duration estimation was never asked for explicitly. Therefore, even if duration was estimated, it was estimated retrospectively. Following on the logic of the evaluability effect, Ariely and Loewenstein (2000) argued that when encoding experiences, particular attention is given to salient attributes, which in most cases do not include duration because this is not an important attribute to which one is attending. However, when making decisions about future events, the picture changes. Decision makers take into account both expected intensity and expected duration. The reason is that when choosing between two sequences, duration is an important attribute that should be compared, and therefore attention is allocated for its evaluation. These predictions were empirically supported.

Temporal relevance refers to the degree to which taking duration into account is essential for interpreting the meaning of a situation or for making optimal decisions in terms of adaptation to a relevant environment (Zakay, 1992). On the basis of the above-mentioned arguments and findings, we suggest that whenever temporal relevance is high, duration neglect will not be found. In other words, whenever duration is relevant, attention is paid to it and therefore it will be taken into account. This hypothesis directly leads to a prediction that if duration is estimated prospectively, duration neglect should be eliminated. This prediction was empirically supported by Rinot (2000), who asked participants to evaluate the degree of discomfort created by sequences of tones while also prospectively judging the duration of the sequences. Rinot found that the overall hedonic value of each sequence was mostly influenced by its duration, and the impact of the peak and end levels of loudness have much lower impact than that of duration. As expected, the higher the loudness and the degree of discomfort of a sequence, the longer was its estimated duration, probably because participants wanted the unpleasant situation to end as soon as possible and therefore they paid more attention to time than when the level of discomfort created by the tones was reasonable.

Zakay (2002) asked participants to evaluate the overall degree of suffering expected in regard to different scenarios of dental treatments. Dental treatments were described by the following four binary parameters: treatment's duration, peak pain level, pain level at the beginning of the treatment, and pain level at the end of the treatment. All 16 combinations of these parameters were evaluated. A conjoint analysis revealed that treatment duration was the strongest predictor of the hedonic value attached to each sequence, followed by the peak and end levels of pain. Somewhat similar findings were reported by Gilbert, Pinel, Wilson, Blumberg, and Wheatley (1998), who found that people tend to overestimate the duration of their affective reactions to negative events, like the dissolution of a romantic relationship or a rejection by a prospective employer. They called this the *immune neglect effect*, analogous to the way that people minimize the strength of their physiological immune system. We suggest that this finding, which indicates paying a high level of attention to duration, is caused by the explicit demand to judge duration as well as by the high relevance of duration in the type of episodes studied in this research.

As for the cases in which episodes are evaluated separately and retrospectively, it might be that duration is actually being retrospectively estimated but this is not taken into account because the temporal relevance of duration for evaluating the hedonic value of a single past event is not high.

Interestingly, the peak-and-end heuristic represents an important characteristic of retrospective duration judgment. Cognitive models of retrospective duration judgment are based on the assumption that the more contextual changes occur during an episode (Block, 1990), such as changes when the episode is segmented by high priority events (Poynter, 1983, 1989), the longer is its remembered duration. Undoubtedly, the starting and ending events of an episode are involved with two important contextual changes that also segment the episode and are easy to remember. Thus, regardless of the actual duration of an episode, the starting and ending events have a high impact on both the retrospective hedonic level attached to the episode as well as on its retrospective duration estimation. This hypothesis should be empirically tested. Some support for it might be found in a study conducted by Ariely and Zauberman (2000), who addressed the question of the impact of temporal spacing of an episode on its overall hedonic value. They found that breaking an episode into smaller pieces by the inclusion of short pauses moderated the duration neglect bias. They hypothesized that the breaks cause the individuals to perform interim evaluations of the episode segments, such that in retrospective judgments these evaluations rather than the instant utility levels are aggregated. We argue that by segmenting the episode its remembered duration also increased, and its impact on the overall hedonic value of the episode became emphasized. If this is the case, then perhaps duration is not really neglected. Instead, its impact on the retrospective hedonic value of a single past episode is not revealed because of the low level of duration relevance in such evaluations.

The duration neglect phenomenon illustrates broader characteristics of both prospective and retrospective duration judgments. For prospective judgments, duration neglect is a result of the high dependency of prospective duration judgments on the allocation of attentional resources for timing (see later). Whenever attentional resources are not allocated for timing, duration is neglected because fewer pulses enter the accumulator. (For an explanation, see our earlier description of the attentional-gate model). Temporal illusions — such as when a duration filled with a demanding cognitive task is prospectively judged as shorter than an equivalent time interval filled with a less demanding cognitive task — may be a result of duration neglect in the first case attributable to the attentional resources required by the demanding task.

For retrospective judgments, duration is neglected whenever there are few contextual changes, and this is reflected by temporal illusions, such as when an interval filled with contextual changes is perceived as retrospectively longer than an otherwise equivalent "empty" interval.

Although the role of remembering in retrospective duration judgment is critical, it is of interest to note that memory systems also play an important role in ongoing (prospective) duration judgments, but in this case the main role of memory is exhibited not so much in processes of retrieving information from long-term memory as in ongoing processes that mainly involve short-term (working) memory.

12.3. Timing the Present: Evidence

In experiments on how people time present durations, they are asked to judge the experienced duration of an episode while it is in progress, and the paradigm is called the *prospective paradigm* (see Chapters 2 and 4). In this kind of temporal judgment, people are aware that timing is relevant (Zakay, 1992). In many dual-task experiments, a person must time a duration while also performing either a difficult, an easy, or no secondary task. If a person must perform a simultaneous nontemporal task during a time period, experienced duration varies with the difficulty of the attentional demands that are required by it. Thus, if the processing task is more difficult, experienced duration decreases, as revealed by longer productions or smaller verbal estimates of duration (Hicks, Miller, & Kinsbourne, 1976; Zakay, 1993; Zakay & Block, 1997). In everyday life, prospective timing usually occurs in a dual-task condition in which attention is shared between nontemporal and temporal information processing. Nontemporal information processing involves external stimuli (along with accompanying internal cognitions), but excludes temporal attributes of those stimuli. Temporal information processing involves time-related aspects of external stimuli, as well as time-related internal cognitions (such as what is called *attending to time*).

Many findings reveal that temporal information processing requires access to some of the same working-memory resources that are needed for attending to nontemporal information (Brown, 1997). If a person is able to allocate relatively more attentional resources to processing temporal information, experienced duration increases. For example, if a subject must track the duration of several concurrent events, timing accuracy decreases as a function of the number of events that must be timed (Brown, 1997). If a subject is told how much attention to allocate for temporal information processing and how much to allocate for stimulus information processing, experienced duration depends on the relative allocation of resources (Brown, 1997; Macar, Grondin, & Casini, 1994; Zakay, 1992, 1998; see also Chapter 4).

For these reasons, most theorists emphasize the role of attentional resource allocation, along with working-memory processes, in experienced duration (e.g., Block & Zakay, 1996; Brown, 1997; Zakay & Block, 1996). The attentional-gate model described earlier (see Figure 12.2) emphasizes these component processes. Consider, however, whether there may be an alternative way to account for prospective timing without needing to assume an underlying pacemaker-accumulator system. Block (2003) proposed that interval timing may involve a comparison of apparent ages of events. Assume that the apparent age of an event (which is the inverse of its apparent recency) increases as a negatively accelerated function of physical time, just as Friedman and Kemp (1998; see Figure 12.4) and others have found. When a person is producing a duration, he or she terminates the production when the apparent age of the start (duration-onset) signal matches the average apparent age for that approximate duration, an average that has been learned in the past. When a person is verbally estimating a duration, he or she compares the apparent ages of the start-of-duration and end-of-duration (or the present) events in memory, and then translates this information into numerical time units based on verbal translations learned in the past and retrieved from long-term memory. These comparisons may involve impressionistic information about the apparent ages of the events, a distance-based process (Friedman & Kemp, 1998; see also Chapter 11).

Block (2003) further noted that if prospective timing involves comparing the relative ages of the start and end events in memory, the process by which attentional demands during the duration influence the comparison must be clarified. If there are few attentional demands during the time period, the usually assumed process involves attending to time (such as by opening the attentional gate wider or more often) and, as a result, encoding more temporal information. Block's alternative suggestion is that attending to time involves effortful retrieval of automatically encoded information concerning the apparent age of the previous act of attending to time. Because the apparent age of a past event increases as a negatively accelerated function of physical time, if age information is retrieved more frequently, the accumulated age information increases in an unusually large way. Thus, the process involves accumulating samples of relatively large differences in relative age. In contrast, if a person attends to time less often, apparent age of a past event (such as a start-of-duration event) is only retrieved a few times, and the power-function aging process is nearer to an asymptotic level. This model, which Block called a *memory-age model* of prospective duration timing, is a plausible alternative to pacemaker models of interval timing.

A process that underlies the memory encoding and retrieval of age information was originally called *study-phase retrieval* (Hintzman, Summers, & Block, 1975) and more recently has been called *recursive reminding* (Hintzman, 2004a). Recursive reminding is the relatively automatic way in which information associated with an earlier event is retrieved by the same event or a similar event. The retrieved information includes contextual associations, which contain information on apparent recency or age of the previous occurrence. Thus, when a person attends to time, that action will automatically retrieve information about the previous action of attending to time, including the apparent age of that earlier action. More frequently attending to time, such as when timing is relevant and attentional demands are relatively low, therefore increases experienced duration (shortens productions and lengthens verbal estimates) by means of this recursive retrieval process, and perhaps also by increasing the segmentation of the duration.

12.4. Timing the Future: Evidence

Duration-judgment processes are also sometimes needed in relation to future acts. For example, if a person decides at 19:30 to listen to the news at 20:00, he or she should monitor the elapsing time in order not to miss the news. This type of cognitive activity is traditionally called *prospective memory*, and it is usually defined as remembering actions that need to be performed in the future (Einstein, McDaniel, Richardson, Guynn, & Cunfer, 1995), or as memory of future intentions (Rude,

Hertel, Jarrold, Covich, & Hedlund, 1999). Another definition of prospective memory is that it involves "the ability to formulate intentions, to make plans and promises, and to retain and execute them at the appropriate place and time" (Graf, 2005, p. 305). Thus, it requires a process of retrieving from long-term memory a person's intentions for future actions (Park, Hertzog, Kidder, Morrell, & Mayhorn, 1997).

There are two types of prospective remembering: event based and time based. In event-based prospective remembering, the intention is to perform an action when a specific event occurs (e.g., tell my colleague something important when I encounter him or her). In this case, what is needed is to successfully recognize the event (perception of my colleague), and then to successfully retrieve from memory the intention (the important information). The event, in this case, serves as a retrieval cue.

In the case of time-based prospective memory (e.g., remembering to take a medicine 30 min from now), the main goal is to remember to perform an intended act at a specific future time. Time-based prospective remembering is a central cognitive ability that is needed for ensuring optimal daily activity (Brandimonte, Einstein, & McDaniel, 1996). A process of duration judgment should start such that when an interval (such as 30 min) has elapsed, the intention is retrieved, and then the intended action is performed. Thus, timing has a central role: A cue, based on a prospective duration judgment, must retrieve the intention in order for the person to perform the action.

Harris and Wilkins (1982) were the first researchers to suggest that time-based prospective remembering is related to duration judgment. They proposed a test-wait-test-exit model according to which an effective time monitoring is a key to a successful performance of the prospective memory task. According to this model, a person monitors time in a series of feedback loops, until he or she decides that the appropriate time for performing the task has arrived. Einstein et al. (1995) reported empirical support for this model. They found a high correlation between the number of times a person looked at an external chronometer during a time-based prospective remembering task and the amount of success in actually performing the intended prospective task. This test-wait-test-exit model, however, does not specify the cognitive processes that underlie this correlation. Observing an external chronometer is simply a behavioral indication of some internal cognitive processes. Indeed, Ceci and Bronfenbrenner (1985) found that with 10–14-year-old children, number of clock checks did not predict success in a time-based task. They claimed that task success is predicted not by the number of clock checks but by their effective and strategic allocation toward the end of the task. In addition to that, they found that children failed more in a home context than in a laboratory context. A plausible explanation for this finding is that the laboratory context enabled fewer attentional distractions than the home context since the laboratory context itself is a cue of the task and thus children's resilience to potential distractions is higher than at home. This explanation is supported by Craik's (1986) argument that prospective remembering depends on self-initiated attention-demanding processes. Einstein and McDaniel (1990) proposed a similar explanation.

Graf and Uttl (2001) argued that successful prospective memory requires both prospective and retrospective components, or stages. In the prospective stage, the cue for retrieving an intention from memory must be noticed and recognized, and in the retrospective stage the intention must be successfully retrieved. Thus, the basic difference between event-based and time-based prospective remembering is in the prospective stage. Graf and Grondin (2006) claimed that the domains of time perception and of prospective memory are connected and involve at least some of the same high-level cognitive processes or mechanisms. They suggested that time-based prospective memory is composed of several distinguishable components or functions. They argued that clock-checking strategies and time-related processes are likely to be critically involved in only some of them. Block and Zakay (2006) argued that the test-wait-test-exit model is not adequate in that it does not explicitly address several questions, such as exactly what is being tested. They also suggested that prospective remembering does not involve any special cognitive or memory systems. Instead, they said that "prospective remembering relies on the functioning of well-known attention and memory systems" (p. 25). Regarding time-based prospective remembering, at least when it involves short-term periods in the range of seconds and minutes, they said that a process of prospective duration judgment is automatically evoked by the intent to perform an act after a certain interval. This claim is related to the notion of temporal relevance (see p. 383). Undoubtedly, temporal relevance is high in time-based prospective remembering situations.

Thus, it is possible to describe the process that underlies time-based prospective remembering as the encoding of an intention to perform action after a specified interval has elapsed. This intention automatically initiates a prospective duration-judgment process that continues until the person perceives that the interval has elapsed. When this happens, the intention may (or may not) be retrieved from memory, and the intended action is (or is not) performed.

Observing an external clock is nothing more than an external behavior that indicates the allocation of attention for prospective duration judgment. However, there are individual differences in the translation of the allocation of attention to the external behavior, and consequently the correlation between the number of clock checks and the quality of the performance of the intended action is not a good indicator of the internal process. In addition, failure to perform the task may result from either a failure in the prospective duration-judgment process or in the retrieval of the specific intention. In both cases, the major potential source of failure is attentional distraction. For example, if one decides to take his or her medicine after 30 min and during that interval the person is engaged by a television program, he or she might be surprised after the 60-min program has ended that more than 30 min has elapsed. This is an example of the impact of attentional distraction (the television program) on prospective duration judgment, which is well explained by the attentional-gate model or the memory-age model. However, it might be that even if the person accurately judged the 30-min interval, he or she will not remember what the intention was, and this failure might also be a result of the distraction by the television program.

Evidence reveals that some of the same processes are involved in event dating and duration timing, including those that are implicated in time-based prospective remembering. One process used in event dating depends on retrieving contextual associations that were automatically encoded along with the event. Similarly, the main process used in retrospective duration timing is one that depends on changes in contextual associations that were automatically encoded during an episode. In prospective duration timing, attention to time and the retrieval of information about previous, similar durations from memory is required. In prospective remembering, especially those that are time based, similar kinds of attentional and memory processes are required, along with retrieval from memory of the intended action.

12.5. Summary and Conclusions

We reviewed theories and research on several ways in which timing and remembering are intimately interrelated. We focused mainly on the encoding and retrieval of temporal information. Various theories, or models, dating back to Hooke's (1705/1969), make various proposals about processes by which people: (a) date past events — that is, remember the autobiographical temporal location (or recency) of events; (b) estimate the duration of past episodes (encoded either without or with prior awareness that timing is relevant); and (c) time intentions for future actions. Some of the theoretical models make similar claims, although the differences among them have been difficult to test, and some major issues are still unresolved.

In this chapter, we reviewed evidence on timing the past (including recency and retrospective duration judgments), timing the present (prospective duration judgments), and timing the future (time-based prospective memory actions). We have highlighted that some similar processes are implicated in each of these situations, although there are also some important differences. However, a grand unified model that accounts for similarities and differences among these timing and remembering situations remains somewhat elusive. Any unified model should consider the following general findings:

1. People use two kinds of information in event dating (i.e., remembering when a past event occurred): contextual associations (a location-based process), and age-related properties of memory traces that do not involve contextual associations (a distance-based process). Some recent evidence reveals that memory traces inherently contain time-related information, although contextual information is also used to make temporal judgments about past events.
2. A process of remembering contextual associations, and a comparison of differences between them, is also involved in retrospective duration timing: Remembered contextual changes are used to estimate past durations. In addition, event dating and duration timing may both involve acts of reconstruction based partly on logical inferences.

3. Contextual information may also be involved in prospective duration timing, at least according to the memory-age model (Block, 2003).
4. Viewing duration neglect as a general characteristic of duration-judgment processes suggests that unlike objective time, subjective time is not continuous, and is used only when it is relevant and when it falls within the range of an attentional spotlight. While reading an interesting book during a vacation, duration is neglected because it is not relevant. In other words, subjective time does not "flow" unless it is relevant and therefore receives attention.
5. Time-based prospective remembering apparently involves many of the same processes that are required for prospective timing (Block & Zakay, 2006).

Any unified model of temporal remembering must also take into account the inherent variability of the underlying processes and the resulting variability of time judgments. Just as chronobiological timing displays "sloppiness," or lability (Campbell, 1990), so does psychological timing. People can remember approximately when past events occurred, but lability attributable to scale effects and other contextually based errors in dating events is common (Friedman & Wilkins, 1985). People can estimate durations both retrospectively and prospectively, but those judgments are notoriously variable, as revealed by measures such as the coefficient of variation (Block & Zakay, 1997). The peak-and-end heuristic in hedonic judgments also reveals violations of temporal monotonicity (Ariely & Zakay, 2001). People often perform time- or event-based actions at approximately the correct future time, but failures to do so are all too common (Block & Zakay, 2006).

Although Aristotle worded it differently (McKeon, 1941), timing requires remembering, and remembering involves timing. This is illustrated in Salvador Dali's famous painting, "The Persistence of Memory." Both timing and remembering rely on complex interactions of processes and consequently are fluid, sloppy, and labile. Nevertheless, research reveals important overall effects, which we have highlighted in this chapter and which must also be highlighted in future, more unified models.

Acknowledgment

We thank Douglas L. Hintzman, Simon Grondin, and Scott W. Brown for helpful comments on an earlier version of this manuscript.

References

Ariely, D., & Carmon, Z. (2000). Gestalt characteristics of experiences: The defining features of summarized events. *Journal of Behavioral Decision Making*, *13*, 191–201.

Ariely, D., & Loewenstein, G. (2000). When does duration matter in judgment and decision making? *Journal of Experimental Psychology: General*, *129*, 508–523.

Ariely, D., & Zakay, D. (2001). A timely account of the role of duration in decision making. *Acta Psychologica, 108*, 187–207.

Ariely, D., & Zauberman, G. (2000). On the making of an experience: The effects of breaking and combining experiences on their overall evaluation. *Journal of Behavioral Decision Making, 13*, 219–232.

Auday, B. C., Sullivan, C., & Cross, H. A. (1988). The effects of constrained rehearsal on judgments of temporal order. *Bulletin of the Psychonomic Society, 26*, 548–551.

Bartlett, F. C. (1997). *Remembering: A study in experimental and social psychology* (Original work published 1932). Cambridge, England: Cambridge University Press.

Block, R. A. (1974). Memory and the experience of duration in retrospect. *Memory and Cognition, 2*, 153–160.

Block, R. A. (1978). Remembered duration: Effects of event and sequence complexity. *Memory and Cognition, 6*, 320–326.

Block, R. A. (1982). Temporal judgments and contextual change. *Journal of Experimental Psychology: Learning, Memory, and Cognition, 8*, 530–544.

Block, R. A. (1986). Remembered duration: Imagery processes and contextual encoding. *Acta Psychologica, 62*, 103–122.

Block, R. A. (1990). Models of psychological time. In: R. A. Block (Ed.), *Cognitive models of psychological time* (pp. 1–35). Hillsdale, NJ: Erlbaum.

Block, R. A. (1992). Prospective and retrospective duration judgment: The role of information processing and memory. In: F. Macar, V. Pouthas & W. J. Friedman (Eds), *Time, action and cognition: Towards bridging the gap* (pp. 141–152). Dordrecht, The Netherlands: Kluwer Academic.

Block, R. A. (2003). Psychological timing without a timer: The roles of attention and memory. In: H. Helfrich (Ed.), *Time and mind II: Information processing perspectives* (pp. 41–59). Göttingen, Germany: Hogrefe & Huber.

Block, R. A., & Reed, M. A. (1978). Remembered duration: Evidence for a contextual-change hypothesis. *Journal of Experimental Psychology: Human Learning and Memory, 4*, 656–665.

Block, R. A., & Zakay, D. (1996). Models of psychological time revisited. In: H. Helfrich (Ed.), *Time and mind* (pp. 171–195). Kirkland, WA: Hogrefe & Huber.

Block, R. A., & Zakay, D. (1997). Prospective and retrospective duration judgments: A meta-analytic review. *Psychonomic Bulletin and Review, 4*, 184–197.

Block, R. A., & Zakay, D. (2006). Prospective remembering involves time estimation and memory processes. In: J. Glicksohn & M. S. Myslobodsky (Eds), *Timing the future: The case for a time-based prospective memory* (pp. 25–49). River Edge, NJ: World Scientific.

Brandimonte, M., Einstein, G. O., & McDaniel, M. A. (Eds). (1996). *Prospective memory: Theory and applications*. Mahwah, NJ: Erlbaum.

Brown, G. D. A., Neath, I., & Chater, N. (2007). A temporal ratio model of memory. *Psychological Review, 114*, 539–576.

Brown, S. W. (1997). Attentional resources in timing: Interference effects in concurrent temporal and nontemporal working memory tasks. *Perception and Psychophysics, 59*, 1118–1140.

Campbell, S. S. (1990). Circadian rhythms and human temporal experience. In: R. A. Block (Ed.), *Cognitive models of psychological time* (pp. 101–118). Hillsdale, NJ: Erlbaum.

Ceci, S. J., & Bronfenbrenner, U. (1985). "Don't forget to take the cupcakes out of the oven": Prospective memory, strategic time-monitoring, and context. *Child Development, 56*, 152–164.

Church, R. M. (1978). The internal clock. In: S. H. Hulse, H. Fowler & W. K. Honig (Eds), *Cognitive processes in animal behavior* (pp. 277–310). Hillsdale, NJ: Erlbaum.

Clayton, N. S., & Dickinson, A. (1998). Episodic-like memory during cache recovery by scrub jays. *Nature, 395*, 272–274.

Clayton, N. S., & Dickinson, A. (1999). Scrub jays (*Aphelocoma coerulescens*) remember the relative time of caching as well as the location and content of their caches. *Journal of Comparative Psychology, 113*, 403–416.

Craik, F. I. M. (1986). A functional account of age differences in memory. In: F. Klix & H. Hagendorf (Eds), *Human memory and cognitive capabilities: Mechanisms and performances* (pp. 409–422). Amsterdam, The Netherlands: Elsevier.

Einstein, G. O., & McDaniel, M. A. (1990). Normal aging and prospective memory. *Journal of Experimental Psychology: Learning, Memory, and Cognition, 16*, 717–726.

Einstein, G. O., McDaniel, M. A., Richardson, S. L., Guynn, M. J., & Cunfer, A. R. (1995). Aging and prospective memory: Examining the influences of self-initiated retrieval processes. *Journal of Experimental Psychology: Learning, Memory, and Cognition, 21*, 996–1007.

Eisler, H. (1976). Experiments on subjective duration 1868–1975: A collection of power function exponents. *Psychological Bulletin, 83*, 1154–1171.

Fortin, C., & Breton, R. (1995). Temporal interval production and processing in working memory. *Perception and Psychophysics, 57*, 203–215.

Fraisse, P. (1963). *The psychology of time* (J. Leith, Trans.). New York: Harper & Row. (Original work published 1957).

Fredrickson, B. L., & Kahneman, D. (1993). Duration neglect in retrospective evaluations of affective episodes. *Journal of Personality and Social Psychology, 65*, 44–55.

Friedman, W. J. (1991). The development of children's memory for the time of past events. *Child Development, 62*, 139–155.

Friedman, W. J. (1993). Memory for the time of past events. *Psychological Bulletin, 113*, 44–66.

Friedman, W. J. (2001). Memory processes underlying humans' chronological sense of the past. In: C. Hoerl & T. McCormack (Eds), *Time and memory: Issues in philosophy and psychology* (pp. 139–167). Oxford, England: Oxford University Press.

Friedman, W. J., & Kemp, S. (1998). The effect of elapsed time and retrieval of young children's judgments of the temporal distances of past events. *Cognitive Development, 13*, 335–367.

Friedman, W. J., & Wilkins, A. J. (1985). Scale effects in memory for the time of events. *Memory and Cognition, 13*, 168–175.

Gibson, J. J. (1975). Events are perceivable but time is not. In: J. T. Fraser & N. Lawrence (Eds), *The study of time II* (pp. 295–301). New York: Springer-Verlag.

Gilbert, D. T., Pinel, E. C., Wilson, T. D., Blumberg, S. J., & Wheatley, T. P. (1998). Immune neglect: A source of durability bias in affective forecasting. *Journal of Personality and Social Psychology, 75*, 617–638.

Graf, P. (2005). Prospective memory retrieval revisited. In: N. Ohta, C. M. MacLeod & B. Uttl (Eds), *Dynamic cognitive processes* (pp. 305–332). Tokyo: Springer.

Graf, P., & Grondin, S. (2006). Time perception and time-based prospective memory. In: J. Glicksohn & M. S. Myslobodsky (Eds), *Timing the future: The case for a time-based prospective memory* (pp. 1–24). River Edge, NJ: World Scientific.

Graf, P., & Uttl, B. (2001). Prospective memory: A new focus for research. *Consciousness and Cognition, 10*, 437–450.

Harris, J. E., & Wilkins, A. J. (1982). Remembering to do things: A theoretical framework and an illustrative experiment. *Human Learning*, *1*, 123–136.
Hicks, R. E., Miller, G. W., & Kinsbourne, M. (1976). Prospective and retrospective judgments of time as a function of amount of information processed. *American Journal of Psychology*, *89*, 719–730.
Hinrichs, J. V., & Buschke, H. (1968). Judgment of recency under steady-state conditions. *Journal of Experimental Psychology*, *78*, 574–579.
Hintzman, D. L. (2000). Memory judgments. In: E. Tulving & F. I. M. Craik (Eds), *The Oxford handbook of memory* (pp. 165–177). New York: Oxford University Press.
Hintzman, D. L. (2003a). Judgments of recency and their relation to recognition memory. *Memory and Cognition*, *31*, 26–34.
Hintzman, D. L. (2003b). Robert Hooke's model of memory. *Psychonomic Bulletin and Review*, *10*, 3–14.
Hintzman, D. L. (2004a). Judgment of frequency versus recognition confidence: Repetition and recursive reminding. *Memory and Cognition*, *32*, 336–350.
Hintzman, D. L. (2004b). Time versus items in judgment of recency. *Memory and Cognition*, *32*, 1298–1304.
Hintzman, D. L. (2005). Memory strength and recency judgments. *Psychonomic Bulletin and Review*, *12*, 858–864.
Hintzman, D. L., & Block, R. A. (1971). Repetition and memory: Evidence for a multiple-trace hypothesis. *Journal of Experimental Psychology*, *88*, 297–306.
Hintzman, D. L., Block, R. A., & Summers, J. J. (1973). Contextual associations and memory for serial position. *Journal of Experimental Psychology*, *97*, 220–229.
Hintzman, D. L., Summers, J. J., & Block, R. A. (1975). Spacing judgments as an index of study-phase retrieval. *Journal of Experimental Psychology: Human Learning and Memory*, *1*, 31–40.
Hooke, R. (1969). *The posthumous works of Robert Hooke: With a new introduction by Richard S. Westfall* (Original work published 1705). New York: Johnson Reprint.
Howard, M. W., & Kahana, M. J. (2002). A distributed representation of temporal context. *Journal of Mathematical Psychology*, *46*, 269–299.
Hsee, C. K., Abelson, R. P., & Salovey, P. (1991). The relative weighting of position and velocity in satisfaction. *Psychological Science*, *2*, 263–266.
Langer, T., Sarin, R., & Weber, M. (2005). The retrospective evaluation of payment sequences: Duration neglect and peak-and-end effects. *Journal of Economic Behavior & Organization*, *58*, 157–175.
Lejeune, H. (1998). Switching or gating? The attentional challenge in cognitive models of psychological time. *Behavioural Processes*, *44*, 127–145.
Loewenstein, G. F., & Prelec, D. (1993). Preferences for sequences of outcomes. *Psychological Review*, *100*, 91–108.
Macar, F., Grondin, S., & Casini, L. (1994). Controlled attention sharing influences time estimation. *Memory and Cognition*, *22*, 673–686.
McKeon, R. (Ed.) (1941). *The basic works of Aristotle*. New York: Random House.
Murdock, B. B., Jr. (1972). Short-term memory. In: G. H. Bower (Ed.), *The psychology of learning and motivation* (Vol. 5, pp. 67–127). New York: Academic Press.
Murdock, B. B., Jr. (1974). *Human memory: Theory and data*. Potomac, MD: Erlbaum.
Ornstein, R. E. (1969). *On the experience of time*. Harmondsworth, England: Penguin.
Park, D. C., Hertzog, C., Kidder, D. P., Morrell, R. W., & Mayhorn, C. B. (1997). Effect of age on event-based and time-based prospective memory. *Psychology and Aging*, *12*, 314–327.

Poynter, W. D. (1983). Duration judgment and the segmentation of experience. *Memory and Cognition*, *11*, 77–82.

Poynter, W. D. (1989). Judging the duration of time intervals: A process of remembering segments of experience. In: I. Levin & D. Zakay (Eds), *Time and human cognition: A life-span perspective* (pp. 305–331). Amsterdam, The Netherlands: North-Holland.

Redelmeier, D. A., & Kahneman, D. (1996). Patients' memories of painful medical treatments: Real-time and retrospective evaluations of two minimally invasive procedures. *Pain*, *66*, 3–8.

Rinot, M. (2000). *Prospective duration judgment and hedonic evaluation of tones' sequences.* Unpublished Master's thesis, Department of Psychology, Tel-Aviv University.

Rode, E., Rozin, P., & Durlach, P. (2007). Experienced and remembered pleasure for meals: Duration neglect but minimal peak, end (recency) or primacy effects. *Appetite*, *49*, 18–29.

Rude, S. S., Hertel, P. T., Jarrold, W., Covich, J., & Hedlund, S. (1999). Depression-related impairments in prospective memory. *Cognition and Emotion*, *13*, 267–276.

Shum, M. S. (1998). The role of temporal landmarks in autobiographical memory processes. *Psychological Bulletin*, *124*, 423–442.

Wearden, J. H. (2004). Decision processes in models of timing. *Acta Neurobiologiae Experimentalis*, *64*, 303–317.

Wickens, D. D. (1987). The dual meanings of context: Implications for research, theory, and applications. In: D. S. Gorfein & R. R. Hoffman (Eds), *Memory and learning: The Ebbinghaus centennial conference* (pp. 135–152). Hillsdale, NJ: Erlbaum.

Williams, N. (2004). Soul searching. *Current Biology*, *14*, R454–R455.

Wixted, J. T., & Carpenter, S. K. (2007). The Wickelgren power law and the Ebbinghaus savings function. *Psychological Science*, *18*, 133–134.

Yarmey, A. D. (2000). Retrospective duration estimates for variant and invariant events in field situations. *Applied Cognitive Psychology*, *14*, 45–57.

Yntema, D. B., & Trask, F. P. (1963). Recall as a search process. *Journal of Verbal Learning and Verbal Behavior*, *2*, 65–74.

Zakay, D. (1992). On prospective time estimation, temporal relevance and temporal uncertainty. In: F. Macar, V. Pouthas & W. J. Friedman (Eds), *Time, action and cognition: Towards bridging the gap* (pp. 109–117). Dordrecht, The Netherlands: Kluwer Academic.

Zakay, D. (1993). The roles of non-temporal information processing load and temporal expectations in children's prospective time estimation. *Acta Psychologica*, *84*, 271–280.

Zakay, D. (1998). Attention allocation policy influences prospective timing. *Psychonomic Bulletin and Review*, *5*, 114–118.

Zakay, D. (2000). Gating or switching? Gating is a better model of prospective timing (a response to 'switching or gating?' by Lejeune). *Behavioural Processes*, *50*, 1–7.

Zakay, D. (2002). *Is duration really neglected?* Paper presented at the Annual Conference of the European Society for Medical Decision Making, Taormina, Italy.

Zakay, D., & Block, R. A. (1996). The role of attention in time estimation processes. In: M. A. Pastor & J. Artieda (Eds), *Time, internal clocks and movement* (pp. 143–164). Amsterdam, The Netherlands: North-Holland/Elsevier Science.

Zakay, D., & Block, R. A. (1997). Temporal cognition. *Current Directions in Psychological Science*, *6*, 12–16.

Chapter 13

Nature of Time and Causality in Physics

Francisco S. N. Lobo

The conceptual definition and understanding of the nature of time, both qualitatively and quantitatively, are difficult and of utmost importance and play a fundamental role in physics. Physical systems seem to evolve in paths of increasing entropy and of complexity, and thus, the arrow of time shall be explored in the context of thermodynamic irreversibility and quantum physics. In Newtonian physics, time flows at a constant rate, the same for all observers; however, it necessarily flows at different rates for different observers in special and general relativity. Special relativity provides important quantitative elucidations of the fundamental processes related to time-dilation effects, and general relativity provides a deep analysis of effects of time flow, such as in the presence of gravitational fields. Through the special theory of relativity, time became intimately related with space, giving rise to the notion of spacetime, in which both parameters cannot be considered as separate entities. As time is incorporated into the proper structure of the fabric of spacetime, it is interesting to note that general relativity is contaminated with nontrivial geometries that generate closed timelike curves, and thus apparently violates causality. The notion of causality is fundamental in the construction of physical theories; therefore, time travel and its associated paradoxes have to be treated with great caution. These issues are briefly analyzed in this review paper.

13.1. Introduction: Basic Ideas about Time in Physics

Time is a mysterious ingredient of the universe and stubbornly resists simple definition. St. Augustine, in his *Confessions*, reflecting on the nature of time, states: "What then is time? If no one asks me, I know: if I wish to explain it to one that asketh, I know not" (*Confessions*, Chapter XI, Section 17). Perhaps the reason for being so illusive is that being a fundamental quantity, there is nothing more fundamental to be defined in terms of. Citing Alfred North Whitehead, the

Psychology of Time

DOI:10.1016/B978-0-08046-977-5.00013-2

philosopher-mathematician: "It is impossible to mediate on time…without an overwhelming emotion at the limitations of human intelligence." (Whitehead, 1920). However, intuitively, we do verify that the notion of time emerges through an intimate relationship to change, and subjectively may be considered as something that flows. This view can be traced back as far as Aristotle, a keen natural philosopher, who stated that "time is the measure of change." Throughout history, one may find a wide variety of reflections and considerations on time, dating back to ancient religions. For instance, a linear notion of time may be encountered in the Hebrew and the Zoroastrian Iranian writings, and in the Judaeo-Christian doctrine, based on the Bible and the unique character of historical events, which possesses a beginning, namely, the act of creation. In ancient Greece the image of Chronos, the Father Time, was conveyed, and Plato further assumed the notion of a circular time, where the latter had a beginning and looped back unto itself. This was probably inspired in the cyclic phenomena observed in nature, namely the alternation of day and night, the repetition of the seasons, etc. Eastern religions also have a cyclic notion of time, consisting of a repetition of births and extinctions. However, it was only in the 17th century that the philosopher Francis Bacon clearly formulated the concept of linear time, and through the influence of Newton, Barrow, Leibniz, Locke, and Kant amongst others, by the 19th century the idea of linear time dominated both in science and philosophy (see Chapter 1).

In a scientific context, it is perhaps fair to state that reflections on time culminated in Newton's concept of absolute time, which assumed that time flowed at the same rate for all observers in the universe. Quoting Newton from his *Principia* (Newton, 1726): "Absolute, true, and mathematical time, in and of itself and of its own nature, without reference to anything external, flows uniformly and by another name is called duration." However, in 1905, Albert Einstein changed altogether our notion of time, through the formulation of the special theory of relativity and stating, in particular, that time flowed at different rates for different observers. Three years later, Hermann Minkowski formally united the parameters of time and space, giving rise to the notion of a fundamental four-dimensional entity, spacetime. Citing Minkowski (speech delivered at the 80th Assembly of German Natural Scientists and Physicians, September 21, 1908): "Henceforth space by itself, and time by itself, are doomed to fade away into mere shadows, and only a kind of union of the two will preserve an independent reality."

If we consider that time is empirically related to change, which is a variation or sequence of occurrences, then, intuitively, the latter provides us with a notion of something that flows, and thus the emergent character of time. In relativity, the above empirical notion of a sequence of occurrences is substituted by a sequence of *events*. The concept of an event is an idealization of a point in space and an instant in time. It is interesting to note that the concept of an instant, associated to that of *duration*, or an interval of time, is also an extremely subtle issue, and deserves a brief analysis. One may consider duration as an ordered set of instants, contrary to being a sum of instants. A duration is infinitely divisible into more durations, and not into an instant. Now the classical concept of time being a linear continuum implies that between any infinitesimally neighboring instants, an infinity of instants exist, and the flow of instants constituting a linear continuum of time is reminiscent of Zeno's paradoxes. Perhaps the problem can be surpassed by quantizing time in units of the Planck time, 10^{-43} s, in an eventual theory of quantum gravity. Now, a sequence of events has a determined temporal order, which is experimentally verified as specific events — effects — which are triggered off by others — causes — thus providing us with the notion of causality.

In the physics literature, one may find two exclusively mutual concepts of time, which can be characterized as the relational theories and the absolute theories of time. The latter imply that time exists independently of physical spacetime events, contrary to relational theories that defend that time is but a mere relationship of the causal ordering of events, i.e., time is an abstract concept, nonexistent as a physical entity, but useful in describing processes. In particular, an example of an absolute theory of time can be traced back to early 17th century, with Isaac Barrow's refutal of the Aristotelian notion that time is related to change, stating that time is an entity which exists independently of change or motion. This is reflected in his *Lectiones Geometricae*, in 1676, where he states: "Whether things run or stand still, whether we sleep or wake, time flows in its even tenor." His student, Isaac Newton, extended this idea and compared time and space with an infinitely large vessel, containing events, and existing independently of the latter. This notion was, in turn, refuted by Gottfried Leibniz, who defended a relationship between time and an ordering of nonsimultaneous events: "Time is the order of possibilities which cannot coexist and therefore must exist successfully." (Hartz & Cover, 1988).

Now, for an emergent subjective notion of time to occur, it seems that a changing configuration of matter is necessary. For instance, in an empty universe, a hypothetical observer cannot measure time nor length, i.e., in a universe without processes one may argue that the observer cannot experience an emergent notion of time, or for that matter, of space. However, the absolute time theorists defend that the container spacetime, i.e., space and time, still exists. The fundamental question is whether time does exist independently, in the absence of change. Albert Einstein seems to provide the controversial answer: "Till now it was believed that time and space existed themselves, even if there was nothing — no Sun, no Earth, no stars — while now we know that time and space are not the vessels for the universe, but could not exist at all if there were no contents, namely, no Sun, no Earth, and other celestial bodies" (*New York Times*, 3 December 1919). But, in another stage of his life contradicts himself, by stating: "The conceptions of time and space have been such that if everything in the universe were taken away, if there were nothing left, there would still be left to man time and space" (*New York Times*, 4 April 1921). Note that the above ideas further complicate the issue of the flow of time. Some theorists deny the objective flow of time, but nevertheless admit the presence of change, and argue that the empirical notion of the flow is merely subjective. Their opponents defend an objective flow of time, where events change from being indeterminate in the future to being determinate in the present and past.

An interesting example of an absolute theory of time is the "Block Universe" description of spacetime as an unchanging four-dimensional block, where time is considered a dimension. In this representation, a preferred "now" is nonexistent and past and future times are equally present. All points in time are equally valid frames of reference, and whether a specific instant is in the future or past is frame dependent. However, despite the fact that each observer does indeed experience a subjective flow of time, special relativity denies the possibility of universal simultaneity (which shall be treated in more detail below), and thus the possibility of a universal now. Now, if future events already exist, why don't we remember the future? We do remember the past, and this time asymmetry gives rise to a subjective arrow of time. It appears to the "Block Universe" representation that the notion of the flow of time is a subjective illusion. Note that the Block Universe point of view inflicts a great blow to the notion of "free will," as it proposes that both past and future events are as immutably fixed, and consequently impossible to change. A Block Universe advocate may argue that free will is but mere determinism in disguise. We refer the reader to Ellis (2006) for more details on the objections to the Block Universe viewpoint.

An important aspect of the nature of time is its arrow. The modern perspective in physics is that essentially "dynamical laws" govern the universe, namely, given initial conditions of the physical state, the laws specify the evolution of a determined physical system with time. However, the dynamical equations of classical and quantum physics are symmetrical under a time reversal, i.e., mathematically, one might as well specify the final conditions and evolve the physical system back in time. But, several issues are raised by thermodynamics, general relativity and quantum mechanics on the theme of time asymmetry. In principle, the latter would enable an observer to empirically distinguish past from future. For instance, the second law of thermodynamics, which states that in an isolated system the entropy (which is a measure of disorder) increases provides a thermodynamic arrow of time. One may assume that the second law of thermodynamics and the thermodynamic arrow of time are a consequence of the initial conditions of the universe, which leads us to the cosmological arrow of time, that inexorably points in the direction of the universe's expansion. In the context of quantum mechanics, a fundamental aspect of the theory is that of quantum uncertainty, i.e., it is not possible to determine a unique outcome of quantum events. It is interesting to note that despite the fact that there is time symmetry in the evolution of a quantum system, the reduction of the wave function is essentially time asymmetric. These aspects are explored in more detail below.

As time is incorporated into the proper structure of the fabric of spacetime, it is interesting to note that general relativity is contaminated with nontrivial geometries that generate closed timelike curves, and apparently violates causality. A closed timelike curve allows time travel, in the sense that an observer who travels on a trajectory in spacetime along this curve, returns to an event that coincides with the departure. The arrow of time leads forward, as measured locally by the observer, but globally he/she may return to an event in the past. This fact apparently violates causality, opening Pandora's box and producing time-travel paradoxes (Nahin, 1999), throwing a further veil over our understanding of the fundamental nature of time. The notion of causality is fundamental in the construction of physical theories; therefore, time travel and its associated paradoxes have to be treated with great caution (Visser, 1995).

As this chapter is mainly aimed for students and researchers in psychology or neuroscience, the mathematics is kept at a minimum. We refer the reader to the remaining chapters for the psychological aspects of time, and only the objective nature of time will be considered in this chapter, which is outlined in the following manner. In the next section, the relativistic aspects of time in special and general relativity will be considered in detail, where much emphasis will be attributed to spacetime diagrams. It is followed by a section on time irreversibility and the arrow of time, which are treated in the context of thermodynamics and quantum mechanics. In the final section before the conclusion, closed timelike curves and causality violation will be analyzed.

13.2. Relativistic Time

The conceptual definition and understanding of time, both quantitatively and qualitatively, are difficult and of utmost importance. Special relativity provides us with important quantitative elucidations of the fundamental processes related to time-dilation effects. The general theory of relativity provides a deep analysis of effects of time flow in the presence of strong and weak gravitational fields. The general theory of relativity has been an extremely successful theory, with a well-established experimental footing, at least for weak gravitational fields. Its predictions range from the existence of black holes, gravitational radiation to the cosmological models predicting a primordial beginning, namely the big-bang (Hawking & Ellis, 1973; Wald, 1984).

13.2.1. Time in Special Relativity

To set the stage, perhaps it is important to emphasize that one of the greatest theoretical triumphs of the 19th century physics was James Clerk Maxwell's formulation of electromagnetism, which, in particular, predicted that light waves are electromagnetic in nature. Now, as was believed, in Maxwell's time, all wave phenomena required a medium to propagate, and the latter for light waves was denoted as the "luminiferous ether." Thus, it was predicted that experiments would allow the absolute motion through the ether to be detected. However, the famous Michelson–Morley experiment devised to measure the velocity of the Earth relative to the ether came up with a null result. To explain the latter, Lorentz deduced specific relationships, denoted as the Lorentz transformations, which are shown below. Einstein also later derived these transformations in formulating his special theory of relativity. Explicitly, using the Lorentz transformation, Lorentz and Fitzgerald explained the Michelson–Morley null result by inferring the contraction of rigid bodies and the slowing down of clocks when moving through the ether (Ellis & Williams, 2000). It is also worth mentioning that the Maxwell equations were not invariant under the Galilean transformations, i.e., they appeared to violate the principle of Galilean relativity, which essentially states that the dynamical laws of physics are the same when referred to any uniformally moving frame. At first, it was thought that Maxwell's equations were incorrect, and were consequently modified to be invariant under Galilean transformations. But, this seemed to predict new electromagnetic phenomena, which could not be experimentally verified. However, applying the Lorentz transformations, it was found that the Maxwell equations remain invariant.

To make the above statements more precise, we shall briefly consider the Galilean transformations, and analyze the Lorentz transformations in more detail. Note that the first law of Newtonian physics essentially states that: "A body continues in its state of rest or of uniform motion, unless acted upon by an external force." The frame of reference of a body at rest or in uniform motion, i.e., possessing a constant velocity, is denoted an *inertial* frame.

Consider now an inertial reference frame O′, with coordinates (t', x', y', z'), moving along the x-direction with uniform velocity, v, with respect to another inertial frame O, with coordinates (t, x, y, z). The Galilean transformation relates an event in an inertial frame O to another O′, and are given by the following relationships

$$x' = x - vt,$$

$$y' = y,$$

$$z' = z,$$

$$t' = t.$$

Note that the last equation is the mathematical assumption of absolute time in Newtonian physics.

In Euclidean space the distance, l, between two arbitrary points, A and B, with coordinates (t_A, x_A, y_A, z_A) and (t_B, x_B, y_B, z_B), respectively, is given by

$$(\Delta l)^2 = (\Delta x)^2 + (\Delta y)^2 + (\Delta z)^2, \tag{13.1}$$

where Δx, Δy, and Δz are the Cartesian coordinate intervals between A and B. One may infer some interesting properties from the above relationship. First, one verifies that $\Delta l = 0$ if and only if $\Delta x = \Delta y = \Delta z = 0$, which states that both points A and B coincide when the Euclidean distance between them is zero. Now, one may show that both the time difference $\Delta t = t_B - t_A$ and the relationship in Equation 13.1 are separately invariant under any Galilean transformation, which leads one to consider that time and space are separate entities in Newtonian physics.

Einstein abandoned the postulate of absolute time, and assumed the following two postulates: (i) the speed of light, c, is the same in all inertial frames; (ii) the principle of relativity, which states that the laws of physics take the same form in every inertial frame. Considering, once again, an inertial reference frame O′, with coordinates (t', x', y', z'), moving along the x-direction with uniform velocity relative to another inertial frame O, with coordinates (t, x, y, z), and taking into account the above two postulates, Einstein deduced the Lorentz transformation, which are given by

$$t' = \gamma\left(t - \frac{vx}{c^2}\right),$$

$$x' = \gamma(x - vt),$$

$$y' = y,$$

$$z' = z,$$

where γ is defined as

$$\gamma = \left(1 - \frac{v^2}{c^2}\right)^{-1/2}. \qquad (13.2)$$

One immediately verifies, from the first two equations, that the time and space coordinates are mixed by the Lorentz transformation, and hence, the viewpoint that the physical world is modeled by a four-dimensional spacetime continuum.

Considering two events, A and B, respectively, with coordinates (t_A, x_A, y_A, z_A) and (t_B, x_B, y_B, z_B) in an inertial frame O, then the interval, s, between the events is given by

$$\Delta s^2 = -c^2\Delta t^2 + \Delta x^2 + \Delta y^2 + \Delta z^2, \qquad (13.3)$$

where c is the speed of light, and Δt is the time interval between the two events A and B (Hobson, Efstathiou, & Lasenby, 2006). Note that for this case if $\Delta s = 0$, one cannot conclude that $\Delta t = \Delta x = \Delta y = \Delta z = 0$, due to the minus sign associated with the temporal interval. One verifies that Equation 13.3 is invariant under a Lorentz transformation, and as advocated by Minkowski, space and time are united in a four-dimensional entity, denoted as spacetime. Thus, the interval (Equation 13.3) may be considered as an underlying geometrical property of the spacetime itself. The sign Δs^2 is also invariantly defined, so that

$\Delta s^2 < 0$,	timelike interval,
$\Delta s^2 = 0$,	null interval,
$\Delta s^2 > 0$,	spacelike interval.

It is useful to represent the nature of space and time using spacetime diagrams, as depicted in Figure 13.1. The diagrams present a view of the entire spacetime, without a special status associated to the present time, as shown in the figure. For simplicity, in the spacetime diagrams presented, the y and z spatial dimensions have been suppressed. Observers moving with a relative velocity $v < c$ travel along timelike

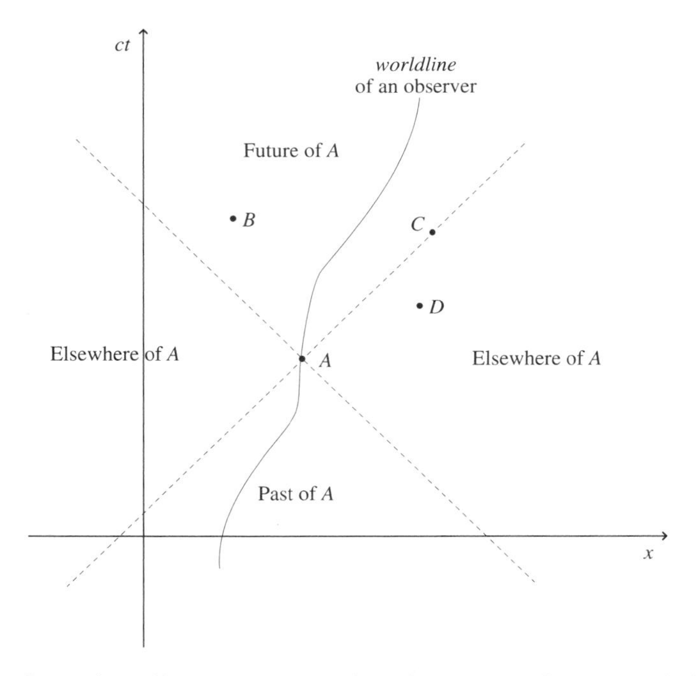

Figure 13.1: Spacetime diagram representing the nature of space and time, where, for simplicity, the spatial dimensions y and z have been suppressed. Events A and B are separated by a timelike interval; events A and C by a null interval; and events A and D are separated by a space-like interval. The curve represents the wordline of a timelike observer. The dashed lines constitute the light cones of A. The exterior of the light cones, denoted the "elsewhere region of A," constitutes the region of events which cannot influence nor be influenced by A. See the text for details.

curves, for instance, as depicted by the curve in Figure 13.1, which is denoted by the *worldline* of the observer. Now, there is a unique time measured along a worldline, denoted as *proper time*. A photon travels along null curves, $ct = +x$ and $ct = -x$, which are depicted by the dashed curves in Figure 13.1, and constitute the light cone of A. Events A and B are separated by a timelike interval; events A and C by a null interval; and events A and D are separated by a space-like interval. All events within the upper light cone of A are in the future of A, and all events with the lower light cone constitute the past of A. Events outside the light cone, such as event D, only become visible to A when it enters the light cone of A.

The interior of the future light cone of A constitutes the region that can be influenced by A with objects traveling with less than the speed of light. The boundary of the future light cone can only be influenced by signals with the speed of light from A. In counterpart, the past light cone constitutes the region in spacetime with events that may influence A. The exterior of the light cones, denoted the "elsewhere region of A," constitutes the region of events that cannot influence nor be influenced by A (Hobson et al., 2006).

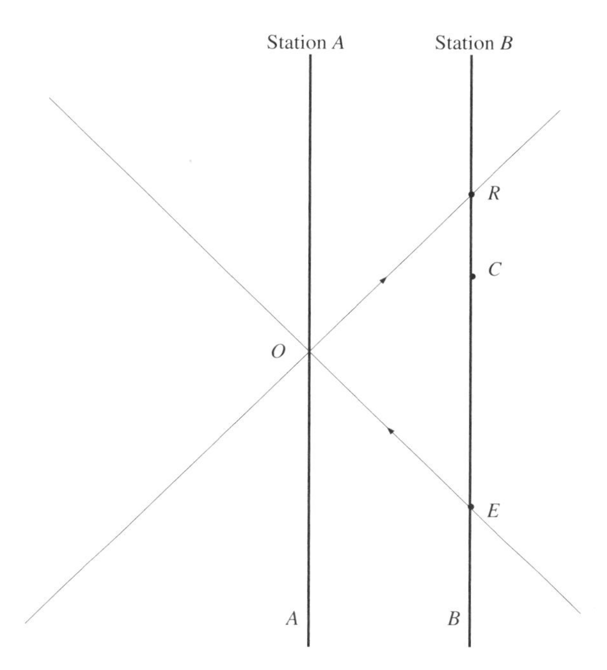

Figure 13.2: Spacetime region representing an example of the "elsewhere region." Consider two stationary space stations A and B, where the former observes event E, representing a threatening asteroid on collision course with the station B. However, as the event C, depicting the collision of B with the asteroid is situated outside the causal future of A, i.e., in the "elsewhere" region, it is impossible for A to warn B of the impeding danger in time to avoid the collision. See the text for details.

To illustrate the latter feature, consider the following example (Ellis & Williams, 2000), which is depicted in Figure 13.2. Assume the existence of two stationary space stations, A and B, respectively. A is observing B using a powerful telescope, and at event O observes event E, a threatening asteroid on collision course with B. Despite of sending a warning signal that arrives at B at event R, it will be impossible to warn B of the impeding danger in time to avoid the collision. This is due to event C, collision B-asteroid, being outside the causal future of A, i.e., in the "elsewhere" region of A. This is depicted in Figure 13.2.

The special theory of relativity challenges many of our intuitive beliefs about time. For instance, the theory is inconsistent with the common belief that the temporal order in which two events occur is independent of the observer's reference frame. To illustrate this fact, consider an inertial frame O′, with coordinates (t', x'), moving along the x-direction with uniform velocity relative, v, with respect to another inertial frame O, with coordinates (t, x). In Figure 13.3, the dashed line parallel to the x-axis represents events for a constant time t, so that events A and B are simultaneous in the observer's O reference frame. The dashed line parallel to the x'-axis depicts simultaneous events in

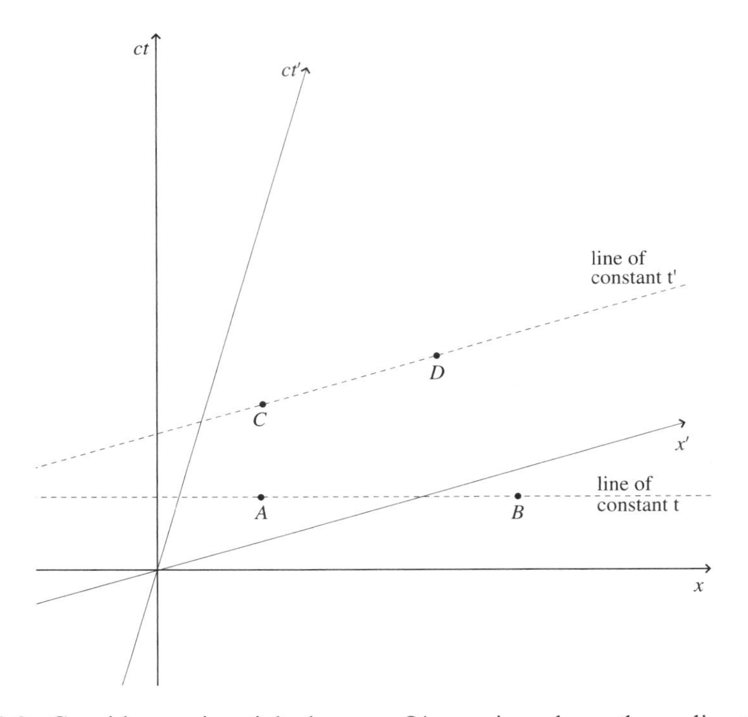

Figure 13.3: Consider an inertial observer O′, moving along the x-direction with uniform velocity, v, relative to another inertial observer O. The dashed line parallel to the x-axis represent events for a constant time t, such that events A and B are simultaneous in the observer's O reference frame. The dashed line parallel to the x'-axis depicts simultaneous events in observer's O′ reference frame. Note that C and D are simultaneous in O′, but C precedes D for observer O. Thus, special relativity denies the possibility of universal simultaneity, and consequently the possibility of a universal now.

observer's O′ reference frame so that despite the fact that events C and D are simultaneous in O′, one verifies that C precedes D for the observer O.

Consider the following example to further illustrate this point, which is depicted in Figure 13.4. Consider two space stations A and B, separated by a distance D. Assume now a stationary satellite O midway between the stations, and a second satellite O′ moving towards station B with a velocity v with respect to O. At the instant that both satellites are midway between the stations, these send out a simultaneous signal, A′ and B′, respectively, as measured from A at event C. However, satellite O′ will receive the signal from station B, at event D, before the signal from A, event E, as depicted in Figure 13.4. Thus, whether a specific instant is in the future or past is frame dependent. *Special relativity denies the possibility of universal simultaneity, and hence the possibility of a universal now.*

This raises the problem of the synchronization of distant clocks in defining simultaneity in spacetime. A simple conceptual definition of a clock will be provided

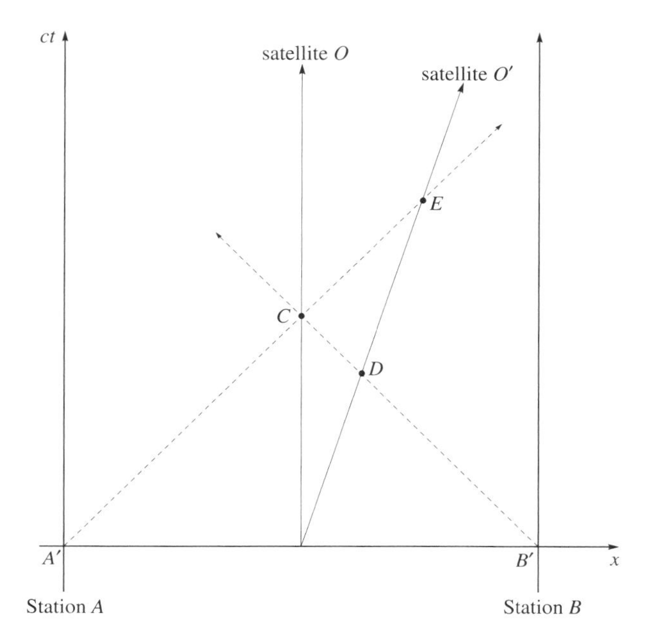

Figure 13.4: Spacetime diagram representing an example of the impossibility of universal simultaneity. Consider two stationary space stations, A and B, respectively, a stationary satellite O midway between the stations, and another satellite O′ moving towards B with a velocity v relatively to A. Satellite O measures at event C simultaneous signals, A′ and B′, sent out by A and B, respectively. On the other hand, satellite O′ will receive the signal from B, at event D, before the signal from A, at event E.

below. Consider two clocks at rest with respect to an observer, located at spacetime points A and B, respectively. Suppose now that at time t_1, A sends out a signal to B, which is reflected and returns to A at time t_2. Taking into account the constancy of the speed of light, A will conclude that the event reflection from B is simultaneous with the time T is his worldline, which is precisely half the interval of travel time, i.e.,

$$T = \frac{t_1 + t_2}{2}. \tag{13.4}$$

This is a simple and practical way of determining simultaneity and of synchronizing clocks, which is depicted in Figure 13.5.

Another feature of our intuitive beliefs challenged by the special theory of relativity is that related with time-dilation effects. For instance, consider the following thought experiment suggested by Einstein. Suppose that an observer travels along a tram moving with a relativistic velocity, while observing a large clock through a powerful telescope. The observer sees the clock, as the emitted light catches

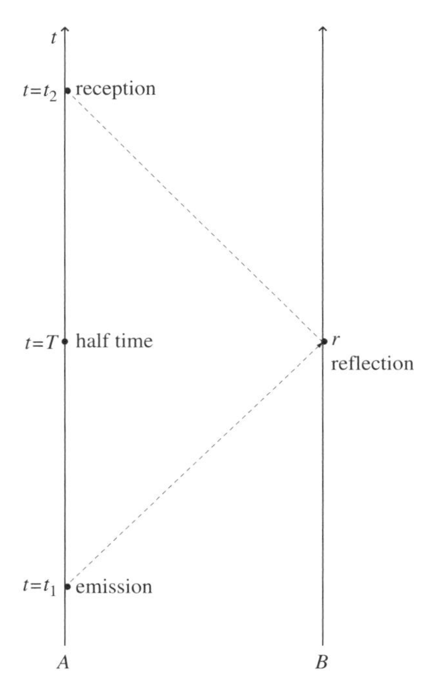

Figure 13.5: Figure depicting the synchronization of distinct clocks and the definition of simultaneity in spacetime. See the text for details.

up with the tram. Now, if the tram moves at a speed close to that of light, the light rays emitted from the clock take longer to catch up with the observer. It seems that time has slowed down as measured by the latter. If the tram now attains the speed of light, then the light reflected from the clock cannot catch up with the observer, and it seems that time would come to a standstill.

One may infer time dilation from the constancy of the speed of light. First, it is useful to provide a simple conceptual definition of a clock, namely, that of a "light clock." The latter is constructed by two mirrors separated by a distance d, with a photon being continuously reflected in between. A "click" of this idealized clock is constituted by the time interval, $2\Delta t'$, with which the photon traces the distance $2d$, as depicted in Figure 13.6. Thus, one deduces the following expression $2\Delta t' = 2d/c$, which implies $\Delta t' = d/c$. Now, consider that this clock is at rest in an inertial frame O′ traveling with a relativistic velocity v with respect to a frame O. From the special relativistic postulate that the speed of light is constant in all frames, the time interval traced out by the photon, as measured by the observer at rest O is $2\Delta t$, and taking into account Pythagoras' theorem, we have

$$c^2(\Delta t)^2 = v^2(\Delta t)^2 + d^2. \tag{13.5}$$

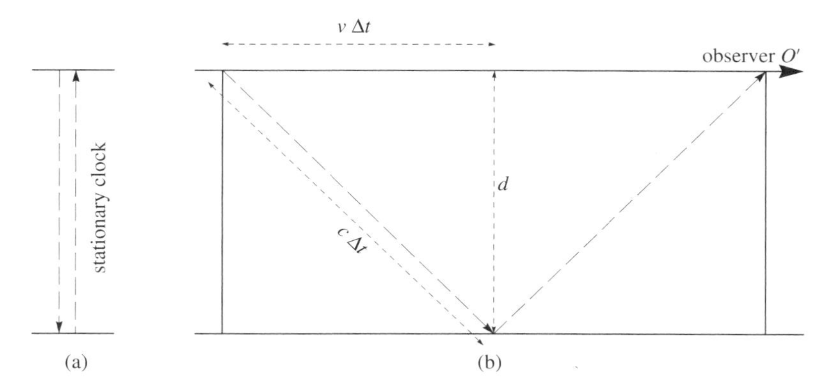

Figure 13.6: (a) A light clock at rest in an inertial reference frame O′. The light is reflected from a mirror at a distance d, and is received after a time $2\Delta t'$ as measured in O′. (b) This depicts a light clock at rest with respect to an inertial frame O′, which is traveling at a speed v with respect to an identical clock on the ground, at rest in an inertial frame O. The latter observer measures a "click" in a time interval $2\Delta t$. See the text for details.

Using $\Delta t' = d/c$, one finally deduces the following relationship

$$\Delta t = \gamma \, \Delta t'. \tag{13.6}$$

As $\gamma > 1$, then $\Delta t > \Delta t'$, so that time as measured by the moving reference frame O′ slows down relatively to O.

The above relationship may also be deduced directly from the Lorentz transformations. Suppose that a clock sits at rest with respect to the inertial reference frame O′, in which two successive clicks, represented by two events A and B are separated by a time interval $\Delta t'$. To determine the time interval Δt as measured by O, it is useful to consider the inverse Lorentz transformation, given by

$$t = \gamma\left(t' + \frac{vx'}{c^2}\right), \tag{13.7}$$

which provides

$$t_B - t_A = \gamma\left[t'_B - t'_A + \frac{v\left(x_B{}' - x'_A\right)}{c^2}\right], \tag{13.8}$$

where t_A and t_B are the two clicks measured in O. As the events are stationary relative to O′, we have $x'_B = x'_A$, so that one finally ends up with Equation 13.6, taking into account $\Delta t = t_B - t_A$ and $\Delta t' = t'_B - t'_A$. We note that the fact that a moving clock

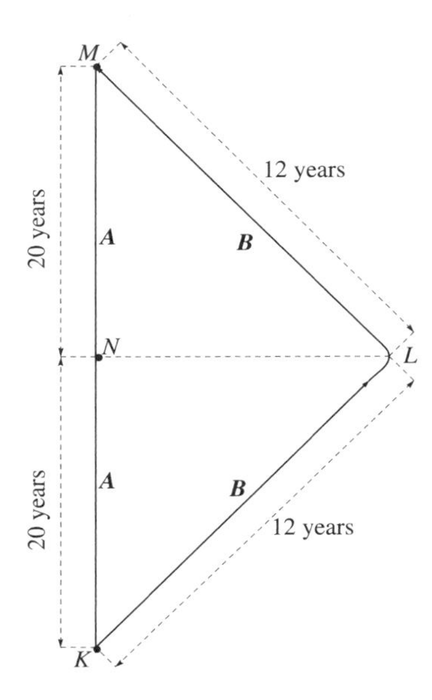

Figure 13.7: Time-dilation effects in the twin paradox. See the text for details.

slows down is completely reciprocal for any pair of inertial observers, and this is essentially explained as both disagree about simultaneity.

An interesting example of the time-dilation effects is the so-called "twin paradox," depicted in Figure 13.7. Consider two identical twins, A and B, respectively, where A remains at rest, while B travels away from A at a relativistic velocity, close to the speed of light. As a practical example, consider that B initially recedes away from A at a speed of $v = 4c/5$ for 12 years, as measured by B's clock, then returns at the same speed for 12 years. Thus, B measures a total journey time of 24 years. One may ask what the total travel time is, as measured by the twin A. To answer this, consider that the event K, relatively to the twin A, is where B begins his outward journey; L is the event when B turns around; and M the event when B arrives back at A. From Equation 13.2, we verify that in both the outward and return journey, we have $\gamma = [1-(4/5)^2]^{-1/2} = 5/3$. Considering that the event N, relative to A, is simultaneous to L, then one verifies that $t_{KN} = \gamma t'_{KL} = (5/3) \times 12 = 20$ years, so that the total travel time as measured by A is 40 years.

However, time-dilation effects are reciprocal between two inertial frames, and one may wonder how it is possible to reconcile the difference between both observers. It is important to emphasize that the difference between both observers, A and B, is that twin B is not an inertial observer, as his trajectory consists of two inertial segments joined by a period of acceleration. It is interesting to note that this feature has been observed experimentally, in particular, in the Hafele–Keating experiment, which we refer to below (Hafele & Keating, 1972a, b).

13.2.2. Time in General Relativity

The analysis outlined above has only taken into account flat spacetimes, contrary to Einstein's general theory of relativity, in which gravitational fields are represented through the curvature of spacetime. In the discussion of special relativity, the analysis was restricted to inertial motion, and in general relativity the principle of relativity is extended to all observers, inertial or noninertial. In general relativity it is assumed that *the laws of physics are the same for all observers, no matter what their state of motion* (Ellis & Williams, 2000). Now it is clear that a gravitational force measured by an observer essentially depends on his state of acceleration, which leads to the *principle of equivalence*, which states that "there is no way of distinguishing between effects on an observer of a uniform gravitational field and of constant acceleration."

The general theory of relativity has been an extremely successful theory, with a well-established experimental footing, at least for weak gravitational fields. Of particular interest in this work are the gravitational time-dilation effects. For this, imagine the following idealized thought experiment, suggested by Einstein (Schutz, 1990), which is depicted in Figure 13.8. Consider a tower of height h hovering on the Earth's surface, with a particle of rest mass m lying on top. The particle is then

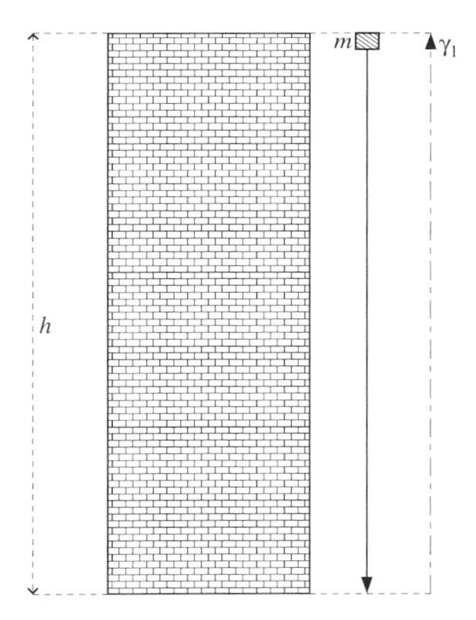

Figure 13.8: Figure representing the gravitational time-dilation effect. Suppose that a particle of mass m is dropped from the top of a tower, falling freely with acceleration g and reaching the ground with velocity $v = (2gh)^{1/2}$. The idealized particle is then converted into a single photon γ_1 and returns to the top of the tower. An observer, at the top of the tower, measures the time interval $\Delta t' = \Delta t\ (l + gh/c^2)$, where Δt is the time interval as measured by an observer at the bottom of the tower. Thus, this shows that time flows at a faster rate on top of the tower than at the bottom. See the text for details.

dropped from rest, falling freely with acceleration g and reaches the ground with a nonrelativistic velocity $v = (2gh)^{1/2}$. Thus, an observer on the ground measures its energy as

$$E = mc^2 + \frac{mv^2}{2} = mc^2 + mgh. \tag{13.9}$$

The idealized particle is then converted into a single photon γ_1 with identical energy E, which returns to the top of the tower. Upon arrival it converts into a particle with energy $E' = m'c^2$. Note that to avoid perpetual motion $m' > m$ is forbidden, so that we consider $m = m'$, and the following relationship is obtained

$$\frac{E'}{E} = \frac{mc^2}{mc^2 + mgh} = 1 - \frac{gh}{c^2}, \tag{13.10}$$

with $gh/c^2 \ll 1$. From the definitions $E = h\nu$ and $E' = h\nu'$, where ν and ν' are the frequencies of the photon at the bottom and top of the tower, so that from Equation 13.10, one obtains

$$\nu' = \nu\left(1 - \frac{gh}{c^2}\right). \tag{13.11}$$

This is depicted in Figure 13.8.

Now, to obtain the important result that clocks run at different rates in a gravitational field, consider the following thought experiment. The observer at the bottom of the tower emits a light wave, directed to the top. The relationship of time between two crests is simply the inverse of the frequency, i.e., $\Delta t = 1/\nu$, so that from Equation 13.11, one obtains the approximations, considering $gh/c^2 \ll 1$,

$$\Delta t' = \Delta t\left(1 + \frac{gh}{c^2}\right). \tag{13.12}$$

This provides the result that time flows at a faster rate on top of the tower than at the bottom. Note that this result has been obtained independently of the gravitational theory.

13.2.3. Experimental Tests

A well-known experiment to test the time-dilation effects in general relativity, in particular, that clocks should run at different rates at different places in a gravitational field, is the Pound–Rebka experiment (Pound & Rebka, 1959), which confirmed the predictions of general relativity to a 10% precision level (Pound & Rebka, 1960). These results were later improved to a 1% precision level by Pound and Snider (1964).

The Hafele–Keating experiment (Hafele & Keating, 1972a, b), realized in October 1971, was an interesting test of the theory of relativity. It essentially consisted of traveling four cesium-beam atomic clocks aboard commercial airliners, and flying twice around the world, first eastward, and then westward. The results were then compared with the clocks of the United States Naval Observatory. To within experimental error, the results were consistent with the relativistic predictions.

A modern application of the special and general relativistic time-dilation effects are the synchronization of atomic clocks on board the global positioning system (GPS) satellites. The GPS has become a widely used aid to navigation worldwide, enabling a GPS receiver to determine its location, speed, and direction. Now, as verified above, general relativity predicts that the atomic clocks at GPS orbital altitudes will tick more rapidly, as they are in a weaker gravitational field than atomic clocks on Earth's surface; while atomic clocks moving at GPS orbital speeds will tick more slowly than stationary ground clocks, as predicted by special relativity. When both effects are combined, the experimental data show that the on-board atomic clock rates do indeed agree with ground clock rates to the predicted extent.

13.3. Time Irreversibility and the Arrow of Time

The modern perspective in physics is that dynamical laws essentially govern the universe, i.e., they specify the evolution of a determined physical system with time, given the initial conditions of the physical state. One normally considers the evolution of physical systems into the future, which are governed by differential equations (Penrose, 2005). In this context, it is not a common practice to evolve the physical systems into the past, despite the fact that the dynamical equations of classical and quantum physics are symmetrical under a time reversal. Mathematically, one might as well specify the final conditions and evolve the physical system back in time. One specifies data at some initial instant and these data evolve, through dynamical equations, to determine the physical state of the system in the future, or to the past, i.e., detailed predictability to the future and past is in principle possible. However, several issues are raised by thermodynamics, general relativity and quantum mechanics on time irreversibility and the arrow of time.

13.3.1. The Arrow of Time in Thermodynamics

A classical example of an irreversible process is the dissipation of smoke from a lit cigarette. In principle, the evolution of the system and its outcome is possible if the microscopic dynamics of each individual particle is possible, but in practice one has little knowledge of the position and velocity of every particle in the system. The overall behavior of the system is well described in terms of appropriate averages of the physical parameters of the individual particles, such as the distribution of mass, momentum, energy, etc. One may argue that the knowledge of these averaged parameters is sufficient to determine the dynamical behavior of the system and the respective final outcome. However, this is not always the case, as in the specific examples of "chaotic systems."

Chaotic systems are classical systems, where a small change in the initial conditions modifies the behavior of the system exponentially, resulting in an unpredictability of the final outcome. This chaotic unpredictability is closely related to the second law of thermodynamics, which states that the entropy of the system increases (or at least does not decrease) with time. The entropy is essentially a measure of the disorder or randomness in the system. For instance, note the increased randomness of the convoluted path of the diffusion of smoke from a lit cigarette. As a simple example, consider a body moving through the air. The body possesses kinetic energy, in an organized form, and as it slows down from the air resistance, the kinetic energy has been transferred to the random motion of the air particles and the individual particles of the body (Penrose, 2005).

Consider the flow of heat from a hot body to a cooler body. The evolution of this system is deterministic in character and predicted by the second law of thermodynamics. If one theoretically considers the time-reversed evolution of the system, then one would have the following scenario: Two bodies of the same temperature evolve to bodies of unequal temperature. It would even be a practical impossibility to know which body would be the hotter, and which the cooler. Note that this difficulty of dynamical retrodiction applies to most macroscopic systems, which possess a large number of constituent particles and behaving in accordance with the second law of thermodynamics.

A particularly interesting example is that of friction (Ellis, 2006). Consider, for simplicity, a block of mass sliding along a plane, and being slowed down by a constant force of friction, consequently coming to rest at a determined instant. One may agree that providing the detailed microphysical properties, such as the distribution of heat on the plane, it may be possible to predict the initial conditions. However, using a macroscopic viewpoint, after the system has settled down, one cannot retrodict the initial conditions. One cannot even reconstruct the trajectory, and one could conjecture if the block came from the left or from the right.

In all of the examples outlined above one may argue that the microphysics is completely deterministic, contrary to the outcome of macroscopic viewpoint (Ellis, 2006). This is essentially because in the macroscopic viewpoint one does not have enough detail of the physical system's microproperties. One may provide a statistical prediction of the eventual outcome, but not a detailed and definite prediction. Note that the total energy of the system is conserved as dictated by the first law of thermodynamics. One may state that the disorder or randomness has increased. Thus, the increase in entropy generically provides a thermodynamic arrow of time. It is also possible to assume that the second law of thermodynamics and the thermodynamic arrow of time are a consequence of the initial conditions of the universe, which leads us to the cosmological arrow of time that inexorably points in the direction of the universe's expansion.

13.3.2. The Arrow of Time in Quantum Mechanics

Quantum uncertainty is a fundamental aspect of quantum theory, i.e., it is not possible to determine a unique outcome of quantum events. Formally, consider the wave function $\psi(x)$ as a linear combination of eigenfunctions $u_n(x)$, given by

$$\psi_1(x) = \sum a_i u_i(x). \tag{13.13}$$

Suppose now that a measurement takes place at $t = t_n$, thus reducing the wave function to

$$\psi_2(x) = a_n u_n(x), \tag{13.14}$$

for some specific value $i = n$. It is important to emphasize that the initial state (Equation 13.13) does not uniquely determine the final state (Equation 13.14). This is not due to lack of data, but is due to the nature of quantum physics. Furthermore, one cannot predict the final eigenstate $\psi_2(x)$ from the initial state (Ellis, 2006). One cannot also retrodict to the past at the quantum level, as once the wave function has collapsed to an eigenstate, one cannot know the initial state from the final state. Thus, despite the fact that there is time symmetry in the evolution of a quantum system, the reduction of the wave function is essentially time asymmetric.

It is illustrative to consider the following example (Penrose, 2005). Consider a photon source S that emits individual photons. The latter are aimed at a beam splitter B, which is simply a half-silvered mirror, and is placed at an angle of 45° to the beam. Thus, if a photon is reflected, it will be absorbed at the ceiling C; if it is transmitted, it will activate a detector D. Suppose that the probability of reflection and transmission is 50%, respectively. Now, suppose that a detection at D is verified, which is equivalent to the reduction of the wave function corresponding to Equation 13.14. Given this, one may ask what the initial probabilities are. For this, the relevant histories would be SBD and FBD, where F is a point on the floor. If a photon were emitted at F, it would be reflected at B and be detected at D. Now, applying the quantum mechanical rules, one verifies that there is a 50% probability that the photon will be detected at D, for the respective emissions at S and at F. This is absurd, as there is a 0% probability that a photon would be emitted from F. From this simple example, one verifies time asymmetry related to the reduction of the wave function in quantum mechanics. This is depicted in Figure 13.9.

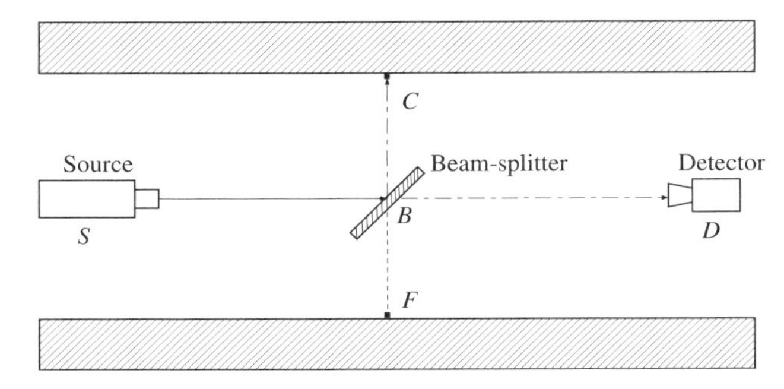

Figure 13.9: Time asymmetry in the reduction of the wave function. See the text for details.

13.4. Closed Timelike Curves and Causality Violation

As time is incorporated into the proper structure of the fabric of spacetime, it is interesting to note that general relativity is contaminated with nontrivial geometries which generate *closed timelike curves* (Visser, 1995). A closed timelike curve (CTC) allows time travel, in the sense that an observer, who travels on a trajectory in spacetime along this curve, returns to an event which coincides with the departure. The arrow of time leads forward, as measured locally by the observer, but globally he/she may return to an event in the past. This fact apparently violates causality, opening Pandora's box and producing time-travel paradoxes (Nahin, 1999), throwing a veil over our understanding of the fundamental nature of time. The notion of causality is fundamental in the construction of physical theories; therefore, time travel and its associated paradoxes have to be treated with great caution. The paradoxes fall into two broad groups, namely the *consistency paradoxes* and the *causal loops*.

The consistency paradoxes include the classical grandfather paradox. Imagine traveling into the past and meeting one's grandfather. Nurturing homicidal tendencies, the time traveler murders his grandfather, impeding the birth of his father, therefore making his own birth impossible. Another example is that of autoinfanticide, where the time traveler returns to the past, and kills himself as a baby. In fact, there are many versions of the grandfather paradox, limited only by one's imagination. The consistency paradoxes occur whenever possibilities of changing events in the past arise.

The paradoxes associated with causal loops are related to self-existing information or objects, trapped in spacetime. Imagine a researcher traveling forward in time and reading the details of the recently formulated, and anxiously anticipated, consistent theory of quantum gravity. Returning to his time, he explains the details to an ambitious younger colleague, who writes it up and the article is eventually published in the journal, where the first researcher read it after traveling into the future. The article on the theory of quantum gravity exists in the future because it was written in the past by the young researcher. The latter wrote it up, after receiving the details from his colleague, who in turn read the article in the future. Both parts considered by themselves are consistent, and the paradox appears when considered as a whole. One is liable to ask as to what is the origin of the information, as it appears out of nowhere. The details for a complete and consistent theory of quantum gravity, which paradoxically were never created, nevertheless exist in spacetime. Note the absence of causality violations in these paradoxes.

A great variety of solutions to the Einstein field equations containing closed timelike curves exist, but two particularly notorious features seem to stand out (Lobo & Crawford (2003a, b)): solutions with a tipping over of the light cones due to a rotation about a cylindrically symmetric axis; and solutions that violate the energy conditions of general relativity, which are fundamental in the singularity theorems and theorems of classical black hole thermodynamics (Hawking & Ellis, 1973; Visser, 1995).

13.4.1. Stationary, Axisymmetric Solutions

The tipping over of light cones seems to be a generic feature of some solutions with a rotating cylindrical symmetry, which is depicted in Figure 13.10. The present work is far from making an exhaustive search of all the Einstein field equation solutions generating closed timelike curves with these features, but the best-known spacetimes will be briefly mentioned. The earliest solution to the Einstein field equations containing closed timelike curves is probably that of the van Stockum spacetime

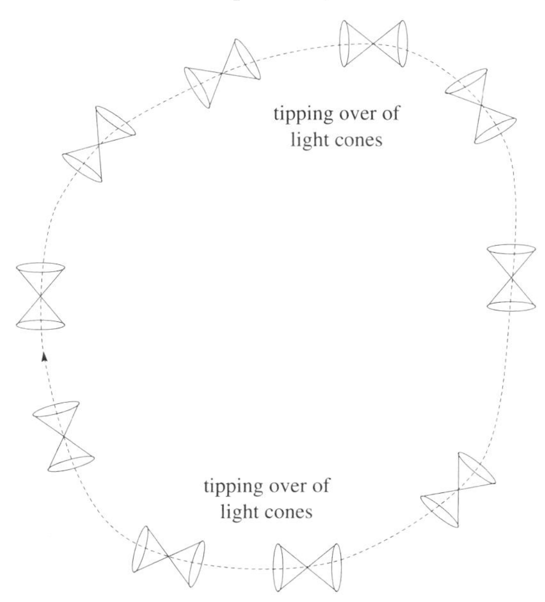

Figure 13.10: The tipping over of light cones, depicted in the figure is a generic feature of some solutions with a rotating cylindrical symmetry. The dashed curve represents a closed timelike curve.

(Tipler, 1974; Visser, 1995). It is a stationary, cylindrically symmetric solution describing a rapidly rotating infinite cylinder of dust, surrounded by vacuum. The centrifugal forces of the dust are balanced by the gravitational attraction. The light cones tip over close to the cylinder, due to the strong curvature of the spacetime, consequently inducing closed timelike curves. In 1949, Kurt Gödel discovered another exact solution to the Einstein field equations consisting of a uniformly rotating universe containing dust and a nonzero cosmological constant (Gödel, 1949). It is possible to show that moving away from the axis, the light cones open out and tilt in the angular direction, eventually generating closed timelike curves (Hawking & Ellis, 1973).

An analogous solution to that of the van Stockum spacetime, although possessing a different asymptotic behavior, is that of an infinitely long straight string that lies and spins around the z-axis (Visser, 1995). These latter solutions also induce closed timelike curves. An interesting variant of these rotating cosmic strings is an extremely elegant model of a time machine, theoretically constructed by Gott (1991). It is an exact solution to the Einstein field equations for the general case of two moving straight cosmic strings that do not intersect. This solution produces closed timelike curves even though they do not violate the weak energy condition, which essentially prohibits the existence of negative energy densities, have no singularities and event horizons, and are not topologically multiply connected as the wormhole solution, which will be considered below. The appearance of closed timelike curves relies solely on the gravitational lens effect and the relativity of simultaneity. However, it was shown that the Gott time machine is unphysical in nature, for such an acausal behavior cannot be realized by physical and timelike sources (Deser, 1993; Deser, Jackiw, & t'Hooft, 1992).

13.4.2. Solutions Violating the Energy Conditions

The traditional manner of solving the Einstein field equation consists in considering a plausible distribution of energy and matter, and then finding the geometrical structure. However, one can run the Einstein field equation in the reverse direction by imposing an exotic geometrical spacetime structure, and eventually determine the matter source for the respective geometry.

In this fashion, solutions violating the energy conditions have been obtained. One of the simplest energy conditions is the weak energy condition, which is essentially equivalent to the assumption that any timelike observer measures a local positive energy density. Although classical forms of matter obey these energy conditions, violations have been encountered in quantum field theory, the Casimir effect being a well-known example. Adopting the reverse philosophy, solutions such as traversable wormholes (Lemos, Lobo, & Quinet de Oliveira, 2003; Lobo, 2005a, b; Morris & Thorne, 1998; Visser, 1995), the warp drive (Alcubierre, 1994; Lobo & Crawford (2003a, b); Lobo & Visser, 2004), and the Krasnikov tube (Krasnikov, 1998) have been obtained. These solutions violate the energy conditions and with simple manipulations generate closed timelike curves (Everett, 1996; Everett & Roman, 1997; Morris, Thorne, & Yurtsever, 1988).

We shall briefly consider the specific case of traversable wormholes (Morris & Thorne, 1998). A wormhole is essentially constituted by two mouths, A and B, residing in different regions of spacetime (Morris & Thorne, 1998), which in turn are connected by a hypothetical tunnel. One of the most fascinating aspects of wormholes is their apparent ease in generating closed timelike curves (Morris et al., 1988). There are several ways to generate a time machine using multiple wormholes (Visser, 1995), but a manipulation of a single wormhole seems to be the simplest way (Morris et al., 1988). The basic idea is to create a time shift between both mouths. This is done invoking the time-dilation effects in special relativity or in general relativity, i.e., one may consider the analogue of the twin paradox, in which the mouths are moving one with respect to the other, or simply the case in which one of the mouths is placed in a strong gravitational field, so that time slows down in the respective mouth (Frolov & Novikov, 1990; Visser, 1995).

To create a time shift using the twin paradox analogue, consider that the mouths of the wormhole may be moving one with respect to the other in external space, without significant changes of the internal geometry of the tunnel. For simplicity, consider that one of the mouths A is at rest in an inertial frame, while the other mouth B, initially at rest practically close to A, starts to move out with a high velocity, then returns to its starting point. Owing to the Lorentz time contraction, the time interval between these two events, ΔT_{B}, measured by a clock comoving with B can be made to be significantly shorter than the time interval between the same two events, ΔT_{A}, as measured by a clock resting at A. Thus, the clock that has moved has been slowed by $\Delta T_{\mathrm{A}} - \Delta T_{\mathrm{B}}$ relative to the standard inertial clock. Suppose that the tunnel between A and B remains practically unchanged, so that an observer comparing the time of the clocks through the handle will measure an identical time, as the mouths are at rest with respect to one another. However, by comparing the time of the clocks in external space, he will verify that their time shift is precisely $\Delta T_{\mathrm{A}} - \Delta T_{\mathrm{B}}$, as both mouths are in different reference frames, frames that moved with high velocities with respect to one another. Time is hooked up differently as measured by through the interior or in the exterior of the wormhole. Now, consider an observer starting off from A at an instant T_0, measured by the clock stationed at A. He makes his way to B in external space and enters the tunnel from B. Consider, for simplicity, that the trip through the wormhole tunnel is instantaneous. He then exits from the wormhole mouth A into external space at the instant $T_0 - (\Delta T_{\mathrm{A}} - \Delta T_{\mathrm{B}})$ as measured by a clock positioned at A. His arrival at A precedes his departure, and the wormhole has been converted into a time machine (see Figure 13.11).

13.5. Summary and Discussion

In this chapter, a brief review on the nature of time in physics has been explored. In particular, it was noted that in Newtonian physics, time flows at a constant rate for

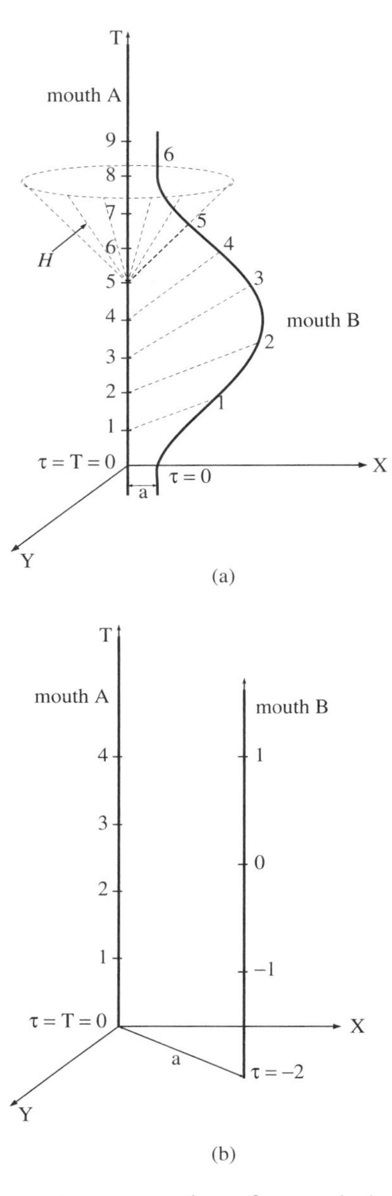

Figure 13.11: Depicted are two examples of wormhole spacetimes with closed timelike curves. The wormholes tunnels are arbitrarily short, and its two mouths move along two world tubes depicted as thick lines in the figure. Proper time τ at the wormhole throat is marked off, and note that identical values are the same event as seen through the wormhole handle. (a) Mouth A remains at rest, while mouth B accelerates from A at a high velocity, then returns to its starting point at rest. A time shift is induced between both mouths, due to the time-dilation effects of special relativity. The light cone-like hypersurface H shown is a Cauchy horizon, beyond which predictability breaks down. Through every event to the future of H there exist closed timelike curves, and on the other hand there are no closed timelike curves to the past of H. (b) A time shift between both mouths is induced by placing mouth B in strong gravitational field. See text for details.

all observers, providing the notion of absolute time, while in the special and general theories of relativity, time necessarily flows at different rates for different observers. It was shown that special relativity denies the possibility of universal simultaneity, and consequently the impossibility of a universal now. In this context, the Block Universe description emerges, where all times, past and future are equally present, and the notion of the flow of time is a subjective illusion. This leads one to the possibility of time being a dimension, contrary to a process. Indeed, intuitively, one verifies that the notion of time as something that flows arises due to an intimate relationship to change. Nevertheless, in relativity the concept of spacetime being an independent entity containing events predominates. Despite the fact of the great popularity of the Block Universe representation in the physics (in particular the relativistic) community, this viewpoint often meets with resistance, and we refer the reader to an interesting paper by George F. Ellis (Ellis, 2006).

Ellis argues that the Block Universe picture does not constitute a realistic model of the universe for several reasons: It assumes simplified equations of state and thus does not apply to spacetimes including complex systems, e.g., biological systems; they don't take into account several issues such as dissipative effects, feedback effects, and quantum uncertainty. Indeed, in our everyday experience, psychological time does contrast to the Block Universe picture, due to the subjective emergent notion of time as a process. Thus, adopting this viewpoint, it is plausible to consider that time is an abstract concept, nonexistent as a physical entity, but useful in describing processes. Contrary to the Block Universe, representing spacetime as a fixed whole, Ellis argues in favor of an Evolving Block Universe model of spacetime (Ellis, 2006), where "... time progresses, events happen, and history is shaped. Things could have been different, but second by second, one specific evolutionary history out of all the possibilities is chosen, takes place, and gets cast in stone." The Evolving Block Universe representation defends that spacetime is extended into the future as events occur along each worldline, which is determined by causal interactions.

A fundamental issue in the nature of time is its arrow. In modern physics, dynamical laws essentially govern the universe, where one considers the evolution of physical systems into the future. Nevertheless, the dynamical equations of classical and quantum physics are symmetrical under a time reversal, and mathematically one may evolve the physical systems into the past. In principle, detailed predictability to the future and past is possible. However, several issues are raised by thermodynamics and quantum mechanics on time irreversibility and the arrow of time. In a thermodynamical context, one may argue that the microphysics of a specific system is completely deterministic, contrary to the outcome of the macroscopic viewpoint (Ellis, 2006). This is essentially because in the macroscopic viewpoint one does not have enough detail of the physical system's microproperties. One may provide a statistical prediction of the eventual outcome but not a detailed and definite prediction. This fact is closely related to the second law of thermodynamics. Thus, the increase in entropy generically provides a thermodynamic arrow of time. It is also possible to assume that the second law of thermodynamics and the thermodynamic arrow of time are a consequence of the initial conditions of the universe, which leads us to the cosmological arrow of time, that inexorably points in the direction of the universe's expansion. In a quantum mechanical context, it was also shown that despite the fact that there is a time symmetry in the evolution of a quantum system, the reduction of the wave function is essentially time asymmetric.

Relative to causality violation, if one regards that general relativity is a valid theory, then it is plausible to at least include the *possibility* of time travel in the form of closed timelike curves. However, a typical reaction is to exclude time travel due to the associated paradoxes, although the latter do not prove that time travel is mathematically or physically impossible. The paradoxes do indeed indicate that local information in spacetimes containing closed timelike curves is restricted in unfamiliar ways. Relative to the grandfather paradox, it is logically inconsistent that the time traveler murders his grandfather. But, one can ask, what exactly impeded him from accomplishing his murderous act if he had ample opportunities and the freewill to do so. It seems that certain conditions in local events are to be fulfilled, for the solution to be globally self-consistent. These conditions are denominated *consistency* constraints (Earman, 1995). Much has been written on two possible remedies to the paradoxes, namely the principle of self-consistency and the chronology protection conjecture.

The principle of self-consistency stipulates that events on a closed timelike curve are self-consistent, i.e., events influence one another along the curve in a cyclic and self-consistent way. In the presence of closed timelike curves, the distinction between past and future events is ambiguous, and the definitions considered in the causal structure of well-behaved spacetimes break down. What is important to note is that events in the future can influence, but cannot change, events in the past. According to this principle, the only solutions of the laws of physics that are allowed locally, and reinforced by the consistency constraints, are those that are globally self-consistent. Hawking's chronology protection conjecture is a more conservative way of dealing with the paradoxes. Hawking notes the strong experimental evidence in favor of the conjecture from the fact that "we have not been invaded by hordes of tourists from the future" (Hawking, 1992). An analysis reveals that the value of the renormalized expectation quantum stress-energy tensor diverges close to the formation of closed timelike curves, which destroys the wormhole's internal structure before attaining the Planck scale. There is no convincing demonstration of the Chronology Protection Conjecture, but perhaps an eventual quantum gravity theory will provide us with the answers.

But, as stated by Thorne (1992), it is by extending the theory to its extreme predictions that one can get important insights to its limitations, and probably ways to overcome them. Therefore, time travel in the form of closed timelike curves is more than a justification for theoretical speculation; it is a conceptual tool and an epistemological instrument to probe the deepest levels of general relativity and extract clarifying views. Relative to the issue of time, one may consider that the underlying question is that of an ontological nature, and quoting Ellis: "Does spacetime indeed exist as a real physical entity, or is it just a convenient way of describing relationships between physical objects, which in the end are all that really exist at a fundamental level?" (Ellis, 2006).

Acknowledgments

I thank Simon Grondin for the kind invitation to write this chapter; Giuseppe de Risi and David Coule for extremely stimulating discussions; and acknowledge funding from the Fundação para a Ciência e a Tecnologia (FCT) — Portugal through the grant SFRH/BPD/26269/2006.

This work is dedicated to my parents, wherever or whenever they may be.

References

Alcubierre, M. (1994). The warp drive: Hyper-fast travel within general relativity. *Classical and Quantum Gravity*, *11*, L73–L77.

Deser, S. (1993). Physical obstacles to time-travel. *Classical and Quantum Gravity*, *10*, S67–S73.

Deser, S., Jackiw, R., & t'Hooft, G. (1992). Physical cosmic strings do not generate closed timelike curves. *Physical Review Letters*, *68*, 267–269.

Earman, J. (1995). *Bangs, crunches, whimpers, and shrieks: Singularities and acausalities in relativistic spacetimes*. Oxford, UK: Oxford University Press.

Ellis, G. F. R. (2006). Physics in the real universe: Time and spacetime. *General Relativity and Gravitation*, *38*, 1797–1824.

Ellis, G. F. R., & Williams, R. M. (2000). *Flat and curved spacetimes*. New York: Oxford University Press.

Everett, A. E. (1996). Warp drive and causality. *Physical Review D*, *53*, 7365–7368.

Everett, A. E., & Roman, T. A. (1997). A superluminal subway: The krasnikov tube. *Physical Review D*, *56*, 2100–2108.

Frolov, V. P., & Novikov, I. D. (1990). Physical effects in wormholes and time machines. *Physical Review D*, *42*, 1057–1065.

Gott, J. R. (1991). Closed timelike curves produced by pairs of moving cosmic strings: Exact solutions. *Physical Review Letters*, *66*, 1126–1129.

Gödel, K. (1949). An example of a new type of cosmological solution of Einstein's field equations of gravitation. *Review of Modern Physics*, *21*, 447–450.

Hafele, J., & Keating, R. (1972a). Around the world atomic clocks: Predicted relativistic time gains. *Science*, *177*(4044), 166–168.

Hafele, J., & Keating, R. (1972a). Around the world atomic clocks: Observed relativistic time gains. *Science*, *177*(4044), 168–170.

Hartz, G. A., & Cover, J. A. (1988). Space and time in the Leibnizian metaphysics. *Noûs*, *22*, 493–519.

Hawking, S. W. (1992). Chronology protection conjecture. *Physical Review D*, *56*, 4745–4755.

Hawking, S. W., & Ellis, G. F. R. (1973). *The large scale structure of spacetime*. London: Cambridge University Press.

Hobson, M. P., Efstathiou, G., & Lasenby, A. N. (2006). *General relativity: An introduction for physicists*. Cambridge, UK: Cambridge University Press.

Krasnikov, S. V. (1998). Hyperfast interstellar travel in general relativity. *Physical Review D*, *57*, 4760–4766.

Lemos, J. P. S., Lobo, F. S. N., & Quinet de Oliveira, S. (2003). Morris-Thorne wormholes with a cosmological constant. *Physical Review D*, *68*, 064004.1–064004.15.

Lobo, F. S. N. (2005a). Phantom energy traversable wormholes. *Physical Review D, 71*, 084011.1–084011.8.
Lobo, F. S. N. (2005a). Stability of phantom wormholes. *Physical Review D, 71*, 124022.1–124022.9.
Lobo, F. S. N., & Crawford, P. (2003a). Time, closed timelike curves and causality. In: R. Buccheri, M. Saniga & M. Stuckey (Eds), *The nature of time: Geometry, physics and perception (NATO Science Series II)* (pp. 289–298). Dordrecht, The Netherlands: Kluwer.
Lobo, F. S. N., & Crawford, P. (2003b). Weak energy condition violation and superluminal travel. *Lecture Notes on Physics*, *617*, 277–291.
Lobo, F. S. N., & Visser, M. (2004). Fundamental limitations on 'warp drive' spacetimes. *Classical and Quantum Gravity*, *21*, 5871–5892.
Morris, M., & Thorne, K. S. (1998). Wormholes in spacetime and their use for interstellar travel: A tool for teaching general relativity. *American Journal of Physics*, *56*, 395–412.
Morris, M., Thorne, K. S., & Yurtsever, U. (1988). Wormholes, time machines and the weak energy condition. *Physical Review Letters*, *61*, 1446–1449.
Nahin, P. J. (1999). *Time machines: Time travel in physics, metaphysics and science fiction*. New York: Springer-Verlag and AIP Press.
Newton, I. (1726). *The principia* (3rd ed.). Translated by I. Bernard Cohen & Anne Whitman (1999). Berkeley: University of California Press.
Penrose, R. (2005). *The road to reality: A complete guide to the laws of the universe*. London: Vintage Books.
Pound, R. V., & Rebka, G. A., Jr. (1959). Gravitational red-shift in nuclear resonance. *Physical Review Letters*, *3*, 439–441.
Pound, R. V., & Rebka, G. A., Jr. (1960). Apparent weight of photons. *Physical Review Letters*, *4*, 337–341.
Pound, R. V., & Snider, J. L. (1964). Effect of gravity on nuclear resonance. *Physical Review Letters*, *13*, 539–540.
Schutz, B. F. (1990). *A first course in general relativity*. Cambridge, UK: Cambridge University Press.
Thorne, K. S. (1992). Closed timelike curves. In: R. J. Gleiser, C. N. Kozameh & O. M. Moreschi (Eds), *General relativity and gravitation* (pp. 295–315). Bristol: Institute of Physics.
Tipler, F. J. (1974). Rotating cylinders and the possibility of global causality violation. *Physical Review D*, *9*, 2203–2206.
Visser, M. (1995). *Lorentzian wormholes: From Einstein to hawking*. New York: American Institute of Physics.
Wald, R. M. (1984). *General relativity*. Chicago, IL: University of Chicago Press.
Whitehead, A. N. (1920). *The concept of nature*. Cambridge, UK: Cambridge University Press.

Subject Index